Teaching Today

A PRACTICAL GUIDE

Fourth Edition

Geoff Petty

 Nelson Thornes

First published in 1993 (Stanley Thornes Ltd)

Second edition 1998 (Stanley Thornes Ltd)

Third edition 2004 (Nelson Thornes Ltd)

Fourth edition published in 2009 by:
Nelson Thornes Ltd
Delta Place
27 Bath Road
CHELTENHAM
GL53 7TH
United Kingdom

09 10 11 12 13 / 10 9 8 7 6 5 4 3 2 1

A catalogue record for this book is available from the British Library

ISBN 978 1 4085 0415 4

Illustrations by Liz Singh
Cover photograph/illustration: René Mansi/istockphoto
Page make-up by Pantek Arts Ltd

Printed and bound in Spain by GraphyCems

Contents

Preface

This book is a straightforward and practical 'how to teach' book. It is intended for those teaching in either schools, colleges, universities or work-based learning – indeed for *anyone* interested in learning and teaching.

Part 1 explores the emotional and practical needs which all learners have. Part 2 gives very detailed advice on the use of the most common teaching methods or learning strategies. Part 3 looks at how to make and use learning resources. Part 4 shows you how to go about planning lessons and courses, how to measure their effectiveness, and how to improve them. Part 5 is about your role and responsibility as a teacher and how you work within your institution. Many teacher training courses start with Part 5, but you will of course find that the earlier parts will greatly help your understanding of Part 5.

For decades I taught an 'ordinary timetable' and trained teachers. So, whilst developing my ideas and writing this book, I have had my nose rubbed daily in the messy reality of learning and teaching. If my ideas don't work – well, my students are the first to make this clear. I hope you will be able to learn from both my successes and my failures, and so take George Bernard Shaw's advice: 'Only a fool learns from experience; a wise man learns from the experience of others'.

I am impatient with jargon, so throughout the book I have used the word 'teacher' to mean any of the following: 'teacher', 'lecturer', 'trainer', 'instructor' or 'facilitator'. Similarly, I have used the words 'student' and 'learner' interchangeably, in places where I could also have written 'pupil', 'trainee', 'course participant' or 'candidate'.

In the lists of further reading at the end of each chapter, particularly useful or noteworthy books are signalled by an asterisk, with an additional comment where appropriate.

I would like to thank Liz Singh for her unshakeable faith, her insistence that I make sense, and for her cartoons and drawings.

This new edition includes some of what I have learned in studying for and writing *Evidence Based Teaching*, so it is informed by research. It has been extensively updated to meet the new standards for teachers in schools, and the new standards for teachers in the 'lifelong learning' or 'post-compulsory' sector.

Geoff Petty, 2008

Help with your teacher training assessments

Before attempting any assessment or assignment, read Chapter 28 which helps you to structure your writing (and that of your students). You are likely to be set assignments on the following topics. In each case I give chapters that will help you.

The legislative requirements of a teacher: see the end of Chapter 7.

Creating and evaluating a teaching resource: Chapters 35 and 36 are obviously relevant, but read about 'graphic organisers' on pages 158 to 162 and 'decisions, decisions' on page 257 too. To evaluate a resource see pages 400 and 409.

Inclusion, personalisation etc. (making sure everyone learns well): highly related are equality, diversity and differentiation. Read Chapters 7 and 47 to see the individual differences and how they are discovered. Chapter 41 considers how to design a course that deals with these differences.

Appendix 2 on differentiation looks at how to design lessons to deal with differences; the introduction to Part 2 deals with modern approaches to learning styles.

Equality and diversity: see Chapters 7 and 41; also consider the chapters under inclusion above.

Embedding functional skills or key skills or thinking skills into your teaching: see Chapters 38 and 42, especially the bits about double-decker lessons on pages 441 and 486; also see Chapter 30.

Communication: see Chapter 4, 'graphic organisers' on page 158; see also Chapters 11, 12 and 13.

Principles of learning: see Chapters 1–4 and 43.

Writing lesson plans and schemes of work: see Chapters 37–40 and 42; see Chapter 41 for a top grade!

What records should I keep?: see Chapter 41.

What assessment methods should I use?: see Chapters 43 and 44; see Chapter 6 is also relevant.

Evaluating my lessons and courses: see Chapters 46 and 49.

Reflective essay, reflective learning journal: read Chapter 46.

Relation of theory to practice: see Chapters 1 and 46.

Professional values and codes of practice: see Chapter 45; see also Appendix 1 on standards which are also codes of practice.

Government policies: see www.dcsf.gov.uk, then try arguing that most are wrongheaded and that we should be following evidence-based practice – see the first few chapters of my *Evidence Based Teaching*!

It really helps to look at the contents page carefully, so you know where to find things.

1

How do we learn?

Learning and memory

What was the weather like on 4 March last year? You knew once! Psychologists are still not sure how we remember and why we forget, but they believe the process of remembering involves information passing from our short-term memory into our long-term memory. Information may be stored in the short-term memory for as little as a few seconds. The long-term memory can store information for a lifetime, but nearly all of what passes through our brain is promptly forgotten.

The short-term memory (STM)

An unfortunate man who has lost his short-term memory (STM), as a result of a head injury in a car accident, can still tell his doctor in great detail what he did in the war. But when asked where he has put his coffee, he asks: 'What coffee?' The accident has damaged his STM.

Our STM stores what we are thinking at the time, along with information that has come from our eyes, ears, etc. After storing and processing this information for a few seconds, the STM promptly forgets nearly all of it. For example, if someone read out five telephone numbers one after the other, you might be able to remember the last one, but you would probably have forgotten the earlier numbers. *The content of the STM is short-lived, and is easily displaced by new information.* That last sentence has important implications for the way teachers should plan their lessons and courses; you might like to think what these implications are. (They will be summarised later in the chapter.)

Sometimes, of course, the contents of the STM are passed on to the long-term memory (LTM). The contents of the LTM are structured. If you try to remember how to do long division, you are not swamped by irrelevant memories concerning other skills you were learning at the time. The LTM is like a super-efficient filing cabinet, with information filed for future access. In order to pass into the LTM, information must first be processed and structured in the STM so that it 'makes sense' to the student. The process of structuring new information takes time; but it is time well spent, because students find it almost impossible to remember something that they do not properly understand.

Thick wall it tea of myrrh seize knots trained

Spend a few moments trying to remember the above group of words before reading on. I will test you later to find out how well you have done!

If a student is given new information too quickly, he or she will not have time to process it properly in the STM, so the information will not be retained. Experimenters tried halving their normal speech rate to students with learning difficulties, and found that the students' retention was doubled.

This vital process of structuring or giving meaning to new information is demanding as well as time-consuming, so we must try to give our students as much help as we can. Learning activities that involve students in using the new ideas will aid clarification.

This search for structure also explains why many learners appreciate being given summaries and well-organised notes.

Suppose you were given five newspaper articles about wine-making in Germany, and you were asked to learn this information for a test. How would you go about studying them? Most people would write notes, breaking the information down into main headings – for example, wine varieties, vine varieties, growing methods, etc. We feel a need to organise and structure what we want to understand and remember.

The long-term memory (LTM)

Once the STM has 'made sense' of the information, it is passed into the LTM where, unless it is subsequently used or recalled in some other way, it is again eventually forgotten! I remember finding my university lecture notes in the attic ten years after graduation. If they had not been written in my own handwriting I would not have believed I had written them! I had not used this knowledge, so my brain appears to have judged it of no use, and thrown it out of my LTM.

What we call 'forgetting' is the brain's built-in technique for ensuring that it is not cluttered up with useless knowledge. Its aim is to remember nothing but useful information. Unfortunately, however, it tends to consider a fact or idea 'useful' in the long term *only if it comes across it regularly*.

Forgetting and remembering, then, are not under direct conscious control; they are automatic. There is only one way to ensure that something is remembered: repetition. As teachers we must make sure that any knowledge we want our students to remember is recalled and used frequently.

There are exceptions to this rule: sometimes a one-off experience will be remembered for a lifetime – for example, an event with great emotional significance. But as far as teaching is concerned, we are at the mercy of the brain's automatic mechanisms, and repetition is vital.

Immediately after the initial learning of a simple idea, or after a review of that learning, our recall is 100%. Then we begin to forget what we have learned, as the graph below shows (note the unusual timescale). However, each recall fixes that learning more firmly in the LTM. As a result, it takes progressively longer for the learning to be forgotten after each recall.

As a result of this forgetting mechanism, we only remember ideas:

- that have been recalled frequently, or
- that we have heard recently.

J. B. Watson, the father of the behaviourist school of psychology developed by B. F. Skinner, said that remembering depended on 'frequency and recency'.

Our knowledge about short- and long-term memories suggests the following advice for teachers, which is dealt with in more detail in later chapters:

- *Don't cover new material too quickly.* If you tend to speak quickly, try to slow down. Also, leave a silence after an important sentence, so as to leave time for it to 'sink in'.
- *Students need activities which encourage them to process new material.* Activities that make students use – and hence develop a personal restructuring of – the ideas you are trying to teach them will make them learn more efficiently than passive activities such as listening.

- *For information to be stored in the LTM it must be used and recalled often.* A teacher cannot expect to teach an idea in September and, without referring to it again, have the students remember it in June.

The three schools of learning

There are three schools of psychology that have contributed to learning theory. Each looks at learning from a different point of view; they supplement rather than contradict each other and often overlap in practice. The cognitivist school looks at the thinking processes involved when we learn. The behaviourist school ignores these, and looks at how teacher behaviour and other external factors influence learning. The humanistic school has an interest in education as a means of meeting the learner's emotional and developmental needs. Let's look at each in more detail.

The cognitivist school: learners must construct their own meaning

I had a friend who taught his tiny daughter Newton's Third Law, 'For every action there is an equal and opposite reaction.' It was astonishing to hear a four-year-old come out with this. But did she understand it? Of course not! It was learning without understanding: 'rote learning' or 'surface learning'. Cognitivists aim to teach for *understanding*, which requires that new learning is built on existing learning.

What does it mean to 'understand' a concept? It means to be able to explain it in terms of *other* concepts. For example, if you look up a concept such as 'division' in the dictionary, it is explained in terms of other concepts such as sharing. So when a child develops a good understanding of how to divide, this is not entirely new learning. It is built upon her existing understanding and experience of cutting up cakes, sharing out bricks and so on. She is not remembering her teacher's concept of division, she is creating her own.

The cognitivist school believes that learning by doing, and asking students challenging questions, will help students make their own sense of what they are studying, and enable them to make use of their learning in real life.

This cognitivist theory called 'constructivism' is now almost universally accepted by all experts on the brain or the mind. They all agree that learning occurs when students construct their own meanings, usually out of their prior learning and experience, and of course out of their instructional experience.

This learning is a physical process. The brain contains billions of tiny brain cells called neurons, and when you learn something new you connect neurons in your brain to create a network which encodes this new learning. Everything we know is written in the brain in the language of neural connections! So when someone asks you to recall this new learning, you go to this network of neurons to 'read it off'! If you *understand* this new learning then it is connected to your existing learning.

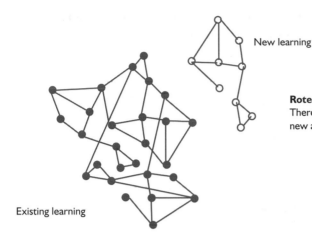

New learning

Rote learning
There is no connection between
new and existing learning.

Existing learning

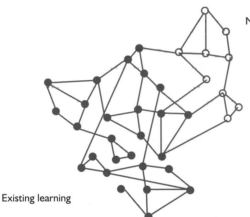

New learning

Deep learning
Learners construct their own
meaning for new learning, and
makes connections between new and
existing learning.
Thoughts travel along these
connections. So once these
connections have been made, the
learner can reason from new to old
learning and vice versa.

Existing learning

Constructivism

New learning is constructed from old

The idea of constructivism is nicely illustrated by a children's story called 'Fish is
Fish' by Leo Lionni. A rough summary of his story goes something like this. Are
you sitting comfortably? Then I will begin.

*There was once a little fish and a tadpole who shared the same pond. They
were great friends and played together every day. But one day the tadpole
grew legs and his tail began to disappear. Eventually the tadpole left the pond
as a fully grown frog.*

*The little fish often wondered where his four-footed friend had gone. But days
and weeks went by and the frog did not return.*

*Then one day the frog splashed back into the pond saying he had seen extra-
ordinary things. 'Like what?' asked the fish. 'Like birds,' said the frog.*

*The frog went on to describe birds as having wings and two legs. What did
the fish make of this? The fish imagined a bird to look just like a fish, with two
frogs' feet and fins for wings.*

5

Our students do not simply remember what we tell them, they construct their own meanings out of their limited experience, in just the same way as the fish!

Bird as imagined by fish

Exercise

Bearing in mind that the fish had only seen fish and frogs, what would he make of the frog's description of cows and people? Please draw your answer and then explain and justify it to someone else.

Suppose you had recently read a novel and someone asked you to recount it. You would not tell the story in the same words as the author. In fact, the author may even disagree with your version of the story. You have forgotten the author's words, and what you have remembered is not her exact story, but your own version of it. The same goes for students making sense of what you teach them.

We are usually unaware of this restructuring process, until it goes wrong.

> *In 1989 a man approached the staff of a railway station, saying he didn't know his name or address and had no idea why he had made a train journey. He had entirely lost his long-term memory. His wife recognised him on television and rang the station to arrange to collect him. It was discovered that he had suffered a blow to his head earlier in the day. Luckily his LTM re-established itself as he recovered. The long- and the short-term memory really do exist separately.*

My stepdaughter once complained of diarrhoea, but said she had not been to the toilet. I was alarmed until I discovered she meant ear ache ('dire ear'). Such misunderstandings are as delightful as they are common, because they show children actively trying to make sense of their world.

But we never grow out of this way of learning. Exam howlers show the same creative hypothesis-making. The following howlers were made by students in a GCSE biology exam:

'A common disease in cereal crops is wheat germ.' The student was never told by his teacher that wheat germ was a cereal disease! He heard a jumble of information about cereals, and then tried to 'make sense' of it. The very phrase 'make sense' alerts us to the fact that learning is a creative process, not a passive one.

'Name a food suitable for pickling.' *'A branston.'* Again, the student was never told that a branston was a fruit used for pickling. She simply 'made up' that piece of knowledge. Nearly all our knowledge is created in much the same way, but usually more successfully! Everything you know you made up.

> *'When I use a word,' Humpty Dumpty said in a rather scornful tone, 'it means just what I choose it to mean – neither more nor less.'*
>
> *Lewis Carroll*, Through the Looking-Glass

Anyone who doubts that learning is active needs only to talk to five-year-olds about their conception of science, God, work or any other 'adult' topic. If the child trusts you enough to answer your questions, you will be well rewarded; he or she will be full of ideas on these topics – many of them insightful, others comically off beam. These five-year-old 'students' are learning by making up what seem to them to be sensible ideas, and only changing them when they are proved wrong. (This trial-and-error method of 'hypothesis and refutation' is also the basis of the scientific method, and of postmodern critiques of the notion of 'truth'.)

Successful learning, then, happens by a process of personal hypothesis-making. This cognitivist theory of learning is sometimes called 'constructivist', because it describes how learners construct their own knowledge. Only when learners have 'made sense' of the topic like this will they be able to reason with it to solve problems and to do other useful tasks.

> *More creative hypothesis-making from exam candidates:*
> *'Worms hold themselves together by the suction power of their little legs.'*
> *'Some bacteria are used as food, e.g. marshmallows and ice creams.'*
> *'How do mammals keep warm in cold weather?' 'They wear cardigans.'*

We need to learn all 'Bloom's bits'

But what does it mean exactly to have a full grasp of a new topic, and to be able to use your learning successfully even in new situations?

One way of answering this question is to consider the skills in Bloom's taxonomy. Benjamin Bloom split learning into a 'spectrum' of tasks or skills which he called a 'taxonomy'. At the bottom, the skills are relatively undemanding, but they get more difficult, more connected and much more useful towards the top. As we will see, learning is only complete for a given topic when all the skills in the taxonomy are attained.

There is a lot to this taxonomy – don't expect to understand all its implications after one reading! We will look at it more fully in Part 4. Look at the diagram on page 9, which I have adapted slightly from Bloom's work. Let's start at the bottom and work our way up. The six sections can all be seen as skills, that is, the ability to recall, explain, etc.; or as tasks that a teacher could set. By this I mean any task: an oral question, a class activity, an essay, a project, a task on an assignment, etc.

Knowledge is just the ability to recall something. The little girl who could recall Newton's Third Law had knowledge of a sort.

Comprehension means you understand the knowledge. In practice, this means that you can explain the knowledge in terms of your existing learning and experience. You have made connections. Actually, comprehension will only be reasonably full when the later skills have also been developed.

You can't comprehend something you don't know, so I have drawn an arrow on the diagram to show that comprehension requires knowledge. The lower skills on the taxonomy are usually required by the higher ones in this way.

Application means doing after being shown how. For example, a maths teacher might show you how to do a certain type of calculation, and then ask you to do very similar calculations yourself.

Analysis is breaking a complex whole into parts, and then looking at the parts in some detail. For example, you might be asked to analyse a lesson that you have observed. There are two ways to analyse: with a knife, or with spectacles!

- To analyse with a knife, you cut the whole into logical parts and then consider each part separately – for example, cutting the lesson up into what happens first, what happens second, and so on – or considering teacher activity and student activity.
- To analyse with spectacles involves looking at the whole, but only from a specific point of view. For example, you might look at the whole lesson using 'spectacles' or questions in mind such as:
  - What resources were used?
  - What was the relationship between teacher and students like?
  - What was the student–student interaction like?

Anything can be analysed by knife or by spectacles. But to analyse well you must choose 'spectacles' that bring important aspects of the whole into focus. Try teaching your students how to analyse in these two ways.

'*Why*' questions ask 'what is the cause of this effect?' Causes and effects are parts of the whole, so 'why' questions are usually analysis questions.

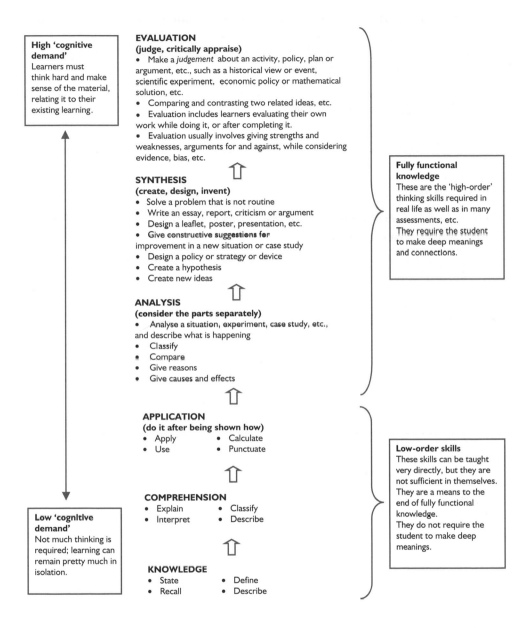

High 'cognitive demand'
Learners must think hard and make sense of the material, relating it to their existing learning.

EVALUATION
(judge, critically appraise)
• Make a *judgement* about an activity, policy, plan or argument, etc., such as a historical view or event, scientific experiment, economic policy or mathematical solution, etc.
• Comparing and contrasting two related ideas, etc.
• Evaluation includes learners evaluating their own work while doing it, or after completing it.
• Evaluation usually involves giving strengths and weaknesses, arguments for and against, while considering evidence, bias, etc.

SYNTHESIS
(create, design, invent)
• Solve a problem that is not routine
• Write an essay, report, criticism or argument
• Design a leaflet, poster, presentation, etc.
• Give constructive suggestions for improvement in a new situation or case study
• Design a policy or strategy or device
• Create a hypothesis
• Create new ideas

ANALYSIS
(consider the parts separately)
• Analyse a situation, experiment, case study, etc., and describe what is happening
• Classify
• Compare
• Give reasons
• Give causes and effects

APPLICATION
(do it after being shown how)
• Apply   • Calculate
• Use   • Punctuate

COMPREHENSION
• Explain   • Classify
• Interpret   • Describe

KNOWLEDGE
• State   • Define
• Recall   • Describe

Fully functional knowledge
These are the 'high-order' thinking skills required in real life as well as in many assessments, etc.
They require the student to make deep meanings and connections.

Low-order skills
These skills can be taught very directly, but they are not sufficient in themselves. They are a means to the end of fully functional knowledge.
They do not require the student to make deep meanings.

Low 'cognitive demand'
Not much thinking is required; learning can remain pretty much in isolation.

Bloom's taxonomy

Synthesis tasks include extended writing and problem-solving. Synthesis requires the student to decide how to do the task. Learners must use whatever skills, knowledge, experience and other learning is relevant to the task. Then they must use these together appropriately to complete the task. If the student is shown exactly how to do the task, then this is 'application', not synthesis.

Evaluation is to give the value of something, to state its strengths and weaknesses. Students can be required to evaluate an argument, policy, plan, solution or experiment, etc. However, they also need to evaluate their own work. Indeed we rather hope they will! Ideally, they will evaluate it while they are doing it, and improve it before we see it. If students cannot evaluate then they cannot take even the first steps towards their own improvement.

Evaluation requires that students know what criteria to consider. If you evaluated a lesson you might use criteria such as:

- **Did learning take place?**
- **Did the teacher check this learning? and so on.**

Such criteria help us to use the 'spectacles' that focus on the important aspects of what we are evaluating.

When students are evaluating their own work they also need to know what criteria to look for, as we will see in Chapter 43.

We have considered cognitive learning above, but a very similar approach can be used for learning practical skills.

The Jabberwocky exercise

Here is a task for you to make what went before a little clearer. Please read this first verse from 'Jabberwocky' by Lewis Carroll and answer the questions that follow. If you get stuck, read the poem very carefully! This is a nonsense poem, so most of the words in it do not have a meaning.

> 'Twas brillig, and the slithy toves
> Did gyre and gimble in the wabe;
> All mimsy were the borogoves,
> And the mome raths outgrabe.'

1 What were the slithy toves doing in the wabe?

2 How would you describe the state of the borogoves?

3 What can you say about the mome raths?

Please do questions 1, 2 and 3 before answering the following questions:

4 Does the student need to understand material in order to answer low-level questions directly related to the texts you give them?

5 Why were the borogoves mimsy?

6 How effective was the mome raths' strategy?

Most people get the following answers:

1: Gyring and gimbling.
2: They are all mimsy.
3: They outgrabe.
4: No!

5 and 6: I've no idea! These are impossible to answer as we cannot understand the text. That is, we can't make a meaning for it which is not pure speculation.

The learners need to understand grammar well enough to pick out the right words. But they don't need to understand the meaning of the text to complete the task successfully.

But here is the most important question for a teacher. Where were questions 1, 2, 3, 5 and 6 on Bloom's taxonomy? Do please work this out before reading on – it will help you make sense of 'constructivism'! (You can ignore question 4.)

Questions 1–3 were knowledge questions. However:

- **Question 5 was 'analysis' as it was a 'why' question.**
- **Question 6 was 'evaluation' as it asked for a judgement.**

Questions 5 and 6 required that you made sense of the poem, which, of course, was impossible. You had not made connections. There were no neural links to your existing learning.

The purpose of that exercise was to show that tasks at the bottom of Bloom's taxonomy do not *require* the learner to make sense of the material. However, tasks near the top of the taxonomy *do* require the student to make meanings, or 'constructs'.

Learning without understanding is called 'rote' or *surface learning*. The learner does not need to make sense of the material to get the right answer.

There is nothing wrong with asking knowledge questions, of course, but you must not stay at the knowledge level. To get deep learning, you must require the learner to operate at the higher levels of Bloom's taxonomy as well as at the lower ones. Then they will make deeper and deeper meanings for what you are teaching them, by making more and more connections to their existing concepts. This will also help them to remember the material.

Let's look at some examples of surface learning to make this clearer. I'm going to use examples from arithmetic, but surface learning arises in every subject, and at every academic level.

Researchers studying SAT tests in schools found that with a calculator 80% of 12-year-old students could complete this task:

- A. $225 \div 15 =$

But only 40% could complete this apparently identical task:

- B. 'If a gardener has 225 bulbs to place equally in 15 flower beds, how many would be in each bed?' (In this case, most of the failing pupils did not know which mathematical operation to use.)

Where are tasks A and B on Bloom's taxonomy? What do they require of the learners? Work this out before reading on.

Question A is an *application* question for many learners, as it asks them to 'do after being shown how'. However, for the weaker learner it might just be a *knowledge* question. These learners might just try to recall how to divide, without comprehending what they are doing – '… now press that key with the line and the dots on it, not sure what it does …'.

Question B, however, is a *synthesis* question as it requires problem-solving. The learner must first recognise the question as an arithmetic question (and not an algebra, grammar or guessing question, for example). Then they must decide which arithmetical operation to use to solve the problem.

Teaching is a bit like giving learners a toolkit of skills. *Application* tasks teach your students how to use each tool ($+, -, \times, \div$, usually one at a time). But *synthesis* tasks require your students to choose the appropriate tool for the job. This is not easy, and requires careful teaching. Page 259 shows an activity to teach this synthesis skill.

It is one thing to teach a carpentry student to chisel, to saw, to use screwdrivers and so on. It is quite another to point at a door that does not close, and ask the learner to fix it; that requires the synthesis skill of deciding *which* tools and skills can be used to complete the job.

Considering the topic of division again, each section of Bloom's taxonomy describes a different skill, and each is vital:

- *Knowledge*: to be able to recognise the divide sign on the calculator.
- *Comprehension*: to be able to explain how to divide with a calculator.
- *Application*: to be able to succeed with $225 \div 15 =$.
- *Analysis*: to be able to break down an arithmetic problem expressed in words and recognise the component parts.
- *Synthesis*: to be able to recognise a question as an arithmetic problem, and decide how best to solve it, e.g. to know *when* to divide.
- *Evaluation*: to be able to check your own working and problem-solving strategies or that of another, and recognise errors and omissions.

Similarly, a history teacher would need to do more than ensure that students could recall knowledge of Henry II. Students also need to be taught:

- *Application*: to use their knowledge of how laws were made in Henry II's time to answer a simple question on this.
- *Analysis*: to scrutinise the detail concerning Henry II's reign using the knife and spectacle approach.
- *Synthesis*: to decide which aspects of this detail are relevant to given essay titles.
- *Evaluation*: Here is an essay on Henry II. Does it meet these criteria for a good history essay? Does it answer the question, for example? Or what are the criteria a baron might use to evaluate Henry II's foreign policy? What would be his judgement?

Weak students can cope with these higher-order skills if the tasks set are attainable, and if the processes involved in analysing, problem-solving, essay-writing, evaluating and so on are taught explicitly, and practised. They also need clear, constructive feedback on their use of these skills.

Let's summarise some key points concerning Bloom's taxonomy.

1   For a given topic such as 'division', learners must have all the skills in the taxonomy to have fully functional knowledge – that is, if they are to be able to use their knowledge to solve problems and make judgements. It is not enough that they have skills up to 'application' only.

2   The lower skills are required for the higher skills. For example, it is not possible to solve a division problem expressed in words (synthesis) if the learner isn't capable of analysis and application.

The problem of students not having synthesis skills occurs in every curriculum area. I used to teach physics and I vividly remember waiting for my A-level students to come out of their examinations. Every year they would come up to me with questions like, 'How was I supposed to do number 12?' When I said something like, 'Well it was just a momentum question', they would say: 'Damn, if I'd *known* that I could have *done* it! I was trying to solve it with Newton's laws.'

The students had learned 'momentum' and 'Newton's laws' up to application, but had not learned *when* it was useful to take these tools out of their toolbag. That was my fault, of course; I had not given them enough synthesis practice.

It is not as hard as it seems to teach all the skills on Bloom's taxonomy, as the lower skills are contained in the higher skills. For example, if you set a synthesis task you will develop in your students better comprehension and analysis skills. Similarly, if a maths teacher asks students to evaluate a given solution to a problem, this will require students to use and develop their knowledge and comprehension of the mathematical procedures.

Surface learning

Researchers asked children and adults the following question:
'There are 26 sheep and 10 goats on a ship. How old is the captain?'
The adults laughed, but in one case more than 75% of the children got an answer. One child said: 'Well, you need to add, subtract or multiply in problems like this, and this one seemed to work best if I add.' (Bransford *et al.* 2000)
This is an example of surface learning, where the child is striving for 'the trick to get the tick' rather than a deep understanding.

Confirmation of the cognitivist and constructionist approach.

Professors John Hattie and Robert Marzarno reviewed a massive quantity of careful research on which teaching methods work best in real classrooms. See page 145 for some findings. These strongly confirm the cognitivist and constructivist approach.

We will look at Bloom's taxonomy again in Part 4, but for now we can conclude:

The principles of learning according to the cognitivist school:

- *Teachers need to set high-order tasks*. That means analysis, synthesis and evaluation. This is to ensure fully functional knowledge, and because the exclusive use of lower-order tasks leads to jabberwocky-style 'surface learning'.
- *High-order skills can be taught and are not God-given gifts*. These skills all involve the application of processes that can be taught explicitly – for example analysing with a knife and with spectacles – essay planning, evaluating with clear criteria, etc.
- *Set ladders of tasks*. It often makes sense to set tasks that gradually climb Bloom's taxonomy as if it were a ladder, or that climb from simple and concrete to harder and more abstract.

 'The question is the answer.'

Jamie McKenzie

Constructivist principles include:

- *Use teaching strategies that* require *all students to make a construct*. Passive methods such as teacher talk do not require students to form constructs; active methods do. When students act, they must create and apply their construct in order to decide what to do.
- *Check and correct*. Learning is a trial-and-error process, so set activities that require students to check for their own and each other's learning errors and omissions, and check for these yourself. When students act they usually make a *product* that should be used to diagnose learning errors and omissions. See also Socratic questioning below.
- *What the learner does is more important than what the teacher does*. Teaching is just a means to the end; it's the learning that counts! This is why Ofsted inspectors are trained to observe learning, not teaching.
- *Make learning fun!* Enjoyable tasks create more participation, concentration, persistence, and more cognitive engagement.
- *We learn by doing*. This is a commonly heard principle often attributed to Dewey, which rather loosely summarises the principles above.

Common cognitivist or constructivist teaching strategies include:

- 'Teaching by asking' or guided discovery.
- 'Diagnostic' question and answer, and use of poor answers to explore and correct misunderstandings ('Socratic questioning').
- Explaining tasks that require students to express their understanding to each other or the teacher, especially if these explanations are formally or informally corrected.
- Group work requiring students to discuss the material, so that constructs are made and peer checking and teaching takes place. This requires high-order tasks and questions.

- Students creating 'mind-maps' or 'spider diagrams' and other summaries that identify the key points and how these parts relate to the whole. See page 127 for an example, and Tony Buzan's website (www.mind-map.com).

See also the more active methods in Part 2.

The behaviourist school: rewards and motivation

Behaviourist psychologists have studied learning in animals by teaching them simple tasks. E. L. Thorndike (1874–1949) caged hungry cats in 'puzzle boxes' within sight of food; the cats learned to pull a string, or operate a lever, to escape from the box and take the food. Skinner (born 1904) taught pigeons, dogs, rats and other animals using a 'Skinner box'; in this there was a lever which, when pressed, delivered food to the animal. Similar techniques were used by experimenters to teach rats to find their way through mazes.

In each case, the animals were taught by rewarding them with food when they did well; much the same method is used to train pets or circus animals. Some of the findings apply surprisingly well to human learning, though they hardly tell the whole story. Here is a simplified summary of behaviourist research findings, which are of particular interest to the teacher. These are, in effect, the principles of learning according to the behaviourist school; they are given in italic, and then commented on below.

Learners require some reward or 'reinforcement' for learning

If one puts a recently fed cat in a puzzle box it will go to sleep. Only hungry cats will learn how to escape. Human learners are also motivated by an expected reward of some kind (such as praise or satisfied curiosity); learning will not take place without it. Nobody learns for nothing!

Effective teachers put huge emphasis on rewarding their students with praise, attention and other encouragement. They set achievable tasks for all their students, and divide long tasks into a number of shorter tasks. This allows students to experience successful completion frequently. Courses are often divided into modules to increase the frequency of rewards.

Reinforcement should follow the desired behaviour as soon as possible

If a rat pushes a lever and food drops immediately into its cage, then it quickly learns to press the lever for food. If reinforcement is delayed, learning takes longer.

A similar effect is seen in human learning. A student whose work is usually marked immediately is more motivated than one who expects to wait weeks for reinforcement in the form of praise, or knowledge of success.

Effective teachers continuously reward and encourage students while they are working, so reinforcement is almost immediate.

Learning proceeds step by step rather than happening all at once, and is strengthened by repeated success

Cats naturally take time to escape from their puzzle boxes, but the time taken steadily diminishes with practice. Similarly, human learning takes time, and past successes provide motivation for present learning. If a learner is never successful in your lessons, he or she will soon give up.

We remember what we have experienced frequently and recently

If you teach something in September, and never refer to it again, it will soon be forgotten.

Effective teachers stress key points and summarise them at the beginning and at the end of classes. They also make use of old learning in developing new learning.

Sadly, much teaching in our schools and colleges violates the behaviourists' findings. Weaker students in some classes are set work that is so difficult for them that they never experience genuine success. Partly as a result, some students rarely, or never, get praise or encouragement. Work may not be marked promptly, and knowledge and skills are often taught and then not referred to again for months. As a result, many learners simply give up.

Learning is a complex process, and the behaviourists, like the other schools of psychology, give us only part of the story. There is more on their approach to learning in the chapters on motivation (5), praise and criticism (6), discipline (9) and learning for remembering (23).

The humanistic school: meeting the emotional needs of learners

In *How Children Fail* (1964), John Holt claimed the school system could destroy the minds and emotions of young children. His blistering attack accused schools of inducing fear in pupils, and of humiliating, ridiculing and devaluing them. Humanist psychologists believe that fear of failure and rejection produces maladjustment. Either learners play it safe and withdraw, feeling crushed and lacking in self-confidence as a result; or they hit out in retaliation, becoming disruptive. Either way, pupils, and their learning, are damaged.

Most teachers have found their own learning to be a reasonably straightforward process. Though you may well have found some learning difficult, you must have been a very successful learner in other areas to have gained the qualifications or skills required to become a teacher. For many people though, learning is a process filled with pain, anxiety and frustration. Thirty per cent of pupils leave school without a GCSE of any grade. It is estimated that between 7 and 10% of people are functionally illiterate – that is, they are unable to read newspapers and road signs or to fill in forms. Learning may have been easy for you, but it is not easy for everyone.

The humanistic school believes that emotional factors, and personal growth and development, are the highest values, and it argues that these are ignored in a society which is unduly materialistic, objective and mechanistic. Humanistic psychologists believe that society, schools and colleges exist to meet the needs of the individual learner, not the other way round. They believe that learners should be allowed to pursue their own interests and talents in order to develop themselves as fully as possible in their own unique direction.

The main principles suggested by humanistic psychologists have been highly influential, especially in adult education and training, and in further education, though they are rarely met in full.

Learners should be self-directed

Teachers are encouraged to help each *learner* choose what knowledge and skills they want to learn, negotiating a unique 'learning contract' or 'action plan' for each individual. The materials, methods and rate of learning are also customised to meet the needs of the individual.

Student choice ensures ego involvement in the learning tasks, and students will be highly motivated by following their own interests and curiosity. An HMI report on Summerhill School, which was run by A. S. Neil on humanistic principles, said the pupils were 'full of life and zest and of boredom and apathy there was no sign'.

Standard curricula and compulsory attendance are either abandoned or given a low priority. While this is a radical approach if adopted in a school, it is commonplace in the teaching and training of adults. Most schoolteachers make at least some use of humanistic principles, however.

If you cannot allow students to self-direct their learning, you can often at least give them some measure of choice in tasks or assignments, enabling them to follow their own interests. You can also set assignments that maximise creativity and curiosity, instead of those that only require the restatement of facts.

> 'The ultimate goal of the educational system is to shift to the individual the burden of pursuing his own education'
>
> 'We think of the mind as a storehouse to be filled when we should be thinking of it as an instrument to be used.'
>
> J. W. Gardener

Students should take responsibility for their own learning

As well as choosing the style and content of their own learning, learners are encouraged to take responsibility for its effectiveness. They are encouraged to be active rather than passive in their attitude to learning, and over-helping by teachers is discouraged as it is thought to encourage dependency. When I was observing a science lesson during my teacher training, a student complained that an electrical meter he was using kept going off the scale. I was surprised by the teacher's reaction, which was to say perfectly pleasantly: 'And what are you going to do about that?' That was a very humanistic response: the student soon found a more appropriate meter, and was delighted by the discovery that he could solve his own scientific problems.

Self-assessment is preferable to teacher assessment

Self-assessment or self-evaluation encourages the self-reliance and self-direction that humanistic theorists prize. Self-assessment is itself a crucial skill for work and for learning. It encourages students to take responsibility for their own improvement, and is the route to excellence in any field. Teachers' tests, it is argued, encourage rote memorising and working for grades rather than real learning and personal development. Teacher assessment can also create fear and humiliation and can lower students' self-esteem. Students will never take responsibility for their own improvement until they learn to be constructively critical of their own work.

Teachers often ask students to evaluate their own assignments or pieces of work, offering a teacher assessment only if the self-assessment is unsatisfactory.

Learning is easiest, most meaningful and most effective when it takes place in a non-threatening situation

Learners should be motivated by a desire to succeed, to explore, to develop and to improve, not by a fear of failure. There should be a 'no blame' policy for mistakes, which should be seen as inevitable and as an opportunity to learn. Students should be allowed to present themselves for assessment when they feel ready, rather than at a predetermined time, and they should be allowed time to improve their work if they have not yet met the assessment standard.

The following cycle uses humanistic principles to encourage students to improve their own learning or performance on a course. Note that it involves self-evaluation, is non-threatening, and encourages students to take responsibility for their own learning and improvement. How does this process compare with a report from the teacher saying how the student should improve? In your comparison of these two approaches, consider the motivation and the likely emotional reaction of the student.

Self-evaluation
Where am I now?
The learner reflects, evaluating his or her own skills, knowledge, values and attitudes.

Goal-setting
Where do I want to be?
The learner considers his or her aspirations, and sets personal goals or targets.

Action plan
How can I close the gap between where I am and where I want to be?

Action!
Carry out the action plan, monitoring its implementation.

The self-directed learning cycle

Chapters 10, 33 and 34 give more detail on the theory and practice of self-directed learning.

Adult learning and 'androgogy'

This humanistic 'self-directed learning' approach has been particularly influential in adult education, though it is also used to teach teenagers and younger learners in certain topics or situations – for example, project work, learning to learn and to meet individual needs. What's different about adult learning?

A teenager or younger learner usually accepts or expects their teacher to take control of what is taught and how. (Sometimes to the extreme of becoming a passive learner; see page 61.) But adults want more control. They usually have very specific and very individual reasons for enrolling on a course – 'I want to paint botanical illustrations of wild flowers'. Teachers need a very flexible approach to satisfy their learners' different aspirations in the same class.

The following helps with this difficult and important topic:

- Chapter 41 looks at how adult learning differs from school and most 16–19 learning, and how courses can be organised to meet the needs of adult learners. Planning courses that don't lead to a qualification is also considered.
- Chapter 34 looks at how to use self-directed learning with adults or younger learners.
- Chapter 33 looks at 'how to manage independent learning', which helps learners move towards self-directed learning.
- Chapter 10 looks at the 'facilitation' approach common in self-directed learning – 'Are you an instructor or facilitator?'
- Page 61 has a diagram which shows the danger of too much teacher control.

Specialist pedagogy and vocationally specific pedagogy

> 'Pedagogy: the … theory or science of teaching'.
>
> Concise Oxford English Dictionary

Yes, but what's the best way to teach my subject? So far, this chapter has considered general principles which will apply whether you teach history or hairdressing, mathematics or dressage. But you will need to apply these principles in ways which suit your subject, you and your students. You will need to answer three questions, and your answers might vary somewhat with course and academic level. Your subject mentor will be able to help you, at least with questions 1 and 2, and your observations of good teaching in your subject will also be useful.

1 What are the most useful and effective general teaching methods for my students? For example, a history teacher might repeatedly use teacher talk,

followed by group work with 'spectacles', and then assertive questioning. There are details on these and many other methods in Part 2. Scan all the methods; some might help more than you expect. Chapters 38 and 39 help you choose methods for a lesson.

2   What is the best way to teach each topic? 'How do I teach nutrition? How do I explain it? What analogies or examples should I use? And, most importantly, which student activities enable my students to develop the concept faithfully?'

> *Try an internet search using 'scheme of work' in quotes, followed by your subject or course. However, only exceptionally will you find schemes that suggest effective teaching methods and any necessary resources. I hope that one day teachers will collaborate online to create these nationally.*

3   How can I teach my students to think in my subject? You must teach your students to think like a historian, hairdresser, or in a way appropriate to whatever you teach. Subject-specific thinking skills are the most powerful legacy you can leave your students. So set tasks that require students to reason in a subject-specific way, and then generate discussion:

'Is that method mathematically valid?'...
'Why?'
'What would be the most appropriate hair dye for this client?' ...
'How do you know?'
'What if she resisted your advice?'

It is important to manage these discussions in ways that maximise participation and thought. See Chapter 14 and especially Chapter 24. Chapters 38 and 42 look at how to plan 'double-decker' lessons, which teach subject-specific thinking skills while teaching content.

Are you being lured onto the rocks of folk pedagogy?

I once taught a lawyer to teach law; she participated with enthusiasm during my session on active learning, but when I observed her teaching I was dismayed that she spent the entire class alternating between lecturing her students and dictating notes.

When I referred to learning theory and my sessions on active learning, she shook her head and smiled, saying, 'Ah yes, but I teach law.'

She was deeply respectful of her own teachers who had all taught her this way. She explained there was simply too much content to cover to teach actively.

This problem of 'folk pedagogy' is not peculiar to law; every teacher must grapple with it.

The facts are that though your teachers might have been inspiring and effective in many ways, you are most unlikely to have been taught as well as you could now teach. We know more about how to teach now. There are now hundreds of thousands of classroom trials of teaching methods, showing that, regardless of your subject and the academic level at which you teach, the best results are gained by active learning on challenging tasks, including dialogue and informative feedback on how well the task was done. This feedback might include self- and peer assessment. See page 506.

In Chapter 22 of *Evidence Based Teaching*, I look at research on what the very best teachers do (best in terms of the value they add to their students' qualifications). They don't cover all the detail in each topic, but use precious class time to climb ladders of tasks (page 14) designed to ensure that students understand the topic deeply. The less important detail can be set for students to study themselves in homeworks and assignments.

> *Too much detail to cover in too much time? See Chapters 25, 33 and 36. If you cover all the detail, students are usually swamped by it, and so unable to understand or remember even important points or skills. 'Coverage' of detail should never have priority over deep understanding. See page 304 of* Evidence Based Teaching.

Who can help or develop your specialist pedagogy? Your tutor and/or mentor will help, and so might subject learning coaches, advanced teachers, advanced practitioners or whoever coaches teachers in your institution. Ask them for their advice – they will be delighted to hear from you.

Social learning: some learning is not taught

If a teacher tells students that one must always wash one's hands before handling food, but doesn't actually do so, then students learn that this hand-washing is not important. Studies show that what we as teachers do is overwhelmingly more influential than what we say. Setting an example in this way is called 'modelling'. What do you need to model in your teaching: enthusiasm? thoroughness? patience? neat presentation? safe practices? Whatever you decide, remember that 'Do what I say, not what I do' simply doesn't work as a teaching strategy.

We also teach unconsciously by our behaviour towards our students. A teacher who talks to, smiles at, encourages and helps students of Asian and European origin equally, is teaching the students to respect everyone, regardless of their origins. Such inadvertent teaching is sometimes called the 'hidden curriculum'.

That list of words

Can you remember the list of words that you were asked to remember on page 2? Is it possible to remember what you can't make sense of? The word list: 'thick, wall, it, tea, of, myrrh, seize, knots, trained' is phonetically almost identical to 'The quality of mercy is not strained.' You would have found the latter much easier to remember – because it makes sense. On the whole we don't remember words, we remember meanings; and these meanings we must make ourselves.

You will find much more on how people learn in other chapters of this book, especially in the next two chapters, and also Chapters 23 (on learning for remembering), 29 (on guided discovery), 31 (on learning from experience) and 43 (on assessment).

Summary

Learning is not the same as remembering; it is an active 'meaning-making' process. Only information that has been structured and organised by the student can pass into the long-term memory and can be used in real life. This organisation process is helped by *doing* rather than listening.

Information will only stay in the LTM if it is reused or recalled often. 'Frequency and recency' govern our ability to recall what we have learned.

Motivation is crucial for learning; it is provided in part by repeated success, and by prompt reinforcement for this success. Learning is more effective if it is motivated by a desire to succeed rather than by a fear of failure. The student should take as much responsibility as possible for learning, assessment and improvement. We teach unconsciously by setting an example.

A common error is to see the teacher's role as mainly to present information to students. To send information is one thing, but to get students to understand this information by making their own meaning of it is quite another.

Checklist

❏ Do your students spend most of their time learning by doing?

❏ What new student activities could you try in the near future?

❏ Do all your students get some measure of success in their learning?

❏ Does this success get quickly reinforced?

❏ Do your students reuse previous learning?

❏ Do you use old learning to help new learning?

❏ Do you encourage self-evaluation and student responsibility?

❏ Do you avoid using threats to get students to learn?

❏ Have you decided what you as a teacher must model?

Further reading

Bransford, J. D. *et al.* (2000) *How People Learn: Brain, Mind, Experience and School*, Washington: National Research Council. This summarises a huge review of research on learning commissioned by the US Government.

*Holt, J. (1995) *How Children Learn* (revised edition), Cambridge, MA: Da Capo Press.

Knowles, M. (1988) *The Modern Practice of Adult Education from Pedagogy to Andragogy* (revised edition), Cambridge Book Company.

*Kyriacou, C. (1998) *Essential Teaching Skills* (2nd edition), Cheltenham: Nelson Thornes.

Pinker, S. (1997) *How the Mind Works*, London: Penguin.

Reece, I. and Walker, S. (1997) *A Practical Guide to Teaching, Training and Learning* (3rd edition), Sunderland: Business Education Publishers.

*Rogers, C. (1994) *Freedom to Learn* (3rd edition), New York: Merrill. On the humanistic approach to education.

Rogers, J. (1989) *Adults Learning* (3rd edition), Milton Keynes: Open University Press.

Any good A-level psychology textbook will deal in outline with memory and the theories of learning.

2

Learning skills by corrected practice

You have been learning all your life. You know what makes you learn, and as a result you know more than you realise about what makes others learn. The problem is that this knowledge is intuitive and unstructured. We need to uncover this unconscious knowledge of how we learn best, so that you can use it to discover how you should best teach.

To examine how we like to learn, we will carry out a 'thought experiment'. It will uncover what helps us to learn a specific intellectual or practical skill, and you will be surprised at the power of your own intuition.

Desert assignment

Imagine you must travel entirely alone, in a Land Rover, from A to B on the map. This involves travelling for hundreds of miles across the Sahara Desert. In order to survive this journey you need to be taught two skills, and it is a matter of life or death that you have learned them effectively.

1 You must be able to dismantle, clean and then reassemble a carburettor

Driving across the desert means that sand blowing into your engine may eventually get into the carburettor. This causes the engine to die. Unless you are able to put this right you will be stranded in the desert with a limited supply of water, and your fate is certain death!

2 You must be able to navigate by the stars

No compass will be provided, so you will need to be able to determine your position and your direction of travel from the stars alone. Star charts and other necessary equipment will be provided. Should you get lost, you will run out of fuel and water, and your fate – yes, again it is certain death!

In each case you are learning a specific skill. Skill learning often requires and includes 'understanding', but goes further than that. You should, for example, be able to understand navigation by the stars; but you should also be able to do it. Skill 1 is *practical*, skill 2 is *intellectual*.

You will be relieved to hear that you are to be taught these two vital skills before your journey! In each case you can choose how you are to learn these skills, and no expense is to be spared. However, remember that it is a matter of life or death that the skills are, without any doubt, properly learned.

What learning experiences would you need, to be sure you had learned these skills? And in what order would you prefer to have these learning experiences? You are at liberty to choose any learning experiences you like. Here are a few examples for you to choose from.

> *Reading*. Students are set relevant reading.
> *Test*. A test may be simple or realistic, marked by the teacher.
> *Class practical or exercise*. The students practise under supervision.
> *Note-taking*. Notes or handouts are given to provide a permanent record.
> *Demonstration*. Students watch a teacher show them how it should be done.
> *Explanation*. Students listen to an explanation given by the teacher.
> *Discussion*. The class discusses informally.
> *Question and answer*. The class can ask questions of the teacher.
> *Watching a video*. Students watch a relevant topic.
> *Summarising*. Students are given a summary of the most important points.
> *Investigation*. Students are asked to research a topic for themselves.
> *Role-play*. Students take part in a realistic simulation.

You may choose any other learning experiences you like; the chapter headings (see the contents list at the beginning of the book) will give you more ideas.

Sit down with a pencil and paper, and try to decide what learning experiences you would choose, and in what order, for each of the two skills. Do this before reading further. (Start with the carburettor.)

It is very noticeable that most people choose very similar learning experiences to acquire these skills, which suggests that there are certain patterns in the way we like to learn. Below is an example of a typical suggestion for methods to learn the carburettor skill.

To learn how to clean a carburettor

1 *Explanation* of the function of the carburettor, where it can be found in the engine, how it works, etc. – with plenty of *visual aids and handouts* specific to the carburettor on our vehicle.

2 *Demonstration* of the removal, dismantling, cleaning and reassembly of the carburettor, including notes containing hints, warnings and tips.

3 *Class practice*, i.e. students do (2) above themselves, under supervision.

4 A realistic *field practice test* in a desert, unsupervised, but assessed by the teacher (and with emergency support, please).

There is an explanation, so that the students understand what they will be doing; and a demonstration, so that they are shown 'doing-detail' – that is, what to do and how to do it properly. Everyone feels the need to practise the skill themselves, and most people take for granted that their performance will be checked by the teacher. We all tend to forget, so we want a handout or a manual or notes, or some other aide-memoire; and to clear up any queries, we need an opportunity to ask questions at some time or at all times during the lessons. Lastly, no one would stake their lives on their carburettor-cleaning skills unless these skills had been realistically tested or 'evaluated' and found to be adequate.

When we learn specific skills our needs fall into this pattern, which is summarised by the mnemonic *educare?* (*educere*, meaning 'to lead out', is the Latin root of the word 'educate').

Learning a specific skill requires that the following needs be met:

E   *Explanation*. The students need to understand why the skill is carried out in the way it is, along with any important background information.
D   '*Doing-detail*'. The students must discover precisely what they are expected to do, and how it should be done. This is the 'doing-detail' which students often best learn by being 'shown how', for example via a demonstration or case study. These provide models of good practice to copy or adapt, and are useful precisely because they provide 'doing-detail'.
U   *Use*. The students must use – that is, practise – the skill.
C   *Check and correct*. Students' practice must of course be checked and corrected by the students themselves, and usually by the teacher.
A   *Aide-memoire*. The students need some reminder or other – for example notes, handout, book, tape.
R   *Review* and reuse of earlier work is required to ensure that old learning is not forgotten.
E   *Evaluation*. Learning must be tested under realistic conditions, if the learner and the teacher are to be confident of the learning.
?   *Queries*. Learners always require an opportunity to ask questions.

The 'use' and 'check and correct' needs are cyclic, and must continue until the skill is mastered. In our thought experiment we imagined a short series of lessons, so review may not have occurred to you, though you may have thought of including a summary. When teaching covers an appreciable length of time, it is very important to revise or reuse old learning, or earlier work will be forgotten.

It is very important to understand that the *educare?* elements are all learning experiences, not teaching methods. For example, the *explanation* can be provided in a multitude of ways. It could of course be provided by 'teacher talk', but just as effectively by the student: through reading, watching a video, carrying out an experiment, discovering for themselves, etc. What matters is that, at some time or other, the student does come across an explanation of why the activity is done in the way it is. How the explanation is obtained is not important, even if they read it on the back of a crisp packet they find on the floor of a bus – they still get the explanation, after all! The same goes for the other elements: the mode of delivery is irrelevant, but *having each need met* is vital.

The needs may be combined – for example, it is often effective for students to get their explanation and the 'doing-detail' at the same time. 'Use' and 'check and correct' are also sometimes experienced concurrently. However, *successful learning requires that all the needs are met*. Other aspects of learning a practical skill are considered in Part 2 of this book, 'The teacher's toolkit'.

Of course, the learner also has physiological, emotional and motivational needs; the *educare?* mnemonic only deals with what could loosely be called *cognitive* needs. What we have discovered are the learning experiences a motivated student requires in order to learn a practical skill effectively and confidently.

However, whether one is learning a specific practical skill or an intellectual skill (including a language skill), one will nearly always need the *educare?* elements if successful learning is to take place. To test this, let's look at the following list of learning experiences, suggested by some trainee teachers, for learning the navigation skill. Compare them with your own.

To learn how to navigate by the stars

1 *Lecture.* Introductory talk on the sky at night, recognising constellations, etc., star charts, what they are and how they are used.

2 *Demonstration* of how to find your position with a star chart, and how to find north, etc.

3 Some *easy class exercises* using the charts, but in the classroom if possible, followed by a question-and-answer session.

4 *Notes* given out, along with a *description of where people went wrong* in their class exercises.

5 A realistic *class practical* – for example, at the Planetarium or actually at night, preferably in the desert so that the sky looks the same, but with help in case we make a mistake.

6 A series of *tests* that are realistic but more difficult, set and assessed by the teacher.

Look through the navigation skills list and see if you can make out the *educare?* elements. Do this before reading further.

Skills and abilities commonly taught

We will see in Chapter 37 on aims and objectives that most learning enables the learner to *do something* that they were unable to do before. It develops skills and abilities. Here are some examples of skills or abilities that are commonly taught in schools and colleges:

The ability to:

- distinguish between conduction, convection and radiation
- answer exam-style questions on soil fertility
- type a business letter in the accepted manner
- add fractions
- blow-dry hair
- recall the most important dates in the reign of Henry V
- recall an outline of how a radio works
- fill in a form correctly
- use the French verb *avoir* correctly in sentences
- make a hotel reservation in Spanish
- use a wood drill correctly
- diagnose a fault in a colour TV
- say 'no' to sex without a condom.

We learn specific skills and abilities like these by *corrected practice*, and the learners will have the needs described in the *educare?* mnemonic.

When teaching a physical skill it is important not to teach too much at once. A complex task is best broken into a chain of steps, each of which is learned separately. These steps should next be practised slowly and accurately until the required speed is attained. Then the steps can be chained together to make up the complex task. For example, a music teacher might teach a student to play a complex four-bar passage in this way, perhaps one bar at a time.

The *educare?* mnemonic can be used to devise learning activities, to check a lesson plan for important omissions, or to help with troubleshooting when learning has not taken place. The next chapter looks at the mnemonic in more detail, and on pages 38–9 you will find a summary of this chapter as well as the next.

Further reading

Bruner, J. S. (1966) *Towards a Theory of Instruction*, New York: W. W. Norton.

*Wilson, B. (1987) *Methods of Training*, Vols 1–4, London: HMSO.

3

The learner's needs

In the previous chapter I used a simple 'thought experiment' to show that when learning a specific skill or ability, physical or intellectual, the learner has certain learning needs. These needs I have called: explanation, 'doing-detail', use, check and correct, aide-memoire, review, evaluation and questions (or queries). They can be remembered by the mnemonic *educare?* These needs or elements are present in the learning of any well-defined skill.

Using the elements of *educare?*

Let's look in detail at each of the learner's needs in turn, to see why each of them is so vital to the effective learning of a skill or ability.

Explanation

Would you be content to follow a procedure for cleaning the carburettor, without having the least knowledge of how the device worked, and why you should clean some parts and leave others untouched? We tend to feel very uneasy when carrying out a procedure we do not understand. We need an 'explanation'. The explanation should include relevant background information: for example, what a carburettor does, and why it sometimes needs cleaning.

You might expect that any teacher would see the need for an adequate explanation, but some teachers eliminate the explanation by teaching a routine. This may occur in the teaching of almost any kind of skill, from filleting a fish to solving quadratic equations. The students are given a list of things to do, and told in what order they must carry them out, without any explanation of *why* each step is necessary, why it is done as it is or what exactly is achieved by each step.

Routines teach without understanding and are soon forgotten; they leave learners unable to cope with the unexpected, or a situation where something goes wrong. Such learners will lack confidence even when they have learned correctly. Learning without understanding is shallow learning indeed – but it is attempted more often than you might realise. There is, for example, a widespread myth that *training* does not require understanding.

Some teachers leave out the explanation because they think it is 'obvious'. However, what is obvious to the teacher is rarely obvious to all the students. Take a look at the average computer manual! Does it explain, or does it just tell the student what to do as a sequence of orders? Computer manuals need not give the learner every detail about the electronics, but they do need to include simple explanations such as:

'Now press the return key; this tells the computer that you have finished entering the name.'

Only students who understand what they are doing, in terms of previous knowledge and experience, will be able to go on learning and developing after your teaching input ends.

If some teachers omit the explanation, others believe this is *all* they need provide. A university-style lecture on its own cannot teach a skill or ability; this requires corrected practice, and fulfilment of the other needs represented in the mnemonic *educare?*

Remember that, as we saw in Chapter 2, explanations are a learner's need, not a teaching method. It is not necessary for the teacher to do the explaining, if the students get the explanation in some other way – for example, by reading or by discovering for themselves. (See Chapters 11 and 12 for more detail.)

'Doing-detail': what we learn from being shown how

Why do learners feel a need for a demonstration when they are learning a skill? It is because they want to know, preferably in concrete terms:

* what they are expected to do
* how they can best do it
* how they can tell when they have used the skill or ability correctly

and perhaps:

* when and where it is appropriate to make use of their skill.

In short, they need 'doing-detail': a concrete definition of their learning task. This can be provided in many ways, but most learners prefer a concrete example of good practice to copy or to adapt. For example, it is almost impossible to imagine being taught how to strip down a carburettor without being shown how to do it at some stage. Discovering 'doing-detail' is vital in any skill learning; it can be done in many ways. Some examples:

By demonstration
* demonstrating how to wire a three-pin plug
* demonstrating how to solve quadratic equations 'on the board', before expecting students to do it for themselves
* demonstrating how to pronounce a word in a foreign language.

By case study
* A teacher in retail training might ask students to watch a video of a salesman dealing with a difficult customer.
* A teacher of accounting might give students examples of bad practice, asking them to deduce good practice from these.

By exemplar

- A teacher of computer programming might show students a correctly constructed program, and discuss this with them to provide 'doing-detail' on program structure.
- Later, the students could be asked to find the faults in bad programs.
- A history teacher wishing to teach essay-writing skills might show students examples of good and bad essays, and discuss these with the class.
- A law teacher might demonstrate the skill of recognising libel and slander by describing a scenario and then arguing aloud to the class whether or not it involves libel, slander or neither. (Examples containing deliberate mistakes can also provide 'doing-detail'.)

By being told how

A teacher may give an ordered list of instructions, for example on how to change an air filter (but 'telling someone how' usually only works if students already have substantial relevant experience).

By discovery

Information technology students can be asked to experiment until they have discovered by themselves how to change the margin settings on a piece of text.

Learning by imitation is one of the main forms of learning, in and out of the classroom, because it is an excellent way of obtaining 'doing-detail'. However, sometimes it is not enough. For example, students may need the teacher's help if they are to learn general rules of composition or colour use from a painting; or how to write a report from an exemplar.

Unfortunately, many teachers, especially of academic subjects, miss 'doing-detail' out of their teaching. As a result, learners are left to discover for themselves – or from each other – what is expected of them. Here are just a few examples:

- A maths teacher says, 'These equations are solved by squaring both sides and then rearranging to make the unknown the subject of the equation', without 'doing one on the board' – that is, without showing how it is done.
- An inexperienced geography teacher expects his students to answer complex map interpretation questions, never having shown (in contrast to told) his students how these questions are best approached.
- A computer teacher says, 'Using the File menu, you can change the printer options to suit your purposes', without gathering the students around a computer screen and demonstrating how this is done.

If you are usually teaching physical skills rather than intellectual skills, you may invariably give 'doing-detail' by means of a demonstration. If this is so, you might like to remember the D element in the mnemonic as 'demonstration' rather than as 'doing-detail'.

Students will find 'doing-detail' useful even if it only confirms their expectations. It gives them confidence that they have understood, and that they really are doing the right thing when they do it for themselves.

Sometimes, when teaching a simple skill, or a skill very like one taught earlier, the 'doing-detail' has already been provided and need not be repeated. For example, a teacher may decide to teach how to poach haddock without demonstrating, if the class has already been taught to poach cod. But beware: most novice teachers overestimate their students, so play safe! When a teacher explains how to find the unknown angle in a triangle by using the fact that the angles add up to 180°, this may as well be demonstrated, even though it only involves simple addition and subtraction; the demonstration gives the students confidence that they have understood, and is more likely to be remembered. (See Chapter 13 for more detail.)

Using the skill

Would you feel able to strip down, clean and reassemble a carburettor, or read a star chart and make deductions, if you had never practised?

Whether we are learning to solve quadratic equations in a mathematics class or deal with difficult customers in a retail shop – indeed, whatever skill we are learning – we need practice. Most students rightly value practice very highly as a method of learning. Unfortunately, many teachers do not rate it so highly as a method of teaching!

I remember a student chemistry teacher who was teaching a class how to tackle questions involving chemical formulae. He explained well and demonstrated the solution of some problems on the blackboard; and the students copied these into their notes. But he seemed to regard student practice as just a luxury. He told me, 'I would love to give them a chance to practise doing some questions themselves, but there just isn't time.' There was time, however, for an hour and a half of explanation and demonstration of how to tackle such problems!

I wonder how he would have felt if there wasn't time for him to practise cleaning his carburettor, because the teacher had spent so long demonstrating how to do it?

We very rarely have as much time as we would like to teach what our students must learn. But this does not mean that we should alter the proportion of total time spent on each of the individual *educare?* elements. How should we divide the time between these activities? It will of course depend on the circumstances, but student practice will frequently be the single most time-consuming activity, often by a very wide margin.

In a later chapter on aims and objectives, we will see that even academic teaching involves teaching learners how to do something (if only answering exam-style questions). This, of course, needs practice. (See Chapter 16 for more detail.)

Check and correct

You probably don't need the carburettor or navigation learning examples to convince you that it is important for the teacher to check a skill as it is practised. The ideal is that every student's work should be checked a number of times every lesson, and corrected with extra explanation and demonstration where necessary. A major aim is to prevent the student from repeating incorrect methods, and thereby learning those rather than the correct version. The check shows the student what needs correcting. It needs to be detailed and specific.

The overall intention is to give students an ability to check and correct their own work, so whenever possible let the learners 'check and correct' themselves. The more responsibility learners take for their own correcting, the better.

However, some caution is needed. Though self-checks can save a teacher considerable time, high-order skills do need also to be checked by the teacher; and in any case, only rarely can students independently check their own (or each other's) work in the early stages of a new area of activity.

The 'check and correct' phase also provides vital feedback for the teacher. Is learning taking place? Am I teaching too quickly? Are they doing it properly? The importance of this feedback cannot be over-stressed.

The 'use' and 'check and correct' phases together form a repeatable feedback cycle which must continue until mastery of the learning has been achieved.

Students should have their work checked and corrected as quickly as possible after its completion, and ideally while it is being done. Wherever possible this phase should be continuous, student-led and teacher-supervised; but this ideal is often difficult to achieve in practice. (See Chapter 16 for more detail.)

Aide-memoire

If you were about to set off to find your way through the Sahara, you would almost certainly want to take a book, notes or some other reminder to make sure you could deal with a mental block or some other unexpected event. Your students too will need a record of what they are supposed to know.

Notes compensate for the fallibility of human memory, but they also have other functions. They can summarise a learning session, and indicate the key points students are expected to understand and remember. (See Chapter 15 for more detail.)

Review or revision

Many teachers seem to follow a 'teach it in September and forget it till June' strategy. Learning needs to be reinforced by recall and practice, not left to be revised right at the end of the course. This important aspect of teaching is considered in more depth in Chapter 23, 'Learning for remembering'.

Evaluation

It is one thing for learners to be capable of a skill or ability when the teacher and other learners are available to help, but can they do it by themselves in realistic conditions? Going through learning experiences does not guarantee learning. There is only one way to be sure, and that is to evaluate the learning, which in this context means 'assess', 'test' or 'examine'.

Suppose you were in a class of students who were being taught to navigate by the stars. What would you need to give yourself confidence that you were sufficiently competent in navigation to let your life depend on your skills? After your programme of lessons you would want a realistic practical test of your skill. You would want to navigate from one place to another without help from the teacher, and you would want this performance evaluated by the teacher. If you managed on your own, and your teacher was happy with your performance, that would give you confidence in your learning.

If this evaluation takes place during a course, then remedial action can be taken where learning is not up to standard. This is a crucial aspect of the teaching process. Tests to evaluate learning can be structured in any number of ways; in very sensitive areas the students may not even know that their learning is being tested. A teacher of adult literacy may just give the student an unfamiliar piece of text to read, and evaluate the student's reading of it. A woodwork teacher may, after teaching the use of the plane, ask the students to make something and evaluate the planing on this.

Evaluation can be done surreptitiously, and it can be done with flags and trumpets; but it must be done, otherwise the teacher will not know if learning is taking place. Novice teachers are nearly always surprised by the results of evaluation; it is not easy to guess who is learning and who is not.

There is more on evaluation or assessment and how it helps learning in Chapters 43 and 44.

Queries: the student's need to ask questions

The last element in the *educare?* mnemonic is the question mark. When one is learning, one may want to ask questions at any stage during the learning process. It is important to realise that some students are too shy to ask questions in front of their classmates; the teacher needs to give such students the opportunity to ask questions in a one-to-one situation. This opportunity is often best provided during the 'use' phase of the learning process, where the teacher usually moves amongst the students, checking and answering individual queries.

Can you imagine being taught to clean a carburettor without being able to ask questions? One of the major difficulties for students studying on their own – for example, on correspondence courses or in 'open learning' – is that this questioning facility is absent much of the time. It is very frustrating to become 'stuck' and have no one there to help, or to be too frightened to ask for help.

Putting the elements together

If you feel sure that your lesson outlines for learning to clean carburettors and navigate by the stars are satisfactory, it is very likely that each of the *educare?* elements will be present in every lesson. They may not be in any specific order, and some may be combined in one activity, but they will all be there.

Shortage of time may mean reduced time for each need represented in the *educare?* mnemonic. But a need should never be missed out entirely, unless you are *sure* it has already been met. A carpenter who has to make a table in a hurry will not miss off one of the legs!

Making use of the *educare?* pattern

Learning can be said to fall into three broad categories or 'domains'. These domains were first suggested by B. S. Bloom and are now widely accepted; we look at them in more detail in Part 4. The three domains are:

* *The cognitive domain*: learning intellectual or thinking skills, e.g. how to add fractions, how to write a report, how to recall specific facts, how to use learning to solve problems or be creative.
* *The psychomotor domain*: learning practical skills, e.g. how to use a wood chisel, or how to do a somersault.
* *The affective domain*: developing values, feelings and attitudes, e.g. learning to value people who are elderly, or learning positive attitudes towards a particular subject.

The *educare?* mnemonic can be used to help choose activities to aid learning in any of these domains, as later chapters will make clear. For example, Chapter 23 will show that the ability to recall facts is a simple skill, learned by the corrected practice of recall.

Suppose your students needed to be able to recall a diagram of the structure of the heart, along with the names and the functions of its parts. This is a specific skill which, like all skills, can only be learned by corrected practice. The students' needs are:

* *Explanation*. They need to understand the events they are learning about.
* *Doing-detail*. They need to know exactly what you expect them to be able to recall, and in what detail. This is obvious to you, but not to them. If an aide-memoire is too detailed, then a revision summary could do this for them.
* *Use*. It is not enough to read the notes over and over, as many students believe. They must practise the skill of recall. This can be done with written and verbal questions, quizzes, tests, games such as 'tennis' (Chapter 19), and so on.
* *Check and correct*. Once students have drawn their diagram, their recall needs to be checked and corrected so that it can be improved. This is often done best by the learner.

The need for the other *educare?* elements is self-explanatory.

We intuitively use the *educare?* pattern when trying to learn by heart a poem or some lines in a play. We use a 'study–cover–recall–check' method. However, students very rarely use corrected practice of recall in order to learn factual material, unless they are *prompted* to do so.

Teaching a skill with *educare?*

Suppose you were teaching your students to solve quadratic equations, write a precis, or answer examination-style questions on a given topic. Choose any one of those three examples before reading on.

How would you start? Perhaps by demonstrating how to 'do one' on the board, explaining the process at the same time by thinking out loud. This provides some 'doing-detail', and the explanation. You may then ask the class to 'do one' collectively. You could use question and answer to step through an example, gradually writing the class's solution on the board as they decide upon it.

Students can then examine exemplar solutions in order to find 'deliberate mistakes', or to discover good practice. It is particularly useful to see a worked exemplar solution for a task one has just attempted oneself. If the task is complex, learners can draw up a checklist of criteria for success. All this provides 'doing detail'. The students are discovering exactly what they are expected to be able to do, and how to do it.

Once the skill is clear, the learners must of course 'do one' by themselves, and this work must be checked and corrected. The 'check and correct' phase will probably involve you, but students can also check their own or each other's work. Ideally, the correction itself should be done by the student. The need for an aide-memoire, and for review, evaluation and to be able to ask queries, is self-explanatory.

The suggestions on the last few pages are not meant to be in any way prescriptive. There is an infinity of ways of teaching or learning any intellectual or physical skill; but whatever methods are used, the learner's needs must be met if learning is to be successful.

Corrected practice without the *educare?* approach

Suppose a history teacher was about to teach a topic such as the reign of Henry V. It would not be sensible to split the topic up into specific skills and then teach them one by one! So in this case, the *educare?* mnemonic is less helpful. However, there is still no doubt that we learn best by doing, so how can this teacher devise activities for her lessons?

She could use a more indirect approach to arranging corrected practice, which is summarised by the diagram, and is considered in detail in Chapter 38.

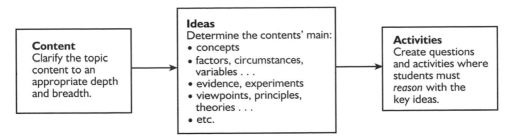

The 'CIA' process

The teacher starts her preparation by outlining the content her students must 'cover' in the topic she will teach. Then she considers the main 'ideas', such as the facts, concepts and principles which the students must become familiar with. However, there is more to teaching than the 'delivery' of such ideas and content.

Students will only learn this new material if they *make their own sense of it*, which requires that they process this information in their own way. If students answer questions, which require them to argue and think with the new material, this will effectively require them to make their own sense of it. This ensures that the material is better remembered and understood than it would be if it were only presented to the student.

Her students must *use* the material she has presented. For example, she might ask her students questions to be discussed in groups, such as, 'What does the reign of Henry V say about his character?' or 'What might have happened if Henry had lost at Agincourt?' Simpler questions could also be asked. Reasoning with the new material, and especially reasoning beyond the material immediately given, will also give her students corrected practice in historical reasoning. Reasoning skills can only be developed by 'doing', or more accurately by corrected practice.

Looking at the new material in terms of *Content – Ideas – Activities* can help to make your lessons more active and enjoyable, as well as more effective.

Summary

To learn a skill, students must know what they are expected to be able to do and how it is best done ('doing-detail'); they must know why it is best done that way, along with relevant background information (explanation). They must have had the opportunity to practise (use); and have had that practice checked and corrected. Our fallible memory means that learners need an aide-memoire and an opportunity to review previous learning. They need to have their learning evaluated, and they need to be able to ask questions.

Each of these needs can be met by a multitude of learning experiences or teaching methods. They can be provided together or separately, and in many different orders. We learn by doing. Even if you cannot see your material in terms of skills to be taught by use of the *educare?* elements, students still need corrected practice in reasoning with the material you are teaching. (There is much more detail on this and related matters later in this book, in Parts 2 and 4 especially.)

Exercise

Have a look at the two lesson summaries below. They were both done by trainee teachers before they were taught how to plan a lesson. Look for the learner's needs in the educare? mnemonic, and see if you can identify which ones are missing. Don't worry if you don't understand the content of the lessons; you should still be able to criticise the learning activities that the teachers have chosen. If you can, re-plan the lessons.

Look very carefully at the objectives of the lessons before you start. The objective states the skill or ability that the students should learn in the lesson. It is this skill that requires the explanation, 'doing detail', corrected practice, etc. These lesson outlines are far from satisfactory; how would you improve them?

Lesson 1

Objective: Students should be able to choose indoor plants suitable for various environments in their own home.

1 Environmental factors that affect plants: humidity, temperature, light, etc.

2 Ferns and other plants that don't mind dark and cold conditions.

3 Plants that need a high humidity.

4 Plants that don't mind direct sunlight.

Lesson 2

Objectives: Students should be able to:

i. read a simple weather map.

ii. interpret it well enough to predict likely changes in the weather.

1 Description of the symbols used on the map. How temperatures and wind direction are shown on the map.

2 Description of high- and low-pressure regions and isobars.

3 Description of how to recognise cold and warm fronts.

4 Direction of movements of cold and warm fronts, and high- and low-pressure regions.

5 I will show how to predict weather changes over 24 hours on a selection of maps from recent newspapers.

Further reading

Bruner, J. S. (1966) *Towards a Theory of Instruction*, New York: W. W. Norton.

*Wilson, B. (1987) *Methods of Training*, Vols 1–4, London: HMSO.

4

Teaching is a two-way process

Here is a game to play. Two people sit back to back. The 'teacher' has a diagram of a structure which is to be drawn by the 'student'. The teacher tells the student how to draw the structure (without showing the student the diagram); however, one-way communication only is allowed. The teacher cannot look at the student's drawing, and the student cannot ask questions or even acknowledge any comment from the teacher.

This apparently simple task turns out to be extraordinarily difficult to complete successfully, and anyone watching is soon in fits of laughter. It is not long before the student misinterprets at least one of the teacher's instructions, and as a result later instructions are often impossible to carry out. The student becomes paralysed by indecision, and by the relentless flow of apparently nonsensical instruction.

The reaction of those playing the game is interesting. The 'teacher' may feel an overwhelming desire to check that instructions are being carried out properly. The 'student' is desperate to ask questions to clarify the instructions, or is itching to tell the 'teacher' to slow down.

It is evident from the game that the process of learning is doomed to failure unless:

* the student can question the teacher to resolve ambiguities or clarify difficulties
* the teacher is given some feedback about the student's understanding.

If teaching were a one-way process, we would learn perfectly satisfactorily from books and videos, and teachers would just be an unnecessary irritation.

The student communicating directly with the teacher, and the teacher checking the student's work, are both examples of 'feedback' for the teacher. Without this feedback the teacher cannot know whether or not understanding or learning has taken place.

Communication and learning requires that the following chain works perfectly:

what I mean → what I say → what they hear → what they understand

Rather like the game of Chinese whispers, the message can be corrupted at each arrow in the above chain. The message sent is not the message received, and what is taught is not what is learned! That is why feedback is so vital.

Learning is a hidden mental process over which the teacher has no *direct* control. Learners develop a personal understanding of the material studied, and the abilities to be acquired. This learning is an approximation; it will usually be incomplete and inaccurate in the first instance. During the teaching/learning process, the learners improve by correcting misconceptions and adding to their understanding, thus achieving an increasingly closer approximation to the ideal learning outcome. This process requires corrected practice, but it is not enough for the teacher to correct the student's work: learners must correct their own understanding. Learning is a private problem-solving process, the student's problem being to create a personal understanding of the skills and knowledge to be learned.

Communication blocks

Achieving the two-way flow of communication which learning requires is no easy matter. In practice, a number of barriers present themselves, preventing or inhibiting effective communication. Which barriers to learning are experienced will depend on the teaching situation, but some of the more common ones are considered below.

Level of work is inappropriate

It is crucial for motivation that the level of work is such that each student feels they have accomplished something of value in your lesson, and gets recognition for these accomplishments. Clearly this can only be achieved if the level of work is matched to the ability and previous attainment of each student, and if the speed of teaching matches the speed of learning. Easy to say, but not so easy to do!

Ask experienced teachers to guide you and, if at all possible, watch an experienced teacher working with the group you will teach, or a similar group. Look at the previous work of your potential students.

Jargon

It goes without saying that teachers should not use unexplained jargon, but again, this is not as easy as it sounds. For a nurse, 'path lab' does not seem like jargon; it is an expression she uses many times a day. The same is true of 'menu' for a computer user, and 'evaluate' for a maths teacher. Teachers must become aware of the special vocabulary they use, and explain it as they use it. Write such words or expressions on the board. Ideally, the first five or six uses of a new word or expression should be accompanied by an explanation. After this introductory period you can ask the occasional question to confirm that students understand the meaning of previously taught jargon: 'What happens in a path lab, Julie?'

Everybody knows what 'menu' means in its usual sense, but a computer user has a special meaning for the word. The words 'power' and 'energy' also have special, very specific meanings for a scientist. This is sometimes called 'hidden jargon'. Is there any in your subject area? If so, jot down all the jargon and teach it. (If there is a lot of jargon you could even produce a glossary.)

Vocabulary and other use of language

Teachers usually have a larger vocabulary than their students. A little informal research I carried out recently showed that above-average 17-year-old students with grade A to C in GCSE English did not understand the following words (among others):

> *facilitate, assign, rapport, define, analyse, spurious, unison, align, postpone, abrasion, credentials, divulge, deduce, effigy, euphemism, flagrant, futile, heathen*

The students were asked to either give a sentence in which these words were used correctly, or explain their meaning. The great majority were unable even to attempt either task for the words given above.

Similarly, teachers may tend to use more complex grammar than their students. Keep your language simple; don't try to impress with over-formal English – it may alienate students instead. Say 'go', not 'proceed'; 'shows', not 'indicates'.

Are you worried about your accent? Given time, your students will soon get used to it; but try to speak particularly slowly and clearly at first if your accent is strong.

Environmental factors

Is the teaching situation distracting or noisy? Is it the last lesson on Friday afternoon? You may need to consider such factors in your preparation and lesson planning. Students who are tired, hungry or thirsty will find learning difficult.

Fear of failure and low student expectations

Imagine you are:

- a school pupil who hates maths, just starting with a new maths teacher
- a woman returning to education, after 17 years bringing up children
- an adult who hated school, undergoing retraining to update computing skills
- a 50-year-old manager of a retail store, being sent to management classes by her new area manager.

How do you feel about your first few classes?

Not having experienced success in maths before, the school pupil will be expecting failure with his or her new teacher. The 'woman returner' will be afraid that she has forgotten how to learn. The adult who hated school will be expecting not to enjoy his new classes. The manager will be feeling resentful that she has been asked to go to classes, and will not be expecting to learn anything new.

In one way or another, many students expect their lessons to be unproductive, and as a result they have a negative or fearful approach to their classes. Such students may also lack motivation.

The cure for such difficulties is first to understand your students. What are their anxieties? What are their motives for attending your classes? Get to know your students by talking with them as a group or one to one; talk with individuals in private if necessary. Ask them questions about their motives, fears and anxieties; only by knowing their problems will you be able to find solutions. Developing a rapport with your students, and discovering how to motivate them, is considered in the next few chapters. The next chapter gives practical strategies.

'Unapproachable' teacher

We have seen in this chapter that 'students asking questions' is a vital part of the learning process; but students, especially shy ones, will not ask questions of an over-formal or forbidding teacher. How does a teacher become 'approachable'? This is not just a matter of personality and dedication; there are a number of techniques and skills that can help, as you will find in Chapters 7 and 8. Chapter 12 deals with the art of explaining.

During the first few sessions with a new class, try to discover what the learners' attitudes and expectations are. Ask each learner to jot down on paper what they hope to get out of their classes, and what they are most anxious about. Make the last question anonymous if you like. (In adult education, you could also ask why they enrolled on your course.)

You will find the replies most helpful in planning the course; the other students will also be interested in the answers.

Other challenges: mixed-ability 'differentiation' and dyslexia

Your students might be very varied in their prior learning, motivation, maturity, and in other respects. You need to teach in a way that accommodates these differences, which is called 'differentiation', and is summarised in Appendix 2.

You might also encounter students with specific learning difficulties such as dyslexia. This is considered in Chapter 7.

Checklist

❑ What barriers to communication do you expect to experience in your teaching?

❑ What jargon will you need to explain?

❑ Do you frequently see the work of your students to discover the extent of their learning?

❑ Are any of your students too shy to approach you with difficulties?

❑ Have you asked your students what they expect to find most difficult about learning what you are teaching them?

If your class is of 'mixed ability':

❑ Do you avoid too much class teaching – e.g. avoid 'chalk and talk'?

❑ Are some of the learning activities easy enough for successful completion by the least accomplished/knowledgeable learners?

❑ Are some of the learning activities demanding enough for the most accomplished/knowledgeable learners?

❑ Is a large enough proportion of the tasks you set open and adaptable to the learners' abilities?

❑ Do you make enough use of group work?

❑ Do all students achieve some success and get some reinforcement?

❑ Finally – and crucially – do you make use of mastery and developmental objectives? (See Chapter 37.)

Reference and further reading

Good, T. L. and Brophy, J. E. (2002) *Looking in Classrooms* (9th edition), New York: Allyn & Bacon.

Tomlinson, J. (1995) *Inclusive Learning* (The Tomlinson Report), Coventry: FEFC.

5

Motivation

You are a fly on the wall of a class of students in a school or further education college. They are on a course preparing them for nurse training. A teacher has just explained to the class that each student is to search in a pile of books to discover the symptoms, incubation periods and typical recovery times for six common childhood diseases. Katrina makes a dash for the pile of books, eager to find the best one to take back to her desk. Rachel remains seated, and slowly turns her head to stare out of the window.

Motivation is regarded by experienced and inexperienced teachers alike as a prerequisite for effective learning, and the greatest challenge that many teachers face is to make their students want to learn. If students do not want to learn, their learning efficiency will be so low that they may learn virtually nothing. If you know how to motivate students, you can hugely increase their learning rate.

Sandra teaches mathematics in a comprehensive school; she tells the following story, but it is such a common experience that you may well have heard a story very like it yourself. Sandra spent years trying to teach elementary arithmetic to Terry, a slow-learning pupil. She claimed very little success, and the boy left school without even a minimum qualification in mathematics. Two years later, Sandra came across Terry scoring for a darts team in a pub. They were playing '501', which involved Terry doing calculations such as $501 - (17 + 11 + [2 \times 19])$ in his head. Terry had no difficulty with this; he could complete such a calculation accurately in seconds. Sandra could barely keep up with him.

She asked him how he had learned to do in his head, in two years, what he was unable to learn how to do on paper in five years. He replied that if he had not been able to score, he would not have been allowed in the darts team; he loved playing darts, 'So I had to learn it, didn't I?'

How can we make a student want to learn? Let's start by looking at the most common reasons that students have for wanting to learn.

The reasons for wanting to learn

1 What I am learning is useful to me

Some students want to be able to swim like their friends, or to be able to speak French on holiday, or to be able to do their own car maintenance; but we have to recognise the fact that most school and college learning has little everyday application for most learners.

2 The qualification for which I am studying is useful to me

Some students want qualifications for a career, or for progression to another course or college. This is a long-term aim for some students, but it is not the main, day-to-day, short-term motivator, even for the relatively few students who know 'what they want to do'.

3 I find I usually make a success of my learning, and this success increases my self-belief as a learner

This is the main motivator for most students (even the not very motivated ones). We all have our self-esteem raised by learning successfully; it gives us a sense of achievement. This is why students are sometimes competitive about their learning, showing at least as much interest in their fellow students' marks as their own. They enjoy challenges for a similar reason – it's fun to succeed. Do you remain motivated in the face of persistent failure? When you set a student a task you provide them with a target. Consider the following cycle:

Target → success → reinforcement → new target → (etc.)

The faster this cycle acts, the more motivating it becomes. The addictive nature of video and computer games is thought to be due to the immediacy of the success and reinforcement they provide. If players learned their score (and which planes they had 'shot down') a week after the game, then the games would not be so popular! Yet students often wait weeks for marked work. Can you make the reinforcement that students get from success more immediate?

4 I will get the acceptance of my teacher, and/or my peers, if I learn effectively

This is also linked with self-esteem. Even if a student does not enjoy learning, he or she will often try to 'keep up' with the rest of the class for the sake of being accepted by the teacher, and/or by other class and family members. Few people enjoy being the class dunce. However, some students gain credence from their peers by rejecting learning and the values associated with it.

5 I expect the consequences of not learning will be unpleasant (and fairly immediate)

'If I fail next week's test, Mr Jones will be furious and I'll have to do extra work.'
'My mother will kill me if I get a bad report.'

6 What I am learning is interesting and appeals to my curiosity

Learning can satisfy the natural curiosity we feel about many subjects, and even appeal to our sense of wonder about the world.

7 I find that the learning activities are fun

Even if we have no great interest in the subject of our studies, we can enjoy the activities the teacher has prepared. They may be novel, light-hearted, fun, or involve us in self-expression or creativity.

> *In October 1992 a Canadian prisoner smashed up his cell, because he wanted to finish a three-month cookery course but was about to be released. He was sentenced to two more years and finished the course!*

Motivators can be long- or short-term. In my list above, no. 1 and no. 2 are long-term, while the others are usually short-term. On the whole, the short-term motivators are more powerful, especially for younger learners. An adult is happy to plant an oak tree, but 16-year-olds get impatient waiting for mustard and cress!

Increasing motivation

Let us examine the seven motivators in turn, to find ways of increasing our students' desire to learn.

1 What I am learning is useful to me

Most teachers do not teach a subject which their students see as being of direct use to them. However, if you are teaching bricklaying to someone who wants to build a garden wall, or astronomy to someone dying to use their new astronomical telescope, your motivation problems will simply evaporate. We need, then, to try to make connections to students' interests.

'What's the point?'

2 The qualification for which I am studying is useful to me

It is generally recognised that schools in areas of high unemployment have a great deal of trouble motivating their pupils. Young people often do not see the point of working for qualifications that they believe will be of no use to them when they leave school. Without a long-term goal for their studies, students become demotivated.

To avoid this demotivating effect, which can occur in most learning situations, it is important that teachers underline the purposes of learning what they are teaching. Preferably, these purposes should be both long-term and short-term. For example, consider students studying surveying on a building course. They should understand the *long-term point* that it is not just surveyors who need to understand surveying; everyone in the building trade should be able to understand a surveyor's plans. Students also need to be clear about the long-term advantages of the qualifications for which they are studying, in terms of career opportunities, etc.

The surveyor students should also be told of the *short-term point* of, for example, studying gradients. They need to be told that you will never understand drainage systems without understanding gradients; and that there is a test on gradients in two weeks, there is always a question in the final exam on gradients, and so on. It may be very clear to the *teacher* why gradients are being taught, but the importance of the topic must also be made clear to the students.

A long-term motivator can become a strong short-term motivator if coursework forms part of the assessment for a course. Students will work much harder on a project if the mark contributes to their final grade.

To be convinced of the purpose of learning, students must look at the world outside their college or school. Work experience, trips, visits and visitors can all help to make learning seem relevant and purposeful. Students need frequent reminders of the short-term and the long-term point of studying what you are offering them. You need to 'sell' what you are teaching.

The carrot

3 I find I usually make a success of my learning, and this success increases my self-esteem

This motivator is the most powerful. It is dominant even when the other motivators are involved. It is the engine that drives the learning process. But it can work both ways.

It's 'human nature' to enjoy doing something you are good at – and *not* to enjoy something you are bad at. If someone produces five wonderful meals the first few times they try, they believe in their ability, they find cookery fun, and before you know it they are trying more and more advanced recipes. Their self-belief gives them the persistence and determination that success requires, and will give them the confidence to shrug off the occasional failure. Nothing succeeds like success.

By contrast, someone whose first attempts at cooking have involved burnt saucepans and consistently inedible meals will tend to avoid cooking if at all possible. Should starvation drive them to the kitchen, they will open the recipe book with trepidation. And, expecting failure, they will usually find it: their lack of persistence, effort and determination will ensure that they will be easily defeated by minor difficulties. In the end they simply say, 'I can't cook'.

In the same way, if a student completed the work in your last lesson satisfactorily, and was given some praise or recognition for this, success will make them approach your next lesson more positively. If they are usually successful in their learning, they will develop a positive belief in their ability to learn in your classes. Beliefs are permissions to switch on our capabilities. They have a way of making themselves true. There is a saying: 'Whether you believe you *can* or you *can't* do something – you're *right!*'

The vicious and the virtuous circle

Success breeds success, by a virtuous circle, as shown in the diagram overleaf. As a result, the effects of success and reinforcement are much greater than many teachers realise.

The learning engine

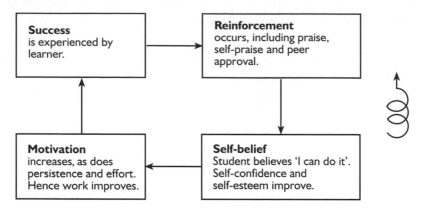

This is the engine that drives all learning. Even if the other motivators are working flat out, failure to get this engine going will mean that the learner is going nowhere. However, engines can work in reverse, producing a vicious circle:

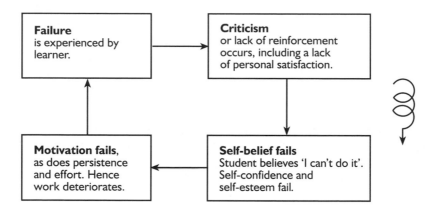

Many students will fall into this vicious circle because of an absence of praise or other reinforcement. Few of us would persist in the face of consistent failure. Praise or reinforcement earned by success is the engine that drives the learning process. The lesson for teachers is:

- Make sure students know exactly what they are expected to do and how to do it, and that help is available when they need it.
- Some tasks must be straightforward, and quickly achievable with sufficient corrected practice so that all students experience success in them. Other tasks can stretch the more able.
- Give lots of praise and other forms of recognition for any success in learning, and give this regularly for routine success, e.g. for finishing a task more or less successfully. This reinforcement should come as quickly as possible after the completion of the activity.

The above three points are crucial to motivation in most teaching situations. They need very careful consideration indeed. Beware the trap of feeling satisfied if you provide success for *most* of your students; success should be routine for *all* of your students, or some will lose the self-belief that makes learning possible. Those who learn are those who believe in themselves. Those who believe in themselves are those who experience success.

But can weak students experience success and reinforcement? Yes! We will see how this can be achieved in the next chapter and in Chapter 33. The chances of success are increased greatly if at least some of the learning tasks are specific, and carefully defined so that the learner and the teacher know when they are met. And the tasks need to be designed in such a way that corrected practice leads to success and reinforcement for all students. For much routine learning, success is a matter of time and effort, not ability. Mastery objectives, as described in Chapter 37 on aims and objectives, are helpful to teachers here.

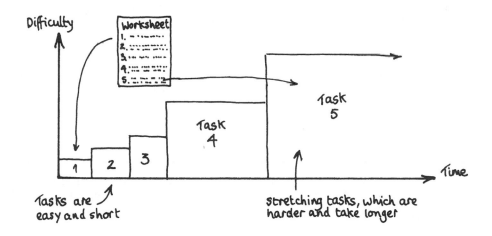

Your students must see the tasks you set as being both achievable and substantial. This is a difficult balance to strike, and varies from individual to individual. You must think carefully about the standards you set. Students will not value reinforcement or gain a sense of self-belief by completing tasks they see as trivial. Nor will they learn from them.

Most novice teachers set tasks that are too difficult. Try to observe the students you will teach, look at their work and talk to their regular teachers. Remember, it is the students' perceptions of the difficulty of the tasks which count – not yours.

Often it is worthwhile to set personal targets for your students, which must of course be reinforced when they are met. For example, if a student's essays are rather short, you might discuss with them how this might be improved – then set a personal target to make the next essay, say, at least two sides long. When personal targets are achieved there should be plenty of recognition and praise. Targets help to make students involved and responsible for their own learning.

> *'The ultimate goal of the educational system is to shift to the individual the burden of pursuing his own education.'*
>
> *J. W. Gardener*

You may remember that pupils in the 'bottom' form at school were not keen on doing schoolwork, whilst students in the 'top' form were on the whole harder-working – and even did their homework! Students who have been successful at learning in the past are always the most motivated students. Imagine a message permanently tattooed on the forehead of your students: 'Please give me regular success and reinforcement'!

Working for the teacher

4 I will get the acceptance of my teacher, and/or my peers, if I learn effectively

Michael Argyle in *The Psychology of Interpersonal Behaviour* points out that 'some students may be motivated by a need to be approved by the teacher'. This is more likely to occur if the teacher has a good relationship with the student; we will look at this further in Chapters 7 and 8.

Students also want approval from their peers, or at least enjoy being successful in measuring themselves against their peers. This is why competitions or challenges can often produce strong motivation in a class of students, even in fairly trivial games. Competition does need to be treated with care, however, or the gain in motivation and self-esteem of the 'winners' may be more than offset by the drop in motivation and self-esteem of the 'losers'.

Another problem with competitiveness is that some students delight in pointing out errors made by their peers, often ridiculing each other without mercy. This can be a measure of their own anxiety about being unsuccessful in learning, and perhaps for this reason it is more characteristic of poor learners than of effective ones. Teachers must not allow this behaviour to develop, as it produces a negative self-image in the criticised students. We need to develop a 'can do' attitude to learning in our students. It goes without saying that a teacher should never ridicule, even in fun, a student or a student's work.

The stick

5 I expect the consequences of not learning will be unpleasant (and fairly immediate)

When I was at school I hated learning French vocabulary, but not as much as I feared Miss Browning. I was fully aware of what she would do to me if I failed to learn this week's 10 words – so I learned them!

I have already mentioned how important checks and tests are in ensuring that learning really has taken place; however, they are also very important as motivators.

I am not, of course, suggesting that you should terrify your students into learning by threat, but do not underestimate the motivating effect of an anticipated test. Even if all the students claim they have not revised for it (which is unlikely to be true), the very fact that you test regularly will encourage them to try to learn in your lessons. Failing a test can motivate, but only if learners believe in their own ability to succeed eventually. Persistent failure is a huge demotivator.

Deadlines are good motivators, but you must be consistent in your management of them.

Increasing student interest

I will deal with how to use the sixth and seventh motivators together.

6 What I am learning is interesting and appeals to my curiosity

7 I find that the learning activities are fun

It is an obvious enough point that students will be motivated if learning is interesting, appeals to their curiosity, or is fun. But how do we make learning like this? Some teachers seem to have a natural talent for making learning enjoyable, but most of us have to learn.

Some years ago I paid a visit to a trainee teacher on teaching practice. I spoke first to the teacher who normally took the class; he said they were a 'difficult' class of 16-year-old students who were studying basic numeracy. Apparently they found this work boring and were poorly motivated.

I came into the classroom after the class had started, and made my way to the back. None of the students paid me much attention; they were working furiously from handouts. Every now and then a student would finish his work, rush over to a classmate to compare answers, and then rush back to his desk. The student teacher was besieged by requests for help from students who were genuinely impatient to succeed in their sums. I looked at the student teacher's lesson plan. At the top was the title for the lesson: 'Percentages'. These students had been taught percentages every year since their first year at school. By rights they ought to have been bored to tears in this lesson.

What was it that motivated the students so much? It was not, as I had first suspected, a challenge or a competition – it was student relevance. The trainee teacher had used data she had collected on football league results, to prepare a handout on 'analysis of team performance'. This was thinly disguised practice on percentages. Each student worked out, in terms of percentages, how often their favourite team won, drew or lost; how often they scored one, two and three goals; and so on. They were fascinated by what they were doing, and enjoyed comparing their figures with those of their classmates. The basic principle is simple here: students, like most people, find something more interesting if it relates directly to their own lives or to their own enthusiasms. The idea is to aim for student relevance in preparing work for them.

Some ways of increasing student interest

- Show interest yourself – be enthusiastic.
- Focus on curiosity-inducing questions rather than delivery of facts.
- Show the relevance of what you are teaching to the real world. Bring in real objects, show videos of applications, go on visits, have visitors, etc.
- Make use of student creativity and self-expression.
- Make sure students are active.
- Change the students' activity regularly.
- Make use of surprises and novel activities.
- Use group competitions and challenges.
- Make the learning directly relevant to the students' lives.
- Give the subject human interest.

In the USA about 10% of adults are classified as functionally illiterate – defined as being unable to decipher a road sign – and 20% of 12-year-olds cannot find their country on a map. Failure to learn is often due to a teacher's failure to motivate.

Try to get into the habit of thinking in terms of student relevance. Give examples that relate to the student's own experiences. Don't ask, 'Why does dilation of the blood vessels cause reddening?' Ask 'Why does your face redden after heavy exercise, or when you are embarrassed?' If you are a science teacher teaching power, don't just do an experiment to measure the power output of an electric motor; get the students to measure their own power output by running up stairs or doing press-ups. If you are teaching geology, talk about the geology of the locality; ask students where they have found fossils or quarries. If you are teaching about muscles and tendons, talk about the sports injuries of the students themselves and of famous sportsmen and women. If something on the TV last night related to what you are teaching, ask students if they saw it – get them to talk about it. Try to make what you are teaching relate to the students' own lives; controversial, ethical or personal topics are particularly motivating. This is not always easy, but when you are successful it will be very well rewarded.

Human interest – or the case study

An important but subtle method for making a topic more interesting is to attack it from the 'human interest' angle; newspaper editors and TV producers do this; so can we.

Any general principle, academic idea, etc., will be made more interesting if seen from the point of view of the individuals it affects. Suppose a TV producer was going to do a programme on the symptoms and treatment of mental disease. An amateur producer might attack this topic by asking psychiatrists, doctors and nurses to explain the subject matter directly. If you were teaching the same topic you might do that too. But a professional producer is trained to attack the topic from the human-interest angle. They would find a 'typical' patient for each disease or condition, and would interview them on screen to discover their case history, treatment, etc.

The trick is to see the phenomenon *in terms of its impact on individuals*. Compare quality newspapers with the tabloid newspapers; compare academic and popular non-fiction. The professionals in the media know the power of human interest. But teachers are professional communicators too. 'Ah,' I hear you say, 'but it's not possible to teach my subject from the human-interest angle. I teach physics, catering, law or typing ...'

But a law teacher who intends covering the procedure of arrest, trial and punishment is not obliged to teach it only from a general point of view. Human interest is provided when the students see a topic from *one* person's point of view, rather than in generalities. So why not pick on one person, perhaps a famous person recently caught speeding, and follow their arrest, trial and punishment through the newspapers, introducing the general principles through this particular example?

If you teach catering, you can tell stories about mistakes and disasters you personally have made, or heard of others making (students love these!), using them to underline the principles you are teaching. If you are teaching hygiene, cut out newspaper articles on food poisoning, get a video of an environmental health officer relating bad practice that he has discovered ...

The limits of the use of human interest are not the subject, but your imagination. Keep an eye on the newspapers, collect anecdotes, try to see your subject from the point of view of the people who practise it – or who are affected or described by it.

Case studies not only make the topic more interesting, they also illuminate general principles very effectively. As we will see later, students learn abstract or general ideas best by examining concrete examples.

Puzzles and controversies

The puzzle is the classic thriller writer's technique for maintaining reader interest. Why was the timid vicar's daughter riding her bicycle at midnight with a revolver in her saddlebag? I must read on! The technique is to present a paradox at the beginning of a chapter, but not give the answer until the end of the chapter, by which time we are given another paradox, and so on.

Teachers can do this too. If you can structure your teaching around puzzling questions rather than around the delivery of facts, this generates curiosity and an intrinsic interest in your subject. For example, a good science teacher does not simply tell students that some materials absorb moisture from the atmosphere and that glycerine is an example. It is better to use a puzzle:

Last week this glycerine weighed 104 g, but now it weighs more! 143 g. Where has the extra mass come from? Any ideas? Also, how could we discover whether our ideas are right?

A good English literature teacher does not just read Act I of *Romeo and Juliet*, but again, uses a puzzle:

Shakespeare wanted to convey that Romeo's love for Juliet was as deep as it possibly could be. So, how does he portray Romeo before he meets Juliet? Does he show him unhappy with another lover, or unhappy because he has no lover at all? No, Shakespeare is far too clever for that! Let's see what he does by reading Act I.

Exercise

How would you teach the following topics, making them interesting by the use of human interest, student relevance, curiosity, etc.? The answer to the first is in a box at the end of the chapter.

1 How to fill out forms
2 The idea that the correct fuse (5A or 13A) should be fitted in the three-pin plug of an appliance to help to protect us from electric shock
3 The paperwork involved with the process of admission, monitoring and discharge of patients in a surgical ward
4 The principle that the simpler a company logo, the more impact it has and the more easily it tends to be remembered
5 At least one topic from your own teaching subject

Learning answers questions. The 'subject' you teach exists to answer questions. But too many teachers give students the answers, without first asking the questions!

Exercise

Teachers often start new topics by asking puzzling questions. 'Why do some trees lose their leaves?' 'What causes unemployment?' 'What is *Romeo and Juliet* about?' 'Why do people use percentages?'

What are the questions in your subject? Choose a topic you are about to teach and frame the questions which that topic answers.

Maslow's hierarchy of needs

Maslow, a humanist psychologist, and one of the greatest thinkers of the twentieth century, has explained 'human nature' in one simple model. He suggested that there are universal, instinct-like needs, which every human being strives to satisfy. Almost all human activity can be seen in terms of these needs.

Maslow gives the needs a hierarchical order. Those needs at the *bottom* of the diagram overleaf are of greatest importance. A need towards the top would only be of importance to someone if the needs lower down were already largely satisfied. For example, a researcher observing a gang noticed that one of its members, who was a very good bowler, deliberately lowered the standard of his game when he played cricket with his gang. He didn't want to humiliate his friends by getting them all out first ball. His need for belonging was greater than his need to boost his self-esteem.

Although we are not fully aware of these needs, they are rather like mental vitamins; if we are denied them, we can never be fully mentally healthy. Maslow observed that if we feel deficient in any of these needs, then problematic behaviour, such as that described on the left of the diagram, often results. If the needs are met, mentally healthy behaviour results, as shown on the right of the diagram.

It is very important to realise that there are no substitutes for these needs, and only gratification of the need can prevent deficiency-type behaviours. For example, when I was a novice teacher I used to 'tell off' students who were attention-seeking or showing off. Then I was advised to give them more praise for attention to task, and give them conspicuous or responsible tasks to do in class in order to raise their self-esteem. I was surprised at this advice – but it worked!

If the two lower needs are largely met for your students, then you can harness Maslow's needs by making sure that:

- All students feel valued, accepted and included, at least by you the teacher; and that a group ethos is developed. There is also an opportunity for group work (belonging needs).
- All students experience success, and get praise and other reinforcement. There are opportunities for students to gain respect from you and other learners (esteem needs).
- Routine tasks sometimes make way for choice, creative work and other opportunities for students to express their individuality and explore their own interests. You foster curiosity and opportunities for students to think for themselves (self-actualisation needs).

Maslow showed that there is only one way of motivating your students. And that is to ensure that your students' belongingness, esteem and self-actualisation needs are nourished through the learning activities you devise. These are the only 'go buttons'.

Maslow's hierarchy of needs

If the need is *not* met the student feels . . .

The self-actualisation needs
- restless and bored, with a lack of zest for life
- life is meaningless, boring and without purpose
- a tendency to avoid growth and development
- listless

- fearful of criticism
- fearful of failure and of risks, e.g. fear of new situations or learning activities
- fearful, frustrated or angry toward those who withhold respect, e.g. a teacher, school or college
- envy and bitterness

Persistent thwarting leads to neurotic compensation, e.g.
- chronic showing off, attention-seeking, arrogance
- shyness and withdrawal

- lonely, rejected and rootless
- strong conformity to group norms
- dislike or hostility towards out-groups

Persistent thwarting leads to neurotic compensation, e.g.
- maladjustment and hostility
- or withdrawal

- anxiety, dread
- fight-and-flight behaviour

- craving for food, water, etc.

Needs

The self-actualisation needs
To make actual what one is potentially. Personal growth and development by following one's own passsions and interests. Self-expression, creative action, need to search for identity and meaning in life.

The esteem needs
Self-esteem: desire for achievement, strength and confidence; adequacy: to be able to cope by oneself.

Respect: desire for recognition, reputation, prestige, status and dignity.

The belongingness and love needs
The need to give and receive love and affection.
To belong, to have roots.

The safety needs
Freedom from pain and injury, security, stability, etc.

The physiological needs
Food, water, air, etc.

If the need *is* met the student feels . . .
- a desire to grow and develop in the direction of their higher values
- creative, positive and energetic
- unselfish desire to make a useful contribution
- curious and open to new experiences
- a desire to think for themselves
- a growing sence of identity

- self-confident, content
- self-belief and self-respect
- prepared to take risks and try something new, e.g. to learn
- cooperative, generous and kindly
- esteem needs lessen and higher needs take their place

- they can love themselves, and others
- they can trust friends and loved ones, and give them freedom
- these needs lessen and higher needs take their place

- physical security
- safety needs lessen and higher needs take their place

- no physiological craving
- these needs die away and higher needs take their place

> *Some teachers think motivation is an end in itself, but it benefits learning because it increases attention to the learning task, mental effort and perseverance in the face of difficulty. If a classroom is noisy and distracting, students may find it difficult to achieve attention, effort and perseverance, despite being motivated.*

Passive and active learners – learners taking responsibility for learning

We have seen that learning is not something done to students, but something students do to themselves. But many students, especially poor learners, seem genuinely to believe that in order to learn, all they need do is attend classes and carry out the activities more or less willingly. They then expect that learning will follow automatically. This 'passive learner' approach is described in more detail in the box overleaf.

Look carefully at the box describing active and passive learners. How can we make our students into 'active learners'? You must encourage your students to realise that they must teach themselves with your help (not sit back and expect to pick it up by osmosis!). It is often worth talking one-to-one with passive learners to encourage them to take more responsibility for their learning.

You can encourage your students to become active learners by:

- discussing the active and passive learning approaches with your students,
- encouraging students to assess their own work and their own learning
- asking students to set themselves targets
- asking searching and puzzling questions as part of your teaching
- avoiding the use of over-controlling 'recipe' style worksheets and activities
- getting students to make their own understandings by the use of the questioning teaching method (Chapter 14)
- getting students to think for themselves – for example, with group work, discussion and the guided discovery method (Chapters 18 and 29).

And perhaps most systematically by:

- independent learning, where students take full responsibility for learning small sections of the course (Chapter 33)
- mastery learning, where students must pass frequent tests or retests (Chapter 43)
- self-directed learning, where learners take control and responsibility by evaluating their own performance, and then striving to improve it to meet their own needs (Chapter 34)
- adopting the facilitating approach (Chapter 10).

Giving the problem to the student

You can encourage students to take responsibility for their learning by *giving the problem to the student*. Here is an example:

'How do you find doing your lab reports, Peter?'

'Oh. Alright I suppose.'

'What do you find most difficult about them?'

'The conclusion bit, Miss.'

'Yes, lots of people find conclusions hard. So what are you going to do to improve them?'

The technique is first to ask for *self-evaluation*. If the student does not volunteer a problem, then ask a *problem-finding question*, such as, 'What do you find most difficult?' Then, when you have found the problem, *give it to the student* by asking, 'What are you going to do about it?'

There are two types of learner:

Active learner	Passive learner

Learning is something I do to myself ...

So success or failure depends on me.

- *I* need to find the right resources.
- *I* need to check my understanding.
- *I* need to find my learning problems.
- *I* need to put these problems right.
- In short, *I* need to take control and responsibility.

... So if I don't learn ...

I need to try harder or change my learning strategy, e.g.:

- try another book
- ask a friend for help
- brush up my prior learning.

Either way, if I take full control and responsibility, I'm likely to succeed.

Mindset: *Empowered*

'I can make a difference.'
'Just try your best.'
Focused on:

- the *process*: 'What should I do next?'
- improvement (rather than perfection)
- the positive (avoids the negative).

adaptive, responsive, self-believing

Learning is something done to me by experts ...

So success or failure depends on factors beyond my control:

- how good the teacher is
- the resources
- my intelligence
- my talent for the subject
- etc.

... So if I don't learn ...

either:

- the teacher is at fault
- the resources are at fault, or, more likely
- I'm stupid.

Either way, the only rational course is to give up!

Mindset: *Disempowered*

'It's all out of my control.'
'I won't succeed, so I'm giving up.'
Focused on:

- likely negative *outcomes*
- the impossibility of getting it perfect
- the negative.

defeatist, fatalistic, despairing

Perhaps it is your attitude and approach that is most crucial. You must see yourself as a learning facilitator or learning manager, and encourage students to *take responsibility for their own learning*. This shows respect for the learner, and develops their self-belief, autonomy and resourcefulness. Conversely, if the teacher always takes responsibility, this can develop the students' feelings of dependency and helplessness, and encourage them to avoid the blame for their own poor learning.

Students can be given at least *some* control over their learning on *every* course, as Chapter 41 on course organisation shows. How this 'facilitating', 'self-directed' approach can be implemented is considered in more detail in Chapters 10, 34 and 41.

Adults will usually feel resentful and alienated if a teacher adopts a command-and-control approach. Many teenage learners feel the insult just as keenly, and can become very uncooperative. The teacher has at least as much to gain as the learner in giving the learner some control.

> *Professor Carol Dweck has discovered that about half of learners at every educational level believe their ability is fixed. The other half believe ability can be increased by learning. Students who believe it is fixed tend to give up in the face of a difficulty, but those who believe it can be increased by learning tend to increase their efforts in the face of a challenge.*
>
> *See the motivation page of www.geoffpetty.com for more details.*

Carl Rogers, in *Freedom to Learn*, quotes research showing that in only 1 per cent of their activities are school pupils given some choice.

How much choice, control and freedom (e.g. creative work) are students usually given in *your* subject?

To what extent can students meet their self-actualisation needs through the teaching of your subject?

The expectancy–value theory of motivation

According to the 'expectancy–value theory' of motivation, a learner's motivation is given by the following formula:

Motivation		Expectancy The extent to which the learner *expects* success in the learning		Value The value of the learning to the learner
	=		×	

In this formula, value and expectancy of success are multiplied by each other, not added together (Feather 1982). This means that if students give their course an 'expectancy' score of zero, then motivation is zero however large the 'value' score. Similarly, motivation is zero if they score 'value' as zero, however high their 'expectancy' score.

How would your students score value and expectations of success? Why not ask them? Get them to score both value and expectation of success on a scale of zero to 10, 10 being the maximum score. If you then multiply the value and expectations marks you will get their motivation expressed as a percentage.

Low 'value' score?

Some learners come from families or cultures that do not value education. If no one in a learner's family got a job or some other advantage out of education, then that family may not value education for their children. We need to 'sell' the value of our courses to our students.

Low 'expectancy' score?

Talk to students about students in past years who have gone on to be successful, or, better still, get these past students to come to the class and to talk to them. Stress that the achievement of these role models was not exceptional when they arrived, but was due to effort.

Also, make sure that tasks allow students to gain early success by using a mixture of mastery and developmental tasks for students. Stress that their success came from their efforts, not innate ability (see Chapters 6 and 43).

You may even be able to arrange for the students to gain an intermediary qualification very early on in their course. This could be a nationally accepted qualification such as a first-aid certificate, or it could be a school or college certificate.

Demotivators

Earlier in the chapter it was pointed out that some factors tend to demotivate students. Emotional factors such as depression or anxiety due to previous failure can demotivate. So can environmental and physiological factors such as cold, noise, hunger, etc. It is also possible to be too motivated! If students are anxious about examinations, for example, they can overwork and tire themselves, or become so anxious that their efficiency falls.

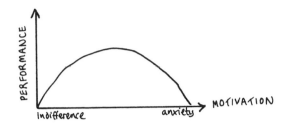

Checklist

Here is a checklist of factors which increase motivation. There is some overlap between them, but they summarise most of the ideas mentioned in this chapter. You can use it during lesson planning or as an aid to troubleshooting. Students will come to your class with some motivation; how you manage in terms of the factors mentioned below will decide whether you increase or decrease this initial motivation. Try to get as many of these factors working as possible.

Success

❏ Is the work you set at the right level and speed for your students?

❏ Do you set tasks of varied difficulty, so that every student can experience some success, yet more able students are challenged?

❏ If students' work is not up to standard, do you allow them to rework it until it is? (Do you then praise or otherwise reinforce their completion of the task?)

Purpose

❏ Do the students understand the personal advantage they will gain from studying what you are teaching?

❏ Do students appreciate the relevance of what they are studying to the world of work?

❏ Do you actively 'sell' your subject, and the topics you cover within it?

❏ Do you negotiate at least some of the content with students so they learn what they want to learn? (Chapters 34 and 41)

Enjoyment

❏ Are your lessons varied?

❏ Do your lessons involve plenty of engaging student activity?

❏ Are the student activities you use often fun, e.g. discussion, group work, games, competitions, challenges?

❏ Do you make use of student relevance and human interest?

❏ Do you excite curiosity by basing your teaching on interesting questions?

❏ Is there an opportunity for students to show creativity or self-expression – for example, in problem-solving or design activities?

❏ Are you enthusiastic in your teaching?

❏ Are students allowed some choice in what they study?

❏ Do you have a good rapport with your students?

❏ Are there opportunities for students to work collaboratively (social needs)?

Reinforcement

❏ Do your students get frequent reinforcement, e.g. marks, comments, praise?

❏ Does your reinforcement or recognition of success come as quickly as possible after the student has completed the work?

❏ Are there opportunities for students to satisfy esteem needs (making presentations, exhibiting work, marks or achieved competences, or other evidence for success)?

Targets

❏ Are the standards you set seen as worth achieving by your students, as well as being achievable by them?

❏ Do you test regularly, and set well-managed deadlines for students' work?

❏ Are the consequences of not learning unpleasant enough to motivate?

❏ Do you set personal targets for learners, and praise them when they are met?

❏ Do you encourage students to take responsibility for their own learning?

❏ Can you encourage your more mature learners to negotiate their own learning needs, set their own targets, and monitor and assess their own learning?

The first letters of 'success', 'purpose', 'enjoyment', 'reinforcement' and 'targets' spell 'SPERT'. If you will excuse the spelling, these factors make your learners 'spert' on to greater achievement! Motivation is also affected by the student's attitude to you, and to learning; so try to encourage active learning and develop good rapport.

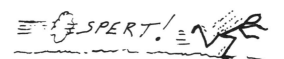

Exercises
Putting the theory into practice

The advice in this chapter expects a great deal of the teacher. It is often hard to motivate students in practice. Indeed, the consistently negative experience of education which some young people suffer gives many teachers an impossible brief. However, much can be done to galvanise the majority. Look at the following teaching situations, and try to formulate a strategy to increase the motivation of the students concerned. Go through the SPERT factors for each case, and consider Maslow's needs and ways of fostering active learning.

1 'I need to teach the stages of child development from birth to the early teens. How can I make that interesting?'

2 'I need to teach the role of the planning department in granting planning applications for new buildings. How can I motivate my students?'

3 'I teach some trainee electronic engineers who come to my college for off-the-job training. I take them for 'Communication', and I have been told to improve their basic writing skills, which are, on the whole, of a very poor standard. They all say they'll never get a job when their training scheme is over, "So what's the point of me bothering?" '

4 'I teach keep-fit in an adult education college. Most of the people who come have shown improvement over the weeks, but Joan, 65 years old, seems to think that she is too old to make any progress. I often wonder why she bothers to come, quite frankly. I admit it would take time, but she is perfectly capable of improving her suppleness and her stamina, both of which she complains about.'

5 'I teach people basic computer skills, mainly at their place of work. The main problem I have is with older people, who come to the classes with the idea that computers are impossible to understand for anybody over the age of 50. The depressing thing is that it turns out to be a self-fulfilling prophecy – they don't really try, so they end up being nowhere near as good as the younger people I teach. Then they say, "I told you so!" '

Answers

Possible answers for Question 1 on page 54

a Choosing a student in the class who needs to fill out a form – for example, a motorcycle insurance form – and talking over the completion of this form with the class (*human interest*).

b Each student could fill out a form that is of direct use or interest to him or her, e.g. an application for a provisional driving licence or an exam application form. A dating agency form would also be of interest to most students (*student relevance*).

c To encourage curiosity, the teacher could hand out incorrectly filled-out forms with non-obvious errors, and ask the students whether they can see the errors made (*paradox or puzzle*).

References and further reading

Argyle, M. (1994) *The Psychology of Interpersonal Behaviour*, Harmondsworth: Penguin.

*Dweck, C. S. (2000) *Self-Theories: Their Role in Motivation, Personality, and Development*. Philadelphia: Psychology Press.

Feather, N. (ed.) (1982) *Expectations and Actions*, Hillsdale, NJ: Erlbaum.

Good, T. L. and Brophy, J. E. (2002) *Looking in Classrooms* (9th edition), New York: Allyn & Bacon.

*Holt, J. (1995) *How Children Learn* (revised edition), Cambridge, MA: Da Capo Press.

Knowles, M. S. (1975) *Self-Directed Learning*, Cambridge University Press.

*Maslow, A. H. (1970) *Motivation and Personality* (3rd edition), New York: Harper Collins.

Petty, G (2006) *Evidence-Based Teaching*, Cheltenham: Nelson Thornes.

*Rogers, C. (1994) *Freedom to Learn* (3rd edition), New York: Merrill.

Any general book on teaching will deal with motivation; Capel *et al.* (2005) has a useful section (see the bibliography).

6

Praise and criticism

Let's try another thought experiment. A teacher training tutor, an experienced teacher, is going to observe every one of your next 30 lessons. Suppose you have just taught one of the first lessons to be observed, and you are packing away your things as the last student leaves the room. It is only the third or fourth lesson you have ever taught, so naturally you are relieved it is over and anxious to hear how you did. Assuming you have no reason to distrust the tutor's judgement, what would be the effect of the following responses on your confidence, motivation and work rate?

1   The tutor walks straight out of the classroom, saying nothing.

2   The tutor praises you effusively, even praising aspects of the lesson that you knew did not go well.

3   The tutor gives you a detailed analysis of each mistake you made, telling you how to put it right and implying that you should try to improve your performance.

4   The tutor praises some aspects of your lesson, but criticises other aspects, and explains what you need to do to improve, finishing off by saying that on the whole you had made a good effort.

5   You get a mixture of praise and criticism, as in 4, but overall the tutor implies that the lesson was rather mediocre.

If every one of your next lessons was received in the same way – that is, each got response 1, or each got response 2, etc. then:

A. How would you feel after 30 lessons?

B. How much would you have learned?

C. Is there anything else you would like in the feedback?

Nearly everyone feels quite strongly that they would be most motivated, and learn fastest, with a response similar in style to 4 above. It is encouraging in that it recognises success, but outlines ways of achieving a higher standard in the future. People often mention in answer to C that they would like an opportunity for self-assessment; hardly anyone asks for their lesson to be graded.

It is most unlikely that the students in your classes will differ from you in their emotional reactions to praise and criticism. They will hate being ignored; they will be encouraged by praise; and as long as their successes are recognised and praised, they will probably find any reasonable, constructive criticism challenging rather than demotivating. Research reviews confirm your gut instinct, as we will see later in Chapter 43 on formative assessment.

How can we make sure students take our criticism positively?

Experienced teachers can criticise a student's work in a way that sounds like advice. Read the examples below: can you see how the teacher does it?

1   *'That's great, your graph has well-chosen scales. Use a pencil, though, then you can rub out any mistakes. All the points look correctly plotted – well done!'*

Compare the above with: 'Don't use a pen to do graphs.'

2   *'That's a great opening sentence, it gets straight to the heart of the issue. Keep it in the future tense, Sheila – can you see where you slipped into the past tense? … Yes, that's it, well done.'*

Compare with: 'Don't mix your tenses up.'

The teacher is mixing praise and criticism, and is giving the criticism in a forward-looking and positive manner (rather than in a backward-looking and negative one). For example: 'Next time check the spelling', not 'There are lots of spelling mistakes here', and not 'Next time, don't make so many spelling mistakes', which is forward-looking, but negative. In the second example, the teacher is leading the student to correct her own mistakes.

In general, learners need:

A medal

Learners need information about what they have done well, and what is good about it. 'That's a great opening sentence, it gets straight to the heart of the issue.' Learners need to know what is right about their work, partly to encourage further effort, but mainly because they often cannot judge this for themselves with certainty.

Medals usually describe positive aspects of the work itself, 'the product'. However, they might also include praise for how the work was approached – for example, the student's planning and effort, the 'process'.

A mark, grade or other comparative comment is not a medal but a measurement, as it does not say what is right or wrong about the work.

A mission

The learner needs information about what needs improving, and how to improve it. This needs to be forward-looking and positive, so that it sounds more like advice than criticism and is easier on the ego. Also, it shows how to improve, not just what is wrong.

Missions close the gap between where students are, and where they are trying to go. That is, between their attainment to date and the goals.

Missions may include how to do a better job the next time the student does a similar piece of work. For example, a comment on an essay might say: 'Try to give more evidence and illustrations to support your points of view.'

However, a 'mission' might also say how to improve the existing piece of work – for example, in the case of a draft. 'Keep it in the future tense, Sheila.'

Clear goals

Medals and missions are related to the goals the student is working towards – for example, the task – and the criteria used to assess their work. Goals should be clarified before students attempt the task, of course. Chapter 43 on formative assessment looks at this in more detail.

If students don't know where they are going, they are hardly likely to arrive! So teachers need to clarify the words they use to set tasks.

Similarly, it is good practice to give learners 'assessment criteria' which tell them what they must do for a good mark or grade. But again, students often find these hard to understand. Come to that, so do many teachers! These need teaching, as explained in Chapter 43.

> *Learners have great difficulty understanding what they are aiming to do. I remember one student telling me with great authority that 'describe', 'analyse', 'criticise' and 'evaluate' all meant the same thing: 'write about'.*

It may seem odd to include goals here, especially as they are given in advance. But the medals are the goals the learner has achieved, and the missions are some goals they still need to work on. For this reason, firm 'goals' are linked to medals and missions.

You can't always include medals, missions and clear goals, especially in a short piece of verbal feedback. Don't worry about this, but make sure that over a period of time, and for any given student, you are not giving medals only, or missions only. However, do your very best to include medals, missions and goals for all substantial pieces of work, as explained in Chapter 43.

If you imagine that learning is like rolling a rock up a slope, then learners need their feedback to be referenced to where they are on the slope, not to where someone else is. That is, feedback needs to be non-judgemental.

Learners need medals for how far they have rolled their rock, and missions for how to roll it that bit further. In practice, research has shown that learners get judgemental feedback, which compares them to each other. Those who do better than most of their peers tend to get medals, but no missions. Learners who do worse than most of their peers tend to get missions, but no medals. In each case, learning is hampered. In some cases, students get neither a medal nor a mission, just a grade or percentage.

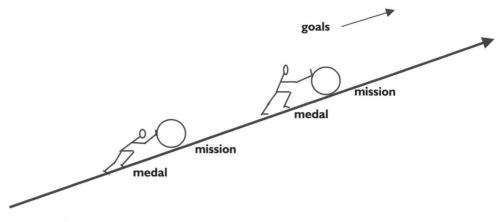

Medals, missions, goals

> *'God himself does not presume to judge a man till the end of his days.*
> *Why then should you or I?'*
>
> Ben Jonson

There is an exception to this rule, however. Students with learning difficulties, and other learners with very low attainment, are often given medals, but no missions. This is because teachers are so concerned to preserve learners' self-esteem with praise and encouragement, that they fail to show them how to improve, or to set them a challenging target. This is a grave mistake, as these learners find it hard to work out a target for themselves.

> *Some teachers suggest that unless you teach English you should correct*
> *grammar, punctuation, etc. in pencil rather than in red pen. The red pen*
> *should be reserved for subject content.*

How can we make sure every student earns a medal?

It is worth mentioning that even weak students can have their minor successes or improvements recognised. If weak students persistently get reaction 1 or 3 in the thought experiment at the beginning of this chapter they will eventually give up – so would you or I! In the previous chapter, on motivation, I mentioned the 'learning engine', which makes it clear that unless the learner experiences success followed by some form of reinforcement, learning will not take place.

If praise, self-praise or any other form of reinforcement is to be awarded, the learner must be at least partly successful in the tasks the teacher has set. Your opportunity to praise or reinforce learning will be maximised if you:

- *Set attainable goals.* Some, but not all, of the learning tasks you set should be attainable by every student in a matter of minutes, given sufficient time or corrected practice. This requires that the tasks be well defined, specific and not highly dependent on previous learning. These include lower-order skills on Bloom's taxonomy, such as recall, drawing and labelling diagrams, simple calculations and some simple intellectual skills – for example, explaining three advantages of terrace farming.

If students are exclusively assessed on their essay-writing or report-writing skills, then success will elude a substantial majority. Such skills take time to develop, are highly dependent on previous learning, and involve high-order cognitive skills. (See mastery and developmental objectives in Chapter 37.)

- *Break tasks down.* Difficult or protracted tasks should be broken down into manageable steps, which are practised and rewarded separately. Only when success is achieved on one step is the next step attempted.
- *Give learning time.* Time should be given for students to practise until mastery of the learning is achieved. Retests and resubmissions should be accepted so that the learners are eventually successful, even if they 'fail' at first. 'Relabel the diagram and show it to me again.'
- *Recognise partial success.* You should look for something positive in every piece of work; you will often find something right if you look very carefully!
- *Recognise the 'process' as well as the 'product'.* Comment positively on how they worked, as well as on what they did. Recognise effort, the strategy used, the time invested, thoroughness, asking for help, and so on.
- *Never restrict praise and recognition* only to those with motivation, aptitude or flair.

> *Two internationally renowned Professors at King's College London, Paul Black and Dylan Wiliam, carried out a review of the research on formative assessment which included how to praise and criticise students. They concluded that feedback on students' work probably has more effect on their achievement than any other single factor. Professor John Hattie has studied the variables that have the greatest effect on achievement; he comes to the same conclusion. See www.geoffpetty.com*

Positive reinforcement

Medals and missions look at feedback to learners from the point of view of the information they need to learn well. Behaviourist psychologists look at feedback from a slightly different point of view. They consider 'positive reinforcement', which is a positive consequence for learning that is likely to increase learning in the future. ('Reinforcement' is not repetition in order to improve learning, as some people think.)

There are many ways of encouraging a student's efforts to learn, as the box below shows; not all of these will work with all learners, of course. Remember that reinforcement should come as soon as possible, and should be experienced by every student.

FORMS OF POSITIVE REINFORCEMENT
Extrinsic (from outside the learner)

The teacher:

- giving attention to the student
- respecting the student as a person, and showing warmth
- listening with interest to a student
- accepting an idea from a student
- using a student's work as an exemplar
- showing interest in the student's work
- spending time with the student
- laughing at the student's jokes
- showing high regard for the student
- writing comments on written work
- giving smiles, eye contact, thumbs-up sign, etc.
- ticking in the margin in response to a good point made in an essay
- exhibiting a student's work on a noticeboard, for example
- giving a special privilege, or a 'merit mark'

Praise from peers, parents and others, including the teacher, of course! Passing a test or exam.

Something useful to take away from the lesson.

(Chapter 43 on formative assessment will show that grades and marks are not good positive reinforcers and can have the opposite effect.)

Intrinsic (from within the learner)

Students:

- studying a topic, or completing a task of interest to them
- satisfying their own curiosity
- discovering something for themselves
- being creative, being in control
- meeting a challenge (especially one set by themselves)
- ticking off competences or a task list
- feeling 'I can do it! – I got it right!' or the 'penny dropping' feeling
- achieving personal objectives, or completing a task they set themselves

---

Mastery learning techniques are excellent for reinforcing learning; they are dealt with in Chapter 43. Some students will see public praise as a slur on their anti-establishment image. However, I have yet to meet a student who will not accept praise privately!

Both reinforcement and criticism can be given informally by non-verbal means – for example, with facial expression, through tone of voice, by ignoring, by gestures.

Intrinsic reinforcement is a better motivator than extrinsic reinforcement, partly because it works when the teacher is not there. It is the glow of satisfaction we get when we feel we have done a job well: 'I've made a widget and it WORKS!' 'I can do FRACTIONS!' It is also the drive we feel when studying something which excites our curiosity or when doing something interesting or enjoyable. Creative activity, or any work where we can show our individuality, generates this intrinsic reinforcement.

Research consistently shows that even experienced teachers think they give positive reinforcement much more frequently than they actually do; and that increasing the rates of reinforcement dramatically improves the atmosphere and work rate in their classes.

From some written work by a 14-year-old boy:

'When I get a piece of work back and I think it is good, and I get a bad mark, I feel like frotling the teacher.'

One of the commonest faults of novice and poor teachers is that they are not positive enough. I've seen hundreds in their first few hours of teaching, and I've never seen one praise or recognise achievement too much. Suppose you start in September with a class of 20 students, whom you see once a week for an hour, and you make a positive comment once per lesson. At best, some students will have to wait until June for their turn! If you want every student to get a little recognition or praise every lesson, then on average you must make a positive comment at least once every two minutes. During student practice, some teachers can recognise success more than once a minute. It seems very odd doing this until you get used to it, but it has a dramatic effect on work rate and atmosphere in the class.

It is common for written comments on students' work to be almost exclusively critical. Your students' mistakes may leap from the page, but don't let their successes be taken for granted.

'Never underestimate the pleasure, satisfaction and educational value which pupils get from satisfactorily completing an action however simple.'

Michael Marland, *The Craft of the Classroom* (his emphasis)

President Lincoln wrote a damning letter to General Meade, criticising him severely for his failure to win a battle in the American Civil War. Lincoln's view was that many men had lost their lives because of Meade's mistake – certainly more than adequate justification for writing the letter.

And how did the General respond to the letter? He didn't, for it was never sent; it was found in President Lincoln's papers after his death. As Dale Carnegie writes in How to Win Friends and Influence People, *Lincoln had learned that severe criticism was almost never productive.*

Attainment and effort

Some students achieve a great deal without trying; others achieve very little despite Herculean efforts. Attainment should, of course, be recorded and acknowledged, but it is effort to achieve that should be rewarded. If you only praise achievement, you will discourage weak students and make the able lazy.

But do weak students deserve praise? The answer is an emphatic YES! Indeed, it is the weaker students who need and deserve it most; they have to battle with work they find difficult and daunting, without the advantage of natural flair or ability, and this struggle rarely brings the rewards of work well done. Also, they must suffer the indignity of watching capable students overtake them with little effort. If some of our students are attempting to scale Everest without oxygen or crampons, the least we can do is to nod politely in their direction from time to time!

> *'I began by thinking I was marking my students, but then I realised I was marking my teaching.'*
>
> A student teacher

Positive reinforcement improves behaviour too

Ideally, then, during every learning session there should be lots of medals and missions for every student in your teaching group. This is expecting a great deal, and not just because of shortage of time. Take snotty detestable little Darren, who smells of grease or worse, and who regularly emits sacrilegious expletives about how boring your classes are. When he finally stops his habit of kicking Sandra while staring vacantly out of the window, and actually puts pen to paper, you must step up to him and offer smiling encouragement. You will not be alone in finding this difficult. But if you can't do it, Darren will never improve; indeed, he will probably get worse, making your life even more difficult.

If you can encourage people like Darren, students of all kinds will come to respect you, and you will enjoy good relationships with your classes. You will also become a more effective teacher. But first you must get used to being pleasant and encouraging to people you fear or dislike. Strangely, if you manage this, you may soon find Darren is less fearsome and detestable than you thought. He may start to respect you, start to do more work and spend less time 'playing you up'.

What you will gain from recognising achievement

Research shows that reinforcement (e.g. medals, praise and other rewards) is one of the teacher's most powerful tools. Reinforcement substantially improves the following, and is usually the single most effective way of improving them:

* learning and attainment
* motivation
* behaviour
* concentration in class
* self-belief or self-efficacy – that is, students' belief in their own ability to improve, to develop and to overcome their own difficulties

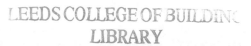

- self-esteem
- attitudes to learning and to your subject
- attitudes to the teacher.

Notice that there are substantial gains for the teacher as well as the student!

You can get students to give themselves feedback with self-, peer and spoof assessment, as in Chapter 43.

How to praise and reward for maximum effect

There have been many hundreds of research studies on 'reinforcement'. The messages from this research show a high level of agreement, but these messages are not easy to implement! It will take time, thought and practice to become a good practitioner in this respect. The most effective reinforcement should be:

Frequent!

Try to give every student at least some reinforcement every lesson. Put students who are a pain or whose progress is slow into 'intensive care' – not by beating them up! This is the teacher's intensive care, and means recognising their effort and achievement at least four times an hour, smiling, talking with them in a friendly manner, etc. Do this for a month, however difficult you find it (and you will find it difficult!), and see the results.

Perhaps you doubt whether you can find enough praiseworthy work to give as many 'medals' as I am suggesting? Don't forget to recognise everyday effort. 'You've finished a question – well done.' If you reserve praise for conspicuous merit, some students will never get any, and they will soon be tail-spinning into the vicious circle I described in the chapter on motivation.

Task-centred not ego-centred

Praise should be earned by, and focused on, the student's work, not on the student.

It should be earned for effort, completion of a task, achievement, the skill shown, an appropriate strategy used, etc.

It should not be given for just being there, or for just listening, say, unless these are achievements in themselves for that student.

Praise should not be ego-centred, such as 'You are very good at this', 'You are a very able student', 'I'm proud of you'. This is because ego-centred praise

- assumes that success is due to personal attributes rather than effective efforts to learn
- teaches students to interpret difficulties in terms of a lack of such personal attributes.

Exercise

Think back to the thought experiment at the beginning of this chapter. What would be the effect on your learning if the tutor graded your lesson, and you found that, compared to your colleagues on your teacher training course, your grade was almost always

a) in the top quarter of your class?

b) in the bottom quarter of your class?

Read Chapter 43 on formative assessment to see if research confirms your view!

Student-referenced

Students should be trying to beat their own record, not someone else's.

Specific

You should specify what the praise is for and indicate the value of the accomplishment. In other words, make it a medal rather than just praise. This is easier to do if it is focused on the task as described above. Saying what the praise is for has another benefit of ensuring that the praise is not seen as 'patronising':

> 'Well done, that's a good way of solving the problem.' Or just:
> 'That's a good way of solving that problem.'
> 'Correct' in response to a correct answer to a question.
> 'All the commas are in the right place, good.'
> 'You are really concentrating well now.'
> 'You've presented the data very clearly.'

Sincere

You should sound spontaneous, and as if you really mean it (even if you hate the wretch). Praise should not sound like a 'reflex action' or a habitual phrase just trotted out for no particular reason. It should not sound to the student as if you are using praise just as a means to control them.

Not easy, is it?

> *Some theorists argue that we should abandon praise entirely and concentrate on self-assessment, and on other medals, in part to increase intrinsic motivation. This may be particularly true for adult learners.*

Exercise

Work out your own policy on medals, missions and other forms of positive reinforcement.

How will you make sure that the points in the summary above and the check-list will be achieved in practice? You could do this after reading Chapter 43.

Do weak students deserve praise?

Checklist

Criticism

❏ Do you accept the student's standard, however high or low, and set about encouraging and improving it in stages, by medals, missions and other positive reinforcement?

❏ Is your criticism forward-looking and positive, and do you mix it with praise?

❏ Do you allow resubmission of unsatisfactory work?

❏ Do you ask your students to evaluate their own work and set themselves targets?

❏ Do you set the most able students the most challenging targets?

❏ Are your students kept informed of how their attainment compares with the needs of the course?

❏ Do you break tasks down into manageable steps, and reward their achievement?

❏ Do students set themselves targets for improvement?

Praise

❏ Do you set each student achievable goals so they all experience some success?

❏ Do you always acknowledge positively a correct answer given to a verbal question?

❏ Are you able to give plenty of medals? For example, can you praise effort, progress and the completion of routine tasks?

❏ Does every student receive some reinforcement and some constructive criticism?

Exercise

1 Ask a colleague to observe one of your lessons, and to count the number of times you reinforce a student. Ask them also to count the number of students who receive no reinforcement.

2 If all the students in a group are having trouble with something, many teachers would blame the group. Others would blame their own teaching. What do you think?

3 What are the relative values of ticks, marks and comments on written work?

4 What are your feelings about having your own work marked? Do you remember your feelings about being marked at school?

5 Can you explain the importance of both extrinsic and intrinsic reinforcement by reference to Maslow's ideas mentioned in the last chapter?

References and further reading

See also the references for Chapter 43.

*Dweck, C. S. (2000) *Self-Theories: Their Role in Motivation, Personality, and Development*. Philadelphia: Psychology Press.

*Good, T. L. and Brophy, J. E. (2002) *Looking in Classrooms* (9th edition), New York: Allyn & Bacon.

*Holt, J. (1967, revised 1983) *How Children Learn*, London: Penguin.

Wright, C. J. and Nuthall, G. (1970) 'The relationship between teacher behaviour and pupil achievement', *American Educational Research Journal*, 7: 477–91.

www.nwrel.org/scpd/sirs/2/cu3.html has a good research review on reinforcement.

7

The teacher–learner relationship and equal opportunities

First impressions

When you go for an interview, you put on your best clothes. Employers are affected by first impressions, but so are you as a teacher. Social psychologists believe that when we meet someone for the first time, we select information from what we perceive, and process it in an attempt to develop a rapid characterisation of that person. We do this because we want to know how to behave towards the person, and how we can expect them to behave towards us. It would of course be fairer to suspend judgement, but few of us manage this in practice.

Individuals differ in the information they use to form this initial characterisation. Typically, impressions are obtained from factors such as dress, hairstyle, facial expressions, posture, gestures, age, ethnic origins and gender, as well as what the person says or how they say it. Teachers may also be affected by a student's handwriting, friendship group, previous attainment, reputation, and so on.

Here are the test marks. All those with neat handwriting and new blazers: A. Everyone else: B. Except scruffy, gum-chewing personal stereo users: fail.

Once these characterisations are formed, they are used to make judgements about the thoughts, feelings, attitudes, goals and traits of the person concerned. The table on the next page shows a teacher's initial characterisations of two students, Samantha and Kevin, both in the same class.

These initial characterisations will of course influence the teacher's behaviour towards Kevin and Samantha.

Name	Teacher notices:	Teacher's personality theory leads him/her to surmise:
Samantha	She is quiet, polite, well-dressed, attractive and middle-class.	She will be interested in study, intelligent, hard-working and pleasant.
Kevin	He is large, ungainly, unfashionably dressed, communicative, with a strong rural accent and a loud voice.	He's 'thick', uninterested in study; working-class; likely to become a farm labourer; could be a troublemaker.

'It is perception not reality which is crucial in determining behaviour.'

Carl Rogers

First impressions stick

The problem with our first impressions, or 'initial characterisations', is that they are resistant to change: rationalisations preserve them from contradictory evidence. For example, Samantha in the table above has been seen as a committed student. Suppose she starts to smile in a lesson. The teacher might then think, 'She's enjoying my lesson. I knew she would be a good student.' If Kevin starts to smile, however, the teacher is likely to think, 'What mischief is he up to?' The same evidence is used to draw opposite conclusions, each confirming the initial characterisation.

If Samantha turns in a poor piece of work – well, 'She must be tired.' If Kevin hands in a good piece: 'Who did he copy?' If Samantha is short-tempered: 'Poor thing, she must be upset about something.' If Kevin is polite and pleasant: 'Why is he trying to butter me up?' I exaggerate for effect, but it is dangerous to believe one is above such rationalisations; I am certainly aware of having fallen prey to them.

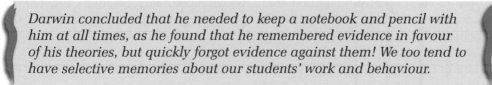

Darwin concluded that he needed to keep a notebook and pencil with him at all times, as he found that he remembered evidence in favour of his theories, but quickly forgot evidence against them! We too tend to have selective memories about our students' work and behaviour.

Both students will become aware of the teacher's appraisal of them. Samantha will get eye contact, smiles and friendliness – and Kevin will notice their absence. This, in turn, will affect the students' behaviour; they are both likely to behave more like the teacher's characterisations of them.

Stereotyping

We all have prejudices and stereotypes. Here are some of mine, though I probably have others I am not aware of. Students with good handwriting and neat presentation are conscientious, while those without are slapdash. Outgoing, communicative students are interested in my lessons; those who are quiet and reserved are not.

Stereotyping is the tendency to attribute, to an individual, traits that we assume are characteristics of the *group* to which we believe they belong. This of course tends to blind the perceiver to the differences between the members of a group. We all have stereotypes, but we rarely see them for what they are, because they are sometimes partially true, and as a result they fall easy prey to our rationalisations and our selective memory. Research shows that teachers, like the rest of the population, have their stereotypes: 'Students of Afro-Caribbean origin are not academically ambitious', 'Girls are no good at science', and so on. If we are honest, many people have stereotypes based on class, gender, ethnic origin, age, learning difficulty or disability. I am not alone in my handwriting stereotype either: research shows that well-presented written work gets disproportionately high marks compared to untidy written work.

The self-fulfilling prophecy

Likes, dislikes, prejudices and stereotyping would matter less if it were not for the effect of the teacher's expectations on a student's learning. Robert Rosenthal and Lenore Jacobson, in a celebrated book *Pygmalion in the Classroom* (1968), describe research in which they deliberately gave teachers false expectations of their pupils. They tested school pupils, and pretended to their teachers that they were able to identify pupils whose attainment was about to improve substantially. In reality, the names of the 'improvers' which were passed on to their teachers were chosen at random.

When the researchers returned a year later, objective tests showed that those reported as 'improvers' had indeed improved! The authors showed that the IQs of the 'improvers' had increased significantly in comparison with the IQs of 'non-improvers'. Thus the prophecy, despite having no basis in fact, was 'self-fulfilling'.

Rosenthal and Jacobson claimed, then, that a teacher's expectations affected the student's performance in the direction of that expectation. In other words, if a teacher thinks a student is 'good', they get better – and conversely, if the teacher thinks the student is 'bad', they get worse. Other researchers have shown the self-fulfilling prophecy at work in almost every conceivable teaching situation, from nursery teaching to the teaching of adult professionals.

Can a low expectation be fulfilled? Indeed it can. Research shows that slow learners are given less time and less help when answering questions; they get less praise and more criticism, less teacher time overall and a less friendly approach – for example, they are smiled at less often. Less work is demanded of them, and their test papers are marked more severely.

This self-fulfilling prophecy is not inevitable. A good teacher will need to make sure that low expectations of a poor student are not conveyed to that student. If they succeed in this, then the process will not occur.

> *'If men define situations as real, they are real in their consequences.'*
>
> W. I. Thomas

The self-fulfilling prophecy places a heavy responsibility on the teacher. It is not easy to share our time, encouragement, smiles and jokes equally. You may not feel like encouraging an ungrateful, morose individual with a funny hairstyle! Teachers of adults may find it difficult to give reinforcement to a student who thinks he 'knows it all'. Yet we have a professional duty to do our best by every student. Everybody needs a sense of dignity, purpose and self-worth. If you can help to provide this for your students, you will get the best out of them. If you don't provide it, you may get the worst.

As with stereotypes and prejudices, it is important for teachers to be aware of their likes and dislikes. What characteristics do you like in your students? Score these from 1 to 5; a 3 means you are indifferent.

Like very much – Dislike very much

	1	2	3	4	5
politeness					
interest in your lessons					
clear handwriting and neat presentation					
very fashionable clothes and hairstyle					
attractiveness and friendliness					
jolly, outgoing personality					
quietness and reservedness					
good personal hygiene					
a know-it-all student					
poor English (second-language speaker)					
students of the opposite sex					
students of your own sex					
students from a very different culture from your own					
students from a very different class from your own					

People like people who are similar to themselves – those who share their basic values and assumptions. Teachers are no exception; they like students who are hardworking, attentive, neat, polite and good-looking! Whatever your likes and dislikes, you should not show them unless there is a sound educational, ethical, vocational or safety reason for doing so. You may, for example, have sound reasons for requiring a student to improve the presentation of his or her work, but this does not give you reason to react towards that student with unreasonable dislike or irritation. Beware any fives or ones in your scores in the questionnaire above.

Rapport requires that you develop the respect of your students. You will achieve this by being professional about preparation, timekeeping, dress, and so on, and by showing that you respect your students as individuals.

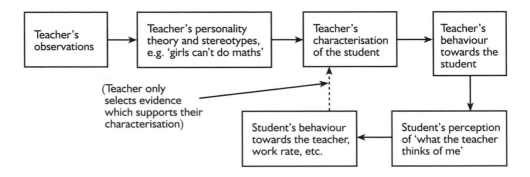

Working towards equal opportunities in the classroom

All students must feel that they are positively and equally valued and accepted, and that their efforts to learn are recognised, and judged without bias. It is not enough that they are tolerated. They must feel that they, and the groups to which they belong (e.g. ethnic, gender, social class or attainment groups) are fully and equally accepted and valued by you, and by the establishment in which you work. Translated into *studentese*, this reads: 'Teachers should be fair, with no teachers' pets, and no pet hates.'

Few teachers intend to give unequal opportunities, yet most do. For example, research has consistently shown that female students get less classroom attention than males, have less access to computers or other specialist equipment, and are marked down if they are very able; and that the offending teachers are unaware of such unequal treatment. Research has also continued to show that Afro-Caribbeans, Asians, other ethnic minority students, and learners with disabilities or learning difficulties also get an unfair deal in the classroom from most teachers. So do students who are shy, working-class, less able or disruptive.

Why is this? Few teachers are deliberately prejudiced; most of the discrimination is unintentional. For example, most of us behave most positively towards students who are able, pleasant or hardworking. This is understandable, but not professional.

Parents who pay their fair share of taxes expect a fair share of educational effort to be spent on their offspring. After all, refuse collectors empty everyone's bin, not just those of pleasant, good-looking, hardworking, intelligent white males! I, at least, have reason to be grateful for their fair-mindedness, and students deserve the same fairness from me – though I hesitate to claim success every time.

Many teachers assume that if they set the same learning activities for the whole class, and give help to anyone who asks for it, they will provide equal opportunities. This is not the case. Shy students need more help than they ask for, and the vociferous less. Every student deserves his or her fair share of your effort, but because students have different needs you will find that you must treat them differently.

Monitor carefully how you ask questions, use eye contact and smiling, crack jokes, give emotional support, and so on, to see whether you behave differently towards different students. It would be very surprising if you found you naturally behave in the same way towards everyone. I am aware, for example, that I tend to joke more with males; I give more eye contact and emotional support to females, especially the ones I like; and I tend to be more serious-minded in my support for students who are disabled. Also, I tend to give less attention to shy students than they need. But my awareness of these tendencies to discriminate at least helps me to compensate for them.

I try not to read the name of a student before I mark his or her work. (Research shows that female students tend to have good work marked down, and poor work marked up. Some universities ensure all marking is 'blind', by giving students code numbers to put on their work.) I also try to vary assessment methods so that no group is unfairly disadvantaged – for example, those with English as a second language.

The reasons for trying to achieve equal opportunities are essentially ethical and professional; we want all our learners to benefit from our teaching. But there are also legal and economic reasons: our economy will not thrive if barriers to opportunity prevent us from making the best of our human resources.

Gender

Research shows that many teachers have different expectations of males and females; that males generally receive more teacher attention; and that males dominate in the use of equipment in science, design, technology and computer studies. Also, males and females leave school or college with different skills and different expectations of their future lives; many females still set their sights lower than males. It is well known, too, that females are under-represented (especially post-16) in maths, physical sciences and technology.

Boys now do less well in GCSEs than do girls, perhaps because they have less-developed study skills, and a less mature attitude to study.

It is important not to be fatalistic about such barriers to opportunity. How can teachers prevent them, or minimise their effect?

Of course, one should be careful with careers advice; it is unlawful to give guidance on gender or racial grounds. But also:

- Avoid characterising your subject as a 'male' or 'female' one. Try to portray such gender assumptions as old-fashioned.
- Make a point of researching and mentioning the role of women and men in your subject area. Mention positive 'role models'.
- Avoid assumptions about traditional roles. For example, if one of your assignments mentions a fictional factory inspector by name, why not make the inspector female?
- If one of your class must operate a video or move a table, don't assume the helper will be male.
- Ensure that your wording in handouts and assignments is not sexist.
- Teach all students effective study skills and discuss attitudes to study.

Non-sexist writing for the teacher

Increasing numbers of women and men are irritated and offended by sexist language, so it is a matter of common courtesy to avoid it (even if you personally find this a trial). First, avoid obviously sexist assumptions in your material:

Not: The ancient Egyptians allowed women considerable control over property.
But: Women in ancient Egypt had considerable control over property.

Not: The prairie farmer was concerned about the price of his wheat.
But: Prairie farmers were concerned about the price of wheat.

Try, at appropriate moments, to work positive role models into your writing:

> *Question 2*: A bus driver has a reaction time of 0.2 seconds and is travelling at 50 km/hr. How far will she move before beginning to brake?

Most commentators feel that 'man' should now only be applied to males. If women are included, use 'people' or 'person(s)'. Here are some expressions which could be held to contain sexist assumptions, along with alternatives:

man in the street	average citizen
to man the office	to staff the office
man-made	synthetic
craftsman	craft worker
etc.	

Use 'woman' rather than 'girl' or 'lady'; avoid reference to 'the fair sex' – and of course any flirtatious behaviour, which offends many women deeply.

Avoiding the pronoun problem

Avoid using 'he' to mean 'he or she'. This is easier than it sounds; take, as an example, the following sentences:

> The student can then identify *his* learning needs if *he* wishes.
> A surveyor should always be insured, as *he* is vulnerable to legal claims.

One can of course use 'he or she', 'he/she', 'she/he', 's/he', and also 'his or her' or 'her or his'; but if, like me, you feel these are often clumsy, try one of the following:

Use plurals

'Students can then identify *their* learning needs if *they* wish.'

'Surveyors should always be insured, as *they* are vulnerable to legal claims.'

Misuse plurals

'A student can then identify *their* learning needs if *they* wish.'

This is ungrammatical as the sentence starts in the singular but then switches to the plural, but some people, including me, use it sometimes.

Address directly with 'you' or 'one'

'One can then address learning needs if one wishes.'

'As a surveyor, you should be insured, as you are vulnerable to legal claims.'

Rewrite to avoid gender altogether

'Learning needs can then be addressed if this is desirable.'

'A surveyor is vulnerable to legal claims, and so requires insurance.'

Ethnicity

It is said that when Margaret Thatcher was visiting an inner-city school, she had a conversation with a young working-class white boy in which he complained of insufficient pocket money. Mrs Thatcher thought he could offer to earn money at home, and suggested: 'Why not offer to clean the family silver?' We all need to be fully aware of our cultural, ethnic and class-based assumptions. If we did but know it, we all share Mrs Thatcher's difficulties in this respect. It is easy to forget (or even not to know) that some of our learners may live in homes where it is improper for women's legs or upper arms to be seen uncovered, and where alcohol or meat consumption are considered sacrilegious. (See also the box on pages 95–6.)

Many teachers believe that we should attempt to acknowledge in our teaching the contributions made by every culture. Arabs developed our number system, the Chinese invented the suspension bridge, and Africans developed writing and the first cities; but you would hardly know this from the ethnocentric curriculum taught in most schools and colleges. Perhaps it is not only government ministers who suffer from ethnocentrism.

Third World agricultural methods, Asian music and cookery, Caribbean and Chinese poetry and African art enliven the curricula in many schools and colleges. Can you do anything to make the teaching of your subject *multicultural*? This is even more important in schools and colleges which do not have a cultural mix. Teachers are important role models; through multicultural education they can teach their students to value cultures different from their own. Conversely, if a teacher or course ignores the multicultural nature of society, it can unwittingly send a message that it is acceptable to be indifferent to, and ignorant of, other cultures.

Anti-racist education seeks to challenge racist assumptions. For example, a science teacher may mention that 'races' are genetically almost identical, and that there are no differences in innate intelligence between races. Can you integrate anti-racist aspects into your teaching?

Can you imagine trying to learn a conceptually difficult subject in your second language? Many teachers mistake *language difficulties* for more fundamental learning difficulties. If you have people in your classes for whom English is their second language, try to make your English particularly clear, and encourage peer-tutoring in the first language. However, encourage such students to use their English, both spoken and written, as much as possible.

The special needs of students with learning difficulties or disabilities

People who have learning difficulties learn in the same way as everyone else. They need to be set a ladder of tasks from achievable to challenging goals, and then they need active, constructivist methods with lots of feedback in order to achieve them.

Research on these learners has shown that they benefit from:

- Individualised assessment of their present skills and abilities, and an individual learning plan focused on learning that will really benefit them in their everyday lives. See Chapters 47 and 48.
- Very deliberate and intensive teaching, focused on very clear goals. It is a myth that these learners only need care and protection. See Westwood (2003).
- Feuerstein's methods – for example, 'bridging' – have been very successful, as described in Chapters 31 and 45. Bridging takes place *after* a learning activity. First the student is asked, 'How did you do that?' in order to confirm the process they used, and then they are asked, 'Where else could you use that approach?' in order to help the learner transfer this process to as many different situations as possible. See Sharron and Coulter (1996).

Challenging goals are often not set for these students; they tend to be given only positive and encouraging feedback, which protects them from learning. See Chapter 43.

There is hardly a page of this book that does not apply to students with either general or specific learning difficulties, though you will need to use your imagination at times to see how to adapt the ideas and principles to their use.

Specific learning difficulties: dyslexia

Some learning difficulties are general, others are more specific, like dyslexia.

You are likely to come across students who are much better at answering questions verbally than they are at writing and especially at reading. In some cases this can be extreme, and the student seems very bright, but is not able to read one sentence or one phrase at a time, and instead seems to labour over each word in turn. However, there are a number of possible causes of reading difficulties, so only a qualified person, often an educational psychologist, is able to diagnose dyslexia.

The US Government commissioned the National Institute of Health to carry out an enormous study of dyslexia. As part of this, 5,000 children aged 4–18 were tested by specialists three times a year. Brain scans, genetic tests and other investigations were also carried out, and thanks in part to this study we now know very much more about dyslexia. For example:

- About 15–20% of people have a language-based learning difficulty, and dyslexia is by far the most common.
- The condition is inherited, and the gene for it has been identified.
- It is the leading cause of school dropout in the US, and probably in this country. The majority of young offenders, and probably the older ones too, are dyslexic.
- Dyslexia is a lifelong condition, but special teaching can greatly reduce its negative effects. This should start as early as possible and certainly at age 5.
- People with dyslexia process language in a different area of the brain than more fluent readers.
- About half the children with dyslexia were found also to have an entirely separate condition called attention deficit disorder (ADD), or the hyperactive version of this condition ADHD.
- Dyslexia is not related to intelligence, and it does not necessarily inhibit achievement. There are a large number of very gifted and successful people who are dyslexic.

> *Some of the most gifted people were dyslexic, including Albert Einstein, Leonardo da Vinci, Beethoven, Muhammad Ali, Walt Disney, Winston Churchill, George Washington and W. B. Yeats, to name only a few.*

The researchers found that the root difficulty suffered by dyslexic children was a lack of 'phonemic awareness'. A phoneme is a sound such as the 'c', 'a' or 't' sound in 'cat'. If you ask a young dyslexic child what rhymes with 'cat' or what the word 'cat' would sound like if you removed the 'c' sound, they can't work this out. However, if phonemic awareness is taught with direct, explicit instruction before the child is taught to read, then the child can learn to read almost normally.

As well as difficulties with reading, a dyslexic student may have 'dysgraphia', which means they have difficulty with handwriting, even to the point where they cannot read their own writing.

Why can you read tihs?

Aoccdrnig to a rscheearch at Cmabrigde Uinervtisy, it deosn't mttaer in waht oredr the ltteers in a wrod are, the olny iprmoetnt tihng is taht the frist and lsat ltteer are at the rghit pclae. The rset can be a total mses and you can sitll raed it wouthit porbelm. Tihs is bcuseae the huamn mnid deos not raed ervey lteter by istlef, but the wrod as a wlohe.

Supporting students with dyslexia

First of all, if students have been identified as having dyslexia, *talk to them*. Symptoms vary greatly from student to student, but those with the condition are often very clear about what helps them. So ask:

* What would help you most?
* Am I delivering material too fast? (This is a very common problem.)
* Do I do anything that you find difficult, or that makes you feel uncomfortable? (Dyslexic students may not like to have to read or write for classmates, for example.)
* Is there anything else I can do to help?

Make it clear that it is not their fault they have dyslexia, and that you understand it causes difficulties. Stress that the student can succeed if 'we work together to find what support you need, and then make sure you get this'.

All students with dyslexia should have a teacher or support worker designated to support them, so speak to this teacher about the student's individual difficulties and ask what you can do to help.

Almost all of the following advice will help all students, not just those who have dyslexia. You could ask your dyslexic students to consider if any of these would help. Let them take it away and think about which measures, if any, would help most. You can download a copy from www.geoffpetty.com

Because a student who has dyslexia often finds it hard to read text or numbers, it may *help if you:*

* Keep information that must be read to a minimum. Keep it concise, clear and very structured, with helpful headings and subheadings, for example.
* Introduce new words explicitly. Write them on the board and explain what they mean with some concrete examples. Give students a glossary.
* Produce handouts that include a mind-map summary of the key points, preferably at the beginning. Use other visual representations, as explained in Chapter 32 and the introduction to Part 2.
* Leave notes on the board for as long as you can.
* Use colour coding of handouts if there is a lot of material.
* Allow students to tape lessons.
* Don't force students to read large amounts of text, and don't require learners to read out loud, as this will embarrass them in front of their peers.

In addition, you may be able to arrange for the students to have someone to read to them during exams, or for them to have extra time in exams, or both.

Because writing and spelling may be difficult for a student who has dyslexia, it may *help if you:*

* Produce written handouts. If the students make their own notes, check that they can read them.

- If you grade work, grade the content, not the spelling, handwriting and grammar.
- Don't judge understanding by writing; students may limit their writing to words that they can spell, and they may use odd grammar.
- Allow students to present their ideas verbally where possible.
- Consider the amount of written work you set. A dyslexic student may take four or five times longer to complete this than your other students – is the workload fair?
- Allow students to use a laptop for written work so they can check spelling and grammar and read their notes easily. They may need careful tuition in how to type, though.
- Accept dictated homework.
- Allow students to use speech-recognition software. This reduces typing time, and also checks spelling and grammar.

In addition, you may be able to arrange for students to have someone to write for them in exams.

Because many dyslexic students are visual processors:

- Use visual and kinaesthetic methods, as described in Chapter 32.

I bet you won't believe this, but I was writing this section on a laptop on a train and I noticed that the man next to me was peering at the screen and laughing. 'Very true,' he said, pointing to the bit about not being able to read your own handwriting. He was dyslexic. One in five people are dyslexic, so it is not as surprising as it sounds.

We discussed his very negative school experience in the 1970s, when very little was known about dyslexia, and even that was often not believed. He said he lived in fear of ridicule from teachers and from students for his bad spelling and writing, and that his brother, who was also dyslexic, was badly bullied. He wrote reams for spelling tests, but this did not help in the slightest and he often got zero marks.

Despite his difficulties, Jeremy Collingwood made a success in the music business and was in the process of writing sleeve notes for a collector's compilation of Bob Marley recordings.

I asked him what would have helped him most. He thought for a bit and said, 'Mind-maps, and just people accepting that I found spelling almost impossibly difficult, no matter how hard I tried. Oh, and never ever being asked to write something on the board!' He said he was always thinking at one level, but having to write at another, because he could only dare write the words he could spell.

Never show impatience with a dyslexic student; they are much more frustrated by their difficulties than you can ever be!

> *Dyslexia may be a gift as well as a disability. Psychologists studying entrepreneurs for* Mind of a Millionaire, *a BBC Two TV programme, found that 40% of the most successful had learning difficulties, mostly dyslexia (Sunday Times, 5 October 2003). If you are not born dyslexic, sadly there is no way of making you so!*

Supporting students with physical disabilities and other special needs

Students who use wheelchairs, or whose hearing or sight is impaired, are at risk of not learning as well as they might. Many other factors can impact negatively on learning. This is not due to the learner's disability, but to a lack of the provision that would meet their needs. Is wheelchair access sufficient? Does the student who is hearing-impaired sit near the front? And does she need you to avoid turning your back on her when speaking to her, or to the class, so as to help with her lip-reading? Will a sight-impaired student need your handouts reproduced with extra-large lettering? Or can she convert your text files into Braille? There is only one way to find out – get the student into your confidence and ask her! Don't 'tiptoe' around her for fear of causing offence; speak frankly and openly, but with respect, and ask what you can do to help.

You won't have to deal with these support issues by yourself; wherever you teach, there will be someone with specialist knowledge to help you – seek their advice too. See also Chapters 47 and 48.

Others whose opportunities are at risk

Do you ensure that all your students get a fair share of your efforts, smiles and good humour, whatever their ethnicity, sex or class, and no matter how shy or self-confident, attractive or unpleasant, cooperative or disruptive, weak or able they may be? This is a high expectation; if you believe you could meet it without considerable effort, you have underestimated the problem. But you have taken the king's shilling in becoming a teacher, and you must do your best, for two reasons: because it is equitable, and because if you value all your learners, they will value your teaching. If particular students are not valued by their school or college, then those students may protect their self-esteem by rejecting the school or college, and the values for which it stands.

Modelling equal opportunities

Many teachers believe that all members of the profession should model the fair-mindedness of equal opportunities to their students. You will have considerable influence on students who respect and admire you; if you come across books, videos or other materials that are discriminatory or patronising, it is important to refer to this – to do otherwise is to condone them. Except in extreme cases, this may be more effective than avoiding such materials altogether.

When dealing with student prejudice, factual rather than emotional responses are most effective: 'That's a sexist remark', or 'Some people would find that joke offensive: or 'That remark suggests that you regard homosexuals with scorn'. Responses of that kind are much better than 'How dare you make such a remark in one of my classes!'

How should one deal with discriminatory behaviour in the class? Suppose, for example, female students are not taking part in a discussion. Don't assume weakness and protect or help. Rather, try to raise awareness of what is happening and leave the women to assert their own independence. Again, a straightforward factual approach is often best: 'I notice that no women have spoken yet' is usually enough to get a response from a female student soon after.

The legal responsibilities of teachers

You won't be surprised to hear that it is illegal for a teacher to sprinkle students with sulphuric acid or hurl them through windows. Less obviously it is also illegal to tell a student who uses a wheelchair that they can't study art because the art room is on the top floor, or to tell a student she shouldn't become an engineer because she's a girl. As teachers, we should, of course, go well beyond what the law requires of us; this chapter, and Chapters 47 and 48 certainly do that. The law only sets minimum standards.

Laws change, and I don't want to give outdated advice, so please use the following websites so you are smack up to date.

Health and Safety at Work Act (www.hse.gov.uk/education)

The most common accidents at school or college are falling off climbing frames, tripping or slipping, or getting hurt during a sports lesson. Often the risks and responsibilities depend on what you teach, of course, and the HSE website allows you to search by risky subjects – though if you are recently qualified you should find you already know most of the risks. Your students won't though, and will lack your skill and caution. Please teach them how to survive!

If your students must handle chemicals and other substances that are potentially hazardous to health, then 'COSHH' regulations apply (otherwise you can ignore these). See www.hse.gov.uk/coshh/

If you teach science, design and technology, information and communication technology, art and design, and/or physical education, then you or your colleagues are legally obliged to teach students to recognise and manage risks. See www.hse.gov.uk/education/qca.htm. All educational institutions will have a health and safety policy, have a look at yours.

If you are involved with school trips, then www.rospa.co.uk has some useful advice.

Go to **www.dcsf.gov.uk** and **www.teachernet.gov.uk** and type in the name of the Act you are interested in. You will then find advice for teachers.

Disabilities Discrimination Act (DDA)

This Act aims to promote equality of opportunity between disabled people and other people, and to eliminate unlawful discrimination or harassment of disabled people. It requires that disabled people's needs are met, and that they are not treated 'less favourably', even if this requires extra effort. This chapter and Chapters 47 and 48 show how.

The Act requires educational institutions, helped by disabled people, to prepare and publish a Disability Equality Scheme, and then to report on this. Ask to see yours!

Data Protection Act

At the time of writing (2008), teachers are required, for example, to keep data that is accurate, relevant and not excessive, and not to keep it longer than necessary. They are not allowed to pass data on to another country without adequate protection.

Codes of practice and values are dealt with in Chapter 45.

Checklist

Ethnic origin

☐ Do you show that you value all your students equally, by treating them with equal respect? It is the little things that count so much in making you a positive role model:

 – same use of students' names (however difficult some might be to remember!)

 – offering and giving equal help

 – same giving of smiles, engaging in casual conversation in your usual way before and after the class, etc.

☐ Do you encourage students with English as a second language to practise their English? For example, encourage them to speak in class (even if it is a bit laboured, or they are uneasy about showing themselves up). Also encourage reading.

☐ Do you maintain high expectations of students from ethnic minorities, and not interpret their limited English as evidence of their being slow learners?

☐ Do you avoid cultural assumptions in activities or assignments, e.g. 'Let's do a Christmas collage'?

☐ Do you adopt assessment methods which do not unnecessarily penalise those with English as a second language, e.g. using plain English and not relying exclusively on written assessments?

Multiculturalism

Do you naturally integrate into the content of your courses, wherever it can be made relevant, material to:

❏ Promote a world view, showing the subject under study as a worldwide activity rather than adopting a narrow Eurocentric approach?

❏ Raise the awareness and appreciation of the contribution made to the study area by non-white, non-Europeans? For example:

- in English classes: study of some Caribbean and some Chinese poetry

- in mathematics classes: an appreciation that our number system is of Asian and Arabic origin.

❏ Actively include non-white peoples in curriculum materials such as worksheets and assignments? For example: use of Asian names in assignments, consideration of the Third World and North–South issues, etc.

❏ Cultivate understanding and appreciation of non-white, non-European cultures? For example: examining the difference between the values and beliefs of different cultures, and encouraging an appreciation of these differences.

❏ Raise student awareness of the experience of being in a racial minority?

❏ Show positive images of people from other cultures, especially the Third World (e.g. active, well-fed people with smiling faces rather than famine victims)?

❏ Avoid exaggerating the underdevelopment of 'developing nations' (some students are genuinely astonished to learn there are skyscrapers in Africa!)?

❏ Encourage mutual understanding between different cultures, religions, etc.?

❏ Can you arrange for a visitor to your class from an ethnic minority to give their perspective on a curriculum issue, e.g. some aspect of a social care or a sociology course?

Anti-racist education

❏ Do you deal with racist remarks by criticising the *opinion*, but not criticising directly the *person* making the remark?

❏ Do you naturally integrate into the content of your courses, *wherever it can be made relevant*, material to:

- raise issues of equality of opportunity in society in your teaching?

- raise the issue of stereotyping and ethnic bias?

- refute racist assumptions, e.g. brain size differences, racial superiority, etc.?

Gender

❏ Are your assignments, worksheets, etc. in gender-free language?

❏ Do your assignments and worksheets include role models which challenge sexist assumptions, e.g. male nurses, female engineers?

❏ If sex-stereotyped material is used, do you point this out, or invite discussion?

❏ Do you encourage students of both sexes to take your subject seriously as a career?

❏ Do you critically explore the issue of sexism where your subject allows this?

❏ Do you try to characterise sexist attitudes as old-fashioned?

❏ Do you ensure that no single sex dominates the use of specialist equipment?

❏ Are you consistent across sexes in your response to such behaviour as lack of interest in your subjects, rowdiness or bad handwriting?

❏ Do you give sensitive moral support to the minority gender in your classes?

❏ Do you deal with sexist behaviour in your students in a firm but fair manner, criticising the behaviour but not the person?

❏ Do you ask questions equally of males and females?

❏ Do you expect both males and females to lead groups or move tables, etc.?

The special needs of students with learning difficulties or disabilities

❏ Do you discover individual needs, and seek advice from the student and from specialist teachers in providing for them? For example, needs due to:

– *dyslexia*: e.g. arranging extra time for assessments

– *impaired sight*: e.g. seating position, lighting, photocopy size increased, etc.

– *impaired hearing*: e.g. seating position, special equipment or support, etc.

– *mobility problems*: e.g. seating position, classroom used, etc.

– *emotional or behaviour problems*

– *needs due to medical conditions*: e.g. due to asthma, epilepsy, or due to taking medication which affects concentration, etc.

❏ Are your assessment and course materials approachable for people with reading difficulties?

❏ Do you ensure that your use of video, board, handouts, etc. does not cause avoidable problems for students with special needs? For example, can the materials or equipment be heard and/or seen?

Others whose opportunities are at risk

❏ Do you make a special effort to help shy students?

SOME IMPORTANT RELIGIOUS LAWS AND CUSTOMS

Adherence to laws and customs varies, but in general:

Hindus

Believe in many gods which are all part of one God. They have a caste system, and believe in reincarnation and karma, a moral law whereby evil deeds will result in accident, failure or misfortune.

Tradition and prohibitions: No Hindu may eat beef, as the cow is sacred. Higher castes have stricter diets – many are vegetarian (as also are Buddhists).

Jews

Their religion is Judaism, from which Christianity and Islam are in a sense descended. They believe in one God, and regard the Old (but of course not the New) Testament as scripture.

Traditions and prohibitions: Meals have great religious significance. Only ritually clean (*kosher*) meat may be eaten. Pig meat is not kosher. Cooking utensils must be especially cared for.

Muslims

Believe in one God, *Allah*, and study the teaching of the Prophet Mohammed. Jesus is accepted as a prophet. Islam lays down detailed laws covering every aspect of life: moral, legal, economic and religious.

Traditions and prohibitions: Only ritually clean (*halal*) meat may be eaten; the avoidance of lard may make bread or ice-cream prohibited, and no alcohol or pig meat may be consumed. During the month of Ramadan (or Ramadhan) no food or drink may pass the lips during daylight hours. Ramadan commemorates Muhammad being sent the Qur'an (or Koran), Islam's sacred book. It follows the lunar calendar, and so occurs ten days earlier each year.

Sikhs

Believe in one God, and freedom and equality for all. Sikhism is an offshoot of Hinduism, but rejects its caste system. Last names are 'Singh' for men and 'Kaur' for women, even after marriage.

Traditions and prohibitions: Men wear long hair and turbans. Their undershorts (*kachh*) and bangle (*kara*) may not be removed for sports. No alcohol, tobacco or other intoxicants.

Christians

Believe that Jesus is the Son of God, and that only through faith in Him can they obtain forgiveness of their sins and go to heaven. Christians believe their sacred book, the Bible, is the inspired word of God. (Muslims also regard it as one of the sacred books, and the Old Testament of the Bible is a sacred text for Jews.)

Traditions and prohibitions: There are a wide variety of Christian churches and organisations, with their own rituals and observations. Traditional festivals are Christmas Day (25 December) and Easter (March/April). Ash Wednesday (February/March) is a day of fasting and abstinence for many Christians. Some Christians avoid alcohol and many would not celebrate Halloween, as the Bible disapproves of witchcraft. Catholics often refuse meat on Fridays. Many do not approve of non-essential Sunday working.

General comments:

In Asian religions, young women are usually expected, for the sake of family honour, to avoid imprudent social contact with men.

Strict Hindus, Jews, Muslims, Sikhs and Christians all reject a secular basis for ethics. They regard moral laws as essentially religious, and based on the detailed teachings of their sacred books. They reject, or at least have distaste for, sex education when they see it as separated from these moral laws.

References and further reading

Baker, G. C. (1994) *Planning and Organizing for Multicultural Instruction*, New York: Addison-Wesley.

Good, T. L. and Brophy, J. E. (2002) *Looking in Classrooms* (9th edition), New York: Allyn & Bacon.

Hargreaves, D. H. (1975) *Interpersonal Relations and Education*, London: Routledge.

*Kyriacou, C. (1998) *Essential Teaching Skills* (2nd edition), Cheltenham: Nelson Thornes.

Mitchell, D. (2008) *What Really Works in Special and Inclusive Education: Using Evidence-Based Teaching Strategies*, Abingdon: Routledge.

Myers, K. (ed.) (1992) *Genderwatch!*, Cambridge University Press.

Reises, R. and Mason, M. (1992) *Disability Equality in the Classroom: A Human Rights Issue* (2nd edition), London: ILEA/Disability Equality.

Rosenthal, R. and Jacobson, L. (1968) *Pygmalion in the Classroom: Teacher Expectation and Pupils' Intellectual Development*, New York: Holt, Rinehart and Winston.

Thorpe, S., Deshpande, P. and Edwards, C. (eds) (1994) *Race, Equality and Science Teaching: A Handbook for Teachers and Educators*, Hatfield: Association for Science Education.

On learning difficulties, including dyslexia:

*Mitchell, D. (2008) *What Really Works in Special and Inclusive Education: Using Evidence-Based Teaching Strategies*, Abingdon: Routledge.

Sharron, H. and Coulter, M. (1996) *Changing Children's Minds: Feuerstein's Revolution in the Teaching of Intelligence*, Birmingham: Imaginative Minds.

*Westwood, P. (2003) *Commonsense Methods for Children with Special Educational Needs: Strategies for the Regular Classroom* (4th edition), London: RoutledgeFalmer. Don't be put off by 'children' in the title; this is highly recommended.

Reports on the US research study on dyslexia can be found on the Internet. Search with 'National Institute of Health' dyslexia.

There is a good deal else on the Internet about dyslexia. For example:

www.brightsolutions.us is an excellent site

www.interdys.org – the International Dyslexia Association

www.dyslexia.com has a great list of famous people with dyslexia (all accessed September 2008).

8

Classroom management

Teacher–student relationships

Good teacher–student relationships are based on mutual respect. The student respects the teacher for his or her teaching skills, personal qualities, knowledge and professionalism; and the teacher respects each student as an individual, and that student's attempts to learn. It is important to realise that respecting each individual student is not the same as some kind of generalised respect for the class as a whole; and that the teacher's respect must be shown as well as felt, otherwise the student will be unaware of it.

Rapport and formal authority

Rapport takes time to establish, usually passing through two phases. In the first phase you achieve a position of power by virtue of your role as a teacher. If your students are never likely to challenge your authority, offer a brief prayer of thanks, and skip this topic by moving on to the next section on rapport and personal authority.

David Hargreaves, a social psychologist in the education field, suggests that a teacher starting with a new class must insist that the students accept his or her 'formal authority'. Teachers must convey that their authority is legitimate, that it exists to maximise learning; and they must show confidence in their ability to enforce their authority.

You cannot expect students to like you from the first lesson; you have no mutual experience on which to build a personal relationship, so – like it or not – you will start in a formal relationship with your class. Being a teacher confers on you certain duties, but with these duties come rights: grasp them with both hands! You have the right to be obeyed on matters of work and behaviour. You have the right to silence when you are speaking. Some learning teachers feel uneasy in this position of power, perhaps because they are unfamiliar with it, and the first time a student obeys one of their orders they can barely hide their surprise. Why should you feel shy or apologetic about the use of the teacher's formal authority, if you are using it for the students' benefit? You are there to teach, and you cannot teach without order; use your authority.

How do you develop and use this formal authority? This depends on your teaching situation. If your students are not cooperative, then you may well find yourself in the following fix: your students will only accept your authority if you apply it with confidence. However, you will only begin to feel confident when they accept your authority. An unfortunate 'Catch 22'.

You never get a second chance to make a first impression. To begin with, you must act. Stride about the room as if you are absolutely confident of your ability to control the group. Appear to be self-confident, relaxed and in control – especially when you are not! This is particularly important in your first few lessons or when coping with a difficulty.

A staffroom adage: 'Never smile before Easter.'

Formal authority is sustained by non-verbal methods. Stand up straight, shoulders back, face students squarely, give orders with a confident tone of voice and expect to be obeyed. If you ask a student to do something, don't hang around with an anxious look on your face wondering what will happen next. Give your order with confidence. If the student has not done what you asked in reasonable time, be confident and emphatic; you might show a puzzled surprise at the impertinence, but never show that you are flustered.

Authority is conveyed principally with body language. For example, compare these two ways of dealing with a student who is not working:

1 Not facing the student, and at five metres' distance saying: 'I want you to stop talking and start working now, Paula.'

2 Walking confidently but unhurriedly up to the student, putting both hands on her desk to lean over and face her, looking her in the eye for three seconds, then saying 'Why haven't you started?' confidently, still holding her gaze.

These two methods produce startlingly different effects on the student; ask a friend to try it on you if you don't believe me!

Of course, you don't need to be quite so extreme in giving every order, but remember that when giving instructions the effect on the student is increased, not by shouting or anger, but by:

- *Proximity.* The closer you are, the greater your effect, especially if you invade the student's 'personal space' and adopt a commanding posture.
- *Eye contact.* That is, sustained eye contact while you are speaking, and for enhanced effect, before and after you have spoken.
- *Posing questions.* It is often more powerful to put the student 'on the spot' by posing a question than to deliver a lecture. However, this is sometimes best done when you have the student alone. For example, 'Why haven't you started?'

The above three enhancements can be remembered by the mnemonic 'PEP' – proximity, eye contact and posing questions. Using them well, you can 'pep up' your message. Usually, proximity and eye contact are enough without posing questions; they should certainly be tried first, with a positive statement such as 'Come on, let's get started', before combining them with questions.

If you use the PEP approach effectively, you will barely need to raise your voice to maximise the effect of your instructions. In fact, you will make at least as big an impression by *lowering* your voice.

If you expect trouble, *never* sit behind the desk; move around the class, and use plenty of eye contact. If there is unproductive talking, move over to that part of the classroom, and use eye contact.

You don't have to be tall. The most effective disciplinarian I have ever seen was a woman no more than five feet high; she just stood up straight and looked confident! Don't over-rely on enforcing formal authority in this way, though; interesting lessons, good relations and proper classroom management are much more effective in keeping order, as you will see in the next few pages. If you have problems, some of the advice on discipline later in this chapter may help. Don't be afraid of making short-term enemies; you must show that you are not afraid of becoming unpopular, if you are to become popular!

Rapport and personal authority

Phase two in developing student–teacher relations is a gradual shift from this formal authority towards the teacher's personal authority. A teacher who wields formal authority fairly and effectively, shows some skill in teaching and shows that they value students and their attempts to learn, will earn the respect of their students. If all goes well, given time, the relationship may shift so that it is based on personalities. The source of the teacher's power becomes the desire of the students to please the teacher, and to build their own self-image through the teacher's approval. This is called 'personal authority'.

How does this personal authority evolve? It takes months rather than weeks; obviously teachers will gain their students' respect by being effective teachers, but the following will also help:

- showing a genuine *interest* in each student's work, and making a point of using praise – especially in recognising a student's individual contributions or attempts to learn, regardless of their previous attainment or innate ability.
- having a clear set of rules and applying them fairly and consistently, without bearing grudges from one class to the next
- using the students' names
- showing ordinary polite respect for students by saying 'please' and 'thank you'
- never using put-downs or sarcasm
- having a professional approach to your teaching and its organisation, e.g. well-planned and organised lessons, good time-keeping, tidy appearance, etc.
- being patient
- choosing teaching methods which allow students to make personal contributions, and reacting positively to these when you can
- showing an interest in students' attitudes, feelings and needs: 'What do you think of the new library, then?' 'Are you worried about the mock exams, Andrew?' 'Are you clear on that now, or would you like me to go over it again?'

And a little later:

- showing an interest in students as individuals, e.g. smiling, using eye contact and speaking to them 'one to one'; recognising each student's individuality, e.g. their personality traits, interests, style of dress, etc.
- developing a relaxed and confident style that is not too formal, using humour where appropriate (this includes being prepared to have the occasional laugh at your own expense); relaxed humour conveys confidence.

Much of the above is simply showing that you *value your students as individuals*, as opposed to trying to be 'one of them'; or valuing them only for their attainment or cooperativeness. If you succeed in establishing rapport, your job will be made very much easier, as well as more enjoyable. The main rewards of teaching are in a teacher's relationships with his or her students.

> '*Remember that a man's name is to him the sweetest and most important sound in the English language.*'
>
> Dale Carnegie, *How to Win Friends and Influence People*

Do you find it hard to learn names? I did; but I had a colleague who knew the name of every student she taught within the first week of a new academic year, so I asked her how she did it. Remember that 'frequency and recency' are the clues to all memory learning. She made a plan of the class, with each student's full name written in the place they sat. She read through this a number of times every day, even if she couldn't remember the face to go with each name. She spent a few minutes with her plan before each lesson – and especially after it, while she could still remember the faces. She openly referred to her plan in the class, and always used her students' names when she talked to them. (Students are not offended if you make a few mistakes, or ask their name, in your first few lessons.)

Unless rapport is established, a 'psychological barrier' is created which stops students taking part in discussions, asking questions or asking for help. It also detrimentally affects student motivation and classroom management. Names, smiles and equal treatment are the most effective ways of ensuring this barrier does not develop.

Don't try too hard with rapport. Be patient. You will be disliked if you are desperate to be liked. And don't expect too much; your students don't want you to become a best friend or confidant. They have these already. All they want is that you should be effective in your teaching and classroom management, that you should be approachable, and that you should have a genuine interest in their learning.

You will never establish a rapport with your class unless you can manage the class effectively, and this is the subject of the next section.

Some don'ts

Canadian university students were asked to say which were the teaching habits they most disliked. Their answers were:

- ignoring students
- discouraging and restricting questions
- ridiculing a student's contributions
- sarcasm, belittlement, hostility or anger
- arrogance
- interrupting a student's contributions
- failure to promote discussion or questions.

This research was not specifically about rapport, but notice that all the disliked teaching habits are in effect expressions of the teacher's lack of respect for, or interest in, the students.

Creating a working atmosphere in the classroom

'Students are the beneficiaries, not the victims, of effective classroom control.'

Michael Marland

One day during my first term of teaching, I was walking down a school corridor when I noticed that one of the classes was in uproar. Students were standing on the tables and bellowing at each other, books were flying through the air, and two boys were fighting in a corner. With my heart in my mouth I stormed through the door, put on my sternest expression and bellowed, 'Sit down quietly and wait for your teacher.' The remark was greeted with a roar of laughter from the class; they gleefully pointed to their teacher, who was tucked into a corner with the two students in the class who *were* trying to work.

Some teachers have terrible discipline problems, while others create an atmosphere in the classroom that is conducive to learning, with little apparent effort. How do they do it? The bridge from chaos to order in the classroom has four spans, each of which must be in place if you are to guide your class across. These are:

- effective lessons based on a well-conceived curriculum
- good organisational skills
- good teacher–student relationships
- effective discipline (which is almost impossible to achieve unless the first three conditions are satisfied).

The first of these points must not be overlooked. Most of the 'discipline' difficulties experienced by teachers in the classroom were created before the lesson started; they were inherent in the lesson plan. The factors involving motivation should have been given very careful consideration. The students' work should be interesting, involving plenty of varied student activity. There should be something for every student to do all the time, and the standard of the work should not be too difficult or too easy for any student in the class. There should be ample and prompt reinforcement, such as praise and encouragement, for students' efforts. This is a tall order, but who said teaching was easy!

Practical help in achieving this balance can be found elsewhere in the book; for the moment, we shall be looking at the other three spans of the bridge. I am assuming in what follows that you are interested in how to deal with a fairly 'difficult' class; if you teach adults or very motivated students, some of what follows can be toned down, or may even be wildly inappropriate – unless you are interested in parenthood, where many of the techniques are very relevant!

Organisation in the classroom

Experienced teachers don't deal with problems, they prevent them occurring. This is why student teachers whose classes are reminiscent of the Sorcerer's Apprentice look in vain for the 'tricks' used by teachers who are able to keep 'difficult' classes working. Good classroom organisation allows the lesson to run smoothly, so that good relationships can grow through positive experiences.

Rules and regimes

Every teacher has rules and regimes, even if they are not overtly stated. Think them out carefully, express them clearly and enforce them consistently. Do you want work handed in on Mondays or Thursdays? Do you want students to put their hands up to answer a question? During practical sessions, are students allowed to talk to their neighbour, to students behind them or to students at the other end of the room?

Your rules and regimes will take time to establish, and should be based on educational, safety and moral grounds, not on personal idiosyncrasies. Despite getting my own back on two occasions, I still harbour a smouldering resentment against a teacher who made me rewrite an essay because I had written it in green biro!

Exactly what is allowed in your lessons will be decided by what you do, not by what you say. If you say that there should be no talking when you are talking, but do not enforce this, then the rule becomes inoperative; and should you then 'jump' on a student for talking inappropriately, your inconsistency will be resented. 'Why pick on me, I'm not the only one.' If you consistently refuse to accept contributions from students who call out, but accept them from students with raised hands, then hand-raising becomes a rule.

Whether or not you make your rules explicit, expect them to be tested, and be consistent in their enforcement. This may seem irritating and time-consuming at first, but it is a vital investment in future order. Rules and behaviour are governed by case law, which will only be established by ruthless consistency. Sometimes rules have exceptions, but not many. Be sure you are being fair, then be very firm. A very effective and experienced teacher once gave me this tongue-in-cheek advice: 'Listen to excuses with concern, interest and compassion – then ignore them!'

It is sometimes worth negotiating rules and regimes with students: 'Would you prefer to hand in work on Mondays or Thursdays?' Some teachers go further and bring problems to the group. 'I'm getting lots of trouble with students not handing their work in. What's the problem? Is the work too difficult?' Be equally consistent in enforcing rules decided by the group. Once the rules are established you may be able to bend them a bit, but be fair and consistent even here.

As far as possible, there should be a similar approach to rules and regimes from all the teachers whom the students experience.

Here is a set of rules and regimes I use for 17-year-old students. Many other sets would be equally valid.

- Absolutely no talking if I am talking. (I try not to go on too long, though!)
- Health and safety rules obeyed, e.g. no running in the classroom.
- When working individually or in groups, students can: talk to their neighbour about work and move out of their place to talk about work with another student.
- Work is handed in on the same day each week. Absence for more than one day is an acceptable excuse for a delay in handing in a week's work.
- No personal stereos, and mobile phones switched off.
- No eating or drinking.
- Students are not allowed to pack away their folders until I say so (whatever the clock says – however, I will accept a reminder about the time).

Ask to observe classes in your school or college, so you get a feel for the sort of behaviour which is acceptable. If your expectations are the same as those of other teachers, this will make your life much easier.

Before they arrive

Arrive before your class, and make sure you have everything you need (and that everything works). If you are a science teacher, you should already have rehearsed any experiment procedure you or your class will be carrying out. Lay out anything you may need for the lesson neatly, so you can find it, and prepare the overhead projector or the blackboard for the first few minutes of the lesson.

When the students arrive, you may like to greet them at the door and watch them as they take their places; appear confident and relaxed, but businesslike. Start on time; waiting for students who are late is unfair on those who have arrived on time, and encourages late arrival in the future.

Getting silence

Gaining and maintaining silence is very important. It is worth being pedantic about this when you first meet a new group; time spent at this stage will be an excellent investment. If you don't get silence in your first lesson you probably never will, and even if students can hear you in subsequent lessons, they will not be listening.

Ask for silence and then *wait* for it, however long it takes. If necessary, repeat your call for silence, and use the techniques below to obtain and enforce it. Don't start until there is a conspicuous silence and all students are looking in your direction. *Never* start your lesson over the class's noise. If you do, students will be given the impression that it is permissible to talk whenever they like; as a result even students who were initially quiet will start talking, and before long virtually the whole group will be talking over you.

If waiting makes you feel panicky, don't show it; never be cross or abusive, as this is counterproductive. It gives the impression you are not in control. Instead, make it seem that they are missing something when they make a noise:

'Everyone's waiting to hear what Sandra has to say.'

'No, I'm sorry; we can't start yet because we're not quiet enough.'

Having achieved silence, let it sink in for a second, and then begin saying what you want to say. If someone talks when you are talking, stop in mid-sentence and look at them until they stop. They are likely to find this an embarrassment and will probably soon stop; but, if necessary, use their name or ask for silence again. Only when you have re-established silence should you continue talking, going back to the beginning of the sentence which was interrupted. Should talking start again, do exactly the same. Soon most students will realise that they cannot talk without immediately drawing attention to themselves, and they will stop trying.

If there is a persistent offender, explain that it is impossible to talk and listen at the same time, stand close to them and, if necessary, threaten to move them. Other techniques are dealt with below, but whatever you do, do not give up. However, don't expect too much; some groups can literally only concentrate on teacher talk for about two minutes, or even less. If you have a group like this, don't rely on using teacher talk with the class as a whole. Talk to them in small groups, and communicate with the board or overhead projector, also using worksheets.

Gaining silence is a common problem for inexperienced teachers, but the approach above will work if you are persistent.

At the start

The first five minutes of any lesson are crucial in setting the atmosphere for the rest of the lesson. If you want to enliven a sleepy class, then start with a bang; if you want to quieten a noisy group down, start quietly.

If a class is particularly noisy, try making the first activity one where the students are working alone, without needing input from you. They could be copying a diagram off the overhead transparency or board, doing an exercise from a textbook, or finishing off something from the last lesson. You can then concentrate entirely on getting quiet; settling the class into a quiet working atmosphere; and dealing with Lucy who has arrived late, having lost her folder. Once the class has been really quiet for five minutes, you have set the atmosphere for the rest of the session.

Giving instructions

Get silence first, and make sure the class are all looking at you. Some teachers, especially those who must compete with noise from machines, have a routine way of attracting attention, such as clapping three times. Be brief, clear and positive. The tone should be firm, confident and pleasant. If you are asking the class to change positions, ask them to remain still until you have finished the instruction. When you have finished, give a summary. Here's an example:

(The teacher claps hands a few times.) 'OK, can I have everybody's attention, please. Julie … Robin, look this way, please.' (The teacher waits for silence.) 'Now, when I tell you, I want one person from each group to collect your apparatus from the front bench, and another to pick up a power-pack from the back of the lab. Whoever's left in your group will be preparing a table for the results. OK? One set of apparatus, one power-pack and one prepared table. Off you go.'

If you often require movement to the front of a class for a demonstration, it is worth considering having fixed positions for students to move to.

> *Tell them what you are going to tell them – tell them – tell them what you have told them!*

Don't make repeated generalised complaints, such as 'Come on, everybody, start work.' Give the generalised instruction *once*, then pick on individuals who are not obeying, by name or by eye contact: 'Come on, Paul, get started!'

Those who give instructions should set a good example. If you want students to be neat and methodical in the way they lay out their work, then take your own advice when writing on the blackboard. If you want them to use certain safety procedures, then use them yourself. Don't allow your students to leave before the end of a class; it sets a difficult precedent. If they have completed your activities, try a revision quiz.

'Withitness'

'He has eyes in the back of his head.' A 60-year-old deputy headteacher finished off some excellent advice on how I should treat a new class by saying, half seriously, that I should keep my eyes on the reflections of pupils in the glass doors of the cupboards that lined the laboratory. If I saw in the reflection a student misbehaving, I should then turn my back on the student before beginning to tell him off. 'It really unsettles the little blighters when they think you know what they're up to with your back turned!'

Inappropriate behaviour soon spreads, unless it is dealt with promptly; this is called the 'ripple effect'. Students are quick to think, 'Why should I behave if no one else is?'

Whatever you or your students are doing, you must make your presence fill the room – every corner of it. Students some distance from you will not feel so strongly under your influence; walk close to them occasionally, and scan all the faces in the room with eye contact from time to time. Be vigilant and be mobile; don't sit behind the desk. Which way are the students facing? Are they listening? Have they got pens in their hands? If particular students are not being productive, give them sustained eye contact; if necessary, walk over and stand close to them. This can be done with no disruption to your teaching, and will usually be enough to stop the inappropriate behaviour.

If you are writing on the board, half-face the room and scan the class every now and then, every five words if necessary. If you are talking to an individual student, don't relax your vigilance; always position yourself so that you can see most if not all of the room. Whilst talking, scan the room frequently – all of it. Vigilance has a way of preventing misbehaviour before it starts: students gain little by behaving inappropriately if they are picked up for it straight away. Who bothers to steal helmets off the heads of policemen?

There are circumstances where it is best to pretend not to notice misbehaviour – harmless silliness that is already settling down. With experience you will know what is best ignored, but you will find yourself ignoring very little.

It is difficult to remain vigilant while teaching; it takes practice. If it seems impossible at first, don't worry; it's like changing gear whilst steering a car – you will soon be doing it automatically. You must also notice *appropriate* behaviour, for students who are working should be reinforced.

Firefighting

If inappropriate behaviour begins, it must be stopped as soon as possible, for three reasons:

* to stop the behaviour spreading to other students
* because it is easier to stop behaviour that has hardly started
* to prevent the student gaining from the misbehaviour.

Students talk when they shouldn't because they enjoy a chat. If they usually manage to get half a dozen sentences in before you deal with them, then they might begin to feel their chats are worth your displeasure. On the other hand, if they never manage to finish the first three words of the first sentence, they have gained nothing of value from their inappropriate behaviour, and they will soon decide that it is not worth trying.

Knowing the students' names is crucial to effective firefighting. You probably remember this technique from your schooldays:

> 'In those days Genoa was a thriving commercial port – wasn't it, Samuel? It wasn't a very big city …'

Even if the name is not said with a disapproving tone, Samuel knows why he was 'picked on', and it is nearly always enough to stop the inappropriate behaviour.

Give the work of offending students some attention. If your vigilance and firefighting succeeds in getting them back to work, find something to praise in their work if you can: 'This is better, now you are getting down to it!' Research shows that praise of appropriate behaviour is more effective than criticism of inappropriate behaviour.

The power of praise

In a famous piece of research, students with 'a high frequency of problem behaviour' were observed for 20 minutes a day, three days a week from November to June. Their behaviour was recorded as 'appropriate' or 'inappropriate' every ten seconds during this time. At the start, some students behaved inappropriately as much as 70% of the time, despite having a competent and experienced teacher.

The teacher adopted various strategies to make the students behave well. Telling them the class rules had little effect; and ignoring inappropriate behaviour made them worse! However, if the students were given the class rules, and their inappropriate behaviour was ignored *but appropriate behaviour was praised*, these very difficult students began to behave well 90% of the time.

*Madsen, C. H. Jr., Becker, W. C. and Thomas, D. R. (1968), 'Rules, praise and ignoring', *Journal of Applied Behavioural Analysis*, 1: 139–50.

Further reading

Download 'Evidence based classroom management and discipline' from www.geoffpetty.com/whatsnew.html (this summarises Marzano below).

Department of Education and Science (1989) *Discipline in Schools* (The Elton Report), London: HMSO.

*Gray, J. and Richer, J. (1995) *Classroom Responses to Disruptive Behaviour* (in the series *Special Needs in Mainstream Schools*), London: Routledge.

*Kyriacou, C. (1998) *Essential Teaching Skills* (2nd edition), Cheltenham: Nelson Thornes.

Marland, M. (2002) *The Craft of the Classroom* (3rd edition), London: Croom Helm.

*Marzano, R. J. with Marzano, S. and Pickering, D. J. (2003) *Classroom Management that Works*, Alexandria, VA: ASCD.

Smith, C. J. and Laslett, R. (1993) *Effective Classroom Management: A Teacher's Guide*, London: Routledge.

9

Discipline and problem-solving

I encountered a young pupil called Mandy in my first year of teaching; she was 13 years old, but I lived in dread of her. I put her in detention once for blatant defiance, and I told her to write me a letter there to explain her behaviour. Her explanation was copious, and included the comment: 'Most teachers are very strict about behaviour; others are not. Mostly I like teachers that are strict about work.' I was astonished by this comment. How could such a badly behaved pupil prefer strict teachers? I had a lot to learn; in this respect she was the rule, not the exception.

In the previous chapter I argued that order in the classroom was created by a combination of four factors: effective lessons based on a well-conceived curriculum, good organisational skills, good teacher–student relationships and effective discipline. Here we deal with the last of these four; prevention may be better than cure for the vast majority of 'behaviour problems', but it does not deal with all of them.

 Only unobservant teachers have no problems.

Finding the root cause of the problem

If students are bored because their work is too simple, no amount of juggling of rewards and punishments will solve the problem. Even if vigilance and threatened punishments keep the behaviour within tolerable limits, the problem is likely to resurface in a new guise, which may well be even more difficult to deal with. If the root cause of the problem is inappropriate work, then the solution is obvious. Unhappily, the diagnosis of behaviour problems is sometimes very difficult, and occasionally impossible.

The 'adult-to-adult' chat style is perhaps the best method for finding problems and their solutions. Use it one-to-one after the class.

1 *Find the real problem*. This is best done by listening. Even if your first instinct is to strangle the student, assume in the first instance that they are willing and able to solve the problem by themselves. Do not jump in with advice or judgements at this stage. You may give another's point of view, but without implying that you yourself hold that view. Show acceptance non-verbally. You are looking for the reasons for the behaviour you want to change. A key reason-finding question is: 'What do you find most difficult …?' For example: 'What do you find most difficult about working with the other students in your group?'

2 *Agree a solution*. Give the student the problem and ask them for a solution. 'So what are you going to do about this problem?' If a solution is not forthcoming,

suggest one yourself, but ask the student if they can think of a better one. Ask for an agreement to carry out the solution, if this is not offered.

3 *Set a target.* For example: 'So we agree that you will talk to Philippa about your disagreement before next lesson?'

4 *Follow up with an evaluation,* to see whether the target has been reached. The student is made aware of the fact that the agreed solution is to be checked: 'Good, let me know before next lesson what you and Philippa have agreed between you.'

If you want to give the student time, omit the target and evaluation, and perhaps talk again later. The most unlikely students respond very well to being treated like adults, even if they don't deserve such treatment! Here's an example. A student is a long way behind with his work, despite exhortations. The teacher has listed the outstanding work; the student says he is still positive about the course. The first letters of the four key elements in an adult-to-adult kind of chat (Find the problem, Agree a solution, set a Target, follow up with an Evaluation) spell 'FATE'. See if you can identify each of the FATE elements in the following dialogue:

Teacher	So what's the problem?
Student	I don't know. I'll just have to work harder, won't I?
Teacher	Is the work too hard, too easy, too boring … ?
Student	No, not really.
Teacher	What do you find most difficult about completing homework?
Student	Finding the time, really.
Teacher	Why is that hard?

(*The student tells the teacher that he works in a pub three nights a week, and that when he finds time for college work he is often too tired to concentrate. The money, it seems, is needed to finance the student's car.*)

Teacher	So what do you plan to do about this problem?
Student	Cut down on the pub work – maybe I could just work weekends.
Teacher	What about the money for the car?
Student	I'll ask my mum if I can get a motorbike, but she's not keen on them.
Teacher	OK, talk to your mum and tell me on Monday what you have decided. But don't tell your mum I said you should have a motorbike!

(*On Monday the student says his mother will lend him money to finance his car, if he will work for her during the summer holidays.*)

One advantage of this method over a 'telling-off' is that the *real* problem is much more likely to be discovered, and students are committed to the solution because they suggested it. A further advantage is that it fosters independent problem-solving in the student.

Beware of expecting too much from this technique if the problem is deep-seated. If the evaluation shows the student has not responded, try making him or her feel guilty: 'I'm really disappointed in you, Charlie. I thought you were the sort to keep your promises …' But be ready to believe Charlie if he makes another promise.

Common causes of persistent 'discipline' problems

Don't let the following alarm you; you may never experience any of them, but awareness of the problem is often enough to avoid it, so I make no apologies for mentioning them.

Inappropriate work

Satan finds work for idle hands to do. Is the work too easy or too difficult? Is it clearly defined? Has the task been going on so long that students are bored? Do the students finish very quickly? You must do your best to make sure every student has something to do all the time, and that you are available to give help where necessary.

Students testing the teacher

This is 'playing up' the teacher. Often students tend to behave increasingly inappropriately until your response is sufficiently firm to prevent further deterioration. They are experimenting to find out where you draw the lines. The 'case law' which results defines what they can 'get away with'.

Be strict but fair, and *never appear flustered*, even when you are angry. If you deal confidently, consistently and firmly with this playing-up, it will soon lose its attraction for the students. Consider carefully the contents of this and the previous chapter.

If you feel uncomfortable about being assertive, then read the following canon immediately before and after every lesson for a week!

1   It is entirely appropriate for me to use my teacher's authority, as long as I use it in the interests of my students' learning.

2   If I use my teacher's authority effectively, I may well upset some students for a short time. If I use it ineffectively, I will upset them all for a long time.

3   If I do my best to be strict but fair, eventually I will succeed.

If you are challenged, or find yourself in a difficult situation, try hard not to over-react – or under-react. You may find it helpful to make it clear that:

• You have a right to be obeyed: 'I am the teacher here, and what I say goes.'
• You are acting in the learners' best interests: 'I am moving you because it is clear to me that you, and the rest of the class, will learn much better if you sit over here.'

Try also to make it clear that your final statements are not negotiable, but that you are prepared to discuss any matter with a student in private after the lesson. You may find the 'broken record' technique helpful here. Keep repeating what you have decided, in a calm but very positive and determined way. It helps to acknowledge the feelings of the student, even if you don't sympathise with them, but keep repeating your decision. Remember to 'PEP' up what you say with proximity and eye contact. Here is an example:

Teacher	John, I asked you to pack the equipment away.
Student	Phil will do it, miss, it's his turn.
Teacher	The lesson's nearly finished and he's still doing his graph. I want you to pack it away please.
Student	But it's Phil's turn!
Teacher	Even though it's Phil's turn, I want you to pack the equipment away.
Student	But only ...
Teacher	(*Faces the student with constant eye contact, confident posture, and close proximity*) If you want to discuss this matter, see me after the class. Meanwhile, please pack the equipment away.

Once students realise that you do not easily change your mind, you will find the broken record even more effective, and eventually almost unnecessary.

This dogged persistence usually works, but if it does, don't gloat – you will only make enemies, and in any case, it is more impressive to take the victory for granted. If it doesn't work, wait in determined silence for a few seconds, then simply walk away (removing the immediate pressure sometimes allows the student to back down without losing too much face). If you do walk away, write something down for a few moments without paying too much attention to the student (though they should know you are recording the interchange). Don't say in detail what you are writing. If the student has still not complied, say very confidently and sternly (do not say 'please' or 'thank you') that you will see them after the class.

Throughout the conversation you must appear, certainly relaxed and confident, maybe stern and determined, perhaps almost menacing, but never flustered or rattled. You should try never to lose that inner stillness that conveys authority. A tall order? Yes, it is! But anger is nearly always counterproductive; it tends to produce an angry response from some students, leading to a situation which is out of control. When you are more experienced, you may be able to put on a stately anger that maintains your dignity and sense of authority; until then, it is better to avoid appearing anything more than very stern. If you don't get angry, it's no fun 'playing you up', and you are less likely to be 'tested'.

Give yourself time and space when dealing with problems; don't leap to judgements. Leave difficult situations until the end of the class, and deal with the students on a one-to-one basis when you are both calmer.

Don't worry too much about outright defiance. It is very rare if you are firm, fair and confident. You say what you want to happen (more than once if necessary).

If you are worried about asserting authority, read a self-help book on assertiveness. Such books stress that:

- You show that you understand and value how the other thinks and feels.
- You say how you think and feel.
- You say what you want to happen (more than once if necessary).

For example: 'I know you think it's unfair because it's Phil's turn, but I'm in a rush to finish the lesson. I want you to pack up please.'

Attention-seeking

Attention-seeking students are usually extrovert, and seem to enjoy the attention of the teacher and the class, even if this attention is negative. Classmates may call such students 'show-offs', while teachers who can't think beyond the inconvenience caused to themselves may categorise them as 'buffoons' or 'class clowns'.

The best strategy is to accept the need for attention, but encourage the student to get this attention through 'legitimate' means. Give lots of attention for learning-related activities, and as little attention as possible for the disruptive attention-seeking behaviour. The latter is difficult, but the former isn't.

Such students can be very difficult to deal with, though their craving for attention makes them easy to 'bribe':

> 'That's quite a good start, Cynthia – a good opening sentence … When you've finished up to question 3, let me know and I'll mark it straight away.'
>
> 'Good diagram started here, Cynthia, I'd like to have another look when it's finished.'
>
> 'I would like someone from your group to take notes on your findings, and report them back to the rest of the class. OK, Cynthia, you can do it if you like. Make sure you keep good notes, so you can tell the rest of the class what your group decided.'
>
> (*After giving a neighbour of Cynthia's some conspicuous attention for having completed a task*) 'Now, Cynthia, have you finished too? No?' (Walks away)

Show a meticulous fascination in every aspect of the student's work and anything that relates to it, and react as little as possible to attention-seeking behaviour. The main difficulty for the teacher is that you must give valuable time and attention to a student you may dislike. Such students give teachers a stark choice: give attention for legitimate activities, or they will steal it for disruptive ones.

The seating position of such students should be thoughtfully considered. They are best placed well away from admirers, and next to students who ignore them.

Remember that for all students being able to sit where they like is a privilege, certainly not a right. Experienced teachers have no hesitation in moving students; inexperienced teachers tend to fear the temporary disapproval this engenders, and so make life much more difficult for themselves.

The teacher uses formal authority ineffectively

If your response to the kind of 'testing' mentioned above is not vigilant or firm enough, you may experience rudeness, open lack of respect and even outright defiance. You may also notice that many students who once behaved reasonably well are beginning to join in, and the riot syndrome – a negative 'ripple effect' – causes the misbehaviour to spread.

This is alarming for the teacher concerned, but it is often just an extreme example of 'testing'. If you are strict in your consistent application of classroom rules, and you refuse to get really rattled, you will eventually establish control. Nevertheless, tell someone you are having difficulties, and seek help and advice. Everyone experiences difficulties from time to time. I certainly have. You needn't feel it is an admission of failure to seek expert advice. We all need help when we are learning! If you hit a problem, re-reading this chapter and the previous one may help.

Student stress

How do *you* behave when you are under stress? I expect you lack concentration, are self-centred and lacking in consideration for others, and are irrational and short-tempered. If this is a perfect description of some of your students, then their problem behaviour may be stress-related. Their stress may be due to difficult circumstances at home.

How can we help a student deal with stress? Understanding the cause of their behaviour difficulties may help, but you can also try one-to-one talking and – most of all – listening. Ask them if they are under stress, but don't take their difficulties on yourself; refer them to their pastoral tutor and, if necessary, to a counselling service.

Talk to them about their problem behaviour the next day when they are calm; this is good practice for any recurring problem behaviour. Ask the student how you should both cope when they 'fly off the handle', and how you could both prevent this happening. They may benefit from being isolated from 'friends' who irritate them. You may be able to negotiate in advance a 'cooling-off' strategy, in which, after misbehaviour, you ask them to sit alone for a few minutes. In return, you agree not to tackle them about the misbehaviour until they have calmed down.

There is a breach of discipline but no culprit

Who threw that paper dart? Who said that swear word? You can try to avoid this problem by 'withitness'; but if it does happen, what do you do if no one owns up? Don't over-react by punishing the whole class, as this will be deeply resented. Don't accuse someone unless you are certain.

Quieten the class and then ask who did it; when (as is almost certain) no one admits to the misdemeanour, do your best to use this to your advantage:

> 'If you haven't got the nerve to say it to my face – don't say it at all.'
> 'I see, so the culprit hasn't got the courage to stand up for what they've done.'

In this way, the perpetrator is seen to be sheepish and cowardly rather than smart, so repeat performances are less likely. Someone might even own up; if they do, thank them for their honesty and deal with them as you feel fit, preferably alone. If there is still no admission, it is usually better to move on and forget it; you can do nothing without cast-iron evidence. But increase your vigilance – you can't afford to let it happen again straight away.

Dealing with problems that won't go away

Before explaining the strategies that can be used to deal with really persistent problems, I will deal with some of the techniques that may be useful.

Talking to students one-to-one

If a problem is persistent, you should obviously talk to the student about it. But how? Try the straight-talking adult-to-adult style first, even if your every instinct is to tell the student off (if not strangle them). Anger is rarely your best adviser.

However, there will be times when an 'adult-to-child' approach is more appropriate.

'Adult-to-child' style

There are times when a student needs a good telling-off! How should this be done? Enormous pressure can be put on a student in this way; the technique needs to be used with care, and in conjunction with problem-solving techniques. (If the student cries, relax the pressure and if possible revert to a more adult-to-adult style, though this might be better accomplished the next day.)

Talk alone. Remember the 'PEP' technique from the previous chapter. Face the student squarely, move too close for comfort, use almost constant eye-to-eye contact. Don't act in an aggressive way, and don't touch the student. If you are flustered, hide it, and think through carefully what you are going to say before you say it.

Ask questions in a stern and extremely self-confident manner. Don't be afraid of silences after your questions; they create a great deal of pressure on the student. Don't launch into a tirade of criticism; your body language and your questions put much more pressure on the student than anything you can say. Never be venomous or sarcastic in anything you say, and relate your criticism to the student's learning or safety.

Make it absolutely clear that you are doing this for the student's own good, not to 'get your own back' or for any self-centred reason. If you are sure the telling-off has been effective, it sometimes pays to extract a promise and then try to end up on reasonable terms. Here is an example.

Emma (13 years old) threw a pencil after being told not to. She was then asked to see the teacher after the class. The teacher speaks more slowly than usual, and tries to appear absolutely in control. Remember, it's the body language that does the real talking.

Teacher	Let's get this straight. If I tell you not to do something – you don't do it. Is that clear?
Student	(*Silence*)
Teacher	Is – that – clear? (*Silence with sustained eye contact; then:*)
Student	Yes, Miss.
Teacher	Do you know why I don't want pencil-throwing in my classes?

Student	Because we're not supposed to throw things, Miss.
Teacher	Yes, but why? (*The student can't think of anything, but you leave a long silence with constant eye contact.*) Well? … Safety, Emma, safety. I am responsible for your safety and that of the class. Now, what's wrong with throwing pencils?
Student	Could get in someone's eye.
Teacher	That's right. And what effect would that have?
Student	(*Silence*)
Teacher	(*After some time with constant eye contact*) What effect would that have?
Student	(*Silence*)
Teacher	How would you feel if your eye was damaged by someone throwing a pencil?
Student	(*More silence – but Emma is clearly upset.*)
Teacher	(*In a more friendly style, but still firmly*) OK. How about a promise?
Student	(*Still no response yet*)
Teacher	(*Quietly*) Well? Will you promise not to throw pencils in future?
Student	Yes, Miss.
Teacher	Good. (*In a friendlier tone*) OK then, Emma, you can go.

Never touch a student during adult-to-child talk; the student may interpret it as an attack and strike you in 'retaliation'. *Don't* show aggression. Never allow a student to walk away or turn away: 'Look at me when I'm talking to you.'

This technique puts far more pressure on the student than any punishment or any 'lecture', but if you find yourself relying on it then you are failing to diagnose the real problem. If you talk to a student like this in the class, make sure they have their back to the class or they might 'play to the gallery'. They may also resent the 'put-down' in front of their peers, and respond badly. Older students will certainly resent this technique if taken too far. If you are fairly sure a student will 'answer back', don't use this technique, especially in front of a class. Instead, use the 'broken record' technique to emphasise an indisputable fact or a well-known class rule. Many students will try to draw you into an argument: don't be tempted. Stay on ground where you know you can't lose, by repeating the fact or rule:

> 'But I was explaining fractions to Paul!'
> 'You know very well you are not to talk when I'm talking.'

In an exchange like this, a good-natured laugh or smile can drop the temperature and show your confidence. Criticise behaviour, never criticise the student.

A summary of three approaches

The figure overleaf shows an expanded summary of what we have been discussing. Three separate approaches are distinguished, but really they form a continuum: for example, the adult-to-adult example on page 110 was a mixture of a 'chat' and a 'word'. To respond appropriately, you must choose the right approach to fit the student and the situation. Beware if your personality gives you a strong bias to a particular approach.

A 'chat'
**Non-directive adult-
to-adult style**

A 'word'
Parent-to-adult style

A 'telling-off'
**Directive parent-
to-child style**

**Teacher's implied
message:**
'I think you are willing and
able to solve your own
problems.'
'I respect you as an individual
and have some sympathy for
your difficulties.'

**Teacher's implied
message:**
'I think you need some
pressure to solve your own
problems.'

**Teacher's implied
message:**
'You are a perishing nuisance
and I don't like you.'
'You can't solve your own
problems.'

Technique:
Ask probing questions and
LISTEN:
'What do you find most
difficult … ?'

Technique:
Set clear targets. Tell the
student the consequences if
the targets are not met.
Evaluate the achievement of
the targets. (A persistent
series of meetings may be
necessary.)

Technique:
'PEP' – proximity, eye
contact, pose questions and/
or use 'broken record':
'Why haven't you … ?'
'Do you realise the
consequences of
this behaviour?'

Style and body language:

supportive/encouraging ⟵⟶ dictatorial
non-judgemental ⟵⟶ judgemental
accepting ⟵⟶ directing
listening ⟵⟶ telling

Likely student reaction:
cooperative

Likely student reaction:
compliant

Likely student reaction:
resentful but compliant

Escalating your response to repeated inappropriate behaviour

If you have a persistent problem with a class or individual, your response to that problem may be ineffective. You must change the response if it doesn't work! This idea is simple but critical, and often overlooked. If you find yourself saying 'For heaven's sake, how many times have I told you not to … ?', then stop and think: why are you using a response you have proved does not work? A response to misbehaviour should not be tried more than two or three times consecutively with the same student. After this, change or escalate your response, or threaten to do so.

> *If you're in a hole, stop digging!*

If you habitually respond in the same way, the students will begin to feel secure about repeating the inappropriate behaviour: 'He only tells you off if you talk, so I'll have another chat with Mandy.' You must gradually increase the severity of your response, until the gain the student experiences from the inappropriate behaviour is no longer worth the unpleasant consequences of being caught at it. Only steady escalation will help you discover what is a sufficient deterrent.

> *If you always do what you've always done,*
> *You'll always get what you've always got.*

Teachers who are very good at maintaining control often have a wide range of reactions to inappropriate behaviour. This means they are rarely at a loss, and are always able to move to a new reaction if a previous one did not work. The list below is roughly in order of severity; it would, of course, be up to you to choose which techniques are appropriate in any given situation. I certainly do not suggest that you work mechanically through the list in every case, but if the strategy you are using is ineffective, try one a little further down the list. (You may like to make up your own list, using this one as a guide.)

- Look at the student.
- Sustain eye contact.
- Move towards the student, maintaining eye contact.
- Remain close to the student.
- Shake your head or frown while looking at the student.

(All these first five techniques can be used without interrupting teacher talk, etc. Bear in mind when reading the following that you can request a change in behaviour, giving the work-related reason, you can insist on the change, then you can threaten undesirable consequences if the change is not forthcoming, then you can carry out the threat.)

- Stop talking and look at the student until they notice your attention; sustain eye contact in silence, then continue.
- Use the student's name without explanation: 'Then, John, I'll look at Act II.'
- Ask the student a work-related question.
- Ask the student to explain some aspect of the work to the rest of the class.
- Stop what you are doing, and ask the student in a firm voice to stop the behaviour.
- This can be done in public, but is best one-to-one.
- Do the above with more non-verbal pressure – e.g. sustained eye contact in silence, stern voice – while standing close to the student. Ask the student a question about the behaviour (PEP).

- Speak to the student after the class, using adult-to-adult style. Set targets and evaluate these. Repeat as necessary.
- Threaten to move the student.
- Move the student.
- Put the student 'on report' – that is, he or she must show you work done at the end of the lesson, or after every lesson in the week.
- Threaten to report the student to a higher authority, e.g. to his or her tutor.
- Report the student. Keep the higher authority updated verbally on the student's subsequent behaviour. Tell the student this. (Don't be afraid to ask for help from experienced staff or from your teacher education tutor. It is not an admission of failure to ask for advice.)
- Record the student's behaviour on paper, sending a copy to a higher authority, keeping your own copy. You could tell the student you are doing this.
- Threaten to ask a senior teacher to talk to the student.
- *In response to misbehaviour that has been constantly repeated, despite every attempt to stop it*. Stop what you are doing. Move away from the student if you are close, and get a piece of paper; ask someone for the date and the exact time. Coolly write down the behaviour on the piece of paper, saying: 'OK. I've had enough. If this is the way you want it, so be it.' *Do not say what will happen to your piece of paper.* If asked, be vague: 'You'll see.' This will almost certainly stop the student misbehaving. Give a copy to the tutor responsible for the student.
- *In response to outright defiance*. As immediately above. This removes you from the confrontation, and some students will 'back down' almost as soon as the pressure is released. It is essential that defiance is reported. It is widely accepted in the profession that you should not be expected to teach students who are not prepared to accept your authority in the classroom, for safety reasons if for no other.
- *Contracts*. The student agrees, in writing, to a code of behaviour. The student should then be 'forgiven' and fully accepted back into the fold.
- In addition to all the above, your school or college may have standard forms of punishment with which you should comply.

Exactly what you do is less important than the fact that you increase the severity of your response, and that you appear confident and in control at all times. Changing tactics leaves the student uncertain of the consequences of repeating a misdemeanour. This uncertainty acts as a deterrent.

Never physically handle or hit a student. Do not send a student out of a class unless you have been told this is acceptable. If you do send a student out of a class, you are responsible for anything the student does in class time.

Don't bear grudges. Try very hard not to *show* resentment towards a student who is causing you trouble. I know this is very hard, but if you show resentment the student may retaliate. A student who believes you dislike him or her will make your job much more difficult.

Having threatened a student, you must carry out this threat to the letter if the student persists; otherwise, your credibility will go down in the eyes of the students, and should you make another threat it will not be taken seriously. Only consistency will give your authority credibility. For this reason, it is very important not to get so angry with a student that you deliver a threat that you regret, or that you could not carry out! Long before you get really angry, pretend that you have reached the end of your tether and 'act angry' with the student; that way you are more likely to appear in control. Use your temper, don't lose your temper.

Sometimes it is better to say 'I will see you about this after the class' than to rush to hasty threats or punishments. This gives you time to think, and the student time to reconsider.

Make sure you have your facts right before you reprimand a student.

ABC

ABC stands for antecedent → behaviour → consequences. Behaviourist psychologists suggest that inappropriate behaviour is triggered by a situation they call the antecedent, and that the behaviour usually has desirable consequences for the misbehaving student. Behaviour can be changed by changing either the antecedent or the consequences, or both.

Avoid the antecedent that triggers the behaviour. If students squabble when they collect equipment, give the equipment out yourself or elect a student to do so. If students arriving late disrupt the teacher-talk introduction to your classes, start the lesson with group or individual activities. If a class cannot maintain concentration for longer than two minutes, then don't talk for longer than a minute and a half at a time. I followed this approach with a particularly difficult group: I communicated with an overhead projector, with handouts, by talking one at a time to a series of small groups, and with the blackboard which I prepared before the lesson.

This transformed the lessons. First, I wasn't frustrated by students' poor concentration or their interruptions; and, second, these methods of communication released me from teacher talk, so I could give my undivided attention to firefighting and to praising and encouraging students who were working well.

Avoid situations you know cause problems. Why struggle over a wall when you can walk round it?

If you can't change the antecedents, see if you can change the consequences. If you repeatedly come across a problem, ask yourself, 'What are the students getting out of this inappropriate behaviour?' – then try to remove these gains. For example, suppose you are having difficulties with students packing up their folders five minutes before the end of the session. You can't change the antecedent, which is that the lesson is near its end, so what are the consequences *for the students*? They do less work! You could change this consequence by asking students who pack up early to summarise the main points of the lesson for you, or to answer searching questions on the lesson. If packing up early begins to mean *more* rather than less work, then this type of work-avoidance behaviour will naturally disappear.

Sandra was repeatedly late to my classes, and she played the class clown when giving excuses for her lateness. The consequences for her were that she got attention from the class. I made it clear that from now on I wanted written excuses for lateness, and the behaviour disappeared. If students don't gain from their misbehaviour, then the behaviour usually ceases.

However, the problem with denying needs is that, however successful in the short term, it leaves those needs unsatisfied, and the student may seek their fulfilment in some other way. Attention-seekers and students who are bored, frustrated or angry are not easily put off; if you close one door, they will soon find another. Can you discover what these students really want – perhaps attention, or an opportunity to be a leader – and give this to them in a legitimate activity?

> Student teachers often complain of the lack of attention of some students in their class while they are talking. What are the antecedents and the consequences for this behaviour? Can you think of solutions to this problem? There are answers in the box on page 115. (No, don't look – think the answer out for yourself first!)

Authority without resentment

There is a difference between authoritarianism and the vigorous use of legitimate authority. The former is resented and the latter is not. Suppose your ship sank on a cruise, and you and the other passengers were marooned with the captain on the proverbial desert island. What principles should be followed by the system the captain might use to maintain 'law and order'? Most people would suggest the following guidelines:

- *There must be equality before the law*. The objective of the law must be to protect the interests of all its subjects equally. It should not be used to the unfair advantage of a privileged minority or those in authority. If subjects believe the law benefits the lawmakers and law-keepers, rather than themselves, then they may well revolt (the 'revolution' syndrome). The law, including case law, should be widely understood.
- *The law must be effectively policed*. Ideally, the policing should be conspicuous and effective, and transgressors should know they stand a good chance of being caught. If a law is not enforced effectively, at least some members of the community will consider the law inoperative. (For example, it is illegal to travel at 75 mph on the motorway, but many travel at this speed, believing the police will not charge them.) If policing is conspicuously absent, then lawbreaking can become widespread; even the usually law-abiding may then take advantage and join in the lawless behaviour (the 'looting' syndrome).
- *Policing should be seen to be fair*. If an element of the community believes it is being 'picked on', harassed or kept down by policing, then respect for the law and its enforcement diminishes, and it can even be seen as an instrument of oppression.

During difficulties in Toxteth in 1988, the police started 'saturation policing'. This caused resentment in the black community, who complained of being harassed. Eventually, resentment at this perceived injustice caused serious riots, and millions of pounds of damage was caused.

- *Subjects should have a right to a fair trial*. Subjects should have a right to a fair hearing, and the decisions of the court should be seen as impartial, consistent and equally fair to all subjects.

In Los Angeles in 1992, a court saw a widely broadcast amateur video showing four white policemen beating a black motorist, Rodney King, whom they had pinned to the ground. The man sustained nine fractures to the skull and was in intensive care for some time. The court found the policemen not guilty on all charges. Riots ensued in which 60 people died.

- *Punishment should be fair and sufficiently onerous*. Likely punishments should also be well known, and they should be severe enough to have a deterrent effect. Where possible, punishment should attempt to achieve rehabilitation of the transgressor. After accepting punishment, the subjects should be welcomed back into the fold without bitterness.

At the end of the First World War the German people were made to give up German land, and to pay reparations to the Allies. Most historians now recognise this as a dreadful if understandable mistake. The German people were seething with resentment at the reparations; they saw them as a humiliation, and looked around for someone to restore German pride. This led to the rise of Hitler, and to the Second World War. If a punishment is perceived (eventually) by the miscreant as being fair, it is effective. If it is perceived as being unfair, it may actually encourage further lawbreaking.

Law and order in the classroom

If the general principles above are applied to the classroom, class rules should be based on educational, moral and safety criteria only. They should not be seen by students as being primarily for the teacher's benefit. The rules and their purposes should be well understood. The rules should be equally applied to all students. It may help to emphasise that the rules are there to benefit the students in the class, not just the teacher.

When you have more confidence, why not try involving your students in rule-making? Agree the class rules in your first few classes, asking for educational justifications for the rules. Punishments suggested by students can be surprisingly tough; you may need to soften them. Then, if a student transgresses, you have the class's authority behind you:

'Ashley, we agreed no talking when I'm talking.'

This democratic approach can be most effective.

Another effective 'democratic' approach is best shown by example. During a practical session a class works well, but is very noisy. Most teachers would stop the class, say the noise is a disgrace, and tell the students to be quiet. An alternative approach is:

Teacher I really can't work in this noise. I like a quiet classroom, I just can't think straight with noise like this. I know it's work noise mainly, but is there something we can do about this please? (*Some students offer to work more quietly.*)

Teacher Yes, but we have tried that before and five minutes later everyone is noisy again.
(*A student suggests a new class rule that students can only talk to someone within a metre of them. This is accepted by the class, and the teacher thanks students for their consideration, but enforces the rule.*)

This approach, of honestly expressing your own feelings, accepting those of your students, and then giving the problem to the students, is both assertive and democratic. It requires good rapport, but may not work immediately with very immature students, though it may be worth a try.

Policing

Make sure you are constantly 'on the beat', enforce the rules conspicuously, and be vigilant. However, don't harass individuals. It is perceptions that count here. If a student feels harassed, or 'picked on', he or she might rebel, making future class management more difficult. It makes little difference if students are wrong in feeling picked on (unless they can be persuaded they are wrong); it is not reality that determines behaviour, but perceptions.

If a student feels picked on, tell other students off for the same offence (preferably within earshot) before repeating a criticism of the 'harassed' student. Escalating your response can avoid the need to nag a student for repeating a misbehaviour.

Fair trial and punishment

Don't punish unless you are clear about the facts. Listen to excuses, don't punish in anger, be consistent. Only those who have transgressed should be punished; don't punish a whole class. After punishment, show that you don't bear grudges – for example, by showing an interest in the student's work, smiling, etc.

> ### Suggested answers to the problem on page 120
> The antecedent is that the teacher is using teacher talk, so use teacher talk less often and for shorter periods. The consequence of inattention is that the student avoids work. If every student who shows inattention is asked a question, then the behaviour actually increases work rate – and so should die out!

Unsolvable problems

> *God, give me the grace to accept the things I cannot change, the courage to change the things I can – and the wisdom to know the difference.*

Don't blame yourself for failing to deal with difficulties caused by factors beyond your control – for example, severe local unemployment, or family and emotional problems. Those who are unloved become unlovable; all we can do is try to treat such unlucky creatures as professionally as we can.

From an NSPCC poster:

> *'He drinks, he smokes, he spits at his teacher ... What he needs is a damned good cuddle.'*

Curriculum problems

Many criticise our school system because it recognises and rewards intellectual skills, but in comparison ignores, for example, manual skills, creative skills and personal skills, even though these are of great personal and economic importance. Students with these non-intellectual skills feel undervalued, and as a result tend to reject the system they feel has rejected them. Many 'behaviour' problems are really curriculum problems.

It is beyond the scope of this book to look into this problem in any detail, but on the next page is an exercise to make the point. Mark each type of skill listed out of ten, first for use and then for value.

Comment on any discrepancy you find between the marks for 'use' and 'value', and its effect on learning – bearing in mind that success is a prerequisite for learning, and that students will tend to value an education which values their skills.

This simple exercise raises more questions than it answers: for example, how teachable or examinable are these skills? To some extent, the problems raised are beginning to be addressed, with the moves towards vocational education and common or core skills.

If, with some groups, discipline is a problem even for experienced teachers, then there is something wrong. Often the problem is that the students do not see the educative experience as being in their own interest. Frankly, they are sometimes correct in this perception. If a curriculum consistently condemns a student as a failure, then the student may well retaliate by condemning the curriculum and those charged with teaching it. The solution for such problems lies in developing a curriculum that is perceived by students as being in their own best interests. This may be done in part by valuing every student's attempts to learn, and by developing a curriculum which recognises such a wide variety of skills that most students have a chance of having some of their abilities recognised and valued.

> '*My argument is that our present secondary school system … exerts on many pupils … a destruction of their dignity which is so massive and persuasive that few subsequently recover from it.*'
>
> David Hargreaves

EXERCISE

Note:
'Use' = usefulness in the real world, e.g. in commerce and industry, or at home.
'Value' = value and reward given by schools and by post-school education.

Use/Value

Intellectual skills. Academic skills in any subject: arts or sciences, humanities.
Manual skills. Any skills that involve coordination of hands and eyes: woodwork, metalwork, electronic assembly, dressmaking, etc.
Creative skills. Ability in design; ability to create, in the visual and other arts; ability to think up new ideas or use established ideas in a new way; ability to be proactive rather than reactive, e.g. entrepreneurial skills.

Self-organisational skills. For example, being organised and dependable, able to work unsupervised.
Interpersonal skills. Ability to work well in a team; ability to lead or to motivate others; sensitivity to others; caring skills; ability to cope with difficult emotional situations; being 'good with people'.
Vocationally specific skills. Knowledge and capability specific to a vocation or profession.

The use of reinforcement

Don't, in your difficulties, lose sight of your most powerful ally, the use of reinforcement for good behaviour. An American-inspired system called 'assertive discipline' has recently been introduced in some British schools. In outline, six rules are displayed in every classroom. Pupils are told they must arrive quietly and on time for lessons; bring everything they need; remain seated unless asked to move; follow instructions the first time they are given; raise their hand before speaking; and treat others, their work and their belongings with respect. There is nothing surprising here, so why are teachers using the system almost universally enthusiastic? Why does it work? Because of reinforcement. Students who obey all six rules get an 'R' for reward in the teacher's register every class. Six letters earn a 'Bronze' letter of commendation, noting their high standards of behaviour, to take home to their parents. Silver and Gold certificates can be earned for more 'R's.

This was a school-wide initiative, of a kind which you will not be in a position to institute by yourself. But the principle is what counts: reward good behaviour with recognition, encouragement and praise.

Below is a 'mind-map' for the topic of discipline. (You might like to ask your students to prepare mind-maps for the topics you teach; research shows they aid understanding and memory.)

A summarising concept map for Chapters 8 and 9. Try using mind-maps in your teaching.

EXERCISE

'Problem page'

Can you solve these real-life problems? They have all been experienced by learning teachers. Some suggested answers are given on page 129.

1 'My class is very difficult to get started at the beginning of a lesson. They are noisy and unsettled every week, and won't concentrate on what I say. I think it's because they have Mr Jones just before.'

2 'The class are reasonably OK when they are doing written work activities, but as soon as they start a practical activity they go barmy.'

3 'I was telling a girl off for being late when there was a comment I didn't hear from someone in the class, and she then collapsed into a fit of giggles.'

4 'I teach firemen first aid. They seem to think it is a blow to their dignity to be taught by a woman, and they do everything they can to question my authority.'

5 'One student in my computer class always finishes before the others; then she causes problems by distracting others in the group.'

6 'Whenever I dismiss the class, Paul always runs out at breakneck speed to get to the coffee machine first. I tell him off, but it makes no difference.'

7 'Kevin is a pain. He wants attention all the time, and he keeps bossing the others about. I've tried but I can't stop him. He's quite able, but can't concentrate for more than a few minutes. When he finishes the task he distracts me from helping the less able students in the group.'

Further reading

Same as the further reading for Chapter 8.

ANSWERS

Note: I am assuming that the lessons are well planned and interesting, and that there is plenty of reinforcement for success. These are skeleton suggestions only.

1 Don't use teacher talk at the start of the lesson. Give them something to do and go round firefighting, praising and settling them.

2 Talk to the class about it, and ask for their cooperation; it sounds as though they enjoy the practicals. Plan activities with great care, and threaten not to use friendship groups. Open a really interesting practical by threatening to withdraw it if they are noisy. Firefight at the start of the practical, praising individual groups for sensible behaviour.

3 Never start a battle you may not win. Tell her you will see her after the class, and to settle down, then do your best to ignore her.

4 Tell them your qualifications. Act in a calm, relaxed and confident way. If you teach well, sooner or later you will get their respect.

5 Give the class an interesting, stretching, 'fun' activity to do when they have completed the routine work.

6 Change the antecedent. Dismiss the class in order of completing the last task, or by rows. Alternatively, dismiss Paul last if he runs.

7 See the section on attention-seeking. Give his work plenty of attention while he is doing it. Can you get him to help the others when he has finished his tasks?

10

What kind of teacher are you?

Some teachers want to be the centre of attention in their classrooms, and are in danger of putting their own needs before those of their students. Others want to be liked, without realising that students like teachers who make them learn. Many unquestioningly teach in the way they were taught themselves. This chapter begins to look at the huge challenge of forging yourself as a teacher. What are your goals and what is your philosophy?

Here is a questionnaire designed to evaluate your approach as a teacher, according to a specific method of analysis. The background to the questionnaire is explained later. Think of your teaching situation or intended teaching situation, and answer the questions from your 'teacher's' point of view. Answer the questions honestly; don't try to guess the 'right' answer. There is no need to tell anyone about your score.

Teacher's self-analysis questionnaire

Tick the appropriate column to show your opinion:

YES! = emphatically yes   Yes = on the whole, yes

NO! = emphatically no   No = on the whole, no

	YES!	Yes	No	NO!
1 On the whole, students come to school or college reluctantly.				
2 Most learners can do well on an appropriate course if the teaching is good.				
3 The subject I teach is rewarding and interesting to learn.				
4 Most learners don't like their work being appraised by the teacher.				
5 Learners can be divided into two groups: those who want to get on, and those who want to get away with as little work as possible.				
6 Most learners can be motivated by an effective teacher.				
7 Every learner works best with plenty of individually given praise and positive reinforcement.				
8 Learners are reluctant to learn unless they are firmly directed.				
9 Most students like an orderly, well-managed environment in which to work.				

YES! Yes No NO!

10 Bright students are difficult to control.

11 It is only natural for students to do as little work as possible.

12 There is always a reason for the way students behave.

13 'What's in it for me?' is a legitimate question for learners to ask about a course.

14 On the whole, if learners fail to learn it is the fault of the teacher, the school, the curriculum or poor resourcing.

15 Most learners learn to their maximum if the teacher is skilled.

16 What learners want and what teachers want is different, therefore they can never see eye to eye about work rate.

17 Work of a low standard deserves strong criticism.

18 Teachers should be prepared to put their foot down if necessary, even at the risk of temporary unpopularity.

19 It encourages inattention if the teacher helps students who don't listen the first time.

20 Teachers should go out of their way to behave positively towards students who they know do not like work.

21 The subject I teach requires natural flair – either you can do it or you can't.

22 Students should be threatened with punishment if they do not work.

23 Learners nearly always accept constructive criticism, as they know it helps them improve.

24 Students welcome work if they are given a chance to succeed.

Scoring

Using the table on the next page, for each question number, please circle the mark corresponding to the answer you chose in the questionnaire. For example, if you answered 'No' to question 1, score 3; if you answered 'YES!' to question 5, score *minus* 5.

1 Add all your positive scores together and put the total in the positive score box.

2 Add all your negative scores together and put the total in the negative score box.

3 Combine your positive and negative scores by addition. For example, $+75 - 25 = +50$.

4 Read off below the table the findings which are appropriate to your final score.

	YES!	Yes	No	NO!		YES!	Yes	No	NO!
1	−3	0	3	5	13	5	3	−2	−3
2	5	3	−3	−5	14	5	5	−3	−3
3	5	5	−3	−5	15	−5	−2	2	5
4	−3	0	3	5	16	−3	−3	3	5
5	−5	3	3	3	17	−5	−2	3	5
6	5	2	−5	−5	18	5	3	−3	−5
7	5	3	−3	−5	19	−5	−3	2	5
8	−3	0	0	0	20	5	3	−3	−5
9	5	2	−3	−5	21	−5	−3	3	5
10	−5	−3	3	5	22	−2	2	0	0
11	−5	−3	3	5	23	5	3	2	−2
12	5	3	−3	−5	24	3	5	−2	−3

Positive score ☐

Negative score ☐

TOTAL SCORE ☐

−100 to −40 Your attitudes are likely to produce learners who do as they are told and nothing more. Please read Chapters 5, 6 and 7.

−39 to zero Your attitudes are likely to produce learners who only rarely show genuine interest in their work. Please read Chapters 5, 6 and 7.

zero to +40 Your attitudes are likely to produce an average bunch of students who will do well on the whole; many of the more able will show some interest and enthusiasm for their work.

+41 to +100 You will produce students who are committed to learning (and to you), and they will find their work enjoyable and rewarding.

If you are unhappy with your score, re-read the chapters on motivation and praise and criticism.

Background to the questionnaire

The questionnaire is very loosely based on Douglas McGregor's analysis of management styles in his book *The Human Side of Enterprise*.

Broadly speaking, teachers have two different assumptions about human nature. We can label those assumptions 'Theory X' and 'Theory Y'.

Theory X
- The average learner dislikes work and will avoid it if possible.
- Learning is difficult and not very interesting.

- Because learning is basically lacking in interest, most people must be coerced, controlled, directed and threatened with punishment in order to learn satisfactorily.
- The average learner is passive, unambitious and prefers to be directed rather than show initiative.

Theory Y
- In most learning situations learners only work to a fraction of their full capacity.
- Learning is rewarding and interesting. Learners have social, self-esteem and egoistic needs which they want to satisfy by their learning. They achieve this satisfaction by gaining respect and recognition for their successes.
- Students do not dislike work. Laziness, and lack of motivation or ambition, are not inherent human characteristics; they are reactions to unsatisfactory learning conditions.
- Learners can become committed to the goal of self-improvement.

Theory Y does not preclude the setting of targets, nor should it encourage low standards. According to Theory Y, the successful teacher must satisfy the self-esteem needs of the learner through activities directed towards the teaching aims. According to Theory X, the learner must be directed and coerced into carrying out these activities. In a strange sense, both of these theories are correct. They both have a tendency to work as self-fulfilling prophecies. Theory X teaching can make students bored, passive and demotivated. Theory Y teaching can be inspiring, motivating students into self-improvement. To some extent, what the teacher thinks will happen is what the teacher gets.

Of course, students also have theories about teachers. Theory A is that the teacher is only in it for the money, and basically dislikes the students and the subject they are teaching. Theory B is that teachers are interested in students, in their efforts to learn and in their subject. If a Theory Y teacher meets a Theory A class, it can take some time to turn the situation into one where learning is productive.

Are you an instructor or a facilitator?

Who should have control over learning, the teacher or the student? This is a central question you must answer. Most teachers operate somewhere between 'instructor' and 'facilitator' described below, depending on the context.

Instructor

Here the teacher is in control. An instructor plans and directs all the students' activities, giving clear, recipe-style instructions for the tasks to be carried out. Attention is focused on putting over a predetermined body of knowledge and skills. There is an emphasis on the *product*, that is, the students' work, which should be neat, tidy and without error. The teacher checks the students' understanding to discover any learning errors or omissions and then helps the students, usually by re-teaching the appropriate material. The teacher is also in charge of assessing and evaluating the students' work.

It may seem a paradox at first, but this approach has been criticised for being too helpful. If you help too much, it is argued, you create 'learned dependency' and 'learned helplessness': a state of mind in the students where they believe they are entirely dependent on teachers in order to learn, and do not have the capacity to help themselves or to overcome difficulties unaided. Consequently, learners fail to take responsibility for their own learning and become *passive learners*, as described in Chapter 5. They 'go through the motions', doing what the teacher requires, but learn only very superficially.

For example, suppose a teacher intends her class to study the attitudes of adults to the unemployed. She gives the students an investigation to carry out, providing recipe-style instructions, references and a questionnaire the students must use in the high street. In this case, students will *not* learn for themselves how to plan, carry out and evaluate their own investigations, though they will learn the 'product' – that is, the attitude of adults to the unemployed.

Facilitator

Consider the alternative approach of giving the students more control. This can be done by 'teaching by asking' rather than by telling. The teacher asks students, 'What is the attitude of adults to the unemployed?' They are then encouraged to conclude that they must carry out a survey to answer this question.

The students plan, carry out and evaluate this survey for themselves. The teacher does not hand *all* responsibility over to the learners. She looks at their plans, she questions them and, if necessary, reminds or guides her students to ensure their survey is effective. But she does her best to ensure that her students do as much as possible for themselves. If a student asks for help she does not give it straight away, but uses questioning to gently prompt students into answering their own questions.

In this way, the student learns the product, that is, the attitudes of adults to the unemployed, but also learns *process skills* such as how to carry out a survey, and how to monitor and evaluate its implementation. Having designed their survey for themselves, the students are likely to be much more committed and interested in their work. They feel a sense of 'ownership' and so are more likely to become active learners during the activity.

The approach described above, of encouraging the students to devise their own survey, is an example of the facilitator approach. Here, instead of the teacher taking control, the students are given control over their own learning, and so learn to teach themselves. The teacher's role is to facilitate (help) this process, by ensuring that students really do take control and responsibility. However, help is given where it is really needed.

Notice that the focus is on the learning *process* (how students learn) rather than exclusively on the *product*, and mistakes are seen as an opportunity to learn, rather than being reprehensible.

Learners often fail to make best progress because of fear and lack of self-belief. So great stress is placed on developing a supportive psychological climate. Consequently, facilitators are encouraged to put themselves into their learners' shoes (develop empathy) and try to become non-judgemental, yet genuine. They should be supportive towards their students, whom they should hold in high regard as people, however slight their accomplishments.

Only when fear of teacher criticism is overcome, and student self-belief is developed, will students have the courage to take responsibility for their own learning.

> *Researchers into management styles have compared managers who delegate responsibility with those who prefer more control. Some managers tell their staff not just what to do, but also how they must do it. Researchers find that the staff of such controlling managers tend to take little initiative, feel less committed, and are less creative in finding and solving problems.*
>
> *However, it is found that managers who delegate a good deal of responsibility get much more commitment, creativity and initiative from their staff.*
>
> *Learners are the same: they tend to take initiative, and develop enthusiasm only when they are given some responsibility and control over their learning.*

The instructor–facilitator continuum

Educationalists and many effective teachers come down heavily in favour of the facilitator approach. However, in practice there is a continuum between 'instructor' and 'facilitator' where control over learning is shared, and most teachers move back and forth along this continuum as the situation demands.

Where should you operate on this continuum? What aspects of teaching or learning should your students have control over and responsibility for? The following diagram is designed to help you answer this question.

Many teachers operate between 'instructor' and 'facilitator' on the continuum

⟵————————————————————————————————⟶

Instructor:
Teacher is in control

Control is
shared
between
teacher and
learner

Facilitator:
Learner is in
control

above, in a style which suits their current purposes. They might adopt the instructor style when introducing new material, but the facilitator style when encouraging students to overcome a difficulty, or revise for an exam. Like many things in teaching the decision is made on the basis of 'fitness for purpose'. However, there is a general consensus that the extreme instructor style, though common, is not effective.

Becoming a facilitator rather than an instructor is not so much about the use of techniques or teaching methods. It is an attitude and a set of values. Facilitators argue that giving students more control over and responsibility for their learning has the following advantages:

- It encourages active and deep learning, rather than passive and superficial learning.
- It develops self-management and 'learning to learn' *process skills* as well as delivering the learning *product*.
- It discourages learned helplessness and learned dependency and encourages the development of self-belief, self-reliance and autonomy.
- It is less stressful and more enjoyable for the teacher, who also gains the students' respect for treating them with respect.

The issues raised here are returned to in the chapters on course organisation (41), independent learning (33) and self-directed learning (34).

Developing your own teaching style

Most novice teachers make these two mistakes:

- They err on the side of the 'instructor'.
- They teach the way they were taught, even if this is not best practice or most appropriate for the situation in which they are teaching.

Are you making either or both of these mistakes? If so, why, and what could you do about it?

Personal goals

What are you trying to achieve by your teaching? This is a very demanding, but when you can begin to answer it, also a very illuminating question. Of course, you want your students to learn successfully, but you may also have overarching personal goals, such as encouraging in your students:

- curiosity and interest in your subject
- self-confidence and self-belief
- critical thinking skills and intellectual independence
- empathy, and a sense of personal moral responsibility

- creativity, self-expression and personal development
- spiritual understanding and development
- appreciation of peoples and cultures other than their own
- appreciation of environmental or social issues.

Which of these personal goals would excite your loyalty and motivate you? Or are there other values which you want to work towards? It may take a year or so before you feel ready to decide on your personal goals, and it may take a lifetime to find effective ways of achieving them. But such personal missions, and others like them, can inspire and direct your teaching, and can allow you to realise your own personal values through your teaching, and so help you to find your work meaningful and rewarding, as well as increasing its effectiveness.

You must, as a teacher, achieve goals that others set for you. Your students must pass, and must not set fire to the classroom! But within these constraints there is still room for you to take control, and achieve your own vision of good teaching and learning.

Further reading

Entwistle, N. (1988) *Styles of Learning and Teaching*, London: David Fulton.

McGregor, D. (1985) *The Human Side of Enterprise* (revised edition), New York: McGraw-Hill.

Martinez, P. (2001) *How Colleges Improve*, LSDA Online. You might find this in your library, but I can't find it online anymore.

Maslow, A. H. (1987) *Motivation and Personality* (3rd edition), New York: Harper Collins.

*Rogers, C. (1994) *Freedom to Learn* (3rd edition), New York: Prentice Hall.

On the humanistic approach to education:

*Russell, B. (1992) *The Basic Writings of Bertrand Russell* (2nd edition), Part 10, London: Routledge. Short essays on education, teaching and its aims.

Introduction

In order to make an informed choice of teaching method or learning strategy, and in order to be adaptable and have a variety of activities for lesson planning, the teacher must know:

* what teaching methods are available
* what are the strengths and weaknesses of these methods
* what purpose each of them can serve
* how each should be used in practice.

This is the purpose of this section of the book.

Which is the best teaching method? You might as well ask a carpenter which is his best tool; he chooses his tool depending on whether he wants to make a hole, remove a screw or cut a piece of wood in two. Every tool has its uses, and good carpenters not only know how to use each tool, but are able to assess which is the most appropriate in a given circumstance. Teaching methods, like carpenters' tools, are chosen on the basis of fitness for purpose. As we will see in the chapters on lesson planning (Part 4), the teacher should first clarify the purposes of the lesson, and then choose activities which will achieve these purposes.

Which learning activities or teaching methods you choose, and how you use them, will not depend only on your purposes. It is crucial to consider also your students, the physical environment such as the room and the equipment available, and the emotional climate. Were they a bit bored last lesson? Have you had a lot of group work lately? Do they find worksheets tedious? All these factors must be taken into account. You must be observant, and responsive to what you observe. You must also know which methods have proved particularly powerful in classroom trials.

Student preference

What teaching methods do students prefer? This is not a deciding factor, but it is certainly a very important one. It is better for students to have 80% concentration on a moderately effective method than 10% concentration on a supposedly brilliant one.

M. Hebditch asked students aged 11–18 years what teaching methods they preferred. The answers to his questionnaire are tabulated on the following page. Look at them carefully before reading on: what do their preferences have in common?

Students' preferences in teaching methods

Style	Like %	Dislike %	Neutral %
Group discussion	80	4	17
Games/simulations	80	2	17
Drama	70	9	22
Artwork	67	9	26
Design	63	4	33
Experiments	61	11	28
Options (choice allowed)	61	4	33
Computers	59	22	20
Exploring feelings (empathy)	59	11	30
Reading English literature	57	9	35
Practical ideas	52	9	37
Laboratory work	50	11	37
Library research	50	24	26
Charts, tables, etc.	46	15	37
Craft work	43	17	39
Fieldwork	43	20	35
Open-ended work	43	20	37
Themes	41	11	48
Creating products	41	11	43
Working alone	41	26	33
Invention	39	20	41
Organising data	37	20	43
Empathy	35	30	35
Observation	30	13	57
Worksheets	28	17	52
Reading for information	26	30	43
Using technology	24	26	46
Deadlines	24	50	26
Time schedules	17	41	41
Analysis	17	35	46
Theories	15	39	43
Essays	13	28	54
Lectures	11	70	19

Data collected from questionnaire submitted to students from 11 to 18 years and provided by M. Hebditch, Gillingham School, Dorset, 1990.

Students like action: talking in groups, making things, being creative, doing things.

Passive methods get an emphatic thumbs-down; bottom of the list is 'lecture'. So don't fall for the commonly believed myth that students are fundamentally lazy, preferring activities which intrude as little as possible into their daydreaming. In general, the more active and engaged students are, the better they like it.

Many teachers develop one or two teaching methods and stick to them. This is a mistake. A variety of methods – as well as increasing student attention and interest – gives you the flexibility to deal with the wide range of challenging and infuriating problems that teachers inevitably encounter. It also helps you deal with the increasing demands of the teacher's ever-changing role. In modern education, as in evolution, the motto is 'adapt to survive'.

Some teaching methods are much better than others

Teaching is embarking on a revolution and I hope you will be part of it. In the last few decades, researchers have tested teaching methods by asking a good teacher to use their usual methods with a 'control' group; and to teach a parallel and nearly identical 'experimental' group. This group is taught in the same way, except that the method being researched is included in an appropriate part of the lesson. Students are then tested to see if the experimental group has learned better than the control group. When a method has been trialled like this many times with different teachers, it is possible to find its average effectiveness and to determine the best way to use it.

Some methods improve students' marks in the test by two grades, and improve the pass rate by more than 30%. To the great surprise of many, the best methods work their magic regardless of the age or ability of the students, or the subject they study. For example, self-assessment works with primary school children learning maths, but also with university students studying English. The potential effectiveness of a teaching method is roughly the same in any context.

Professor John Hattie is a world expert on these experiments and other attempts to measure what most influences attainment. He has collected hundreds of thousands of studies and concludes that the most successful methods share three characteristics:

1 **They set students challenging tasks**: rather than being given exclusively attainable tasks, students are given an activity which involves them in deep thought. See Chapter 1, especially 'Bloom's bits'.

2 **Students and teacher get informative feedback**: this is feedback on what aspects of these tasks was done well, and what needed improving. See Chapter 43.

3 **The task was constructivist**: it required the student to create and improve their personal understanding rather than, say, remember by rote. See pages 4–7.

Here are some methods that have done particularly well in these trials; some come from Hattie and some from Professor Robert Marzano who has done similar work:

- **Whole-class interactive teaching**: active learning using the PAR structure, with assertive questioning and/or student demonstration. See Chapter 24, and the PAR structure on page 444.
- **Feedback**: formative assessment, including self-, peer and spoof assessment. See Chapter 43.
- **Graphic organisers**: students creating and improving mind-maps, flow diagrams, Venn diagrams, matrixes or similar visual ways to organise information. See pages 344–5.
- **Same and different**: asking students to compare and contrast to find similarities and differences in what they are studying, e.g. fractions and percentages. See page 235.
- **Good classroom management and discipline**: making sure that learning is not disrupted, and is efficiently carried out. See Chapters 8 and 9, and a free chapter from my *Evidence Based Teaching*, which can be downloaded from www.geoffpetty.com/evidence_based.htm
- **Strategy training**: teaching 'learning to learn', writing, thinking and study skills by integrating this into your teaching. See Chapter 28. For the detail see Chapters 21 and 24 in my *Evidence Based Teaching*.
- **Decisions, decisions**: see pages 228–30.
- **Hypothesis testing**: a challenging evaluation to develop arguments for and against a hypothesis, policy, etc. For example, a hypothesis such as 'Cromwell was a dictator' or 'TV is the best advertising medium'. This is evaluation really. See the end of Chapter 38.

In *Evidence Based Teaching*, I look at what we can learn from these trials, and other evidence in detail. It follows on from *Teaching Today* and is intended for the last half of your training and for continued personal and professional development.

Note also that by a lucky coincidence active methods are the most enjoyable, and the most effective! Or is it a coincidence?

From learning styles to whole-brain learning

In the last few years there has been a seismic shift in how learning styles are used and understood. Having read this chapter you will be more up to date than most teachers – but try not to appear too smug! Have a look at Herrmann's learning styles on page 149 to get the idea of 'learning styles'.

It used to be thought that everybody had a personally preferred learning style, or even that everybody learned in their own unique way. The idea was that the student should use whatever style suited them best, as each style was capable of leading them to any learning destination. But learning styles didn't turn out to be equivalent and interchangeable roads to the same place.

Instead, the emerging view is that we can all learn in all the styles. We might find some styles easier than others, but we can all learn with them all. Also, learning the same topic with different styles helps us to learn better. Learning styles should not be seen as alternatives to choose from. Instead, they are different ways of learning which are complementary and mutually supportive. Rather like the plan, front and side views of an architect's drawing, they all help our understanding.

You can't talk to me … I'm a visual learner.

In 2004, Professor Frank Coffield and colleagues published the results of a two-year review of over 70 learning style systems. Did any of these systems describe real differences between people? Were their questionnaires reliable? They looked for hard evidence, but found none for most of the systems. These included systems that have been used for years in schools and colleges, such as VAK (visual, auditory and kinaesthetic); Honey and Mumford (activist, theorist, pragmatist and reflector); Dunn *et al.*; and many others.

Miss I'm a pragmatist … is there a question on this in the exam?

However, Coffield did find a few learning style systems for which there was hard evidence. As described immediately below, these were all 'whole brain' in their approach, rather than the old-fashioned 'type and match'.

- *Whole brain*: there are different ways of thinking, and different preferences, but we can all do them all. We learn a given topic best and enjoy learning most, if we encounter all these styles.
- *Type and match*: (an old-fashioned approach) we prefer different learning styles, and we learn best if we are taught in our preferred style. So teachers need to find what style or type a student is, and match their teaching to this.

For example, imagine two students: John likes verbal explanations, and Jill prefers visual explanations. Even if these preferences are real enough, they will both learn best if they both experience both the styles (Dunn *et al.* 1989). Klein (2003) also quotes research that shows that a student's understanding and recall are improved if all styles are encountered. If you teach a student one-to-one, you can start with the student's preference, as this might help, but use other styles too.

By way of analogy we could say that even if one eye is much stronger than the other, it makes no sense to put a patch over the weaker eye! Or a liking for plan views is no reason to ignore the side views.

> *'… instead of trying to teach every learner in the dominant learning style, we must remember to offer our students both variety and choice. It's that simple. The human brain is a multi-processor. It learns in many ways usually at the same time.'*
>
> Super Teaching, *Eric Jensen (an expert on the brain)*

The false idea that each 'learning style' can stand alone, that your preference doesn't change, and that each style provides a complete alternative route to the same learning goal is still strongly held by some teachers. It will take time, but if we follow the evidence there will be a move in the next few years towards 'whole-brain learning' and 'multiple representations'. Let's look at this now.

Multiple representations

The more ways ideas are presented to students, the better they understand them. This is why we sometimes say, 'Can you explain it another way?' when we don't understand something. If a student is having difficulty understanding percentages, they will benefit if they experience it in different ways – for example, visual representations with pie charts, analogies such as 30% is 30p in the pound, practical activities with counters, concrete examples, having to explain the concept without using mathematical words, and so on. This is called 'multiple representations'. Formal definitions, abstract explanations and formulas are not enough for most students.

These different experiences cause the learner to represent the concept of 'percentages' in their brain in different ways, and in different parts of their brain. They can also help to make links between existing concepts and the new concept of 'percentages', and this considerably helps understanding. For example, linking pennies in the pound and percentages.

We now know that at the unconscious level the brain is a 'multiprocessor' which uses all these representations at the same time! The more varied these representations and links, the more likely it is that the learner will 'get' the concept, and gain a full understanding.

Multiple representations in the teaching of mathematics

Berkshire Mathematics is an approach to maths teaching using ideas from Professor Mahesh Sharma. He makes use of at least six representations in developing a new maths procedure.

- New concepts are developed by ensuring every new fact is introduced as an extension of something the child already knows.
- Through a concrete model such as Cuisenaire rods or the Invicta Balance.
- Pictorially – for example, by a sketch or an illustration.

- Only then are mathematical ideas expressed in their usual abstract form e.g. 3 + 4 = 7.
- Then the child is asked to form a number story using this fact. 'I had three apples and then I found four more under the tree. Then altogether I had seven.'
- She is then asked to explain the strategy being used. For example, '3 + 3 = 6, I know 3 + 4 is one more, so 3 + 4 = 7.'

www.berkshiremathematics.com

There is more on this in my *Evidence Based Teaching*.

The new approach to learning styles

Don't dump the idea of learning styles. If you get your students to use all or many learning styles while teaching a topic, then your teaching will:

- **be varied and interesting**
- **provide 'multiple representations'**
- **benefit all your students, whatever style they prefer**
- **develop different skills in your learners.**

Students differ in the teaching methods they do best in, and only a variety of activities will ensure that you play into the relative strengths and preferences of every student at least some of the time. If you always use teacher talk followed by students working alone from worksheets, then students who learn well from visual representations, creative work and group discussion will not fulfil their potential. Some teachers teach almost exclusively in the way they were taught, or the way *they* like to learn. This is unlikely to suit all their students.

Do use learning styles questionnaires, but remember that Coffield showed they are most unlikely to be reliable or valid. Despite this, he said students may still benefit from reflecting on how they like to learn – but encourage them to exploit their strengths and work on their weaker styles.

Coffield's review of learning styles research is the most thorough and authoritative we have. Surface and deep learning, which are the subjects of Chapter 1, came out very well in his review. So did Herrmann's whole-brain model, and a few others I think are less helpful to teachers. These were usually adaptations of the 'right-brain' 'left-brain' model below.

There is no perfect learning style system, but each can help us to see how to explain in more than one way, and each requires us to use more varied teaching methods. I will explain the models that did well in Coffield's review, then look at some systems that are still common in schools and colleges. But first I will look at the 'right-brain' 'left-brain' model. Coffield's report finds no evidence that people have a stable preference for left- or right-brain thinking. But classroom trials suggest we learn best if we experience them both (Petty 2006).

Right-brain and left-brain thinking

Have a look at the right- and left-brain learning diagram below. It is a tempting 'common sense' view that the brain thinks in language and that if you understand something you can express it in words.

But we often solve a problem in a flash, and then stumble for some time in a frustrated effort to express our reasoning verbally. Also, we can know what a word means, yet be unable to express this in words. What is going on?

Thinking verbally, and doing one task at a time in a logical order is called left-brain thinking. But we also have a right brain, which thinks non-verbally. The right brain sees things as a whole (holistically), and right-brain understanding is non-verbal, and visual, or of the immediate 'penny-dropping' type. (Strictly speaking, the 'right' and 'left' brain descriptions are not anatomically correct, but there is little doubt that the brain thinks in these two ways.)

We can all think with both sides of our brain, of course. Yes, even your students! We will learn better if we use our whole brain rather than just one side, though we might need help with the activities that we don't prefer. For example, some students have trouble with sequencing or with mind-maps and need to be shown how to do these.

Right- and left-brain learning

Dr Ross Cooper has developed 'The Learning Styles Interactive Computer Program', which gives students personalised advice on how to improve their learning. Students often find this interesting and helpful. He advises teachers to use both left- and right-brain teaching strategies, and believes that many 'learning difficulties' are often really teaching difficulties. For example, some learners may experience 'learning difficulties' if they are taught in an almost exclusively verbal and sequential manner.

We all need both a right-brain and a left-brain understanding, and good teachers provide both of these.

Left-brain and right-brain teaching strategies

Overwhelmingly we teach using language, breaking topics down into logical sub-units, and then teaching these one at a time. This is a very left-brain approach. If we also taught to the right brain, then fewer students would experience difficulties, and all students would benefit, because they would all be learning using both sides of their brain.

But how can we teach to the right side of the brain? See graphic organisers below and Chapter 32 on right-brain, visual and kinaesthetic teaching strategies.

In practice, we need to teach to both sides, often at the same time. For example, a teacher might give a verbal 'left-brain' explanation providing detail, and step-by-step explanations of some complex relationships. But the teacher might also show

Left brain:

sees things
in parts –
sequential,
language
and logic

Right brain:

sees things as
a whole –
spatial, music
and images

Left-brain learners

(Verbal sequential, or a serialist learner)

You have a preference for learning in a
sequential style, logically step by step. You like
to be organised and ordered in your approach,
doing one thing at a time.

You like to break things down into categories
and to consider these separately. You are good
at deductive thinking, for example using cause
and effect.

You feel more comfortable attending to detail
than dreaming up new ideas. Left-brain
learners do well in the assessment process at
least up to GCSE, as this is very verbal.
However, the ability to think also in a
right-brain way is important for top grades at
level 3 (e.g. A Level) and above.

Left-brain learners like:
- a step by step approach
- working in small steps up to the big picture
- a narrow focus
- to deal with steps in order and in isolation
- rules and structure
- logic rather than intuition
- facts rather than their experience.

Right-brain learners

(Visual holistic learner)

You like to see the whole in context: 'the big
picture'. You need to see the meaning,
relevance and purpose of what you learn.
You focus on similarities, patterns and
connections with former learning. You like to
get a 'feel' for the topic, and see how it all fits
together. You prefer to follow your intuition
rather than work things out carefully. You can
use lateral thinking.

You are flexible, and feel more comfortable
dreaming up imaginative and creative ideas
than you do being systematic and organised.
You may prefer music while you work, unless
the task is very demanding, and to work with
peers in an informal seating style.

Many dyslexic learners have a strong
right-brain preference

Right-brain learners like:
- to see 'the big picture' with a clear meaning
  and purpose
- working from the big picture down to the
  detail
- to explore in an idiosyncratic, personalised
  and intuitive way
- to jump in anywhere
- to avoid rules, structures and details
- making links and relations between topics
  and seeing patterns.

a 'right-brain' schematic diagram, which clarifies understanding by eliminating the
detail and only showing the key points and their interrelationships. This diagram
has different strengths to the verbal explanation. It shows the topic 'all at once' or
holistically, it organises the information, and the learner can search it for clarification. It also aids recall. Neither the verbal explanation nor the diagram alone are
as good as both together. Right- and left-brain approaches are not interchangeable alternatives, they are complementary. We return to this approach in 'Styles
of analysis' below (page 152).

Theorist – the rational self
(males often prefer this)

Likes: Logical, rational, and mathematical activities
(*as opposed to*: emotional, spiritual, musical, artistic, reading, arts and crafts, introvert, or feelings activities)

Learns by:
Acquiring and quantifying facts
Applying analysis and logic
Thinking through ideas
Building cases
Forming theories

Learners respond to:
Formalised lecture
Content which includes data
Financial/technical case discussions
Textbooks and bibliographies
Programmed learning
Behavior modification

Rank:

Innovators- the experimental self

Likes: Innovating, conceptualising, creating, imaginative, original, artistic activities
(*as opposed to*: controlled, conservative activities)

Learns by:
Taking initiative
Exploring hidden possibilities
Relying on intuition
Self-discovery
Constructing concepts
Synthesising content

Learners respond to:
Spontaneity
Free flow
Experiential opportunities
Experimentation and exploration
Playfulness
Future oriented case discussions
Creating visual displays
Individuality
Aesthetics
Being involved

Rank:

Organisers – the safe-keeping self

Likes: Order, planning, administration, organisation, reliability, detail, low level of uncertainty
(*as opposed to*: holistic thinking, conceptualising, synthesis, creating or innovating.)

Learns by:
Organising and structuring content
Sequencing content
Evaluating and testing theories
Acquiring skills through practice
Implementing course content

Learners respond to:
Thorough planning
Sequential order
Organisational and administrative case discussions
Textbooks
Behaviour modification
Programmed learning
Structure
Lectures

Rank:

Humanitarians – the feeling self
(females often prefer this)

Likes: Interpersonal, verbal, people-orientated, emotional and musical activities.
(*as opposed to*: analytical technical, logical, mathematical activities.)

Learns by:
Listening and sharing ideas
Integrating experiences with self
Moving and feeling
harmonizing with the content
Emotional involvement

Learners respond to:
Experiential opportunities
Sensory movement
Music
People-orientated case discussions
Group discussion
Group interaction such as jigsaw
Empathy and role play
Reflection

Rank:

Herrmann's 'whole-brain' model: each person likes *two* styles, but can use them all

148

Herrmann's 'whole-brain' model

Herrmann found that everyone has a preference for two of the four styles shown in the diagram on page 148. However, we shouldn't stereotype students, as we all need to be able to work in all four styles. Coffield's review is positive about Herrmann's model; we each have a real and stable preference for two of the four styles. But Herrmann finds that we enjoy being challenged to work outside our preferences, and benefit from this. However, we need to be taught how to do this in some cases. Whole-brain teaching involves teaching any substantial topic by using all four styles.

Rank the four styles 1, 2, 3 and 4 in order of your own teaching preference. Then ask yourself how you could become a more whole-brain teacher, using all styles equally. There is more on whole-brain teaching in *Evidence Based Teaching* (pages 32–9).

Other learning style systems

The following learning style systems are common, but if you ask your students to complete the questionnaires for these styles, do not take the results seriously. Completing the questionnaire on two different days often gets two different results! So don't use them to stereotype your students.

Herrmann's is the only learning style system with stable results that also gives detailed suggestions to teachers. However, the following learning styles systems identify ways in which you can vary your teaching, and you might find your institution makes use of them, or that they are on your teacher training syllabus.

Visual, auditory and kinaesthetic ('VAK') learning styles

The 'visual, auditory and kinaesthetic' (VAK) system suggests three teaching approaches. You can present ideas using:

* The visual approach: e.g. with diagrams called 'graphic organisers' (below, page 152); videos; demonstrations and so on.
* The auditory approach with teacher explanations, discussion and so on.
* The less common 'kinaesthetic' or 'tactile' approach. Here students encounter ideas through action; they physically make or do something in a hands-on, real-world way, or experience simulations of these. They are often allowed to move around the room as part of the activity.

Chapter 32 on right-brain visual and kinaesthetic methods looks at teaching methods that make use of visual and kinaesthetic learning.

'Multisensory learning' suggests learners should experience all three approaches to learn any substantial concept or topic. This is associated with primary education's 'Montessori method', and has been successful in teaching dyslexic students. NLP (neurolinguistic programming) and 'accelerated learning' also make use of

VAK, but often suggest the 'type and match' strategies described on page 143, which Coffield is against.

Remember that we don't have stable preferences for one style, but benefit from using them all. However, if you ask students what their preference is on any given day you get some surprising results. Paul Ginnis, in his excellent *Teacher's Toolkit*, quotes research on over 5,000 school pupils whose stated preferences were:

- **29% visual**
- **34% auditory**
- **37% kinaesthetic.**

Kolb's cycle and learning styles

Honey and Mumford devised learning styles based on Kolb's cycle, shown below. The idea is that in order to learn, say, how to calculate percentages or how to skin a fish, we do it, review how it went, learn from this review and then apply this insight the next time we do it, and so on.

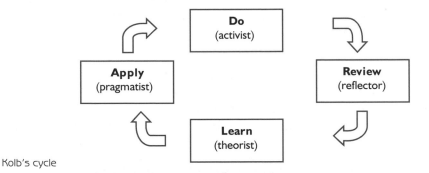

Kolb's cycle

The cycle is explained in detail in Chapter 31. Honey and Mumford argue that each stage in the cycle requires us to work in a different style: activist, reflector, theorist, pragmatist, as the diagram shows. Coffield found no evidence that these learning styles were stable for any individual, so, again, we need to use them all, preferably in the meaningful sequences described later.

Honey and Mumford devised their learning styles approach to promote learning, not to stereotype learners, and believe that all learners should work on their weak styles to improve their learning.

Honey and Mumford collected data on adult professionals working in the field of business and management, and came to the following conclusions:

- about 2% of people are 'fully equipped', i.e. able to make good use of any style
- about 70% of people use only one or two styles.

In an article in the *Guardian* they gave the learning style profile of Jack Straw, the MP and Cabinet Minister; he had a very strong preference for activist and pragmatist, and a moderate preference for reflector and theorist. Peter Preston, editor of the *Guardian* at the time, had a very strong activist preference, and a low, or very low preference for the other three styles.

Kolb believed that good learning requires that we go round the cycle, and so use all the learning styles at appropriate times. If you plan lessons that follow Kolb's cycle, the learning is often well structured and all styles are visited. Let's look at a few lesson plan structures that do this. These do not always go neatly round the cycle, but all styles are present. The styles are given by their first letter, so:

Howard Gardner has proposed that we have at least seven intelligences, and that individuals differ in the extent to which they have each. Schools have concentrated on numbers 1 and 3.

1 *Linguistic intelligence*: skill in using language, both verbal and written.
2 *Musical intelligence*: skill with music and rhythm.
3 *Logical-mathematical intelligence*: skill with numbers and logic, as in maths and science.
4 *Spatial intelligence*: the ability to comprehend maps, plans and to think in 3D.
5 *Bodily-kinaesthetic intelligence*: movement and manipulation skills.
6 *Interpersonal intelligence*: the ability to empathise, and work well with others etc.
7 *Intrapersonal intelligence*: self-awareness, ability to regulate your own thinking.
8 *Naturalistic intelligence*: awareness and ability associated with the natural world.

This approach has been criticised by Coffield, and by those who believe that intelligence is not a fixed attribute but can be learned. See Chapter 45 and Klein (2003).

Try a search on the Internet using: GARDNER – MULTIPLE INTELLIGENCES

reflector is **[r]**, **theorist** **[t]**, **pragmatist** **[p]** and **activist** **[a]**

case study (fairly activist as a whole)

Give students a case study [p]	Ask them to analyse, comment upon, explain and evaluate the case study [r]	Ask students to conclude some general principles of good practice [t]	Ask students to suggest improvements to the case study [p]

problem-solving (fairly activist as a whole)

Give students a problem or design challenge, e.g. write a marketing plan [p]	Students create their own solution or design in groups [p/a]	Students evaluate each other's solutions [r]	Teacher asks, 'What are the key principles here?' and, 'What have we learned?' [t]

practical or student practice (fairly activist as a whole)

Teacher demonstrates a practical, intellectual or social skill [p/r]	Students practise doing it [p/a]	Students evaluate their own and each other's work and methods [r]	Students action-plan how to improve their own skills [p] and justify this [t]

guided discovery (fairly theorist and activist as a whole)

Small groups are asked a 'What's your theory?' question, such as 'What helps teams work well together?'	Groups discuss and agree their answer [a/r/t]	Groups tell the class their answers and agree a collective answer [a/r]	Teacher improves the class answer and explains her additions and corrections [t]

video (fairly theorist and activist as a whole)

Teacher asks questions that students can answer by watching a video [p/t] (depends on questions)	Students watch the video and try to answer the questions [a/r/t]	Class compares their answers to the questions [a/r]	Teacher improves the class answer and explains his additions and corrections [t]

Styles of analysis

There are two ways of analysing a topic, a left-brain, 'atomistic' approach, and a right-brain, holistic approach. We need to use both styles, but many teachers and students only use the left-brain, atomistic method. Both are needed for a full understanding.

Atomistic and holistic analysis

Atomistic and holistic analysis

Atomistic analysis or analysis by parts: You can cut the topic up into discrete bits and look at these one at a time. This includes looking at a sequence of events in history.

For example:

* looking at childhood diseases from the point of view of measles, mumps, whooping cough, etc.
* splitting a scientific experiment up into a sequence of tasks
* splitting the story in a novel, or a historical event, into a series of events to describe 'what happened'.

There is often more than one way of analysing something by parts – for example, a play can be analysed into a sequence of events (plot), and/or into a list of characters.

Holistic analysis – analysis by spectacles: You can look at the whole from different points of view, including different people's points of view or different criteria, reasons, factors, issues, themes, etc.

For example:

* looking at all childhood diseases from the points of view of immunisation, public health, etc.
* looking at a play, novel or poem from the points of view of the different themes or issues it raises, or from the point of view of influences or use of language, etc.
* looking at a scientific experiment from the points of view of criteria such as reliability, validity or methods of improvement, or from a 'what we learned' or a history of science perspective, etc.
* looking at a historical event from the political, economic, religious and social points of view.

Atomistic analysis, or analysis by parts, often produces what teachers disparagingly call a 'descriptive' piece of work. When students have 'covered' all the parts, they often think 'they have finished' and so stop work. If they are taught to analyse using spectacles as well as by parts, the quality of their work can improve greatly.

> Professor John Biggs has researched the characteristics of high- and low-grade work, and shown with his 'SOLO taxonomy' that full (right-brain) relational thinking is a characteristic of high-grade academic achievement. Students must see the big picture and the patterns and links in a subject to do very well in it. This requires a balanced, or a right-brain approach. It certainly requires 'spectacles'. (See Petty 2006.)

The danger of atomistic analysis being used alone, a common fault, is that the learner won't see how the topic relates to other topics or its meaning and purpose. That is, they can't 'see the wood for the trees'.

153

You can teach students to overcome the following weaknesses in their use of spectacles:

- not knowing which are the most useful and revealing spectacles
- not realising that one spectacle can't give the whole answer, and a spectacle can absorb us so much that we are blinded to the other points of view: 'Every way of looking is a way of not-looking'
- not realising that you must balance the views from different spectacles.

Graphic organisers can help students use atomistic and holistic analysis, so let's look at these now. They can be used with almost any teaching method.

Graphic organisers

If you *organise* information in a *graphical* way, you create a 'graphic organiser'. Examples include a flow diagram, a timeline, or a mind-map. Have a look at some of the diagrams below to get the idea. Classroom trials requiring students to create graphic organisers and improve them after feedback have shown an increase in attainment of about two grades compared to good conventional teaching (Petty 2006). Organisers probably work because they force students to pick out key points, see the wood for the trees, see important relations within the material and construct their own meanings. This chapter is only an introduction; once you get the idea, see Petty 2006 and Caviglioli and Harris 2008 for the detail.

A3 paper is twice the size of A4 and gives students more space for detailed organisers. A3 can be folded twice and hole-punched to fit into an A4 ring-binder.

Graphic organisers can be used to describe, compare or show processes and cause and effect. They are also useful aids to creative and evaluative thinking, and for planning writing. Graphs and charts are also graphic organisers, but are too well known to need attention here. 'Spectacles' described above are involved in some organisers.

It is important to choose the appropriate graphic organiser for the task. If you want to compare – use a comparison table, not a description table! Graphic organisers work with learners of any age or ability, and in any subject area (see Petty 2006).

Graphic organisers that describe

You can use more than one of these to describe a given topic; indeed you could use them all. If students are to compare or evaluate, it often helps to describe with one of these first.

Venn diagram: This is a remarkably powerful aid to concept development. For example, suppose you were trying to teach the concept of 'reptile' to young learners. After explaining the basics, the teacher can ask students to place things inside or outside the reptile circle, as follows:

inside put :
- examples of reptiles
- true statements about reptiles
- accurate diagrams of reptiles
- typical characteristics of reptiles
- exam questions on reptiles.
etc.

outside put:
- non-examples
- untrue statements
- innaccurate diagrams
- non-typical characteristics
etc.

The aim of the 'outside' of a Venn diagram is to establish the boundary of the concept and so clear up common misconceptions. For example, many students wrongly think frogs are reptiles, and that reptiles have slimy skins. So 'frog' and 'has slimy skin' would be useful for students to place on the Venn diagram.

Like all organisers, Venn diagrams work at any academic level. You could use them to establish the concepts of 'red', 'quadratic equations', or 'Kantian ethics'. We will see later that Venn diagrams, like all 'describing' organisers, can be adapted to compare two or more concepts.

Reptile
snakes
lizards
scales on skin
cold-blooded
frogs
toads
some are warm-blooded

Atomistic mind-map: This is a visual way to cut a topic into parts. These parts can then be further cut.

A tree diagram is an atomistic mind-map that can describe a hierarchy – for example, in an organisation or among concepts.

passenger ships
sea
cargo ships
transport
land / rail \ road
long haul / air \ short haul

Holistic mind-map: As we saw a few pages above, instead of cutting a topic up, you can look at the whole topic from different points of view, or with different 'spectacles'. Each spectacle can create a different 'arm' on the mind-map.

Computer
personal computers
mainframe computers
super computers
apple mac
microsoft

cost per mile
passenger viewpoint
- regularity
- punctuality
- convenience
transport
environmental impact
CO2
particles
road building
costs < public costs \ passenger costs

Description table: This is a way of structuring notes on a descriptive topic, such as 'The role of the district nurse'. A3 paper is often used. An atomistic analysis cuts the role (topic) into parts 1, 2, 3, etc., e.g. post-operative care, diabetic care.

A holistic analysis looks at the role (topic) from important points of view A, B and C, etc. This might include the points of view of doctors and surgeons, and the economic point of view. Students write bullet point notes in appropriate parts of the table. Chapter 28 looks at this in more detail.

Graphic organisers can be created using word-processing applications or in dedicated programs such as MindGenius®.

description table

target map

A target map can be used to prioritise – for example, to prioritise the features of a poem.

Graphic organisers that compare

These organisers are useful for topics such as

- *compare and contrast*: e.g. viral and bacterial infections; alkanes and alkenes
- *with and without*: e.g. how do computers aid stocktaking?
- *before and after*: e.g. what effect did the Russian revolution have on peasant life?

The descriptive mind-maps and Venn diagrams above can be merged to compare two or more concepts. It sometimes helps students to describe things with graphic organisers before they compare with them.

A description table with a line down the middle becomes a comparison table. Sometimes there are only 'spectacles' and no 'parts'. Students find these challenging, so use them on familiar material first, perhaps as a revision exercise. Or compare something they know with something they are learning.

Point of view ↓	district nurse	practice nurse
patient		
doctor		
surgeon		
economic		

comparison table

Whether or not assessments require students to compare; it is one of the most powerful ways of developing a concept well enough for students to be able to understand it accurately.

Of course, comparison tables can compare more than two things. For example, you could compare many different computer printers with criteria such as price, speed, colours, paper handling, etc. As the same criteria are used, the comparison is fair and rigorous.

Graphic organisers that show processes, including cause and effect

These are useful for describing 'what happens' and 'why it happens':

comparison table comparing more than two things

- **How is stocktaking carried out?**
- **What were the main changes caused by the Crimean War?**

A flow diagram can show a process or procedure, such as how minerals are extracted, or how an election is planned and carried out. They can show cycles, of course, such as the water cycle. Flow diagrams can also display the structure of an argument, such as a justification for a social policy. See, for example, the visual essay-planning diagram on page 352; this is a very useful student activity.

flow diagram

storyboard

Events may have more than one cause! For example, the Crimean War is thought to have caused inflation in Russia, but there were other causes for this inflation, which should also be shown on the diagram.

A timeline can show a change with time, as can graphs and charts, of course. A 'storyboard' is a series of images which show changes with time. It is sometimes useful to combine organisers on the same timeline.

Graphic organisers are brilliant ways to plan writing (see Chapter 28).

How to use graphic organisers

They have many other uses described below, but, ideally, graphic organisers are used to structure information in students' heads. So they work best if students create them individually or in groups in class, for homework or assignments. Here is an approach to try:

1 Present students to with new material in your usual ways.

2 Ask students to create a suitable organiser to summarise the topic, or answer a question about it. You can either stipulate the type of organiser or leave them to choose the most appropriate one.

3 When their organiser is nearly complete, ask students to leave them on their desk, and move around to look at everyone else's. The aim is to learn how to improve your own organiser.

4 Students improve their organisers.

5 Students self- or peer-assess organisers. Give them your own model organiser, or some assessment criteria to do this with.

You can do this electronically too; see graphic organiser ping-pong on page 397.

Other uses of graphic organisers include:

- To summarise what a class *already* knows about a topic before you teach more of it.
- To create a summary of what they are *about* to learn, called an 'advance organiser' (see page 175). Students can add their own notes to this during the class.
- Students can create flip-chart-sized organisers which can be posted on the classroom noticeboard to be referred to later.
- They can also be used as the basis for card-sorting games, as described under 'Decisions decisions' on page 248. For example, statements such as 'has dryDskin' or 'lays hundreds of eggs' could be placed on a 'same and different' diagram comparing reptiles and amphibians – great for interactive whiteboards.
- Groups can record and report their findings to the class using organisers.
- Also useful for Microsoft PowerPoint® and whiteboard presentations, displays, etc.

Case study

Here's a good way to show students how to structure writing with organisers. A teacher introduces a description table by asking students to use one to write a note for her lesson on the impact of Internet shopping on retail in the UK.

- After studying the topic, students work in threes to complete an A3 description table, first deciding on parts such as Internet shopping sites, methods of payment, etc. Then they choose spectacles such as customer and retailer perspectives and the impact on high streets (see spectacles above, page 153).
- Then they write conclusion and introduction notes, in that order.
- The teacher visits groups as they work and each presents an aspect of their table at the end of the lesson.
- The teacher then 'bridges' by saying, 'You have just planned an essay – how did you do that and why? Where else could we use a description table?'

The table constituted a good activity for the lesson, and provides a great note as well. But this was a double-decker lesson, teaching Internet retail *and* essay writing at the same time. (Chapter 38 has detail on double-decker lessons, and Chapter 28 looks at planning writing.)

Do show students how to create organisers, especially complex ones like comparison tables, by demonstrating on the board while thinking out loud.

Some students may be resistant initially: tell them that research shows they help everyone, and ask them to give organisers a fair try for a bit. Most people convince themselves of their value after a few weeks. If they remain unconvinced, require them to use the same structures as the organisers above, but just in writing with very clear headings.

More methods for more skills, and more enjoyment

Different teaching methods develop different skills in the learner. Worksheets require students to develop carefully the skills of reading and of attending to detail. Design work develops their creative flair. Teacher talk develops the skill of listening attentively, and group work develops the skills of discussion, persuasion and working with others. Independent learning develops the skill of learning how to learn, and so on. These 'process skills' may not be a formal part of your course content, but they are crucial. Long term, they may be more important for many of your students than the subject-specific facts and skills you are teaching. Not every science student becomes a scientist, and in any case, these high-order skills are required for success in assessments, and make the subject more interesting.

A variety of teaching methods makes the teacher's job more stimulating and enjoyable. One-method teachers bore themselves as well as their students. When it comes to trying out new teaching methods, one could hardly do better than to take Sir Arnold Bax's advice: 'You should try everything once – except incest and folk dancing.' Teaching being what it is, though, to find out what works you need to try everything *three* times, learning, adapting and improving as you go. Once may be an accident, twice could be a coincidence, but three times begins to look like a pattern.

Try as many teaching methods as you can. Use different approaches for different classes. Be bold; as Chapter 31 on learning from experience makes clear, it is only by risk-taking experimentation that you will discover which methods suit your purposes.

Don't be worried if you find that you can't make the methods work well the first time, or that students are initially reluctant to vary their diet. Keep practising and you will soon make them work. And remember, if you don't have the occasional disaster when you are learning how to teach, you are not experimenting enough.

Further reading

Biggs, J. (1987) *Student Approaches to Learning and Studying*, Camberwell: Australian Council for Educational Research.

Bransford, J. D. *et al.* (2000) *How People Learn: Brain, Mind, Experience and School*, Washington, DC: National Research Council. This summarises a huge review of research on learning commissioned by the US Government.

Buzan, T. (1990) *The Mind Map Book*, BBC Books.

Caviglioli, O. and Harris, I. (2008) *Wiseguide to Visual Tools: A Practical Classroom Guide for Raising Achievement*, Stafford: Network Educational Press.

Coffield, F. *et al.* (2004) 'Learning styles and pedagogy in post-16 learning: a systematic and critical review'. Download from www.lsrc.ac.uk/publications

Coffield, F. *et al.* (2004) 'Should we be using learning styles? What research has to say to practice'. Download from www.lsrc.ac.uk/publications

Cooper, R. (1997) 'Learning styles and staff development', *Journal of the National Association for Staff Development*, 37: 38–46.

Honey, P. (1989) 'Trials and tribulations', *Guardian*, 19 December.

Jensen, E. (1998) *Super Teaching* (3rd edition), San Diego: Brain Store. Good on VAK.

Klein, P. D. (2003) 'Rethinking the multiplicity of cognitive resources and curricular representations: alternatives to "learning styles" and "multiple intelligences"', *Journal of Curriculum Studies*, 35, 1: 45–81. A cogent criticism of some interpretations of learning styles, and a bid to replace them with the idea of 'multiple representations' or something like them.

Kyriacou, C. (1997) *Effective Teaching in Schools* (2nd edition), Cheltenham: Nelson Thornes.

*Kyriacou, C. (1998) *Essential Teaching Skills* (2nd edition), Cheltenham: Nelson Thornes.

Marzano, R. J. *et al.* (2001) *Classroom Instruction That Works: Research-based Strategies for Increasing Student Achievement*, Alexandria, VA: ASCD.

Petty, G. (2006) *Evidence Based Teaching*, Cheltenham: Nelson Thornes.

Sperry, R. W. (1968) 'Hemispherical deconnection and unity in conscious awareness', *Scientific American*, 23: 723–33. A historic account.

Westwood, P. (2003) *Commonsense Methods for Children with Special Educational Needs: Strategies for the Regular Classroom* (4th edition), London: RoutledgeFalmer. Don't be put off by 'children' in the title; this is highly recommended.

Try also:

On learning styles:

Type 'Herrmann whole brain' or 'Allinson and Hayes' into your favourite search engine. Professor Coffield's review found these among the best learning styles systems.

www.outsider.co-uk.com Here you can try Cooper's 'Learning Styles Interactive Computer Program'.

www.pz.harvard.edu/index.cfm This is Howard Gardner's site.

More general sites on teaching methods:

www.eduref.org/ This is a gigantic, searchable database of authoritative papers on educational matters.

http://adulted.about.com/ On adult education.

www.acceleratedlearning.com/ Colin Rose's site – not much about styles, but useful.

www.geoffpetty.com/links.html has many more links.

11

Teacher talk

> *'If telling were teaching, we'd all be so smart we could hardly stand it.'*
>
> R. F. Mager

Teacher talk involves the teacher standing in front of the class and giving a verbal input. A teaching session may, of course, include many other activities besides teacher talk, but we will consider this teaching method in isolation here.

Teacher talk is the most commonly used teaching method, on average occupying at least 60% of most lessons. Certainly, it can help to provide explanations and 'doing-detail'; but crucially, it cannot provide for corrected practice and the other learners' needs outlined in Part 1. Devoting 60% of a lesson to teacher talk is clearly far too much. Good teachers know when to shut up!

Teacher talk is a teacher-centred or 'didactic' teaching method. What are its main advantages and disadvantages?

Advantages
- It is a convenient method for delivering an explanation.
- Unlike a book, it can be adapted to the correct 'level' for the class, and the content can be tailored to the needs of the class.
- It can be inspiring.
- Little preparation or resourcing is required for the experienced teacher.
- It is a rapid method of presenting material.
- It is a more personal method of communicating than written methods.

Disadvantages
- The student is not *required* to form an understanding or 'construct'.
- There is no feedback on whether understanding has taken place.
- Retention is very low, so backup is required to ensure that information is understood and remembered.
- The teacher must go at the same pace with the whole class.
- Inexperienced teachers tend to deliver material too quickly.
- It can be boring.
- There is no active student involvement.
- Students' concentration span is shorter than for other learning methods.
- It assumes consenting students.
- Students are not given the opportunity to use the ideas being taught.

> *'When all can read, lectures will be unnecessary.'*
>
> Ben Jonson (1573–1637)

The talk trap

Most people talk at about 100 to 200 words per minute. At that rate, a one-hour lecture could contain up to 12,000 words – a short book!

Here is a simple calculation that compares the rate of delivery of material using teacher talk with the rate of student comprehension:

Even at a moderate rate, a teacher could read aloud to a class the whole of a typical GCSE textbook in about 10 hours, covering the entire syllabus in this time. The average GCSE course includes about 200 hours of teaching time. This means that, very roughly, teacher talk can deliver (even very appropriate) material at about twenty times the rate at which students are expected to learn it!

Is it any wonder that inexperienced teachers often 'lose' their classes when they use teacher talk? Teaching with teacher talk is rather like herding cows in a Ferrari.

Imagine going to an evening class to study GCSE biology, and finding that the teacher simply read from a textbook, or sounded as if he or she was doing so. Why would this be unsatisfactory? Our short-term memory would soon be swamped, and with no time to process the new information, it would never become structured enough to pass into the long-term memory, and so it would quickly be forgotten. Nor would we have any chance to practise *using* the ideas that we were learning. There is much more to teaching than telling.

Concentration span

The concentration span of some students while they listen to teacher talk is less than 5 minutes; that of undergraduates and sixth-formers is perhaps 15 to 20 minutes.

> *A lecture is an event where information passes from the notes of the lecturer into the notes of the student, without passing through the brains of either.*

This short concentration span puts the near-exclusive use of teacher talk in some educational circles into a rather alarming perspective. Many former university students will remember the eerie experience of revising from lecture notes that are entirely unfamiliar, but in one's own handwriting!

163

Remember that, in effect, the short-term memory soon gets filled up, and any new material simply displaces earlier material. Even if a teacher-talk session is of moderate length, the teacher cannot guarantee the concentration of all the members of the class all of the time. During a ten-minute teacher-talk session, almost every student will 'dream off' at least once, perhaps at a crucial point in the explanation. If you don't believe me, try maintaining 100% concentration through-out a 30-minute radio documentary.

You must imagine that, for any given student, it is as though your teacher-talk session has had sections cut out of it at random: from that student's point of view, your performance is rather like watching a video that is 'on the blink'. Yet your lesson *must* make sense to them, despite these random omissions. Clearly, repetition of the most important points will be necessary – though these repetitions should of course be disguised as far as possible, to avoid boring the students who do listen well. Our inability to sustain 100% concentration is one reason why students appreciate summaries.

Teacher-talk technique

As we have seen, many teachers use teacher talk too much; but most teachers use it a good deal, so it is worth looking at how to improve your technique.

It is fascinating to watch really effective teachers use teacher talk. Often they owe their effectiveness not to what they say but to the way they say it – in particular, their use of body language. They never sit behind a desk or bench, but stand close to the class, unless they are using the board a great deal. They move around the classroom, facing first that group, then this, constantly making direct eye contact with students. The pitch and the volume of the voice change a great deal to add emphasis, and there is much use of gesture and facial expression.

If a student should start to talk, they move over to stand next to them and stop them talking without a break in their delivery. Their presentation appears to be 'off the top of their head'; they will not be found reading, with their face buried in a sheaf of papers. A new sentence or a new paragraph is usually signalled by a long pause, and a new section by a change of posture or position. Key points are stressed by expressive gestures, and a pause before and after.

Inexperienced teachers, by comparison, are self-conscious and rather flat in their presentation until they gain in confidence.

> *Experienced teachers – indeed, able public speakers of any kind – tend to vary the pitch and volume of their voice at least three times as much when 'performing' as when they are not.*

When we are depressed, we talk more slowly than usual, and with a lower pitch; when we are excited, we talk faster and higher. If you want to convey enthusiasm, you must be prepared to use your voice for that purpose. Listen to Jeremy Paxman, David Attenborough, your favourite radio personality or some other effective communicator – but don't listen to what they say, listen to *how* they say it. They have an excellent voice technique, they vary pitch and volume enormously, they convey enthusiasm by their lively delivery. Try to learn from these examples, but note that their style is natural and informal. Don't put on a formal 'announcer's voice'; this tends to distance you from the students.

> *Hypnotists can put people to sleep with a monotone.*

A problem many learning teachers have is that they repeat, over and over again, phrases such as 'OK?' or 'All right?', or they 'um', 'ah' or 'er' too much. To 'er' is human, but try not to overdo it. I once caught students recording with a five-bar gate the number of times a student teacher said 'Right, then'. They told me they had counted 82 in their one-hour lesson, but they were disappointed it wasn't a record! Gestures or verbal habits that become mannerisms can be very distracting, but you may need someone to observe your teaching before you become aware of them.

Don't stare down at your boots or at the ceiling. Students feel 'included' if you look at them and if you face in their direction (eye contact and body-pointing). This requires that you rake the class with eye contact, and change the way you are facing from time to time – one reason why it is not a good idea to read from notes. If you must use notes, put them on the overhead projector or on the board before the lesson. The students will think you put them up for their benefit, when really they are there to jog your memory.

Without eye contact the class feels rejected. I remember a story, which I hope is an exaggeration, of a history lecturer at Edinburgh University who delivered a lecture to 200 students with his eyes closed throughout. It was a mannerism of his which he thought gave him the air of someone deep in intense concentration. At the end of the lecture, he opened his eyes to find his students had all gone!

Clearly, *interest* must be considered very carefully when preparing for teacher talk, which most students agree tends inherently to be the most boring teaching method. This topic was dealt with in detail in Chapter 5 on motivation, where techniques such as human interest, student relevance, curiosity and puzzles were described.

Summaries help enormously; these are worth repeating often, but are particularly useful at the end of lessons, and then repeated at the beginning of the next lesson.

Humour is greatly appreciated by nearly all students, except when they are the butt of your jokes. You don't have to be a professional stand-up comic to make a class laugh. I have heard them roar with laughter at the following:

'King John was a sod.'
'I will now demonstrate how to rip your arm off with a lathe.'

Don't hide behind a dour style; try rhetorical questions, humour, anecdotes, quotations, curiosity-inducing questions, catchphrases, exaggeration, understatement – and don't be afraid to experiment. Let the real you come out!

Making the material easy to understand

First of all, make sure you avoid unexplained jargon and an over-sophisticated general vocabulary – we looked at this in Chapter 4. Try to become familiar with the working vocabulary of the students you are teaching; alarm bells should ring when you go beyond this. Most teachers have at least twice the vocabulary of the average 16-year-old. (Of course, you should not be afraid to *teach* the meaning of unfamiliar words if they are genuinely important.) The next chapter deals with the art of explaining and should be read in conjunction with this one.

Enhancement

Teacher talk can be made very much more effective by the use of visual aids: whiteboards, overhead projectors, models or other objects brought into the classroom. These are dealt with in later chapters.

One of the main methods of enlivening teacher talk is the use of questioning. This involves the students, and so overcomes some of the disadvantages of the basic teacher-talk technique (see Chapter 14). Chapter 24 on whole-class interactive teaching shows you how to extend student concentration, and encourage participation, by integrating teacher talk with other strategies.

How do you know if your teacher talk is effective? What is the students' body language? Are they attending, or staring out of the window and shuffling in their seats? Look at the feedback mentioned in Chapter 4: can they answer questions? does their work demonstrate understanding?

Questioning also gives instant feedback on whether students are understanding you.

Help! I have too much material to teach!

The exhaustive delivery of your entire knowledge base on the topic you are teaching is rarely necessary, even when it is possible. Be guided by your students' need to know.

It is common, however, to prune your input to the bare bone, and still find you are using too much teacher talk. If so, beware the assumption that everything your students are to learn must first pass through your mouth! Or that everything you say, they will learn.

Seriously consider:

- independent learning: see Chapter 33
- sending your students pre-lecture briefing packs or notes to read before your class
- using your lesson to establish *understanding* of the key points rather than coverage, and then setting reading homework. Reading will be easy once the topic is basically understood, and has a better recall rate than listening – even listening to you! See Chapter 40.

Checklist

❏ Do you know your students' concentration span, and do you avoid exceeding it?

❏ Do you make your voice sound lively?

❏ Do you use eye contact and body-pointing?

❏ Do you use straightforward words in short sentences?

❏ Do you use humour and human interest?

❏ Do you use student relevance?

❏ Do you appeal to curiosity with questions, paradoxes and puzzles?

❏ Do you stand close to students and move your position occasionally?

❏ Is your voice loud enough?

EXERCISES

- Listen to how professionals in the media use their voice; pay special attention to variation of pitch, volume, etc.
- Try testing the vocabulary of your students with the list of words in Chapter 4.
- Comment on the efficiency and use of the university-style lecture.

Further reading

Brown, G. and Hatton, N. (1982) *Explanations and Explaining: A Teaching Skills Workbook*, Basingstoke: Macmillan Education.

Kerry, T. (1982) *Effective Questioning*, London: Macmillan.

Marzano, R. J. *et al.* (2001) *Classroom Instruction That Works: Research-Based Strategies for Increasing Student Achievement*, Alexandria, VA: ASCD.

Petty, G. (2006) *Evidence Based Teaching*, Cheltenham: Nelson Thornes.

12

The art of explaining

Early in my teaching experience I encountered a student in my tutor group who regularly complained that one of her teachers had very poor explaining skills:

> 'If you ask him to explain, he just says the same thing over and over.'
> 'When I say I don't understand, he just says, "You should have listened the first time" – but I was listening.'

Most students on the course complained about this same teacher. One day I made the mistake of pointing out that the teacher was exceptionally well qualified in his subject. I was astonished by the anger in her reply: 'I'm sure he knows his stuff, but his brain doesn't appear to be connected to his mouth.'

Her frustration and bitterness demonstrated to me two points that are confirmed by almost every teacher's experience: that students consider explaining to be perhaps the teacher's single most important skill; and that a teacher's subject knowledge alone will not make him or her into a good explainer. So when your students don't understand, don't complain that they are 'thick'; develop your explaining skills.

In the 1930s, A. W. Hollis asked 8,000 pupils what characteristics they most valued in their teachers. Very near the top of the list came 'the ability to explain difficulties patiently'.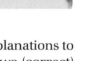

But how does one learn to explain? Let's look at some examples of explanations to discover what makes them effective – or ineffective! Compare these two (correct) explanations of how to get to Charles Street:

Explanation 1. 'Straight on to the roundabout, where you take the third exit signposted to Durham. Half a mile later, fork right, and it's the first on your left. So it's right at the roundabout, right at the fork, then first on the left.'

Explanation 2. 'Charles Street is right off Comberton Street. That's if you're travelling towards the city centre, so it will be left as you approach it. So, carry on past Carrington's, they've got a sale on now, actually, three-piece suites for less than £500 – worth going to; past the railway station, that's not the main railway station, of course, it's Farringdon Street, you know, that one on the Euston line. Keep going on the same road until you get to the Bull Ring, about a mile before the town centre, you know. Turn right. Then on your right you'll see the floodlights for the football ground – they call it the stadium, heaven knows why – anyway … after that you're in Comberton Street. I explained earlier how to get to Charles Street from there.'

What are the good and bad features of these two explanations?

The second has *redundant information* which lengthens and confuses the explanation. It also assumes knowledge in the learner – for example, that the learner will recognise 'the Bull Ring'. It isn't logically ordered, as the last direction is explained first.

The first is *logically ordered, concise* and includes a summary of the more important points; particularly important points are emphasised.

A good explanation should:

* contain *only* such information as will be sufficient to give a reasoned, logically ordered description of the point being explained
* be exclusively built on knowledge that the student already possesses
* be tailored to the intended audience, *even if this means missing out what an expert on the subject (such as a teacher) might call important detail*
* be carried out persuasively and patiently.

It is important to recognise that a statement of fact, such as 'When starting a car from rest, the clutch should be released slowly', is not an *explanation*. Understanding requires that the student knows the 'why' as well as the 'what'.

Explaining is a skill that you must prepare for, and practise – on your own as well as in the class. There follow some techniques for you to practise. Throughout, I assume the teacher is attempting to explain a concept or idea that students tend to find difficult to understand.

Start from the student's existing knowledge and experience

This is harder to achieve than one might think. It requires an intimate knowledge of the subject being taught, as well as of the learner's ability and previous learning. It also requires careful planning.

The diagram below illustrates the point that a new understanding is built on old learning. But remember that the process shown in the diagram goes on inside the student's head. Explanations that do not relate to our foundation of present knowledge are not just inadequate, they are meaningless.

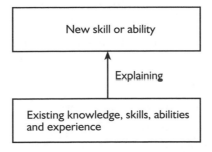

Relevant recall questions

If students already know a little about what you are about to teach, then here is a great activity to start the topic.

Ask students to write down everything they can remember about the topic in very summarised form (one or two minutes). They then compare notes in pairs (one or two minutes), in each case agreeing a summary set of points. Lastly, you ask the foursomes, in turn, to give one of their points, and write good points on the board. If you discover any misconceptions you challenge them then, or later in your explanation.

This 'snowball' takes only about five minutes, but has been found to save more time than it takes (Black 2003). Alternatively, you could discover what they know with an assertive questioning-style discussion (Chapter 24). Recalling relevant prior learning has been found to be exceptionally powerful in trials (see Petty 2006).

If students don't know anything relevant to the topic you are about to explain, then think of an analogy for the topic that is in their experience. Then ask questions about that. For example, electricity is like water flowing through pipes. Questions on water flow will help them recall their present understanding of flow, and build their understanding of electricity onto this prior learning: *'What would happen to the current if the water pipe forked?'*

Metaphors are powerful. A state is like a family, so: *'Is your family autocratic or democratic?'* … *'What is an autocratic family like to live in?'* Cash flow is like the water left in a bath if the taps are on, but the plug is out. So: *'What would happen to cash flow if inputs increased?'*

Whatever you ask students to recall, it is worth referring back to this during your explanation. *'So increasing the voltage is like increasing the power of your water pump.'* Make sure any misconceptions are corrected if you find any.

Simplify

During an explanation, the teacher's enemy is often the limited *size* of the student's short-term memory. Don't feel you have to mention everything you know about the subject; only include information *vital* for understanding the point being explained.

Don't be afraid to simplify to the point where you are distorting the truth somewhat. You can always mention the exceptions and oddities later, once the basic idea is understood.

Extreme simplification is often used by teachers of science and mathematics to establish a principle. Here is a teacher explaining the equation:

distance = speed $\times$ time

Teacher	Say you were travelling at 20 mph. How far would you travel in one hour?
Student	20 miles.

Teacher	How far would you travel in two hours?
Student	40 miles.
Teacher	And how far in five hours?
Student	100 miles.
Teacher	Good. How did you work that out?
Student	Multiply the speed by the time.
Teacher	Very good! So distance = speed × time.

If the teacher above wants to mention how Donald Campbell got the land speed record, or the speed of the fastest running mammal, it should be done after the basic idea has been explained and understood; or beforehand, as part of the introduction. Explain new ideas very, very simply, preferably getting learners to persuade themselves rather than be persuaded by you; *then* fill in the detail. *Warning*: simplification is a very difficult technique for the teacher; it needs careful preparation.

> *On being asked whether the theory of relativity was too difficult to explain to a school pupil, Einstein is said to have replied that any scientist who cannot explain what he is doing to a reasonably intelligent 14-year-old is either incompetent or a charlatan.*

Level of complexity

Simplicity requires that we avoid unnecessary complexity. One way of achieving this is to think in terms of 'black boxes'. One is aware of what goes into each box, and what comes out of it, but one does not worry about how it works inside. A child, an unmechanical adult, an amateur car mechanic and a professional mechanic all see the car at different levels of complexity. However, no individual understands a car in its entirety – for example, an expert on the thermodynamics of combustion may not understand the ergonomics of seat design. Most things, for most people, are understood in terms of 'black boxes'. *So do not try to give every detail about what you are trying to teach*; choose a level of complexity that is as simple as possible, while still being sufficiently detailed for your students' needs.

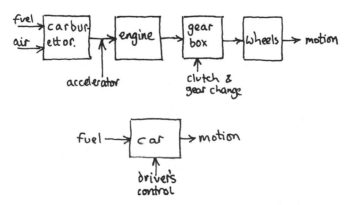

The car, in two different levels of complexity

Simplification can only be achieved by careful thought and planning before the lesson.

Focusing

When a speaker is confusing we often think, 'What is the point of what they are trying to say?' We might understand each sentence, but we are left unsure of where the sentences are leading.

Even a fairly concise explanation might last ten minutes, in which case you will deliver over 2,000 words. Are all these words or sentences of equal importance? A student struggling with a new idea often has difficulty in isolating the point you are trying to make from the explanation you are giving in support of it. Even if students are intelligent and motivated, without help they may well miss important points amongst the detail.

Depending on the nature of the explanation, you may need to focus on a key phrase, a list or a chain of reasoning.

A key phrase

Can you boil down your explanation to a simple sentence or formulation that is the kernel of the teaching point(s) you are trying to make? Don't be afraid to use the vernacular; it gives students confidence if the idea you are trying to teach them can be stated in simple language. It is essential to prepare this 'key phrase' in advance, and to repeat it to the students often. Here are some examples:

'Voltage is the push on the electrons.'
'If we don't shutter trenches, we may end up digging our own graves.'

To focus attention on this key phrase, you can use:

* emphasis
* gesture
* repetition
* silence before and after the phrase.

You can write the phrase up on the board or overhead projector (OHP), and leave it there during the discussion; give the phrase in handouts or in notes; or say, 'Listen to this carefully – it is very important …'

Use questioning to check whether the point you are focusing on has sunk in.

A list

Many explanations are best summarised as a list. For example:

The overhead projector

Advantages over whiteboard are:

- Transparencies can be prepared in advance.
- Transparencies can be updated and kept for future use.
- Accurate drawings can be presented immediately.
- 'Overlay' and 'reveal' techniques can be used. [etc.]

Emphasise and display the list during the explanation, as with the key phrase.

Chain of reasoning

If an explanation cannot be summarised as a list or as one key phrase, it can usually be summarised in a chain of reasoning. For example, when a science teacher is explaining why hot air rises, she might focus on, or 'point' to, the following reasoning:

> A gas expands when it is heated.
> This expansion reduces the density of the gas.
> Less dense materials float in more dense fluids (like cork in water). Therefore hot air floats in the surrounding cold air.
> That is to say: 'Hot air rises.'

Each of the four statements needs explaining carefully in its own right, but in order to understand why hot air rises, the overall chain of reasoning must be understood. After convincing or reminding the students of the four separate statements, it is necessary to repeat this chain of reasoning in its shortened form a number of times. It is as though all four statements need to be understood separately, and then need to be in the short-term memory together, for the students to be able to connect up the chain of reasoning and 'understand' why hot air rises. It's that constructivism again!

Whether you summarise your explanation as a key phrase, as a list, or as a chain of reasoning, it is important to emphasise and repeat your summary. This is sometimes called 'pointing'.

> *'His speech was like a tangled chain; nothing impaired, but all disordered.'*
>
> Shakespeare, *A Midsummer Night's Dream*

Structure and orientation

Suppose you were asked to study a play entirely on your own. You have seen the play twice, and read it twice; you are anxious to do well in an examination on the play in two days' time. How would you prepare for it?

Most effective students would write organised notes, with headings and subheadings, mentioning the most important features of the play. These notes could be in time sequence; they could be broken down by character, by events in the play, by acts and scenes, by plot and subplots; or perhaps each theme in the play could have its own heading. Different students will choose to organise their notes in different ways, but effective learners will all organise them.

We need to impose a *logical structure* on what we want to understand and remember. It is as though our long-term memory is like a filing cabinet, requiring information to be divided into drawers, files and sub-files. Even students who do not resort to pen and paper are likely to 'structure' the play in their understanding in some way. Only structured material can pass from the short-term into the long-term memory.

Good explainers make sure their students have the explanation in a structured form, usually by doing the structuring for them, but alternatively by ensuring the students develop their own structure.

Explainers make it clear at all times where they are in the structure; this is called 'orientation'. For example:

> We have been looking at the reasons for the introduction of compulsory schooling in Britain. So far we have isolated a number of economic reasons for compulsory schooling: shortage of clerks, shortage of skilled labour, and so on. But economics did not provide the only reasons for compulsory schooling. Let's have a look at some of the others.

The diagram on the next page shows how information can be shown in a *tree structure*; the headings and subheadings in this chapter could also be displayed in that way. Such a structure makes information easier to remember.

Orientation and structuring avoids the explanation becoming a vast, seamless, incomprehensible mass; and it breaks the argument up into easily understood and assimilated portions. Structure can be shown on the whiteboard or OHP, or in headings in the students' notes.

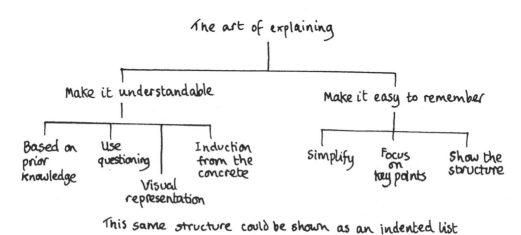

This same structure could be shown as an indented list with headings and subheadings.

Advance organisers

An advance organiser is a summary in advance, along with a persuasive case for the importance of the topic. It seems strange to summarise in advance, but it really helps students to know where they are going before they set off. The bullet points on page 170 are an advanced organiser for this chapter.

You could show your summary in advance graphically, using a mind-map, flow diagram, or similar device. See the illustration on page 347 and pages 154 to 159.

To conclude this section, then, a good explainer makes plain both the structure and the hierarchy of importance in the content of an extended explanation.

Abstract and concrete explanations

How would you explain the meaning of the word 'superstition' to an eight-year-old? Would you say: 'A superstition is an untrue belief, based on the idea that certain actions can affect our luck by magic'? Whilst the eight-year-old might understand all the words in that explanation, I am prepared to bet that they would not understand the sentence. It is an abstract explanation: 'superstition', which is itself an abstract idea, has been explained in terms of other abstract ideas, such as 'luck', 'magic' or 'untrue belief'.

Hopefully you would also explain the idea of 'superstition' with a concrete explanation; that is, by means of concrete examples of superstitions, preferably those with which the eight-year-old is familiar, such as:

It is superstitious to:

- cross your fingers in the hope it will make a wish come true
- believe a rabbit's foot can help you pass your examinations
- expect trouble on Friday 13th.

Non-examples are also very helpful: 'It is superstitious to cross your fingers before crossing the road, but it is not superstitious to look both ways'; 'To believe that the earth is flat is not superstitious; that is an untrue belief, but not one that involves luck or magic'; and so on.

Concept learning and corrected practice

Concept learning like this is best done by corrected practice. Students are given suggestions such as 'I believe the earth is flat'; 'I don't believe in swimming out of my depth'; and 'The full moon helps you if your birth sign is Cancer'. The teacher then classifies these as superstitious or not superstitious by reasoning out loud (or by Socratic questioning).

'That's not an untrue belief, so it can't be superstitious, can it?' This gives the doing-detail and the explanation in *educare?*.

Students are then asked to classify similar suggestions in the same way. Ideally, some of the suggestions are borderline cases, or are based on common errors.

The same technique can be used to help students differentiate between similar concepts, such as superstition, delusion and myth, or 'quality of life' and 'standard of living'. The technique can be used in any subject, at any level. The 'Decisions, decisions' game in Chapter 19 is an excellent method for such learning.

Learners feel a strong need for concrete examples (and non-examples) of abstract ideas. This seems to be the way they like to form new concepts. Another way of putting it is that they like to move from the particular to the general.

Interestingly, a child who has learned to use the concept of 'superstition' correctly may not be able to explain it! Concepts seem to be formed in the right half of the brain, which is non-verbal. In learning at all levels, understanding comes first, and the ability to verbalise the understanding comes later. This in itself should warn us against explaining purely through abstract explanation.

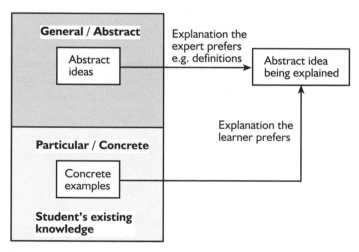

Two ways of explaining a difficult concept or idea

For learners of all ages, the ideal introduction to an abstract idea is often through concrete, specific examples from their own experience, with an abstract explanation to summarise. *Good explainers use both abstract and concrete explanations.* Venn diagrams exploit this idea and are an excellent way to learn concepts (see page 154).

The fact that learners and experts prefer to think in different ways during explanations explains why experts are often bad explainers; they cannot make themselves think from the concrete to the abstract. The diagram opposite presents this idea in visual terms.

The strengths and weaknesses of concrete explanations

Concrete explanations are easily assimilated, but inexperienced teachers often omit them; they think it is 'talking down' to give concrete examples of phrases like 'adequate precautions' or 'protein-rich foods'. But experienced teachers would give (or ask for) examples to make the meaning of such abstract phrases clear.

Consider the concept of friction: 'Friction is a contact force which opposes motion.' We can view a concept as a kind of mental box in which we keep examples. In our 'friction' box we might keep:

> Friction is rubbing hands; it stops bike wheels from turning for ever; it makes it hard to pull a box on level ground … and so on.

The box labelled 'friction' is useless to us until we have something to put into it! Then we begin to see what the examples in the box have in common, apart from the opposition to motion:

> Friction is reduced by wheels, by oiling or by ball-bearings; friction causes heating; friction causes wear; friction provides grip … and so on.

The best way to develop this new 'box' in students' minds is to give them plenty of things to put into it. A good explainer helps students to 'fill their concept boxes'.

How would you teach the concepts of 'a raising agent'; 'mean and mode'; or 'cash flow'?

The strengths and weaknesses of abstract explanations

Abstract explanations tend by their nature to be concise, accurate and widely applicable, and so are much prized by teachers. For example:

> A psychological complex is a group of (repressed and forgotten) ideas or impressions to which are ascribed abnormal mental conditions and abnormal bodily conditions due to mental causes.

You are unlikely to have understood this last sentence!

Definitions are abstract explanations, using abstract concepts. If the concept being explained is 'difficult', the learner will usually feel that such an explanation is vague, or even completely meaningless. Definitions are often an end point rather than a starting point for the teacher.

Learners prefer to form a concept by induction, and then test and improve their concept by using or testing it:

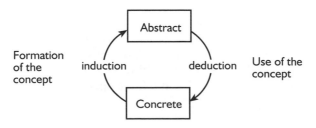

If I were trying to explain a psychological complex as defined on page 176, I would not start with the definition. Instead, I would give examples of complexes, and ask students if they could see the similarities between them (induction). That would form the concept, and enable us to draw out the definition. Then I would ask students to use this definition to categorise other examples as either 'complexes' or non-complexes (deduction). This would require students to use the concept, so

177

that I could check they were using it correctly (and thus infer that they had understood it). So we have involved both the abstract and the concrete, both induction and deduction.

More tools for explainers

Questioning

Questioning is a very powerful way of bringing about understanding; it is also a vital technique for checking that learning has taken place. (It is dealt with in detail in Chapter 14.) 'What would happen if …' questions are particularly helpful when explaining. For example, when teaching the process of making bread:

> 'What would happen if I didn't use strong flour?'
> 'What would happen if I poured the boiling water over the yeast?'
> 'What would happen if I used twice as much yeast?'
> 'What would happen if I covered it in a dry cloth instead of a wet one?'

Effective teachers use student questioning, and invariably make use of the rhetorical question as well, especially at the start of an explanation. This creates curiosity, and encourages students to interrogate and process the material.

Reductio ad absurdum

This is a method of 'unteaching' an erroneous idea, by showing it leads to a clear absurdity. The last sentence gave an abstract explanation of an abstract idea, and no doubt you will find a concrete example helpful! So here goes:

Suppose a student thinks that $4 \times 0 = 4$. (This is a common misunderstanding.)

Explanation: 'I have a fleet of cars that carry four people each. How many people can be carried by two cars?' ($4 \times 2 = 8$) 'How many people can be carried by one car?' ($4 \times 1 = 4$) 'How many people can be carried by zero cars?' ($4 \times 0 = ?$)

This technique is particularly useful in science and mathematics. Here is a science example. A student states that the smaller the diameter of a chimney, the faster the smoke in it rises. The teacher knows this is true only up to a point, not as a generalisation. So she replies: 'Suppose I had a chimney with a near-zero diameter. Your theory suggests the smoke would rise at a huge speed. Is that likely?'

Visual representation

Even abstract ideas and relationships can be represented visually – a mode of communication that has a very powerful impact and is easily remembered. Use mind-maps, flow diagrams, tree structures, graphs, tables and other pictorial representations, as described in the introduction to Part 2. These show the whole all at once. They explain in a right-brain 'holistic' way.

Kipling analysis

I keep six honest serving men

They taught me all I knew,

Their names are What and Why and When,

and How and Where and Who.

The six questioning words in this verse by Rudyard Kipling can be used to break down any topic into sensible sections. Suppose you had to explain gyroscopes. By the time you had explained *what* they were, *why* they worked, *when* they were used, *how* they worked, *where* they were made or were used, and *who* found them useful, there wouldn't be much else to say. Remember that 'when' refers to both appropriate times and circumstances.

Expressing yourself unambiguously

Words such as 'it' and 'they', and phrases such as 'the system' or 'the method', all refer to a word or phrase mentioned earlier, usually in the same sentence. This can be confusing or even ambiguous, so for maximum clarity in worksheets and in verbal communication they should be avoided. For example, in the last sentence 'they' could mistakenly be taken to mean 'worksheets', but is actually intended to relate to 'a word or phrase mentioned earlier'.

What's this explanation for? – setting tasks in advance

Some students need a reason to concentrate, or even to listen. Give them one! Set a task in advance of your explanation, which will have an audience that gives feedback. For example, 'When I have explained the role of the district nurse, you will devise a poster which summarises the role. Then everyone will display their poster. I will give you key points that each poster should have mentioned. Then you will use these to peer-assess each other's posters.'

A good task set in advance can concentrate the minds of your less-motivated students, and give a purpose of your explanation. In trials, this strategy has improved students' attainment very markedly (see Petty 2006).

Some general advice

Try to hear what you are saying through your students' ears. Use simple language in short sentences, explaining all your jargon, and remembering that what is jargon to the student may be everyday language to you. Watch out for body-language clues indicating 'lost' students: if someone is finding it hard to understand, they may lean forward and frown. Try to devise more than one way of explaining difficult ideas, and don't forget that explanations are never enough in themselves. Students must *use* the concepts or ideas being taught before they will really understand them. Don't go on too long.

Giving summaries

Summaries help to consolidate learning by giving an overview of the main ideas and their structure. For example:

> An explanation should be based on the student's existing knowledge and vocabulary. It should be concise and logically structured, and this structure should be made clear. The explainer should focus on the vital components of the explanation by pointing, and should use both abstract and concrete explanations. Before an explanation it helps to find out what students already know about the topic, to summarise its key points, and to set a task in advance.

Checklist

- ❏ Do you base your explanation on existing knowledge?
- ❏ Do you give your explanation a logical structure and make this clear to the student?
- ❏ Do you focus on the crucial points by 'pointing', e.g. emphasis, repetition?
- ❏ Do you simplify, adding detail later?
- ❏ Do you avoid unexplained jargon?
- ❏ Do you use the concrete, giving examples and non-examples?
- ❏ Do you use the abstract, but do so referring to the concrete?
- ❏ Do you give analogies and visualisations?
- ❏ Do you use questioning to explain and to monitor learning?
- ❏ Do you give students a chance to use the ideas you are teaching?

No one sets out to be a poor explainer, but many become one. Good explainers improve their explaining by clarifying their ideas, inventing explanations and evaluating their effectiveness. They don't blame the students if they don't understand, or even themselves; they get busy working out how to do it better. There is more advice on explaining in Chapter 14 on questioning. Persuading is dealt with in Chapter 39.

EXERCISES

1 *The dictionary game*. Get a friend to read out the definitions of reasonably well-known words from a dictionary, and try to guess the word being defined. You will find it harder than you think; this shows that our understanding of concepts is not verbal, and, consequently, that abstract definitions are poor explainers. At times, definitions are so poor at explaining that we don't even recognise an abstract definition of a concept that we understand very well.

2 How would you explain 'communication' or 'irrational' to a seven-year-old child?

3 In your own subject, choose a concept or topic that is difficult to explain.

4 Look back over this chapter, and use it to prepare two alternative explanations of this topic or concept.

References and further reading

Black, P. and Wiliam, D. (1999) 'Inside the black box', download from www.pdkintl.org

Black, P. *et al.* (2003) *Assessment for Learning: Putting into Practice*, Maidenhead: Open University Press.

Brown, G. and Atkins, M. (1988) *Effective Teaching in Higher Education*, London: Routledge.

Brown, G. and Hatton, N. (1982) *Explanations and Explaining: A Teaching Skills Workbook*, Basingstoke: Macmillan Education.

Kerry, T. (1982) *Effective Questioning*, London: Macmillan.

Marzano, R. J. *et al.* (2001) *Classroom Instruction that Works: Research-Based Strategies for Increasing Student Achievement*, Alexandria, VA: ASCD.

Petty, G. (2006) *Evidence Based Teaching*, Cheltenham: Nelson Thornes.

13

The art of showing

Demonstrating physical and intellectual skills

Perhaps the most natural way to learn is by imitation. This, after all, is how children learn to speak their first language – and the method is almost 100% successful! How can teachers make use of this method of learning?

If we accept that a demonstration is 'showing how' by example, then it is clear that this method can be employed by a teacher of any subject. As we saw in Chapter 3, it can be used to teach physical (psychomotor) skills, such as how to fillet a fish or weld mild steel; but it can also be used for intellectual skills – such as how to use Pythagoras' theorem, how to write an appreciation of a poem or how to analyse critically a theory in sociology. Most demonstrations will of course be followed by an opportunity for student practice. This chapter considers the demonstration of physical and intellectual skills separately.

Demonstrating a physical skill or ability

Learning teachers are often terrified of demonstrations; they remember the science teachers whose experiments never worked and expect a similar humiliation. But there is nothing to fear if you have practised in advance.

The aim of most demonstrations is to provide students with a concrete example of good practice to copy or adapt. This provides the 'doing-detail' that, as Chapter 3 showed, is so vital for learning physical and intellectual skills: it shows how the task is carried out, what the task achieves, to what standard it should be carried out, the indicators that the task has been carried out successfully, and so on.

'Doing-detail' can occasionally be provided by an exemplar (i.e. a model of good practice); for example, a typing teacher can show students a well-laid-out table of figures, and a catering teacher can show a well-presented dish. Examples of bad practice can also be useful. 'Here are two business letters; they each have four layout mistakes in them. See if you can find them!'

Science teachers sometimes demonstrate a phenomenon by experiment. The intention here may not be to encourage the learner to imitate the teacher; indeed, that might be dangerous. These demonstrations should be carried out in much the same way as is described below.

Preparation

Make sure the students are ready: have they been introduced to the necessary background information, and do they know what the demonstration achieves? If the demonstration is likely to be long and involved, can it be broken down into parts to be learned separately?

It is nearly always necessary to move students for a demonstration, but even then, will the whole class be able to see? If not, it would be better to break it down into smaller groups. Will you let students arrange their own positions, or will you direct them? Whatever you decide, get them as close as is practicable. Some teachers who often do demonstrations have a routine position for students around the demonstration bench – for example, the students from the front row on the teacher's right, the second row to the left, and so on. This avoids students jostling for position. If you are in a science laboratory, decide in advance whether some students will be allowed to sit on top of the bench immediately in front of the demonstration bench. If this is allowed, arrange for the front-row students to sit in front of that bench, rather than in their usual places behind it, to avoid the other students sitting on their folders, etc.

Student placement for a demonstration in a science laboratory

Will there be a mirror-image problem? Students will see your left hand on their right. This is not normally a difficulty unless you expect students to copy *while* you are demonstrating, as some keep-fit or dance teachers do. If this is the case, demonstrate the movements in mirror image so that students see you as they would see themselves in a mirror – see the illustration overleaf. (Are you left-handed, or are any of your students left-handed, and if so will this make any difference?)

How will you involve your students? This can be done by asking questions, but a student can also be asked to copy or adapt your demonstration in front of the rest of the class, before the general student practice session. In science experiments, students can be asked to take readings.

Always practise a demonstration before doing it in front of the class, and make a note of all the equipment you need, including any extras you may need to repeat the demonstration if this is necessary. Can you talk and work at the same time? Does the demonstration take longer than you expected? If so, you may need to use the *Blue Peter* trick: 'Here's one I prepared earlier.'

The demonstrator as a mirror image

It is important to decide in advance on the key points you want to make during the demonstration; these can often get lost in the welter of detail. Have a summary ready for the board or overhead projector. Finally, are you certain that you have considered all the safety factors carefully?

Execution

Arrange the equipment in advance, well away from any confusing clutter, so that it is facing the students if at all possible. Once students are aware of what they are about to see, and why, move them into their new positions. Don't start until they are all settled.

Explain as you demonstrate if you can, preferably using questions. 'What should I do next?' 'Why am I doing it like this?' 'What should I be careful of here?' 'What would happen if … ?' Make sure your students understand the purpose of each action; they should understand the 'why' as well as the 'how'. Emphasise your key points carefully.

Do it slowly, and if necessary do it at a more realistic speed later. If there is more than one method and you wish to demonstrate them all, it is usually better to show only one at a time. Show the other method(s) in a separate demonstration if necessary. It is very difficult to demonstrate, talk, question and use eye contact with the group at the same time – but try; if you can do it, this will increase the impact of the demonstration enormously.

Now you need some feedback. Have they learned what you have taught them? Do they understand the *how*, the *what* and the *why* of the technique? To discover this, repeat the demonstration, but ask your students to 'talk you through one'. Follow their instructions, asking them questions as they tell you what to do. 'What for?' 'Why must I do that first?' and so on. Without this feedback step, there is a grave danger that any student practice which follows will be badly done, and not understood.

If necessary, repeat the demonstration a number of times, until you are sure that they understand. If students are about to have a go themselves, ask them to look out for particular points which will show whether or not they are doing it properly. These 'performance indicators' are important: here's a woodwork teacher finishing off a demonstration on planing wood.

> … You should hardly need to push at all; the shavings should be so thin that you can see light through them; and there should be no score marks left by the plane.

This is important 'doing-detail', because it helps students to check and correct their own work.

If you make a mistake, laugh it off and, if possible, make a teaching point out of it. 'You see how important it is to do it slowly! You will have more time, so I will expect a better job from you!' For long or complex demonstrations, consider giving students a demonstration observation sheet where they record relevant details, describe the technique, record what they have learned and record what they must remember when they do it themselves.

Learning by imitation or 'modelling' takes place even when you don't intend it. It is well known that students take more notice of what teachers *do* than what they say. If you tell your students to turn off the power pack before changing their circuit, or to wash their hands, or to be courteous to patients – then do so yourself. If you want your students to employ safe practice, to lay out work tidily or to be thorough or enthusiastic, you must do the same! Think carefully what a teacher in your subject area needs to model, and make sure you set a good example.

Some techniques you might like to try are:

The silent demonstration. Here the teacher explains that the coming demonstration will be without explanation, and asks the students to watch carefully, as they will later be asked exactly what was done, and why. This can often create intense student concentration, especially if some aspect of the technique is unexpected or puzzling.

The 'how not *to do it' demonstration*. We can certainly learn from deliberate mistakes, but be careful that your students do not become confused, or learn the wrong technique. The students are of course asked to watch out for the mistakes. If safety is involved, this technique should be avoided. With humour, this method can be most effective, a good example being the John Cleese videos showing how not to behave at an interview. (Those videos show, incidentally, that it is not just practical skills that we can learn by example.)

The Socratic demonstration. You ask the class to tell you how to do it right from the start, and follow their instructions, asking questions for clarification as you go. This approach can be very amusing if their instructions don't work. Then you can feign tears and complain it doesn't work!

The student demonstration. Students can demonstrate too, and not necessarily before you have demonstrated yourself. This technique is fully explained in Chapter 24.

Checklist for demonstrating a physical skill

❑ Did you ensure that the students could all see?

❑ Did they know what they were seeing and why it was done that way?

❑ Did you involve students by question and answer?

❑ Did you do it slowly enough and a sufficient number of times?

❑ Did you get feedback to check their understanding?

❑ Did you consider safety?

❑ Did you give performance indicators so students could self-check during their practice?

Demonstrating an intellectual skill or ability

If you teach intellectual skills or abilities you can still teach by showing. This method of teaching is underused and underestimated by many teachers of intellectual skills. There are two main methods of 'showing how'.

Showing by exemplar

The teacher shows a model of good practice from which students can copy, adapt or learn technique. You can show your students good essays, intelligent critical appreciations, well-constructed computer programs, good assignments, worked solutions, effective designs, etc. The source of these may be the teacher, books, former students or even peers. The exemplar is then examined carefully by the learners, and perhaps assessed against assessment criteria, as explained in Chapter 43 on formative assessment. With care, they can learn from both good and bad examples. (However, don't use a *student's* work as a bad – or even a good – example, if this will cause embarrassment or offence.)

Showing the exemplar is often not enough. The student must be clear how it was done, and understand *why* the exemplar is effective. Discussion and questioning may bring this out, but if not the teacher must provide all the information.

Sometimes it is helpful for students to prepare checklists of criteria defining good practice, based on the examples.

Give some thought to the number of examples you will show your students. Usually it is a case of 'the more, the better'. If the examples are very different, so much the better, as this helps the student see what the examples have in common, and how to use the skill in different contexts. It is particularly helpful for students to study an exemplar solution of a task soon after completing an identical task: an exemplar laboratory report or translation, for example; or an 'A' grade essay on the same title as a recent assignment. See spoof assessment and peer assessment in Chapter 43.

Showing by demonstrating

The skill or ability being taught can be carried out by a teacher in front of the class. For example, a mathematics teacher might demonstrate how to solve a problem in geometry; an English teacher might demonstrate how to write a critical appraisal of a poem; or a doctor might carry out a diagnosis. Demonstrating an intellectual skill like this usually requires that the teacher 'thinks out loud'. This takes practice. Watch a good mathematics teacher at work; not only is the correct thinking shown, but students are warned against common errors, and the class are often involved in the process by the careful use of questioning:

> 'I bet some of you think the answer is simply 12. But it's not! Can anybody see why? …'
> 'What should I do next? I can't find the height h, so it looks like I'm completely stumped. Or am I? …'

After showing by demonstration, many teachers 'do one on the board' in a different way – by following instructions from the students. This gives the teacher feedback on knowledge and understanding and enables students to practise the skill under close supervision, before a 'solo flight'. Mathematics and science teachers often do 'worked examples' in this way, using questioning to elicit instructions from the students: 'Right, so I've found the relative molecular mass; now what? …'

> *'Learner case studies' are excellent methods of teaching by showing. They are commonly used in the teaching of professionals. For example, nurses being trained in a new care technique can report back to their study group on how their use of the new technique is going in practice. This can generate valuable discussion, and each student's experience can be used to demonstrate to the others on the course how to use, or how not to use, the technique being studied. The nurse trainer can also offer practical help as her students use the care technique they are studying.*

Teaching by example is a most effective and inspiring way of giving students 'doing-detail': what students should be able to do, and how they should best do it. But be sure you do not teach the method by rote, without students really understanding the 'why' as well as the what and the how.

You can of course let students work out the 'doing-detail' for themselves; such 'guided discovery' is an excellent strategy, but needs to be handled carefully (see Chapter 29). But if you leave out the 'doing-detail' thoughtlessly, weak students will flounder, but able students will do well, because they are bright enough to work out what you want.

Students often spend some time discussing 'doing-detail' amongst themselves: 'What does he want? … How long does it have to be? … Is this OK, do you think? … How have you done it?' These questions are often best answered by showing how, or with careful use of guided discovery. They should not be left to guesswork.

Teachers of social sciences, English literature and a number of other subjects must develop their learners' ability to create their own informed opinion. Even high-order cognitive skills such as this can be learned by showing. Indeed, they are taught almost exclusively, if unconsciously, in this way. Exemplar opinions can be studied and criticised – for example, the views of experts or peers, opinions from a textbook, etc.

The teacher can argue out loud whether such and such an opinion is consistent with the facts, explaining why it is or is not valid, and showing why a different view is not tenable. From this, students can learn the characteristics of a well-argued opinion, and so develop their ability to create their own informed opinions. Much of this learning is done unconsciously; it is then called 'modelling'. However, try to make a conscious use of the technique, 'thinking out loud' to exemplify these high-order thinking skills.

If you are involved with this form of teaching, it would help your students enormously to explain and make explicit the criteria for a well-reasoned opinion. Science students are not left to discover for themselves how scientific laws can be induced from experimental data. Science teachers rightly regard the laws of scientific reasoning as far too subtle and difficult to be left solely to self-discovery. Yet humanities students are often left to divine the much more complex laws of reasoning in their subjects completely unaided.

Showing and telling

Showing is not always necessary. If the skill or ability is a straightforward adaptation of a well-practised technique, then simply telling students the 'how' of the skill may be enough. If the technique is well practised, they already know the 'doing-detail'. (Students who are practised at algebra may be happy with 'Divide the two equations and then solve for the unknown'. Those less practised would like to see one done on the board.) However, if the skill is complex, or must be developed over an extended period of time, then 'showing how' is important.

Showing and telling are not really equivalent methods of giving the same information. The two techniques involve the learner in quite different mental processes. *Showing* is concrete and holistic; it involves the learner in analysis of the examples, and looking for similarities in the examples of good practice. It involves learning by induction. In contrast, *telling* is abstract, and involves the learner in synthesis and learning by deduction. Cognitively they are mirror images of each other; they probably even involve different halves of the brain.

As was mentioned in the previous chapter on the art of explaining, when we are learning a concept we like to be given examples of its use; the definition is not enough. We like to be *shown* how to use the concept, as well as being *told* how.

Learning seems to require both the concrete and the abstract, both induction and deduction (though it is possible that some learners learn better from one than from the other).

Don't ignore learning by imitation; it is immensely powerful. Incredibly, we can learn complex skills such as grammar or the laws of reasoning in this way, without being told – or even formally understanding – the rules that govern these processes! Perhaps the reason for the power of this kind of learning is that our species learned to imitate before it learned to speak. Have our brains perhaps evolved to learn best in this way? Who knows; but no teacher can afford to ignore its power.

Checklist for demonstrating an intellectual skill

❏ Do you show your students examples of good practice?

❏ Are the examples you show numerous and varied?

❏ Do you 'think aloud' to your students to show the reasoning in your subject?

❏ Do you let students examine bad as well as good examples?

❏ Can you make use of case studies to show how the ideas you are teaching are used in practice?

❏ Do you get feedback on their understanding?

EXERCISES

1 Work out strategies for teaching the following by demonstration:
   • How to use inverted commas or apostrophes.
   • How to write an application letter for a job.
2 Practise 'thinking aloud' while showing how, and then make use of the technique in one of your classes.

Further reading

Petty, G. (2006) *Evidence Based Teaching*, Cheltenham: Nelson Thornes.

14

Questioning

The advantages of questioning

Most experienced teachers use questioning a great deal, in talking to classes and groups, as well as when talking to individual students. Questions are of course used in both verbal and written form; but this chapter will focus on the teacher asking questions verbally. Many experts on education, including many experienced and effective teachers, consider verbal questioning to be one of the teacher's most potent tools. Why is this?

To help us answer this question, let's compare two teachers developing the same teaching point. They are both teaching students of catering how to display cakes in a self-service cafeteria.

The first teacher's approach is to use teacher talk.

Teacher   Now, in cafeterias it is important to make sure that the cakes on display do not go stale over a period of time. This is particularly important if there is a large selection of cakes, or where the cake is kept in warm conditions. Unfortunately, warm conditions are all too common where food is being cooked and served. So we must pay a great deal of attention to the display of cakes in a cafeteria environment.

When choosing a cake for cafeteria display, bear in mind that it should be an iced cake, as these go stale less quickly. Also, it should not be left near an oven, coffee urn or other source of heat. It should be covered, of course, and a cake display cover like this one could be used to good effect here. So, during your practical this afternoon, I want to see cakes in suitable display conditions.

The second teacher uses questioning to develop the same teaching point.

Teacher	Why does fruit cake go stale?
Student 1	Currants go off, sir.
Teacher	Currants keep for years, actually.
Student 2	Flour goes off, sir?
Teacher	No, flour keeps for ages too! *(Silence)* How would you tell fresh cake from stale cake?
Student 3	Fresh cake is nice and moist, and stale cake is all dry.
Teacher	Good! So if stale cake is dried-out cake, how could we store cakes to stop them going stale?
Student 1	Put them in a plastic bag, or an airtight tin … *(Teacher nods and smiles.)*

Student 2	Or use one of those glass covers.
Teacher	That's right, like this one. Now – plastic bags, air-tight tins, glass covers … Why would these all stop the cake going stale? … Tracy?
Student 3	Because it stops the cake drying out.
Teacher	Good. And what effect would icing a cake have on the staleness?
Student 1	It would stop it going stale so fast, because it covers most of it up.
Teacher	Good, so going stale means drying out. Now, in our practical this afternoon, would you choose an iced or an un-iced cake for display?
Students	Iced.
Teacher	And where would you store it?
Student 2	Away from the oven.
Student 3	Away from anything hot.
Teacher	Yes, away from the oven, the heated display counter, the coffee urn and so on. Because … ?
Student 3	Because heat dries cake out, makes it stale.
Teacher	That's right! Well done.

There is a crucial advantage to the questioning approach, and that is that the knowledge gained in such a lesson is 'transferable'. Imagine asking the two classes who experienced these lessons the following question:

'How should bread be stored overnight to prevent it going stale?'

The class who were given the 'teacher talk' lesson would probably say, 'We haven't done bread.' (One hopes they would not suggest icing it!) However, the class taught to *understand* the process of going stale would probably have some correct suggestions; they would be able to transfer their understanding to this unfamiliar problem. It is important to teach for understanding, rather than just for knowing. Questioning teaches students to think for themselves.

Does anything else strike you about the differences between these two approaches? Most people would agree that the questioning approach would be more interesting for the students; they are actively involved rather than passively listening, and the questioning style tends to stimulate the students' curiosity – why *does* cake go stale? Moreover, the students are made to *think* in the questioning-style lesson; the logic of the subject is exposed and they are encouraged to use it: 'How could we store cakes to stop them going stale?'

The emphasis in the questioning-style lesson tends to be on understanding rather than simply knowing. In the teacher-talk lesson, the students were simply told what they had to know; they were not encouraged to understand it, and are less likely to remember it. This is constructivism again, as we saw in Chapter 1.

As a result of the questioning, the students had their assumptions and prior knowledge challenged and corrected. Beforehand, some of the students had thought that 'going stale' meant 'going off'; but in the course of the lesson they found out it means something closer to 'drying out'. This process of having incorrect assumptions corrected is sometimes called 'unlearning': as we have seen in earlier chapters, correction is a vital part of the learning process. Many students come to our classes with incorrect assumptions and 'common non-sense' notions that need challenging. Questioning helps enormously here.

Notice also that the teacher who used questioning was being given instant feedback on the understanding of the students, while the lesson proceeded.

More teacher questioning

A history teacher has asked her students to discuss in pairs the problems that landowners might have experienced immediately after the Black Death (a plague that killed a high percentage of the adult population in Britain and elsewhere). One group has realised that landowners would get less income from their cottages because some of them would be empty, but they are now 'stuck'; they cannot think of any other economic consequences the plague might have had for a landowner.

Teacher What do landowners do with their land?
Paula Hunting?
Teacher Yes, anything else?
Emma Grow wheat and stuff. They would farm it.
Teacher Good. Now, what problems would farming landowners have after the Black Death?
Paula No one would want to work on their farm, because they would catch the plague from the other workers.
Emma No, the plague is over now.
Teacher That's right, but Paula is half right in a way. The landowner would find it difficult to find workers, but not for the reason that Paula gave. It's obvious, really.
Paula Some of them have died. There are fewer workers.
Teacher That's right; well done, Paula. Now, what would the landowner have to do to make sure he got workers to bring in his harvest? (*Silence*) All the other farmers need workers too, but there's a shortage.
Emma Pay good wages?
Teacher That's it. And would the landowners be pleased about that?
Paula No!
Teacher So, what are you going to write down on your list of effects of the plague? Get it right – I'm going to ask you to explain it to the rest of the class in a bit.

Knowing only involves remembering – understanding requires that students 'own' the reasoning.

There is another crucial advantage of using questioning as a teaching technique. When we were considering motivation, it was pointed out that students need to know they are making a success of their learning. Nothing motivates quite as much as the glow of satisfaction that a student gets when he or she answers a question correctly and immediately gets warm praise from the teacher.

To summarise, then, the advantages of questioning as a teaching method are that it:

- displays the 'logic' of the subject and passes it on, encouraging understanding rather than rote remembering
- ensures that learning is built on prior learning in a constructivist way (Chapter 1)
- produces transferable learning
- gives instant feedback (to teacher *and* student) on whether learning is taking place
- ensures the lesson moves at the student's pace
- is an active and interesting activity for the students
- gives students practice in *using* the recently acquired ideas and vocabulary you have been teaching
- uncovers incorrect ideas and assumptions, allowing 'unlearning' to take place (i.e. it supplies the 'check and correct' elements of learning)
- can be motivating, as it gives students a chance to demonstrate their success in learning
- offers, in one-to-one questioning, a chance for the teacher to diagnose the difficulty a 'stuck' student might be having
- can be used to discipline a student
- allows the teacher to evaluate learning
- encourages the development of high-level thinking skills.

The disadvantages are that it:

- can be a time-consuming activity
- makes it difficult to involve all students in the group
- is not an easy technique for the teacher to master.

Questioning technique

How should we use questioning? A good questioning technique should encourage *all* the students in the class to think. It should avoid an 'I'm trying to catch you out' atmosphere, and should give students a chance to get some positive feedback, demonstrating their success in learning.

After posing a question, wait; most of the students should then be trying to puzzle out the answer. When they have had reasonable time to think, ask someone to answer. If you nominate someone to answer *before* posing the question, the rest of the class will be mentally in neutral, if not actually asleep! A helpful mnemonic is: 'Pose – Pause – Pounce!' The longer you pause, the more thinking the students do, and the longer their answers will be when they come.

Encourage responses to your questions by asking simple ones at first, especially with a new group. Without going overboard, show that you are grateful for the responses you are offered, and *always praise correct answers*. If an answer is given in a quiet voice, repeat it to the class.

How do you deal with incorrect responses? Re-read the example at the beginning of this chapter, and see how the teacher involved dealt with the problem. He did not ridicule the incorrect answers; instead, he tried to show the reasoning that would have given the correct answer. If a response was incorrect, he simply stated why it was wrong (without giving away the answer), and then asked another question to get the student(s) on to the right track. He also used the incorrect answers to correct misconceptions.

It will take practice for you to develop your questioning skills to this level. But in time it will happen, and you will enjoy doing it.

This technique of leading students through the reasoning can also be used if they are unable to answer a question at all. Here is a driving instructor's response to an error made earlier by one of her students. Look at her technique carefully. You might like to cover this dialogue with a sheet of paper and reveal it line by line, thinking of questions the teacher might ask before revealing what she actually says.

Teacher	You started signalling too early just then. Say you wanted to turn right, when should you start signalling?
Student	(*No response*)
Teacher	Can you signal right too early?
Student	Not sure … I suppose so.
Teacher	What would happen if you signalled right a mile before the junction in a city centre?
Student	Other drivers would think you were turning right before you really were.
Teacher	That's right, so when should you start signalling if there are lots of junctions about?
Student	Just after the junction before?
Teacher	That's right!

The student's confidence is boosted by the praise and smile from the teacher, and a potentially negative experience for the student is turned into a positive one. You might not have asked the same questions, but that does not matter, as long as your questions would make the student think out the reasoning for himself.

Distributing questions

When questioning a class, try to distribute the questions as widely as possible:

> 'How about someone on the back bench answering this one?'
> 'Have *you* any idea, Simon?'
> 'How about someone who *hasn't* answered a question yet answering that one.'

The plan of a classroom shows what is sometimes called the 'arc of vision' of the teacher. Students within this are more likely to feel involved in the lesson, and are therefore more likely to answer a question.

Students who do not want to participate in a lesson choose to sit out of the teacher's arc of vision. You may remember from your schooldays the scramble for seats at the back of the class in the less popular lessons!

It is too easy to ignore quiet students at the back of the class. Try to include them. Responses can often be obtained from reticent students by 'body-pointing' or by eye contact. Suppose, for example, two students on your left have not yet answered a question. If you move closer to them, and keep looking from one to the other after you have asked the question, one of them will answer if they can.

Don't be afraid to leave plenty of time for students to think; this is not wasted time. Smile while you are waiting, if you are worried about putting too much pressure on them.

> **Teacher** Why did we go to war? As a merchant, how would you feel? And how was your trade affected by the Napoleonic War?

What answer do you think the teacher got? I expect you guessed: he got no answer at all. Make your questions short and simple – and ask them one at a time!

Avoid questions which are so vague that there could be any number of correct answers. I have heard many novice teachers ask such 'guess what I'm thinking' questions. Here is an example. A keep-fit teacher had asked a student to demonstrate an exercise to the rest of the group, to review what the students had learned the previous week. The teacher noticed that the student had her arm in the wrong position, so she pointed vaguely to the student and asked: 'What do you see here?' The question was so vague that no student felt confident enough to answer. A better question would have been: 'Can anyone see anything wrong with her position?' The question 'What do you see here?' was not a genuine question at all, but an invitation to guess what the teacher was thinking. She would have been cross if one of the students had – correctly – answered this question with: 'Susie in a green leotard.'

If a question leads into a conversation between you and a student, use eye contact and body-pointing to include the other members of the class. Give your own comments to the whole class, and repeat the student's points if they are made too quietly for all to hear.

If students are reluctant with their answers, then first make sure your questions are simple enough, that you wait long enough, and that you praise or thank students for their responses. If you still have problems, use pair work as follows.

Using pair work

If your students are very unresponsive in question-and-answer sessions, or if your questions are challenging, try the following pair-work strategy. Ask your question and write it on the board, and then ask pairs to discuss it, giving them a time limit of literally a minute or two. If necessary, check there is attention to task during their discussion. Then ask for their answers, praising sensible responses. Pair work gives students time to think, and allows them to check their answer with their partner. This increases their confidence and so increases their responsiveness to your questions.

The assertive questioning technique described in Chapter 24 can also hugely increase student concentration and participation.

Experienced teachers usually pepper their teacher talk with between one and four questions per minute. When explaining a difficult point that involves reasoning, their presentation is often virtually 100% questioning.

Comparing questioning strategies

The table shows six questioning strategies, and gives each a star rating for five important criteria. The exact rating will vary depending on your class and exactly how you use each strategy – for example, how long you wait between asking a question and getting an answer.

Imagine a weak, poorly motivated student 'Jo' in your class while you use 'Q & A: volunteers answer'. Jo will soon learn that she need do nothing during your Q & A, just keep her hands down! She won't participate, and you won't know of any difficulty she has.

But if you habitually use 'Buzz groups: nominees answer', Jo will realise you might ask her to respond for her small group. She will participate now, ensuring she can explain her group's answer. If after a response you often ask, 'Why did your group think that?', she will also ensure she understands her group's answer. Groups don't like being misrepresented, so there is peer pressure to engage with your questions, and report the group's answers faithfully.

Any Q & A strategy may be appropriate at some stage in your lessons. Even Q & A: volunteers is useful sometimes. But when you are homing in on important points and the thinking behind them, you need methods towards the bottom of the table. Chapter 24 deals with assertive questioning, a vital questioning skill.

Which questioning strategy?

Excellent ***   good **   weak *   poor !!

Questioning strategy (The scoring assumes that the students are used to the strategy, and expect the teacher to use it.)	Participation rate The proportion of students who are engaged in trying to answer the question is high. There are few 'passengers'.	Teacher's feedback The teacher gets representative feedback on the quality of students' understanding and reasoning.	Student's feedback Each student gets feedback on their thinking. This can come from dialogue with other students.	Thinking time Each student spends a good deal of time thinking about the question and the quality of their answer.	Student comfort Students are not 'put on the spot'. They don't feel humiliated by the teacher or by others in the class.
Q&A: volunteers answer Students volunteer to answer questions.	!!	!!	!!	!!	***
Q&A: nominees answer Students nominated by the teacher answer questions.	**	*	*	*	!!
Buzz groups: volunteers answer Students work in small groups to answer a thought-provoking question. Teacher asks each group in turn to contribute part of the answer. A volunteer answers for their group.	**	**	**	*	*

Questioning strategy (The scoring assumes that the students are used to the strategy, and expect the teacher to use it.)	Participation rate The proportion of students who are engaged in trying to answer the question is high. There are few 'passengers'.	Teacher's feedback The teacher gets representative feedback on the quality of students' understanding and reasoning.	Student's feedback Each student gets feedback on their thinking. This can come from dialogue with other students.	Thinking time Each student spends a good deal of time thinking about the question and the quality of their answer.	Student comfort Students are not 'put on the spot'. They don't feel humiliated by the teacher or by others in the class.
Buzz groups: nominees answer As above, but the teacher nominates the student in each group who will contribute that group's answer(s).	***	**	**	**	*
Assertive questioning Groups work on a thought-provoking question. Teacher asks individuals to give their group's answer, says 'thank you' and then asks the rest of the class to discuss and agree a 'class answer'. Only then does the teacher 'give away' the right answer. See Chapter 24.	***	***	***	***	**

***		**		***	**	**
Pair checking Students work alone to answer a question. Pairs then compare their answers, giving their partner one good point and one way their answer could be improved. The teacher then gives the correct answer. Pairs now suggest another improvement to their partner's answer. Teacher looks over shoulders throughout.						

Varying the type of question you use

Open and closed questions

Closed questions have only one satisfactory answer, which is usually very short. For example:

> 'Should it be "Yours sincerely" or "Yours faithfully"?'
> 'Is there a danger of the plant drying out?'

Open questions require a more detailed response, and there is often more than one correct answer. For example:

> 'What did merchants have to gain from this war?'
> 'How could we improve the apparatus to make our experiment yield a more accurate value?'

Open questions make students think, and tell the teacher much more about what the students have learned. By contrast, closed questions, such as 'yes/no' questions, usually require little thought. They are likely to be guessed with at least 50% success, and so have low 'diagnostic power' – that is, the teacher cannot assume for certain that a correct answer means that successful learning has taken place.

Some students can manage a 100% success rate on 'yes/no' questions, without understanding the first thing about the subject of the questions. Their technique, perhaps unconscious, is to put on a thoughtful expression after the question has been asked, and then shake their head from side to side to give the impression they are about to say 'no'. Whilst doing this they look carefully at the teacher's expression. If the teacher smiles and raises his or her eyebrows, the student completes the answer as a 'no'. If, however, the teacher lowers the eyebrows or shows no expression during the student's head-shaking, the student feigns a sudden flash of insight and converts the answer to a 'yes'!

A similar student technique is to give an immediate answer, for example a 'no', and watch the teacher's non-verbal reaction. If this is unfavourable, the answer is immediately changed before the teacher has had a chance to respond verbally. Most students use this second technique quite unconsciously. If you don't believe me, try the following. Ask students some reasonably difficult 'yes/no' questions. On receiving a correct answer, say nothing, and make no facial expressions or other bodily movement – just wait. Unless the student is very sure of the subject, I will wager that within three seconds he or she will have changed the correct answer to an incorrect one!

Questioning levels

> 'What are the names of the bones in the upper arm?'
> 'What would happen if human beings didn't have a skeleton?'

Some questions simply require that students recall facts. Such questions certainly have their uses: reinforcing earlier learning, practising recall, 'pointing' to the most important facts in a topic and informing the teacher of what students can and cannot remember.

However, there is more to learning than remembering. Even the most hard-boiled teachers would acknowledge that most examination syllabuses award less than half of their marks for the recall of facts. The majority of marks are awarded for higher-order skills, such as the ability to comprehend and apply the concepts and principles associated with the course of study. Although it is not recognised formally, marks are, in effect, also awarded for more general 'thinking skills', such as the ability to sift through the memory and choose only the information relevant to a particular question.

Fact questions do not by themselves develop understanding, and they do not let students apply their knowledge, let alone practise the higher-order thinking skills. There are plenty of types of question that are more demanding.

Trevor Kerry (1982) listed a number of different question types. His suggested categories are shown below.

Question type	Example
Data recall	What is the capital of France?
Naming	What is the name of the bone in the thigh?
Observation	What colour was the litmus paper?
Control	Will you sit down, John?
Pseudo-question	(An open question but the teacher expects only one answer): What do you see here?
Higher-order question types	
Speculative hypothesis	What would happen if all the trees in the world were cut down tomorrow?
Give reasons	Why do people in the Third World choose to have so many children?
Evaluation	What evidence is there for and against the existence of an afterlife?
Problem-solving	How can we drill the wood without overheating the drill?

While facts are often soon forgotten, higher-order thinking skills tend to be retained, because such skills are more generally applicable and therefore more often used. The dates of Henry VIII's reign, for example, will soon be forgotten unless recalled from time to time. In a culture such as ours, the importance of higher-order mental skills can hardly be overstated; once developed, such skills can be applied in any field of human endeavour. For the majority, who find little direct use for most of the factual knowledge gained during their education, these skills are the main benefit of their many years in school or college. These precious thinking skills can only be developed by the effective use of questioning. Their use also ensures understanding of the content.

Education is what remains when you have forgotten what you have been taught.

Sadly, research shows that 70–80% of questions asked by teachers require only factual recall. Researchers suggest that many teachers are simply not skilled enough to ask higher-order questions. Have another look at Bloom's taxonomy in Chapter 1; do you use questions at every level?

The uses of questioning

In terms of the *educare?* elements of learning, questioning can be used to provide students with an *explanation*, to let them use the knowledge you are teaching, and of course to *check and correct* and indeed to *evaluate* their learning. It can also be used to *review* or revise earlier work.

An explanation should display the logic of a subject and pass this thinking on to the student; questioning is an excellent way to do this. Here is an example of the use of questioning to give a student an explanation for hot air rising. The student has already studied density and expansion.

Teacher	Why does cork float on water?
Student	Because it's less dense than water.
Teacher	Good. Now, when you heat air, it expands. What effect does this expansion have on the density of the air?
Student	It makes it less dense.
Teacher	That's right. So, what happens to hot air when it is surrounded by cooler air? *(Silence)* Well, what happened to the less dense cork when it was surrounded by water?
Student	It floated.
Teacher	Yes, so what will happen if hot air is surrounded by cool air?
Student	It will float too.
Teacher	Good; and why?
Student	Because the hot air is less dense than the cold air.
Teacher	Well done. So hot air floats in cold air. Can you think of an example of this 'convection' happening?
Student	A hot air balloon?
Teacher	Exactly. And that's why we say 'hot air rises'.

The teacher could of course give this reasoning by teacher talk. However, there are a number of advantages in making the student provide the steps in the logic. The explanation is done at the student's pace; there is an opportunity for the student to use the ideas, and have the use checked; and when the student eventually 'gets it right', the success is motivating. It also ensures that the learner creates their own understanding and the logical links in a constructivist way.

It is important to realise that the interchange on hot air rising could have been carried out with a class as a whole, with a group, or with an individual student.

Questioning can be used to evaluate any relevant prior learning that students require to understand a new topic.

If you have trouble thinking up thought-provoking questions, try those which start with 'why' or 'how'. Putting one of these words in front of almost any statement can help change it into a question. 'What would happen if … ?' is also a useful phrase for the start of a question. Try making the following statements into questions:

Rain tends to fall in mountainous regions.
Thomas More was executed.
Increasing the temperature increases the rate of the chemical reaction.
This bacteria needs air to survive.
Jesus told parables.

It is often possible to make more than one question from each factual statement. For example, you could ask 'Why was Thomas More executed?', 'How was Thomas More executed?', 'What would have happened if Thomas More had not been executed?', etc.

Questioning can also be used to wake up an inattentive student. Paul is gazing out of the window:

Teacher	So, how would you tell a good precis from a bad precis? … Paul?
Paul	What? (*Some laughter in the class*)

Another important use of questioning is in the diagnosis of a student's difficulty. When students are 'stuck', how should a teacher respond? It is tempting to help them over their difficulty as quickly as possible by *telling* them what to do, but it is better teaching to find the cause of the blockage and put this right – or better still, let the student *discover* how to put it right. Questioning students is perhaps the only way of discovering the misunderstanding or knowledge gap that has caused their difficulty. The driving instructor dialogue we looked at earlier is an example of this use of questioning.

Teaching by the use of questioning only is sometimes called the 'Socratic method'. Socrates claimed he knew nothing (this may partly explain why he never wrote his ideas down); he simply questioned his students in order to show up any inconsistency in their beliefs. He was not rewarded for this humility, however, but was put to death for 'corrupting the young'. Moral: don't ask questions that are too difficult!

Questioning does not come naturally to most people, because novice teachers are used to thinking in terms of answers rather than questions. As a result, many novice teachers find it very difficult to sustain a lengthy bout of questioning, requiring as it does the ability to 'think on your feet' in order to field an unexpected answer and turn it into the next productive question.

It is advisable to think out in advance the questions you are going to use in a lesson, especially the thought-provoking ones. However, it does not take long before you are able to think up questions 'on the spot'.

Trevor Kerry (1982) thought the main faults inexperienced teachers showed when using questioning were that their vocabulary was too complex; they did not leave enough time for students to answer; they did not use enough reinforcement (e.g. praise); and they were often unable to prompt a student into producing a useful response by, for example, using a simpler question. Most learning teachers are unaware of these faults, so it is advisable to start by over-compensating: make your questions very clear and concise, leave more answering time than you think necessary, and give more praise than you think necessary.

P. Groisser (1964) said that questions should be clear, purposeful, brief, stated in a natural and simple language, thought-provoking and distributed widely; there should be a balance between 'fact' and 'thought' questions.

Summary

Questioning is of paramount importance. It would be impossible to develop genuine understanding, or other higher-order mental skills, without it. It teaches students to think for themselves, and produces high-quality, transferable learning.

It allows students to practise using the concepts and principles they are being taught, and it gives the teacher the opportunity to check immediately and correct this use. It also gives teachers feedback on whether learning is taking place, and ensures that they do not 'lose' the students.

Students tend to find questioning an active and enjoyable activity, especially as answering correctly gives them confidence and a feeling of success. Even the students who are not chosen to answer the question will gain in confidence if they are able to think of the correct answer for themselves. This confidence and success, along with the praise and approval which should accompany it, fuels motivation.

However, questioning is an unfamiliar technique for most of us at first, though after a little practice it soon comes quite naturally.

Questioning skills checklist: the 'ten commandments'

1   Do you ask questions which students can answer successfully?

2   Do you leave time for students to think, by using pair work, for example?

3   Do you use body language (eye contact, smiling, raising the eyebrows, nodding, etc.) to encourage responses?

4   Do you always thank, praise or otherwise acknowledge responses?

5   Do you avoid ridiculing students' answers?

6   It no answer comes, are you able to ask a simpler question that leads to the answer to the original question?

7   Do you make questions short and clear, using straightforward language?

8   Do you avoid using solely fact-based questions?

9   Are you able to distribute questions widely around the class or otherwise get all students participating?

10 Are you able to ask questions, say, twice a minute during teacher talk?

EXERCISES

1   Take a simple teaching point that needs only a minute or so, and requires reasoning, and try teaching it entirely by questioning. Prepare your questions in advance. Use 'why … ?', 'how … ?' and 'what would happen if … ?' questions.

2   Think of a process or skill you know well, which requires reasoning to explain it – say, wiring a three-pin plug or repotting a pot plant. Think of a series of questions that could be used to teach a student the skill.

3   Write down five ways to encourage answers from reluctant or shy students.

4   Write down five ways to help distribute questions widely around the class.

References and further reading

Groisser, P. (1964) *How to Use the Fine Art of Questioning*, Englewood Cliffs, NJ: Teachers Practical Press.

Kerry, T. (1982) *Effective Questioning*, London: Macmillan.

Marzano, R. J. *et al.* (2001) *Classroom Instruction that Works: Research-Based Strategies for Increasing Student Achievement*, Alexandria, VA: ASCD.

Petty, G. (2006) *Evidence Based Teaching*, Cheltenham: Nelson Thornes.

15

The aide-memoire: note-making

Earlier chapters, in considering the *educare?* mnemonic, have explained that students regard 'aide-memoires' as vital. The aide-memoire is usually a summarised record of what is being learned. This may be provided by textbooks, handouts or intranet pages; alternatively, the teacher can use dictation, or students can copy written notes from the board or screen. The aide-memoire is needed to clarify what has to be learned, to compensate for the fallibility of memory, and to provide material for revision (though ideally you should also provide a separate, very concise set of notes for students to commit to memory – see pages 275–6).

When students are learning an exclusively practical skill, such as bowing a violin, an aide-memoire may not be necessary, but even here many teachers like to offer one to prevent the student getting into bad habits during unsupervised practice.

Have you ever tried writing and listening at the same time? Sadly, many teachers (especially in higher education) still leave their students to write their own notes during lectures. As a result, universities are full of students who cannot concentrate in their lectures because they are too busy writing over-detailed and inadequate notes. At bottom, the justification for this practice is: 'If it was good enough for me, it's good enough for my students.' A wider application of the same argument would have kept us in the Stone Age. If a lecturer provides a summary, students can concentrate on the lecture itself.

Getting students to write their own notes is a great teaching method, as we will see. But most teachers communicate their notes directly; let's see how they do it

Aide-memoire by textbook

If a well-written, readable textbook or handbook comprehensively covers every aspect of the course you are teaching, this may well fulfil all your students' aide-memoire needs. You are also very lucky! If the textbook is too comprehensive, it is sometimes possible to indicate to students which sections they may omit, or better, they can be asked to mark the sections of the textbook relevant to what is currently being studied. If you are going to use a textbook like this, ask students to bring it to your sessions and refer to it in class.

Most teachers do not have the luxury of a text that suits all their needs, or prefer their students to have a personal record of their studies.

Writing notes for your students

Writing notes for your students has many obvious advantages, though it can be very time-consuming. Whether they are communicated by handout, by writing on the board/OHP or by dictation, make them:

* *Concise*. A summary is better than a full explanation. Refer to textbooks (giving page numbers) if necessary. Stress the key points.
* *Simple*. Don't try to impress by an over-formal style. Use as simple a vocabulary as you can, and explain all technical terms. Keep your sentences shorter than 20 words whenever you can. (See Chapter 12 on the art of explaining.)
* *Attractive*. Take care with layout. Use clear, simple diagrams whenever you can. Try to get your handouts produced on a computer. Don't overcrowd the page; unattractive handouts are not read.

Making your notes clearer

Avoid words such as 'it', 'they', or 's/he' which refer to other words; avoid ambiguity by replacing them with the word to which they refer, for example:

Not: Wood, like coal, creates pollution, though it is a renewable resource.

But: Wood, like coal, creates pollution, but wood is a renewable resource. (Students may think that 'it' in the first sentence refers to coal.)

Avoid complex sentence constructions.
Avoid negatives; positives are often clearer, for example:

Not: Seldom does the machine fail to jam when the cotter is not lubricated.

But: Lubricate the cotter or the machine may jam.

Aide-memoire by handout

Handouts save valuable teaching time and can be made to suit your needs exactly; however, they can be very time-consuming to produce. Weak students collect handouts assiduously, but rarely read them unless they are set an activity that requires it.

It is common for teachers to give out handouts, and then to find that students are reading rather than listening. If possible, give them out after the topic has been covered, and talk students through the handout as a way of summarising the topic for them.

Alternatively, students can be led through the topic with constant reference to the handout – but make sure you have their attention when you need it.

Whatever you do, make sure you have used the handout with the students. Some teachers produce uncompleted handouts: diagrams that are not labelled, headings with missing text, questions without answers, and so on. Completing the handout then becomes a useful lesson activity, which 'personalises' the handout for the student. Encourage students to annotate their handouts with their personal notes.

Death by a thousand handouts is a common fault of many courses for professionals. Don't try to write a textbook – write references to other people's books instead. Don't give out more than one double-sided A4 handout per hour; any more will be treated with exasperation. And do get your handouts copied double-sided rather than single-sided. Modern photocopiers can manage this entirely automatically, and if all teachers did it, we would collectively save at least one tropical rain forest a year.

Using the board or OHP for notes

Note-taking need not be a passive, fruitless activity. Teach the topic first, and then use note-taking to get the students to summarise what you hope they have learned.

Suppose, for example, a science teacher is about to give the following note on power after teaching the topic:

Power

Power is the rate of transforming energy, and it is measured in watts. One watt is one joule per second. So, for example, if an electric motor used 18 joules of energy in three seconds, the power would be 6 joules per second or 6 watts.

$$\text{power} = \frac{\text{energy transformed}}{\text{time taken}}$$

Rather than writing this all down at once, after writing the title, the teacher can ask the class for a definition of power, with its unit. A satisfactory answer should give the first sentence of the note, which can then be read out and written up. Then the teacher can ask, 'What do we mean by a watt?' This should give rise to the note's second sentence. Next, the third sentence can be written, up to 'the power would be …'; and the teacher can then ask someone to complete the sentence. Finally, the teacher can ask, 'What is the equation for power?', and a correct answer completes the note. Students enjoy being involved in composing their notes, and it gives them confidence in their learning when they are successful. Try to use their wording where you can.

If an OHP is used, the note could be progressively revealed as students answer the questions and complete the sentences. Alternatively, it can be written up at the time, which is more likely to give the students a feeling of involvement with the process. If you have access to an interactive whiteboard, then see Chapter 35 in the resources section.

Dictation

Dictation is the bête noire of teaching methods, but students often find it quicker and easier than copying. However, dictation is a disaster for slow writers, bad spellers, most dyslexic students – and for students whose pen has just been lost! Nevertheless, the status of great dictator is not as difficult to achieve as the history of the Third Reich suggests. The solution is to dictate the note while it is being written on the board or screen.

Use a slower, more deliberate voice than usual, and give the punctuation; students can check their own spellings from the board.

Notes as a teaching method

Write headings

Try giving your students a set of notes with the headings missing, but with space for these, and ask them to write their own headings in the form of sentences. This requires the learner to read and understand the material, and results in headings such as 'The heart is a blood pump' or 'The heart increases its speed in response to the needs of muscles'.

Note-making

Here is an old-fashioned method I remember from my school days. The teacher leaves five minutes or so at the end of a short topic for students to write their own notes in their own words, perhaps under headings given by the teacher. This method has been abandoned by most teachers in favour of giving handouts, but in classroom trials, student note-making raises achievement by an average of two grades! Also, it is by far the most common method used by the most expert teachers (see Petty 2006).

However, students' notes need checking! Ask them to leave large gaps between paragraphs and in the margins where they can improve their notes. After note-making, ask the class for key points that the notes should cover. Confirm these, then ask your students to improve their notes. Also, encourage them to create 'graphic organisers' (see page 154).

If you look at notes created this way, I guarantee you will be shocked and your toes will curl! But the aim of the method is not to create faultless notes on paper. The aim is to create a personal understanding in the student's *head*, and then to improve this with feedback. This is very constructivist! (Chapter 1) Good student notes are only created by making bad ones first. The same goes for student understandings. Giving them handouts they don't read won't improve their understandings, even if it makes you feel better!

Peer-explaining

If your students are weak writers, or very reluctant ones, then use peer-explaining instead. Split the short topic into two, put your students in pairs, then:

> The student in your pair nearest the door will explain how the district nurse works with patients. The one furthest from the door will explain how she works with doctors.

Give students a minute to prepare their explanation by writing bullet points, then a minute each to peer-explain, then a minute to improve each other's bullet points. Then you give key points for them to check against. This, also, has been a highly effective method in trials (see Petty 2006).

All these methods work best if students are expecting them, of course!

Reviewing skills as well as content: So far we have just considered content, but what about the skills used in the lesson, such as evaluating or data analysis? These will need a note too – see Chapter 23.

What are notes for?

Don't give notes if your students will never need to use them. Give them sections of notes to learn, and then test them (see Chapter 23 on learning for remembering).

Don't overdo notes; they should just be a summary. If there is a lot of detail, give reading references instead.

Further reading

Marzano, R. J. *et al.* (2001) *Classroom Instruction that Works: Research-Based Strategies for Increasing Student Achievement*, Alexandria, VA: ASCD.

Petty, G. (2006) *Evidence Based Teaching*, Cheltenham: Nelson Thornes.

16

Supervised student practice

We owe almost all our skills and abilities to corrected practice, so this is an obligatory teaching method. It gives students an opportunity to develop their skills, and the teacher an opportunity to get feedback, and so discover whether the students have learned anything, and whether this learning requires improving. Here are some examples:

* students completing a series of exercises from a worksheet or textbook
* students carrying out an experiment
* learners in an adult education dressmaking class, making a garment chosen by themselves
* engineering students practising a welding procedure
* humanities students discussing the best method of reducing unemployment.

Note that students in the same class may not be doing the same thing. In the dressmaking class, for example, there is an element of personal choice, so that the individual interests of the students and their differing attainments can be accommodated. This is very motivating, but it is not always possible.

In this chapter we will look at the practice of practical and intellectual skills separately, but before doing so, we will consider some aspects that are common to both. (An alternative approach to student practice is the discovery method described in Chapter 29.)

In terms of the *educare?* elements, at the very least this activity lets the students 'use' the skill, and gives an opportunity for a 'check and correct' phase; it also offers students a chance to get their queries answered (the '?' phase).

Supervised practice makes students work harder than any other learning method, so the cynical might expect it to be unpopular. However, if it is well prepared and managed, students enjoy this method of learning more than most.

Preparing for the activity

If student practice is to be used effectively, before the activity starts:

* The students must have been adequately introduced to the activity, so that they understand the aim of the work they have been set. They must be fully aware of 'doing-detail' (what they are expected to do and how best to do it). They will also need to know why things are done this way.
* The activities must be at the right level for all the students. (This might involve different activities, or different expectations, for different students – for example, stretching activities for students who finish early.)

- Students should have had the opportunity to ask questions about the activity.
- If the activity consists of a series of tasks, these should usually be available to the students in a written form, and broken down into subtasks. For example, 'When you have finished, write a report' may be too vague for many students; try itemising subtasks – for example, what the report should contain. Alternatively, get students to devise such subtasks themselves – for example, by action-planning before they start.

I will now look in more detail at managing students while they practise intellectual skills; class practicals are dealt with later in the chapter.

Managing the practice of an intellectual skill

The crucial first few minutes

Describe the activity with care, giving it to the students in written form. Before allowing anyone to start, ask if there are any questions; when everyone seems clear, summarise the activity one last time before they start. For almost any activity, each student's work should now be checked as soon as possible after the start of the practice, to make sure no one is completing it incorrectly. Communication in the classroom is so tenuous that, however carefully you explain, in most groups at least one student will get the wrong end of the stick, or will have no stick at all, or will not be aware there is a stick!

> *I once saw a student maths teacher set his class a series of exercises on fractions. The class seemed to be working well, and the teacher moved about answering queries. About forty minutes later at the end of the class, the work was handed in, and the teacher noticed that one student had completed all the exercises incorrectly. Understandably the student felt frustrated, angry and demotivated. What was more, she had spent forty minutes practising an incorrect method which might be difficult to unlearn. A quick initial check avoids such disasters.*

You can check students' work by moving systematically round the class, looking over their shoulders; by asking students to self-check or peer-check; or by giving the answer to the first few questions. This initial check is important, and should usually take priority over answering individual queries. Those most in need of help are least likely to ask for it. It also establishes that everyone is working!

Here is a teacher of geometry 4 minutes into a 20-minute activity. She has stopped the large class and asked for silence:

> Everybody has finished the first question now, so let's make sure we are all on the right lines. I want you to check three things. First: does your construction fill the page? Second: is it labelled like the one on the board? Lastly, did you get 8.7 metres as the answer to question 1? See me if you have any queries.

Even better, she could ask the students to supply the checking criteria, and having established these, ask the students to use them to check their own or each other's work.

Once you are under way

Once you have established that all students are working along roughly the right lines, your role as teacher is to praise and encourage, to be permanently available to help students with any difficulties, and to continue the checking process. In some classes, it is also important to check on the work rate of all the students.

Unless the activity is very short, it is often wise to check *every* student in the class briefly from time to time (though in large classes this can be very difficult). Apart from allowing monitoring of student work rates and prompt correction of errors, the checking process also gives students positive feedback; this provides motivation and gives them confidence in what they are doing. If your criticism is constructive and if you use plenty of praise, students will enjoy the attention of regular checks, and find them motivating.

Never ridicule a student's work. However silly or appalling their mistake, do not even show surprise, let alone laugh, or you will discourage help-seeking in the future. For the same reason, discourage students from ridiculing each other's work. We all make mistakes; we could hardly learn without them. Of all the attributes of able teachers, the most prized by students is patience. Not that effective teachers are really patient; it's just that they learn not to show their irritation. Cultivate the ability to smile through clenched teeth, and keep a punch bag in the staff room!

Reluctant learners

Try:

> When you have finished down to question 4, let me know and I will mark it for you straight away.

Instant knowledge of results like this is very motivating, even for students whose work rate is usually very low; mark with the student present, and find something to praise if possible. Students enjoy your undivided attention as much as the marking. If the class is large, then offer to mark part of the work on the spot, but all the work of those who are least motivated.

How do you deal with students whose work rate is low because of low motivation?

- Check work rate often. You may need to make a mental, or even a written, note of where students have 'got up to' in their work at the beginning of the work session.
- Use eye contact between checks.
- Praise what you can in their work.

- Set targets: 'I'll come back in five minutes, and I'll expect to see question 4 completed.' Make sure your targets are realistic, that you remember to check whether they have been met, and that you praise their achievement.
- In extreme cases, put students 'on report' – that is, they must bring their work to you at the end of each lesson.
- Read the chapters on motivation and praise and criticism in Part 1!

You may need to keep an eye out for trouble. As you move round the class or give individual help, try to arrange yourself so that you face the majority of the class, and scan the whole room from time to time.

Helping students 'one to one'

How should you correct a student's error? There are all manner of approaches: the wrist-slappers, the shoulder-shruggers, the move-over-and-let-me-do-iters.

> *When a stroke victim is left paralysed down one side, they must relearn how to carry out such everyday tasks as opening a jam jar. Seeing someone who is struggling to open a jam jar produces in most people an overwhelming desire to 'help' by opening it for them. But the families of such stroke victims are told that to help is to hinder. To become independent, the victims must be left to practise by themselves, no matter how long it takes. Sometimes it is most helpful not to help.*

Inexperienced teachers often over-teach when sorting out a student's difficulties: their approach is to say, 'No, do it like *this*', and then to take over. It is much more effective to encourage students to recognise their problem and to work out their own solution. The aim here is to make students independent of the teacher, by developing their ability to *evaluate* their own performance, *diagnose* problems and *solve* them on their own. Such skills are crucial if students are to learn how to improve their performance. The aim is to produce a 'reflective practitioner', that is, a student who reflects on his or her performance with a view to improving it.

In general, when correcting students' work, try to get them to do as much of the correcting as possible:

- Ask if they have any questions or difficulties, and listen carefully to their reply.
- Try to get the students to recognise the root cause of their difficulty, using questioning if necessary.
- Having discovered the problem, ask them if they can see the solution.
- Only when this fails should you explain and demonstrate how the error should be corrected.

It has to be said that with large classes there often isn't time for this process – especially if you are besieged with queries because the work is too difficult or the class is not well prepared!

Do you want your students to help each other, or should all difficulties be referred to you personally? Most teachers encourage peer tutoring.

If a lot of students have similar troubles, get them in a group; this can save you the trouble of saying the same thing over and over. You can say:

> Quite a few of us are having trouble with question 7. If you'd like some help with this one, gather round the board; I'll go over it with you. The rest of you can carry on.

Students find working alone hard work, and although this activity can often go on for very long periods, beware of tiring them out.

Worksheets

Worksheets are usually a series of exercises or practical tasks for the students, but they may also include summarised notes.

Commercial publishers market worksheet masters with a copyright waiver, which usually authorises the purchasing institution to photocopy the sheets for use within that institution. However, most worksheets are produced by the teacher for his or her own use. (See the section on handouts in Chapter 35 on visual aids.)

When writing your own worksheets:

* Graduate the work very carefully. Students need more than one question to practise a difficult idea, and they like to climb one step at a time.
* Make the first few questions very simple to give confidence.
* Whenever possible, break tasks down into subtasks, giving each a unique question number. Order tasks with great care.
* Worksheets should give students the opportunity to demonstrate the skills and knowledge they have been learning in a straightforward way. Don't aim to catch students out. Leave the more difficult questions until the basics have been well established and practised. Success is the key to motivation.
* Make at least the last question *open*, so that students who work quickly don't end up with nothing productive to do.
* Consider student relevance, human interest puzzles, challenges, etc.
* Make your worksheets as attractive and interesting as you can. Type them; include diagrams and photographs; don't cram too much into them. (Look carefully at commercially produced worksheets and see how they do them.)

The Jabberwocky exercise in Chapter 1 showed that students can appear to do quite well without understanding what they are doing. Worksheets which require students only to fill in missing words, or mine handouts for answers, have little value. Start with such questions by all means, but then ask more searching questions, higher on Bloom's taxonomy, which require students to:

- *Make decisions*. Were the borogroves right to feel mimsy?
- *Give reasons*. Why were the toves in the wabe?
- *Evaluate*. How effective was the mome raths' strategy?
- *Hypothesise*. What would have happened if it was not brillig that day?

Such questions, and others like them, require students to process the information and come to an understanding. They require genuine thought about the subject matter, and provide you with feedback as to whether it is comprehended. They make the material more interesting, better understood and better remembered. They also develop important thinking skills.

Have some simple text-based questions by all means, but move on to ask searching questions. Do your worksheets suffer from the Jabberwocky or 'surface learning' problem?

Don't rely too heavily on worksheets, especially if other teachers on your students' course use them widely. Overuse makes for tedium. If you are provided with a coursebook or a large collection of worksheets for a course you are teaching, don't feel tyrannised into using them to the exclusion of all else.

Checking progress

In most teaching situations the work can be marked by the teacher. If so, the results should be given to the students as soon as possible, as this maximises motivation. In subjects such as mathematics, where there is often only one correct answer, students can be asked to check their own answers; however, don't over-rely on self-checking. Always mark some of the work yourself to check on work rate, methods used to obtain answers, copying, etc. Copiers are easy to spot, especially if you collect and mark work in classroom seating order; they use identical layout and make identical mistakes. But some copying is genuine collaboration, so investigation may be necessary. Regular testing, such as in 'mastery learning', soon uncovers those who copy and those who collaborate.

I will probably be shot for saying this, but if the student work rate exceeds your ability to mark it, then consider marking only a sample of each student's work – for example, the last four questions of the worksheet only. Ideally everything should be marked, but ideal practice also requires that you are given adequate time and resources. Even better, make use of peer assessment as described in Chapter 43 on formative assessment.

'Has anybody any queries?' is better than 'Is anybody stuck?' In learning, errors are both inevitable and necessary for advancement, so try to adopt a shoulder-shrugging 'no blame' policy towards them.

Some teachers use individual student practice almost exclusively – for example, those teaching the use of standard computer application packages through work-books; or practical classes such as dressmaking, where students are working on their own projects. Over-reliance on any one teaching method can be tedious for the students, so try hard to introduce variety. The dressmaking students will enjoy grouping round each other's work and hearing from the teacher about each other's special difficulties, techniques employed, etc. The computer students will benefit from seeing demonstrations of practical uses of the application they are learning, or acquiring some general background to the equipment they are using.

The plenary

'What have we learned from this activity? What are the key points?' The plenary helps students to see the wood as well as the trees. Students usually need to reflect on the activity, discuss it and have common difficulties cleared up; summary notes are often given after this process.

After work has been marked, it is of course vital that you (or preferably the student) correct any errors, and that you go over any common difficulties with the group.

Managing a practical activity

At their best, practicals are an enjoyable and active 'hands-on' experience. At their worst, they are frustrating episodes where not even the teacher knows what is supposed to be happening, and where half the equipment is malfunctioning or missing. As with so much in teaching, success depends on planning.

Are the students well prepared for the activity? Will they be following a procedure defined by you, or using a 'discovery' approach (Chapter 29)? Will they be working separately or in groups (Chapter 18)?

However you elect to organise a practical activity:

1   It will take much longer than you think, so allow *plenty* of time.

2   Unless the activity is very routine, try out the practical yourself (with the equipment the students will use). Try to see it from the students' point of view, making a note of the following:

    –   the procedure, and *all* the equipment required

    –   what can go wrong

    –   any 'performance criteria', giving students clear goals

    –   (especially) any safety precautions.

3   Order the equipment well in advance (before anyone else 'bags' it!).

4   Ask experienced teachers for tips, tricks and traps on handling the practical before planning the lesson.

If you have a shortage of equipment, divide students into groups and either extract groups from a class activity to do the practical, or have a 'circus' of different activities (see Chapter 18). If students are extracted from other activities one at a time to use specialist equipment, then student number five will benefit from watching student number four, and so on.

Decide on exactly what you hope to achieve in the lesson, and then plan the activity with more than usual care. Is there anything you especially want your students to notice? Do you want them to write up the activity in any way? Will the students need a demonstration? Have you emphasised safety considerations? Make sure everybody has something to do all the time; you might like to consider an open-ended stretching activity for those who finish early.

Unless a discovery method is to be used, put special emphasis on clarity of instruction; make sure the activity is described for students in written form on a worksheet, board or overhead projector screen. These instructions will not be read unless they are concise, and are best written up before the class.

If preparation is critical – for example, whisking egg whites before adding to a soufflé mixture, or setting up an electrical circuit before starting a science experiment – it sometimes pays to get the learners to check their preparation with you before continuing.

As soon as the activity is under way, check that each individual or group has started correctly. Are they getting the results you would expect? Pay special attention to safety factors. While supervising the activity, especially if safety or misbehaviour is likely to be a problem, try to remain facing most of the group even when talking to individuals. Scan the whole class with eye contact every few seconds.

The plenary session is often very important in practical work. What should the students have learned? What conclusions can be drawn? Can any anomalous experiences or results be explained away? Students often appreciate a summarising note at this stage. They may also profit from seeing each other's work and discussing it. Common problems need dealing with.

If you expect practical work to be written up, make it clear how this is to be done, and let students see good examples of such write-ups. Allow plenty of time, with the accent on repetition, which should be deliberate, accurate and unhurried. 'Doing-detail' should include performance indicators where these are appropriate, so that students are in a position to self-check their work. It is not true that practice makes perfect; it is *correcting* practice that makes it perfect.

When teaching a physical skill, it is important not to teach too much at once. A complex task is best broken into a chain of steps, with each step learned separately. Particularly in the case of a physical skill, these steps should then be practised *slowly* and *accurately* until the required speed is reached. Then the steps can be chained together to make up the complex task. For example, a music teacher might teach a student to play a complex four-bar passage in this way, perhaps one bar at a time. (Chapter 2 also deals with the teaching of a practical skill.)

Experimental work in science

One cannot imagine science being taught satisfactorily without experimental work; but however necessary, such work is not sufficient. Students also require an opportunity to use the scientific idea you are teaching to solve problems, and to answer questions verbally and on paper. It is one thing to understand an experiment involving, say, 'diffusion' and then write a laboratory report. It is quite another to be able to use the concept of diffusion to answer, say, examination-style questions. This latter skill can only be developed by corrected practice in question-answering. Such practice provides the teacher with feedback, so that errors and omissions in the use of the concept can be corrected.

When used well, experimental work is active, fun, enlightening and engaging. If used badly it can result in bored and confused learners. Research (see next paragraph) shows that even directly after completing a conventional practical exercise, many learners cannot say what they did, why they did it or what they found out!

Uncritical and unfocused use of experimental work has received heavy and well-deserved criticism in the Association for Science Education's journal (see Hodson 1990 and 1992).

It is crucial to be clear about your objectives when using experimental work. These may include learning:

- about a particular example of a scientific fact, principle or concept
- how scientific investigations are carried out
- how to interpret data, e.g. how relationships between variables are discovered
- how to deal with anomalous results
- how to carry out error analysis (etc.).

Especially early on in a science course, learners are sometimes expected to cope with all these objectives at the same time. This can overwhelm, or at least confuse, all but the most able. There is a lot to be said for at least *introducing* each of the above objectives *one at a time*, with an activity which allows the clear and unambiguous exploration of the objective. This introductory activity may or may not involve experimentation.

You can develop scientific concepts and principles by providing students with a variety of concrete examples of the concept or principle. Methods for providing such examples might include practical demonstrations, teacher talk, discussion of students' suggestions, textbooks, computer simulations, videos, etc., as well as experimental work.

It is important to be sure that your science practicals do not always involve your students in blindly following a procedure laid down by you as the teacher. Constant use of this 'recipe' method bores students, as it reduces their need to think. If they are to develop skills in planning and designing experiments, they must practise those skills! Try asking students what they expect the experiment will show before they carry it out, then ask them to compare their results with their expectations.

Try to avoid time-consuming, repetitive work; it is often possible to share out sections of an experiment. Different groups can investigate different variables, or different values of the same variable, and then report their findings back to the class. For example, each group can find the solubility of a salt at a different temperature, and the result can then be combined on to a master graph.

Even if students are carrying out identical experiments, there is something to be said for this reporting back of results to the group. It is motivating, and encourages students to take responsibility for their work. The averaging effect of taking all the results from a class can also produce more reliable results.

Make sure you leave time to tidy up and collect the apparatus, and for a plenary session. This plenary is vital for experimental work. Make clear what the student should have learned from the experiment, explain any anomalous results and drive home the objective with a will. Make sure the students are aware of the laws of valid inference from experiment.

Common problems for inexperienced teachers

Work too difficult

Are you surrounded by a forest of hands? Are you saying the same thing over and over? Have you decided the class is a bit thick? Don't worry; setting work that is too difficult is a very common mistake for learning teachers! Get advice on the level of work from teaching colleagues and teacher tutors. Make sure the students really know how it should be done, and why it is done that way. Show them plenty of examples – that is, do a demonstration. Compare the work you set with the level of work set by their other teachers. Don't assume knowledge or skills the students lack.

Task too vague

Are they missing things out? Are they 'doing it all wrong'? Does everyone look bemused? Break the task down as far as possible; write it down very clearly in simple language.

Some students finish early and have nothing to do

Make at least the last task 'open-ended', and perhaps a little more demanding.

Everything takes them much longer than you expected

This is quite normal! As long as they can cope and are not wasting time, you probably don't need to worry.

See also Chapter 18 on group work and student talk.

Checklist for managing student practice

❑ Are students prepared – for example, are they aware of the 'doing-detail'?

❑ Did you ensure that the necessary resources and sufficient time were available?

❏ Is the task sufficiently broken down, achievable, and clearly and concisely defined in writing?

❏ Were there at least some questions which required genuine thought?

❏ Did you check and correct each student at the start of the activity?

❏ Can you help students without 'doing it for them'? (See Chapter 14.)

❏ Did you look out for safety and discipline problems by facing the majority of the class as you checked and corrected, helped and circulated?

❏ Do you always have a plenary, so that no student is left in doubt about what they should have learned?

For experimental work

❏ Will students get paper practice and other opportunities to develop the scientific ideas you are teaching?

❏ Do you avoid constant use of the 'recipe' approach? (See Chapter 14.)

Further reading

Hodson, D. (1992) 'A critical look at practical work in school science', *School Science Review*, 73, 264: 65–78.

Kyriacou, C. (1997) *Effective Teaching in Schools* (2nd edition), Cheltenham: Nelson Thornes.

*Kyriacou, C. (1998) *Essential Teaching Skills* (2nd edition), Cheltenham: Nelson Thornes.

Marland, M. (1993) *The Craft of the Classroom*, London: Croom Helm.

Marzano, R. J. with Marzano, S. and Pickering, D. J. (2003) *Classroom Management that Works*, Alexandria, VA: ASCD.

Petty, G. (2006) *Evidence Based Teaching*, Cheltenham: Nelson Thornes.

17

Discussion

We all love a discussion. The media has been quick to catch on to this, even if some teachers have not: it is hard to avoid discussions now on radio or TV, be they panel-based, phone-ins or involving a studio audience.

Discussion is used as a method of teaching more often than you might realise. It involves a free-flowing conversation, giving students an opportunity to express their opinions and ideas, and to hear those of their peers. Some teachers use short, spontaneous discussions as a natural extension of their questioning technique, but this chapter concentrates on their deliberate use in a class or large group.

Try doing the exercise at the end of this chapter now. Then read the chapter to see if you gave effective answers.

When to use discussion

Discussions are generally considered to be of value in the following situations:

1   Where the students' opinions and experiences need to be known by the lecturer, or are valuable and interesting to the other students in the group. For example:

    –   in a workshop where experienced health workers are evaluating old methods of working and considering new methods

    –   in a personal and social education (PSE) class discussing bullying.

2   Where the topic involves values, attitudes, feelings and awareness, rather than exclusively factual material. For example:

    –   while exploring sex-stereotyping

    –   while trying to develop or change attitudes to safety in an engineering workshop.

3   Where it is necessary to give students practice in forming and evaluating opinions. For example:

    –   discussing the character of Hamlet in an English literature class

    –   discussing some effects of unemployment in a sociology class.

Uncontroversial, fact-based topics are of course not suitable for discussion-based learning. It is important to recognise that many teachers are, in effect, encouraging their students to develop their own informed opinions about the material being studied. This is where the discussion comes into its own. Opinion-forming and persuasion are considered in Part 4.

Imagine you manage a high street chain store, a job you have held for eight years. Your head office sends you on an updating store-management course, and one of the sessions concerns intentional and unintentional racism in your staff's attitude towards customers. Think about your reaction if the session involved:

1 A lecturer being critical of the racism he has discovered in his research, and prescriptively describing in detail how store managers should change their practices in order to improve matters.

2 A discussion where a lecturer first details factual material concerning intentional and unintentional racism in stores, and then asks you and your fellow participants what you feel about it as store managers, and what could be done about it.

Many people would react to the first session I have described by rejecting the implied criticism. 'What does he know about running a store?' 'The lecturer is just a careerist on a bandwagon.' The result would, if anything, be a hardening of attitudes – quite the opposite of the lecturer's intention.

The reaction to the second session is likely to be more positive, and not only because students enjoy expressing their opinions. If students' views are accepted with interest, they will respond by being open-minded rather than feeling threatened and defensive. They are then more likely to change their opinion and practices, especially if they find that other course participants do not agree with them.

It might be objected that a discussion will only encourage students to express 'wrong' opinions. However, 'wrong' opinions can only be changed if they are challenged, and for this they need to be out in the open. (You might, though, want to make an exception in the case of a very personal topic such as personal hygiene.)

Using discussion as a teaching method carries a hidden message – the teacher is in effect saying to his or her students: 'I value your experience and I am interested in your opinions.' By contrast, the unspoken message of a lecture in teacher-talk style is that the students know nothing of value about the topic.

Well-managed discussions are interesting, absorbing and active. They produce a safe environment for students to examine their opinions, and where necessary change them (although opinion changes often occur later, as a result of reflecting on the discussion). There is an opportunity for students to use high-order cognitive skills such as evaluation and synthesis. They are useful for affective education – for example, establishing empathy, examining social and moral values. They also offer an opportunity for students to get to know each other, which is important if they are to feel at ease and become communicative.

> Make a list of topics for discussion in your teaching situation.

Planning a discussion

For anything other than a short, ad hoc discussion, the discussion leader needs to have objectives that he or she hopes to achieve during the session. Once these are decided on, a plan must be produced; the plan may simply take the form of some factual material to start the discussion off, and then an ordered list of key questions. Effective discussions are usually structured very carefully, though the participants may not be directly aware of this. A well-structured discussion critically examines evidence, beliefs and values, and then asks students to form opinions based on this. Many popular television programmes encourage participants to vent opinions without justification; this is hardly a model appropriate for education, but some students may need weaning from it!

DISCUSSION PLAN

Planning policy: trees in urban landscapes

What are the advantages of trees in urban environments?

What are the disadvantages? How many of these can be dealt with?

Where are trees used in practice? Where are they most effective?

Where can they most easily be added to an existing urban landscape?

What should be the local planning policy regarding the urban use of trees? (Advantages and disadvantages of students' proposals should be discussed.)

Note that to ensure the opinions arrived at by students are sound:

- Relevant issues need to be considered first, before the main question for discussion is asked.
- Both the advantages and the disadvantages of any issues, proposals or alternatives should be discussed.

Some discussions are genuinely open-ended, and the teacher will be more interested in listening to the students' ideas than in achieving predetermined learning. For example, a teacher may start a weekend gardening course by asking each student to describe their own garden, with the aim of learning a little about each member of the group. Similarly, a teacher of English literature might ask students to discuss the motives of a character in a novel. Open-ended discussions like these are dealt with under 'opinion-forming' in Chapters 38 and 39. It is still worthwhile to prepare a list of questions in advance, though you may not stick to them.

Other discussions have clear objectives. Consider a discussion on safety at work, designed to establish the main risks to health and safety in an engineering workshop and how these risks can be minimised. In discussions such as these, a list of questions will not in itself ensure that the objectives are achieved. There will be important conclusions that need to be reached during the discussion, and it is advisable to write these conclusions down as they are made, preferably in a place where the students can see and refer to them. You certainly need to prepare a clearly worded summary of each of the key ideas you want to get across.

Choosing appropriate questions

As we saw in Chapter 14, there are two types of questions:

Closed questions have only one appropriate answer, as in 'yes/no' questions. For example: 'Is spilt oil a risk?'

Open questions require a more detailed and more personal response. For example: 'When do you find yourself most tempted to take risks?'

Clearly, open questions are more useful for getting a discussion going. If a student gives a short answer to an open question, use eye contact, nodding, etc., to encourage a longer answer.

Make sure the sequence of questions and conclusions leads you to fulfil the objectives that you set for the discussion. If the discussion is not planned, then it will degenerate into an aimless airing of views; the students will learn nothing of value, and the experience will be a waste of time for all concerned. The discussion plan needs to be written down; no one minds a discussion leader having a prompt sheet in front of them setting out their plan (they do it on TV, so it must be OK!).

Which of these questions would be suitable for inclusion in a discussion on safety in the workplace?

1 Is safety important in the workplace?
2 Could anyone tell us about any unsafe practice they have seen in the workplace?
3 In your opinion, is too much importance placed on safety procedures?
4 What would you think are the greatest risks to health and safety in your working environment?

To produce the best response, try open, controversial and personal questions. Question 1 is closed, impersonal and uncontroversial, and is therefore hopeless for a discussion. Question 2 is personal, question 3 is personal and controversial; both would be suitable for a discussion as long as 'yes/no' answers were not expected. How would you classify question 4?

How to lead a discussion

Give the topic, and then sit back and wait until it is all over? No! It takes skill to develop a successful discussion, especially if specific objectives are to be covered.

First consider seating; participants need to be able to see each other's faces easily, so the circle is the best seating arrangement. If this is out of the question (because of fixed benches, for example) try one of the seating plans below, where most students only have to change the way they are facing.

The start

Has relevant factual material been presented? Opinion should be consistent with fact! Starting a discussion is sometimes difficult, especially if the participants are shy and reticent because they have not met before. It often helps if the leader of the discussion produces some factual material to start it off. If the topic is a matter of dispute, the introduction should be as unbiased as possible; give both sides of the argument – for example, by reading a few paragraphs from relevant sources. Don't give away your own opinion on the matter, as this may inhibit students from expressing the opposite opinion.

Conventional seating   Discussion seating

Or you could permanently rearrange the seating in this discussion style.

Seating plans for discussions

After this initial input it is helpful for the leader to ask a question. The question should be open, clear and concise, not a jumble of related questions. In order to make sure the discussion 'warms up' quickly, it helps if the first question is either controversial or requires an answer from each member of the group, as in the examples below:

'Would each of you in the group just like to explain briefly the responsibilities you have in your company?'

'Do you think revision is a waste of time for a good student?'

Don't ask vague questions such as: 'Well, you have most of the important facts now; what do you think?'

Questions which require answers from every member of the discussion group are called 'rounds', and can be used at any stage of a discussion. For example:

'How would you deal with this situation?'

'What most troubles you about this procedure?'

Make sure you respond positively to the contributions.

Encourage students to give fuller answers by asking supplementary questions. 'That's interesting, and why do you think that?'

In large groups there is a tendency for the more self-confident students to dominate discussion. For this reason, some teachers split their students into smaller groups. With more than about 12 students, it is difficult to run a discussion where most students contribute. However, short discussions can still be valuable in such larger groups.

Too often, discussions are like a game of ping-pong, with comments passed back and forth like this:

teacher – student – teacher – student – teacher …

Ideally, student–student communication should also take place.

You can encourage responses from students non-verbally:

- While a student is talking, use eye contact and nod your head.
- When a student appears to finish, leave a silence with sustained eye contact to encourage a longer contribution.
- When you are talking, scan all the members of the group with eye contact.
- When you have finished asking a question, fix an individual who has not contributed yet with eye contact, and wait. They will feel strong pressure to answer.
- *Don't* talk in a quiet, restrained manner. This 'drops the temperature'. Use a strong voice, and show interest and enthusiasm!

You can also encourage responses verbally by controversial questions, and by:

- Saying 'That's interesting – can you explain that more fully? … What makes you feel that way? … Could you say a little more about that?'
- Playing devil's advocate or exaggerating a student's opinion (with a smile): 'So you believe even white people with non-white marriage partners are racist?'

If discussions tend to go badly with a group, talk to them about it directly – ask them why. If they find that everybody in the group is as nervous as they are, this sometimes helps. Ask them how students should behave in order to make discussions fun. Get a list of this behaviour, then ask the group members to promise to try it out!

Credit the source of ideas during the discussion:

'As Paul said, there is no point in …'

This shows you genuinely value contributions and so encourages participation.

The style

Most people distinguish between a debate and a discussion. In a debate, the style is competitive; in a discussion it is, ideally, non-competitive and exploratory. There should be a cooperative attempt to come to a mutually held conclusion, and members of the group should not attack each other's views in an adversarial style. Unlike a debate, a discussion should leave people free to speculate, and to change their point of view.

You may like to establish ground rules with your group, such as: no interrupting; no one speaks for more than one minute at a time; all points of view must be respected; no negative personal comments.

If all the students are in agreement, it is sometimes hard to get a lively discussion. Try being a 'devil's advocate': express an opposing opinion regardless of whether or not you hold that opinion yourself. This often enlivens discussion:

'But if other nations manage without nuclear weapons, why can't we?'

The role of the discussion leader during the discussion

You can include yourself: 'What do we think about …?'; or exclude yourself: 'What do you think about … ?' During the discussion, it helps if you watch out for the points in the Checklist (see page 230).

The summarising role is very important, to ensure that students are clear about what they have learned during the discussion; the main points should be reinforced by note-taking or by handouts, otherwise they will soon be forgotten. For similar reasons, discussions lasting more than half an hour are of questionable value.

Some people find it difficult to 'shut up' students who hog the discussion, but you will gain everyone's respect if you are brave enough to intervene on the group's behalf. Be polite: 'Clive, you've made some interesting contributions already, but I'm anxious to hear everyone's opinion …' Try nominating someone who has not spoken to answer the next question; or just say, 'How about someone who hasn't contributed yet?' Some teachers advocate doing a 'round' of all the students who have not contributed at the end of a discussion. If students know this will happen, it encourages them to get involved before the end. One teacher I know routinely 'rewards' a particularly good or full answer from a student with a five-minute ban on further contributions!

It is almost always best for you not to express your opinion on the matter under discussion until the very end, if at all. If you must, use assertive questioning, as in Chapter 24. It is considered unprofessional to give away your political opinions during a discussion.

See also 'the skill of opinion forming' on page 429, summarised by the three-legged stool diagram on page 433.

Summary

Discussions are fun. They can involve students in high-order cognitive skills such as evaluation, and can be used to develop their opinions, attitudes and values. They can be left open, but usually need to be structured, perhaps by means of a series of questions. The questions should be open, personal and controversial if they are to elicit strong responses, and they should be clearly and concisely stated.

Student response can also be encouraged by praise, interest and acceptance of students' opinions; and non-verbally by eye contact, waiting at the end of a response, or nodding.

If a teacher uses discussion, this demonstrates that he or she values the students' knowledge and opinions. Therefore it is a vital method for use with adults, and for attitude-changing in any age group. Avoid verbal bullying, time-hogging and clamming up, by making it clear you value all opinions and want everyone to contribute.

Encourage decision-making and summarise the main points as they are covered or agreed, moving on once consensus is found or when a point is exhausted.

Summarise at the end, perhaps with an aide-memoire.

Checklist

☐ Do you make sure only one person speaks at a time?

☐ Do you clarify what someone has said if it was not well expressed?

☐ Do you encourage decision-making, and summarise the main points as they are covered or agreed?

☐ Do you move on once consensus is found, or when a point is exhausted?

☐ Can you ensure that one person does not dominate the discussion, and that everyone feels involved, even if they don't make a contribution?

☐ Can you make sure there is no verbal bullying?

☐ Do you keep your eye on the clock and on the objectives?

☐ Do you encourage participation by praise and acceptance, and by non-verbal means?

☐ Do you listen hard, and summarise and conclude the discussion at the end?

Exercise

Consider a 10-minute, whole-class discussion carried out by an effective teacher. What will she do to avoid these common problems?

1 They all talk at once.
2 Some don't talk at all.
3 One student dominates.
4 They go off at a tangent.
5 They get angry with each other.
6 The class gets confused because ideas are expressed so unclearly.
7 They will be unclear about what they should have learned.
8 Students express poor and prejudiced opinions as they are unaware of the facts.

Further reading

*Jaques, K. (1991) *Learning in Groups*, London: Kogan Page. Mainly HE-focused.

Kyriacou, C. (1997) *Effective Teaching in Schools* (2nd edition), Cheltenham: Nelson Thornes.

*Kyriacou, C. (1998) *Essential Teaching Skills* (2nd edition), Cheltenham: Nelson Thornes.

Marland, M. (1993) *The Craft of the Classroom*, London: Croom Helm.

Marzano, R. J. *et al.* (2001) *Classroom Instruction that Works: Research-Based Strategies for Increasing Student Achievement*, Alexandria, VA: ASCD.

Petty, G. (2006) *Evidence Based Teaching*, Cheltenham: Nelson Thornes.

*Wragg, E. C. (ed.) (1984) *Classroom Teaching Skills*, London: Croom Helm.

18

Group work and student talk

Why use groups?

Think of an activity you really enjoy, and I will wager it either *requires* other people, or would be made more enjoyable by involving them. Think of an activity you hate, and I am prepared to bet that doing it in company would make it less odious. *Homo sapiens* is a social animal, and even that arguably distinct life form *Studens quasi-sapiens* enjoys working in groups – so long as the teacher is able to direct activities meaningfully.

Peer through the window into a science lesson, or into a primary classroom, and you are more likely to find learners working in fours or fives than being taught as a whole. Why do teachers use groups? Is it just fashion and fun? Let's look at some examples of teachers splitting students into groups. See if you can guess the teacher's motives.

Case A

A humanities teacher has just explained the principal factors affecting the growth of European towns during the Industrial Revolution. She splits the class into groups of four, giving each group the details of a different fictional town. 'OK, I want you to use the ideas we have been talking about, to prepare an argument that will convince the rest of the class that your town will grow fastest. You have just five minutes to prepare your case.'

Later, one person from each group shows the map of their town, and argues the case for its growth to the class.

Case B

Some maths students have just completed a graph. 'Now,' says the teacher, 'remember the 10 points to look out for when drawing a graph? In a moment I want you to work in your groups to check each other's graphs against those 10 points. If you find an error, explain how to put it right.' Later the teacher asks the groups which errors they discovered. A similar graph is set for homework.

Case C

An accountant is running a one-day course for middle managers in a newspaper business. He has just described two alternative accounting procedures. He asks the course participants, working in groups of four, to write down the main advantages and disadvantages of these two systems.

Later, the teacher gathers the class together and asks each group in turn to give one advantage and one disadvantage, until he has been given all the suggestions. During this process he accepts legitimate points and summarises them on the board.

Group work is active. It gives the students a chance to use the methods, principles and vocabulary that they are being taught. Shy students who will not contribute to the full class can usually be coaxed into contributing to a group. What is more, there's a built-in self-checking and peer-tutoring aspect to most group work, where errors in understanding are ironed out, usually in a very supportive atmosphere. Students can often do together what they could not achieve alone, with each member of the group providing part of the 'jigsaw' of understanding.

Group work involves learners in task-centred talking. As well as being an enjoyable activity in itself, this provides huge opportunities for learning. It requires that learners process the new material, and make personal sense of it, as we saw in Chapter 2. Good group work hands the responsibility of learning over to the students.

In terms of the *educare?* elements, bearing in mind 'peer tutoring', group work provides all but the aide-memoire of these learners' needs (and could be adapted to provide even this). Students get a chance to practise high-order mental skills such as creativity, evaluation, synthesis and analysis. They also practise 'common skills' such as the ability to work with and communicate with others.

In addition, group work gives students a universally welcomed opportunity to get to know each other. It can also arouse group loyalty, especially if there is an element of competition; this can produce strong motivation (as in Case A above).

The teacher is given an opportunity to make use of the views and experiences of students. Consider the middle managers' lesson. Students in groups are more likely than individual students to think of all the major advantages and disadvantages of the accounting system; and more likely to get them right. Partly because of this self-checking factor, group members have confidence in group suggestions, and so offer them for discussion more readily. If the teacher had asked for individual contributions presented to the whole class, he would have been given fewer suggestions, and these would have been less well thought out.

The use of groups improves rapport between students, giving all your classes a more trusting and supportive atmosphere. Social activity is so universally enjoyed that group work promotes a positive attitude to your teaching, and to your subject.

> *In group work, students' opinions are being valued and accepted; in teacher talk they are being ignored. This has important implications for all teachers, but especially those who are teaching professional people, or those trying to change attitudes, values or prejudices. The 'hidden curriculum' underlying group discussion, as against that for teacher talk, was examined in the previous chapter on class discussion.*

Most of the activities in Cases A, B or C above could have been carried out individually by students, but a high proportion of the advantages outlined would then have been missed. Group work is an adaptable and powerful teaching strategy, with marked advantages; it is an essential feature of almost all modern teaching.

Limitations of group work

Groups can go off in the wrong direction, and they can be hijacked by a determined individual. Some group members may become passengers, letting others take the lead. Whole groups or even whole classes can become 'free riders' if the teacher does not ensure that they take responsibility for their work – for example, by effective monitoring and by demanding feedback.

Difficulties with group work can nearly always be overcome by using well-devised tasks, and good classroom management along the lines described below. However, like all teaching methods, group work becomes ineffective when used indiscriminately, or when used too often or for too long. Be clear what you are trying to do, and make sure that group work is the best way of achieving this.

> *'Garrulousness far from guarantees insight.'*
>
> Mike Ellwood, *Times Educational Supplement*

Seating is an important consideration. If students are working in a group they need to be able to make eye contact with each other. If seating is fixed in a face-forward style, as in many lecture theatres or laboratories, then ask some students to turn round, moving their chairs if possible, to work with those behind for group work. (Conversely, if students are working on solitary tasks, arranging them in groups makes concentration difficult for some.) If seating is arranged to suit your purposes, and your students, then attention to task can be greatly increased.

Group work activities

Single tasks

Groups are asked to carry out a task or sequence of tasks – for example, design an experiment; answer a question; make an evaluation; carry out and check a series of calculations; research a set of books for specific information.

The task needs to be very clearly stated, and broken down if necessary.

If possible, set individual tasks as well as group tasks – for example, by requiring each student to record the group's findings for themselves. If you include a stretching activity for individual work after the group work, this will help 'teach to each'. For example, after designing their experiment, individuals could be asked to look for ways of improving the design. More able students will then look for ways of improving the accuracy of the measurements, the less able for more straightforward improvements.

Same, selected and different tasks

The task can be identical for each group, or selected by the group from a list of options. Alternatively, different related tasks can be entrusted to each group. For example, each of six groups can research the main manufacturing industries in one of six different cities; their findings can then be reported back to the class as a whole. Students often respond well to the trust implied in giving them a unique task to carry out for the class.

Look again at Bloom's taxonomy in Chapter 1, and try to set at least some high-order tasks. In any case, open-ended tasks should be used – or at the least, one open-ended task should be given as the last activity. For example, after finding the manufacturing industries for their city, the students could be asked to 'prepare a case for other manufacturing your city could do'. If the task is 'closed', you may find one group will have finished and have 'nothing to do', before other groups have even worked out which way up to hold their pencils!

Group challenges and competitions

'Can you find at least four pieces of evidence on your map that this is a fast-flowing river?'

'You will design a poster that summarises the role of a district nurse; then I will show my 10 key points. Your challenge is to cover as many of my key points as you can on your poster.'

'Your challenge is to find at least three ways to do this problem, stating the mathematical principles used in each case.'

Challenges motivate more students than competitions because everyone can meet a challenge, but only one can win a competition. Classroom trials have found that challenges, at least those tackled cooperatively, create a better social climate and more self-esteem, as well as better achievement (see Petty 2006, page 151). This has nothing to do with 'political correctness', just effectiveness.

The best challenges are open. See the last example above: 'at least three ways' is better than just 'three ways', as it will stretch the most able, and so differentiate better.

The circus

The 'circus' is routinely used in science lessons, but is now finding extensive use elsewhere. A set of tasks is carried out by each group in a different order – thus, at any given time, each group is carrying out a different task; but by the end of the circus, all the groups have completed all the tasks.

This allows classes to complete tasks for which full class sets of materials are not available: science apparatus, for example, or computers, or reference books. The two tables below outline examples of how this system can be used with three groups, A, B and C. The first table involves three tasks of equal duration; the second accommodates five tasks, one of which takes twice as long as the others.

Group	Task		
A	1	2	3
B	2	3	1
C	3	1	2

minutes   15   30   45

Three tasks of the same duration with a change-over every 15 minutes

Group	Task					
A	1	1	2	3	4	5
B	2	3	4	5	1	1
C	4	5	1	1	2	3

minutes   15   30   45   60   75   90

Task 1 takes 30 minutes; the other tasks take 15 minutes. There is a change-over every 15 minutes.

Circus tasks can be of different durations if this is planned for carefully

The tables may look complex, but they work easily in practice.

Libraries will find a selection of books on a given topic for you if you give an indication of the level of work, but they will need adequate notice. You can then use these as reference materials for tasks.

'Buzz groups'

Students are asked to discuss (usually in pairs or threes) in order to answer a question, solve a problem, draw up ideas for a design, decide on their attitudes to a scenario, etc. It is usual for the teacher to provide relevant factual material, and perhaps to outline the main arguments as an introduction. As with any discussion, the topic should not be purely factual.

Make sure the topic is clear, concise and structured. Asking buzz groups to 'discuss safety on the building site' is too vague to be productive, even if the students have had some experience of building sites. Break the task down:

1   Has anyone in your group heard about (or experienced) an accident on a building site? If so, tell your group.

2   What safety procedures are apparent in your place of work?

3   What do you think are the five most common accidents on building sites?

The task breakdown should be displayed for students during the group work; it could be written on the board, provided on a handout or card, etc. If the task is too vague or too abstract, the discussion may 'stall' or become directionless.

Try asking different but related questions of each group, with the group's findings to be reported back to the class. This is motivating, as it gives each group a special responsibility. For example, different groups of trainee teachers could discuss when to use questioning; how it should be used; its advantages as a teaching method; and its disadvantages.

Arrange seating so that students are facing each other. Buzz group sessions usually work best when they are kept short – a maximum of five minutes. It is usual then for the teacher to ask for feedback; students will be interested in expressing their findings and in hearing those of the other groups. As students have had time for critical appraisal of their ideas, the quality of their responses will probably be quite high, certainly higher than in question and answer; but if you are disappointed, try not to be too critical of the responses. Accept those you can, perhaps summarising them on the board or overhead projector (OHP). It is very important for the teacher to reflect on and summarise the main points at the end of such a session – though indeed this is true of all group work.

Some teachers ask buzz groups to produce outline answers to old examination questions. Students appreciate the practice.

Buzz groups are named after the noise made when a class starts discussing; so don't be alarmed. If the discussion is task-centred, what you are hearing is the sound of learning. However, if you are dealing with reluctant learners, make sure you have established ground rules with them before using this method.

If some group members are time-hoggers, try to invent activities which share group discussion time out among the group's members. You can say, 'Start with each group member expressing their ideas in turn. Talk for about a minute each, without interruption. Then embark on a general discussion.'

Buzz groups are very popular with students, but use a time constraint; if you wait for everyone to finish you will be there for ever. Don't be afraid to keep it short; some simple questions can be quite deeply discussed in no more than one or two minutes. Buzz group discussions are an excellent way to break up a long explanation.

Activities to try with buzz groups
Compare and contrast

This involves looking for similarities and differences in two or more concepts, ideas, theories or approaches. For example, students could compare two marketing plans, organisational theories, or two different business letters. They could also compare osmosis and diffusion, fractions and percentages, or presidential and parliamentary systems, perhaps making a reasoned choice between them.

This method has been found to improve students' understanding of a topic by more than two grades (see Petty 2006). This is a challenging activity, made easier if students compare something familiar with something new; or if they revise by comparing two familiar concepts. The same and different diagram on page 156 helps enormously.

Hypothesis testing – evaluative thinking

A hypothesis is a suggestion; the most useful in teaching is often a hypothesis that is partly true and partly false, or only true in certain conditions.

> The more sunlight a plant gets, the faster it will grow.
> *Macbeth* is about ambition.
> This solution is mathematically valid.

Students work in groups to find fully justified arguments for and against the proposition. Later, students can devise their own hypotheses and evaluate these. Teach students to test hypotheses by asking, 'What would be the consequences if this were true?' and then to check whether these consequences are indeed true. For example, if plant growth only depended on sunlight, then there would be no slow-growing plants in hot deserts. But some cacti grow slowly, so the hypothesis cannot be entirely true. See the end of Chapter 38 for a graphical approach. Students can, of course, evaluate designs or policies as well as hypotheses.

Pros and cons

This involves looking for the advantages and disadvantages of different approaches.

'What's your theory?'

This type of buzz group session is greatly enjoyed and highly adaptable. Rather than the teacher telling the students the accepted theory or 'correct' opinion on some matter, students are asked to discuss their own opinions in groups, and then report their ideas back to the class as a whole. Only then are the textbook ideas introduced by the teacher. For example, trainee managers could be asked to draw up guidelines on how to run a good meeting, before teacher talk on the topic. The group can write their findings on an OHP transparency, or on flip-chart paper, for later display to the class.

This is an example of 'teaching by asking' rather than 'teaching by telling', and has the considerable educational advantages of the guided discovery method; see the case study in Chapter 29 for help in devising suitable questions.

This method is overused in professional in-service training, but very underused elsewhere. It discovers prior learning, and then enables you just to teach what is missing or incorrect, instead of wasting time delivering it all.

Snowballing

This is a way of extending buzz groups. After a buzz group session in pairs, two pairs combine to make a foursome in order to complete a related activity. If necessary, these groups of four can then combine again to create groups of eight.

Here's an example. A mechanical engineering lecturer has just described ARD, a new method of creating plastic mouldings:

Five-minute buzz groups. Working in pairs, trainees isolate the likely problems with the ARD production process.

For 10 minutes. After joining pairs to make fours, the trainees combine their list of problems into a master list, and then think of ways of overcoming two of the main problems they have isolated.

For 5 minutes. Combining groups of four into groups of eight, the trainees compare the work they have done in fours, and then decide whether or not to recommend the adoption of the new production process, or to recommend its adoption with reservations.

Snowballing works best if the activities at each stage are more than just combining lists, and (as in the example above) develop in a logical sequence.

Brainstorming

Brainstorming is a method of producing a large number of creative ideas for subsequent evaluation. The rules are that:

* All ideas are welcomed, however offbeat or daft (wild ideas can often suggest more practical ideas, or be tamed to produce useful contributions).
* The group aims for quantity, not quality.
* *Judging* ideas is not allowed.
* Ideas are common property; combining or improving previous ideas is encouraged.

The first time you use brainstorming, you must explain the philosophy very carefully, and an example session can help to establish the idea. Get your class to think of as many uses for a house brick as possible. Initially you will get suggestions like 'doorstop' and 'support for shelves'; when you get suggestions like 'anaesthetic' and 'window remover', you know they have got the right idea!

Once brainstorming is understood:

1 Carefully define/agree the problem, issue or topic to be brainstormed, e.g. 'How could a retail store increase sales at Christmas?'

2 Brainstorm for ideas, writing them down on the board or a flip-chart. You could ask your students to take turns at doing this writing, as it is a full-time job! Everyone should be able to see the suggestions:

   advert in the paper; give the stuff away; Christmas tree outside the shop; give people free coffee; offer a Christmas present ideas service …

3 If they flag, give them a one-minute 'incubation' period and then start up again.

4 Once the brainstorming session has dried up, choose the most useful ideas. If there is no consensus, choices can be made by each student ticking their favourite five, or by awarding points (rather like the Eurovision Song Contest). Alternatively, ideas can be chosen for satisfying agreed criteria, e.g. 'Must be cheap to implement; must not require special training; must not involve extra staff'.

5 Now the ideas themselves are brainstormed to decide how they can be implemented in practice:

'*How* would a "Christmas present ideas service" work?'

'*How* could the store go about giving people coffee?'

6   There is a vote for the two daftest or funniest suggestions, e.g. 'Give the stuff away'. Now ask, 'Is there any sense at all in this suggestion?' Discussion might then lead to the idea of giving away one free present to anyone spending more than £20.

7   Evaluation of the ideas is best done on another day.

Brainstorming is great fun, but surprisingly, research shows that people can produce almost twice as many effective ideas when working alone (see Taylor et al. 1958). So why not snowball?

A simplified version of the above, where there is just one brainstorming session, is sometimes called a 'bull session'. (See also Chapter 30 on creative work.)

Peer tutoring and peer checking

Peer tutoring involves students helping or teaching each other. This goes on informally much more than most teachers recognise; finding a whole class with an identical misconception in a piece of homework is not uncommon. On the whole, most teachers look on peer tutoring very positively. It allows the faster learners to teach the slower, and gives the slower ones a chance to query misconceptions without embarrassment.

Peer checking is one method of peer tutoring, and is an underused activity. Immediately after completing a calculation, a diagram, or some written work, students are asked to check each other's work in pairs or in small groups. The students must of course be very clear on how the work should be evaluated. An example might be:

Now each of you check the other's letter – are the addresses both in the right place? Is it dated? Has the right ending been chosen? Is it well placed on the page?

Asking students for a list of criteria to check each other's work is in itself a very useful activity. Peer tutoring or peer checking encourages students to develop *and* use the skills required to check or evaluate their own work, and to clarify in their own minds the criteria that need to be met for the task at hand – prerequisites for future improvement.

Give prior warning that the activity will be peer checked – this will concentrate students' minds wonderfully. The activity is usually carried out in a very good-humoured way; if you find it is not, use self-assessment instead. Students who prefer it can self-assess while the rest of the class peer-assesses.

Presentations

Each group researches a different topic and makes a presentation to the rest of the class. The 'research' could be extensive in both time and scope, or as simple as a five-minute group discussion. The presentation usually involves one member of the group, or indeed all of them, explaining the group's conclusions to the class with the aid of notes written on an OHP transparency.

Advocacy

A debating topic is argued in pairs. After three minutes or so, the pairs are asked to switch 'sides' in their argument. Clearly the topic must be contentious if this activity is to be a success. Here are some possible examples:

> 'Euthanasia could never be reconciled with a nurse's professional duty.'
> 'Who was responsible for the deaths of Romeo and Juliet?'
> 'Unless there is a global ban on nuclear weapons, one day they will fall into the hands of someone ruthless enough to use them.'

Unless the group is very able, it is important to ensure that its members are acquainted with at least some of the relevant arguments, and of course the relevant facts. It is often worth telling students which point of view they will be arguing, and giving them time to prepare notes before the persuasion session.

Some topics are best approached by describing a scenario or a case study to a group, and then asking it to debate a point arising from this. For example, after describing details of Mr Jones's behaviour and his treatment by his employer, you could ask them to debate: 'Was Mr Jones wrongfully dismissed?'

Optionally, the pairs can feed back to the class any new arguments or debating points for class discussion. The session can end with a vote. This activity could also be carried out in groups of four, with two people taking each side at any given time. If they are able students, it is fun for the teacher not to warn the students that they are going to be asked to change sides halfway through. This is an excellent activity where students need to be aware of the arguments on both sides of a contentious issue.

A variant of this game is for students to take turns in picking a statement out of a hat and then defending it against the rest of the group. Usually some preparation is necessary.

Empathy

You can ask buzz groups to create a detailed empathy profile of someone – for example, nurses discussing how a new arrival on a surgery ward might feel, or teachers considering the possible feelings of someone returning to study after 20 years.

Alternatively, each person in a group takes on a character, and the other members of the group interview these characters in turn. This is a useful activity for any topic to do with human interaction: aspects of management, work in the caring professions, character analysis in English literature, etc. Here is an example:

A case study concerning strike action is read out. Groups of three are formed, and each member of the group is allotted a character: the employer, or the union official, or a 'blackleg'. Students are given time to make notes about how it feels to be the character they have been allotted.

Each character is then 'interviewed' by the other members of the group. The other group members can either keep their roles during the interview phase – or better still, they can take the role of a sympathetic outsider or newspaper reporter. (See also 'Role-play' in Chapter 20.)

J'accuse

This is similar to advocacy. The class is divided into four groups: A, B, C, D.

A and B are prosecution and defence in one 'case'; C and D are prosecution and defence in another. The 'cases' involve accusing a person (or process) of something or other; for example:

'Hamlet is accused of being a self-obsessed procrastinator.'
'The box construction girder bridge is accused of being an outmoded design.'

While A and B are acting as lawyers, C and D act as jury – and vice versa. One person can be appointed judge. Taking this further, there can be 'expert witnesses' who have researched a particular aspect of a case in detail; cross-questioning and points of order are allowed. It's fun to think of a humorous sentence if a conviction results.

Groups will need substantial preparation time, and this preparation needs to be checked by you before the 'case' is tried.

'J'accuse' is ambitious, but active and fun; students remember what they have learned, as the activity usually makes a big impression.

Any more ideas?

Students can be asked to make a decision, to evaluate an idea or approach, to find a solution to a problem, to compare and contrast, to hypothesise with a 'what would happen if … ?' question or to answer examination-style questions. The only limit to group activities is your imagination. (Many more suggestions can be found in Chapters 19 and 20 on games and simulations.)

Planning the activity

First decide on your objectives, and be sure these can be genuinely met with the use of group work. Choose an activity that your students can complete with only very infrequent help from you. Don't overestimate them. Is there some preparatory activity that will make the group work easier and more productive?

Choose short activities at first; if you are going to have a disaster, it may as well be a small one! Group work can often last as little as a minute. Make sure the task involves putting something down on paper, so that you will have something to check.

Make sure your activity is concrete, clear and structured, and decide on concise wording for it.

Collect and prepare your resources. Group work is an admirable opportunity to use books, magazines, videos and specialist equipment that students would not otherwise see. Don't forget to leave time for the plenary, where the activity (and what was learned from it) is discussed and summarised.

The plenary

It is important to ask for feedback from the groups, then to reflect with the class as a whole in order to summarise what has been learned. Commonly, the scribe from each group reports back their findings, and these are written on the board by the teacher. To increase participation consider nominating the group member who will report back only after their work. This requires all the learners to get clear what their group thinks. If groups have brainstormed ideas or their answer is a list of some sort, then ask for just one idea from each group at a time, so every group can make a contribution.

You can praise and thank students for their comments, or alternatively you can withhold your judgement, so that the class can exercise theirs. Only when the class have *agreed* their collective answer do you say whether it is correct. This 'assertive questioning' approach is described in Chapter 24.

Occasionally it is possible to summarise with each group individually, immediately after the completion of each task.

Leave the class in no doubt what they should have learned from the group activity.

Grouping

What size should your groups be? This may depend on the activity.

The *larger* the group:

- the greater the confidence the group will have in its findings, and the more likely it will be to challenge the tutor's opinions
- the more likely it is that the group will interpret the task correctly
- the more experience the group will have to draw on
- the less time it will take you to visit all the groups
- the slower the decision-making process, and the greater the difficulty in achieving consensus.

The *smaller* the group:

- the more activity there will be –

and therefore:

- the fewer passengers there will be
- the faster decisions will be made.

Pairs more or less guarantee that every student is active. Groups of between two and five are very common. Groups greater than about four tend to require or develop leaders. Groups larger than about seven tend to become increasingly unwieldy, and passengers become common unless very specific roles are allotted. Up to six and many hands make light work; over eight and too many cooks spoil the broth!

How do you decide which student goes into which group?
Random grouping

For example, allot each student a group number by counting and pointing round the room: 1, 2, 3; 1, 2, 3; 1, 2, 3 ...

Random groups might be a little shy with each other at first – which may or may not suit your purposes.

Friendship grouping

Students will soon group themselves if you ask them to; but be clear and firm about the maximum group size.

This is popular with students, but friendship groups may not share your lesson objectives, and they can be resistant to awareness-raising or attitude change. There is often no gender or ethnic mixing, and cliques or exclusions can develop. Students will not increase their pool of acquaintances.

Achievement or experience grouping

This could be strictly by achievement, with a top, a middle and a bottom group; or those with a specific weakness (e.g. maths) can be grouped together so that they don't become (maths) 'passengers', and can together be given the specific help they might need. Shy students are sometimes grouped together for similar reasons.

This approach allows the groups to go at their own pace; it can produce rivalry and resentment, but this is by no means always the case. It is commonly used in adult language classes, where students often place themselves in a 'beginners' or 'improvers' group within the same class.

Deliberate mix

You may want a mix of experience, backgrounds, ages, genders or abilities.

This is useful in preventing bias, and allows students to learn from each other's experiences. It is helpful, too, for awareness-raising and attitude-changing. Mixed-ability groups can create an opportunity for peer tutoring.

Proximity grouping

This is the most commonly used method. But don't choose groups of people who sit beside each other; make groups of those who sit behind and in front of each other. This makes it easier for the group to arrange itself so that members can see each other's faces, which is most important. Grouping like this can be carried out in a lecture theatre or laboratory, as well as a classroom.

Managing group activities

Bear in mind Chapters 7, 8 and 9 on classroom management. If you use groups a great deal, you may like to rearrange the furniture, but check with others who use the room, or finish the class by putting it back as you found it. If you do decide to move furniture, give very clear instructions before allowing any movement.

It helps to have a scribe, and perhaps a spokesperson and chairperson for each group. Ask for 'someone who hasn't done it before', so that everyone gets a turn. Make sure the task is clearly explained, and draw the attention of the class to the all-important task summary, which should be permanently available to the group. Ideally, the task(s) should include some individual activity, such as making notes of the group's decisions. If the task is not demanding, can you include a stretching activity for the more able? Don't allow any activity until you say so, and give a time limit: 'Right, off you go; you have five minutes.'

To begin with, leave them to get on with it, but remain obviously in attendance. Unless the activity is only going to last a minute or two, it then becomes important to visit the groups. (If the activity lasts more than three minutes, this is vital.)

1   Check that genuine progress has been made:

- What has the scribe written down?
- Have they interpreted the task correctly?
- Have they missed some important points?

2   Ask if there are any queries.

Don't talk to the entire class during group work unless it is unavoidable. If it is, then stop all activity; make sure you have everyone's attention; and make your point clearly and concisely. Groups dislike being interrupted.

Body language

As you visit, make sure you don't get stuck with one group, however interesting their work might be. Body language is important. Get your head down to their level, and smile to signal cooperation rather than judging. Some teachers ask each group to leave a spare chair for them, but position themselves so they can see the other groups. Check the group is on task by asking to see what the scribes have written down. Every now and then, ask if they need more time.

Getting feedback

When the activity is over, ask each group to report back one of its findings to the class. Go round from group to group until you have harvested all the ideas. The groups will usually be interested in each other's work. Alternatively, ask each group to summarise their findings on an OHP transparency or on flip-chart paper for display to the class. Thank the groups for their responses as soon as their ideas are expressed, and add your own arguments in support of their ideas if you wish, but do not overdo this. It's their time, not yours. Ideally, use assertive questioning (see Chapter 24).

Remember that it is *vital* to summarise what the class should have learned from the activity. Inexperienced teachers often ask groups to carry out tasks for which they are not prepared; they fail to define the task clearly in writing; and neglect to visit groups or to clarify learning.

EXERCISE

Pointers for success in group work or individual student practice

Summarise advice for each 'box' in the flow diagram below to ensure effective student practice.

Checklist for the use of group work

❏ Do you define the task very clearly, and leave a summary of the task on the board?

❏ Do you visit each group as it is working, to check on progress and to help where necessary?

❏ After the activity, do you nominate individuals to summarise their group's ideas to the class?

❏ Do you acknowledge the ideas of each group – for example, by thanking them and/or by putting them on the board?

❏ Do you hold a plenary to summarise what students should have learned from the activity?

❏ Do you use group work as often as you could?

References and further reading

Brown, G. and Atkins, M. (1988) *Effective Teaching in Higher Education*, London: Routledge.

Jaques, K. (1991) *Learning in Groups*, London: Kogan Page. Mainly HE-focused.

Marzano, R. J. with Marzano, S. and Pickering, D. J. (2003) *Classroom Management that Works*, Alexandria, VA: ASCD.

Petty, G. (2006) *Evidence Based Teaching*, Cheltenham: Nelson Thornes.

Taylor, D. W. *et al.* (1958) 'Does group participation when using brainstorming facilitate or inhibit creative thinking?', *Administrative Science Quarterly*, 3: 23–47.

19

Games and active learning methods

During my schooldays, learning was regarded as a serious and difficult process; if laughter ever burst from a classroom, passing teachers would peer in with anger and suspicion. Yet games can produce intense involvement, and a quality of concentration no other teaching method can match. What is more, the increase in interest and motivation produced by a short session of game-playing can produce positive feelings towards the subject (and the teacher) which last for weeks.

The basic assumption of this chapter is that learning and enjoyment are not mutually exclusive. The 'Further reading' section at the end of the chapter directs you to subject-specific games, of which there are many. But I will start by considering 'games for all seasons': that is, generic games which may be adapted to almost any topic or subject area. Most of these games can be played by students as individuals or in groups. There were other examples of games and active learning techniques in the previous chapter, on group work.

If cards need to be made, remember that any photocopier will copy on to thin white or coloured card in the usual way. Then you can guillotine these copies to cut your game cards to shape. If you hole-punch cards, you can keep sets together with the 'treasury tags' used to keep examination scripts together.

Keep sets of cards on 'treasury tags'.

Games for all seasons

Decisions, decisions

Students usually work in pairs or small groups for this game, though they can work alone. The game will make more sense when you have seen a few examples, but in general, each group is given a set of cards which have on them: words, sentences, short descriptions of vocational scenarios, diagrams, photographs, mathematical expressions – almost anything in fact.

Grouping cards

The task is then to match, group or rank these cards in some way, or to treat the cards as labels and place them on a diagram, map, mind-map, computer program, worked example, photograph, painting, etc.

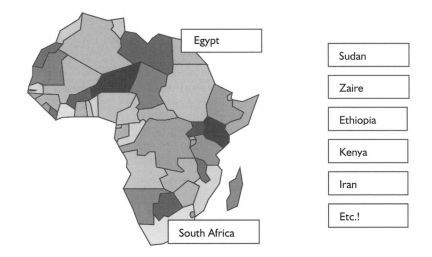

You are quite right, Iran is not in Africa! But well-chosen 'spurious' cards act as 'distracters' to really test learning, make good learning points, and they make for more fun. Use them in all 'decisions, decisions' games.

Matching games: some examples

Science students are given a set of cards describing energy transformations, and another set describing processes. They have to match each 'process card' with the appropriate 'energy change card'. So they end up with many pairs, such as:

A rock falling off a cliff	Gravitational potential energy Being converted into Kinetic energy

Students can also be asked to match:

- questions and answers
- words or technical phrases, with their descriptors parts or tools, with their functions
- equivalent mathematical expressions, etc.

Get students to write your question and answer cards for you; they love it and they learn more that way. Don't forget the spurious cards!

You can match:

Technical terms and their meanings ...

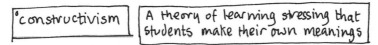

°constructivism | A theory of learning stressing that students make their own meanings

Equivalent mathematical statements ...

°$y = x - 7$ | subtract 7 from x and that gives you y

Parts and their functions ...

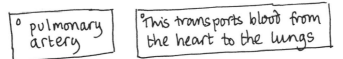

° pulmonary artery | °This transports blood from the heart to the lungs

Grouping games: some examples

Students are given a set of, say, 30 cards, each of which has a different phrase with an underlined word – for example, 'The fox ran <u>quickly</u> into a hole.' Students work in pairs to sort the underlined words into nouns, adjectives, adverbs or none of these. Each group has the same set of cards.

Similar games can be devised for students to practise classifying:

- metaphor, simile and personification, and none (spurious card)
- examples of conduction, convection and radiation, and neither
- igneous, sedimentary and metamorphic rocks, or neither
- valid and invalid arguments for the increased crime rate in cities
- errors in punctuation under 'comma'; 'full stop', etc.
- valid and invalid evidence for competences, etc.

Classifications of statements that are useful include:

- true; sometimes true; false
- often; sometimes; never
- agree; don't know; disagree.

For example:

- Groups of social workers and probation officers on an AIDS awareness course are given cards on which are described various sexual practices. They are to sort them into three piles: 'safer sex', 'unsafe sex' and 'don't know'.
- Maths students are given cards with expressions such as '$x + 3 > 2$' or '$y - 7 < y - 2$', and they have to sort these into three groups: always true, sometimes true and never true.
- Students with learning difficulties are given photographs and drawings of clothes, etc., that they might or might not take on a trip. These are grouped as: 'everyone needs it'; 'no one needs it'; 'our group only needs one of these'.

Grouping is good for 'question typing'. For example, physics students are given cards with examination-style problems on them. They are *not* asked to do the problems, but to sort them by what principle they would use to solve the problem – for example, 'use momentum', 'use conservation of energy', 'use equations of linear motion'. This develops the synthesis skill of deciding how to solve a problem considered in Chapter 1.

Question typing to develop synthesis skills

Make cards by using the table feature of your word processor with, say, 2 columns and 10 rows. There is usually an 'autofit' feature to make the cells in the table the same size. Computers and photocopiers copy on to thin card with no trouble. You can colour code if it helps. Get your students to make question and answer cards and then keep them for revision.

Ranking by time: some examples

- Students of first aid are revising how to respond to a medical emergency. They are given cards with phrases such as 'ring 999', 'check airways and breathing', 'turn off the electricity', and must place them in the correct order.
- Students with learning difficulties are given photographs of various stages for making a cup of tea. Each stage has a short descriptive phrase, such as 'boil the water'. Students must place these in the proper time order.

If you suspect the person has had an electric shock...

turn off the electricity

check their breathing

give mouth-to-mouth respiration if necessary

ring for an ambulance

check circulation

rejected spurious cards

wear rubber gloves

Sequencing cards

- Plumbing students are given cards that describe the process of fitting a new central heating system. They must place them in the order that the tasks would be done.

Ranking on a continuum or 'spectrum': some examples

Students can sort cards into orders of priority, or characteristics; for example:

'Place these diseases into order of infectivity.'
'Place these wines in order of sweetness.'
'Place these care plans in order of effectiveness and then in order of cost.'
'Place these marketing strategies in order of ease of implementation.'

> These games are very 'constructivist' and involve students in high-order thinking. They can be played with cards, or with text boxes on a computer screen.

Mastery games and 'mountain climbing'

This is less rigorous than mastery testing in Chapter 43, but more fun. I will describe a version of this game for level 2 learners, but it can easily be adapted for more advanced learners.

You split the past week or two's teaching between teams of students, who write three or four mastery questions (low on Bloom's taxonomy) with answers for their subtopic. You check these questions and answers, making sure they are on vital material, are truly mastery questions, and have good answers. Groups make enough copies of their cards for what follows.

The following are examples of question cards for a game on the topic of mastery learning. The students who have *written* these questions and answers have already learned a good deal. The questions can be typed into a table in a word-processing application. (If you set 'autofit' to 'distribute rows and columns evenly', all the cards become the same size.) You can then print on thin card, with a different colour for each topic if necessary, and cut into question cards. Alternatively, they can be handwritten.

Question: Give two key characteristics of a teaching method that make it 'constructivist'.	**Question:** Give two key differences between a mastery test and a conventional test.
Answer: accept any two from: It requires the learner to make a construct. It requires learners to find errors and omissions in their constructs and to correct these. It must require learners to actively make use of their understanding.	**Answer:** accept any two from: The students must do *remedial* work if they don't pass. *Everyone* passes eventually. There is no mark, just 'pass' or 'not yet passed'. All questions are low on Bloom.

Students can pass their group's questions on to the next group so every group gets a set of questions, and the sets rotate.

Alternatively, students work in pairs with a *complete* set of the cards. They take it in turns to ask each other a question. If the students get it right, they move their counter up one square on a game board with a mountain drawn on it. There are almost as many squares up the mountain as there are question cards. If a student does not get their question right, they keep their 'wrong card' and can study the correct answer during the game. One square before the summit of the mountain is a 'base camp' where students must take a second attempt at all their 'wrong cards'. The object of the game is for the *team* of two or more 'climbers' to both get to the top of the mountain, not for the individual to be first to the top.

This is about twice as much fun as it sounds, yet it has a very serious purpose. Mastery games can be used by themselves, or can of course be used to prepare for mastery tests.

Research cited in Black and Wiliam's (1998) review on formative assessment showed that asking students to generate their own questions and answers for each other produces marked improvements in achievement. Perhaps because it is constructivist, active and fun.

Mountain climbing

The quiz

Quizzes are usually arranged as a competition between groups; they are a popular means of checking learning or enlivening revision. Most commonly, the teacher asks the questions; alternatively, students can make up questions for their competitors to answer, though these questions need to be cleared by you to ensure fairness.

Split the quiz up into different sections, along the following lines:

- Groups answering questions in turn. (Will conferring be allowed? Will unanswered questions be offered to another group?)
- Questions for individuals (two points for a correct answer, one point if there is conferring with other team members).
- Questions for groups, where challenges from other groups can gain them double points if they challenge correctly, and a loss of a point if they challenge incorrectly.
- Difficult questions for the first raised hand (with referring to notes allowed).
- Questions which are very difficult to begin with, and then become progressively easier (but score fewer points) as more information is given.

In a more elaborate version of this activity, groups make up questions for each other on a given topic, with model answers. These questions and their answers are checked by you as you visit the groups. Then the groups ask each other their questions in turn in a quiz format; you do the scoring. Make sure you decide on the rules about conferring, etc., before the quiz starts.

Try reviewing the last lesson at the beginning of the next using a two-sided quiz, with one half of the class against the other. Ask: 'What can you remember about last lesson's topic?' Each side gives one point in turn; the aim is not to be the side that cannot think of anything more to say about the topic.

Agree the format and scoring system in advance, and stick to it! Try to do the quiz in a spirit of fun.

Tell me more

This is a recall game for a class to play. Imagine, for example, that your last lesson was about safety legislation. You divide the class down the middle into left and right, and ask one side to think of one thing they can remember about safety legislation. Once a student has responded, it becomes the turn of the other side to think of something else they can remember about the topic. Statements alternate from left and right until one side loses because it cannot think of anything else to say about the topic. This simple game can make an enjoyable but useful start to your lesson.

Tennis

If students share a summarised mind-map or set of revision notes, they can test each other's recall by playing 'tennis'. Students play against each other in pairs, asking questions of each other, *from the revision notes*, alternately. This 'rally' goes on until one student makes a mistake, when a point goes to the other. They take turns to 'serve', and scoring is like tennis: love, 15, 30, 40, game, with a 'deuce' at 40–40. This game can be introduced in the classroom, but is best played outside it. My students tell me they particularly enjoy mixed doubles!

The exhibition

You give groups the same topic or different subtopics, and they must produce wall posters and other exhibits to demonstrate their ideas and the key points. This can be shown on the classroom or corridor noticeboard, or some other public space.

Modified TV/radio games

Students often find it amusing to play an adaptation of a well-known TV or radio game show. Some examples might be *Blockbusters*, *Who Wants to be a Millionaire*, *Any Questions/Question Time*, *Gardeners' Question Time* – all offer formats which may be adapted to your subject area.

For example, I once saw the *Gardeners' Question Time* format (where a panel of experts answer questions from the floor) being used to great effect on a management training course. Course leaders formed the 'expert panel' on the first day; but on the last day of the course the panel were course participants, and the course leaders were among the audience.

The challenge

Almost any activity can be made into a game by turning it into a challenge:

> 'Can you separate the following chemicals without using filtration?'
> 'Can you devise a computer program to do the following, in less than 20 lines?'

'Can you devise a marketing strategy for this charity that costs next to nothing?'

'Five factors causing urbanisation are mentioned in the video – I bet no one gets them all!'

Treasure hunt

A search for information can become a simple game by making it into a race, or a competition – for example: 'Find as many examples of the use of percentages as you can in your newspaper. Let's see which group can find the most!'

Spectacles

Some topics can be looked at from different points of view, or by using different 'spectacles'.

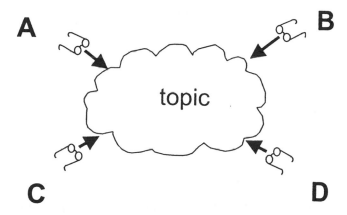

For example:

- looking at five childhood diseases from the points of view of infection process, symptoms, immunisation, long-term risk, etc.
- looking at different themes or issues raised in a play, novel or poem
- looking at scientific experiment from the points of view of criteria such as: reliability, validity, methodological weaknesses, methods of improvement, error analysis
- looking at a historical event from the political, economic, religious and social points of view
- looking at methods of saving, considering: risk, ease of withdrawal, rate of return, etc.

The 'spectacles' used should not be the *main* content being studied, but just the means of looking at key content. Students are given the same materials and one or two 'spectacles' to look at this material.

This will take some time. Students then report back to the class on their findings. The rest of the class will have studied the same material and so will be able to critically appraise the contributions of other groups. This is a method of 'teaching without talking', as the teacher does not present the material by teacher talk, but leaves the students to study it. There are other similar methods on www.geoffpetty.com

Ice-breakers

Games or activities are often used to introduce members of a new class to each other. Here is one example often used for the first meeting of an adult education group (though it could be adapted for any class):

> The class is split into pairs. The members of each pair ask each other a prepared list of questions: 'What is your name? Where do you live? Why did you come on this course? Where do you work? What are your hobbies? Have you any children?' and so on.

> The pairs then form into foursomes. Each person in each pair then introduces their partner to the other pair, giving the partner's answer to each of the questions. Fours then form into eights; each pair introduces the other pair in their foursome, and so on. This develops listening skills!

Another ice-breaker is to ask each person to find someone in the room with a particular characteristic: someone who is a vegetarian, who doesn't like coffee, who sleeps without pyjamas, who has been to Africa … These will need to be on a handout, and at least a few should be slightly silly!

Board games

Commercially made board games on many topics are available from educational publishers.

Using games in practice

There is too much seriousness and not enough levity in most of our lives, so be brave and try using games. If learners are used to a very dull diet, they may get a little overexcited or show initial reluctance. But games are universally enjoyed, and encourage real attention to the task, and intrinsic interest in the subject matter.

References and further reading

Gibbs, G. (1989) *Learning by Doing: A Guide to Teaching and Learning Methods*, London: FEU.

*Jaques, K. (1991) *Learning in Groups*, London: Croom Helm. Mainly HE-focused.

Marzano, R. J. with Marzano, S. and Pickering, D. J. (2003) *Classroom Management that Works*, Alexandria, VA: ASCD.

Petty, G. (2006) *Evidence Based Teaching*, Cheltenham: Nelson Thornes.

Powell, R. (1997) *Active Whole-Class Teaching*, Stafford: Robert Powell Publications.

Swann, M. and Green, M. (2002) *Learning Mathematics through Discussion and Reflection LSDA*. (This is a brilliant video and CD-ROM with 'decisions, decisions' games and other activities for students learning elementary algebra. Colleges were sent a free copy. See also the standards unit materials 'Improving Learning in Mathematics.' Your department may have a copy.

20

Role-play, drama and simulations

Role-play

In this activity, learners take on roles and act out a given scenario. For example:

- A class of trainee teachers is split into pairs. One in the pair takes on the role of a student with persistent attendance problems; the other takes the role of the student's teacher. Later the teachers swap roles.
- Trainee hotel receptionists take on the role of a receptionist dealing with an irate couple whose room has not been cleaned. Other students play these customers. The rest of the class watch, taking turns to be the receptionist.
- Three students take on the roles of characters in a novel they are reading. They are interviewed by the class about their motives.
- Two students take on the roles of Muslim women, talking of their fears about sending their five-year-old sons to school for the first time.

Role-play is very useful for developing the 'interpersonal skills' of learners – for example, for training in the caring professions, the police, the retail trades, or for management training, and so on. It gives learners an opportunity to practise skills in a risk-free environment. Other uses include sex and relationships education; indeed any situation where students must learn to negotiate in an assertive yet respectful manner.

As well as helping students to develop social skills, role-play can help students explore emotive issues. (The last role-play activity bullet point above is an example of this.) Other examples might include teen pregnancy, smoking, puberty or the Factory Acts.

Several groups of students can carry out the same role-play activity simultaneously, as in the case of the first bullet point above. This has the advantage that it allows every member of the class to practise the social skill. It also reduces stage fright! However, it is not suitable for repeated performance of these role-plays to the whole class, as the repetition becomes too tedious.

Alternatively, the role-play can be a single performance viewed by the rest of the class, often taking the form of a playlet or social skill demonstration. In this case, it is sometimes possible to give the observers a specific role: 'And this group: look out for the use of assertive techniques.'

Another way to include the 'audience' is to invite them to offer to step up and replace one of the 'actors', perhaps in a 'replay', to show another approach. This can be a hugely popular activity, and even excitable students can be persuaded to curb their exuberance because they don't want the exercise to stop! It is fun to introduce additions to the plot as the activity proceeds; however, this needs planning.

There is of course a lot to be said for having a demonstration role-play followed by a class practice.

Planning the role-play activity

Be clear about what you are trying to achieve, and design the activity towards these ends. If a skill is to be practised – for example, interviewee skills – you could explain any background information or techniques to participants first, and perhaps show them an example of good (or indeed bad) practice.

Alternatively, you could use the discovery method (Chapter 29), and learn entirely from the role-play activity itself. If you are using role-play as an empathy exercise, then research and group discussion can be used to develop a profile of the players before the role-play itself begins.

The scenario is best provided on paper; different versions are usually required for each player. For example, in the case of the first bullet point on page 258, the 'teacher' should not know everything the 'student' knows. Emphasise the goal for each role, and make the instructions brief; the players will enjoy filling in the detail. Don't define characters; the players will feel more involved if they do this themselves. Avoid stereotyped or extreme characters. Consider providing supporting documents, such as mock letters or newspaper articles, to give background.

Can you give every member of the class a role in the play, or a special observing role? Observers can be assigned a particular player, or given some other specific observing brief – for example, they might be given a checklist. These observations can then be used as a focus for the debriefing session.

Clearly, the players will need to be given background details about the scenario being played out, perhaps including briefing on what they know about the other characters. In empathy-related role-playing, the background research might be considerable.

Sometimes adults, and occasionally teenagers, are reluctant to take part in role-play, especially if they don't know one another well. This can be because they see themselves as 'no good at acting' and feel self-conscious. To overcome this, put them in friendship groups, and tell them that most people really enjoy this activity. Don't ask for a commitment to take part from the start, but do require even the reluctant ones to work out a role-play from their scenario. Let them watch the others have a go first, and with a bit of encouragement they will often join in.

Running the role-play activity

Give players time to study the scenarios, and don't start until they are ready. If well planned and prepared for, role-play activities should run themselves; indeed, you should intervene as little as possible. However, you might like to add new information while the activity is running – for example, a memo or message could arrive for one of the players. Such interventions can be designed to prevent the action becoming too one-sided, but usually need to be prepared in advance.

Consider allowing a character the opportunity to stop the role-play activity at any point. This 'time out' can give the person concerned time to consult others, or to think out how to proceed. Once the student is ready, the play continues from where it left off.

If skills are being practised, and the players are reasonably confident and used to role-play, you could consider videoing the session. This allows for self-evaluation, and supplies detail for the debriefing session; but it may inhibit the players.

Debriefing or plenary session

Debriefing should be done straightaway if possible. It is usually the most important and time-consuming part of the activity. The aim is to reflect on the role-play, and to reach some general conclusions. You might like to prepare a list of questions to be considered by individuals and/or groups, and then by the class as a whole. For example:

> Skills practice. What went on? Why did it go like that? How could it have been done differently? In what way was it realistic – and unrealistic? Can you relate what you saw to theory or technique? How did each player feel as the play progressed? What were their motives, and were they justified? …

In the case of skills practice, it will be necessary for learners to criticise themselves and each other. Handle this carefully. Ask for self-evaluation first. Try asking the class for 'two goods and one improvement' – that is, two creditable aspects of the performance, and one way in which it could have been improved. You must tease out from the experience both good and bad practice, and thus move towards generalised criteria for future success. Chapter 31 on learning from experience has more detail on this.

If the experience has been intense for any player, or for the group as a whole, feelings should be discussed. Ask players how they feel on a one-to-one basis, while the rest of the class are preparing for the debriefing session; and give any support they might need.

Drama

Drama raises self-esteem and self-confidence, often allowing hitherto unremarkable members of your class to shine. For all students it encourages empathetic understanding and identification with the characters portrayed. It is a very powerful method for affective education. If you tell students to avoid early pregnancy they may simply nod in bored agreement, but let them watch a play about it, and you may have them in tears of sympathy.

The subject matter clearly needs to have emotional content. If students are writing their own playlet, you will usually need to give them a brief. This should be a very bare outline – for example, 'Perform a play about the effect of having a baby on a 14-year-old girl'. The drama can be improvised along lines agreed by the group, or written down so that the lines can be learned. The latter may not be worth the extra time, but this depends on your purposes.

Sort students into groups, and give them time to plan their story, perhaps with a 'stick man' storyboard. They need to concentrate on conflict between characters and the agony of their decision-making if the plot is to have real drama. Let them rehearse in private a few times before the show, avoiding complex costumes, sets or props. This activity can have real impact, and may become the highlight of their term. If you do not feel confident with drama, start with role-play, and then do very short dramas of about five minutes' duration.

Simulations

An elaborate role-play activity is often called a simulation. Examples include war games; playing Chancellor of the Exchequer with a computer simulation of the British economy; flight simulators; and business in-tray games. Micro-teaching is another example, where trainee teachers deliver a short lesson to their peers.

Simulations can introduce an element of realism into our teaching, perhaps giving students experiences it would be impossible for them to have 'for real', and allowing them to develop skills without suffering the real-life consequences of their errors. By condensing time, and by eliminating non-essential distractions, they often provide powerful tools for teachers. They are now widely used in teaching and training in business studies, economics, stock market operations, political science and medical diagnosis.

Simulations can be home-made or obtained commercially: see the 'Further reading' below. Simulations inevitably simplify, and students need reminding of this.

Further reading

Hopson, B. and Scally, M. (1989) *Lifeskills Teaching Programme No. 4*, Otley, Lifeskills Associates.

Lewis, R. and Mee, J. (1981) *Using Role Play: An Introductory Guide*, Cambridge: Basic Skills Unit.

21

Games to teach language and communication skills

I feel very envious of teachers of foreign languages. Almost any activity they fancy will be educationally valuable, so long as it involves the use of the language they are teaching. So why not play games? They produce an overwhelming desire to communicate, and so are excellent teaching methods. The following games can be used to teach any language, but there are thousands more games and activities; make up your own, or look for more in books on teaching English as a foreign language (TEFL). The games in this chapter, then, are just to get you started; they may seem tame on paper, but once you have tried teaching languages with games, I promise you will never abandon the idea. Unless otherwise stated, it is assumed that learners will speak only in the target language (i.e. the one they are learning).

Picture recognition

Cut-out pictures from colour magazines are spread out on a table at one end of the classroom. Arrange the class into groups, and place them away from the table; identify each group as A, B, C ... etc., and number each group member 1, 2, 3 ... etc. No. 1 from each group is shown by the teacher one of the pictures on the table; the teacher makes a note of which picture has been allocated to which group. The No. 1s then attempt to describe their picture (in the target language) to their group. Meanwhile, the picture placements on the table are shuffled by the teacher.

No. 2s then go to the table and attempt to choose the correct picture. They can if they wish go back and ask questions of No. 1 (who for the moment must leave the group). When they feel sure, the No. 2s bring the picture they have chosen back to their group (which No. 1 has not yet rejoined). If the group agrees this is the right picture, it is submitted to the teacher.

If their decision is correct, No. 2 is shown a new picture to describe; and so on round the group. Groups race to finish, say, two circuits round the group members. This game can generate real excitement and an intense desire to communicate. Students run excitedly to and fro (so check there are no floor obstructions).

Depending on the similarity of the pictures, this game can suit any level, from elementary to advanced students. I have seen advanced students of sign language use this game to describe head-and-shoulder portraits of men and women in formal dress; they found it a difficult and hugely enjoyable challenge.

Variations

Sedate version. Each student is given a magazine picture in an envelope, which they are not allowed to show the others. Each describes their picture to their group. When the descriptions are complete, the pictures are shuffled and placed on a table, and identified with a letter. The group must work out whose picture was whose.

Advanced sedate version. The game can be made more difficult by requiring every group member in turn to identify each picture.

Stories

Chain stories

With the group sitting in a circle, the teacher or first group member gives the first line of a story, provided from a card. The next student in the circle makes up the next line, and so on round the circle. Very simple 'stories' are used; for example:

> 'He liked the picture very much.'
> 'It was a painting of his daughter.'
> 'His daughter didn't like the picture; she said it made her look ugly.'
> 'One day the daughter threw the picture away.'

Variation

A more difficult variation is for the beginning line and the end line of the story to be given. The group then provide one line at a time, until they link the two lines logically. This can be hilarious if the lines are amusing and/or have no obvious connection. For example:

> *Start*: 'The dog was learning the trumpet.'
> *Finish*: 'My grandmother hates spaghetti.'

Mime stories

The teacher mimes a simple story. The students then take turns to describe the story as it is mimed. For example:

> He was eating a meal. He dropped some food. He called the dog. The dog ate the dropped food. He patted the dog.

The whole class repeats the story at the end. The teacher claps once if the class is to repeat only the last line; twice if he or she wants the whole story repeated from the start, with students taking a sentence each.

Card stories

Each student has a story in English on a card, and must translate it to the class or group. The class/group must repeat the story back to him in English, sentence by sentence. Use simple stories.

Dice and card games
Dice games

Simple dice games are excellent for teaching numbers. Here is a game for threes. You will require counters or tickets, and one or (usually) more dice for each group.

Student 1 throws the dice, and the other two attempt to be first to say correctly the total number thrown. Alternatively, two dice are thrown and both numbers and their addition must be called out. The student who first correctly says the number(s) picks up one counter; however, if he or she makes a mistake, one counter is *forfeited*. The dice are then thrown by student 2, and so on round the group of three. When all the counters are gone, the student who has the most wins. This game generates more excitement than you might think, and teaches numbers in no time.

Variations

Students can take turns to say the numbers thrown, which gives them more time. In addition, where two or more dice are used, the students can either say all the numbers separately, or add them to practise higher numbers, or both.

Card games

Cards can be used to teach vocabulary. Pairs of students are given about fifty cards, with target-language words on one side and their translation in smaller writing on the other side. Each card is revealed in turn, target-language side up, with the translation hidden from view by a blank card. The first student in the group (including the dealer) who gives the correct translation gets that card. If students make a mistake, however, they must give a card to their opponent. The student with most cards at the end wins.

Variation

The pile of cards is placed in the centre of the table and students take turns, round a group of three or four, to give the correct translation for each card; if they get it right, the card is put on the bottom of the pack. If they get the card wrong, they keep the card and must learn it during the rest of the game. At suitable intervals, each student gives his or her pile of cards to a neighbour, who reveals them one by one; the students who previously got these cards wrong must now attempt to get them right. If they still get it wrong, they continue to keep the card. The student who has the fewest cards at the end of the whole game is the winner.

It helps to have piles of cards on different topics (numbers, money, months and days, the kitchen, shopping, etc.); then groups can swap packs of cards.

Student presentations
Talk

Each student must give a short talk on his or her interests, hobbies, favourite music, favourite dish, etc., to the group. This helps members of the class get to know each other better. Give learners a week or so to prepare.

Objects

All the students are asked to bring an unusual object into the classroom the following week. They show the class their object, and the class have to guess what it is. Students usually bring something to do with their hobbies or interests.

News story

Students choose a story from a recent newspaper, and report it to their group. They prepare this during the week. Optionally, the group can then discuss any issues the story raises.

Variation

This game can be made into a competition between two teams, as in the radio game *Just a Minute*, with a referee changing the speaker to one from the opposite team if hesitation or repetition takes place. The speaker left speaking at the end of the minute wins a point for their team.

Role-play

Role-play was considered in more detail in Chapter 20; it has obvious value for students of a foreign language. The teacher can give each of a group of students a role, which they then act out. For example, one student in each pair could be a hotel receptionist, with their partner playing a speaker of the target language who wants to make a booking. Students can take turns to play each role. It helps to provide scenarios, such as 'You want a quiet double room for a week'.

Drills

Repeated hearing (and repeated use) of a particular language item is very helpful in language learning. As a form of repetition, drills enable us to focus sharply on particular points of grammar, vocabulary or pronunciation; and they can be fun, especially if you are lively and enthusiastic about drilling, and you don't do it too slowly. Give the word, phrase or sentence, and then let the class respond to you. Repeat each item up to six times only, and then give something new to drill. Never drill for more than one or two minutes, and keep this method for really useful learning.

You can ask individuals to respond rather than the whole class; if so, don't go round the class in a predictable order.

To provide variety, some of the following ideas can be helpful.

Changes

Make up a sentence that can be changed very easily – for example, 'Where is the butter?' The teacher gives the sentence, and the class repeats. Then you change the noun – for example, 'Where is the cat?' Alternatively, go round the class, with each student adding their own noun at the end of the sentence.

Ping pong

The teacher gives a sentence. The students must reply with an appropriate question:

> 'I went to the cinema.' – 'Did you enjoy going to the cinema?'
> 'I rode my bicycle.' – 'Did you fall off your bicycle?'

Teaching new vocabulary

Try to teach new words by using them in sentences. The students learn them much more easily this way. Teach new vocabulary items in groups. For example, you can group together things found in the kitchen:

> 'Where is the dishcloth?' 'Where is the mixing bowl?' 'Where is the spoon?'
> 'I need a new kettle.' 'I need a new saucepan.' 'I need a new …'

Make sure you teach the words that the student really needs. It is much easier to translate from the target language into your native language than vice versa. So you could practise drills translating the easy way first, then the harder way. Revision is essential.

Flash cards

There are published sets of these, but you can also make your own. Each card has a picture on it. Students respond to what they see on the card, with words, phrases or whole sentences. Try to make them so that they get harder and harder: 'Small dog', 'Big dog', 'Black cat', 'White cat', 'Small white cat', and so on. Good for revision.

Other games and activities

The pyramid

Students work in pairs to find out, for example, how many brothers or sisters their partner has. The pairs now make groups of four. Each person then tells the group how many brothers and sisters their partner has. Then the groups of four make groups of eight …

I spy

A student chooses an object in the room, revealing only its first letter. Other students ask questions about the object: 'What colour is it?' 'Is it bigger than my briefcase?' When a student guesses correctly, it's his or her turn to think of another object, and so on. This game can be made into a competition by dividing the class into groups, and giving each student an 'I spy' object on a card (an identical set of cards is given to each group). The first group to guess all its objects wins.

Variation

The teacher describes an object, and the students have to guess what it is. For example: 'It is heavy', 'It is made of glass', 'You could put it on a table'.

What's my job?

A student thinks of a job, or is given a card with the job title. Other students ask questions: 'Do you have to travel?' 'Do you earn a lot of money?' The same competitions and variations can be used as for 'I spy'.

Interpreter

One person must use the first language only, another only the target language, and the third interprets between them. The two single-language speakers take on parts – for example, a French speaker wishes to find the way to the local railway station, and an English speaker is asked to provide the directions.

Video

A video is played with the sound turned down, and learners take it in turns to add a radio-style commentary.

Just a Minute

Many radio or TV games can be adapted to teach languages; *Just a Minute* is only one example. Students pick a topic out of a hat, and then speak about it without marked hesitation or repetition. Students usually appreciate being given time to prepare for their 'minute'.

Granny's basket

The group sit in a circle or horseshoe. Students take turns round the circle to repeat objects given in previous turns, whilst adding one more. For example:

'In Granny's basket I found a banana.'
'In Granny's basket I found a banana and a bottle of wine.'

In a large group, this can be a real test of vocabulary and memory.

Posters

The class is shown a poster or large photograph with plenty of detail in it. The teacher then asks questions based on the poster: 'Where is the dog?' 'What is under the table?' The class or individuals respond appropriately: 'In the field', etc. (If you wanted to focus on grammar rather than meaning, you could ask for full sentences, e.g. 'The dog is in the field'.) To practise past and future tenses, a card with 'YESTERDAY' or 'TOMORROW' on it could be pinned below the poster.

What am I doing?

Best done in groups. A student is given a card describing an activity – for example:

> You are ironing your wedding dress for your wedding tomorrow.

The student then mimes the activity to the rest of the group, who must guess what is being done by asking questions which require only a 'yes' or 'no' answer.

Your own games and drills

New games and drills can be invented to suit your particular groups, and your own style; the activities described here are only a start. Try asking students to invent their own, or invent them yourself.

Wherever they come from, though, *do try games*; they create that intense desire to communicate which is the prerequisite for learning any language. And they make your lessons fun.

However, don't play any one game too often, or for too long.

22

Seminars

A 'seminar' is a timetabler's word, not a teaching method. It is an opportunity for between 8 and 20 students to have a searching intellectual discussion on reasonably well-defined subject matter. It is not usually intended to be a wide-ranging general discussion; and it should not be confused with a tutorial, which is usually an opportunity for individual students to clear up personal or intellectual queries or difficulties.

Be clear about what you are trying to achieve, and choose activities to suit. Teaching methods described elsewhere will work very well in seminars – particularly discussion, group work (especially buzz groups), games (notably 'Decisions, decisions') and role-play or simulation. Some other methods are shown below. Beware of turning the session into a mini-lecture; the main aim of the seminar is usually to allow students an opportunity to arrive at the personal meanings which are the products of real learning. This requires that students should have corrected practice in forming their opinions. The process is necessarily slow, and requires student activity.

Student or group presentation

This is the most common seminar activity. An individual or group can be asked to make a presentation to the class; you should define the topic with care, and give references. It is usually very important to discuss the group's findings with them before they make their presentation. The presenter(s) may need help preparing the presentation – and some emotional support! An overhead projector transparency is a useful prompt for the presenter, and handouts circulated before the presentation can considerably improve any subsequent discussion.

In the discussion which usually follows the presentation, the presenting students may feel confident enough to lead; if not, however, they could offer statements for a discussion to be led by you.

This method is useful for exploring different aspects of the same topic, one aspect being taken by each group. You could ask second-year students to present to first-years. If presentations are to be assessed, ask students to take part in this by filling in, for each presentation, a questionnaire based on previously agreed criteria.

Agreeing 'statements worth making'

In *Learning in Groups*, Jaques suggests asking the students who lead a seminar to formulate 'six statements worth making' about the topic under study. These should be well grounded, non-trivial, and not obvious; they should aim to be concrete and useful, rather than vague and abstract. The statements should be agreed with the tutor before the seminar.

The student introduces the statements to the class, and a free and informal discussion follows. Then the student who has made the statements attempts to get unanimous agreement for each statement in turn. The student or the tutor may need to suggest amendments; the aim is to satisfy critics and retain support, and yet leave a statement which is worth making. If compromise proves impossible, the dissident members are left to compose a 'minority view' statement. One student is charged with writing up the minutes of the discussions, making notes of the statements which were agreed. This process requires students to make decisions about the topic under study, and so increases involvement.

You against the rest

As a variant of 'statements worth making', the lecturer can refrain from being involved at all while the group members are deciding their statements. As well as the student presenter and scribe, another student is appointed to chair the discussion. Make it clear that the group must be absolutely agreed and committed to clear written statements; but don't join in the discussion.

Once statements have been agreed, however, you play devil's advocate for all you are worth. A few deceitful arguments will help to raise the temperature! It is now 'you against the rest', and if the students are genuinely committed to reasonable statements, a very lively and reasonably evenly matched discussion should ensue. The session will need a plenary.

Especially if they fear assessment, students can collude in avoiding any forceful criticism of each other's presentations or ideas, preferring to leave this to the lecturer. 'You against the rest' should minimise this tendency. Some seminar leaders would suggest that the lecturer leaves the room during the students' discussion; this heightens the 'us against the lecturer' atmosphere.

It helps to agree ground rules and discuss difficulties with a seminar group. How long should presentations, handouts or discussion contributions be? Who should lead discussions? Have disagreements been genuine or due to personal rivalry? Some sensitivity may be required here!

Witness session

This is usually a less adversarial activity. The 'witness', who may be the lecturer or a student, makes a previously prepared 15-minute presentation on a topic. The witness then leaves the room while the audience forms into groups to formulate questions for the witness. This can take some considerable time and is a most valuable activity in its own right, as it clarifies issues and isolates difficulties. Once the questions have been clearly formulated, the witness is called back into the room and the questions asked in turn.

As an optional extra stage, groups can share their questions and reformulate them, where necessary, before asking them. Again, optionally, questions can be formulated by the group outside of seminar time, in preparation for the next meeting of the seminar group.

Fifteen minutes may seem too short, but the questioning often takes three or four times as long, and in my experience all important aspects of the topic are aired. This method has the huge advantage of giving the students control over proceedings, forcing them to isolate their own issues and difficulties, and then forcing the witness to deal with them. Straightforward aspects of the topic are passed over quickly and most time is usually spent on difficult or problematical areas.

It helps to act as the witness yourself before asking students to do so. If student witnesses lack confidence, questions could be presented in written form, and the witness allowed to confer with you over them before answering to the group. This is a highly recommended activity.

Assertive questioning

This technique, fully explained in Chapter 24, greatly increases the concentration and the participation rate of students. The technique is usually associated with the teaching of younger students, but for no good reason I often use it with adult professionals, who enjoy it very much.

Peer consultancy

This is used at the end of vocational training days for adults in work. Participants are paired up and take it in turns to ask the following questions and to act as consultants, by listening and asking supplementary questions. The main questions are:

* What did you learn today?
* What are you going to do differently as a result?

Further reading

Biggs, J. (2007) *Teaching for Quality Learning at University* (3rd edition), Buckingham: Open University Press.

Jaques, D. (2000) *Learning in Groups* (3rd revised edition), London: Kogan Page.

*Ramsden, P. (1992) *Learning and Teaching in Higher Education*, London: Routledge.

23

Learning for remembering: review and recall

This chapter looks at techniques you can use to ensure students remember what you have taught them. The ability to recall given information is a simple skill, and, like all skills, is learned by corrected practice. Reading notes or listening to summaries is not enough; it is *practising recall* that counts. Intellectual and physical skills are also best retained by reuse, rather than by more passive methods.

As with all teaching, it is vital to set achievable objectives and reward achievement well. But beware – don't turn learning for remembering into a mechanical process; if new material is not understood it will be forgotten very quickly, so teaching for remembering should take place after the material is already well understood. Also remember that learning requires arousal and involvement, not *just* repetition; anything you do to make learning interesting and active will hugely increase recall ability.

Have you ever played 'Kim's game'? Players are shown a tray of objects for a minute, and then try to recall as many of them as they can. If you are like me, you will not be able to remember all the objects; but when you are shown the tray again at the end of the game, you *always recognise the objects you were unable to recall.* The memory was in your mind somewhere – you were just unable to find it! The mind is rather like a library, with our memories as the books. The book is in the library somewhere, but an index system is needed in order to find it. For a given memory, the mind's index system is only established by sufficient recall attempts.

Think of the process of learning a poem by heart. It often takes many failures to recall a line before we can recall it at will. Don't think of these failures in a negative way; they are a necessary part of the learning process. Some recall learning requires two failures; more difficult learning might take ten or more. The mind is developing its index system, and the failed attempts are needed in order to establish or correct it.

Research suggests that anxiety and effort can hamper memorisation. When you set learning for homework, tell your students to settle down with some music and browse over revision notes in a relaxed frame of mind. They should keep attempting recall until they achieve success. It is not *effort* that counts; more important is the *time* spent in corrected practice of recall. One might even claim that anyone can remember anything, if they have tried to recall it often enough!

Some psychologists believe that we never truly forget anything – we simply lose the ability to recall it. The brain surgeons Dr Wilder Penfield and Theodore Rasmussen found in 1950 that if the exposed brain of a conscious patient is stimulated by a mild electric charge, the patient can recall incredibly detailed memories of long-forgotten events, only ever experienced once. Similar experiences occur under hypnosis. (However, I do not suggest that you try either of these techniques in the classroom!)

If the ability to recall given information is seen as a skill, then the learner's needs for corrected practice apply:

- *Explanation*. In order to remember, we must first understand. Otherwise, recall can only be achieved with very great difficulty, and what is recalled is of little use to the learner.
- *'Doing-detail'*. Students like to know exactly what they should be able to recall, and in what detail. This is obvious to you, but not to them. They cannot be expected to recall every word you say, so key facts for learning must be limited and very carefully defined. Specific learning notes can provide this detail. Once key facts are recalled, they act as reminders for associated information.
- *Use*. Students must practice recalling. Many learners believe that reading and re-reading their notes is sufficient, but corrected practice of recall is vital.
- *Check and correct*. The recall must of course be checked for completeness and accuracy; if 'doing-detail' is carefully enough defined, this can be done by the learner.

The need for an *aide-memoire*, and for *review*, *evaluation* and *queries*, is self-evident.

Research suggests that students learn a large number of new words (e.g. the names of the bones in the hand) more quickly if they say the words out loud.

'Within 24 hours of a one-hour learning period at least 80 per cent of detailed information is lost.'

Tony Buzan, *Use Your Head*

Study–cover–recall–check

This is the best way for students to revise, but few seem to know this! Many students just read their notes and are then surprised when they can't recall them.

Study. Students look at the material, making sure they understand it. Summarising mind-maps are very helpful here. The student should perhaps do something else for an hour or two before the next stages.

Cover. The files and books are closed.

Recall. Students write down all the key points that they can recall for the topic.

Check. Students open their files and books again and check that the recall was both correct and complete.

This makes a great homework!

Continuous review

Good teaching programmes provide some of the necessary revision by using knowledge and skills taught earlier to help in the teaching of new knowledge and skills. In this way, previously gained knowledge is maintained without sacrificing time for new learning. Review should be integrated into a course of study, to make sure that earlier learning is not lost. Otherwise, rather like trying to fill a bath when the plug is out, our students will forget old material almost as quickly as they learn the new. Repetition and reminders do work, up to a point, but review should involve students in actively searching their memories for previously learned facts, and actively reusing their previously acquired physical and intellectual skills and knowledge.

> *The Japanese regard repetition of learning experiences as vital. In mathematics, the average 15-year-old Japanese student achieves an equivalent of the British A-level standard. They have an average IQ of 111–115, and 10 per cent have an IQ of over 130. The other side of the coin, however, is that Japanese education has been accused of putting less emphasis on understanding and on higher mental faculties.*

The advantages of this 'review as you go' strategy are:

- More learning is retained.
- You save revision time, enabling more productive activities to be carried out at the end of the course.
- More reliable use can be made of old learning to aid new learning.
- Students are more likely to see the course/subject as an integrated whole, and more likely to see the patterns and similarities which are important for deep understanding.

Given the forgetting mechanism of the human memory, you might expect this 'review as you go' strategy to be common practice. However, many teachers teach Henry V while their students forget about Henry IV. It seems that review is rather like death: it may be unavoidable, but everyone is against it. A teacher of any subject needs to plan for 'review as you go'. Look out for ways of teaching new ideas by using old ones. Allow time for review in your schemes of work and lesson plans.

Some teachers advocate a 'spiral syllabus' in which, rather than finishing off a new topic at once, topics are returned to again and again throughout the course, each time at greater depth or breadth.

You will meet teachers who tell you that they do not have time for review. Yet it only takes a minute to review what it took an hour to learn. And would these same teachers plant out new seedlings, saying that they have no time to water the ones they planted last week? If there is no time to revise, there is plenty of time to forget.

Wright and Nuthall (1970) investigated 62 variables which they thought might influence teacher effectiveness. Two of the five teaching techniques that turned out to improve learning most were:

- providing an informative summary at the end of a discussion (rather than at the beginning)
- providing comprehensive revision at the end of lessons.

(The three other factors involved asking clear questions, spreading them widely, and thanking students for their responses.)

Try this systematic approach: make a habit of taking your last lesson plan into your next class, and reading out the objectives. Then ask questions to discover whether those objectives were achieved.

Summaries

Students can't be expected to remember every word that every teacher says in their 30-lesson week – so get students to remember only key facts. This is crucial to understanding as well as memory. You can prepare key facts for them in summaries, or get them to prepare their own (though these will need checking). Key facts act as reminders for lesser facts, because our memories work by association. Once a key book in the library has been found, other associated books can be found next to it. Every memory does not need to be indexed separately.

Some teachers advocate summarising the last lesson before each new lesson, and the last topic before each new topic. This is all excellent practice, especially if it is done with questioning so that student recall is involved. Research shows we remember most from the beginning and the end of a lesson, so summarising at these times maximises learning.

Mind-maps and the other graphic organisers on pages 154–57 are very helpful here. These make use of association, and present information in a partially visual way, which mimics the way our memory works. Colours and shapes can be used to classify key facts, and diagrams can be used to represent information visually. Have a look now at the example at the end of Chapter 9. Get your students to make a mind-map for a topic and see if you or they like the idea.

Some students like to prepare revision cards – one card for each topic, containing, say, five or six key facts.

Review questions

Quizzes are always popular; they are enjoyable, arousing and involving – all of which serve to increase their effectiveness. Some teachers of examination subjects choose a past paper and get their students to work through it, question by question, in the course of the year. The questions are chosen to review former learning. This has the added advantage that it makes clear to students what they should be able to do, and familiarises them with the examination. Students recognise the importance of doing past-paper questions, and experience a feeling of achievement if they can answer them correctly.

> *In Harbin, China, Gou Yan-ling once memorised more than 15,000 telephone numbers. Bhandanta Vicitsara recited 16,000 pages of Buddhist canonical text from memory in Burma in 1974.*

Revision tests

You can also ask students to learn for a short test: this works best if the 'doing detail' is very precise. For example, don't say, 'Revise for a chemistry test next week.', but 'I want you to learn the formulae for the following chemical reactions for next week …'. I often tell students in advance what the questions in their learning test will be; then there is no excuse for failure! If the learning task is well defined, is achievable by the great majority and is based on well-understood work, the chances of success are high. This success, of course, should be well rewarded with praise and recognition. Students get a real feeling of achievement from success in learning tests, and this fuels future motivation.

Try producing a summary learning sheet for tests. I produce a set for my GCSE physics students; it summarises the key points of the whole syllabus on six sides of A4. Here is an extract covering about two weeks' work. (I ask older students to produce their own revision sheets – but I check them.)

Springs

The bigger the load on a spring, the bigger the extension. *Hooke's Law* states that the extension is proportional to the load. A graph of load against extension will be a straight line (as every extra newton produces the same increase in extension).

When a spring is stretched beyond the *elastic limit*, it does not go back to its original length, and the graph is no longer a straight line.

My summary sheets include diagrams, important reasoning and example calculations, not just facts. Don't forget that visual information is easier to learn than verbal. I test the learning from these sheets by two- to five-minute tests, where I verbally ask simple questions, such as 'What is Hooke's Law?' or 'What is the elastic limit of a spring?' At first, students mark their own papers; this gives them feedback on what they can recall. Then they prepare for a test where I note the mark each student gets.

Summaries indicate key facts that students must be able to recall at will; they are much shorter than 'notes' or the aide-memoire. They also consolidate learning, and if students understand a summary, they are left with a feeling of confidence about that topic.

Mnemonics

'Richard Of York Gained Battle In Vain' can be used to remember the colours of the rainbow – red, orange, yellow, green, blue, indigo, violet. Make up your own mnemonics. Students enjoy making up their own too, but unless you are unshockable, don't ask for them to be repeated to you!

More adventurous review methods

How about using some of the methods in Chapters 18 and 19 on group work and games, respectively? 'Tennis' is particularly useful. You could also use the independent learning approach of using 'study buddies' to test each other's recall, or putting students into 'learning teams'. These teams are collectively responsible for getting each other through recall tests.

'Old learning is never completely lost. Relearning efficiency is the virtue of education.'

Bergen Bugelski

Choosing activities for learning facts

Here is a 'topic plan' for teaching students about the human eye. Note that it stretches over a number of lessons which might also involve other topics not mentioned here. It is a somewhat simplified scheme for readers who are not biologists!

TOPIC PLAN TO TEACH THE FORM AND FUNCTION OF THE HUMAN EYE

Objective: Students should be able to draw a diagram of the eye, and to state the names and functions of the main components.

To present material to be learned: Teacher talk, overhead projector transparency, model, video of dissection of a bull's eye, students take down a note, etc.

To give familiarity and understanding: Verbal question and answer. Student groups are given little cardboard pointers labelled 'retina', 'iris', etc., which have to be placed correctly on a diagram of the eye.

Student groups are also given a set of cards with names, e.g. 'eye lens', and another set of cards with 'functions', e.g. 'to focus light on the retina'. They must match the appropriate names and functions. This is checked by reading out the answers.

Questions to check understanding (written): For example, 'What would happen if the pupil contracted?' 'How would the iris respond if you stepped into the dark?'

Next lesson

Students practise and self-check recall: Students are asked to draw and label an eye, and to write down the functions of each part. The answers are then given for them to self- or peer-check. They are told a mastery test next week will test their ability to do this.

Next week

To assess each student's learning of the objective: Mastery test where students are asked to 'Draw a diagram of the eye, and state the names and functions of the main components.'

Other activities could be used: making posters, quizzes, homework activities, reading, and so on. Note that recall is practised and tested.

Some teachers persist in believing their sole role is to present new material – don't become one of them! Ask yourself: Why am I teaching these facts? What are students supposed to be able to do with them? Usually you will find that they need to be able to *use* facts to *make decisions, solve problems, answer questions requiring more than recall, explain other facts*, etc. The phrases in italics involve higher-order abilities than simple recall, which themselves require corrected practice.

See also mastery learning in Chapter 43.

Recalling skills

Suppose you have just taught your students about marketing plans, and the lesson involved students evaluating a number of alternative marketing plans. Most teachers would review the content (marketing plans) at the end of the lesson. But what about the skill of evaluating? That needs reviewing too! See 'double-decker' lessons in Chapter 38.

Warning

Students accept that not all learning can be fun. However, don't alienate them by intensive and over-ambitious review programmes; this will only demotivate those who can't keep up, and do considerably more harm than good.

> *Victorian educationalists were rightly criticised for an over-emphasis on factual learning. Charles Dickens mocked them in* Hard Times:
>
> *'Now what I want is, Facts. Teach these boys and girls nothing but Facts. Facts alone are wanted in life.'*
>
> *Many educationalists still believe that the modern curriculum is too fact-oriented, and places too little emphasis on skills which are less likely to be forgotten – thinking skills, for example.*

People sometimes think that students will find summaries or other forms of review boring, but in my experience they will appreciate review activities, especially if they are successful at them. But do try to make review less necessary – make your lessons interesting, active and fun, and less will be forgotten!

Checklist

❑ Is the teaching involving, arousing and active?

❑ Do students gain an understanding of key facts before they are expected to be able to recall them?

❑ Is what students must commit to memory clearly defined – by learning notes, for example?

❑ Do students practise recall (not just read, or hear it over again)?

❑ Do they have their recall individually checked and corrected (by themselves or others)?

❑ Is failure to recall tolerated as part of the learning process (as long as satisfactory progress is being made overall)?

❏ Is sufficient time allocated to learning for remembering, on a 'little and often' basis?

❏ Is all relevant previous learning and all current learning reviewed?

❏ Have you tried mind-maps, revision cards and similar techniques?

EXERCISES

If you believe that review is unnecessary or its importance overstated:

Summarise this chapter without re-reading it, and then go back over it, seeing how much you missed.

If you believe review is important:

Devise a review strategy for the next topic you teach!

References and further reading

Bransford, J. D. *et al.* (2000) *How People Learn: Brain, Mind, Experience and School*, Washington, DC: National Research Council.

Buzan, T. (1984) *Use your Memory*, London: BBC Books.

Marzano, R. J. with Marzano, S. and Pickering, D. J. (2003) *Classroom Management that Works*, Alexandria, VA: ASCD.

Petty, G. (2006) *Evidence Based Teaching*, Cheltenham: Nelson Thornes.

Rose, C. (1985) *Accelerated Learning*, Great Missenden, Buckinghamshire: Topaz.

Wright, C. J. and Nuthall, G. (1970) 'The relationship between teacher behaviour and pupil achievement', *American Educational Research Journal*, 7: 477–91.

24

Whole-class interactive teaching – assertive questioning

If you learn one thing from this book I hope it is this method. Why? We saw on page 197 that conventional questioning techniques have severe limitations, with many students not participating and you not getting feedback on your students' understanding or misconceptions. The method in this chapter can fix those problems if used with skill, and can be used in any subject and at any level. It is also an excellent way to develop subject-specific thinking skills.

I look at this in detail in my *Evidence Based Teaching*, but we also know:

- Teachers whose results, in terms of value added, are routinely in the top 1% nationally, almost all use this method towards the end of each topic.
- The nations that do best in international education tables rely heavily on this method.
- In rigorous trials, the method raises students' attainment by almost two grades compared to good conventional teaching. Professor Hattie (2008) has shown this method improves achievement more than almost any other single factor.

The method is also great fun for students and teachers. That's the good news. The bad news is that you are unlikely to have been taught this way, and trainee teachers tend to teach the way they were taught themselves. It takes skill, and it takes time and practice to teach this way, but any teacher can master it.

In whole-class interactive teaching the teacher is in control, but it is a very active method for students, who are very much involved in reasoning and in making their own sense of the ideas and skills they are learning. Some students may also participate by demonstrating the skills being learned, while their peers decide whether this demonstration is sound. The atmosphere should be collaborative and supportive throughout, but with a positive expectation that all students will participate.

While you read what follows, try to keep in mind a context which is familiar to you. If you are a mathematics or science teacher, it might be how to do a specific type of calculation; for an English teacher, how to punctuate correctly a piece of text; for a history teacher, the reasons for the rise of Cromwell, and so on. A concrete example like this will help you to understand the method.

Whole-class teaching strategy

What follows is an approach to whole-class interactive teaching which works well in the West, but differs in detail from Pacific Rim practice. I describe its strongest flavour, but this can be diluted to taste. The basic strategy is to create a dynamic mix of teacher talk (about 40 per cent), constantly peppered with bouts of:

- *Student activity*. For each topic, the student tasks start by being short and easy, and then get longer and more challenging.
- *Assertive questioning*. This is described below, and is intended to maximise participation, active learning and the linking of new learning with old.
- *Student demonstration*. Students display their developing skills on the board or overhead projector (OHP), while their peers decide whether this has been done correctly.

Throughout there is an active scrutiny of the arguments and procedures being learned. The class is encouraged to take collective responsibility for working out the new learning, while the teacher confirms, summarises and emphasises the new learning, making links and comparisons with prior learning.

Assertive questioning

Though assertive, this questioning style should never become antagonistic or have an 'I'm trying to catch you out' atmosphere. There should be no put-downs – but no passengers either. During the following description, I assume that students are asked to write down their answers in rough, perhaps on a handout, but a verbal answer may suffice for some questions.

The assertive questioning procedure, which you may need to explain to your class, is summarised in the flow diagram on page 283. Look at this before reading on, to get an overview.

Ask the question

First a question is asked or a problem set:

'How should the next sentence be punctuated?'
'Who would have supported Cromwell and why?'
'Can you factorise $3x^2 + 4x + 1$?'

The question needs to be clear, concise and sufficiently searching to take students at least a minute to answer. *The question must require the students to reason or act in some other substantial way*. Ideally, the question needs to be simple enough to be largely attainable by nearly all members of the class, but open and high-order so that the more able are stretched. It is often best to write the question on the board. Support material may be provided – for example, for the Cromwell question – but should not give the answer away directly and simply.

Tell students whether they are to work individually or in pairs in the first instance. It works well for students to work separately at first, say for one minute, and then to show and explain their answers to each other in pairs. The aim is for the pair to come to an agreed answer. From first posing the question, to the pairs agreeing their answer, might take only one to three minutes. However, some questions may take longer – for example, the history question above – but with younger learners at least, try not to lose the sense of urgency which makes this method work best.

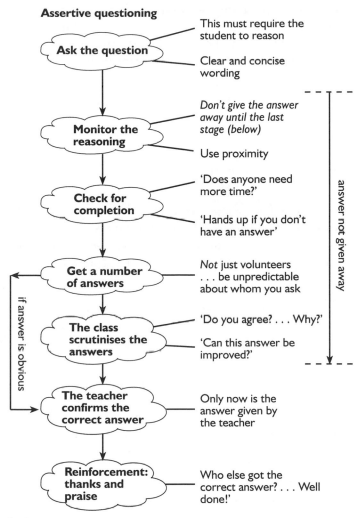

Assertive questioning

Ask the question
- This must require the student to reason
- Clear and concise wording

Monitor the reasoning
- *Don't give the answer away until the last stage (below)*
- Use proximity

Check for completion
- 'Does anyone need more time?'
- 'Hands up if you don't have an answer'

Get a number of answers
- *Not* just volunteers . . . be unpredictable about whom you ask

The class scrutinises the answers
- 'Do you agree? . . . Why?'
- 'Can this answer be improved?'

The teacher confirms the correct answer
- Only now is the answer given by the teacher

Reinforcement: thanks and praise
- Who else got the correct answer? . . . Well done!'

if answer is obvious

answer not given away

Assertive questioning

Monitor the reasoning

While the students work, ask if there are any queries and check they are writing down their answers, but do not comment on these. Use proximity to ensure attention to task. You may have a little time to give hints to students who are resolutely stuck, but don't tell them the answer. If the task is hard, drop a hint: *'Some people are remembering last lesson and using semi-colons.'*

Check for completion

Are they ready? Ask: 'Does anyone need more time?' and 'Has everyone got their answer now?' or 'Hands up if you haven't got an answer.'

The aim here is to get students to own up if they do not have an answer; this is important for the next stage. They will need to show hands at first, but if you use assertive questioning often, they will learn to let you know quietly without owning up in front of the class. If the initial question was appropriate, the great majority of students should have an answer of sorts. If they usually find your questions too difficult, try to break them down into shorter and simpler questions. If they need more time, give help or hints, but without giving away the answer.

If there is no single correct answer, this method still works well. For example, if you ask, 'What was Macbeth's motivation in Act 1?', you will get a most productive discussion with this method.

Get a number of answers

Explain the rules of the game: all students must either have an answer, or have admitted to you that they don't have one.

Now ask for an answer from someone who has one. Don't ask for volunteers; nominate the person who will answer. Even if they are working in a pair, nominate the person who will give their pair's answer. Get at least half of your answers from the weaker half of the class, and spread answers about the class as much as you can.

Once all the students realise you might ask *them*, they will refrain from 'free-riding' or losing concentration.

It is most important to thank the student by name for their answer at this stage, but without saying whether the answer is right or wrong; do not even send a non-verbal signal to this effect. You will find this difficult, especially for dreadful answers!

Ask the student to explain their answer to the rest of the class, and then ask for some other opinions. Again, this should be done whether the answer is right or wrong: 'Has anyone got anything different?' If the class is complacent but the answers are unsatisfactory, you might like to hint at this. 'You're not halfway there yet!'

Some more responses to try:

Do you agree with Clive? Why?	Who agrees with that answer? Why?
Why do you think that?	Who has something different? Why?
What do you mean by that?	Could there by alternative answers?
Can you be sure?	*(To non-responder)* So what do you think?
How did you get that answer?	
Is this what you first thought?	What changed your mind?

If you give the correct answer away too early, you will not be given incorrect answers by students. This lowers the quality of your feedback, and you lose opportunities to correct errors later.

If a student who earlier claimed to have an answer does not have one, give them sustained eye contact. Ask them to 'play the game', reminding them of the rules if necessary.

The class scrutinises the answers

You could skip straight to 'confirmation and reinforcement' if students find the question very simple.

The class is now given collective responsibility for scrutinising the answers in order to check and improve them and so come to a collective answer. Put the students' suggested answers on the board if it helps. Ask, 'Does anyone agree with that answer? ... Why?' or 'Does anyone disagree with that answer? ... Why?' and towards the end of this process, 'Is everyone prepared to commit to this answer?'

Ask nominees and volunteers to explain their opinions. Thank them for their contribution, but, again, do not say whether it is right or wrong.

Try to get:

* *the truth*: 'Is that answer correct?' Or if there is not one correct answer: 'Can that answer be justified?'
* *the whole truth*: 'Is there anything missing in that answer?'
* *and nothing but the truth*: 'Is there anything not quite right about that answer?'

Do your best to develop a sense of pace, suspense and curiosity – what is the right answer?

In most classes, try to get the students to scrutinise the answer without implying a criticism of the student who made it. Allow 'I don't think the $4x$ bit is right', but not 'Carla's got the $4x$ bit wrong'. The answers belong to the class, not individuals. Ideally, the scrutiny should be forward-looking and focused on improvement, not backward-looking and focused on error. 'It's an easy mistake to make. How could you avoid making it next time?'

More mature and confident students can enjoy the cut and thrust of attacking and defending each other's answers, so use your judgement here. The deciding factor is perhaps the spirit in which any criticism is made, and taken.

While the class debate the improvement of their answer, hint at your approval or disapproval of any adjustments only if you are sure your help is necessary. Try to get the class to agree their answer, or to state their differences clearly.

> *When you and the class are more practised, or the students are confident with their answer, you can play devil's advocate. Ask leading questions towards incorrect lines of reasoning, or otherwise attempt to throw the class off the scent. Make sure you don't succeed, of course! This might seem a perverse strategy, but it is great fun and helps 'inoculate' students against poor reasoning and common errors.*

Confirmation and reinforcement

Now, and only now, do you give the correct answer, explaining the reasoning clearly, concisely and persuasively. Praise the thought and effort of the contributors, or if they were wildly wrong, at least thank them. If there is no correct answer, comment on the quality of student opinions and their justification.

This completes the assertive questioning procedure, and you are now ready for the next question, for the next activity or for more input by teacher talk. This approach works best if you use it frequently. It is possible to use it many times in one lesson, and students can become very involved if it is handled with pace and enthusiasm by the teacher.

Students will take a little time to learn the protocol, especially if it is new to them, but this investment will be very well rewarded.

Student demonstration or student answers

This can be a separate activity, but it can also be used as the 'give answer' part of assertive questioning. It can be adapted for almost any teaching. For example, students could write on the board or OHP their answer to the history question considered above. It works particularly well for mathematics.

The teacher sets the task, writing it on the board. If necessary, students can be given time to consider their approach to this problem, working first individually and then peer-checking in pairs. This could be done exactly as in assertive questioning above. If you can, give short time limits for these activities, perhaps one or two minutes. Monitor students' progress as for assertive questioning, discovering those who do not have an answer.

Once you are confident that most students have an answer, choose a student to do the demonstration. Start by asking for volunteers, but when your use of this method is well established, consider the more assertive technique of letting students decide answers in pairs or small groups, and then nominating students at random to give their group's answer. Give prior warning that you will do this, and don't choose students who need more time, or who have made it clear they are unable to carry out the demonstration. Do not always choose students who have brilliant answers!

Students write their answer up on the board. It is usually best if the student and the class see this student as just the scribe for the whole class; their role is to write up the class answer bit by bit and allow the class to discuss. In assertive questioning the teacher does this. The teacher could still facilitate the discussion or it could be left to the student, as you choose.

An alternative is to ask, say, three students to write their different answers up side by side, so the class can compare them. Choose students who have got answers worth discussing, or that compare interestingly.

The session now runs exactly as for assertive questioning, with the class scrutinising the answer(s) and then the teacher confirming it.

Advantages and limitations

The main advantage of assertive questioning and student demonstration is that, by comparison with other teacher-centred methods, they involve the students a great deal, and so ensure concentration and provide you with feedback. It really is very difficult for students to coast or become passengers. No student knows who will be asked to answer, and often a very high proportion of the class will be asked for their view at some time or other for each question. Students don't want to be caught out, so they have to form a construct. However, if they work in pairs or small groups they get the help they require. Consequently, this method ensures that even the less motivated or less able student forms an understanding, and so is good for differentiation.

Because this method discovers errors and omissions in students' learning fast, allowing teacher and students to correct these straight away, it creates a 'self-correcting classroom'. More conventional questioning methods create a 'blind classroom', where teacher and students do not discover misconceptions in 'real time' like this.

It is very important to be clear about your motives for using these approaches. If you use them because you like being the centre of attention and find group or individual work boring, then you will use them inappropriately, and the students will not have their needs met.

Do try assertive questioning when you are confident enough, and in the meantime try nominating rather than asking for volunteers to answer your questions. You may surprise your class, but you might also surprise yourself.

> **Curiosity**
>
> *If a teacher wrote a murder mystery she would probably write in the first paragraph of the first chapter:* 'Well it was the Bishop that did it, in the pantry with a candlestick, and this is how it happened ...' *We wouldn't want to read on, because we now know the answer! What makes us curious is not knowing 'who done it'. Teachers can learn from this! If we withhold the answer, and the reasoning to it, then we make students think, but we also make them more curious about our subject. Curiosity is surely the most precious gift a teacher can bestow.*

Further reading

Muijs, D. and Reynolds, D. (2005) *Effective Teaching: Evidence and Practice* (2nd edition), London: Paul Chapman.

Petty, G. (2006) *Evidence Based Teaching*, Cheltenham: Nelson Thornes.

Powell has also done an 'Active Whole-Class Teaching Interactive CD'; the details are at: homepage.ntlworld.com/robert.powell810/CD_AWCT.html

25

Reading for learning

You would not be reading now if you did not believe one can learn from the process. A decent textbook can be a gold mine of varied and useful activities, but this chapter concerns itself specifically with students who are reading in order to gain knowledge and understanding.

The use made of reading as a teaching method is increasing, but very variable. In many schools and colleges, some learners never trouble their library, and some textbooks are issued only to be returned unopened a year later. Other textbooks are so extensively used that they could do with annual replacement. Until recently, however, reading for learning has often been regarded as old-fashioned outside higher education. Now, partly because of the move towards assignments and project work, some teachers are using it very widely. Some use it systematically, with independent learning assignments as described in Chapter 33, or by giving students 'briefing packs' which summarise basic factual information. In this way, precious contact time can be used for more productive and interesting activities than information delivery.

It is best not to approach this topic with starry-eyed idealism. Reading does not guarantee learning. We have all had the experience of reading something for some time, only to realise with irritation that we lost concentration and learned nothing. I hope it is not happening to you at this moment!

However, if you teach in an active way to encourage students to really understand the key concepts, then you might not have time to 'cover' all the detailed content. In this case, reading tasks are an excellent way to make good this deficiency.

Approaches to reading

In Chapter 1 we considered the surface and deep learning; these ideas were developed by Marton and Saljo (1976), who identified two distinctive approaches to reading:

1 *Surface-level processing*, where students take a passive approach and are concerned with:
   - covering the content
   - how much they have learned
   - finding the right answers
   - assimilating unaltered chunks of knowledge
   - learning verbatim.

2   *Deep-level processing*, in which students take a mentally active approach and are concerned with:

– the central point

– what lies behind the argument

– the whole picture

– what it boils down to

– what it is connected with

– the logic of the argument

– points that are not clear

– questioning the conclusions.

Deep-level processors were shown to be more successful in exams and to be more versatile. I would add a third level:

3   *Zero-level processing*, where the learner simply goes through the motion of reading the text, believing that understanding will automatically follow by some osmosis-like process. The student is concerned with:

– getting it over as quickly as possible

– what's for tea!

How can teachers maximise the chance that students will learn from their reading? In Chapter 1 it was pointed out that learning involves producing a personalised meaning for the information presented to the learner. Reading should be an active process, where learners interrogate the text to form this personalised version of its message. This can be encouraged by, for example:

• *Interesting reading activities*. A challenge to discover the answer to a puzzle, problem or intriguing question is more motivating than 'Read Chapter 23'. It also ensures that students are trying to understand rather than just get it over and done with.

• *Expecting reading notes*. Ask your students to produce a precis, a summary, a mind-map, a set of key points or even a full set of notes. This should be done in the students' own words.

• *Reorganising the material into a different form*. For example, a text which looks in turn at the function of different agencies in a process could be reorganised to give the information chronologically.

• *Reading for information*. Ask students to look for specific information, such as the answers to specific questions; this information should preferably need to be 'dug out' of the text.

• *Reading for criticism*. Ask students to take a critical view of the text they are reading: What is the author's point of view? What is the evidence for and against this point of view? What's missing? What would other authors or theorists think of the points of view expressed?

• *Expecting to make a presentation*. Ask students to read different material in groups and make a presentation to the rest of their class. In higher education, students are expected to present and defend their views on what they have read to a 'seminar' consisting of fellow students and an experienced tutor. Similar techniques are used in further education and in schools. Students can be expected to produce reading notes for their fellow students, perhaps checking these with the tutor before duplication.

- *Expecting a discussion.* Students can be asked to read a set text to prepare for a class discussion. You could give some challenging discussion questions in advance to focus attention on important points, and to make it clear that the reading must be done.

Reading requires that the learner takes responsibility for understanding and learning, and it has many of the advantages of individualised learning. It allows learners to study at their own pace, so that the keener can go further and deeper, and the weaker can take their time with a text personally chosen for simplicity.

It also:

- develops the very important skill of learning from reading, which will never be accomplished without practice
- helps to develop library and book-searching skills
- acquaints learners with their textbooks and with other important texts, which they are then more likely to make further use of in their private study.

Whatever you teach, there are bound to be some excellent texts available, and you are ignoring a valuable source if you don't encourage your learners to make use of them. If the texts you would prefer are not available in the quantities you would like, it may be possible to devise a group-work 'circus', where texts circulate and groups carry out different activities with each of the texts (see Chapter 18). Don't forget non-book material such as journals, newspapers, CD-ROMs, the Internet and so on.

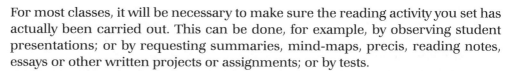

Some research has shown that university students given a textbook, enrolled on a course and told the exam date have done as well as those attending lectures.

For most classes, it will be necessary to make sure the reading activity you set has actually been carried out. This can be done, for example, by observing student presentations; or by requesting summaries, mind-maps, precis, reading notes, essays or other written projects or assignments; or by tests.

Reading is an essentially solitary activity requiring quiet concentration. Many students find it difficult to read for more than a few minutes in class, preferring to read at home or in private study. It is an excellent homework activity, as the ratio of learning value to marking effort is high.

Try producing a reading guide for your students. This should list useful books, with comments from you such as 'Dull but thorough' or 'Better on X than on Y'.

Library and information-searching skills

A university biology lecturer told me that she once set an essay on hawks for first-year students. She provided a book list including a 2,000-page alphabetical reference guide to birds in Europe and North America. When she asked for the essay from one student, he replied, bleary-eyed, that he was still working his way through the book list, and was currently reading the previously mentioned reference guide. He explained sheepishly that so far he had only read up to 'E'!

In her excellent book *Teaching and Learning in Higher Education*, Ruth Beard describes annually finding science and mathematics students researching topics in psychology books by meticulously searching from page to page. 'A suggestion to consult the index invariably caused initial surprise, and some of these postgraduate students needed to be told where to find it!'

It is tempting to laugh at such students, but the derision is better directed at their schools and colleges. Every student should be taught information-searching skills, including the effective use of the full facilities of libraries. This is perhaps best done by a tutor librarian as it is a complex skill. Have your students been taught to skim or to speed-read?

The lecture is the primrose path to intellectual sloth.

Making full use of your library

If they are given sufficient notice, most libraries will assemble a box of books on a given topic for you to take to your class. They may also have a 'desk loan' system, where books in great demand are removed from the shelves and can only be borrowed for use in the library.

You may like to consider writing digests or summaries of some texts for your students – but why not get your students to do this for themselves? Some university lecturers organise 'reading deals', where students share out the reading list and then share their reading notes.

The Internet is also of a great resource, course. Recommend sites, but also ask your students to find them, putting them on the classroom noticeboard (you might like to check them first!).

Readability

Are the books you recommend easily readable by your students? There are a number of methods for estimating the readability of text, usually based on the average sentence length and the average number of syllables per word. These methods can only give a rough idea of the readability, so it is still desirable to supplement them with the use of your own judgement. The 'FOG index' is an example; this calculates the reading age as follows:

1   In a representative section of the text, select five to eight complete sentences. Find the total number of words 'n' in the 's' complete sentences.

2   Calculate the average number of words per complete sentence $A = n/s$

3   Select a passage of continuous text of exactly 100 words within your sample. Find the number of words of three or more syllables, 'W', in your 100-word sample. Don't count the 'ed' or 'es' endings of verbs, so that the word 'realised' counts as only two syllables, despite being three syllables.

4   Calculate the reading age as follows:

   Reading age $= 0.4 \times (A + W) + 5$ years

For somewhat greater accuracy, select three or four passages from the book, and find the reading ages of these, and then average them. This is called the FOG index, which stands for the 'frequency of gobbledegook'.

The average TV guide has a reading age of about 6 years; 17 years is very tough reading indeed, and only suitable for postgraduates.

The 'reading age' of text is the age at which the average person can read it. This means that many people of that age could not read it of course! So the reading age of your material may need to be lower than the chronological age of your students.

To reduce the reading age, simply shorten sentences, simplifying their grammar, and 'translate' difficult words into more common language, adding the formal word later if this helps, e.g. *'makes them feel they can make a difference – that is, empowers them.'*

Reading techniques

Some commentators suggest that reading should follow the 'SQR[3]' process:

Survey	Skim-read the chapter, noting content and organisation.
Question	Before reading each section, stop and ask what is being covered and what you want to extract from it.
Read	Read the text, but think about the material as you do so, and try to answer the questions mentioned above.
Recite	At the end of each section, stop and recite the major points to yourself.
Review	At the end of the chapter, review the whole of it, paying special attention to the way the author organised the material.

There are a number of teaching strategies that are based on students learning from reading, called 'teaching without talking', on my website (www.geoffpetty.com). Try jigsaw, for example.

Checklist

❏ Do you encourage students to make use of their textbooks?

❏ Do you set reading that encourages students to process information rather than simply read it?

❏ Do your students know what books are available, and their strengths and weaknesses?

❏ Do you evaluate whether reading has been done, and whether learning has resulted?

❏ Have your students been taught information-searching skills?

References and further reading

Beard, R. and Hartley, T. (1984) *Teaching and Learning in Higher Education* (4th edition), London: PCP.

Lunzer, E. and Gardner, K. (1979) *The Effective Use of Reading*, Oxford: Heinemann Educational Books.

Marton, M. and Saljo, R. (1976) 'On qualitative differences in learning' (two articles), *British Journal of Educational Psychology*, 46: 4–11, 115–27.

Petty, G. (2006) *Evidence Based Teaching*, Cheltenham: Nelson Thornes.

26

Private study and homework

When I was a student I hated homework, and when I became a teacher I saw no reason to revise my opinion. At the end of an evening marking classwork, preparing for lessons and dealing with a mountain of administrative work, the last thing I want is 30 homework assignments to mark. Then, one year, my new timetable involved me in teaching eight classes of 25 students. Every week I would be setting and marking 200 pieces of homework; at 10 minutes each, simply marking them would take me 33 hours a week! Slowly it dawned on me that the aim of homework is to get the student to work at home, not the teacher.

Many learning activities are best done alone, and are therefore much more suited to private study than to work in the classroom. Ideal homework should:

- involve the student in a genuinely useful activity that is best done alone – or at least does not require teacher support
- be of a kind which makes it possible to check that it has been completed satisfactorily
- require a minimum of teacher effort
- (usually) provide a mark
- not be too onerous.

Which student activities best fit these criteria?

Reading. Most, or even all, homework could simply be reading the textbook; but take note of the previous chapter on reading and set a specific series of pages to read. Give a short five-question 'slip test' to check that the material has been read and understood. If students mark each other's papers, the test need only take three minutes. Alternatively, ask students to produce a summarising mind-map; this can be very quickly marked. Reading familiarises the student with the textbook, and develops self-study skills, as well as direct subject learning.

Preparation for a lesson. This may take the form of reading, revising relevant material covered earlier or answering questions which orientate the student. For example, learners might be asked to outline five purposes of stocktaking, before a lesson on the subject.

Preparing revision notes. Summaries, mind-maps, mnemonics or revision notes are often best produced by the learners themselves, and make an excellent activity at the end of a topic. Revision notes don't take long to mark.

Learning revision notes. Nearly every subject has basic factual material which must be remembered by heart: vocabulary in language subjects, formulae, definitions, procedures, etc. Make sure students understand what they are expected to learn, however – see Chapter 23 on learning for remembering.

Revision. An often neglected activity which is usually too vital to be left to the whims of student motivation. (See Chapters 23 and 43 for further discussion of review and mastery learning.)

Whatever the homework, if it is set, it must be seen, marked or tested by the teacher, otherwise it will be evaded. (Do you need separate homework marks for reports or record cards?)

Finishing off classwork is the most commonly set homework, but it is often not the most suitable. It will not be appropriate if the student is likely to get stuck, or needs special books or equipment unavailable at home; or if separate homework and classwork marks are required. It is a useful way of ensuring that slower students catch up, but it doesn't require anything of students able or fast enough to complete the work in class time.

In general, don't set anything more difficult than the students have practised in class. If you do, some will get stuck, and others will use the difficulty as an excuse for not doing the work, even when they could.

Try to follow a rigid regime for the setting, collecting and marking of homework. It is advisable to require students to write something as part of the homework activity – and for you to have thought out a response for the following:

> 'Sorry, miss, I forgot.'
> 'Sorry, miss, I didn't know there was any homework.'
> 'Sorry, miss, I left it at home.'
> 'Sorry, miss, I spent all evening taking my Granny's budgie to the vet ...'

Checklist for homework

❑ Are you aware of the homework policy and practice for your school or college?

❑ Do your homework assignments combine maximum learning value with minimum marking effort?

❑ Are they genuinely useful?

❑ Are you rigorous about setting, collecting and marking homework? And do your students' parents know this?

Further reading

Marzano, R. J. *et al.* (2001) *Classroom Instruction That Works: Research-Based Strategies for Increasing Student Achievement*, Alexandria, VA: ASCD.

Stern, J. (1997) *Homework and Study Support: A Guide for Teachers and Parents*, London: David Fullton.

27

Assignments and projects

Assignments and projects are the big guns in the educator's arsenal. They can have a powerful effect – if correctly aimed. Few teaching methods enable the teacher to develop a greater range of skills; and few offer greater opportunity to waste time in ill-directed activity. If you are going to involve students in an activity that takes, say, 10 hours, then it had better be well thought out!

What exactly is a project or assignment? It is a task or set of tasks for students to complete – usually individually, but sometimes in groups. Usually the students can exercise considerable autonomy over how, where, when and in what order the tasks are carried out. Projects are usually more open-ended than assignments.

Terminology varies, but the following is common:

0 to 1 hours	an exercise
1 to 8 hours	an assignment
8 to 50 hours	a project
over 50 hours	a dissertation or a thesis.

The rest of this chapter mentions only assignments, but applies equally to projects. Assignments give the students an opportunity to use – that is, to practise and to apply – their skills and knowledge, and so come to a deep understanding; often this is in a fairly realistic context. Some courses are assignment based, but many other courses do not make enough use of them.

Assignment type	**Example**
A series of academic exercises	Carry out a series of calculations.
A design or development problem	Design a self-watering flowerpot and produce a prototype.
A literature search	Research and write a report on owls.
A work-related or real-life activity	Design and make a range of practical cosmetics and market them within the college.
Skill practice	Make a bowl on a wood lathe.
Creative activity	Design an advertisement for a specified computer. Problem-solving Suggest methods for reducing wastage in an industrial process.

| An encounter with the real world | Visit a builders' merchant and interview staff on modern developments in building materials. |

Assignments often involve a sequence of such tasks. A useful strategy is to build the assignment around a question such as 'Does our town swimming pool meet the needs of young people?' or 'What access do disabled people have to our college?'

Assignments give students some control and responsibility over their learning. Unlike many learning activities, they give students an opportunity to use higher-order intellectual skills, such as creativity, problem-solving, evaluation, synthesis and analysis. There is also an opportunity to develop key skills such as communication, application of number, the use of information technology and learning how to learn. Other important 'real-world' skills are also developed, such as self-management, working in a group, information-seeking, and so on. On some courses, such skills are separately planned for and assessed, but any assignment should aim to develop them.

Devising an assignment or project

Your assignments may have been written for you, but often not. Writing an assignment is a creative process. It is not possible to be precise or prescriptive, but the process will usually involve the following:

Decide on objectives. What do you aim to achieve with the assignment? Be sure that an assignment really is the best way of achieving your objectives.

Consider resources. Is there enough time? Are specialist equipment or rooms available where these are necessary? It is most helpful to talk to library staff about useful resources well before the assignment is set; they often find inspiring material you never knew existed.

Will all your students be clamouring for a limited supply of specialist books? If so, warn the library, and arrange for relevant books to be put on 'desk loan'. The library removes the relevant books from the shelves, and students inquiring at the library desk may borrow the books but cannot remove them from the library. You will need to give your students a list of the books available on desk loan.

Consider skills needed. Do your students know how to research in a library? Can they search a CD-ROM? Do they know how to approach an assignment? Are they adequately prepared for all the tasks?

Devise activities. Make sure your activities achieve your objectives. Most assignments benefit from being very carefully described, with tasks broken down and sequenced where necessary. Demotivated students tend to do best with short assignments.

Motivation was considered in detail in Chapter 5. Ensure the activities:

- *Interest the students*. Make the activity genuinely useful: relate it to their interests, make it thought-provoking, intriguing or involving, and remember Maslow's needs. Include self-actualising or esteem-enhancing tasks, where students can make a personal contribution through problem-solving, design, arguing their own opinions, surveys, interviews, making presentations and so on. Try also to meet 'belongingness and love needs' through group or pair work. Including such opportunities to meet Maslow's needs can hugely increase student motivation.

- *Offer an opportunity to practise skills in 'real-life' or work-related circumstances.* Develop realistic scenarios or case studies; give students roles; get the students out of the classroom into the real world; involve them with visits or in having visitors.
- *Are active and varied.* No one wants to spend three weeks researching in the library. Aim for a number of contrasting tasks in a long assignment or a project.
- *Are well defined*, so students are confident that they know what you expect.
- *Set an achievable target which is rewarding to meet.*
- Sequence tasks so they climb Bloom's taxonomy, go from easy to hard or create a 'ladder'.
- Give students' work an audience, using noticeboards, intranet pages or student presentations.

You may like to give staff and students roles – for example, Mrs Smith is the design house manager, Mrs Brown is the customer commissioning the design, students are the designers and have daily meetings with both Mrs Smith and Mrs Brown. If students are working in groups, do you need to define their roles (leader, scribe, journal keeper, etc.)?

Problem-solving assignments

Problem-solving should go through the following series of stages. If you plan to set a problem-solving assignment, tell students about this process and use it as a guide to the tasks included.

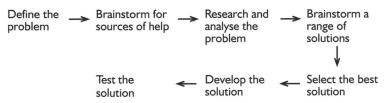

Those affected by the problem and/or the solution should usually be consulted throughout.

Note: 'Brainstorm for sources of help' may sometimes be omitted, but this can lead to 'reinventing the wheel' or to impractical solutions. If, for example, the problem is to reduce wastage in an industrial process, brainstorming may suggest talking to the relevant machine operator, contacting the makers of the machine, etc.

Why not have some tasks or assignments that are student-devised but negotiated with you? This allows learners to follow their particular interests.

Devising assessment criteria

I remember the first time I set an assignment. My class of 14-year-old science students hummed with contented activity for hours. I was delighted – until they handed it in. One lad, and he was not the only one, had made an appalling attempt at the meat of the assignment, but had produced a magnificent front cover. He had meticulously copied illustrations from the box of books the library had provided, combining them into a breathtaking piece of artwork. I pointed out it was a science, not an art, assignment and gave him a low mark. He (correctly) pointed out that I had asked for illustrations, and was incensed.

Now I use assessment criteria! This is common practice in further education (but, sadly, not always elsewhere).

The assessment criteria tell students what is being assessed, and how. They must be given to the students before they start work on the assignment.

ASSESSMENT CRITERIA FOR A CHEMISTRY ASSIGNMENT

Distinction. The water content is measured to an accuracy of plus or minus 3%. The report is well written, and includes a clear indication of all the main sources of error and how these could be reduced.

Merit. Plus or minus 5% accuracy of analysis. Clear indication of the main sources of error, and some idea of how some of these could be reduced.

Pass. Plus or minus 8% accuracy of analysis. Adequate report; the student needs help in determining all the sources of error and their means of reduction.

Refer. If the above criteria are not met, the assignment will be handed back to the student for completion.

Skill development

Use of computers. The assignment is to be written up on computer; marks will be awarded for use of bold, underline and similar effects. Text should be well laid out and fully formatted.

Self-management. Marks will be awarded for finishing on time, and keeping adequate records.

If you don't like this format, design your own, but tell students what you expect. General National Vocational Qualification (GNVQ) and other courses require that assignments are presented and assessed in a very specific manner; make sure you have up-to-date guidance.

Assessment criteria increase student motivation markedly, and they ensure that their time and effort is focused in the direction you intend. Moreover, if students know what to aim for, they are more likely to be successful; this is as important for long-term motivation as it is in achieving the objectives of the assignment itself.

If students are completing assignments in groups, should each group member get the same mark? Some teachers advocate letting each member of the group grade themselves, or each other. Students are often brutally truthful when asked to grade themselves, but a little over-generous with others. Whatever you decide, this must be made clear from the start.

Debriefing and reflection sessions

It is vital that after – and preferably also during – the assignment, students are able to evaluate their performance, decide how it could be improved, and come to firm conclusions about what they have learned. This is true both for subject learning and for more general skills such as learning to learn and working with others.

Reflection can be arranged in a number of ways. It can occur during a debriefing session after the activity, where the teacher and class mine their experience for learning. Alternatively, students can reflect individually with the teacher; or one task in the assignment can be for students to reflect individually or in groups, and report their findings to the teacher or to self-assess. See Chapter 33 for a systematic approach.

Designing the assignment briefing sheet

Every assignment needs to be described to students in detail and in writing. This is usually done on a typed handout containing:

* an introduction which sets the scene for the assignment
* a clear statement of the aims and objectives of the assignment, though not necessarily in formal language
* a clear statement of the tasks, broken down where necessary
* a clear outline of what will be assessed, and how
* background notes, e.g. roles of staff, references, desk loans available; debriefing session
* the launch date and date for completion; usually with a penalty for late completion (e.g. maximum of half marks).

Planning for evaluation

How will you decide whether the assignment was a success, and whether there are ways of improving it? Keep a monitoring copy of the briefing sheet in your folder, on which you can write suggested improvements as they occur to you. You will never get an assignment right first time.

Role of the teacher during assignment work

Assignments are usually completed in students' own time. But what if they do one in class time? You have devised your assignment and briefed the students on it.

'OK,' you say, 'you can start.' The students enthusiastically make their way to the library, and you are left in a classroom which is empty except for two students who are discussing how to approach the assignment. It's a strange feeling. Can this be right? What exactly is the role of the teacher when students are working on assignments, whether they are done in class or in students' time? There is more to this than answering queries, assessment, debriefing and evaluation of the assessment's effectiveness. The teacher must become a learning manager and a facilitator, rather than just an instructor. Students who are going to the library should be asked to write their names on a dated class library sheet. But then what?

If students are left entirely to their own devices, it is very common for them to misinterpret or misread the assignment, or fail to read it adequately. In addition, you may not have described the tasks as clearly as you hoped. If you do not check on the students' progress, they may proudly offer you inadequate assignments after many hours of hard work. This is very depressing and demotivating, for them and for you. Check work is up to standard while it is being done, and request improvement straightaway where necessary – then all work will be successful and motivating.

Except for short assignments, it is common to arrange an appointment system so that you can check on each student's progress, otherwise some students will be missed. Leave a space after each task on the assignment sheet for the teacher (or student) to write comments such as: 'You need more detail here', 'Good effort on this task', or 'Don't forget the *Times* CD-ROM'. Make positive comments where you can! Monitoring motivates those students who find it difficult to sustain effort over a long period.

Procrastination

Parkinson's law says that a job expands to fill the time available; and in the case of assignments, twice the time available! Procrastination is sometimes caused by a lack of confidence on the student's part; this can be overcome by praising or accepting the standard of work in progress.

Some teachers advocate a 'reciprocal supervision' arrangement for long projects. Each student supervises one other student, but not a close friend. The supervisor can be given a fairly detailed brief to monitor against assessment criteria and tasks, and made partly responsible for the prompt submission of the work, or simply asked to meet occasionally to discuss progress.

To be fair on the students who have submitted their assignment on time, it is common practice to deduct marks from those handed in late. Prior warning of this arrangement needs to be given.

If procrastination is a problem, try letting students start an assignment off in class.

Feedback and copying

What should you do with marked work if some students have not completed an assignment? Some teachers give the marked assignments back so students can see their grades and comments, but then they collect the assignments back in again so they cannot be copied.

Students should not copy textbooks or Internet resources either; tasks should require them to put the ideas into their own words. This ensures they process the information and make their own sense of it.

Your comments should be as detailed and as constructive as possible, of course, and if it is practical, try to talk to students about their work as you give their assignments back. This can be arranged if students have a new task to do as you hand their work back.

Integrated (or synoptic) assignments

The aim of an integrated assignment is to encourage students to experience their programme of study as a coherent whole. For example, a student on a built environment course may study a number of 'subjects': materials, science, surveying, technical drawing, mathematics, and so on. An assignment to design a small bungalow would enable students to integrate the skills and knowledge gained in these different 'subjects', and see their interrelation and relevance in the real world.

It is usual for the course team to develop an integrated assignment in such a way that every part of the curriculum is adequately represented. The assignments are often realistic and work-related; and indeed for students on work experience or on day release, the assignment may be suggested by their workplace, and wholly or partly carried out there. Otherwise, a realistic scenario or case study underpins the assignment.

> **Improving your assignments and students' assignment writing**
> Evaluate your assignments just after they have been completed and make notes for next year on a monitoring copy. Ask students how they could be improved. Show students model assignments and involve them in self-, peer and spoof assessment (Chapter 43).

The limitations of assignments

In the flurry and excitement of devising projects, it is easy to forget that they only rarely provide all of the *educare?* elements discussed in Chapter 2. This is especially true of key skills, which are sometimes assessed without being taught. For example, students often fail to complete assignments on time because they have not developed the skill of self-management or time management. It is not enough to give students repeated practice in this skill. That may simply allow them to learn their mistakes. The skill needs to be actively taught with the use of all the *educare?* elements. They need:

- *An explanation.* 'When you first get an assignment, draw up a timetable allotting times to each of the tasks. Plan to finish one day early. Refer to this timetable as the assignment progresses ...'
- *A demonstration* to show them by example: 'For example, let's draw up a timetable together for your present assignment. How long do you think each task will take? ...'

As well as *use*, the student needs a *check*. You can provide this during the assignment: 'We are halfway through the assignment now; are you keeping to your timetable?'

You may feel students can do without an aide-memoire, but they will need review and evaluation until the skill is developed. See the learning tuner approach in Chapter 33 on independent learning.

The same principle goes for skills other than key skills: completing a task does not in itself guarantee learning. For this reason, most teachers combine assignments with other teaching and learning methods. Although careful use of assignments can avoid most of the disadvantages mentioned above, it must surely be a mistake to base an entire course on back-to-back assignments. Students need variety.

Checklist for using assignment-based learning

❏ Was the assignment well defined in writing, with tasks broken down in sufficient detail?

❏ Was assessment transparent, and were criteria given in advance?

❏ Was it enjoyable, with a clear purpose?

❏ Were students adequately prepared for the tasks?

❏ Were resources adequate?

❏ Did you check on, and encourage, both general work-rate and the content of the students' work while it was in progress?

❏ Have you got an annotated monitoring copy of the assignment?

❏ Did all students succeed in completing the assignment satisfactorily?

❏ While marking, did you comment on both good and bad features of the work, as well as awarding a grade? (See the next chapter for further discussion of this point.)

❏ Did debriefing confirm what students should have learned?

Further reading

If a course is assignment based, get up-to-date information from the validating body on how assignments should be designed, used and assessed. This guidance changes rapidly, so make sure you are up to date. Teachers, internal verifiers and library staff will be able to help.

28

Essays and reports

Have you ever written what you thought was a great essay – only to get a really low mark? I am prepared to bet that you felt resentful, and wondered what the teacher was looking for.

By 'essay' and 'report', I mean any extended piece of writing required of your students, including dissertations, reviews or assignment tasks. I call all these 'essays' below. But never mind the students – what about you? You might not have written an essay for some time, or ever! I will also describe how you might tackle the assignments or essays required on your teacher training course.

Essay writing must be taught directly. Students need an explanation of how to go about writing an essay, and they also need to know exactly what is expected of them – in general and for each particular essay. They need to read and discuss good examples; they need practice; and they need informative, constructive feedback on the strengths and weaknesses of each of their attempts. This is particularly important for such a difficult skill, and it is addressed directly in Chapter 43.

What do you want me to do?

Everything that was said about assignments or projects in Chapter 27 also applies to essays. For example, I would argue strongly for detailed guidance notes, and that assessment criteria should be made clear before the essay is started. There are some examples in Chapter 43.

Guidance notes focus student effort in the direction you consider most productive; they can also be changed from year to year to minimise the occurrence of common misunderstandings or omissions. Guidance notes and assessment criteria tell students what to include, not what to leave out, so they are unlikely to be so prescriptive as to hamper an original approach to an essay. Time spent in clarification of the points listed, early on in a course, will be an excellent investment.

How can I best do it?

Make sure you discuss the process of essay writing with your students. College students are often recommended to follow a process similar to that outlined below. Notice that it is a ladder of tasks that climb Bloom's taxonomy.

A simpler version could be devised if that would suit your students better. The students may or may not have been introduced to the topic they must write about.

How to structure writing

If writing darts about from point to point, without any logic or purpose, it is very hard to follow. Writing needs a logical structure. Well-structured writing is easier to write, easier to read, more coherent, less likely to miss important points and much more likely to get a good grade.

In the introduction to Part 2 we saw that there are two ways to analyse a topic, which means to look at it in detail. An atomistic analysis cuts the topic into logical parts which we can number 1, 2, 3, etc. A holistic analysis looks at the whole topic with different 'spectacles' on. That is, we use different perspectives, or points of view, A, B, C, etc. Read pages 152–3 if you are not clear on this.

I will now look at a general approach to structuring writing, then consider some alternatives. This will take some concentration from you, and you may need to read it twice.

The three structures

One of three basic structures will suit almost any essay title, depending on whether the essay requires you:

1   to *describe* or explain something

2   to *compare* two things or evaluate something

3   to *explain* cause and effect.

I am indebted to Oliver Caviglioli, Ian Harris and Janice Evans for this insight, but their approaches differ slightly from mine. Let's look at these three structures in turn. In each case, the structure is best shown visually.

Structuring writing that describes or explains

Consider an essay which asks you to describe, explain, account for or outline something. For example:

>   'Describe the role of the district nurse.'
>   'What is stocktaking and why is it important?'
>   'Outline the legal responsibilities of the teacher.'

Atomistic analysis: Let's take the district nurse example. First, we could cut the role of the district nurse into parts, saying a little about each. Suppose, for example, the parts of the role include: assisting recovery after surgery, caring for the terminally ill, health education for those with diabetes, etc.

The legal responsibilities of a teacher include the following parts: health and safety, the Disability Discrimination Act, equal opportunities legislation, etc.

Holistic analysis: Many people stop after completing an atomistic analysis, but we should also look at the whole topic through useful spectacles.

In the case of the district nurse, the role could be considered from the point of view of the patient, the patient's family, surgeons etc., and also with more abstract spectacles, such as cost or reducing admissions into hospitals.

The teacher's legal responsibilities could be seen from the points of view of the teachers, the students, their parents, or the school or college. Other spectacles may be relevant, depending on the precise question – for example, the government's point of view, inclusion, etc.

A useful way to plan the writing is to use a description table (see page 156 for the detail), which has a row for each part in the atomistic analysis and a row for each spectacle in the holistic analysis. Relevant points are placed in these rows as bullet points. There is also a space for a conclusion. The introduction is best completed *last*, when you know exactly what you are introducing! Once the description table is completed, it is an easy task to write the essay, by working from the introduction downwards, expanding each bullet point into a sentence or paragraph. This is best done the next day, to allow time for the incubation of new ideas.

Many students regard such planning as a waste of time – but, in fact, it saves time. They don't believe it improves the quality of their writing either, but chief examiners disagree – they say the best marks are always achieved by well-structured writing. John Biggs showed that high-grade work always use spectacles (see 'SOLO' in Petty 2006).

If you are not used to planning, you might need to do it a few times before you are really successful. Don't be afraid to add new ideas during the writing process – in the right place. Then, on another day, this draft will need rewriting. See Chapter 30 on creativity.

Structuring writing that compares

Now let's consider writing that compares, contrasts or distinguishes. This includes 'with and without' or 'before and after' questions. For example:

> 'Compare the roles of district nurse and practice nurse.'
> 'What impact did bar codes have on stocktaking?' (comparing before and after bar codes)
> 'Why do teachers use individual learning plans (ILPs)?' (comparing with and without ILPs)

Here, a comparison table (page 156) is useful for planning the writing. This is created by splitting a description table in two. (Alternatively, you can create two separate description tables.) Either way, you can put the two things being compared side by side.

If it is meaningful, the same parts, or at least the same spectacles, can be used for both things being compared.

An alternative approach is to use a 'same and different' diagram (page 156). This works especially well for distinguishing between two things. The distinguishing features are the parts of the diagram that don't overlap. But don't forget to use spectacles too.

Structuring writing that evaluates

Evaluation asks, 'How good is it?'

'Critically appraise the care of the patient in this case study.'
'Evaluate the government's fishing policy.'
'Evaluate the teaching resource you have created.'

Let's take the evaluation of a teaching resource as our example. These questions are often structured by listing strengths and weaknesses. These can be written side by side in a sort of comparison table, but don't forget to use spectacles. An alternative is to first establish criteria which the resource should meet. For example, a teaching resource should:

* **explain clearly**
* **be easy to use**
* **require the student to make sense of it**, etc.

These criteria can then be used in turn as spectacles to look at the resource. As part of any evaluation, you should also consider:

* **alternatives** – other resources that do the same or a similar job
* **fitness for purpose** – does the resource do what it is supposed to do?

This approach – devise criteria, then use the criteria as spectacles – can be used to evaluate anything. Do consider 'alternatives' and 'fitness for purpose' in all evaluations.

Other evaluation criteria or spectacles for evaluating teaching resources are shown on pages 386 and 395.

An alternative approach is to use other graphic organisers, such as mind-maps (page 155) or visual essay planning (pages 352–3). Petty 2006 has a more detailed account of how to structure an evaluation.

Sometimes students are required to evaluate the truth of a statement; this is considered at the end of Chapter 38. Often it helps to describe what you are evaluating before evaluating it, in which case you might use non-evaluative spectacles, such as 'use of colour', before evaluative ones such as 'effectiveness'.

Structuring writing that describes causes and effects

In what way does nutrition affect child development?
What were the main causes of the Second World War?
What factors help to ensure a teaching course is inclusive?

These are all cause-and-effect questions, so description tables or comparison tables won't help, unless you want to describe one of the causes or effects in detail before tackling the main question. Instead, a flow diagram showing the chains of causes and effects can help structure the writing. Once the diagram is completed, it is usually a simple matter to follow the flow of the diagram, expanding each bullet point into a sentence or more. As with other structures, headings may help.

Sometimes it is not easy to decide which of the three structures to use. For example, 'analyse the contribution made by computing to modern teaching methods' could be tackled using any of these three structures because it could be seen as:

- *a description* – describe the 'contribution made'
- *a comparison* – compare computing and non-computing methods
- *a cause and effect* – how can computers cause learning?

So, in this unusual case, you could use all three approaches – one at a time though! Usually, you will be pleased to hear, one structure will do.

Structuring writing is an art rather than a science, so be prepared to be flexible, but do use headings and other pointers to show the reader where they are in your structure – for example, 'So let's now consider the importance of fatty acids in a child's diet.'

> I once saw Janice Evans, a brilliant history teacher, teach this lesson – one of the best I have ever observed. She gave her A-level students a list of 20 or more essay titles from past exams and asked whether a description table or comparison table should be used for each. The students had difficulty with some of them. She asked what the difficult titles had in common, and students realised they were all cause-and-effect questions. She set a homework for students to decide a structure for a cause-and-effect question. Try this lesson yourself!

Using bridging to establish the writing process

Your students will already think they know how to write a report or essay, and you need to improve this conception rather than teach a new one over the top of it. Otherwise they will only revert to their bad practice in times of forgetfulness or exam stress.

The best approach is to get students to write, or at least plan, their first report or essay in class. This is a very useful investment of time and will help them learn the content they write about, as well as the skill of writing. I will describe the use of process proformas like the report-writing help sheet shown on page 310. However, you could adapt the following approach to teach students to structure writing with graphic organisers, as described above.

Hand out the brief with the assessment criteria, but *not* the process sheet shown overleaf, and then ask, 'What should we do first?' They will probably suggest collecting information – hopefully they won't say, 'Find the top-left hand corner of the paper and start writing'! Then you can say, 'But what should we do *before* that?' Once the appropriate task is established, you can ask, 'Why?' and 'What would happen if we had forgotten to do this?'

In this way, you can step your way through the process, after each phase asking, 'What should we do next?' and 'Why?' This should gradually change their conception of how to plan and write.

When you have finished this process and the essay or report is written, or at least planned, ask the bridging questions:

'How did we do that?' Stress that they did a good job, and then ask why they were so successful. This should result in their giving the process back to you. If they miss a stage, say, 'But what should we do before that?' as above. Again ask, 'Why?' and 'What would happen if we missed that stage out?' Get the class to explain and justify the process, using their own names for each stage. When they have finished, you can ask:

'Is there anywhere else we could use that process?' Make them realise that the process was not peculiar to the topic they were writing about, and could be used for any report or essay, or any extended piece of writing. The next time they do a similar piece of writing, remind them of their successful process, and ask them to self-assess how effectively they used it.

You probably won't like the report-writing process shown overleaf – that's fine! Change it or develop your own. But do use bridging to teach whatever process you decide on. It is one of the main methods that Feuerstein uses to add 20 or 30 IQ points to his students.

Alternatively, you could use the ICEDIP processes outlined in Chapter 30. There are still other approaches on www.geoffpetty.com on the generic skills pages.

> *Ten per cent of articles submitted to the quarterly* Journal of Experimental Psychology *are judged to be so unintelligible that it is not possible to decide what experiment (if any) has been carried out! If mature research students find difficulty in expressing themselves, don't expect your students to pick up the skill without help.*

Marking essays

It is vital that your students get good feedback on their essay or report writing in order to learn this difficult skill. See Chapters 6 and especially 43 for the detail on this.

Report-writing process: help sheet
GNVQ Health and Social Care team

Use this process for all reports in all units. When you can use this process well, write
your report without this help sheet, *but still using the process.*

Read, think and plan
Read the assignment brief or title and make sure you understand it thoroughly. Re-read it often.
What will it include? Where could you find information?
When must you hand it in? Plan the report-writing process.

Research and brainstorm
Brainstorm sources of information and points to mention. Then gather information relevant to
the topic. Consider using: library; CD-ROM; Internet; visits; ask people; etc. Re-read the
assignment brief!

Check relevance
Check your information for relevance. Re-read the assignment brief.

Classify
Use an ordered set of headings or mind-maps to sort your information into groups, e.g.:
- topics and subtopics
- strengths and weaknesses
- arguments for and arguments against.

The categories you use will depend on the report title, so re-read it before you start classifying.
Look at the material with different key spectacles or questions in mind.

Draw conclusions and get evidence
What do you want your report to say? For example, what are the strengths and weaknesses of
what you have been investigating?
- *Summarise* your main conclusions.
- Get *evidence* for each of your conclusions.

Plan the report
Make a mind-map or series of headings based on your classification stage. Make notes of what
you want to say. Make sure you do all the tasks or questions.

Write the report, then leave it for a day or so.

Proofread the report, making changes where necessary.

Present the report (one time!).

Report-writing process: help sheet (Health and Social Care team)

> *Try putting one tick in the margin for an important point, and a double tick for a well-made point.*

Coda

In most areas of study, students must understand the rules of clear thinking if they are to write an effective essay – that is, what is and what is not evidence; when generalisations can be made, and when they cannot; the dangers of oversimplification and bias, and the tyranny of labels; and so on. Reasoning is a hugely difficult skill – nobody fully masters it!

There seems to be an invariable law in education that the time spent teaching a skill is in inverse proportion to its importance. We spend a great deal of time teaching facts that can easily be looked up in reference books. We spend very little time developing creative thinking and problem-solving, though our students will be involved in these activities all their lives. But the importance of reasoning is so great that it is usually not taught at all! (See 'The skill of opinion forming', starting on page 429 of this book.)

Checklist

☐ Was the essay well defined in writing, with guidance notes?

☐ Was assessment transparent, and were criteria given in advance?

☐ Were students adequately prepared for the essay?

☐ Have you developed an essay- or report-writing process with your students?

☐ Do students see exemplar essays (not too wonderful), preferably after attempting an essay on the same title themselves?

☐ How would you change the title or guidance notes if you set the same essay next year – have you made a note of these suggestions?

☐ While marking, do you give students medals and missions, or use learning loops, as explained in Chapter 43?

☐ Did a debriefing session confirm what students should have learned?

References

Beard, R. and Hartley, T. (1984) *Teaching and Learning in Higher Education* (4th edition), London: PCP.

Caviglioli, O. and Harris, I. (2008) *Wiseguide to Visual Tools: A Practical Classroom Guide for Raising Achievement*, Stafford: Network Educational Press.

Petty, G. (2006) *Evidence Based Teaching*, Cheltenham: Nelson Thornes.

Sharron, H. and Coulter, M. (1994) *Changing Children's Minds: Feuerstein's Revolution in the Teaching of Intelligence*, Birmingham: Imaginative Minds.

29

Guided discovery: teaching by asking

Welcome to an educational minefield, and a delightful teaching method! But before considering the case for and against discovery learning, let's look at what this teaching method involves.

There are two approaches to teaching: *teaching by telling* and *teaching by asking*.

Teaching by telling. This is teacher-centred or 'didactic' teaching, where learners have the new learning explained to them, and then they are expected to use and remember this new material.

Teaching by asking. The teacher asks questions or sets tasks which require learners to work out the new learning for themselves – though usually with some guidance or special preparation. This new learning is then corrected and confirmed by the teacher. Guided discovery is an example of this latter approach. It may seem perverse, but huge educational advantages are claimed for this method.

'Teaching by asking' can only be used if learners can puzzle out the new learning from their existing knowledge and experience. For example, business studies students could use reason and experience to decide on the various purposes of product packaging. History students could also reason out why the Archbishop of Canterbury, Thomas à Becket, was murdered, given the events leading up to his death. Their answers may need correcting, but the reasoning required by 'teaching by asking' is greatly enjoyed by students, develops their reasoning skills, and provides the teacher with feedback on the students' skills and understanding.

Let's consider some examples. How could a discovery, or 'teaching by asking', approach be used to teach the following?

1. For a circle of any size, the ratio of the circumference to the diameter is 3.14 $(= \pi)$.

2. The time for small swings of a simple pendulum depends on the length of the pendulum, but not on the mass of the bob or the width of the swing.

3. The main motives of adult learners enrolling on adult recreational courses are to develop skills important to their life or career; to gain intellectual stimulation; to follow a hobby or interest; and to enjoy social contact and a change from their home environment.

4. The advantages and disadvantages of laser and inkjet computer printers.

5. How to use French railway timetables.

6. How to solder electrical components onto printed circuit boards.

Let's take each of the above topics in turn:

Topic 1. Assuming the learners are familiar with the concepts of circumference and diameter, the teacher could say: 'Measure the different-sized circles I have given you, and see if you can see any patterns in your data.'

Topic 2. The teacher could ask the learners to guess what variables might affect the time for one swing of a pendulum; and to devise an experiment to investigate each variable in turn, and so discover how they affect the time for one swing.

Topic 3. The teacher could ask the learners to investigate the motives of adult learners, and, if they did not think of it for themselves, be asked to devise and administer a questionnaire to obtain the information for themselves.

Topic 4. The teacher could ask the learners to use such printers themselves, and to survey advertisements in computer magazines to discover the advantages and disadvantages.

Topic 5. The teacher could give the learners copies of French maps and railway timetables, and challenge them to discover, without help, how to travel from Calais to Burgundy.

Topic 6. The teacher could ask the learners to experiment with different types of solder and soldering iron, and with different techniques; and to use this experience to draw up guidelines for soldering.

Which method would you prefer to be taught by: the didactic or the discovery approach? (Note that searching out information from books is not discovery learning.)

Discovery activities are usually carried out in groups. They require high-order thinking skills in order to puzzle them out, and because learners are developing their own meanings, learning is of a high quality. Each member of the group can provide their part of the 'jigsaw puzzle' of understanding for the topic being investigated.

> *Discovery methods are used by many primary teachers, and by many science teachers – for example, the Nuffield Science programme has made extensive use of the method. However, discovery can be used by teachers of all disciplines.*

Effective use of the discovery method

When well devised and managed, the discovery method offers active learning and an achievable challenge which engages interest. Consequently, discovery activities motivate all but the most apathetic students. They are also very effective in developing the learners' understanding. However, it must be stressed that if the activities are poorly thought out, or ineffectively managed, the result can be lack of learning, confused and frustrated students, and a waste of time and goodwill.

How should the method be used? The following are the most important considerations:

Learners must have any essential background knowledge and techniques they need in order to make a success of the discovery activity.

Learners must clearly understand what is expected of them.

It usually helps to have the task precisely and concisely written on the board.

The great majority, if not all, of the learners must be able to make a success of the activity.

This effectively means that guidance must be given where necessary. For example, before starting their soldering activity (topic 6 above), students could be shown how to test a soldered joint. By means of question and answer, the class could also be introduced to the factors which may affect the soldered joint: size of soldering iron bit, where it is placed, time it is in contact, type of solder used, whether flux is used, and so on. The teacher could even suggest experiments for the class to carry out in detail, if they failed to think of their own.

This is 'guided discovery'. Too much guidance, and the students feel cheated of the chance to make their own discovery; too little, and they are floundering in frustration. Clearly you must know your students' capabilities before using this teaching method. Often some groups need more guidance than others, but don't leap in with guidance until the learner(s) have had a chance to think things through for themselves.

In practice, nearly all discovery is guided; it is just a matter of how much guidance has been given. If it took science 2,000 years to arrive at Galileo's ideas about dynamics, one can't expect 2B to do it in an hour and a quarter!

Students' work must be carefully monitored.

Because of their inevitable lack of understanding at the start of the activity, students can spend hours on fruitless activity if left entirely to their own devices. Ask them what they have decided to do. If the method is unsatisfactory, it is usually best to use question and answer to improve it. Here is a teacher who has found a group trying to measure the circumference of a circle by following it with a ruler.

Teacher	How accurate is that method?
Student	Not very; it's hard to do.
Teacher	Try measuring the same circle twice, and see if you get the same answer. (*A little later*) 12 cm and 15 cm for the same circle? That's miles out, isn't it! Can you think of a better way?
Student	Use string? John says we should cut the circles out and roll them …

It sometimes helps if students bring their ideas to the teacher before embarking on them. This gives you the opportunity to check that methods are feasible, and to ensure vital steps or data are included. Alternatively, visit each group in the first few minutes to check they are on the right track.

Sometimes students learn a good deal by being left to see the consequences of their own errors, but this can be counterproductive; guidance is often the safest option. If they waste hours chasing a wild goose with a clutch of red herrings, guess who will be blamed when they find out!

Choose a topic where reasoning is required, but where students are very unlikely to know the answer in full.

It is galling to outline a discovery activity, only to have one or two students shout out 'the answer', even though the activity may still usefully consolidate and confirm their prior knowledge. If you suspect some students do have such knowledge, ask them to keep their ideas to themselves for the sake of the others. If you can, develop a 'stretching activity' for those who finish quickly.

Leave plenty of time.

About twice as much as you expect should do!

Summarise what students should have learned at the end.

This is critical. Some 'discoveries' will lack clarity, and others may be entirely wrong-headed. It is crucial that you summarise the main teaching point(s) of the activity, explaining it fully by reference to their findings. The best way is to ask them what they have learned, and then correct and develop this. If you want students to write their own summaries, then try: 'When you have agreed your conclusion, tell me about it before writing it up.'

> *Students used to teacher-centred methods may need a little practice in the discovery method before they can use it to its full effect.*

Strengths and weaknesses of the discovery method

The discovery method has been criticised for leading students to discover 'the wrong thing', and for leaving learners confused. This, however, is a criticism of the way the method is implemented, not a criticism of the method itself. Every method has such traps, and it is the business of the teacher to avoid them, though it must be said that this method is one of the more difficult for an inexperienced teacher to use. If you are worried by this, show your plans to an experienced teacher or to your tutor/mentor, especially if you have had limited previous contact with the group you will be teaching.

The method is slow, but even this disadvantage can be largely overcome if enough guidance is given.

A far more important limitation of the discovery method, often ignored even by experienced advocates, is that, like all methods, it may not be sufficient by itself. For example, it is one thing to 'discover' an equation describing the oscillation of a simple pendulum; it is another thing to be able to use this equation to predict a pendulum's behaviour. Discovery provides an understanding, but rarely provides corrected practice for all the skills required.

The main advantages of the discovery method, appropriately used, are that:

- It is active, involving, motivating and fun. The questioning involved fosters curiosity, and intrinsic interest in the subject matter.
- Students must 'make their own meaning' – that is, create their own understanding of the subject matter. Consequently, they will understand it, and its links to their prior learning. It is the pre-eminent 'constructivist' method!
- Students are likely to remember what they worked out for themselves.
- It involves the students in high-order thinking: evaluation, creative thinking, problem-solving, analysis, synthesis, etc. By contrast, teacher-centred methods often involve the learner only in low-order skills, such as attending and comprehending.
- As with other student-centred teaching methods, students are encouraged to see learning as something they do to themselves, rather than something that experts do to them. Some teachers believe this 'hidden curriculum' is the method's most important attribute.
- It allows students to enjoy the fun of puzzling things out for themselves, and so arguably it develops their intrinsic as opposed to their extrinsic motivation.

The method does have some limitations. It can be slow, and there is no practical way of using it for some topics – for example, simple, fact-based topics or those where the student is highly unlikely to be able to make the discovery required. As in much group work, there is also a danger of 'passengers' – students who watch rather than participate. You can, however, avoid passengers by nominating students to explain their group's findings after the group discussion, rather than asking for volunteers. This is important, and is explained in Chapter 14 and especially Chapter 24.

The discovery method is still very popular amongst leading theorists; for example, David Ausubel believes that new learning requires appropriate background knowledge, and must be organised by the learner and then integrated into his or her existing knowledge. He sees discovery learning as an excellent method of producing this integrated learning.

Case study: making use of discovery

A media studies lecturer is teaching the historical development of printing in a 90-minute lesson. She is using the CIA process to decide on questions so she can use discovery, or 'teaching by asking'.

Content

Decide on the content you will cover. In this case, it would include the dates of inventions, Acts of Parliament and similar developments affecting printing.

Ideas

What do you want students to notice in this content? What are the main ideas, classifications, concepts or ways of looking at this material? This may include rival interpretations, and the ideas of well-known theorists. Your lesson objectives should mention some of these ideas. In this case of the history of printing, the lecturer decides that the main ideas include:

1   Historically, printing has met the needs of the author, but also those of its intended audience. For example, political pamphlets are a means of campaigning for the author, but a means of information for the populace.

2   You can see the history as a series of technological developments, which governments then attempt to control in their own interests – for example, putting stamp duty on printed matter.

Activities

Now questions are framed to encourage the student to invent, or at least make their own use of, these ideas. For instance, students could be given a factual summary of the history of printing, but with no mention of the 'ideas' above. They could then be asked to consider in groups questions which raise these ideas. For example:

> Looking at the outline historical account, and in your opinion:
>
> In whose interest is printing carried out? (*a hard question based on idea 1*)
>
> (*and/or*) Why did authors publish pamphlets, and why were they read? (*an easier question based on idea 1*)
>
> How have governments reacted to new developments in printing? (*a hard question based on idea 2*)
>
> (*and/or*) What examples of attempted government control over printing do you notice in the historical account, and why did they take place? (*an easier question based on idea 2*)

It is crucial to appreciate that this approach will only work if students are initially given an account which does not include the key ideas you wish to develop. They need the facts without the interpretation, preferably in written form. You can add these interpreting ideas later, once students have carried out their activities. It requires discipline on the part of the teacher not to let these ideas slip out during teacher talk.

Clearly the exact choice of question will depend on the abilities of the students. If discovery is too difficult, you can ask questions which require students to use the ideas rather than discover them. For example:

> Find as many examples as you can in the historical account of:
> (a)   technological developments
> (b)   government reactions to these developments.
> 'For writers such as Swift, pamphlets were a means of campaigning, but for his readers they were a means of access to information.' Is this true? Is it true of today's newspapers? Find evidence for and against.

This is called 'hypothesis testing', (see the end of Chapter 38). It has greatly improved students' attainment in trials (see Petty 2006).

Alternatively, you can use hard questions to begin with, and then use the easier questions to guide weaker groups during the group activity. Try to use the CIA mnemonic to develop a 'teaching by asking' approach to a topic in your own subject.

> *Students do not like being told what to believe. Consequently, the teaching of beliefs and attitudes is usually most successful when guided discovery is used. For example, when exploring sexism with 11-year-olds, a teacher might devise an activity, such as a story or case study, which first uncovers the students' personal desires for fair treatment and freedom from stereotyping. Then, via another case study, the students are asked to say what they think about sexist attitudes. In this way, new attitudes towards sexism are grounded in the students' existing value system; they then 'own' these attitudes, and so they are more likely to be understood and accepted. See Chapter 39.*

Recent controversy

Recently, it has been argued by politicians and the media that 'modern teaching methods' such as the discovery method are a trendy throwback to the permissive 1960s, and are wrong-headed. The discovery method is criticised for not providing enough guidance, and is seen by the critics as confusing for learners. Teachers, it is argued, should go back to 'chalk and talk' methods.

The discovery method is hardly new; it goes back to Socrates, and constructivism has made teachers realise that it is a very natural and effective teaching method.

The diagram on page 19 is worth looking at again here. Discovery is one of the few methods that requires the student to build their constructs on to and out of their prior learning. It discourages rote remembering and the surface learning considered in Chapter 1.

But there are other advantages of this method. Most of the facts we are taught are forgotten, because we don't make repeated use of them. What 30-year-old, for example, remembers the principal exports of Belgium, or the industrial method for the production of sulphuric acid, unless this knowledge has been used since being taught? However, the skills we used while gaining this knowledge are largely still with us, because we make use of such skills almost every day of our lives. I refer to thinking skills such as the ability to learn new ideas and express them concisely; to order and structure our knowledge and understanding; to puzzle out a procedure so it can be expressed in terms of previous knowledge and understanding; to solve problems and evaluate; and so on. These, of course, are the very skills used in discovery learning.

> *Those in the cognitive school think highly of bafflement. They suggest that bafflement motivates the learner to utilise previous learning to come to an understanding.*
>
> *'We think of the mind as a storehouse to be filled when we should be thinking of it as an instrument to be used.'*
>
> J. W. Gardener, *Self-Renewal* (1963)
>
> *'Education is what survives when what has been learned has been forgotten.'*
>
> B. F. Skinner

Early cognitivists argued that education should concentrate on teaching learners concepts, relationships, creative thinking, problem-solving and other thinking skills, and should not simply teach facts. They warned against rote methods which, though they might get quick results initially, were soon forgotten and did not produce genuine understanding. John Dewey (1859–1952), the champion of learning by doing, said that 'mechanical drill' would 'strengthen traits likely to be fatal to reflective power.'

Jerome Bruner (born 1915) expressed the view that 'expository teaching' deprived students of the chance to think for themselves. He said the modern curriculum should strip away all but the bare facts, and leave time for teaching thinking skills. He thought intelligence was the 'internalisation of cognitive tools', and believed it could be improved by appropriate teaching.

The cognitivists were hardly expressing a new idea. For centuries, an education in classics was considered suitable preparation for almost any employment, on the grounds that it 'trained the mind'; and the Civil Service has always recruited graduates of any discipline. Perhaps one day we will have a curriculum based on cognitive skills, rather than an exclusively knowledge-based curriculum.

Now virtually all educationalists believe that useful learning:

- is not the same as remembering facts and techniques – it is making constructs or personal meanings
- must be organised by the learner and then integrated into the learner's existing knowledge
- involves developing cognitive skills such as the ability to reflect critically, to evaluate, to analyse, to think creatively and to solve problems.

> *If learning is just remembering, why are people who do well in intelligence tests usually better learners than those with excellent memories? (IQ tests measure the abilities of pattern recognition, non-verbal and verbal reasoning, and problem-solving.)*

How can we teach a history student to think like a historian, or a science student to think like a scientist? These students will only learn to reason *by reasoning*. It is only by asking students thought-provoking questions that these crucial thinking skills can be developed. When these history and science students have forgotten their dates and formulae, and are working as hotel managers, carers or entrepreneurs, it will be their thinking skills which will be the true, and untarnishable, legacy of their education. As a consequence, many teachers consider that the way we teach (the learning *process*) is at least as important as *what* we teach (the learning *product*).

If a history teacher *tells* their students why the Archbishop of Canterbury, Thomas à Becket, was murdered, then students will be using and so developing the skills of comprehension and recall. However, if they are only told of the events leading up to his death, and then asked to reason out 'who did it, why and with what likely consequences?', they will also be developing the ability to create and sustain a historical argument. Furthermore, they will be more deeply engaged in the subject matter and so will be more likely to remember and comprehend the facts.

So what are we, as teachers, to make of the controversy between guided discovery and 'teaching by telling' methods? Professor John Hattie has collected together and analysed over 140,000 experiments attempting to raise student attainment. He finds that the experiments which worked best all set students challenging tasks, not attainable tasks (see Petty 2006). Some research on guided discovery has had spectacular results. The 'Cognitive Acceleration through Science Education' research project (CASE) was specifically designed to develop thinking skills through discovery learning; with very little science curriculum time, it was shown to improve examination results markedly. Interestingly, the improvement was not just in science subjects, but in mathematics and English as well. Despite further success in other subjects and at primary level, the ideas developed in the project have not been adopted in the national curriculum.

The characteristics of the modern world, such as job mobility, the knowledge explosion and the pace of change within jobs, all require students to have adaptable cognitive skills, rather than a mastery of a narrow set of low-level knowledge and skills.

Discovery is fun, it is motivating and it develops thinking skills in our learners – and research seems to show it has value. It is a very natural way to learn; children and animals spontaneously learn in this way, so it fits with the way our brain has evolved. You must decide for yourself whether to use guided discovery, but most informed opinion now considers that what happens in the learning 'process' is at least as important as its 'product'.

Teacher
controlled

    rote-memorising
    lecture

    questioning

    practical work

    individual work

    group work

    discussion

    guided discovery

    independent learning

    student-directed learning

Student
controlled

(The positions of the teaching methods on this continuum are only approximate, as they depend on context.)

Further reading

*Adey, P. and Shayer, M. (1994) *Really Raising Standards*, London: Routledge. Describes the effectiveness of the CASE programme, and the theoretical background to cognitivist ideas.

Ausubel, D. (1978) *Educational Psychology: A Cognitive View*, New York: Holt, Rinehart & Winston.

*Inhelder, B. and Piaget, J. (1958) *The Growth of Logical Thinking from Childhood to Adolescence*, London: Routledge.

Petty, G. (2006) *Evidence Based Teaching*, Cheltenham: Nelson Thornes.

Shayer, M. and Adey, A. (2002) *Learning Intelligence*, Buckingham: Open University Press.

30

Creativity, design and invention

Ask reasonably motivated students to make notes on the dangers of drug abuse, and they will politely comply; ask them to design a leaflet on drug abuse for distribution in their college or school, and they will be fired with enthusiasm. Creative activities are fun, and increase the learners' sense of self-worth. Whatever your subject discipline, you cannot afford to ignore their motivating effect.

Creativity is often seen as the exclusive territory of the creative arts; yet just stand in a modern department store and look around you. You are surrounded by the products of the creative imagination. In the 'real world', creative skills are vital. They are required for product initiation and design, marketing, packaging, management, childcare, teaching, engineering, house decorating and housekeeping, architecture, cooking, writing, research and development, entrepreneurial development, window dressing, store layout ... Indeed, creative skills are necessary for anyone involved with thinking up new ideas and techniques, or with problem-solving. Creativity is a teachable skill, not just a gift or talent, and, like all skills, it improves with corrected practice.

Creative work is important for the teacher of any subject, for four main reasons:

* *To develop our students' ability to think creatively and to solve problems.*
* *To enable students to use knowledge productively and meaningfully.*
* *To increase motivation.* Creativity satisfies a deep human need to make something and to gain recognition for this. Maslow's hierarchy of human needs places emphasis on self-esteem and self-actualisation, both of which can be satisfied by creative work. Being creative is fun.
* *To provide an opportunity to explore feelings and develop skills in self-expression.* There is more to education than learning facts and work-based skills. Students need to exercise their imagination, and explore feelings and perceptions. They need to make personal meanings of their experiences, and to express these to others.

A New York school was dismayed by discipline problems so extreme that armed guards were employed to roam the corridors. They consulted a curriculum expert, who suggested they introduce creative work into the school. The students were encouraged to paint, put on plays and musicals and do other creative work. Within a year there was no need for the guards.

Planning for creative work

Whilst creativity is a mysterious process, it is not beyond understanding or influence. With the right preparation and activities, the quality of your learners' creative work can be massively improved.

What are the needs of learners when they are involved in creative work? First, they need an introduction to the use of the basic tools and skills. They need to know how to use the wood-lathes, paints or inverted commas that will be the medium for their creative expression (though the creative work itself can of course be used to develop these skills further). Let's suppose this initial need has been at least partially met.

Encouraging creativity

The creative process is complex and variable, and only a simple outline of activities which can improve creativity can be given here. I deal with this fascinating and important topic in more detail in *How to Be Better at Creativity*. The process can be seen as consisting of six phases: inspiration, clarification, distillation, incubation, perspiration and evaluation. (The first letters of the six phases can be arranged to produce the mnemonic ICEDIP.) In the course of producing a single piece of work, each phase may be encountered many times, and not in any particular sequence. However, at any given time, the learner will usually be concentrating on one phase or another. Let's examine each of the phases.

Inspiration

This is the research phase, and involves an uncritical search for ideas. The process is an uninhibited exploration and is characterised by spontaneity, experimentation, intuition, untrammelled imagination and risk-taking improvisation. Very much as in the first stage in brainstorming (see Chapter 19), the idea is to develop as many ideas as possible, however off-beam or impractical they may seem initially. In the field of the creative arts, this phase is often associated with a voice, and with an attempt to conjure up deep sympathy, spirituality or empathy with the subject matter.

If students 'can't think of anything', they could be having difficulty with this inspiration phase. Encourage them to try out 'any old thing', without being in any way self-critical. This is not the stage for worrying about form, composition, practicality, rhyme or metre, etc.; the aim is to think up as many imaginative ideas as possible. If most of the ideas produced are workable, not enough risks were taken.

Henry Moore often roamed the seashore, picking up curious pebbles and shells that fed his current interests, and his work seems to have been in part inspired by the weathered shapes of pebbles.

Picasso's painting was inspired by a visit to an exhibition of carved African masks. He abandoned his literal realistic style, to adopt the symbolic non-representational style of the masks in his paintings. This created an artistic revolution, and a furious public reaction!

Clarification

The idea here is to clarify the purpose or objective of the work. It is characterised by the question: 'What am I trying to do or say?' When a student is stuck for the next sentence in an essay, try asking 'What do you want the line to say?' Often they have no idea, and rather than dreaming up a stream of alternatives they need to consider carefully where the sentence, paragraph or essay is going. A similar argument holds for other forms of creative work. In this phase, the student is being logical, analytical and purposeful, and has his or her eye on the horizon.

Distillation

Here the ideas thrown up by the inspiration phase (or the perspiration phase – see below) are sifted through and evaluated, perhaps in the light of the findings of a clarification phase. The best ideas are chosen for further development. This is a self-critical editing phase. It requires cool analysis and judgement rather than spontaneous idea generation. However, it should not be so critical as to inhibit productivity entirely.

Incubation

It is often difficult to achieve this in practice, but ideally there should occasionally be a few days of inactivity while working on a creative project. This gives time for the subconscious to work on any problems encountered, and provides the learners with a chance to get some distance between themselves and their ideas, so that they are better able to evaluate them. Incubation is particularly useful after an inspiration or a perspiration phase, or if a problem has been encountered. Whilst there is no formal activity during this phase, learners should be encouraged to mull over what they are doing. Creative people rarely snatch at their first idea, and they are content to let half-baked ideas, loose ends and inconsistencies brew away in their subconscious until 'something turns up'.

> *Whenever Sir Isaac Newton had a particularly thorny problem, he worked on it just before he went to sleep. He said, 'I invariably woke up with the solution.'*

Perspiration

Once ideas have been chosen, they are worked on to produce a first draft, though this may well involve further inspiration, clarification and perspiration phases.

> *'Genius is 1% inspiration, 99% perspiration.'*
>
> Thomas Edison

Evaluation

Here you examine the draft for strengths and weaknesses, and consider how it can be improved. Then there will be another perspiration phase, where you implement the improvements to make a second draft. There may be many drafts and redrafts before you judge the work complete.

Remember that though the first letters of the six phases can usefully be ordered to spell ICEDIP, the phases are unlikely to occur in this or any other order, and each phase may be experienced many times in a given piece of work.

Mindsets and creative blocks

One of the main difficulties of the creative process is that the different phases require radically different 'mindsets'. These are described below:

Inspiration. Uncritical, deeply involved, spontaneous, fearless, risk-taking, self-believing, intuitive, joyful, 'slap-happy' and improvisational. Judgement is suspended almost completely.

Clarification. Strategic, purposeful, unhurried and not afraid to ask difficult questions.

Evaluation. Critical of the work, but positive about your vision and your ability to realise it. Willing to learn.

Distillation. Positive and intrepid about the potential of ideas rather than how well they are worked out at present, and strategic about choices.

Incubation. Trusting of yourself to find a way forward, unhurried and forgetful.

Perspiration. Persevering, uncritical, enthusiastic and responsive to evaluation.

Many people find it very difficult to switch from one mindset to another, especially if they have an overpoweringly prevalent mindset. Fewer still realise that switches in mindsets are necessary.

If a student approaches a phase with the wrong mindset, they are almost bound to be ineffective. It is no good being critical and perfectionist when searching for ideas, and it is no good being uncritical and 'slap-happy' when choosing from alternative ideas. It is common to find learners who are strong in one phase and weak in another. One student will be full of ideas, but unable to evaluate them critically; while another will have a dearth of ideas on which to apply their good judgement.

Most 'creative blocks' are due to people trying to use an inappropriate phase, an inappropriate mindset, or both.

Learners and the creative phases

In contrast to the complex process described in the phases above, 'uncreative' people will tend to latch on to the first idea that comes to them, and quickly and uncritically bring it to completion without serious thought about what they are trying to achieve. How can we encourage learners to go through all the phases mentioned, and so increase their creative potential?

One of the teacher's roles during creative work is to help learners manage whichever are their weaker phases. This is done by choosing activities which help them cure their creative constipation or design diarrhoea, and by *explaining and discussing the creative phases with them*. Tell them about ICEDIP. Make it clear that their first idea will not necessarily be their best; that ideas can be worked on; that even for the greatest, great ideas almost never come in a flash; that it is important to have a clear idea of what one is trying to achieve; and so on. Make it clear that the creative process is the same for painting and for engineering, for business management and for poetry. There are handouts and questionnaires to help you in the Chapter 24 downloads at: www.geoffpetty.com/evidence_based_downloads.htm

Anyone can make use of the creative process, and anyone can improve their application of it. The ability to think and act creatively is a skill all students need, no matter what walk of life they follow, no matter what their hobbies or interests. Also, exercising their creative muscle can be a hugely rewarding part of your students' lives.

It can be a route to self-fulfilment and happiness for many, and a way of making a meaning of their lives for some. Creative action is one of life's greatest challenges, and so one of its greatest rewards. So why not teach our students how to do it?

> *'Imagination is more important than knowledge.'*
>
> Albert Einstein

Encouraging the inspiration phase

Sometimes one can provide students with an activity which helps them generate ideas. This is often best done at the start of the creative session. For example, if students are expected to write some prose about the sea, they could browse through books relevant to the subject, or look at paintings or photographs of the sea, noting down as they do so any words, phrases or observations which strike them – without any preconceptions about whether or how these ideas might be used. They could be asked to recall personal experiences or read examples of good writing on the subject.

Word association is another method for generating material. Students could be given two minutes to write down as many words or phrases as they can think of on the subject of the sea. A variant of this is to write down word chains, where each word is suggested *only* by the immediately previous word in the chain – for example, 'Sea, saltwater, tears, cry, shout, danger …' Carefully looking at such chains can suggest useful ideas and associations; this process is particularly useful for creative writing.

> *An uninhibited personal brainstorming session often generates useful ideas.*

It often helps if the inspiration phase forces students away from what would otherwise be the conventional-thinking route to an obvious or clichéd piece of work. 'Kick-start' material, with only an oblique relevance to the subject matter, is often surprisingly productive, as it encourages a more unusual approach. A magazine article about a tidal barrage, or a coastguard safety leaflet, will suggest more original words or approaches to the sea topic than examining a description of the sea in a novel. The more material the better; rifle the library!

More advanced students can try lateral thinking techniques pioneered by Edward de Bono. These techniques may seem oddball and most unlikely to produce ideas with any merit; but all I ask is that you try them seriously yourself for half an hour. Further recommendation from me will then be unnecessary! Here are a few of them.

Random association

This has the advantage of throwing one off well-trodden paths. Words are chosen at random from the dictionary, and then word association is used to work towards the desired subject matter. Here is an example of this technique as used by a student who is looking for ideas for the subject of a painting, to be entered for a competition in the category 'Human Group'. The words on the left are those generated at random from the dictionary. They then try to work towards 'group' from this random word:

recite → poem or reading → group as an audience at a poetry reading

revelation → religious revelation → angel appearing to group of shepherds

glove → hand → handshake → group of people meeting for the first time

glow → fire → group of people round a camp fire

Don't let students give up on one of these chains too easily. However, around 70% of the chains probably won't work.

This technique can be used in almost any creative work, whether devising the plot for a short story, problem-solving or dealing with design problems. In the following example, a student uses the technique to consider ideas for a device that will automatically water plants when the owner is on holiday:

spark → fire → fires can be thermostatically controlled; could a plant pot have a humidity detector that automatically turned on a water supply when a certain level of dryness was reached?

impale → spike → could a spike or pipe which slowly releases water be stuck in the soil?

purse → money → paper → soggy paper; could some kind of highly absorbent material be soaked and placed under the flowerpot to prevent it from drying out?

There is no end to these random and oblique-relevance approaches:

- To look for colour combinations for a wallpaper pattern, try throwing cut-out shapes from magazine pictures on to a white background.
- Try cutting out lots of words and phrases that appeal to you from a newspaper, and then randomly ordering them to produce ideas for a story or poem. (David Bowie has used this technique when writing lyrics.)
- To find interesting shapes for a fabric design, try looking at photographs of microbes.

> *Beethoven is said to have used the rhythm of the hooves of a running horse passing his window when writing a movement of a piano sonata. Using random or oblique sources for inspiration ensures that one escapes the obvious. Why not encourage relatively advanced or motivated students to keep a journal or scrapbook of ideas that interest them? This can then be used for inspiration.*

CAP

This stands for 'consider all possibilities'. For example, if one 'did a CAP' on how the automatic plant waterer could be powered, one might come up with electricity, elastic band, gas, compressed air, clockwork, compressed spring, hamster wheel, petrol, battery, wind, gravity … Every possibility is considered, feasible or not. Each idea suggests a different approach to the design, some practical, some not. CAP forces one to consider possibilities which would otherwise be passed over for no good reason. A musician could 'do a CAP' when working out what bass note would best harmonise a short melodic passage; a whole series of notes would simply be tried in turn.

Po

'Po', as used by de Bono, stands for 'provocation'. A provocative statement is made which is clearly ludicrous, but would be very convenient or interesting. Rather than rejecting the statement, it is worked on to see if it yields any useful or productive ideas. For example:

> 'Po: suppose the plant could water itself.' After a little thought, this leads to the possibility of water transpiring or evaporating from the plant's leaves being put back into its soil. This might lead to the idea of putting a plastic covering of some kind over the plant, so that water would not be able to escape from the plant and pot.

'Po' is particularly useful in group work.

Backtracking

If one is at a dead end, it is often helpful to go back a few paces and take a different route. To take the plant-watering example again, if the design team was experiencing difficulty developing a cheap electrical design, they could 'backtrack' and look at a gravity-fed design which would probably be cheaper. This may seem an obvious strategy, but it is often ignored in practice, as one does not like abandoning an idea in which there is a large investment of time or emotion.

When encouraging inspiration, concentrate on novelty and quantity. The ideas will generate more ideas, and sooner or later something useful comes up. The vast majority of the material generated will be rejected, but what remains is likely to be sound, as well as imaginative.

Creativity is like mining for diamonds: most of what you dig up is thrown away. But that does not make the digging a waste of time!

Encouraging the remaining phases

The other phases in the creative process are more easily encouraged; one simply needs to set appropriate tasks:

Clarification phase. 'I want you to produce a clear statement of exactly what you want your leaflet to achieve. When your group has agreed it, write it down and show it to me.'

Distillation phase. 'Now rifle through your notes and decide on your best ideas; then see if you can choose which ones you want to work on.'

Incubation phase. Here it is simply a question of making the necessary time available – though with crowded curricula, 'simply' may not always be the right word!

Perspiration phase. 'Now you have decided which ideas you like, get going on them and produce a rough first draft.'

Evaluation phase. 'Now look at your draft and ask yourself what are the strongest and weakest aspects of it; see if you can see how to learn from this, and how to make your second draft better …'

> *'In some cases creativity has been abused by being allied with a vague permissiveness, with the notion that whatever happens in the classroom should be allowed to happen without the constraints of moral, critical or imaginative judgements. In other cases, teachers, with a primitive conception of inspiration, have urged children to write spontaneously but without consideration of an attentive audience. This may, of course, be a way of beginning – but if imaginative work stays at this level it will quickly deteriorate into mass cliché and private rhetoric.'*
>
> Peter Abbs, *Root and Blossom* (1976)

Creativity in practice

Creative work never follows a strict pattern, so it is not easy to plan for. However, consideration of the ICEDIP phases can help to make your creative lessons more productive. Let's look at some case studies that make use of ideas in this chapter. Even if the case studies are not in your subject area, you can still learn from the teacher's general approach. You might like to work out your own approaches to the cases before seeing the teacher's solutions.

Case 1. An embroidery class with adult learners who are reasonably experienced at 'embroidering by numbers'. Their teacher, Valerie, is keen to get the class to generate their own ideas, despite their lack of confidence in design. She wants each student to develop his or her own simple abstract design.

Case 2. An English language class of fairly able students. Their teacher, Hilary, has allowed each student to choose a title for a poem about an animal, or to make up his or her own title. We will take Clive as an example; he has chosen the title 'On finding a dead fox'. The other students in the class will follow a similar process with their titles.

The use of the phases described below is in outline only, making the process seem simpler and more logical than it really was.

Valerie's class (Case 1)

Clarification and 'doing-detail'. Valerie shows the group five pieces of original embroidery work and asks them to work in teams of 'judges', as if they are judging a competition. Each group is asked to agree what constitutes a good abstract embroidery design. Eventually, each student uses this as a basis to draw up a personal design brief (e.g. bold simple shapes, strong colours, etc.).

Inspiration. The next week she takes to the class a number of photocopies of a photograph of a stairway. This high-contrast photograph looks almost like a complex geometrical design in itself. She shows the students how to place two mirrors on their photocopy so as to produce a kaleidoscope effect. Moving the mirrors over the photocopy generates a very wide variety of symmetrical designs. Others cut out a small rectangle in a large piece of card, and move this over the photocopy to generate unsymmetrical designs.

She asks each student to use ideas obtained from the mirrors and card to produce four designs, and to sketch these out roughly.

Distillation. With the help of their design criteria, students choose the best of their four designs.

Perspiration. They produce a first draft of the basic shapes, ignoring colour.

Evaluation. They are then asked to isolate this design's main strengths and weaknesses, and to modify the design (*perspiration*) to put this right. (This takes many drafts and redrafts in some cases.)

Inspiration. Students look through colour photographs of garden flowers, lichen, shrubs, wild birds, etc., to get ideas for a colour scheme for their design. The first coloured draft of the design is then produced, using paints and paper.

Hilary's class (Case 2)

Inspiration. Clive is given a 'homework' to go to the library to find books containing colour photographs of foxes. He is told to read about his subject matter, and make notes of facts, ideas, words and phrases that appeal to him. He is also asked to do a word-association list using the words suggested by his title: 'dead', 'fox', 'find'. He finishes up with two pages of words and phrases.

Clarification. After the class has studied some poems with clear central ideas or messages, Clive and the rest of his class are asked to read through their notes and decide on a central idea or message for *their* poems. They are asked to produce three different ideas (but Clive is only able to produce one that he is keen on).

Distillation and perspiration. Clive is asked to take his favourite idea and produce four opening lines, making them as striking as possible; to do this, he makes use of some of the best ideas from his two pages of words and phrases.

Creativity as a 'how to' skill

Some people consider creativity to be an unteachable gift. This is nonsense. Whether the medium is painting, fabric design, engineering design, creative writing, original experimental work, musical composition, creative problem-solving, creative management or some other field of creativity, learners can improve their skill. This requires attention to both process and product.

Learners certainly need to become aware of the creative process that I have tried to describe in this chapter, and must learn to manage it effectively. But they also have to learn about the medium in which they are working, to discover how to make an effective painting, poem, design or whatever. This is a 'how to' skill, so it is useful to examine the elements in the mnemonic *educare?* (see Chapter 2) to see how it could be developed.

Explanation. Students need the theory of the medium in which they are working. For example, they may need some notion of the ideas of form, structure and rhythm in poetry; composition in painting; economy, boldness and simplicity in engineering design; and so on. Do they understand something of their discipline, along with its traditions and schools?

'Doing-detail'. Concrete examples of good practice (e.g. the work of experts/masters in the chosen field) can be analysed to good effect. From this, students should be encouraged to discover the general principles of good practice in the medium they are studying. They will need your guidance here. Students may not all agree on these principles, of course; but if they develop their own ideas, so much the better. Even the great masters learned from, and were inspired by, previous great masters. Students can also learn what not to do from bad practice!

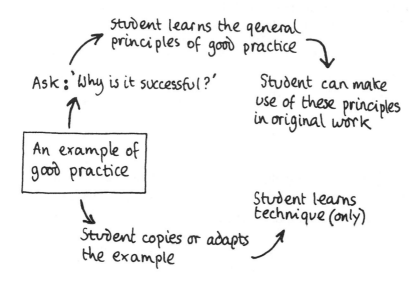

Use. Learners need time to experiment and develop their ideas.

Check and correct. It is even more important in creative work than in other forms of learning that learners criticise and correct their own work. However, a teacher can obviously help enormously, especially in technical matters. It helps if the teacher and the learner are both aware of what the learner is trying to achieve.

Aide-memoire. This often helps to clarify techniques and principles.

Evaluation. Learners gain immeasurably from evaluating their own and each other's work, especially in open discussion with peers and/or a teacher. Appeal to general principles should be encouraged, rather than simple statements of taste. Severe criticism of each other's work is probably counterproductive.

? As always, it is helpful to be able to share difficulties and queries in a supportive atmosphere.

In a further case study, let's examine an example of how *educare?* might be used to choose activities for a design class.

Case 3

Students are to produce a new design for a supermarket's carrier bag.

Explanation. The functions of carrier bags must be explained or discussed.

'Doing-detail'. A varied selection of 'concrete examples of good (and bad) practice' are examined critically by the class. This process is then used to agree on some criteria for good carrier bag design – for example, strength of handles, simplicity and boldness of graphics, biodegradable plastic … This makes really clear what is expected of the design – and of the learner.

Use. Students produce some designs.

Check and correct. Students are asked to evaluate their own, and perhaps each other's, designs against their design criteria.

Aide-memoire. The design criteria are likely to be written down.

Review. What relevant ideas can students use from previous learning?

Evaluation. Ideally, learners should be involved with the evaluation of their completed designs, to sharpen their critical faculties – and therefore their self-critical faculties. Perhaps there could also be a public showing of the work, with a comments book?

The atmosphere should be supportive, with learners able to get their queries answered.

It is not enough to give students the brief and then leave them to it! Creative work rarely follows a smooth path to completion, and people like to work in different ways. As a result, it is impossible to be prescriptive about the process, but I hope that the ideas above will at least help you to devise useful activities.

Perhaps the best way to teach the creative process is by bridging, as described in Chapters 28 and 31; this will be more effective than teaching ICEDIP directly.

Checklist for encouraging creativity

❑ Have you explained the ICEDIP phases and their associated 'mindsets' to your students?

❑ Do you make conscious use of the ICEDIP phases in your lesson plans?

❑ Have your students been shown, and carefully examined, work of a high standard in order to learn the general principles of good practice?

❑ Are students encouraged to use general principles when creating their own work?

❑ Are students encouraged to use general principles in the criticism of their own work, and the work of others?

EXERCISES

Use the *educare?* mnemonic and the ICEDIP phases to develop learning activities to help students do one of the following:

1 Develop a T-shirt design for the 'Grannies for Fitness Campaign'.
2 Write a short story with the title 'Ambush!'
3 Design a jar opener for people with arthritis.
4 Think of ways of collecting money for a local charity.
5 Design an experiment to measure air pollution.

Further reading

*Maslow, A. (1993) *The Farther Reaches of Human Nature*, London: Penguin Arkana. On the psychology of creativity.

Moseley, D. *et al.* (2005) *Frameworks for Thinking*, Cambridge University Press.

*Petty, G. (1997) *How to Be Better at Creativity*, London: Kogan Page. Explains in detail the ICEDIP model, mindsets, tools, blocks, etc. See also creativity pages on www.geoffpetty.com

Petty, G. (2006) *Evidence Based Teaching*, Cheltenham: Nelson Thornes.

*Vernon, P. E. (1970) *Creativity: Selected Readings*, London: Penguin Educational. See the Carl Rogers essay in particular.

31

Learning from experience

In his history of the First World War, A. J. P. Taylor graphically describes the terrible carnage resulting from wave after wave of Allied assaults on the heavily defended German trenches. The tactic, though fruitless, was repeated by the generals with chilling determination. Taylor concludes that 'Nothing had been learnt from previous failures except how to repeat them on a larger scale.'

Experience in itself does not guarantee learning. In order to learn from experience, we must reflect on our experiences; try to relate them to theory; and then plan how we might do better next time. After carrying out this plan, we need to reflect again, and so the process continues. This cyclic 'experiential learning' process is much the same whether we are learning military strategy, coronary care or how to write essays. We also learn to teach by following this cycle.

The 'experiential learning cycle' was first suggested by Dewey, but developed by David Kolb. A learner can start the cycle at any point, but the stages should be followed in sequence.

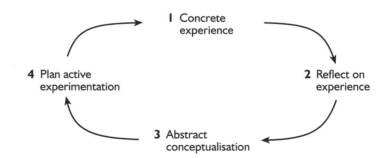

Let's illustrate the cycle with an example. Suppose you wanted to grow prize carrots. You might start on this learning process by (2) *reflecting critically* on your carrot-growing achievements to date. This would lead on to (3) *abstract conceptualisation*, where you consider your experience in the light of theory – for example, soil type, soil pH, spacing, variety of carrot grown. This would lead you to a plan of how to grow better carrots next year – that is, *planning active experimentation* (4). You then have the *concrete experience* (1) of carrying out this plan, which again is reflected on (2), and so on.

Note that the learning process is cyclic, and can go on indefinitely. Whether consciously or not, virtually all successful learning from experience follows this cycle. Let's look at an example of a teacher choosing and ordering learning experiences to follow the experiential learning cycle. This should maximise the learning that takes place from experience.

A case study

A catering lecturer is teaching students how to organise a restaurant kitchen. The students experience one four-hour session every week working in a training restaurant, preparing meals for members of the public. This experience is realistic and intense!

After a session in the training restaurant (1), the teacher holds a debriefing session where students discuss this practical experience. The teacher starts by encouraging the students to reflect on the experience (2). First, facts are established: how did the practice go? Then discussion moves on, with students addressing such questions as: What were the group's successes and failures? How did you all feel during the practical session? What would have happened if … ? How did you feel at the time? Did you work well when you were rushed? Was anybody resentful about their role? The aim is an honest but non-accusatory evaluation of performance, where mistakes are seen as inevitable and even valuable. It's all right to fail, if you (and others) can learn from your mistakes.

 In Chinese, the word for disaster also means opportunity.

Having reflected, the teacher steers the discussion on to 'abstract conceptualisation' (3). What are the general principles that the group can learn from their experience? The teacher may well need to act as midwife here, establishing principles from apparently unconnected events, such as, 'If a task needs doing, someone must be made responsible for it', or 'Unless preparation is comprehensive for each dish, serving will be delayed'. In practice, great stress should be given to these 'learning outcomes'. General principles like these should find their way into the students' notes and, more importantly, should be adopted by them in future practice. Without the teacher to 'mediate' like this, many learners fail to learn.

The next stage is active experimentation (4), where the students are asked to plan how they will organise themselves for the next session. The design could be carried out in some detail, with students assigning themselves responsibilities for the session, and personal action plans being devised. For example, John agrees to read up the recipes in advance, Paula resolves to be less shy about asking for help when she knows she is behind, and so on.

A discussion such as this is a time-consuming process; 10 minutes of concrete experience can generate hours of reflection, abstract conceptualisation and planning active experimentation. Sometimes it is necessary to restrict discussion to one or two themes.

The four stages are now examined in more detail.

1 Concrete experience

Experience can be realistic – for example, students using a woodwork lathe, or taking part in a work experience programme. Alternatively, and usually less effectively, the experience offered can be a substitute for a 'real-life' one. Here are some examples of the latter:

Observing an experienced practitioner (live or on video), e.g. a trainee shop assistant observing someone serving in a shop.

Case study, e.g. doctors discussing case notes, or management trainees discussing the strike record of a company.

Students discussing each other's experience, e.g. interviewing each other about how they approach essay writing; listening to each other's experience of work shadowing; etc. (Student diaries or logbooks are sometimes helpful for this activity.)

Games and role-play, e.g. students of industrial relations acting out an industrial dispute, in which they take the parts of employers and employees.

Simulation, e.g. nurses working on a computer simulation for intensive care.

Demonstration, i.e. the students watch a teacher demonstration.

'Concrete experience' should be used by students to test out ideas, methods and plans, rather than to repeat well-known procedures mindlessly. For example, when students are writing a poem, welding a joint or observing an experienced social worker, they should be trying out a new technique or approach, or looking for something they have not paid particular attention to before. Ideally, the 'concrete experience' should be informed by sessions of 'planning active experimentation' (stage 4).

Learning from work experience

Graham Gibbs, in his excellent book on experiential learning, *Learning by Doing*, suggests that substitutes for direct work experience are useful in order to:

- practise skills in safe contexts
- illustrate theory in action
- develop interpersonal skills
- increase personal involvement in learning and enliven topics
- derive theory or general principles from examples
- prepare learners for work experience
- focus attention on experiences which are difficult or impossible to provide in any other way.

---

2 Reflection on experience

Reflection involves a systematic and objective evaluation of the student's 'concrete experience', perhaps along with an examination of his or her feelings at the time. This may largely be undertaken by or with the teacher at first, but the long-term aim should be to get the students to carry out the process by themselves.

Reflection through self-assessment

There is a danger in students relying solely on their teacher for the evaluation of their performance. If they are never trusted to evaluate their own experience, they will not acquire the habits and skills of reflecting on their performance, and so they will not develop the ability to improve themselves. The aim must surely be to produce a student who has the confidence and skill to reflect and evaluate independently of the teacher. Give students confidence in their ability to learn from their own experience, and when your teaching finishes, their learning continues. The student becomes a 'reflective practitioner'.

You can encourage self-assessment during debriefing sessions by asking questions such as, 'What were the main difficulties your group had?' rather than saying, for example, 'Lack of preparation was your main problem'. Try to avoid the temptation to help too much.

You can also encourage self-assessment by asking students to draw up a self-assessment checklist, preferably in advance of the experience. This serves the dual purpose of aiding reflection and focusing the students' efforts in the right direction. It also encourages the students to analyse the process carefully and to ask questions. For example, before carrying out a welding operation, students could write a checklist of objectives that define a satisfactory weld. This could be checked by the teacher. The students then carry out and assess the weld. Students are often harsher in evaluating their own performance than the teacher would be.

A self-assessment checklist by a student learning how to chair a meeting:

1 Did I stick to the agenda?
2 Did I maintain everyone's interest?
3 Did I prevent red herrings?
4 Did everyone get a fair share of the time to express their views?
5 Was I able to summarise the decisions?

Self-assessment encourages reflection and purposeful activity towards useful goals, as well as encouraging learners to become responsible for their own learning. (See Chapter 43 for self- and peer assessment.)

Peer assessment

Peer assessment is another means of encouraging reflection. Checklists can be used in a similar way as for self-assessment, and the advantages of peer assessment are similar to those of self-assessment.

Diaries and journals

Here is a further way of encouraging students to reflect on their experience. Students are provided with a diary folder and asked to write in it every day when still reasonably fresh. Diaries are perhaps particularly useful where emotional responses are strong, as, for example, with students of social work, teaching or nursing.

After completing a day on a geriatric ward, a student nurse could record factual material about her experiences first, and then her emotional responses; then, what she found difficult or rewarding; what made her feel uneasy; what she felt her strengths and weaknesses were. If she describes problems, she is asked to say how these could have been avoided.

Before starting the 'concrete experience', it sometimes helps if students agree probing questions which they will answer in their diaries. These diary entries can then be used later at a debriefing session with other student nurses. It's amazing how much students forget after they complete placements or work experience; diaries are a useful way of salvaging experience for later use by the student or the group as a whole. You are very likely to be using a learning diary or journal yourself, and Chapter 46 deals with this; everything there relates to your learners as well as to yourself, of course!

The importance of trust

An atmosphere of trust between teacher and student is usually necessary before students are prepared to evaluate and reflect on their strengths and weaknesses honestly. For this reason, the reflection process is often best separated from any assessment of the student. The aim of reflection is to learn, not just to evaluate, which brings us to the next phase. Very many teaching activities stop here and miss the next stages. For example, a student may write an essay and have this evaluated by the teacher and the process may stop there. (Learning loops, as explained in Chapter 43, are a way of taking the process onward.)

3 Abstract conceptualisation

The aim in this stage is for *the student* to relate his or her 'concrete experience' to theory. A learning teacher might ask why students were more motivated in one of her lessons than in another; a design student might ask why a circuit does not behave as expected; a graphic designer might ask why his new design is particularly effective.

Whatever the student is learning, the questions are much the same, though they take less time to ask than they do to answer:

> Why were the successes a success? Why were the failures a failure? How should it be done? Why should it be done in this way? What would happen if it were done in a different way? The more general the learning point, the better.

Students may well need to change the way they think about the process that they are learning. Alternatively, their concrete experience may simply confirm their ideas about theory, in which case this stage may not take long.

4 Planning active experimentation

Having reflected on past experience and attempted to relate this experience to theory, the learner's next task is to ask, 'How can I do it better next time?' The answer to this question can then be tested during a subsequent 'concrete experience'. No one gets better at doing anything other than through this process.

If the student's area of study involves human relations, this stage may require some conscious risk-taking. Trainee doctors may need to ask questions of their patients that make them feel uneasy; student teachers may need to try unfamiliar teaching methods; trainee social workers may need to use more assertive techniques. In many areas of study, it is a matter of 'nothing ventured, nothing gained'. The aim is to encourage the 'active learner' mindset described in the motivation chapter, with students taking responsibility for improvement by being responsive, adaptive and self-believing.

It is often helpful for students to put ideas down on paper. This can take many forms: an action plan, a list of objectives to be achieved, a design for a biology experiment, a checklist of criteria to be used later for the self-assessment of an interior decoration project. These are all ways of setting targets for 'how to do better next time'. Here are some more detailed examples. (See also learning loops in Chapter 43.)

Case 1

Students learning how to program a computer-controlled metal-cutting machine write out an action plan based on what they have learned from previous attempts.

Here is their action plan:

1   Examine the drawing and decide on the cuts necessary to fashion the required shape.

2   Decide on the best order of these cuts.

3   Decide on the depth and speed of each cut.

4   Work out the coordinates for each cut.

5   Write the program.

Case 2

Students learning how to design a newspaper advertisement draw up a list of criteria to be made by the design. This could come from self- and peer assessment of previous attempts, or from looking at examples of good practice.

The advertisement should:

1   be uncluttered and eye-catching

2   include the company logo in a prominent position

3   have an attention-grabbing phrase in the largest type

4   have an explaining phrase in the next largest type

5   have the minimum possible number of words

6   have a design style in keeping with the company image.

Further learning experiences

Some students may decide that in order to do better next time, they need certain learning experiences. They may decide they have had enough of the present activity and want to move on, or that they need more practice in some other activity. Adult learners especially enjoy having some control over their learning.

Stages 2, 3 and 4 in the experiential learning cycle sometimes merge into one another, but there should always be a clear statement of 'how I will do it better next time' as a plan for the next 'concrete experience'.

> **Learning styles**
>
> *Kolb suggested that individuals may have preferences for certain stages in the reflective learning cycle. This gives rise to the 'learning styles' of 'reflector', 'theorist', and so on, described in more detail in the Introduction to Part 2.*

Bridging

The famous educationalist Reuven Feuerstein argues that students with learning difficulties – indeed, any learners struggling with a difficult skill – often fail to learn from experience because their mind ('working memory') is so swamped by the immediate concrete experience of the learning activity. As a consequence, they fail to see 'the wood for the trees' or the general learning points in the concrete detail. For example, a student writing an essay will be so swamped by the details of Henry V's reign that they will fail to learn how to plan and write essays. More essays on new topics will not help, as the skills and processes are still not seen for the content. The learner sees each experience as almost unique, fails to make links between similar situations, and so cannot learn, or learns very slowly.

Feuerstein and other cognitivists argue that the teacher needs to help the learner focus on the general skills and processes common in the tasks they do, and see the key general learning points amongst the detail. This is called 'mediation', and it greatly helps students at all levels. One mediation strategy is called 'bridging'.

Bridging takes the learner right round the Kolb cycle; see if you can see the Kolb stages in what follows:

A: The student 'does it', e.g. writes an essay.

B: The student thinks about what they have done and considers the teacher's feedback on content and process. (Many learning experiences stop here – they shouldn't!)

C. Now that the student's 'working memory' is relatively empty of content, the teacher asks the student to focus on the process, rather than the content or the concrete reality. They do this by asking:

> 'How did you do that?' Why were you successful? (or not)

The student explains, and the teacher uses Socratic questioning to draw out the 'doing-detail' or 'how' of the skill or process.

D: The teacher now asks:

> 'Where else could you use this (skill or process)?'

The student usually answers by saying that in a near-identical situation they could use the same skill or process. The teacher, however, encourages the learner to see more general applications with Socratic questioning. For example, the essay-writing process could be used not just for Henry V, not even just for history, not even just for essay writing, but also for report writing.

E. The student actively uses the process they outlined in C, above, in another context, and the teacher can then discuss this process again. Feuerstein uses bridging over and over again with his students, and this strategy must explain in part his phenomenal success with students who have learning difficulties; they often have average intelligence two years after completing his two-year programme.

There is an example of bridging being used to develop essay writing in Chapter 28. Learning loops are another example of bridging (see Chapter 43).

Conclusion

Experiential learning is as old as learning itself, though it is only recently that theorists have made the process explicit, enabling teachers to choose and to order learning experiences which follow the cycle. Adopting experiential learning techniques need not require a revolutionary approach to teaching and learning. However, the techniques require that students admit their mistakes honestly and willingly, and have the courage to try out new ideas. This is demanding of the learner and requires sensitive teaching.

The reflective learning cycle also describes how you will learn to teach, whether consciously or not. The emotional demands mentioned above also apply to you as a learner. How will you fare in learning from experience? Chapters 45 (on evaluation) and 46 on the reflective practitioner consider this, and there is a questionnaire to help you discover in which phase of the experiential learning cycle you are likely to be weakest.

> *When I first started teaching, I asked a senior member of staff how I should teach a certain topic. It turned out to be bad advice, and a head of department berated me for taking it. I defended myself by pointing out that the teacher whose advice I had sought had 30 years' experience of teaching. 'He has not,' said the head of department crossly. 'He's had one year's experience 30 times.'*

Training design

A great deal of training, especially in the professions, is limited to the 'abstract conceptualisation' phase of the cycle. Theory is taught without relating it directly to the learner's concrete personal experience. In such circumstances, the trainee often cannot apply the theory in practice, even when it is well understood. Even when they can, they are likely to hit some problem later which they cannot solve, and will then 'revert to type', and do things in their old accustomed way.

Some trainers address this problem by designing exclusively practical courses. Here the student is likely to accept techniques uncritically, without any understanding of why these are used or what the alternatives might be.

> *Bruce Joyce and Beverly Showers looked at 200 studies of in-service training courses for teachers. They found that many courses followed the pattern: explain the theory, give a demonstration and then ask staff to try out the new idea. This had no long-term effect on classroom practice! Some courses did affect practice, however; these all involved meetings where teachers reflected on experience, and coached each other over difficulties. The staff, like their students, needed corrected practice, and to follow the Kolb cycle. 'Input' was not enough.*

In short, many teaching programmes concentrate almost exclusively on one or two of the stages of the experiential learning cycle, instead of recognising the importance and interdependence of them all. The strength of the experiential learning cycle is that it develops in the student an understanding of how theory and practice are linked.

I once oversaw a novice teacher who was training experienced working nurses in a new care plan for diabetics. She met her trainees for a short session half a dozen times over a period of some months. She described the new plan, and asked them to try it out on some of their patients.

Each did so, and reported their experiences back to the teacher and the other trainees. The trainees suggested ways of overcoming each other's problems, and congratulated each other on their successes. The teacher put right any misunderstandings, answered queries and gave concrete advice on how to overcome difficulties. The trainees' 'working theory' was corrected and developed by this process.

Theory and practice were welded into one, and the learners soon became confident in the use of their new techniques. All the reflective learning cycle was there; all the learners' needs for corrected practice were met. Compare this with a two-day lecture course!

Checklist

❏ Is your students' concrete experience realistic and productive?

❏ Can skills be practised wherever possible?

❏ Do students evaluate their own performance?

❏ Is this evaluation checked by the teacher?

❏ Are successes and failures related to theory and 'how to do better next time'?

❏ Are students encouraged to experiment bravely and systematically?

❏ Do students draw up checklists of criteria for success?

❏ Do students use theory to work out how to do better next time?

❏ Are students supported emotionally if risk taking or painful reflection is necessary?

❏ Are mistakes seen as opportunities to learn?

❏ Do students take responsibility for their own learning?

EXERCISE

Plan a series of learning activities which follow the experiential learning cycle for:

• someone learning how to do a three-point turn
• students developing their essay-writing skills and techniques
• students developing their study skills.

Further reading

Gibbs, G. (1989) *Learning by Doing: A Guide to Teaching and Learning Methods*, London: FEU.

Joyce, B. and Showers, B. (2002) *Student Achievement through Staff Development*, Alexandria, VA: ASCD.

Sharron, H. and Coulter, M. (1996) *Changing Children's Minds: Feuerstein's Revolution in the Teaching of Intelligence*, Birmingham: Imaginative Minds.

32

Whole-brain, visual and kinaesthetic methods

We saw in the Introduction to Part 2 that the concept of learning styles has been replaced by 'whole-brain learning' (see the diagram on page 147). Most teaching strategies are structured, sequential, logical and language-based, and so are on the left of Herrmann's diagram. Whole-brain learning requires that we also work on the right of Herrmann's diagram, so students use holistic, creative, social, visual and experiential learning strategies. We are after variety, so I also include some kinaesthetic methods in this chapter. Other chapters dealing with the right-hand side of Herrmann's diagram include Chapters 17–21 and 29–31.

Nearly all teachers use *some* of the teaching strategies that follow, but very few use them enough for whole-brain learning. Many of the activities do not take a great deal of time and yet are very powerful, as they help students to consolidate and structure their learning. These methods are particularly useful for learners who have not learned well with conventional methods, or who need a new approach. Many also challenge the most able. Graphic organisers (page 156) are particularly useful.

We will begin by considering general ideas, and then look at some examples of more specific teaching strategies.

Holistic methods: showing 'the big picture'

- *Summaries, reviews, overviews, key points, etc.* provide overviews that students find very helpful. For example, why not display the key points throughout the lesson and point to them from time to time. At the end of the session, take the key points away and ask students to summarise and explain them in their own words, then improve these summaries.
- *Persuasive explanations* of the purpose and relevance of the learning.
- *'Advance organisers'*, i.e. summaries of what is about to be covered given in advance; ideally these are visual – for example, a mind-map (see Chapter 11).

All of the following are most powerful when the student uses or does them:

- *Case studies, demonstrations, illustrations, examples and anecdotes, etc.*, which show 'the whole' in context. Get students to study these with questions in mind.
- *Studying exemplars* (examples of good pieces of work). This is a special case of the above, but is a very powerful way of showing what the students should be aiming to produce. (See also self-assessment.)
- *Models, systems, sayings, flow diagrams and other graphic organisers etc.*, which describe the whole succinctly. Get students to study these with a question in mind, or, better still, to design and make their own.

Advance organiser

- *Symbolic events*: events, e.g. in history, which succinctly demonstrate or dramatise a key point.
- *Making links within a new topic*, or between the present topic and another topic, such as tasks that involve the student in relating similarities and differences, e.g. between measles and chicken pox or between percentages and fractions.
- *Using representations that point out similarities*. Metaphor, analogy, simile and symbol are all very powerful explaining tools, as they represent new material in a vivid and easily assimilated way. They build new learning on existing learning, so they are very 'constructivist', as explained in Chapter 1. They point out links and similarities, and give students the 'big picture':

  'Electricity is like water flowing in a pipe.'
  'Our DNA is like an assembly manual for our body', etc.

	different		same
fractions			
percentages			

Graphic organisers help show 'the big picture'

Seeing and creating visual representations

All of the following are most powerful when made by the learner; quite powerful when carefully scrutinised by the learner with questions in mind; and only moderately useful when experienced passively. Ideally, there is an audience for what the learner produces (other than you!) – for example, it is presented to the class and then pinned up for a few weeks on a classroom or corridor noticeboard.

Get students to make or use:

- *Mind-maps and other graphic organisers*, especially when used to summarise a topic. Learners' attempts are relatively easily improved after they have compared theirs with a model mind-map provided by you. Learners can present their maps to each other or the class. See page 156.
- *Images*, pictures, photographs, posters, diagrams, shapes and patterns, drawings, cartoons, overhead projector transparencies, graphs, charts, symbols, icons, logos, leaflets, etc., which make useful or important points (their value is in their power to explain and persuade and affect, etc.).

made by the learner....

.... scrutinised by the learner with questions in mind....

... experienced passively.

- *'Timelines'* that show the development of something with time pictorially.
- *Colour coding* for related but different concepts, e.g. for handouts, transparencies or projected images. Students' folders can be labelled or indexed using coloured card or paper, sticky coloured blobs or icons.
- *Colour* for impact.
- *Videos* and CD-ROM images.
- *Models* and the real thing.
- *Visually interesting websites*, animations, computer simulations and other computer visuals, Microsoft PowerPoint® presentations that are not too text-dependent. Get the students to make all these and show them to the class. Then they can go on the intranet or Internet. (See Part 4.)

We return to visual representations below.

Other methods on the right of Herrmann's diagram include the following:

Making use of acting/role-play/simulation

These methods are explained in more detail in Chapter 20. You could also give students teaching, checking or board-writing roles.

Giving students tasks that evoke feelings

Making use of emotion, humour, and appealing to senses, personal feelings and associations:

- What do you think would most anger you if you were a wheelchair user?
- What would it have been like being poor in London in the 1830s? What do you think the smells and tastes would have been like? What would have most worried you?
- What might worry a customer when they first checked in to your hotel?

Giving students tasks that require them to use their imagination

- What would it have been like to be a monk in an abbey?
- Imagine you are a water molecule in a heated saucepan …
- What would happen if … ?
- Problem-solving tasks, etc.

Giving students direct experiences

- Doing things physically, hands-on: manipulating, moving, etc. Practicals, experiments, explorations, research, etc. Moving about the classroom.
- Handling primary sources and real objects.
- Multi-sensory experiences that include seeing, handling, smelling, tasting and hearing, sounds, rhythm and music, etc.
- Excursions, visits, field trips, 'shadowing' someone at work, etc. (see the short account later in this section).
- Finding out for themselves.

Examples of activities to create visual representations

What follows are just to give you the idea; do devise your own approaches. Note that:

- These activities are all active rather than passive.
- There is an audience for the product that the students make.
- In order to make a visual representation you must first understand the topic, so the method is 'constructivist', as explained in Chapter 1.

The tasks below should be set before the topic is taught, so students can begin thinking about how to represent the material visually while it is being learned.

Importing images from the Internet

The Internet stores a vast treasury of images that can be used to assist the following activities. There will be images for any topic imaginable; I found hundreds of images for unlikely search words such as 'invoice', 'alliteration' and 'diarrhoea'!

Professionally produced images such as photographs, cartoons and diagrams can be found using Google (and other search engines) by clicking on 'images' near where you type your search terms. Many of the images will come from web pages, of course, and can be referenced in the usual way to avoid at least some copyright problems. Students can copy and paste them into most computer applications. They can then contribute to posters, web pages and handouts; they can usually be made much bigger or smaller, if necessary, to create a really vivid and impressive piece of work.

Creating a flipchart poster or model

Part 1: Students work in groups, each creating a visual representation that summarises the key points of a topic that they have just completed. This could be in the form of a 'concept map', flow diagram or other graphic organiser, or could illustrate a metaphor. Students can create posters on A3 paper, on flip-chart paper, or can create a cardboard model. If each group first plans what they will make in outline, individual students can work separately and then stick their work together to make the complete poster or model. See the diagram opposite.

Part 2: Each group presents and explains its work to the class. This will usually require preparation to decide who will say what. You might like to give them specific tasks so the presentations are not too similar: 'I want you to explain this osmosis diagram very carefully.'

The work can then be displayed using the class noticeboard for a few weeks, and then used for review activities. The work could also be displayed on a corridor noticeboard or other public display space. It could even be displayed in an appropriate venue in the community – for example, a poster on childhood diseases could be displayed in the foyer of a health centre. A real audience for students' work really motivates them.

Creating an intranet website

Students create a website that explains and summarises the key points of a topic, using imported images as described above. Again, with careful planning and co-ordination, a group of students can parcel out different pages of their site for individual group members to create. This is a great homework, and the results can be displayed on the institution's intranet, or on the Internet.

Again, consider a 'Part 2' like that above, where students use a laptop and data projector to display and explain their site.

Creating an exhibition or video

Students, or a whole class, can create an exhibition on a topic to be displayed on exhibition boards. This can be displayed in the college corridors or in other public spaces. If you make it a focus for parents' evenings, your students might even persuade their parents to come!

Alternatively, students can create a video that summarises their work on a unit. Computers can now be used to edit videos quite easily, though the process can be very time-consuming.

Groups can create visual representations

Visual essay planning: 'Let's see what we think'

This method works at any academic level and is excellent for teaching students to explore a complex topic or to plan their writing.

1   The teacher gives the class a meaty question, essay question or assignment task.

2   Students work alone to brainstorm relevant ideas, facts, issues, etc., looking back over their notes and using other sources.

3   Students get into pairs to compare their ideas, and together they write agreed points onto sticky message pads. They could use colour coding – for example, green pads for arguments in favour, and red for those against.

4   Working in pairs or fours or even as a whole class, students now stick their message-pad points on to a whiteboard or noticeboard, or on to flip-chart paper.

Students love to show their Microsoft PowerPoint® presentations and web pages – but check them first!

5 Students now structure their points, by putting related ones together into clusters. They then encircle these clusters and label them. They can also draw arrows, etc., to show relations between points and clusters, such as cause and effect.

6 Once their points and arguments are structured, they can make a personal copy in the form of a mind-map or other essay plan. This essay may or may not be written; the planning is an excellent learning activity in its own right!

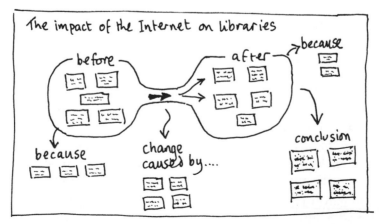

Visual essay planning

There are many advantages in representing ideas and points as mobile objects. Shy students are often happy to write what they dare not say to the class, so it captures ideas from everyone. They make our thinking visible and this promotes discussion. Labelling clusters and showing the relations between them helps students to generalise and deal with other abstract thinking. Clusters can themselves be clustered to create very generalised groupings and concepts. Again, these need to be labelled.

It is often much easier for learners to organise ideas and arguments by moving objects, rather than in their head!

If you like this approach, see www.inspirationresources.com for software and hardware to assist the process.

> *From brain expert Eric Jensen's* Brain-Based Learning *(2000):*
> *'Knowledge about the brain and standard education practices have traditionally been born of different worlds; it's time for a marriage.'*

Learning strategies that are kinaesthetic

Kinaesthetic methods involve students in bodily movement, as we saw in the Introduction to Part 2. I start with the most easily used strategies. Some teachers worry about the loss of control involved with the later strategies, but if they are well managed they can work very well and can get great concentration and involvement from learners. Many students hugely enjoy these strategies and remember them vividly. Consider a careful verbal review after using these strategies: 'What have we learned?'

Again, we will consider some very general strategies first.

Sedate kinaesthetic methods

Manipulate or manage information

- Underline or highlight key points in a piece of text.
- Play 'Decisions, decisions': these are card-sorting exercises (see page 248). These can also be adapted to match, group or rank real objects.
- Research and collect materials to create an exhibition.
- A student manages a group of students while they complete a task.

Practicals

- Class or individual practical activities of any kind.
- Make a model or the real thing, handle it, or take it apart to see how it works, etc.
- Use tools, computers, phone, etc.

Peer teaching

- Doing a demonstration for other students to watch.
- Giving an explanation or giving a presentation using OHTs, etc.
- Writing on the board, flip chart or OHP, etc., for the class.
- Operating an OHP; laptop and projector; video, etc., for you or the class. Some students like to have a class responsibility, and will happily give out or collect materials and equipment, for example.

Full movement methods

Take on physical roles: Here is an example of this approach from office studies. First, students take on roles such as 'invoice', 'purchase order', 'credit note', and parts of the classroom are labelled 'accounts department', 'company bank account', etc. Then students must arrange themselves or move in accordance with the situation described by the teacher:

'I'm raising a purchase order for £600 for computer equipment.'
'The computer supplier is submitting an invoice for the £600.'

Students must then move to show the flow of documents and money.

Students can then rank or group themselves in response to other teacher demands:

'I want all company-generated documents over by the window and all customer-generated documents over by the door.'
'Now put yourselves in the order you would be generated if a customer put in an order.'

Similarly, students can take on the roles of enzymes, hormones and organs in the body and act out the flow in situations given by the teacher. Students are allowed to instruct and correct each other: 'Hey, you're created in the pancreas, what are you doing in my hypothalamus?'

Kinaesthetic 'decisions, decisions'

'Decisions, decisions' was considered in Chapter 19, but here we match, group or rank students rather than cards, rather like the example above. Students are given roles, marked by a hat or a big badge, and they must match, group and rank or sequence themselves depending on your orders.

Visitors and visits

Visitors and visits are amongst the most vivid, enjoyable and best remembered of teaching methods. Students love them, as long as they are well planned. They bring the real world into teaching and learning, provide specialist experiences and expertise, and reveal real issues and debates.

Visitors

Studying urban crime? Why not ask a policeman to visit? Studying suicide? Why not ask someone from the Samaritans to talk to your group? Thousands of organisations can act as a living resource for you: what about Oxfam, Action on Smoking and Health, or the British Association for the Advancement of Science? There are many expert speakers eager to get their message across – why not use them?

Why not get the *students* to arrange the visit, perhaps setting this as an assignment. They will enjoy the responsibility, and their sense of being in control will help make them feel committed and positive about the visit.

Who will write the letters or make the phone calls? How will the visitor be briefed before she comes? Who will meet the visitor? Who will make her coffee? Who will introduce her? Who will thank her on behalf of the class after her talk?

She may need a map, and will need to know where to go and whom to ask for when she arrives. She will also need to know something of the group, its size, prior learning and age. She may also need specialist equipment, and will certainly want to know for how long she will be expected to speak.

The group will need time to prepare for the visit. What questions will they ask their visitor, and who will ask them? It is better to spread the questions among the class members than have one or two students asking them all. Questions need to be open rather than closed, and you will need a strategy that prevents embarrassing silences. If students are arranging the visit, have a brainstorming session to 'discover' the points raised in the previous paragraphs. Then the group can decide how to meet these needs and who will compose the briefing letter.

It may be advisable to monitor your students' arrangements, to avoid embarrassments!

Visits

Talk to the school or college management to resolve such issues as levels of supervision, insurance, consent forms and so on. Such details are very important, but vary considerably from institution to institution, so I do not cover them here. It is sensible to take students on a visit only if you have the agreement of a senior member of staff in your school or college, and if you follow the institution's procedures for visits. Having said that, the procedures are usually very well documented and easy to follow, and there will be plenty of advice if you need it.

A pre-visit will help you to make successful arrangements. Many places to visit have education officers, who will do the teaching for you! Others have official guides, or activity sheets and other helpful resources, but you need to know about these before the visit. If such help is not available, consider devising your own activity sheets, or at least giving students questions they can answer by investigations during their trip.

Before setting off, ensure you have a full list of party members, with their home addresses and phone numbers. Consent letters may not be necessary, but if they are, make sure you have them from all students. Take any letters confirming essential arrangements and details of the trip, along with insurance forms and a first-aid kit. It is usual to have at least one extra teacher or adult helper on a visit, unless the group is small.

References and further reading

Buzan, T. (2003) *How to Mind-map*, London: HarperCollins. Anything by Buzan is worth a look. Try his site too: www.mind-map.com

Ginnis, P. (2002) *The Teacher's Toolkit: Raise Classroom Achievement with Strategies for Every Learner*, Carmarthen: Crown House Publishing.

Jensen, E. (2008) *Super Teaching* (4th edition), Thousand Oaks, CA: Corwin Press.

'A Good Practice Guide: Health and Safety of Pupils on Educational Visits' can be downloaded from the DCSF website: www.teachernet.gov.uk/wholeschool/healthandsafety/

33

Independent learning

This is an advanced teaching method, and you will need practice with conventional assignment work before you can make a success of it.

How can students learn with minimum teacher involvement? You can replace the teacher with instructional material – this is the approach of 'resource-based learning', 'distance learning' and many computer learning packages. But independent learning (IL) adopts a radically different approach: there is no teacher, and no specially designed educational technology; instead, the students teach themselves – and each other. It is the best teaching method for making use of information and learning technology (ILT) or information and communications technology (ICT).

By independent learning, I mean your students learning a short topic which is defined by you, but which you *don't* teach. Students may collect material and write notes and answer questions, but this work is not marked by you. Instead, you assess the *learning*, perhaps with a short test.

There is a subtlety here that is crucial and often missed. Students focus on what is assessed. So if you assess their notes towards the learning goal rather than the goal itself, weak students will often focus on copying notes at the expense of understanding the material. If you only assess the goals, students focus on these, and rightly see the preparatory work only as a means to an end.

If you set a series of independent learning assignments, you can give increasing responsibility to the students until they become able to learn unaided. During this time, you coach them in independent learning skills, but not in the topic they are studying. At first, you may tell students of suitable resources and monitor their work, but the eventual aim is true independence. This requires that your students learn how to find their own resources, how to discover and then correct their own learning deficiencies, and how to monitor their own learning by their own standards.

Independent learning can help to reduce the detrimental effects of having too much content to cover in too little time, and yet provide unique educational gains.

IL can be used on any course, as a one-off experience or for, say, 20% of the content. It is a difficult teaching method to use, but it will work if enough care is given to task design, monitoring and assessment, which need to be 'tuned' to the topic, and to the capabilities of the students. IL produces a rich harvest of educational and logistic gains which I consider at the end of this chapter.

Making use of independent learning

Decide on a section of your course that is straightforward, factual and well resourced, i.e. where good textbooks, websites, videos, etc., are available on the topic. Break the topic down into sections which your students could complete in, say, one to four weeks. Research the resources available before writing the independent learning assignment. Consider the 'tuner' on page 363 to tune your use of IL to the group, as explained below.

Some teachers set an IL assignment in preparation for a discussion, so students are not left to their own devices for the more difficult aspects of a topic.

Designing the independent learning task

For a given topic, independent learning tasks can be directed or non-directed.

A *directed* task might be a detailed assignment giving a carefully planned sequence of tasks, or a set of worksheets with carefully chosen book references with page numbers. The students are told exactly what to learn.

A *less directed* task might be a requirement to produce a set of revision notes on the topic, using the set of references provided, and some relevant past-paper questions.

A *non-directed task* might be to prepare notes on a given topic, the students being provided with the relevant part of the syllabus.

The more directed the task, the less likely students are to get stuck or misinterpret the task, so it is worth being very directive at first.

Time allowed for and difficulty of the learning task

The major difficulty for students is that there is no one to help if they get stuck. So the task needs to be easy or moderately easy. Finding and then learning to recall and explain straightforward factual material is ideal.

To start with, make the assignments short, say, one week or two. A useful sequence of tasks is outlined below.

- Compose and type up revision notes, including a summarising 'graphic organiser'.
- Compare your notes with those of at least two other students.
- Suggest improvements to each other's notes, and act on suggestions you find helpful.
- Test each other's ability to recall the contents of your revision notes, in preparation for a short test.

Students get bored if your tasks are exclusively solitary, and 'book-and-biro'. Consider setting the following tasks as part or the whole of an independent learning assignment:

- To prepare for and deliver a presentation on the topic or some aspect of the topic to the rest of the student group. The whole topic is studied by all, but each student only presents five minutes on an aspect of the topic. (*Which* aspect need only be made clear after the study.)

- To visit somewhere of relevance to the assignment, e.g. a shop or leisure centre, in order to make observations.
- To complete a design or solve a problem.
- To watch a given video in the learning resource centre/library and answer questions.
- To make use of a computer-based learning package.
- To read a given section of a given book or explore a website and make notes in preparation for a class discussion. (This rewards the reading or research very well, as students usually enjoy discussions very much.)
- To discuss a given topic in pairs or groups and make notes on their own and others' opinions and conclusions. This might include requiring students to decide on the central questions, values, evidence and suchlike, for a later class debate or discussion.

Number the tasks, and make sure any difficult or thought-provoking tasks are right at the end of the assignment, so as not to provide a ready excuse for non-completion of the easier parts of the assignment.

Whatever tasks you set, painful experience suggests that you should request that the students present their material *in their own words*, and that students should *not include in their submission printouts from CD-ROMs* or the Internet, excepting diagrams perhaps.

It is worth setting the tasks to conform to the presentation of material in the students' textbook, rather than the order given in the syllabus. I suggest you write the assignment with the textbook open in front of you. The success or otherwise of an independent learning assignment is very sensitive to the precise nature of the task. It must be tuned to the group.

Study skills and self-assessment

Independent learning requires that you do *not* mark the work students do towards their learning goals. You will, however, assess the achievement of these goals, once this work is completed – for example, with a short test. Not marking preparatory work or notes may seem alarming at first, but it is crucial to appreciate that students cannot learn the vital skill of independent learning without actually learning independently! However, a useful question at the end of an assignment is 'How do you know you are ready for the test?' Activities which can help this self-assessment process include:

- Providing self-assessment questions which enable students to gauge their progress and their understanding of the topic. These should be clearly worded, fairly simple, written in informal language and easy for the student to self-mark, i.e. closed rather than open questions. You could require students to present this work to ensure they complete it, but don't mark it.
- Giving students 'study–cover–write–check' tasks or peer-assessment tasks.
- Providing answers to numerical questions on your worksheets, so students can check their own or each other's work.

- Providing the students with model answers or worked solutions, after they have completed the worksheet. The students can then use these to mark their own or each other's work.
- Later, leaving students to find suitable self-assessment questions with answers for themselves. There are plenty of published question books and revision aids which provide these. You may ask students to present such work, but again, don't mark it.
- Asking students to state and evaluate their self-assessment strategy as part of the IL assignment. It is helpful if they provide examples of the self-assessment work they carried out. There should be evidence of corrected practice of recall of key facts, not just written work.
- Giving students a 'teaching' role, making them responsible for their 'study buddy' passing some aspect of the test or assignment.

Later in this chapter we look at ways of teaching independent learning skills.

Resources

Resources can be provided, clearly signposted, vaguely signposted or not even mentioned in the IL assignment; again, this needs to be tuned to the group.

Consider the following:

- *A topic box*. This is a box of resources such as books, magazines, press cuttings, handouts, etc., available from the library loan desk for reference only. Your library will probably help produce this if you provide an assignment brief, and give them *plenty* of advanced notice. Students and staff can be encouraged to add materials to the topic box. They usually do.
- Putting useful but scarce books on desk loan in the library.
- Providing an intranet page of useful Internet links. Invite students to suggest additions, but check them.
- Providing videos, CD-ROMs, computer-based packages, etc.
- Providing an outline summary of the topic which students must supplement.

You could, of course, simply issue a reference list with the assignment; you could even provide page numbers and a brief review of the value of the resource. But don't over-help students, as your aim is to develop the skill of finding resources independently. As part of the assignment, you can ask students to provide a bibliography of the resources they found. You could also ask them to self-evaluate their resource-finding skills – for example, by comparing the resources they found with those found by their peers.

Monitoring

This is a crucial investment, at least to begin with, but the aim is to develop self-monitoring skills. Monitoring could be done in tutorial or portfolio time, and can be close or distant. Again, this needs to be tuned to the needs and characteristics of the group. Err on the close side to begin with.

You can encourage self-monitoring by providing students with a checklist to tick off as they cover the various aspects of the topic, and by expecting them to provide, with the assignment, an action plan showing how they will complete the assignment on time. Learning teams can help too, see the box on page 364.

The 'improve own learning and performance' key skill is a very useful vehicle for driving the work along. You can set or negotiate targets for the weaker ones. If you do issue a checklist with your independent learning assignment, students can tick this off as they go, and you could ask to see it. In my experience, lazy students can't even be bothered to forge these, so they are a fairly accurate indication of progress even for them.

Students should be clear that developing their independence is the main purpose of these assignments. Your monitoring should only take a minute or less per student ideally. Resist the temptation to help them (until they have shown themselves irredeemably incapable) or they will just rely on your help, and so not develop their independence.

You could tell them that you will check their work half way through the assignment, giving a mark for 'conspicuous progress'. Don't mark it, just count pages under your breath with an interested expression on your face!

Alternatively, you could ask to see rough work. Ideally, though, the students should monitor their own performance, or each other's, by using self-tests and checklists, initially provided by you and later created by themselves. You may wish to see the first few checklists your students design. Providing the self-devised checklist could of course be part of the assignment.

Assessment of independent learning

Assessment can be *low heat* or *high heat* and needs to come quite soon after the IL assignment. Like all aspects of independent learning, assessment needs to be tuned carefully to the characteristics of each group. Some groups barely respond to low-heat assessment: 'But sir! If it was proper work, you'd teach it.'

Low-heat assessment includes: self-marked tests; quizzes, etc.

High-heat assessment includes: presentations; tests or exams. Highest heat of all is a system of tests and retests called 'mastery learning'. (See *Evaluation to Improve Learning* by B. S. Bloom *et al.*, or Chapter 43.)

You will probably need to give some students extra time to complete the independent learning assignment or retake tests, so don't run the assignments 'back to back'. Leave a fortnight or more for catching up.

The independent learning 'tuner'

I have stressed the importance of 'tuning' – for example, the task, monitoring and assessment – to the capabilities of the group. Remember also that independent learning skills will only be developed if you gradually remove your help.

The 'tuner' (opposite) is a conceptual aid to help you in this process. For example, if your first IL assignment is not successful, a suitable adjustment to the settings on the tuner will improve your next IL assignment. You may decide to have closer monitoring and higher-heat assessment, and perhaps to reduce help with resources. Your students' performance is your guide, and your aim is to develop independent learning skills. (The tuner can be used for any assignment-based learning.)

Do not give up on IL; the skill is vital. If students don't succeed with it, then they need more practice, not less!

Teaching independent learning skills

We need to *teach* the skills and attitudes required for independent learning. They do not spring magically from maturation. Kolb's reflective learning cycle (see Chapter 31) is useful here, as shown in the diagram on the next page.

After an IL assignment and its assessment, students are asked to reflect on how they got on. This self-evaluation can be aided by a competence checklist, or by answering a questionnaire:

> 'Did you find adequate resources?' 'What did you do if you got stuck? 'Can you search a CD-ROM?'

A questionnaire for self-evaluation is included at the end of this chapter. Ask students to put a '1' instead of a tick on the questionnaire the first time they use it, and a '2' the second time on the same sheet. Then progress is easy to see.

After this self-evaluation, the student may decide, or negotiate with the teacher, goals for improvement. For example:

> 'I plan to find more than just one book on the topic … ask for help from friends more determinedly when I get stuck … find out how to search a CD-ROM with key words …'

These goals become the action plan for the next IL assignment. They can be written at the top of this new assignment in a space specially provided for the purpose.

Attaining the goals can then become *part* of the next IL assignment, and can be self-evaluated by the student; the teacher may also provide feedback on the attainment of these 'learning to learn' goals.

> *Peer tutoring is a useful contribution to independent learning. For example:*
>
> *Study buddies are temporary pairs of students who help each other with specified IL tasks, such as testing recall, assessing each other's work, comparing notes, discussing given questions, playing 'tennis' (Chapter 19) and so on.*
>
> *Learning teams are more permanent groups of students who take collective responsibility for getting each other through IL and other tests. They arrange to meet outside of ordinary class time to help each other study. They have a chairperson and a secretary who keep minutes which describe the attendance, work and times of meeting of the group. The teacher discusses these papers with the team or chair. Teams work best if the teacher chooses the members, making them mixed in ability, social background, ethnicity and so on, and if they are set up very soon after a new class is formed. (See Halpern 1994.)*

Although you are not teaching the IL assignment topic, you can teach the learning to learn skills. This can be done in short one-to-one sessions or with small groups. Once the students are able to learn independently, this support should become unnecessary, though you may still decide to ask students to set themselves learning-to-learn goals.

Why use independent learning?

Great educational and logistical gains are bestowed by independent learning. At first, the time saved by not teaching some material will be used in monitoring and coaching students on their IL assignments. Eventually, however, substantial time can be saved. I hope the gains outlined below comfort you, if, like me, you suffer the indignity of discovering that your students sometimes prefer IL to your teaching.

* It reduces the pace and pressure of teaching, thus enabling the teacher to deal with difficult material more slowly, and increase the proportion of time spent on active, student-centred activities.
* It increases motivation. The coaching involved encourages students to take full responsibility for their own learning; it challenges passive attitudes to learning and it teaches the active learner's coping strategies and mindset.
* Students develop independent learning skills and attitudes which are of vital importance for educational development and progression, e.g. from FE into HE and the world of work, where increasing job mobility and job transformation require independent learning skills and active-learner attitudes.
* Students can learn at their own pace, and in a manner which suits their own preferences and learning style.

- It **is a** change, and students very much enjoy it. It becomes a preferred learning method.
- It can encourage 'deep' rather than 'surface' learning if assessments focus on understanding. Graham Gibbs in a research study (1992a) gave nine factors which encouraged a 'deep' approach. These included: independently learning a topic of the student's devising, independent group work, developing learning skills, reflection, project work and other common features of IL.
- Students discover they can learn without a teacher.

Independent learning skills questionnaire

Questionnaire and competence record ....

Name: ....

When I am studying...

	Can't or don't do	I do this sometimes	I can do this well
Study skills			
I read in an interrogative way (with questions in mind)			
I skim-read			
I speed-read			
I underline key points			
I make notes from my reading			
I make notes from my computer searches			
I produce mind-maps or other summaries			
Coping strategies			
If I can't understand:			
I try harder			
or change resources			
I recognise when I am stuck and change strategy			
I have the courage to ask:			
a fellow student for help			
a lecturer for help			
If I can't find suitable materials			
I ask a librarian			
or a fellow student			
or a lecturer			

There is a consensus amongst management theorists that giving employees control over how they work greatly increases their sense of responsibility, motivation and effectiveness. Unsurprisingly, giving students control over their own learning empowers them in the same way.

Independence is not an arbitrary foundation for a teaching method: it resonates with a deep human need – the need for freedom; the need to be in control. This is a need felt most strongly by adolescents, and by adults in search of personal development and a sense of identity.

It is depressing and salutary to keep the advantages of IL in mind while considering much resource-based learning or computer-based learning. Too often these attempt to replace the teacher with highly structured educational technology, often denying the learners' needs to work with others and to take control. It must surely be better to harness these needs than to struggle against them – especially when the educational gains of doing so are so profound.

Below is a competence questionnaire for self-evaluating learning to learn independently. Not all the questions will be relevant to every independent learning assignment.

The full questionnaire of independent learning competences can be downloaded from the chapter 24 downloads at: http://www.geoffpetty.com/evidence_based_downloads.htm

References and further reading

Bloom, B. S., Madeus, G. F. and Hastings, J. T. (1992) *Evaluation to Improve Learning*, New York and London: McGraw-Hill.

*Boud, D. (ed.) (1988) *Developing Student Autonomy in Learning* (2nd edition), London: Kogan Page. Mainly HE-focused.

*Gibbs, G. (1992a) *Improving the Quality of Student Learning*, Oxford Centre for Staff Development, Technical and Educational Services.

Gibbs, G. (1992b) *Independent Learning with More Students*, Teaching More Students Project, No. 5, Oxford Centre for Staff Development, PCFC.

Knowles, M. (1988) *The Modern Practice of Adult Education: From Pedagogy to Andragogy*, Cambridge Book Company.

Maslow, A. H. (1987) *Motivation and Personality* (3rd edition), New York: Harper-Collins.

Petty, G. (2006) *Evidence Based Teaching*, Cheltenham: Nelson Thornes.

*Rogers, C. (1994) *Freedom to Learn* (3rd edition), New York: Merrill.

34

Self-directed learning

Self-directed learning gives control and responsibility for learning to the learner, though there are three important conditions. Unfortunately, these conditions are sometimes ignored, and often require learning-to-learn support similar to that described in the last chapter on independent learning. The conditions are that the learner must:

- want, or at least be prepared to accept, the degree of autonomy given them
- have, or be quickly developing, the skills and attitudes required to manage this autonomy
- be able to learn reasonably effectively with the degree of autonomy given them.

Teachers vary enormously in the amount of autonomy and help they give their students. If learners accept some autonomy and learn to use it effectively, learning is very effective and great educational advantages follow. The amount of autonomy and help given should depend on the needs of the learner, not the beliefs of the teacher. Having said that, self-directed learning is real-life learning and thus is the prime goal of education; consequently, we must coax and coach our student towards it.

'It does not seem reasonable to impose freedom on anyone who does not desire it.'

Carl Rogers, *Freedom to Learn*

Self-directed learning is a humanistic approach in which the teacher takes on a facilitating role. It is a key strategy in personalised learning. In order to facilitate, the teacher needs to understand the theoretical background (described in Chapters 1, 5 and 10) and plan its use, as described in Chapter 41 on course organisation, which should be read before this chapter.

The advantages of self-directed learning are that it strongly encourages active learning, develops student autonomy and gives the responsibility for learning to the student. A self-directed learning approach is widely used when teaching adults, especially adult professionals, where it underpins the idea of the 'reflective practitioner'. However, it is being used increasingly to teach younger learners – for example, in the key skill of 'improving own learning and performance' and in other aspects of vocational education.

It might help your understanding of this chapter if, while you read, you bear in mind self-directed learning in a context you are familiar with, or in one of the following contexts:

*   encouraging students to improve their essay-writing skills
*   encouraging a manager to improve his or her understanding of marketing principles
*   a fine art lecturer developing a student's painting
*   a one-to-one tutorial between tutor and tutee.

Self-directed learning may be used for a whole course, or for just one aspect of a course, such as individual coursework. Effective use of self-directed learning requires the use of the following cycle, each phase of which is considered below. An alternative approach is to use the reflective learning cycle described in Chapter 31.

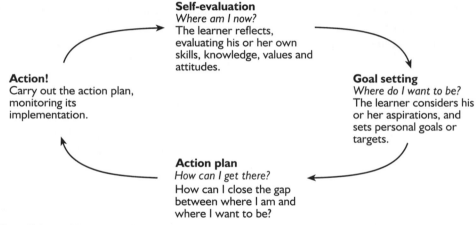

The self-directed learning cycle

Self-evaluation

Self-evaluation is usually the first activity when starting a new cycle. It creates ego-involvement in the learning process and is the only route to self-improvement. There could hardly be a more crucial skill or habit to instil in your students.

Students need to be critical enough to see the need for learning, but not so critical that their self-belief is reduced, or they begin to despair of the task ahead. It is the facilitator's role to ensure that evaluation is positive as well as constructively critical, and begins to suggest attainable goals. If students are over-critical, ask them to look forward to methods of improvement, rather than backward at mistakes or inadequacies. Mistakes should be seen as an opportunity to learn.

Many teachers, or 'facilitators', argue that all evaluation should be carried out entirely by the student. But if *you* intend evaluating your students' work, do this *after* their self-evaluation. This develops the students' self-evaluation skills and gives you valuable feedback on their thinking. In addition, students find their own criticism easier to take than their teacher's.

Strategies

Use question and answer to encourage reflection by using problem-finding questions such as 'What do you find most difficult … ?'; but also encouragement with questions such as 'What are your strengths?' 'What difficulties have you overcome?'

You could systemise this process by using a 'SWOT' analysis, where students record their strengths, weaknesses, opportunities and threats.

A self-evaluation checklist or questionnaire can be very powerful. You can use your questions to focus the attention of your students on the really crucial issues, and so point them in the direction of improvement, yet without criticising them yourself.

Students can look back at marked work and other feedback to help them assess their capabilities. You could also use pre-tests, aptitude tests or even psychometric testing. But most facilitators just use question and answer, perhaps prompted by questionnaires or checklists.

Goal setting

If self-directed goals or targets are being set at the beginning of a course then 'What do you hope to get out of this course?' is an excellent question. You may need to refer learners to careers advice or to other specialists to ensure their aspirations are realistic. Goal setting occurs most naturally when it is a response to self-evaluation.

Self-improvement or self-development goals must be achievable, yet substantial enough to be attractive; this is a difficult balance, and the facilitator needs to help strike it.

Some goals may be reactions to weaknesses shown up during self-evaluation:

> 'I need to improve my punctuation' (an A-level literature student).
> 'I don't know a thing about the theory of customer loyalty' (a marketing NVQ candidate).

Some goals may be defined by external factors:

> 'I'll lose marks if I don't improve my spelling.'
> 'I need to get this competence to finish the unit.'

It is a common mistake to rely exclusively on goals defined by weaknesses and such external factors. Intrinsic goals are much more motivating. Try to encourage students to form their own aspirations and vision, by asking them what they value or what inspires them. A question such as 'What writing do you admire?' or 'What marketing has impressed you lately?' might lead to motivating goals such as:

> 'I want to put more wit and more searing criticism into my writing.'
> 'I want my marketing to create a lively, young image for my company.'

Strategies

Make sure the goals negotiated are achievable, not too long-term, available in writing to the learner and to you, and have a date when achievement might be expected. If long timescales are unavoidable, monitoring will be necessary. Consider negotiating a learning contract, as described in Chapter 41.

Action planning

This process often occurs immediately after goal setting. The aim of the action plan is to think of concrete activities which will help achieve the learner's goals, and so devise ways of closing the gap between where the learner is now, and where they want to be.

Action plans should be in writing, and should be available to you and the learner. But how should activities be decided?

Strategies

As ever with self-directed learning, it is best to ask first. The student will be much more committed to their own ideas than to yours, and will also develop their action-planning skills. However, you may need to negotiate changes to the plan.

Action!

Learners may find it difficult to work alone, and there is a danger that bad practice will be consolidated rather than corrected without a teacher to check and correct. If you can remain available to monitor the learner's progress, this will help. Alternatively, arrange for peers to support each other.

The next self-evaluation should include an evaluation of the learner's working methods: how did they find working alone? What was most difficult about it?

The teacher as facilitator

In self-directed learning, the facilitating role of the teacher is crucial and not well understood. Too many teachers simply pass over full responsibility to students who are not yet ready. The role of the teacher is to be ready to help the student towards independence, but not to help where there is no need. A useful facilitation strategy for any stage in the cycle is to ask the student first, then to use question and answer to lead the student to make good any deficiencies in their suggestions. Only when this fails should you take more control. In this way, the teacher and student become a partnership, but the student is always given the lead initially. Here is a teacher acting as a facilitator with a management trainee who is self-evaluating.

Student   ... so I think my main strengths are organisational, and my main weaknesses are that I am not so good with people, especially those older than myself.

Facilitator	Not good with people?
Student	Well, I'm not bad with most of them I suppose.
Facilitator	Your last piece of work certainly suggests you are excellent with some of them.
Student	Okay, so it's mostly problems with those who are older than me.
Facilitator	Why is that, do you think?
	(Student explains.)
Facilitator	So what could you do about that then?
	(Student makes a suggestion, setting herself a challenge.)
Facilitator	Resources. What might help you in this challenge?
	(Student looks blank.)
Facilitator	Can you think of any other young managers at work who you could talk with about managing staff older than yourself?

This coaching or facilitating role is very far from leaving the student to flounder alone. The teacher is 'leading from behind', and helping the student learn not only the immediate topic of how to manage older staff, but also how to learn independently.

Note that in the above exchange, the facilitator:

* asks for a difficulty, but then gives it to the student: 'what could you do about that then?'
* encourages the student to recognise her own strengths, as well as her weaknesses
* shows that they value the student.

'Bridging' is an excellent strategy to finish off a facilitation session (see page 342).

Carl Rogers suggests that if students are to develop the self-belief that makes self-directed learning possible, the emotional climate created by the facilitator is crucial. The facilitator must empathise with the student, must be non-judgemental and must show that they value the student as an individual. Many teachers would praise the student for taking initiative in the learning process, but Rogers would probably not agree, preferring intrinsic to extrinsic reinforcement. Instead, he would encourage learners to recognise their own successes.

There is a continuum from teacher-directed to self-directed learning, as shown in the diagram below, and students may need to move along it gradually, rather than be thrown in at the deep end. Consider using independent learning before self-directed learning. Students may also find it easier to be self-directed about resources or monitoring than about setting themselves goals or self-evaluating.

Why use self-directed learning? The ability to learn by oneself is the greatest gift any teacher can give a learner; indeed, it is the ultimate aim of all education. The educational gains for self-directed learning are the same as those described in the previous chapter for independent learning (see pages 362–4). These gains are very impressive, and in any case, the ultimate purpose of teaching is to make all students into self-directed learners, so why not give them some practice?

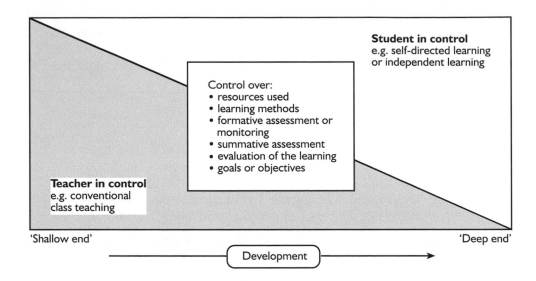

'Shallow end'   'Deep end'

Development

Further reading

See the further reading section for Chapter 33 on independent learning, together with:

Knowles, M. S. (1975) *Self-Directed Learning*, Cambridge University Press.

Petty, G. (1997) *How to Be Better at Creativity*, London: Kogan Page. Deals with the emotional difficulties of self-evaluation and self-improvement.

Rogers, C. (1994) *Freedom to Learn* (3rd edition), New York: Merrill.

35

Visual aids, Microsoft PowerPoint® and interactive whiteboards

The verbal channel of communication is the most used in teaching, but for many purposes visual information is more effective. In pages 149–52, we saw that trials have shown that if students create mind-maps, flow diagrams or other 'graphic organisers', their understanding is improved by about two grades! This is, in part, because visual representations can help us 'see the wood for the trees', by summarising key points and showing how these are related to each other. Information needs to be structured like this to go into our long-term memory.

Getting students to summarise their understanding in a visual way and then to check this is a great way to learn, and was considered in Chapter 32. But we can also use the visual channel to present new information to students in a way that is easy to digest. Some researchers say information enters our brain in the following way:

87% by eyes
9% by ears
4% by other senses

Try to display information visually.

The main advantages of visual aids

- *They gain attention.* You cannot teach without the attention of your students, no matter how carefully prepared your lesson may be. A new picture on a screen is difficult to ignore – a new sentence in a speech is not. Gaining attention in the age of television and computer games is not easy, and we need all the help we can get! Moreover, while the student is looking at your visual aid, he or she is not distracted by competing visual stimuli – the view out of the window, for example.

- *They add variety*.
- *They aid conceptualisation*. This is a major advantage of visual aids. Many concepts or ideas are understood visually rather than verbally – for example, 'practical skills' like soldering. If knowledge is understood and remembered visually, you should transmit it visually. How a table is laid for a seven-course dinner is best shown by means of a picture, or better still the real thing. Most novice teachers realise this; but they often fail to grasp that many *abstract* concepts such as 'fractions' or 'cash flow' are also best conveyed and understood in a visual way. This idea is explored in more detail in pages 149–54.
- *They aid memory*. Research shows that most people find visual information easier to remember than verbal information.
- *They show you care*. Going to the trouble of preparing visual aids shows students you take their learning seriously.

Displaying non-visual information in a visual way

Non-visual abstract ideas can be displayed by a huge variety of methods. Treat the 'graphic organisers' on pages 149–52 as an 'idea bank' of techniques for representing information visually. Next time you are planning a lesson, check through it for ideas. (Consider also maps and tables of figures.)

The advantages of the visual channel to teachers are enormous, but you would be surprised how often poor teachers ignore it.

Types of visual aid

1 Handouts

Modern photocopiers can reproduce newspaper articles, including photographs. They can also increase or decrease size to suit any requirement. If you want a poster-sized copy of a postage stamp, or an architect's drawing reduced to the size of a postcard, it can be done. With careful use, they can cope surprisingly well with faint masters, often making copies which are better than the original. Most colleges and schools have photocopiers which will automatically print on both sides, collate and staple. There are pressing environmental reasons for copying back to back.

You can photocopy on card or on coloured paper. Colour photocopying is also now available (though still expensive).

Masters for worksheet handouts can be obtained commercially, and these are often excellent value for money. The masters are supplied with a copyright waiver allowing the purchasing institution to photocopy the masters, usually for use within that institution only.

Making your own handouts

Handouts can give information, or they can be in the form of a worksheet; sometimes they combine these two functions. You can cannibalise magazines, websites and brochures, and photocopy or computer-scan diagrams from textbooks, adjusting the size if necessary – but beware the copyright restrictions described below, and acknowledge sources. Then this material can be 'cut and pasted', either physically or on computer, together with linking text in type or neat handwriting, to produce a handout with impact.

- Try 'gapped handouts', where space is left for students to answer questions, fill in words and phrases, or label a diagram.
- Don't forget that overhead projector transparencies can be photocopied as a handout, or handouts made into a transparency.
- If you can, word-process your handouts. (But don't be afraid to draw your own diagrams – I have for this book!)
- Leave 2 cm margins on both sides of the page, or you will hole-punch text!
- Don't overcrowd; if handouts are unattractive they will not be read. Pay attention to layout – for example, use indenting and bullets, as in this list. Would it help to present your handouts in the form of a booklet?
- If your school or college has an agreement with the Copyright Licensing Agency (CLA), there will be notification of this displayed near the photocopier. It usually allows you or your students to copy the following for any one course in one academic year. However, you may only make one copy for each student, and one for yourself.
  - Up to 5% or one complete chapter of a book published in stated countries.
  - A single article from a journal or periodical (some journals and periodicals are excluded from this arrangement, so check before copying).

Using handouts in class

Talk your class through the handout, or ask them to use it for individual or group work. Ask them to highlight important parts of the text. In this way, they will become familiar with its contents; otherwise they are unlikely to be read later.

Handouts don't teach. Students learn a great deal by writing their own notes in their own words, or by explaining to each other in pairs (Petty 2006). Do this in class and distribute handouts later. Students learn most from handouts when they have to do something with them: ask students to underline key points or summarise the content with a graphic organiser. Ask questions in your handouts and leave spaces for the answers.

Handouts can save a great deal of time, for you and your students, but don't make them overlong. If you feel more information may be required, set reading homeworks from books or journals.

One last word: don't forget to save trees by using handouts only when they are necessary, and always copy on both sides.

2 The whiteboard

Some use board work like a huge scrap-pad for jottings and sketches; others see it as a neglected art form. Some use it for putting up notes for the students to copy. Others use it to draw attention to the landmarks in the lesson, displaying only the key ideas as they are covered. Some write a five-point summary of their lesson before the class arrives, and barely touch it during the lesson. Maths and science teachers use board work to demonstrate how to solve problems, and to give instructions for experiments. Some teachers prefer to do their board work before a lesson, others during it. Most feel lost without a board of some kind, but some think it should be consigned to the museum.

No teaching aid is more adaptable to the teacher's style, and perhaps this is its real strength. You must decide for yourself how to use it; try the different approaches described above, then choose, combine and adapt to develop your own style. Interactive whiteboards make the device even more adaptable – this is considered in the next section.

General advice

- Always start with a clean board; if necessary, ask for cleaning fluid.
- Make sure you are using a dry marker pen, not a flip-chart or other type. Some markers have a chisel end, allowing you to control the thickness of the line. Hold the markers like a pencil.
- All colours show up quite well, but black or blue show best.
- Make sure it really *is* a whiteboard: a projector screen is irreparably damaged by pens!
- Don't use your usual handwriting, or block capitals which are difficult to read if used exclusively; use a print style. Novice users tend to write too big rather than too small; in most cases, lettering with capital letters about 3 or 4 cm in height is best. Try it out from the back of the class.
- Until you get used to it, plan what you are going to put on the board before the lesson.
- Don't stand in front of the board, and make sure there is no glare on it.
- Talk to the students, not to the board; you may need to raise your voice a bit.
- Use colours only for a specific purpose; use black and blue for writing the main information.
- Don't get the board cluttered; erase unwanted material – but not too quickly.

The technique

The main problem is keeping your lines of writing horizontal. To achieve this, shuffle your feet sideways as you write, keeping your hand at the same height relative to your shoulders for the entire line. This is easier with a roller board, where most teachers write at about eye height, moving the board up every line or two. It's almost impossible to write below chest height; kneel down if you must, but can they see it?

The 'whiteboard shuffle'

To draw a straight line without a ruler: relax and draw with confidence, keeping your eyes *on where you want the line to end – not on the marker*. Use a similar technique for drawing a circle, or alternatively use a piece of string with a loop in it, in which you place the marker. Board compasses, protractors, etc., are usually available if you need them.

If you are concerned about discipline, look over your shoulder every few words, or better still use a data projector or overhead projector (OHP).

Some tricks and traps

Some classes have a Pavlovian reaction to anything written on the board: they write it down in their notes. If you intend to use the board as a scrap-pad, you must tell the class beforehand that they should not copy unless you tell them. They might need reminding until they get used to this. (If you have two boards, you can use one as a scrap-pad and the other for notes.)

If a whiteboard eraser smears, it needs washing with meths/alcohol or cleaning with a proprietary whiteboard cleaner. Board writing is a messy business; think carefully about the clothes you choose to teach in.

If you have a roller board, you can prepare the board before a lesson and roll it out of view until you need it.

Any board work that you intend the class to copy sets an example for the class. If you work untidily, don't expect them to be neat.

Warning! There is an unwritten rule in most schools and colleges that you should always leave the board clean for the next teacher. If you intend to ignore this rule, you would be well advised to attend self-defence classes.

3 Microsoft PowerPoint®, interactive whiteboards and OHPs

Microsoft PowerPoint®, Apple Keynote™ and similar applications enable a computer or interactive whiteboard to display a series of screens called 'slides'. These can contain text, images, graphics, sound and video clips, or any combination of these. The slides can be displayed on a computer, on a classroom screen via a digital projector or on an interactive whiteboard. These presentations, like any other computer file, can be saved on your institution's intranet, enabling students to access them at any time, including from home (see the next chapter).

The most effective use of this medium from the learning point of view is asking students to create their own Microsoft PowerPoint® shows. Many students find this more motivating than a conventional writing task. It also develops ICT skills and, if presented to the class, communication skills. Students can share their shows on your institution's computer system, as explained in the next chapter.

The most common faults with presentations using computer, interactive whiteboards or OHP are:

- *Too much text on the screen* – six lines is a maximum; use a sans serif font such as Ariel or Tahoma, as it is easier to read. Use 28 point or larger. Check you can read it from the back of the room.
- *Not enough images or graphic organisers* (page 149 – a picture is worth a thousand words – especially during a thousand words!
- *Failure to exploit the medium* – don't forget to use reveal, overlay or animation, as described below, and to insert video clips.
- *Overuse of gimmicks* – slide transition animations and complex background designs can distract your audience from your main message; so can changes of font or colour without a clear purpose. The goal is to explain rather than to impress or distract!
- *Too passive!* – the commonest fault with presentations is that they are too long and don't contain student activities, even simple ones such as questions. This can be a fatal weakness, causing students to fail to make sense of the material.
- *Too many bullet points*. Bullets are a valuable device, but can be monotonous if overused.

A failure to exploit the medium

Presentation software can lure you into creating an overbearing deluge of information which students call 'death by PowerPoint'. OHPs are no less deadly. But don't despair: these media can be most effective if you include activities, and make at least some use of the following techniques.

http://excellence.qia.org.uk/ the QIA excellence gateway has lots of Microsoft PowerPoint® shows to download.

www.intute.ac.uk has Microsoft PowerPoint® presentations on hundreds of topics and student tutorials.

www.actden.com/pp has tutorials on using Microsoft PowerPoint® which you or your students might like.

Over-use of gimmicks

Presentation techniques

Use these with presentation applications such as Microsoft PowerPoint®, with interactive whiteboards, with overhead projectors, in computer-based instruction and even with conventional whiteboards – indeed, with any presentation device.

Graphic organisers

Mind-maps, flow diagrams and other 'graphic organisers' can summarise and explain topics with few words and great power.

Reveal and overlay techniques.

It often helps not to show the whole slide or diagram at once, but to reveal it in stages. Suppose, for example, you have designed a slide with a title and two bullet points.

Slide 1

Title

Slide 2

Title
• Information

Slide 3

Title
• Information
• More information

The reveal or overlay technique is shown forwards, but *created* backwards:

1   Create a complete slide with the title and both bullet points on it (slide 3).

2   Duplicate this twice.

3   Leave slide 3 complete, but delete the last bullet point from slide 2.

4   Delete both bullets from slide 1, to leave just the title.

Now each slide reveals one extra line.

A similar process can be used to display diagrams or graphic organisers in stages. Again, work backwards. Start with the completed diagram and delete from this in stages until you are left with the bare outline. When the slides are shown in sequence, the bare outline appears first, and each subsequent slide adds a little more detail. This is called ' reveal' or 'overlay'.

You can use a similar technique to show changes with time, such as a piston moving in a cylinder, or the growth of a plant. If you use overlay a lot, your files will have a lot of slides. Changing slides can keep you manacled to your computer. But small, hand-held remote control devices are available which change slides with a click.

If you are using an OHP, you can 'overlay' by placing a sheet of paper under the OHP slide and reveal it a line at a time, while still being able to see the covered text by looking at the slide itself. Or you can cover text with those sticky office message slips.

The combination technique

This is ideal for an interactive whiteboard or OHP. A master slide is shown – for example, a map of the British Isles. Then details, such as weather fronts, are added to this master. Then the details can be removed, leaving the master untouched, which can be used again to show other weather fronts.

This is great for annotating a diagram, painting or maths worked example. A sequence of slides can create a similar effect in Microsoft PowerPoint®.

If you are using an OHP, create the master with permanent pens. Then add the details with water-based pens, which can then be erased, leaving the master untouched. The master can then be used another day.

Annotating a diagram on an interactive whiteboard

Animation

You can create a limited 'freeze-frame' type animation with a series of slides shown quickly one after the other. More sophisticated animations can be created using presentation software. Ask someone to show you how, or experiment after searching the on-screen help under 'animations'.

Sectioning the presentation

Some topics contain subtopics. If you are using Microsoft PowerPoint®, you can mark a change in subtopic by switching to a different slide background. Avoid red text on a green background, or green on red, as 8% of men are red-green colour-blind. Alternatively, ensure you have a strong dark-light contrast when these colours are used next to each other.

Video and sound

Music and video can be added to your presentation, but your computer or interactive whiteboard will need speakers or a full sound system. Again, consult on-screen help.

Hyperlinks

On any slide you can put single-click links to other slides, or to websites, videos or sound. Use on-screen help to find out about hyperlinks and action buttons.

Creating a great presentation

See Chapter 11 on 'Teacher talk' for a full account, but don't forget the following when designing and using any presentation, whatever the media. Start by reminding yourself why the students are studying this topic – what should they be able to do with the information you will convey? This is a great focus for student activities during the presentation.

1   At the very start of your presentation, set a task for your students which requires that they understand what you are about to explain. This could be some questions to answer or a problem to solve. Hypothesis testing (pages 443–4) also works well, as does 'peer explaining' and the 'one-minute summary' described in Chapter 11. Students realise they must complete these tasks immediately after your presentation. Later, students will also need a more substantial task to apply the learning.

2   During your presentation, include slides that ask questions for students to complete in pairs or, better, to 'snowball'. For example, 'Why is a lever needed? Work alone first, then tell your partner your answer.' You can now reveal the answer and let students self-assess against it.

3   Summarise the main points on a summarising graphic organiser, or centre your entire presentation around one if you can.

4   Use reveal, overlay, animation and video clips, as described above.

5   Search the Internet for suitable images and video clips to illustrate your main points and learn how to insert these into your presentations. You can choose to search specifically for images or video using most search engines. Look carefully at the home page of your search engine to see how to do this. Then you can include these as slides or create hyperlinks to them. When you have the basics, there is more detail in a download on the 'What's new' page of www.geoffpetty.com called 'Evidence based ICT'.

Don't use presentation software all lesson, and whatever you do, don't use it to display a script for you to read.

Peer explaining after a presentation

You can interrupt your presentation for activities, etc. by pressing the 'B' key to turn the screen black, or the 'W' key to turn it white. Pressing the key again returns you to the same slide.

 If in doubt – leave it out.

Interactive whiteboards

These consist of a computer linked to a data projector, with a large, touch-sensitive screen. It can display text, images, graphics or videos. Most boards can convert handwriting to type, which can then be printed as a handout. They can do so much more than show Microsoft PowerPoint® slides! Each model is different, so get someone to show you the ropes, and experiment with:

- Hiding and revealing text or graphics, asking questions and then revealing the answer.
- Enlarging or zooming into parts of a diagram or image.
- Annotating diagrams, images or calculations with a pen – for example, drawing great circles round important parts and labelling them (or getting students to).
- Playing 'decisions, decisions' games, as described in Chapter 19. These can be based on graphic organisers (pages 149–52).
- Saving sessions, and tracking back through them to review or revise the lesson. Ask questions while you do this, to check understanding.
- Student contributions. Students can express ideas on paper, then a special digital camera can display their work on screen.

Use the assertive questioning style described in Chapter 24, so your use of the board is genuinely interactive.

'Has she got it right?' – 'Decisions decisions' on the interactive whiteboard

Evaluating a resource – making it effective and inclusive – assignment HELP

You might have an assignment to evaluate a resource you have made. Whether your resource is a Microsoft PowerPoint® presentation, a set of cards to sort (Chapter 19), or a worksheet – do ensure it works for all your students.

'There is nothing so practical as a good theory', said Kurt Lewin. Because theories apply in almost every case, they can help in your case. Here are some theories worth considering when creating and evaluating your resources.

Constructivism (Chapter 1, pages 5–15; principles, pages 14–15): Your resource should require students to create their own understanding and should correct misunderstandings. It should require them to reason with the content. Good resources have activities built into them, or designed to be used with them. Then the resource will teach, rather than just tell. This helps make the resource 'interactive'.

Evidence-based teaching: The best resources include the most effective student activities found by research. This includes student dialogue. Can your activities require students to work in small groups? How students use your resource is often more important than the resource itself.

Whole-brain learning: Resources sometimes present material bit by bit in a 'left-brain' way. Students also need 'right-brain', 'holistic' explanations. See page 142 and Chapter 32.

PAR: If your resource teaches an entire topic to students working fairly independently, it should follow the PAR structure explained on page 445.

Equal opportunity: Is your resource accessible to students with disability? Does it make unwarranted assumptions about their prior learning or cultural background? Also, is the language level and readability appropriate? See Chapter 25 'Reading for learning', especially 'readability' on pages 291–2.

Fitness for purpose: Last, and most important, what was your resource designed to do, and does it do it well? Ask your students, look at their work, and reflect!

4 Models – and the real thing

If a picture is worth a thousand words, how many for a model? And what about the real thing?

Models can be commercially produced or made by the teacher. A language teacher may bring cooking utensils into the classroom; an engineer may gut and adapt an old alternator for classroom use. A biology teacher may show her class the heart and lungs of a pig. Models and real objects bring the world into the classroom. (Real objects are often referred to in teaching literature as *realia* – Latin for 'real things'.)

Objects have far more impact than words or pictures, especially if they can be handled. This idea permeates the whole of science teaching, but should not be forgotten by other teachers.

If you intend making a model yourself, the following factors need to be considered:

- *Scale*. Is it helpful to scale the size up or down? (It is often useful to scale up, so that students can see without getting out of their seats.)
- *Dismantling*. Some models can be dismantled and reassembled by the students, and/or the lecturer. Some models are sectioned – i.e. part of the model is cut away or made of transparent material so that the inside can be seen.
- *Simplification*. Models can omit non-essential detail which would otherwise confuse the students. In addition, parts of the models can be coloured so that they can be picked out more easily.
- *Scale speed*. A moving model of the solar system would be useless if it only ran at the real speed! So, for opposite reasons, would a model of a four-stroke petrol engine.
- *Can you use or adapt the real thing?* Bringing real objects into the class-room usually excites interest. 'Real things' can be sectioned, labelled, partly dismantled and so on, to aid your teaching. For example, bird skeletons can be labelled; a computer disk can be butchered so that it may be taken apart; an old barometer can be sectioned or dismantled and adapted for use in the classroom. You may even be able to use the real thing without adapting it. Your imagination is the only limit.

If a model is too small to display to the whole class, take or pass it round – prefer-ably when you are not talking to the class. Alternatively, let them view it in groups. It is sometimes important to tell students the differences between the model and the real thing, otherwise the model may confuse rather than illuminate. A huge range of models can be obtained from educational suppliers, though very effective models can be made at home, or by students. Can you think of a model that would be useful in your teaching?

Best of all, get your students to design and make models. This is engaging, has a deep impact on memory, and often requires, and so develops, deep understand-ing: 'What's in the nucleus?' The models can be left on display in the classroom for review, revision and for other groups.

5 Charts and posters

Design is very important for charts and posters; in particular, many are rendered useless by an attempt to display too much information.

They can, of course, simply be pinned up, with students left to read them at their leisure; but students usually have better things to do than read a poster, so it is advisable to use it as a teaching aid. For example, you can gather the class round the poster and use it as a focus for part of a lesson; it can then be left up as a reminder. Posters are particularly useful for teachers of foreign languages.

How about using one noticeboard in your classroom for a regularly changing poster display?

Making your own posters

Aim for simplicity, not complexity or comprehensiveness. Less clutter means more impact. You can of course draw your own, but you can also use a 'cut and paste' combination of colour pictures from magazines; brochures and other advertising material; illustrations from books or computer printouts, increased in size by photocopying; photographs; newspaper cuttings; and so on. Bear copyright in mind. Alternatively, you could set your students the task of making the poster!

Key points to consider:

- **Can the whole class read it?**
- **Is it simple enough for the message to be clear? When in doubt – leave it out!**
- **Is it attractive?**

If you have gone to a great deal of trouble to make a poster that you will use over and over again, you can get it laminated. This covers the card with plastic, both protecting it and enabling you to write on it with a dry marker whiteboard pen.

Write to manufacturers for ready-made posters. For example, if you are teaching computing, write to computer manufacturers and ask for any posters they may have.

6 The DVD or video recorder and video camera

Students consider the television to be a source of entertainment. But don't assume that this means they will automatically watch your DVD (or video) with rapt attention; they may be used to chatting, doing their homework and cuddling their boyfriends or girlfriends while watching TV. You will have to work hard to make your students attend to a programme, and learn from it.

On most DVD or video machines, you can fast-forward to the sections that interest you; pause the programme to talk about what the class has just seen; and rewind to replay a particularly important section. Some machines have a 'freeze-frame' feature, enabling the picture to be stopped and a still frame retained on the screen. Practise with these features on any machine you intend to use, before the class begins. (If you want to dim the room lighting, could you still operate the machine in that situation?)

Always preview anything you intend to show, and decide what you hope your students will learn from it. Read the teachers' notes if any are provided. Then ask your students to look for the features you have highlighted as useful. For example, you might say: 'I am going to show you a video about the role of the health visitor. I want you to use it to answer the questions on the board.' The questions might be:

1 How are health visitors trained?

2 Who organises the visits?

Asking students to look out for prescribed information will increase their attention markedly.

Don't feel obliged to show the whole of a programme; in many cases, it is better just to show selected sections. Avoid the tendency to hand over the teaching to the technology.

Before the class:

- Check everything works. Are the plugs in, and have you chosen the correct video channel on the monitor (i.e. on the TV)?
- Ensure the monitor can be seen by everyone in the class, and that the volume is correctly set.
- Use the counter to work out the sections you want to show on, and write down the appropriate counter numbers or time on the real-time display; wind to the first section you wish to show. (*Warning*: counter numbers may vary on different machines; don't assume, for example, that those on your home machine will be the same as on the one at work.)
- Read any notes that come with the video cassette.

During the video:

- You may like to dim the room lighting.
- Look interested, even if you've seen it a hundred times; if you look bored or walk off, don't expect your students to find it interesting. (In most teaching situations you are legally obliged to remain in the room.)
- Check students are attending.
- Don't forget to use the pause or rewind features to make teaching points during the video.

Video cameras create instant excitement and are extremely easy to use. You just point and press! Try videoing student presentations or role-plays, or let students use them out of college or school to make their own videos. Editing videos is a very time-consuming process and requires special equipment, though many educational establishments will have this. You can make effective videos without editing, as long as you avoid shots of short duration; don't pan too much, and pan very slowly. Avoid indoor shots pointing directly at the window.

7 The slide projector

Slides are still the best way to produce very high-quality images, and can be projected on to any reasonably white surface; but a proper screen is best, especially for a large audience, as it has special reflective properties. Try to dim the room lighting if you can.

Before the class:

- Read any teacher's notes, then preview the slides, editing out any that aren't useful.
- Acquaint yourself with the slide projector; many have a 'zoom' feature, allowing the size of the image to be adjusted. (Smaller images are brighter.)

- Set up the screen and test the projector's alignment. If the image is too small, move the projector further back or adjust the zoom.

When showing the slides, you may well want to dim the lights in the room – but can you still read your notes? (A pencil beam torch might be useful.)

8 Other teaching aids

Games and simulations were dealt with in Part 2; and the computer will be considered in the next chapter. Quite apart from these, there are also audio tapes, tape-slide programmes, interactive video materials and endless other teaching aids. Some are dealt with in the next chapter.

Having read this far, you will have a good idea of how to prepare to use these. Read the notes; find out how things work; acquaint yourself with the material, adapting and editing it to fit your own purposes; try to guess any possible problems, and think of ways to avoid them; and then try things out.

Further reading

Attewell, J. (2002) *Distributed and Electronic Learning: A Review of the Literature*, LSRC Research Findings, available online from www.lsrc.org.uk

DELG (2002) *Report of the Learning and Skills Council's Distributed Electronic Learning Group*, www.lsc.gov.uk

Hill, C. (2003) *Teaching Using Information and Learning Technology in Further Education*, Exeter: Learning Matters. You can download a sample of this excellent book from www.learningmatters.co.uk

McNaught, A. (2004) *Exploring E-learning for Literacy, Numeracy and ESOL Teachers*, Coventry: Ferl/Becta.

MORI (2002) 'E-learning at Home and School', executive summary. Available from www.campaign-for-learning.org.uk/ofi

36

Students learning with computers: e-learning, ICT and ILT

Computers are an extraordinary presentation device for teachers, as we saw in the last chapter. But they are also a potent tool for learners. They offer a library of resources so vast it defies the imagination, and nearly all students love using them.

But more than that, a great deal of real-life learning now involves computers – for example, a motor mechanic learning a new procedure using a computer tutorial, or a mother finding out about her child's eczema on the Internet. If we don't teach our students how to find trustworthy computer resources, and how to learn from these, then we are not preparing them for real life, or for 'lifelong learning', or for progression on to their next course.

And more even than that: there is hardly a job or a hobby now that does not involve using computers. At work, most of your students will swim in an environment dominated by word processors, spreadsheets, databases, and email and Internet searches. If you don't prepare your learners by showing them how to make natural use of such powerful tools, you are not preparing them for work.

And there is more to all this than just computers. Don't forget digital cameras, video cameras and mobile phones; these can also be very useful resources for students and teachers. You can excite your learners by recording their efforts with a digital camera and put the images on the Internet, and then text the mobile phones of those that didn't attend to ask where they were, and set them their homework!

In what follows, don't be dazzled by the technology; ask yourself, 'What am I trying to teach?' and 'Will this help me?' Also ask, 'What will the students do'? It is what students do that creates learning, not what technology does.

The Internet

The Internet links tens of millions of computers, allowing them all to communicate, and to access a colossal and chaotic library, including the World Wide Web (www). Material is provided largely for free, from every corner of the globe, by government departments, companies, organisations, museums and galleries, voluntary groups, charities, experts, enthusiasts and potty individuals in search of attention. Anyone may create a website on any topic, and unless the content is exceptionally outrageous, there will be no attempt to edit, let alone censor it. Consequently, quality is uneven and searching or 'surfing' the web is a frustrating waste of time, or a delight and a revelation, depending on your search skills – and your luck!

What should you do in the face of such a huge resource? In order to make the best use of everything that ICT and ILT can offer, you will need to set off on five parallel and overlapping explorations. Set this as a project for yourself, accepting that it will take some time. As with almost everything in teaching, you will never arrive, but the journey is fascinating, if sometimes rather frustrating. Let's look quickly at the five strands of your exploration first, before looking at them in more detail.

A GARDEN OF JARGON!

IT Information technology. This is the computer kit not yet connected up.

ICT Information and communications technology. This is the computer kit connected up so it can search the Internet and send emails, etc. It can also mean digital cameras, video cameras, etc.

ILT Information and learning technology. This is ICT being used to assist learning, or to assist an educational institution. This includes students learning with ICT, but also students enrolling at a college electronically.

Website A page, or linked set of pages, on the World Wide Web (www), which is part of the Internet. More loosely, a set of pages on the Internet.

Internet A network of computers called 'servers' that are left on permanently and that store websites and other resources for us to search.

Intranet A website only accessible to those within an organisation.

VLE Virtual learning environment. A sophisticated network that operates on most or all of the computers in an institution. Students can log on to any computer at home or in school or college, and access their work in chunks. This work is then assessed and their progress is tracked, and information sent to their teacher. It also enables the learners and teachers to communicate with each other.

MLE Managed learning environment. This is the VLE, if there is one, plus all other information systems and processes in a college or school, that contribute directly or indirectly to learning and the management of learning. This includes, for example, student records. See Hill (2003).

Develop your ICT skills

This is the first strand. Don't worry if you are not yet computer literate; modern personal computers are so user-friendly that even an adult can learn how to use them! It helps to be shown the ropes by someone who already has the skills, but you can learn a great deal by just playing around. That's how kids do it. The main problem is knowing what to do when you get stuck. My strategy is to save what I have done so far, and then to experiment fearlessly. If my material is saved, neither it nor the computer can be damaged by anything I am likely to do. If the experiment has made a mess, I don't save these changes. Then I try on-screen help. If I can't solve the problem by myself, I ask a nearby student, who can usually help me. If not, I ask an expert. If all else fails, I read the manual.

If you don't know the way in a strange town, do you feel humiliated if you have to ask for directions? Adopt the same attitude if you are lost in ICT. There are plenty of people to help. Your institution will probably have an 'ILT champion' you can talk to. You could also do a computer course either at home or at college. The links at the end of this chapter have other suggestions.

Search for useful resources

This is the second strand in your exploration, which, like the others, you can start straight away. There are absolutely tons of ILT resources out there on the Internet, on CD-ROMS and elsewhere. This might require you to learn how to search effectively on the Internet, but other teachers like you have done this searching already, and placed links to the most useful resources in 'web directories', 'gateways' or 'portals' on the Internet. Teachers or editors continually update these for you. If you find these sites you can save yourself and your students a great deal of time, and make your lessons, homeworks and assignments more exciting and effective with little effort.

Do surf the Internet for yourself as well, but make sure your search skills are really up to the job. It is not just a case of typing a topic into a search engine and having a look at what comes up. There are more effective ways of looking through the billions of sites available, as we will see.

Create a personal resource bank

Another strand in your exploration is to collect together the most useful resources you find topic by topic, so that you can find them easily, and you don't forget about them from one year to the next. This requires you to know which resources will help your students and you the most. What are the characteristics of a good ILT resource?

Design student activities that make use of your ILT resources

This strand is the whole point, of course, but it is easy to lose track of this. Never mind the dazzle of the technology, the glittering images, and the clever graphics and funny animations – what about the learning? It is not what technology, or teachers, do that creates learning, it is what students do. We need to devise tasks using ICT as a resource, that meet the criteria we considered in Chapter 1 and elsewhere in this book. They must also meet your aims as a teacher. I am always impressed that experts in ILT always stress the learning, and see the technology as a means to this end.

Reflect on your progress in ILT

You will of course have to reflect on, and evaluate, your use of ICT and ILT, thinking how you can move further forward, but this reflective practice is true of everything in learning and teaching.

Let's look at these strands again in more detail. It is outside the scope of this book to develop your ICT skills, but there are links at the end of the chapter that can help you do this. Let's look at the second strand.

Search for useful resources

There are three main ways to search the Internet. You can use a search engine such as Google, which searches virtually all the billions of websites on the Internet, with no thought to the specific needs of teachers or students – for example, the readability of the site or the prior learning required to understand it. Google tries to put the most popular sites at the top of its listing, but these might not be the best sites for your students, or for you.

A better bet is to use a web directory that is compiled by editors. The best-known example is www.yahoo.com. You can also try searching Google with, for example, 'web directory' biology, to find suitable web directories in biology.

You can also go to a gateway site which is edited by a subject specialist, usually with education in mind, or to some other site that has collected educational resources. These are sometimes very large indeed and you will need time to explore them. You could, of course, search with Google for gateway sites in your subject, with, say, 'gateway biology'. Whatever you do, please try the following, which are vast collections of sites and other resources chosen by teachers, for teachers:

> http://excellence.qia.org.uk/
> www.intute.ac.uk/
> www.bbc.co.uk/learning/
> www.curriculumonline.gov.uk/

There is a list of gateway sites at the end of this chapter; they are vast collections of useful sites. Spend time on them. If you don't find what you need, you are probably not looking in the right place within them.

You will need to develop your own and your students' search skills, the 'intute' site above has subject-specific tutorials for you and your students.

I remember watching a student searching with Google as part of an assignment. He typed in 'food poisoning' as his search words, and found over three million articles matching his enquiry! Most of them did not relate to his assignment task, which was about the health risks when cold meat is not stored correctly in a refrigerator. Arsenic poisoning was hardly relevant. Most students think they know how to search on a CD-ROM or the Internet, but many can't!

If you type in 'food poisoning +refrigerator +meat uk', you only get about 4,000 sites. Putting a plus sign immediately followed by a word finds only those sites that mention that word. Adding 'uk' gives you only United Kingdom sites. This 'narrows' the search, and the sites at the top of the listing are much more likely to be useful. It is worth looking at 'search help' and 'advanced search' on the home pages of your favourite search engines to develop your own and your students' search skills.

COMPUTERS AS LIBRARIES: THE CD-ROM

The main educational use of CD-ROMs is storing reference material in an easily searchable form. This includes, for example, encyclopaedias, newspaper and journal archives, art images, question banks, textbooks and databases such as university course information. CD-ROMs can also store software courses, or 'courseware', which teach students directly.

Evaluating the resources you find

There is often a huge gulf between what ILT could do, and what it actually does. Many programs are just 'page turners', which simply display screen upon screen of information, and so are inferior to a well-indexed reference book. Even some of the more interactive resources offer only repetitive rote drill, which does not require understanding. Some of your students may play computer games that are highly interactive, have striking and varied graphics, and are great fun to play. They will find some educational material deadly dull by comparison.

Don't be too cynical, however; your students may spend more time looking at a computer screen than a book! When choosing material for use with students, bear the following points in mind:

EVALUATION CRITERIA

(See also page 386 in chapter 35.)

- Does it do something that needs doing?
- Is the material of the correct depth (difficulty) and breadth (having sufficient but not over-detailed content)?
- Does it assume prior learning some students don't have?
- Is the resource *interactive*? 'Page turners' soon bore students.
- Is the resource multi-sensory? Does it make use of the visual and perhaps the auditory channel?
- Is the language level appropriate?
- Value for effort: Is it going to take so long for the students to learn how to use the material that the educational gains are not worth their effort?
- Can students get a printout if this is necessary?

And for computer programs that teach students directly:

- Have you got the minimum hardware necessary to run the program?
- Are there technical or copyright restrictions on the number of students who can use the program at the same time?
- Is the program foolproof? Is it *student*-proof?
- Do you know how to load the program/reload it if it 'crashes' (goes wrong)?

You can find out more on sources of information on ILT resources if you:

- *Ask*: library and other learning resource staff, other teachers of your subject and people you meet at conferences.
- *Read*: reviews in subject-specific teaching journals (there is one for every teaching subject imaginable, e.g. the *Journal of the Association for Science Education*); reviews in your library's editions of the educational press, such as the *Times Educational Supplement*, the Tuesday *Guardian* and *Educational Computing*, etc.
- *Search*: the websites at the end of this chapter.

An authoritative report (DELG 2002) found that 'a great deal of content exists, but much of it needs customising; is badly designed; is merely reworked paper material not exploiting the potential of ICT; does not cover the whole curriculum; is not accessible to people with disabilities or basic skills difficulties … and/or is too expensive'. However, a great deal of new material has been developed since the report; see, for example, the 'intute' site mentioned earlier.

Create a personal resource bank

As you find websites, images, video, interactive learning materials, useful documents, weblink pages, materials for VLEs and so on, you should begin to store these in an organised way. Find out about computer 'housekeeping'. This is keeping your files in folders, and folders within these folders, all arranged by topic and subtopic. You will also need to use informative filenames, so that you can recognise what is in a file some months after creating it.

You could create an image gallery for students and you to use to enrich your presentations. You may well be able to put all or some of this material on your institution's intranet so that students can access it; if not, you could give them this on a CD. You could add assignments, schemes of work, handouts, exam papers and examiner reports, and work by former students and by themselves. For example, if students create a slide presentation using a computer program such as Microsoft PowerPoint®, this can be saved so students can access it online.

Many teachers stop here; after all, the material is available to students – what more is there to do? They miss out the last and most important step.

Design student activities that make use of your ILT resources

You can use your ILT resources in a number of ways. Let's look at these before we consider what activities you can set your students.

A single computer in the classroom

A single computer is a great resource. Students can take turns to get data, use an interactive resource, fill in a data table or answer questions you have given them by looking at an Internet site. In science classes they might use the computer to capture data during an experiment. Students might then print out a record of what they have done.

If there is only one computer in the class, then students will usually need 'off the computer' activities while they wait their turn, and after they have had their turn. After their turn, they can of course use what they have printed off. This may sound problematical, but it can work very well if the activities have been thought out in advance. You could make the computer a part of a circuit of activities or 'circus', as described in Chapter 18.

Computers used with resource-based learning (RBL)

Here, every student, or every pair of students, has their own computer, usually in a 'resource centre'. RBL is considered in Chapter 41. Students work at their own pace through activities designed to be reasonably free-standing. This often requires specially written materials that can be very time-consuming to produce or expensive to buy.

Using computers out of class time

If you set activities that require your students to make use of computers outside of your classes, then a number of advantages follow. It allows your students to work at their own pace, at a time and in a way that suits them. They will also be able to develop the real-life learning and ICT skills vital for their future. It also makes them use at least some of their private study time productively!

Remember that if students do not have a computer with Internet access at home, they will have access to one at your institution, and at their local library.

The best way of ensuring that students really learn from out-of-class activities is to set an 'independent learning' assignment, as described in Chapter 33. In many ways this is the ideal way to use ILT.

An alternative strategy is to set a homework that requires students to hand in what they have done, either on paper or by email. A VLE can be used in this way. Logging on to a VLE does not guarantee that a student has been using it productively; you may need better evidence of learning than that. Why not play ping pong?

Graphic organiser ping pong:

Here students make a graphic organiser (see pages 149–52) which 'ping pongs' between them and you:

1 You give the students the task of answering a question, or summarising the key points for a topic by creating a graphic organiser (mind-map or comparison table, etc.). You may give websites and other resources, or leave the student to find these unaided.

2 Students study the topic using resources such as websites and DVDs. You might ask them to print out documents and highlight them.

3 Students create their graphic organiser using Microsoft® Word, a mind-mapping software, or similar. Links to websites can be included in this document. They may add some notes too, written in their own words.

4 Students e-mail their graphic organiser and note to you.

5 Then you send them your graphic organiser, asking the student to self-assess their graphic organiser using yours as a model, and then to improve their organiser in red.

6 They e-mail their improved organiser to you. You check there are indeed improvements in red.

7 They take an online quiz on the topic summarised by the organiser.

You can of, course, stop at point 4. You can also ask students to peer-assess by e-mailing organisers to each other. They can all upload their organisers onto a common VLE or website page, and compare their work with that of others. They can also present their organisers using Microsoft PowerPoint®, on shared web pages, or on interactive whiteboards.

 There are many more methods like ping pong in a download called 'Evidence Based ICT', which you can get from www.geoffpetty.com/ whatsnew.html

A third approach is to set an activity that requires the student to learn something using a resource you have found, in preparation for a short test or presentation, etc., but without the ping-ponging. This is 'independent learning' (Chapter 33).

Why not get your students to prepare a presentation, as described in Chapter 32?

Limit them to, say, five slides; this makes their thinking concise and requires them to find the key points – no bad thing! You could also require that they use, perhaps, at least two images from your image gallery. Groups of students could each present one subtopic of the main topic.

Whatever you do, you will need some way of checking their learning. Making the ILT resource available is not enough. After all, there are books in the library, but does that mean all your students make good use of them?

Examples of activities that use ILT

An underestimated use of computers is to use them in a realistic context. The teacher sets a task making use of computer 'applications' such as word processors, spreadsheets, databases and desktop publishing (DTP) software. These applications are tools which students must become familiar with, so that they know when and how to use them in employment and at home. These skills may be part of their course.

Students often greatly enjoy this natural use of computers, even if it appears a bit dull to you, and at least the younger learners are usually quick on the uptake with unfamiliar software. Some older learners may lack confidence, however, and will need plenty of support and reassurance while they learn. You will need to learn how to use such applications yourself, of course!

Word-processing and desktop publishing

Students can word-process assignments and revision notes, which can then be easily amended and augmented. They can also desktop-publish mind-maps, posters or leaflets they have designed. This is a good activity after a web search, enabling students to capture what they have learned.

Creating interactive worksheets

You or, even better, your students can create interactive worksheets with Microsoft® Word or with a similar word processor. These worksheets can then be put on your institution's intranet or VLE, or displayed with a data projector and completed as a class exercise, or emailed to students.

You can put links to websites or to other documents on handouts (Insert   Hyperlink). Don't forget to put a link in the document you link to, that goes back to the original document. You can also put 'callout' signs that draw students' attention to parts of the worksheet or its diagrams (use the drawing toolbar.)

This is a callout

Typical tasks on interactive worksheets include:

- *Electronic 'decisions, decisions'*: We saw in Chapter 19 that cards can be matched, grouped, sequenced, ranked or used to label a diagram. It is easy to create 'text boxes' to replace cards which can be dragged and dropped to play these games electronically. Students can then save or print out their completed game as a revision aid or to hand in. Great fun and genuinely interactive. Students could be required to do this in pairs, to encourage peer explaining.
- *Highlighting*: You can highlight key points in yellow, just as you can with a conventional highlighter. Give students a handout and ask them to highlight the key points.
- *Drop-down boxes*: You can create a gapped handout for students where they must choose between, say, four optional words in a sentence. The students click on the drop-down box and choose the word they think fits. (See on-screen help or, better still, get someone to show you how, for this and for 'Forms' below.)
- *'Forms'*: This allows you to create an electronic form for the learner to fill in; this can then be e-mailed back to you. Students can use this to fill in their answers to questions. If you use drop-down boxes in forms, you can create a multiple-choice test.

Activities using databases

Databases can be used in any number of ways; the only limitation is your imagination. Information is stored on 'records', each record having the same format. These records can then be sorted or searched for specific data; for example, records of student sporting activities could be searched to discover how many girls play more than three games, or how many boys play both football and rugby. I have seen students use databases in the following ways:

- Chemistry students storing data on dangerous chemicals, such as the names of the chemicals, the hazards they represent, means of disposal, storage and so on.
- Hairdressing students storing data on the various products that they might use in a salon.
- Secretarial students making a database of employment possibilities after their present course.

- Humanities students making a database of recommended library books.
- Electronics students making a database of electronic devices and their uses.
- Computer studies students (in order to keep up to date) extracting and storing data about magazine articles from a computer magazine, with key words that would enable a student to search for an article on a particular subject for an essay. (Every vocational subject has its trade magazine.)

Activities using spreadsheets

Professional accountants, engineers, architects, mathematicians, statisticians, scientists, economists and stockbrokers all make full use of spreadsheets, so teachers in these areas and in related areas should use them too. They are particularly useful for processing numerical data, and for performing calculations and recalculations that would otherwise be too laborious to contemplate. Spreadsheet applications allow the user to draw graphs and pie charts, etc., using their data.

Some uses of spreadsheets I have seen are described below.

- Students design a questionnaire which they give to each other, or to people outside their class, to complete. They then use a spreadsheet to analyse the data collected. For example, health studies students found out how often students cleaned their teeth and for how long. They then compared this data with the number of fillings and extractions the same students reported. (Can you think of a topic for a questionnaire in your subject?)
- A case study exercise on the accounts of a small fictional company.
- Investigating mortgages, compound interest, etc.
- Experimenting with the economics of various livestock-feeding strategies.
- Exploration of the factors affecting the heat losses from a building.
- Investigating the resonance effects in electronic circuits.
- Costing a meal from a menu.
- Investigating any equation from any discipline, using a spreadsheet. For example, students could use the spreadsheet to produce graphs to show the effect of increasing the dimensions of a cube on its surface area, volume and mass.
- Using a graph plot of the equation $y = mx + c$, to carry out 'what if' investigations, to see the effect on the graph of changing the values of 'm' and 'c'.

EXERCISE

How could you use databases, spreadsheets or word-processing programs to devise assignments for students in the following areas?

1 Students looking for employment in the building trade

2 Business studies students studying office machinery

3 Horticultural students studying diseases in vegetable crops

4 Engineering students studying workshop practice

5 Science students doing an assignment on the rates of acceleration of motorcycles

6 An area of study you will be covering with your own students

Web-searching activities

You can, of course, set students a task, an assignment or an independent learning assignment which requires them to search the Internet for information. Your students will love this, as long as they have the search skills. At least for the first assignment, consider being reasonably directive, but gradually hand over control to your students in subsequent assignments. Over a series of assignments, consider taking students through this series of challenges:

1   Requiring students to use specific sites which have a number of useful links, and which you know to be of reasonable quality and relevance.

2   Requiring students to search with web directories such as www.yahoo.com

3   Asking students to check their key words with you before using www.google.com

4   Once students have experienced success with the directed activities above, letting them loose on a free exploration to see what they can find! Expect excitement – and frustration!

5   Asking students to critically evaluate websites. (This is a great assignment task, because it overcomes the problem below, of students copying and pasting website material and claiming it as their own.)

Students can very easily copy text, graphics and pictures from websites, by downloading. Consequently, they can produce a very impressive word-processed assignment in minutes, on any topic, without understanding a word of it! They may use CD-ROMs in a similar way. So stress that students must present work in their own words. Most teachers are happy to let students download at least some material, especially visual material, but require this to be acknowledged and its source given. This policy has the bonus that you learn about useful websites!

Open or closed searches?

If you set off in search of very specific information, you may be disappointed. Reference books and textbooks can often be the best resource for such 'closed' searches for a missing piece in your information jigsaw. However, if you indulge in an open search in an area of interest, you will make surprising and unpredictable discoveries, and exhilarating creative connections to your line of study. Also, more websites will be relevant to an open search such as 'where might tourists visit in Paris' than a closed search such as 'what are the opening times of the Louvre?'

You and your students will probably get most out of the Internet if you alternate between exploration – by experimenting with key words in your line of interest – and a hard-nosed clarification, by asking yourself from time to time: 'What does this do for me?' and 'What do I need exactly?' At its best, the information on the Internet is smack up to date, vividly presented, and, even on the most obscure topics, ludicrously plentiful. Searching is active and fun, and develops students' information-seeking skills and powers of discrimination – these are vital skills.

Activities to teach search skills

Don't treat search skills as an irritating distraction from 'proper' teaching. We live in an age of information overload, and the ability to search with skill and discrimination is vital. A fun and effective way to teach these skills is to set students search tasks requiring them to find specific information you know they will be able to find. A treasure trail of search tasks of increasing difficulty will gradually develop their search skills in a most enjoyable way. These skills will be as useful for CD-ROMs as for the Internet. Beware, however, as each CD-ROM and each Internet search engine will use slightly different searching protocols. Teach a couple of these, but expect students to work the others out for themselves. Ask students what search terms they used and discuss these.

Activities to encourage students to learn from the Internet and other ILT resources

- You can set a task to prepare for a quiz on a given topic and give them useful sites (or not).
- Ask learners to study some sites and then complete an interactive worksheet that they e-mail to you. You can then mark it, or e-mail back model answers for them to mark their own.
- You can set tasks that require students to make presentations (computer-generated slide presentations or websites) which can then go on the intranet or be given in class. (See Chapter 32.)
- You can record students' practical work using a digital camera or video camera.
- Many digital cameras can take a burst of images in a short time, to record students displaying, for example, their craft or sports skills. Some digital cameras can even take short video clips. Once in the digital format, these images can be edited and stored on a PC hard drive, or on the course pages of the intranet. They can also be displayed on classroom or corridor noticeboards. They can later be used for revision and for other activities. Students get a real kick out of their work being recorded in this way.
- MindManager®, MindGenius® or just Microsoft Word® can be used to create mind-maps that summarise what students have learned, from a web search, for example.
- Learning teams, as considered in Chapter 33, can swap their mobile phone numbers and then text or ring each other for help, or if they don't turn up to a class.
- You can create multiple-choice quizzes or tests using Hot Potatoes™, for example. You may be able to find suitable quizzes or tests on the Hot Potatoes™ site, or on the intute site or elsewhere. You can also create quizzes or tests in Microsoft Word®, of course. This can check learning outside of class time well.
- You can give a class some thought-provoking questions, then project a suitable website that answers them, not too directly, using a digital projector or interactive whiteboard. Groups then take it in turns to navigate the site to find the answers to the questions.

- Students can work in groups to create an interactive handout on the topic; each group gives its handout to the next group and hands it back to them for marking.
- Students can create mind-maps or posters by hand, and these can be scanned into a computer for storage on the intranet and for e-mail distribution.
- Students can do a Google search for images, get permission and then put them on to a class CD.
- Students can create an online gallery of images of their work, and images of them doing the work.
- 'Evidence Based ICT' has many more examples. Download it from www.geoff-petty.com/whatsnew.html

Note that the effective use of ILT requires more imagination than it does ICT skills in many cases. Make sure you are not infringing copyright – though educational use of most Internet resources is considered 'fair use' if no money changes hands. See the links for up-to-date information on this, or ask for guidance at your institution.

Activities using e-mail and discussion groups

Many institutions give all their students a free e-mail address. Hotmail and Yahoo! also offer free e-mail accounts.

You can use e-mail to send activities to your students, and to send them links to resources. This is often better than handouts, as students can mis-type Internet addresses (incredible but true) and then loudly complain about your duff typing!

You can also require students to e-mail their completed ILT activity or other work to you. Ask them to reference the sites they visited, with a brief description of each; then you can add the good ones to your collection with a copy and paste.

You can also use e-mail for tutorial support; this can seem impersonal to some students, so make sure you use their name in the communication.

What is it like living in an Islamic country? What do American students think about their nation's contribution to global warming? What do Japanese students think about nuclear weapons after Hiroshima? What are the favourite recipes in Mongolia? The potential of the Internet in this respect is awesome.

Pen-palling for language teaching is being revolutionised by e-mail, which is so fast that it enables virtually live conversations to take place. Video conferencing requires special equipment, but enables language students to converse live with native speakers of the language they are studying while seeing them on screen. There are also special-interest discussion groups or news groups, which communicate with each other by e-mail. Unfortunately, these may be joined by people who take advantage of the relative anonymity of the web, and use bad language and worse. However, some news groups are 'moderated', which means someone checks the material that goes out to subscribers. Most subscriptions are free, and you can unsubscribe if you get fed up with it. Start looking for likely groups at www.tile.net

If you can set up a means for students to discuss their work, this can help them a great deal. Consider allowing students to 'post' anonymous questions for the rest of the class to answer; this can help students who are shy of admitting difficulties, but it also allows students to be offensive, so agree ground rules and use your judgement.

Blogs, wikis and more

Once you are familiar with the most useful ideas above, download 'Evidence Based ICT', which has many more suggestions on activities, from: www.geoffpetty.com/whatsnew.html

Writing your own materials

Multimedia 'authoring' applications allow you to design your own 'screens' and websites, with text, graphics and sound. You can also determine how the screens will respond to the mouse or the keyboard, and so how the user will interact with the material. For example, you can produce a diagram of a heart on which the user clicks with the mouse to gain information, or to start an animation. You can create simple websites using most word processors; simply use 'Save as web page'.

When deciding on a topic worthy of the effort of creating your own materials, or getting students to create theirs, consider the following evaluation criteria (see also pages 395–6 on evaluating resources):

*   *Time stability*. Will you be able to use the resource in subsequent years?
*   *Value for effort*. Will both designers and users be learning something useful?
*   *Need to know*. Ideally, the topic should be indispensable.
*   *Multi-use*. Could the resource be used by more than one group or course?
*   *Interactivity*. Will the user be able to interact with the resource in some way?
*   *Ease of use*. Will users be able to navigate and learn how to use the resource intuitively?

Reflect on your progress in ILT

It is remarkably common for teachers to create a huge list of weblinks that the students are not then required to use. They 'put it all on the intranet'. Vast stores of text documents, such as assignments and handouts, can be useful because they make materials available to students who may have missed a class, for example. But this is not a substitute for effective use of ILT.

What creates learning is what goes on in the learner's head, not what appears on screen or what is available on an intranet. If you read documents from Becta or Ferl and other ILT organisations, it is striking that they are interested in the learning, not just the technology.

EXERCISE

You are a medieval teacher at the time of the invention of the book. You were trained to teach by talking. How should the invention of the book change what you do? Consider:

- How will you find good books?
- What student activities will you use to:
  - ensure that students use the books that are available to them in the library?
  - check their learning from these books?

Some useful Internet addresses

Helping you to develop your ILT activities and skills

www.vts.intute.ac.uk/
Subject-specific training in searching the Internet.

www.hotpot.uvic.ca/
(Hot Potatoes™) For making tests and other interactive activities.

www.rdpslides.com/pptfaq/
This is where to get your Microsoft PowerPoint® queries answered.

www.learningtechnologies.ac.uk
For professional development in e-learning.

Gateway sites and other educational links to resources

The following sites have links to educational resources in almost every subject area. They are vast and repay the time spent searching. Use the BBC site to search for forthcoming educational TV programmes worth videoing in your subject area.

http://excellence.qia.org.uk/
The excellence gateway is truly vast.

www.intute.ac.uk/
This is vast too.

www.bbc.co.uk/learning/
You must have a look here.

www.curriculumonline.gov.uk/
National curriculum-based site, but some materials are very suitable for many non-school teachers.

www.jisc.ac.uk
ILT- and ICT-related matters; some for HE only.

www.sheffcol.ac.uk/links
Award-winning links pages.

www.channel4.com/learning
Not as big as the BBC, but worth a look.

http://curriculum.qca.org.uk/
The national curriculum online.

www.keyskills4u.com
Interactive key skills materials for use by students.

www.amazing-grades.com
More materials worth exploring … have I exhausted you yet?

www.tile.net
Has discussion group listings and lists of mailing lists.

Get that question answered

http://encarta.msn.com/
A searchable encyclopaedia.

www.askjeeves.com
Type in a question and get an answer.

www.wikipedia.org/
An online encyclopaedia to which you can contribute.

Some useful general-interest sites

www.teachernet.gov.uk

www.ofsted.gov.uk
Why not inspect the inspection body's site?

www.dcsf.gov.uk/index.htm
Government Department for Children, Schools and Families.

www.eduref.org
Search a vast database of education literature – lesson plans too.

www.lsneducation.org.uk/
Learning and Skills Network – useful publications.

www.qia.org.uk/
Quality Improvement Agency for research in post-compulsory education.

www.lsc.gov.uk
The funding body for the post-compulsory sector.

www.geoffpetty.com
My own site, which has lots of free downloads on it and many more useful links.

www.rqa.org.uk
Search their database of development projects in the post-compulsory sector.

www.futurelab.org
Includes a list of online journals on ILT.

Further reading

Attewell, J. (2002) *Distributed and Electronic Learning: A Review of the Literature*, LSRC Research Findings, available online from www.lsrc.org.uk

DELG (2002) *Report of the Learning and Skills Council's Distributed Electronic Learning Group*, www.lsc.gov.uk

Hill, C. (2003) *Teaching Using Information and Learning Technology in Further Education*, Exeter: Learning Matters. You can download a sample of this excellent book from www.learningmatters.co.uk

McNaught, A. (2004) *Exploring E-learning for Literacy, Numeracy and ESOL Teachers*, Coventry: Ferl/Becta.

MORI (2002) 'E-learning at Home and School', executive summary. Available from www.campaign-for-learning.org.uk

37

Aims and objectives

A large insurance firm in New York was having trouble with its 20-storey skyscraper. The managing director wrote to engineering firms, telling them of the repeated complaints he had received from his employees. They were complaining about the length of time they had to wait for the lift, so he was asking for quotes for the installation of a new lift shaft.

The managing director received a number of quotes for tens of millions of dollars, along with one from an engineer who said he could solve the problem for $9,000. This quote was rejected out of hand at first, but the director was intrigued. Finally, he telephoned and asked, 'How can you fit a lift shaft for $9,000?' The engineer pointed out that the real aim was not to fit a lift shaft, but to reduce employee frustration. His plan was to create comfortable places for employees to wait for the lift, with easy chairs, potted plants, mirrors, fish tanks, magazines and piped music. This solution still works well to this day. Moral: think very carefully about your aims before starting your plans.

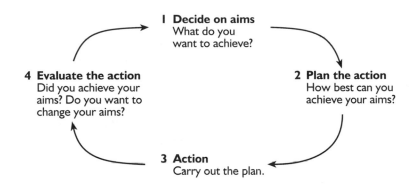

I Decide on aims
What do you want to achieve?

2 Plan the action
How best can you achieve your aims?

3 Action
Carry out the plan.

4 Evaluate the action
Did you achieve your aims? Do you want to change your aims?

Almost any purposeful human activity can be said to fall into the pattern shown in the diagram above – everything from arranging your holidays or cooking fish pie to setting up a business or going shopping.

Teaching falls into the same pattern. Teachers first decide what they hope to achieve (aims and objectives), then plan the lesson, then teach the lesson – i.e. carry the plan out. Then they need to evaluate the lesson, asking themselves whether they did indeed achieve the aims set. Assessing what the students have learned helps answer this question. This evaluation may lead to a change in the aims for the next lesson, or for the next time this same lesson is taught, so the process is cyclic.

What are aims and objectives?

'Aims' or 'educational goals' are clear and concise statements that describe what the teacher hopes to achieve. These statements of intent are usually expressed in a rather broad and generalised way – for example:

- To improve the students' ability to communicate effectively in formal written English.
- To develop an understanding and appreciation of the world's major religions.
- To create opportunities for students to engage in creative self-expression.
- To develop a knowledge and understanding of scientific investigative procedures.

Some people advocate expressing aims from the point of view of the teacher or the course, rather than from the students' point of view. For example:

- The aim of the course is to consider the basic principles of retailing.
- The training package will introduce the basic elements of computer programming.

It is usually impossible to achieve aims absolutely. Students could work on achieving most of the above aims for a lifetime, and still have plenty to do! Aims are so general and all-embracing that there can be as few as four or five for a full-time one-year course.

Aims are like compass directions, indicating the general direction in which the teacher wishes to travel. As such, they are vital; but they are not specific enough to help the teacher pick learning activities, or assess whether learning has taken place. There is no general agreement about how to decide aims and objectives, or precisely how they should be written. But there is agreement that aims are vitally important.

Where do aims come from?

Aims may be provided by an examination syllabus, by a programme of study, or by the awarding body for a qualification. Later we will see that they may in some circumstances be provided by a 'needs analysis', by 'task analysis' or by negotiation with the students on the course. However, teachers decide most of their own aims, even if they are not written down formally.

What are you are trying to achieve by your teaching? Do you take an entirely functional view that education provides students with the means to earn a living and to cope in our society? Or do your aims go beyond this? Some aims will come from your own values (see Chapter 45).

Learning outcomes

Aims may point you in the right direction, but they don't tell you how to get there, or when you have arrived. So intentions must be described in a more detailed way with what are variously called 'specific objectives', 'behaviourist objectives', 'competencies' and/or 'specific learning outcomes'. In this book, I shall call them 'learning outcomes'. They are testable statements describing what you intend your students to learn – for example:

- The student should be able to use inverted commas correctly.
- The student should be able to solder electronic components on to a circuit board.

This is much better than teacher-centred aims such as 'to describe how to punctuate correctly' or 'to show students how to solder'. If you examine the latter carefully, you will see that these statements can be satisfactorily met whether or not the student has learned anything! We must shift the focus from teaching to learning.

Doing so has a number of advantages. It makes clear what students have to practise, and avoids a lesson dominated by teacher talk, where little real learning takes place. It makes lesson planning easier by suggesting learning activities (e.g. corrected practice of soldering or dialogue writing). Moreover, if you know precisely what students should be able to do, it is much easier to assess whether or not they can do it. This enables you to evaluate how successful your lessons have been.

The crucial point is that the outcomes precisely describe observable learner performance, shifting the focus on to what the students will be able to do as a result of their learning, and away from what the teacher will do. For example:

The student should be able to:

- State three advantages of the diesel engine over the petrol engine.
- List the main methods of pest management in Indonesia.
- Distinguish between fog, smog, mist and cloud.

Most people have difficulty in writing objectives at first, tending to think in terms of what the teacher will do rather than what the student will learn. Are these specific learning outcomes?

- To introduce the idea of percentages.
- The Peasants' Revolt.

The answer is no – they aren't. Could you change them so that they were? Have a try before reading further.

Specific learning outcomes or specific objectives should:

- specify precisely and in concrete terms what the student should be able to do
- be written in such a way that it is possible to determine whether or not the objective has been achieved
- usually be short-term
- be drawn up by the teacher to suit the resources, the teacher and the students
- optionally, define the circumstances under which the objective is to be demonstrated and/or what constitutes an achievement, e.g. 'Translate passage 6d in less than five minutes, making fewer than four minor mistakes'.

Some like the mnemonic SMART, standing for specific, measurable, agreed, realistic and timebound.

Here are some legitimate objectives for the topics mentioned above. Notice that they identify skills or abilities, and so suggest 'use', 'check and correct' and the other elements of learning.

Students should be able to:

- express one number as a percentage of another
- calculate a given percentage of a given amount.

Students should be able to:

- state and explain the main events running up to the Peasants' Revolt
- explain three economic consequences of the Peasants' Revolt.

Ineffective teachers say they will 'cover percentages' or 'talk about the Peasants' Revolt', or 'do fractions'. But effective teachers always focus on what the student should be able to do. Writing 'specific learning outcomes' or 'specific objectives' is an intellectually demanding task, and it requires a great deal of time and effort. But outcomes are vital; they are the stepping stones which take the learners in the direction of our aims.

Classification of objectives or outcomes

B. S. Bloom's 'Taxonomy of Educational Objectives' attempts to classify all learning into three domains, and, within each domain, into skills or abilities of different types or difficulty. We also met it in Chapter 1. It is written from a learning objectives point of view, and describes 'how the learners are expected to be changed by the educative process'. It was first developed in 1951 and has had an enormous influence.

The three domains and some of their subsections are described briefly below in a simplified version. Typical verbs used to write objectives are given for each section of the taxonomy.

The cognitive domain (intellectual skills and abilities)

Bloom arranged the categories which follow in order of difficulty, with the easiest first. However, easy, high-order tasks are possible, indeed vital, as we saw in Chapter 1. Without higher-order objectives in your teaching, these skills will not be developed, and neither will fully functional knowledge or full comprehension.

Knowledge. *To be able to:*

state; recall; list; recognise; select; reproduce; draw …

e.g. to recall Newton's Laws of Motion.

Comprehension. *To be able to:*

explain; describe reasons for; identify causes of; illustrate …

e.g. to give reasons for seat belts by referring to Newton's Laws of Motion.

Application. *To be able to:*

use; apply; construct; solve; select …

e.g. to use Newton's Laws of Motion to solve simple problems.

Analysis. *To be able to:*

break down; list component parts of; compare and contrast; differentiate between …

Synthesis (this involves choosing, using and putting together diverse skills, abilities and knowledge to accomplish a particular new task). *To be able to:*

summarise; generalise; argue; organise; design; explain the reason for …

Evaluation. *To be able to:*

judge; evaluate; give arguments for and against; criticise …

The affective domain

This domain concerns itself with attention, interest, awareness, aesthetic appreciation, moral, aesthetic and other attitudes, opinions, feelings or values. For example:

> *to listen to … to appreciate the importance of …*
> *to have an awareness of … to respond with personal feelings …*
> *to have an aesthetic appreciation of … to have a commitment towards …*
> *to recognise the moral dilemmas involved in … to believe in your own ability to …*

The psychomotor domain

This includes motor skills or physical skills, including sense perception, hand-and-eye coordination, etc. For example:

> *to plane; to draw; to throw; to weld …*

Note that 'to know …' or 'to understand …' are not acceptable beginnings for specific objectives, which should describe abilities that are directly observable and testable. What does it mean to say that a student 'knows', say, the story of Lazarus? Does it mean that the student is able to recognise the story and name it? Or recall it in outline? Or recall it in detail? Or describe its significance? The objective needs to state what the student should be able to do in an easily testable form; it could become, for example:

> To recount in outline the story of Lazarus.

Unlike 'To know the story of Lazarus', this is clear, it is testable, and it suggests what the student needs to practise.

Similarly, what does it mean to 'understand' osmosis? Does it mean to be able to describe its significance? To explain how and why it takes place? To be able to use the idea to explain novel occurrences of the phenomenon? Or some combination of these abilities? Often what is required is for the student to be able to answer examination-style questions on the topic; if so, what abilities do such questions demand? Examining textbook and examination questions in the topic you are teaching can help you to see what students should be able to do with the material you are teaching. To say that they should 'know' or 'understand' the material is too vague.

General objectives

Many teachers describe their intentions partly in a form which is somewhere between an aim and a specific learning outcome. Such intentions are variously described as short-term aims, general instructional objectives, or non-behaviourist objectives. Examples might be:

- **To introduce students to some aspects of modern telecommunications.**
- **To outline modern stock-control methods.**

If you choose to describe your intentions in such a way, make sure that you include in each statement both the content itself and what will be done with such content. Make your statements clear and simple. For example:

- **To develop an appreciation of Handel's *Messiah*.**
- **To recognise the importance of safety checks on building sites.**

These general objectives are then used to generate specific learning outcomes. For example, the safety objective above could be broken down as follows:

> *General objective:*
> To recognise the importance of frequent safety inspections.
> *Specific learning outcomes:*
> To list the main checks made during a safety inspection.
> To state the main dangers to health and safety on a building site.
> To recognise and correct the improper use of a ladder.

An aim may encompass many general objectives, and, in turn, each general objective will generate a number of specific learning outcomes.

Developmental and mastery objectives

General objectives are of two broad types: mastery and developmental. Mastery objectives are relatively 'easy'. When in the cognitive domain, they typically involve only knowledge and comprehension. They are designed to be mastered by all students, and form the minimum requirement for passing the course. As a result, their achievement depends more on time spent trying to master them than on innate ability, flair or aptitude – every student can master them if he or she tries hard enough for long enough. The specific learning outcomes developed from them usually describe skills or abilities which can be attained in a short timescale, perhaps a matter of minutes. They can then be assessed easily with a simple test. For example:

Recognise and name the main constituents of a simple cell.

Far from being trivial, targets such as these, which are attainable by all the students in a group, have inestimable value. Mastery objectives give rise to straightforward learning tasks which are time- rather than ability-dependent. They offer the teacher an opportunity to give weaker students the success, reinforcement and motivation which is a precondition for their present and future learning (see Chapter 5).

By contrast, some general objectives, called *developmental objectives*, may never be fully achieved. For example:

* Write a clear, scientifically argued laboratory report ...
* Evaluate the importance of full to high employment in Western societies.

Such objectives are highly dependent on previous learning; require high-order thinking skills; cannot be easily and objectively assessed; and take considerable time and effort on the part of the learner before any noticeable improvement in their execution is shown. Their importance lies in their ability to maximise individual development, and to stretch the more able. Continuous development rather than complete mastery is expected.

No finite list of specific learning outcomes will entirely describe a developmental objective; it is greater than the sum of its parts. However, a representative sample of specific learning outcomes can usually be written, describing typical abilities that a learner will have once the developmental objective has been achieved. For example:

General objective:
Write a clear, scientifically argued laboratory report ...
Specific learning outcomes:
The student should be able to:
* break the report into the usual categories of apparatus, method, etc.
* refer directly to the results when writing the conclusions.

These specific learning outcomes or objectives are not usually taught and tested one by one, as can be the case for mastery objectives. Can all general objectives be broken down? For example, can the objective 'To gain an appreciation of the war poets' be expressed in specific objective form? Some teachers think not. But what does 'appreciation' mean? If you consider that appreciation involves, at least in part, the learner coming to a personal opinion about the meaning and importance of the poems under study, then it is possible. Personal opinion-forming is a high-order skill in the cognitive domain, which is learned by corrected practice (see Chapter 38, where teaching methods are suggested).

> *General objective*:
> To gain an appreciation of Wilfred Owen's poem 'Insensibility'.
> *Specific learning outcomes*:
> The student should be able to:
> * express a personal opinion of the meaning of the poem
> * write a personal evaluation of the poem
> * critically appraise an appreciation of the poem written by another.

Mixing developmental and mastery objectives

Most teaching should involve a mixture of developmental and mastery objectives; for 'differentiation' or 'mixed-ability' teaching this is especially vital. If a teacher habitually assesses his or her students by their essay or scientific report-writing skills, some students will continue to score badly even when they try hard. Both mastery and developmental objectives must of course be recognised, reinforced and assessed, or the mix will be in vain. It helps, however, to concentrate reinforcement on the mastery objectives when motivation becomes a problem.

Sources for objectives

For most courses, objectives may be drawn up by reference to one or more of the following: the course aims, the syllabus, the programme of study, the unit specification, the 'scheme of work', attainment targets, performance criteria or statements of competence. If you are devising your own course from scratch, deciding on aims and objectives is a crucial part of the process; this is dealt with in Chapter 42, on planning courses.

If you are teaching to the national curriculum, you will follow a programme of study which describes which topics to cover, and attainment targets which are rather like detailed objectives. For example, Attainment Target 2 in Science 2 'Life processes and living things' has eight levels. Level 6 includes:

* describe the structure of a simple cell
* identify differences between simple animal cells and plant cells.

These describe what students should be able to do, so they are 'learning outcomes'. Topics described in syllabuses, or in programmes of study, are often less detailed and rather like general objectives. They need to be read very carefully, and then expressed in terms of specific learning outcomes.

The content of National Vocational Qualifications (NVQs) is described in terms of 'competences'. For example:

* Fit a four-way junction box (*in an electrician's qualification*).
* Make recommendations for expenditure (*in a manager's qualification*).

The aim–objective continuum

Learners are expected to gather evidence to show that they have carried out the tasks described in the competences successfully. NVQs are explained in more detail in Chapter 44, on summative assessment.

Competences nearly always involve a good deal of learning, so it is frequently necessary to break them down into specific learning outcomes. Again, read them very carefully first.

If you have difficulty writing objectives, look at assessments for the course. What do examiners or assessors expect learners to be able to do? These skills and abilities must of course be among your objectives. When a course is planned, assessment questions are devised from the objectives, not the other way round! But for a new teacher working on an existing course, assessment tasks often clarify what students should be able to do, and so help considerably in clarifying lesson objectives.

Devising objectives is no easy matter, but the process of clarification it encourages is crucial to effective teaching.

Embedding aims and objectives

Why do experienced teachers often do without formal lesson plans? As teachers become more experienced, some begin to define objectives less formally but more fully. I no longer formally write objectives for many of my lessons, but I have spent years embodying them in worksheets, assessments, practical activities, etc. For example, I do not write down, 'Students should be able to use the principle of moments to solve simple problems'. I find this too vague. Instead, I write question sheets and assessments with examples of such problems, and expect students to achieve a minimum mark on them. The worksheets and assessments, along with other learning activities, are carefully devised to cover what I know from experience students must be able to do. In a sense, I have embodied my very detailed objectives in a comprehensive set of learning activities, worksheets and assessments.

I'm not the only one. Many teachers of computing ask their students to work through workbooks specifically designed to teach their students how to use the computer system they are learning. Similarly, engineering teachers design a programme of 'jobs' for their students to make, which introduces them to a carefully considered series of skills and techniques.

If you use a ready-made system like this, don't hand responsibility over to it entirely. Completing a learning task, even a student-centred one, does not guarantee learning; in particular, students may not understand what they have done.

Process and product

Objectives describe *what* students will learn, and this is sometimes called the learning 'product'. At least as important as *what* students will learn is *how* they will learn it; this is often called the learning 'process'. For example, if students in a geography class are simply told about the historical development of cities, this will require them to listen and to remember. If, however, they are taught the same topic by examining historical evidence, guided discovery, Socratic questioning, and group work, they will *also* develop their ability to interpret evidence, to form hypotheses, to reason, to evaluate arguments and to work in a group. We saw particularly in the chapters on questioning and guided discovery that it is not factual knowledge and low-order skills that are the most valuable legacy of an education, but the high-order thinking skills developed *while* the student learns.

So if the process is more important than the product, why not define the purposes of a lesson in terms of this process? This is a very legitimate approach of emerging importance. Some whole courses, such as General National Vocational Qualifications (GNVQs), are organised at least in part along these lines. The assessment of such courses effectively requires students to undertake certain activities, such as to visit a place of work, study certain aspects of it and write a report. The students learn about the place of work, of course, but they learn much more as well – for example, how to plan, gather evidence, come to their own understanding, check this, communicate it in writing, evaluate their own performance and so on.

EXERCISE

The intermediate GNVQ in health and social care

Unit 2 of the above qualification, which is equivalent to a GCSE, is called 'Promoting health & well-being'. It is assessed by coursework only. The unit stipulates what students should know, but the assessment requires that the student 'produce a plan for promoting health and well-being for at least one person who is at risk.' This is to include information about risks, and to consider factors such as physical, emotional, social and intellectual health and well-being.

This is essentially a 'process' approach, as the unit stipulates what students will do, as well as what they will learn.

1 In addition to the learning about nutrition and food hygiene, what extra learning will come about by the process of researching and writing the report? Be as specific as you can.
2 Compare this with a product approach that stipulates only what the students should know, and then assesses this by an examination.

Many teachers use a mixture of process and product objectives. Here are some examples of process objectives; notice that the learning outcome is not described at all.

- The students will design an experiment to measure the energy stored in a stretched spring.
- The students will improvise an imaginary interview between Henry V and a modern journalist.
- The students will reflect on their learning to date and set themselves targets for improvement.
- The students will debate the strengths and weaknesses of care in the community.

Process objectives are particularly useful when you can't tell in advance what your students will learn. Think, for example, of student nurses writing a journal on their ward experiences, an art class visiting a new exhibition, or a hairdressing student who must provide the styling which her client requests.

At best, only a few objectives can be written in such situations; but if the activity is self-evidently valuable, then write it down as the intention for the lesson.

If student learning is often unpredictable – for example, while serving in a shop on work experience – then learning can be described as a series of competences, which are 'signed off' on student record cards as they are mastered. Alternatively, students themselves can 'own' and tick off their card; I've seen this work well for courses in adult recreational photography, and for woodwork courses.

The limitations of aims and outcomes

There is a danger in concentrating exclusively on learning outcomes. They are almost always short-term and defined by content. What about long-term learning and skills? Skills are vital for real life and for assessment success, and are more transferable than content knowledge, but they can be ignored – for example, skills high on Bloom's taxonomy, such as essay writing, critical thinking skills, study skills, learning how to learn and the development of creative thinking. Ideally, the content is taught in a way that requires the students to practise these transferable skills in double-decker lessons (explained in the next chapter). How you teach is more important than what you teach. It is what the students do that decides what skills they learn, not the topic.

And what of developing motivation, appreciation, interest and curiosity? What about ethics, joy, beauty and the human spirit? You may feel you have nothing to offer here, but many people put their teachers amongst those who have been most influential in their human development. And if we are we putting our students off learning while we teach them, are we doing them a service in the long term?

Most learning has as its ultimate aims the satisfaction of material needs: giving students the ability to obtain and keep a job, and the humdrum skills and abilities we all need if we are to cope in our everyday world. But there is more to being human than being fed and watered, and we are in danger of forgetting this if we over-indulge in 'short-termism'.

This chapter has included some difficult but influential ideas; I suggest you read it again from time to time during your teaching practice.

Summary

You will never achieve your purposes if you are not clear what these are. However, the clarity of your thinking is much more important than agonising over the precise categorisation of your aims, objectives or outcomes. The following diagrams summarise some important aspects of this chapter.

The planning cycle

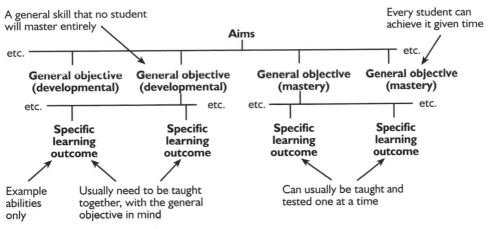

The tree structure of aims and objectives

Checklist

☐ Do you describe your intentions clearly, in the form of aims and of more specific, testable objectives?

☐ Do you have a mix of objectives that (a) can be easily mastered, and (b) give an opportunity for development?

☐ As well as specific objectives, do you pay attention to overarching aims such as motivation, curiosity, interest, appreciation, reasoning skills, creativity, etc.?

Further reading

Most of the general teaching books in the bibliography deal with this topic.

38

Choosing activities for the lesson

So, after days of agonising, you have decided on your aims, objectives and specific learning outcomes: the next step is to choose activities to achieve them. This is more of an art than a science, requiring simultaneous consideration of all the ideas mentioned previously in this book. Remember particularly that learning requires each student to make a personal version of what they are being taught; and that they must improve and expand this incomplete understanding through corrected practice.

Experienced teachers and other educationalists disagree about many things, but there is a rare consensus here: the activities you choose must be related to the objectives you have for the lesson, and they must involve plenty of student activity. But which activities best suit your objectives? There are two models to guide your choice: *educare?* and CIA.

The *educare?* approach

If learning is to be focused on acquiring specific skills, then the *educare?* mnemonic best guides your choice of learning activities. The activities themselves, such as demonstrations and student practice, are described in Part 2. The choice of activities to meet students' needs is covered as listed below.

- *Learning physical or intellectual skills*: See Chapters 2 and 3.
- *Learning facts*: See Chapter 23 on learning for remembering.
- *Learning concepts*: See Chapter 12 on the art of explaining and 'Decisions, decisions' in Chapter 19.
- *Opinion-forming and affective learning* are dealt with below and in Chapter 39.

If you find it helpful, you can see all objectives as requiring corrected practice, and therefore requiring the satisfaction of the learner's *educare?* needs (Chapters 2 and 3). You can use the mnemonic either as a checklist to ensure that learners' needs are met by the activities you have chosen, or as a way of suggesting activities. Try it out for a few lessons, but if you don't find the approach helpful, you are not obliged to use it!

In any case, don't slavishly follow the mnemonic; use your common sense. Sometimes earlier learning will already have satisfied some of these learners' needs. For example, activities designed to achieve one of your objectives may also help to achieve another. But beware of omitting useful activities; most inexperienced teachers overestimate their students. And remember, each learner's need can be satisfied by any number of activities; the mnemonic is not a list of teaching methods, but of learners' needs.

Each learner's needs can be provided in many ways:

Explanation: teacher talk; discovery; questioning; reading; homework; discussion; video; visual aids ...

'Doing-detail' (being shown or discovering in concrete terms what I am expected to do and how to do it): teacher demonstrating the ability; inspecting examples of good work; discussing criteria for success; teacher thinking out loud to demonstrate how to approach a problem; self-, peer or spoof assessment; students working out how to do it for themselves; examining a case study; students watching a video of someone doing it ...

Use (student practice of ability): individual work; group work or discussion; practicals; answering questions (written or oral); essays; games ...

Check and correct: teacher marking work; self-check (with or without given criteria); peer check; questioning; comparing work with an example of good practice; seeing if the device works ...

Aide-memoire: handouts; personal or teacher's notes; booklets; textbooks; reference books; audio tapes; video; mnemonics ...

Review: questioning; tests; quizzes; examinations; practical sessions; homework; games; all the activities mentioned under 'Use' ...

Evaluation: examinations, or any other activities where students work alone.

?: teacher and/or peers available and approachable, especially during the 'Use' phase.

(Methods such as projects, group work, games and questioning are so adaptable that they can provide any or all the elements for a given objective, if used appropriately.)

The CIA approach: corrected practice without *educare?*

Not all cognitive learning is easy to see in terms of the *educare?* elements, especially if it is not focused on specific skills. Here is a more indirect approach to arranging corrected practice, which is summarised by the diagram.

First, the teacher determines the content which must be taught. Course documentation will describe this, but rarely in sufficient detail. You will get some help from 'schemes of work', course-specific textbooks and past examination questions, and

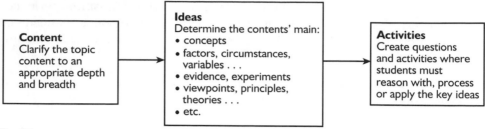

The CIA process

from other teachers' worksheets and handouts. Don't be afraid to talk to teachers about their approach; it is a strength, not a weakness, to ask for advice if it might help you.

Once you are familiar with the material, try to isolate the most important content. Ask yourself: 'What are the key ideas here?' Use the literature mentioned in the previous paragraph for guidance. Make a note of the facts, data, events, people, concepts, principles, viewpoints and other ideas which are central to an understanding of the topic. You might like to write your own notes for the topic at this stage.

Now comes the most difficult stage. You must frame questions, tasks or activities which require the students to reason with, process or apply the ideas in the content. If you are not clear how to do this, look at questions in textbooks or examination papers. Eventually you will get the idea and be able to develop more appropriate questions, tasks and activities by yourself. If you look at Bloom's taxonomy on page 9, you will see many tasks suggested under each high-order skill.

Think also of the academic or vocational relevance of the topic. What should your students be able to *do* with the content you are teaching? Should it enable them to design a marketing strategy, diagnose a fault in a circuit, or give guidance to a customer? Then why not devise an activity which requires your students to do just that? You could base questions on a scenario or a case study. Knowledge is a means to an end. If you focus your tasks on this end, your lessons become real and relevant. Examining the content and ideas may well suggest specific skills, like using a microscope or giving guidance to a customer. The *educare?* model can then be used to generate useful activities.

Consider also the reasoning skills your subject seeks to develop. You must think this through for yourself, and it is a fascinating journey, but examples might include:

* *history:* evaluating evidence, giving reasons for and evaluations of events, determining the views of historical characters by examining evidence such as their writings and actions, etc.
* *science:* interpreting experimental data, using scientific principles to explain phenomena, forming hypotheses and then testing them experimentally, etc.
* *social sciences:* explaining human behaviour in terms of social or psychological theories, empathising with others, etc.

Your subject is a way of thinking, not just a body of facts, and this way of thinking will only be developed by corrected practice. So set tasks which require your students to reason. Get them thinking like real scientists, historians or social scientists. The ideal way to do this is to use double-decker lessons, as explained below.

It is most important to recognise that delivering the content and ideas of your topic is not enough. You are not a petrol pump attendant filling the students' empty tanks! A closer analogy is that you are an athletics coach, developing your students' abilities through the students' *own* exercise and practice. You may be structuring the exercise programme, but like athletes, it is the students who must do the practice, provide the effort and so create the gains.

We 'learn by doing', to use John Dewey's phrase. Students need to reason with the content, they need to use it, to process it and to argue beyond what was immediately given. Why is this? When students begin using the content and ideas, as opposed to simply reading or listening to it, vital advantages follow:

* Students must make their own meaning of the material and come to their own understanding of it. This *is* what we call learning.
* Students become actively involved in their learning.
* Students will remember what they think about, but may forget what they hear or read.
* The teacher gets some feedback on whether students understand the material.
* There are opportunities for both teacher and student to check and correct understanding.
* Reasoning is more demanding than reading or listening, so students are stretched.
* Students develop their reasoning skills, as well as the factual knowledge of the subject matter. These reasoning skills are often more important than the factual knowledge, as facts may go out of date, or may have no direct use for the student in later life.
* Students are encouraged into deep-level rather than surface-level processing, as described in Chapter 25.
* Reasoning is more fun than listening. More fun even than listening to *you*!

Devising activities for your students is not easy, especially if you were taught in a very instructional style yourself. If you were, try not to teach the way you were taught, but to make your lessons more active and effective. Get your students to reason about their world, to solve problems, develop arguments, design or create something, analyse, evaluate and so on. This is exciting teaching as well as exciting learning.

AN EXAMPLE OF THE USE OF THE CIA PROCESS

A health studies lecturer is to teach her class about the human heart. She looks at course documentation, textbooks and past-paper questions to discover the breadth and depth she must cover. Then she composes a handout, with the basic facts illustrated with diagrams. She decides how to use models and computer simulations of the heart to explain its function.

Then she makes up questions for students to answer in groups, which make her students *process* and make *use* of this information. Her plans include the following.

She decides to base some questions on the symptoms of heart disease, as this has vocational relevance, human interest and often comes up in exams. She bases her questions on case studies such as:

Mrs Everett has a narrowing of the arteries which feed the muscles of her heart. Explain, with reasons, what effect this would have on:

a her heart rate at rest

b her maximum blood-flow rate

c her ability to climb stairs

d the likelihood of (i) a stroke and (ii) a heart attack.

She decides to ask the groups, 'What would happen if' questions to test their understanding:

What would happen if ... the pulmonary artery was heavily 'furred up'? ... the wall of the left ventricle was weakened?', etc.

She decides that the specific skill of labelling a diagram of the heart is important, and so devises a labelling game to develop this skill, and a short test to assess it.

A poor teacher would simply 'deliver' the facts about the heart. A good teacher sets activities which require students to process this information and make their own sense of it.

(Look also at the other examples of the use of the CIA process in Chapters 3 and 29.)

This three-phase process of *Content   Ideas   Activities* (the CIA process) should help you to make your lessons more active and interesting for you and your students. How to implement these activities in the classroom is the subject of Part 2 of this book.

If neither the *educare?* approach nor the CIA approach suits you, don't lapse into a teacher-centred approach. Take the following very varied list of objectives. Can you see that in each case the student needs corrected practice? When a specific skill is described, *educare?* should help. If not, corrected practice in reasoning with the content and ideas in the topic is required, and CIA should help. Which model is best for which objective?

The student should be able to:

1 Calculate the volume of a sphere or a cone.

2 Outline the workings of a car's ignition system.

3 List and evaluate the principal ways in which the coming of the railways affected the lives of people living in Victorian times.

4   Use the French verb *avoir* correctly in simple sentences.

5   Make use of the concept of socialisation to explain everyday observations.

Remember in Chapter 1 we found students must have open challenging tasks and informative feedback to learn effectively. Page 146 has some particularly effective tasks to try.

Double-decker lessons

This is the most rigorous CIA approach, but you may need to have taught a few lessons before you try it. First, consider the skills required by your subject, and by the assessments your students must take. Then draw up a list of the skills your students must acquire. For example, suppose you are a business studies teacher. You decide that two skills required of your students are the ability to *evaluate* a business practice and the ability to *plan an essay*.

Now you look at the content you have to teach in your lesson – suppose the topic is marketing plans for small businesses. You now plan a lesson that requires your students to practise a subject-specific skill on this content. For example, you could teach students about marketing plans by asking them to *evaluate* some marketing plans provided by you.

At the end of the lesson you review the content: 'What have we learned about marketing plans?' and you review the skill (*evaluation*) separately. Skills are best reviewed by 'bridging', which involves focusing on the skill and asking two questions:

'You have just evaluated some marketing plans ...'
1. *'How did you do that?'* (This question focuses on the evaluation process. For example, thinking of strengths, weaknesses and ways of improving each marketing plan.)
2. *'Where else could you use that process/skill?'* (For example, the same process could be used to 'critically appraise' or to 'consider the effectiveness of ...' etc.).

In another lesson, students might learn about quality systems by planning an essay entitled 'What is a quality system?' They might not write this essay, just plan it. (The plan doubles as a good aide memoire.) The essay-planning skill would be reviewed by bridging: 'You have just planned an essay; how did you do that?', then, 'Where else could you use that process?', e.g. report writing. This process is described in detail in Chapter 28.

Many double-decker lessons are required to develop any given skill.

See Chapter 42 'Embedding skills into your scheme of work' for more on double-decker lessons. *Evidence Based Teaching* has the fullest account.

The rest of this chapter will show you how to choose activities in order to teach objectives involving opinion forming.

Choosing activities for divergent opinion forming

Teachers of English literature, history of art, music, social and the other human sciences, philosophy and many other subjects are amongst those who often aim to encourage their students to develop their own informed opinions; for example:

Students should be able to:

- give a critical appreciation of Shakespeare's imagery in *Romeo and Juliet*
- consider the role of the United Nations in peacekeeping since the Gulf War.

Students are not all expected to develop the *same* opinion, so this is divergent learning. Like all learning, it can be seen as a process of corrected practice, and the usual learners' needs apply. As always, these needs suggest learning activities.

Let's look at some of the *educare?* elements:

Explanation. The student needs the background factual information relevant to the opinion being formed.

'Doing-detail'. The student benefits from being shown example opinions on the subject matter – for example, the opinions of experts, interested parties, peers, former students, yourself as teacher (you can put forward a variety of points of view for discussion). The more varied the opinions, the better.

Use. Students put forward their own opinions orally or in writing, in a form that is at first tentative and exploratory, but becoming progressively more committed and complete.

Check and correct. Students' opinions are criticised by themselves, peers, the tutor, etc. As a result of this criticism, the students should modify their opinions towards a progressively more informed, better-argued and more defensible position. Corrective feedback should not be overcritical, otherwise the student will develop defensive or withdrawal postures which will prevent constructive modification of their opinion – i.e. prevent learning. The tutor should limit criticism to matters of fact and consistency, and should be tolerant of opinion different from their own.

The other learners' needs – i.e. aide-memoire, review, evaluation and query answering – are self-explanatory. Opinion forming requires high-order reasoning skills, and consideration of factors such as reliability of evidence and bias.

The teaching methods suggested by the above needs include reading, question and answer, small-group and larger-group discussions, debate, essay writing, etc. Many activities mentioned in the chapters on groups and games would also be relevant.

Suppose, for example, that a social studies teacher has the following objective:

> Students should be able to express an informed opinion on the causes of high urban crime rates.

This objective could be achieved by:

Explanation. Giving the students a lecture on relevant statistics and other relevant background facts.

'Doing-detail'. Asking students to read the opinions of police commissioners, politicians, community workers, criminologists, journalists, etc.

Use and *Check and correct*. Asking groups to prioritise 10 alleged causes of urban crime, each being printed on its own card (with some fallacious 'causes' included). Groups could play the role of political advisers to the prime minister and make presentations to the class. There could be class discussions, debates, buzz group discussions, etc.

Evaluation. These activities could be concluded by students writing an essay which is marked by the teacher.

The skill of opinion forming

What follows is an attempt to outline how opinions should be formed on difficult or controversial issues; this is itself a controversial issue, and what I am offering is a personal view, intended to help you clarify your own ideas.

Opinions should be developed on the basis of accurate facts, but they arise also from those fundamental values and beliefs which we consider self-evident or uniquely authoritative. These fundamentals fall into the following overlapping categories.

Ethical beliefs

These are our beliefs about the main purposes of life – for example, to bring about the general good by increasing the sum of human happiness and fulfilment, and decreasing suffering. Included, of course, are the beliefs that one should keep promises, tell the truth, respect the law, not steal and so on. Perhaps the most general ethical belief is 'Do unto others as you would have them do unto you', as practically all other genuinely ethical beliefs can be derived from this. This 'do as you would be done by' principle is accepted by practically all religious and secular groups, and consequently can be seen as, in effect, a moral absolute and used to help clarify ethical controversies. Do not let your students confuse this principle with 'do unto others as they did unto you'. This is the 'tit-for-tat' principle, and is hardly a moral one.

More specific ethical rules are not so absolute, and may indeed conflict: for example, you might break an appointment (a promise) in order to give first aid to a road accident victim. Particular ethical situations, then, can lack clarity; how you decide in such cases will depend partly on matters of fact, such as what you believe will be the consequences of your actions, but may also depend on your value system. It is important to distinguish between relevant matters of fact and matters of value, when deciding ethical controversies.

Matters of fact can often be impartially decided, perhaps by appealing to expert opinion – for example, 'Does beating up a bully make him more or less likely to bully in the future?' This is a matter for psychology, not personal bias. By contrast, there is no universal court of appeal for matters of value: either classical music has value for you or it does not. The difference between matters of fact and value is all too rarely appreciated.

Persuasion in matters of value is difficult, but not impossible – though there will never be general agreement. However, it can be argued from 'do as you would be done by' that one should always give some value to that which others value.

There is little doubt that while ethical reasoning is learned by corrected practice, it is also learned by example, and the teacher has a huge responsibility in this respect.

Some questions on ethical beliefs

What is the constituency included in 'Do as you would be done by'? Does it include other races, other nationalities (the Third World, for example), animals, foetuses, those not yet born, those who have behaved unethically themselves, etc.? Many ethical controversies are due to disagreement on these matters.

Normative beliefs

These are beliefs about what is normal or acceptable; they can vary considerably from culture to culture and from decade to decade. Examples might be attitudes to the role of women, dress, sex, etiquette, who should have the vote and so on. Normative values and beliefs are very important, because they create social cohesion and stability – though they can also cause dissent, especially if they are not seen for what they are. They are not absolute – for example, there was outrage in the 1960s when a 'mixed-race' couple were shown kissing on TV, but this would now be considered entirely unremarkable.

Normative beliefs can be unethical – for example, most of us today would say that the eighteenth century's normative beliefs about slavery were unethical. However, by definition, only a minority of people see the immorality of a normative view in their own time. Normative opinions vary from subculture to subculture. Incorrectly, they are often regarded as ethical opinions by their defenders.

Some questions on normative beliefs:

Should teachers promulgate dominant normative beliefs, to maintain loyally the established traditions which underpin our society?

Or should teachers encourage critical appraisal of normative opinions in the light of ethics, in order to encourage the moral development of individuals and society as a whole?

Religious and spiritual beliefs

These, of course, vary from religion to religion, though there are marked similarities. It is worth mentioning here that science, once thought to have perfect knowledge, is now considered by all philosophers and historians of science to have only 'today's best guess'. History shows that even the most cherished scientific beliefs can be usurped.

Hence, even if science had shown belief in God to be false (which it has not), this might be shown later to be an error. The pure scientific view, if it is relevant, is to be agnostic rather than atheist.

Some questions on religious and spiritual beliefs:

Should teachers value different religious beliefs equally; or should they give precedence to Christianity, to their own religious/non-religious opinion, or to the majority religious opinion in the school or college?

Should teachers critically question religious belief or lack of belief?

Psychological and philosophical beliefs

These include such opinions as: 'People are born evil and are civilised by society'; 'People are born good and corrupted by society'; 'Society's needs are best served by cooperation' (or 'by competition'). These are the beliefs that often underpin political opinion.

Some questions on psychological and philosophical beliefs:

Are such beliefs undecided, or even undecidable, matters of fact?

Are they oversimplifications of complex issues best left to behavioural sciences such as sociology, economics, psychology, etc.?

Aesthetic beliefs and values

These include taste in art, architecture, music, etc. They are partly normative, in that they vary with culture and time; but many argue that they also include an absolute element, because research shows that there is more agreement than most suppose, amongst expert opinion from diverse cultures, on the merits of exceptional work.

Helping students with opinion forming

Our opinions, then, are based on the fundamental values and beliefs outlined above, and on matters of fact or, more correctly, evidence. There should be an attempt to discover the root cause of any disagreement over controversial issues. Is it due to differences on matters of fact, or value, or belief? Is it due to a disagreement over means and ends, over the likely consequences of certain actions, and so on? This can be discovered by asking students *why* they hold the opinions they do.

Such discussion is very widely enjoyed if it is carried out without recrimination. From the learning point of view, the reason an opinion is held is at least as important as the opinion itself. Again, ask students to justify their opinions by asking 'why?'

Students should be encouraged towards awareness that:

* Some of their fundamental beliefs are parochial and changeable, whilst others are at least *comparatively* fixed and universal. They should also learn which are which – and why.
* Disagreement over controversial issues may be due to differences in beliefs and values – for example, 'Should opera be subsidised?' But they may also be due to differences over matters of evidence or theory – for example, 'Which is the best way to prevent criminals re-offending?'
* There is no short cut to certainty, and history shows that science, religion, authority and the majority have all been wrong at times.
* Opinions which satisfy a strong emotional need have an immense pull – for example, 'They should give people such as me a better deal'. When false, such opinions can lead to rationalisation, bias, prejudice, scapegoat hunting, injustice and worse. We see such self-serving in others rather more clearly than we see it in ourselves, of course!
* Everyone has a right to have their opinion respected – and consequently a duty to respect the opinion of others – and a duty to think their own opinions out fully, especially if they affect others.

Helping students to form coherent opinions is difficult but not impossible. I must state a personal prejudice at this stage. I believe that the skill of opinion forming is of incalculable importance. Unwarranted certainty can lead to prejudice, injustice and irresponsibility – even to wars, terrorism and other violence. Students will develop opinion-forming skills only by corrected practice, and by example. The teacher must foster a critical open-mindedness and a willingness to accept doubt where this is necessary. If learners are encouraged to accept certain views with blind loyalty, they have no opportunity to practise their opinion-forming skills and their mental progress is hampered. They may then come to crave certainty where they cannot find it, which is no service to them or to society, and which can have deeply damaging repercussions.

Earlier I was irreverent enough to suggest that the time allowed to teach a skill is in inverse relation to its importance. Sound opinion forming is necessary both for a stable society and to enable individuals to steer their own lives. As a consequence of its overwhelming importance, it is usual for no time to be allowed for the overt teaching of this skill! Were you taught it? If not, do you wish you had been?

As we saw in Chapter 17 on discussion, if there is a disagreement, try to isolate the reason for this. Is it due to differences of fact, belief or values?

Take a look at the diagram below. To challenge Jo's argument, one must remove either one of the three legs supporting Jo's argument, or the reasoning from these foundations. If one leg fails the stool falls. If the connection between the legs and the opinion fails, again the stool falls. Share this three-legged stool approach with your students, getting them to present their arguments in this visual way on wall posters, presentations and handouts.

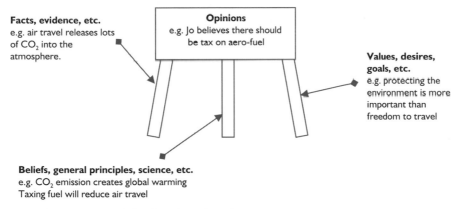

Facts, evidence, etc.
e.g. air travel releases lots of CO_2 into the atmosphere.

Opinions
e.g. Jo believes there should be tax on aero-fuel

Values, desires, goals, etc.
e.g. protecting the environment is more important than freedom to travel

Beliefs, general principles, science, etc.
e.g. CO_2 emission creates global warming
Taxing fuel will reduce air travel

Examining disagreement with the three-legged stool

Hypothesis testing

Venn diagrams are helpful in testing hypotheses such as:

1 To what extent did the Treaty of Versailles cause the Second World War?

2 Prisons do work.

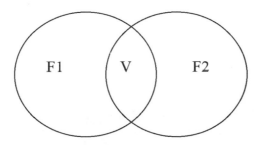

F1   V   F2

In the first case, the circle on the left could be the Treaty of Versailles, the circle on the right the causes of the Second World War. The overlap, V, represents causes of the War due to the Treaty. This verifies the hypothesis. F1 is aspects of the Treaty that did not cause the War. F2 is causes of the War not due to the Treaty.

With 'Prisons do work', the circle on the left describes the nature of prisons, and the right-hand circle describes what it means to 'work'. The extent to which prisons work is shown by the overlap. The hypothesis is verified by this overlap 'V'. Aspects of prisons that don't work is F1. Aspects of 'working' not provided by prisons is F2. Both these falsify the hypothesis. The diagram helps direct thinking towards any evidence that confirms, but also any evidence that denies the hypothesis – great for assertive-questioning-style class discussion, based on an interactive whiteboard diagram.

Further reading

De Bono, E. (1978) *Teaching Thinking*, Harmondsworth: Penguin.

Jepson, R. W. (1948) *Clear Thinking: An Elementary Course of Preparation for Citizenship*, London: Longman.

Marzano, R. J. with Marzano, S. and Pickering, D. J. (2003) *Classroom Management that Works*, Alexandria, VA: ASCD.

Nisbet, J. and Schucksmith, J. (1986) *Learning Strategies*, London: Routledge.

Petty, G. (2006) *Evidence Based Teaching*, Cheltenham: Nelson Thornes.

Thouless, R. (1990) *Straight and Crooked Thinking*, London: Edward Arnold.

39

Choosing activities to achieve affective objectives

Every teacher is involved in achieving affective objectives. Bloom's taxonomy (see Chapter 37) effectively splits the affective domain into two parts. The first of these involves encouraging students to attend and to show interest in their studies – for example, to develop an interest in scientific experimentation.

Developing in students a positive attitude to study has been a major preoccupation throughout this book; relevant factors, such as teacher enthusiasm, motivation, reinforcement, human interest, student relevance and relevance to the real world all play their part, and have been dealt with elsewhere.

The other half of Bloom's affective domain concerns raising awareness in learners, and changing or developing their beliefs, attitudes and feelings. Typical objectives might be:

- To *develop* a positive attitude to non-smoking.
- To *value* a multicultural society.
- To *appreciate the importance of* fibre in a healthy diet.

In the caring professions the affective domain is very evident, and this objective would be typical:

> To *empathise* with newly admitted patients, and recognise the therapeutic value of making them feel comfortable in their new surroundings.

Such objectives require more than knowledge of facts: they require value or importance to be given to these facts. It is one thing to learn that fibre is important in diet; it is quite another to begin to eat it!

The learning described by such objectives can be seen as opinion forming. If the learners develop a sufficiently high opinion of the benefits of dietary fibre, they will change their eating habits accordingly. Values, attitudes and beliefs can all be seen as personal opinions, so affective learning can be seen as a high-order cognitive skill: that of personal opinion forming.

Have you a feeling of unease about changing attitudes and opinions? I hope so. It raises a fundamental ethical question. What topics has a teacher the right to be persuasive about? Perhaps only issues where informed opinion has arrived at a virtual consensus. Opinions associated with matters such as health (e.g. diet) or safety (e.g. use of a lathe) might well fall into this category; but opinions on many political or moral issues (e.g. full employment or abortion) would not. It is part of the teacher's professional duty to remain neutral in areas of political, religious, moral and commercial controversy. Persuasion in these areas is a gross violation of professional ethics.

For some topics, then, the teacher will be encouraging learners to adopt a particular accepted opinion (persuasion, or convergent opinion-forming); and for other topics, the learners will be expected to make up their own mind on the matter – this is divergent opinion forming, and has been considered in the previous chapter.

Persuasion (convergent opinion forming)

So how are learners to develop or change their values, attitudes or beliefs? This requires them to clarify, adapt or change their opinion – and perhaps, as a result, their preferred behaviour. Once again, the skill of opinion forming is involved.

The following approach is based on a model by Kathleen Reardon (and others). It suggests that messages likely to be persuasive may be founded on three factors: image, consistency and effectiveness (let's call it the 'ICE' model). Imagine, for example, that you are attempting to develop a positive attitude to non-smoking in your students. The students will consider:

Image. 'Does the new opinion or behaviour fit in with my image, e.g. with family, friends and peers? Does it fit in with my image of myself?' In the case of smoking, questions which students need to address would be:

> Will I lose or gain credibility with friends, acquaintances and family if I do/ don't smoke? Do I value the image of being a smoker? Am I happy to think of myself as a nicotine addict?

Consistency. 'Is the belief or behaviour consistent with my other beliefs and behaviours?' Smoking-related questions might be:

> How can I smoke if I believe in keeping fit?

Effectiveness. 'How does the belief or behaviour affect any of my long- or short-term goals), e.g. does it bring about any desired ends?' Possible questions here:

> If I don't smoke, how much money will I save? Will I find it harder or easier to get a girl/boyfriend? Will I be better at football? Will I get cancer later in life?

Which of these ICE categories is most influential will depend on the individual and the issue, so teachers should address all three in most cases. In any case, there is considerable overlap between them. It is common but fatal for teachers to ignore 'image' and 'effectiveness' when dealing, for instance, with social issues such as sexism, racism, etc. Thinking in terms of the ICE model helps to generate questions for group or class discussion. Suppose, for example, you intended to develop a positive attitude towards safety at work on the building site. What questions would the ICE model throw up? Think this through for yourself. (Some suggestions appear in the box on page 438.)

Coping strategies

Some researchers believe that learners need to rehearse mental and verbal responses if they are to feel comfortable with a new opinion or attitude. They need to develop coping strategies to deal with a new belief, or they will revert to former attitudes.

What would I do if I heard a friend make a racist remark?

How could I refuse a cigarette offered by a friend?

Role-play is often used to good effect here, and devising coping strategies in small-group discussions is an excellent group activity. It is almost always best for the students themselves to be involved as much as possible in the development of these coping strategies. They know best what would be likely to work, and will be more committed to their own ideas than to yours. It might be useful to add S for 'strategies' to the ICE mnemonic, to make 'ICES'.

Activities to develop affective objectives

The activities and teaching methods used to explore values, attitudes and behaviour must involve the emotions as well as reason, and must offer an opportunity for corrected practice in opinion forming. Commonly used methods are shown in the following box:

Teaching methods commonly used to achieve affective objectives

The most effective overall strategy is guided discovery, as described in Chapter 29. Useful activities include: class discussion assertive questioning style (Chapter 24); small-group discussion; attitude questionnaires (such as that in Chapter 10 of this book); group work; games, simulations and role-play; debates; and surveys of students and others. Active experiential methods are particularly powerful – though sometimes difficult to arrange.

Activities involving learner experiences, human-interest stories (be they in video or in written form) and activities which involve empathy and identification with particular characters are also powerful. For example, you could read out a short story in which a schoolgirl, Julie, refuses a cigarette but eventually accepts it when it is offered repeatedly. Then you could ask the students: 'Has something like this ever happened to you?' 'What do you think Julie was thinking?' 'What would you have done?' ...

All the teaching methods mentioned above were considered in detail in Part 2 of this book.

Changing attitudes takes time and patience, especially when changing ingrained, long-held views. Do not expect overnight success; opinions change a little at a time, usually when the persuader is not present. A dietician persuading a pensioner to change from white to wholemeal bread, or a social studies teacher confronting a pupil's racist views, cannot expect instant results. During discussions, listen rather than talk; watch out for verbal and non-verbal signals of attitudes and feelings, and follow these feelings up. As ever, try to see things from the learner's point of view. How do they think? Why are these perceptions important to them? Why do they think this way?

STRATEGIES FOR PERSUASION

The examples focus on a health worker teaching elderly people modern dietary advice.

Legitimate

Appeal to authority. If you quote statistics or research, it is usually better to give detail rather than just the bare findings: 'Doctors and dieticians believe wholemeal bread is best. Research shows that ...'

Appeal to majority. 'Most people nowadays realise the value of wholemeal bread.'

Moral appeal. 'You owe it to your partner to feed him/her well.'

Request for moderate change. 'Why not buy a little wholemeal bread as well as your usual white?'

Illegitimate?

Confrontation. 'You're not telling me you eat white bread!'

Ridicule. 'White bread? You'll be telling me you live in a cave next!'

Assuming agreement. 'Of course, you all eat wholemeal bread and this provides some of the necessary fibre.'

There are bound to be counter-arguments against the belief you are advocating, though your students may be afraid of voicing them:

> My Grandad smoked for 80 years and it never did him any harm.
> Heroin isn't addictive unless you use it five or six times.

These are often best dealt with directly. It is generally recognised that students need to be 'inoculated' against these counter-arguments, or they may be seduced by them later. This should be done with considerable care, especially with less attentive or intelligent students, or you may give the counter-arguments credibility simply by mentioning them.

As persuader, you must provide relevant factual material, but this alone is not enough: you must also affect emotions, to provide the motivation for the learners to change their own thinking. They must be given the opportunity to explore the belief or behaviour under consideration *in terms of their own existing values and beliefs*.

Self-persuasion is the only real persuasion. 'You are wrong and I am right: you must change your thinking and adopt my ideas' is an approach which leads learners to attack your views, or adopt a defensive, face-saving stance. Rather, the teacher must show that the new belief or behaviour is in line with the learner's existing values and 'self-concept'.

'Sensible people don't want to waste money, destroy their health and put off boyfriends/girlfriends. You are a sensible person. So you don't want to smoke, do you?' is a persuasive strategy. By contrast, 'I believe smoking is bad for the reasons I have given, so you must not smoke' is unlikely to win converts.

The difference is subtle but crucial. Changing one's attitude because someone else advocates a different one implies loss of face; changing to a new attitude because this is more in line with the 'real me' does not. This is why guided discovery is the best strategy for affective learning; students need to 'discover' for themselves that the opinion (which you are 'teaching') is the one that best fits in with their existing values and opinions.

> *Peer education is an emerging approach to affective education, where small groups of students prepare and deliver a whole lesson on an affective issue after special training.*

Ask students *why* they hold the opinions they do. Then you might get responses such as:

> I want control over my own body, I don't want to be an addict.
> I want to spend money on positive things that give me a good time.

When students start asserting their own high values in defence of the new opinion, this can be very powerful. Such statements must come from the students themselves, of course.

Carl Rogers, in *Freedom to Learn*, argues that you must accept and respect the students and their existing values, or they will soon reject you. However, in doing so, you must remain true to yourself and trustworthy. This is not always easy to achieve!

> *Jesus Christ was an inspired teacher in the affective domain. He used parables, perhaps because they examined issues without accusing the listener of wrongdoing; made their point clearly; and offered human interest.*

A case study

> *Research quoted in the* Times Educational Supplement *of 22 November 1991 showed that 25% of 16- to 18-year-olds were prepared to have unprotected sex with a new partner, and that 82% of young people believed that sex education at school bore little or no relation to issues that they faced.*

What activities could be used to help achieve the following objective?

To raise awareness of, and develop positive attitudes towards, safer sex.

You have two one-hour sessions, one of which will have 40 minutes taken up with basic factual material concerning safe and unsafe sexual practices, the nature of HIV and AIDS, etc. The group are 17 to 18 years old; they have elected to come to the lessons.

Use the ICES model to choose some activities for the session. Then (and only then!) take a look at the suggestions in the box below.

Activities which could be used to help achieve the objective: 'To raise awareness of, and develop positive attitudes towards, safer sex'.

A *video* of an AIDS victim recounting his/her story. (*human interest*)

An *anonymous questionnaire*, with percentage responses made available for discussion in the following session. Questions such as:

- How would you feel if your partner insisted on/refused a condom? (*image*)
- Is it macho not to use a condom? (*image*)
- What (if anything) do you believe is worth risking death for? (*consistency*)
- Can you list enjoyable safe sexual practices? (*effectiveness*)
- Do you agree with any of the following: 'Young people hardly ever have AIDS'; 'Only homosexuals and drug addicts have AIDS'; etc. (*dealing directly with counter-arguments*)

(Many more questions would be worth dealing with.)

Small-group work. In groups of same sex, students are asked to devise strategies for dealing with a situation where their sexual partner does not want to use a condom. What would they say or do in this situation? (*coping strategies*)

There are, of course, many legitimate methods of dealing with this difficult topic; these are only suggestions.

Developing a positive attitude towards safety at work on the building site (see page 436). Questions developed by reference to the ICES model.

Image. 'What would you think of someone who took a few minutes to tie up a ladder properly?' 'Do you think it is macho to ignore safety rules?' 'What would your workmates think of you if you suggested that they changed to a safer practice?'

Consistency. 'Do you think of yourself as a risk taker?' 'Would you take risks if you were alone?' 'Would you use faulty electrical equipment at home?' 'Who gains if you take risks at work, you, your boss or neither?'

Effectiveness. What would happen to your wages if you were injured at work and had to take a week off?' 'If you weren't wearing a hard hat, what would happen to you if a brick fell one storey to land on your head?'

Strategies (for coping). 'What would you say to someone who said you were wasting time by tying up a ladder?'

Further reading

Reardon, K. K. (1991) *Persuasion in Practice*, London: Sage.

The Government's Sex and Relationship Education Guidance can be downloaded from: www.dcsf.gov.uk/sreguidance/sexeducation.pdf

40

Writing the lesson plan

Now you have some idea about the activities that will achieve your objectives, it is time to plan the lesson on paper. You will find this a very time-consuming activity at first. Most teachers plan lessons for the class; some prepare individualised learning programmes. This chapter deals with a lesson plan for whole-class teaching. The planning process to follow if your students are not being taught together as a class is described in Chapters 41 and 34.

Lesson planning is an art, not a science; there is no ideal lesson to achieve any given set of objectives. However, the following points always remain important:

- The lesson should be planned to achieve the objectives.
- The purpose of the lesson should be clear to students.
- Final practice of skills and abilities should be as realistic as possible.
- The lesson should be logically structured.
- There should be a variety of student activities and teaching methods.
- On the whole, students should be active, not passive.
- The plan should suit the characteristics of the students. Have a look at the initial diagnostic assessments of the group, as described in Chapter 47.
- Teacher talk should be illustrated with a visual presentation where possible.
- Motivation (remember 'SPERT': success, purpose, enjoyment, reinforcement, target setting).
- Interest (human interest, student relevance, challenges, puzzles, games …).
- Most activities will take much longer than you expect.
- Have a stretching activity for students who finish an activity early; alternatively, use open-ended activities which always provide something for everyone to do.
- Always prepare too much; there is nothing worse than running out of material! (Preparation time is rarely wasted; there is always next lesson.)
- Don't forget that activities can go on in series, or in parallel, in different groups.

To fail to plan is to plan to fail.

Lessons often follow a 'beginning – middle – end' structure:

Beginning. Links are made with earlier work, and students are orientated to the lesson's content. The purpose of the lesson is made clear; some teachers advocate reading the objectives out, but most explain them in a less formal way. Consider the starting activity with particular care: do you need to start with a bang, a quiet settling activity or an activity which accommodates varied arrival times?

Middle. The student activity is introduced. If teaching is focused on specific skills, then students obtain any necessary explanation and are made aware of the 'doing-detail'. That is, they discover the what, why and how of what they are expected to be able to do. Students then practise with the aim of developing the abilities outlined in the objectives.

If the lesson is focused on content rather than skills, the students are given activities requiring them to process or reason with this content. This requires the student to form constructs, as we saw in Chapter 1.

It may be possible to check and correct the students' work in some way as they proceed. Even better, give them some way of checking it for themselves.

End. What has been learned is made clear, summarised and perhaps noted down. A pointer is given to the next lesson.

Of course, you may not be able to complete an objective in one lesson, as this pattern assumes. You can also structure your lesson plan by stating 'content' and 'method', or 'teacher activity' and 'student activity'.

Present, apply, review

An alternative approach to structuring the lesson is the 'present, apply, review' or 'PAR' approach. The idea is that you must present new material, get students to apply this learning, and then you must review what has been learned. There is no expectation that you go from present to apply to review and then stop, visiting each phase only once, though this can work sometimes. In most cases, you will see each of the three phases many times in a single lesson. PAR is another three-legged stool: each phase must be there if the lesson is to stand up. See the summary diagram on page 444.

Lesson plan format

Most teachers use a similar format for all their lesson planning; a blank plan is photocopied and filled in for each new lesson or a word-processor template used.

The format design depends on your individual needs, but should certainly include: title of lesson; aims and objectives; reference to the paragraphs of the syllabus being covered; student activity teaching aids required; other resources required; evaluation of how the lesson went.

It may also include: date, day and time of lesson; room; course title; subject; exam board; validating body; course tutor; etc.

Activities and timings are then added to this blank format for each new lesson, and the lesson plan kept in a folder along with relevant worksheets, etc., for possible future use.

The lesson plan overleaf is for a lesson on a simple topic. Before reading on, look at the construction carefully. Do the activities follow from the objectives?

Present Maximum 35%?

Orientation: the learners are prepared for learning:
- recall learning of last lesson
- recall other relevant prior learning
- persuasive account of the relevance, importance and value of the learning
- advance organiser to structure the new content
- **challenging goals** are given or negotiated.

New material is presented:
Knowledge, reasoning, theories, etc. are explained to students or learned in some other way. Abstract ideas are illustrated with concrete examples.

Practical and intellectual skills are demonstrated, e.g. how to use a tool or formula, or punctuate a sentence. This stresses both process and product. Key points are emphasised. Showing how on the board. Students studying 'exemplars' (good work).

Typical learning strategies:
- listen to teacher talk or watch a video
- watch a demonstration
- study exemplars, e.g. spoof assessment
- 'teaching by asking' (rather than by telling)
- 'teaching without talking' strategies, such as learning from ILT and other resources.

Feedback for learner and teacher:
Learning in progress is checked and corrected, e.g.::
- interactive question and answer (chapter 24)
- other interactive dialogue e.g. in group work
- Students demonstrating on the board, followed by class discussion, etc.

Apply Minimum 60%?

Students work towards their challenging goal. The task(s) require them to apply the knowledge, theories, skills, etc. that have just been presented. This involves them in reasoning, not just reproduction, e.g. **problem-solving, making decisions and creating things such as mind-maps, etc.**

Typical learning strategies:
When learning a practical skill:
- Practical task to carry out the skill.

When learning cognitive skills:
- answering questions on a case study in groups
- exercises, questions, worksheet, essay, etc.
- class discussion to develop an argument or answer a question, etc.
- decisions, decisions game
- student presentation
- critical evaluation of exemplars, e.g. are these sentences correctly punctuated?

Feedback for learner and teacher:
This may not be a separate activity and may involve the students more than the teacher. The aim is:
- inform learners of what is good, and what not! (medals and missions)
- provide support for those who need it
- check attention to task, quality of work, behaviour, etc.
Common strategies include: self-assessment; peer assessment; class discussion; teacher comments, etc.

Review Minimum 5%?

Were the goals met? **Summary and clarification** of what was to be learned. Emphasis on the **key points** and **structure**, etc.

Learning strategies
- note-making
- create a mind-map, poster or handout that summarises the key points
- class discussion
- advance organisers revisited and more detail added
- reviews at the beginning of a lesson with a short task
- peer-explaining of key objectives followed by check by the teacher
- quiz, test, etc.

Feedback for learner and teacher:
Learning is checked and corrected, e.g:
- question and answer in an interactive dialogue to discover and clarify weak learning
- class discussion on difficult points, etc.
- peer and self-assessment

Structure for teaching a topic: the PAR model. From *Evidence Based Teaching* (2006) Geoff Petty

---

Lesson plan P. Wright

Class: Office studies Yr. 1   **Room:** G 12   **Date:** Tuesday 4.9.04

Syllabus content: Filing, paragraphs 8.2; 8.3

Objectives: Students should be able to:
- search for relevant information from an alphabetical listing
- organise information into alphabetical order.

Time	Content and teacher activity	Student activity and resources
	State objectives: Tell them how important it is and that it is not as easy as it sounds. Review last week's lesson quickly.	Intro: OHT
5	Do any of you use alphabetical order for address books or CDs, etc.? Do we all know our alphabet? (Which comes first? game): m or l?, t or q? etc.	Q&A
10	How are alphabetical listings organised? Class asked to discover the rules from their activity and the telephone directory. Including numbers, Mc/Mac, Saint, St, and initials.	Discovery telephone directories
20	Students look for the following phone numbers in the telephone directory (as a race): 1st Choice Parcels; BCL Builders; St. Clare T.S.; Saint Claire Salon; AVS Video; MacBride P.M.; McKie S.L.; 1940s Cafe; de la Siva P.	Student practice
30	Class give rules.	
35	Rules summarised on the board and summarised in students' own words.	Discussion Note-making
40	I go over sorting exercise on OHT to show use of rules.	Demo: OHT
45	Alphabetical filing exercise (3 card sets): Cards given out to pairs of students, played as a race. Bring to me to check the order.	Student practice filing-game cards
57	Summarise rules; tell them about room change.	Summarise by Q&A

(if time)(Filing Worksheet questions 1,3,4,5, plus past-paper questions)

Evaluation: Went well. Discovery phase took much longer than I expected. Some still confused about Mc and Mac, believe it or not. Did I emphasise this well enough in the summary? Races really got them motivated! Must try this again.

Look at the objectives for the lesson again. The lesson plan fits these well, and the activities are motivating and develop important skills. Active methods have been chosen where possible – for example, the discovery method rather than teacher talk was used to find the rules of alphabetical sorting. Most of the learning elements were necessary – and provided.

More advanced lesson-plan formats might require you to state how learning is checked, or where mastery tasks and high-order open tasks are set to ensure differentiation.

A variety of student activity is vital to maintain concentration. The diagram below shows the concentration of a student during a one-hour lesson. Note the complete lapses of concentration occasionally, especially during teacher talk. Note also that changes of activity produce an increase in concentration, and that concentration is maintained for longer when the student is active.

In practice, one may need to stray from the lesson plan. If, for example, students are having difficulty, you may wish to explain further; or if they are bored with an activity, you may want to shorten it. It is very common to run out of time before all the activities are completed. If the lesson does not go to plan, this is not a failure on your part (as long as you have not been induced to chase after a 'red herring'!); if there were genuine immediate needs, the failure would be not to respond to them.

> *Military strategists' saying:*
>
> 'Always have a master plan – and if necessary, use it.'

It is not advisable to plan more than one or two lessons in advance, in any detail. Decide on objectives and choose learning activities, but don't arrange timings for them. Lessons often do not finish where you expect, so detailed subsequent plans would need to be revised. Some teachers like to prepare 'topic plans'; a topic might cover two or three lessons, and can be kept from year to year to help in lesson planning – see the box on page 278 for an example.

Meeting individual needs

Most of your lesson plan will describe what happens to the class as a whole. But what if some students have individual needs? For example, you might negotiate targets with students because they are dyslexic, or have behaviour problems, or missed the last lesson. If only one or two students are involved, you can have a special place in your lesson plan where you note this down. If a number of students are involved, read Chapter 41.

> *As you get more experiences try teaching double-checker lessons as described in chapter 38*

Lesson evaluation

Each lesson should be evaluated. Chapter 31, on learning from experience, made it clear that experience is not enough to guarantee learning; there must be reflection on this experience in the light of theory. This evaluation is very short, which is only appropriate for a teacher with some experience. Only people who reflect on, and learn from, past successes and failures are able to improve, as we will see in Chapter 46.

If you are too self-critical you will lose confidence and fail to experiment; if you are too self-confident you will think improvement unnecessary. Either way, you will fail to learn adequately from experience and will not improve.

> *'Only the mediocre are always at their best.'*
>
> Jean Giraudoux

Don't be depressed if a lesson doesn't go well; it takes a good teacher to recognise a poor lesson, and we all have occasional disasters. Read back over your evaluations occasionally: can you see any patterns? Do you, for example, often make the same mistake?

Your first few lessons

> *'The human brain starts working the moment you are born
> and never stops until you stand up to speak in public.'*
>
> Sir George Jessel

Before teaching practice, find out about:

Resources: photocopying; the library; resources for general use, such as worksheets, etc.; what rooms you will teach in; whether they have permanent data projectors, whiteboards, and/or OHPs; how one orders specialist equipment e.g. videos; coffee arrangements in the staff room.

The people you will teach: their names and previous attainment, along with any special needs. Sit in on some of their classes if you can. Look at their work with an experienced teacher. Can you make a seating plan in advance?

The courses you will teach on: course content; rules and regimes regarding homework, coursework, etc.; work experience and exam dates; internal and

---

external assessment procedures; what they have studied before you start teaching them. Agree in detail what you will teach, and write this down.

The college or school: term dates, name and phone number; names of relevant members of staff and their responsibilities; discipline procedures; the general approach and philosophy; provision for special needs.

Don't read from notes. Put up some major headings on the OHP and use these as reminders; this also serves to direct attention away from you. Some people prefer cue cards.

It may help if you introduce yourself, saying what your qualifications and experience are; try not to mention that it is your first lesson or that you are a learning teacher.

Take in a glass of water if you wish.

Check the room, and all equipment, before the lesson.

Try to see the class in session with another teacher before your class; read their work, and talk to experienced teachers about your lesson plans.

EXERCISE

Below you will find an unsatisfactory lesson plan. What is wrong with it? (A suggested answer is printed upside down at the bottom of the next page.)

What is wrong with this lesson outline?

Learning outcome: Students should be able to repot a house plant.

Introduction, aims of session. Question and answer to review last session.

5 min   Why and when repotting is necessary. Show students a pot-bound plant.

20 min   Materials: types and sizes of plant pot, types of potting compost.

OHT plus examples of pots and compost to show them. Importance of choosing the right plant pot and compost.

30 min   Demo: removing pot-bound plant from existing pot.

Take care!

35 min   Demo: repotting a large, a medium and a small plant.

55 min   Give out handout and recap.

Further reading

Most of the general books on teaching in the bibliography deal with this topic; for example:

Kyriacou, C. (1997) *Effective Teaching in Schools* (2nd edition), Cheltenham: Nelson Thornes.

*Kyriacou, C. (1998) *Essential Teaching Skills* (2nd edition), Cheltenham: Nelson Thornes.

Marland, M. (2002) *The Craft of the Classroom* (3rd edition), London: Croom Helm.

Marzano, R. J. with Marzano, S. and Pickering, D. J. (2003) *Classroom Management that Works*, Alexandria, VA: ASCD.

Petty, G. (2006) *Evidence Based Teaching*, Cheltenham: Nelson Thornes.

ANSWER

There is no corrected practice for students, whether in deciding when reporting is necessary, in choosing pot size and compost for a given plant, or in the actual reporting process itself. Too 'teacher centred'.

41

Flexible and inclusive course organisation and record-keeping

The three modes of teaching

Before you decide how to plan your course, you need to decide how you will organise it. There are three main modes described below. For a given course you may use one mode, or a combination of modes for different parts of the course. Combining modes greatly increases flexibility and effectiveness; first, though, we will look at the strategies in isolation

Whole-class teaching. Here, all students learn the same thing at more or less the same time and rate. Most teaching and learning is designed in this way.

Resource-based learning (RBL). Here students learn the same thing but learn at different rates, and may start the programme at different times or at different starting points. Consequently, at any given time, different students in the same class will be working on different tasks. An example of RBL would be a class learning how to use a computer by each student working at their own pace through a series of workbooks. However, RBL does not need to be used in isolation. A health studies course could be taught by whole-class teaching, except for an RBL module on how to search the Internet. Mixing modes is a powerful way to include all students by being flexible.

Self-directed learning. Here students learn different things at different rates. Students set their own goals and decide their own learning activities during negotiation with the teacher. The teacher's aim is usually to meet each individual student's needs rather than to deliver a preconceived body of knowledge and skills. This is the humanistic approach. An example of this might be an adult education recreational course in photography. This approach is often used on otherwise very conventional courses for developing difficult skills such as essay writing, creative work or study skills, by negotiating individual targets with students, as we will see.

The diagram opposite illustrates these three teaching modes by making an analogy between teaching and walking. In *class teaching*, the teacher takes all the students for the same walk, keeping the walkers together. In *resource-based learning*, students join or perhaps leave the walk when it suits their needs, and walk at different rates, but they all walk the same route, that is, they are all working towards the same objectives. In *self-directed learning*, each student walks a different, self-devised route.

Each mode has different characteristics, making it more or less appropriate for a given course or part of a course. They also have different record-keeping requirements. Let's examine each of them in turn.

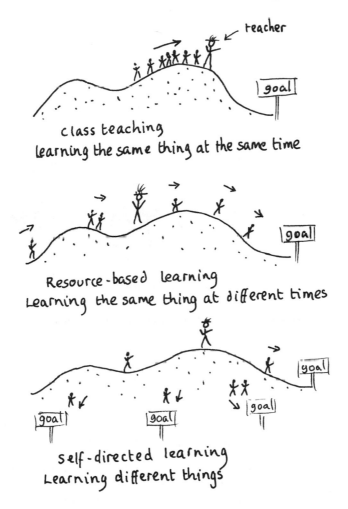

class teaching
learning the same thing at the same time

Resource-based learning
Learning the same thing at different times

self-directed learning
Learning different things

Class teaching

Example: Typical teaching of A-level history

Here the aim is to pass on a predetermined body of knowledge and skills to a group of learners who have similar abilities, attainments and aspirations. The group is mainly taught together, with students following the same learning experiences at more or less the same time.

The learning aims and objectives originate from a source such as a syllabus, or they are decided by the teacher. This course content is arranged by the teacher into a scheme of work which plans what will be taught when, over the length of the course or academic year. Lesson plans are then devised by reference to this scheme of work.

Lesson plans, schemes of work, tests, resources and so on are produced to meet the objectives, and the teacher assesses and tracks the students' progress throughout the course.

"I'm slower than my classmates at programming. I know much more than they do about spreadsheets. I'm in a rock band. How can you personalise your course for me?"

How can you personalise your course for me?

The records kept by the teacher are fairly obvious here, and include schemes of work, lesson plans and, most importantly, marks for each student in a markbook. Monitoring copies of handouts and worksheets are annotated with suggested improvements during the course. The teacher may or may not keep their own record of student attendance, but there is likely to be a centrally kept register.

The problem with class teaching is that students cannot easily learn at their own pace, or learn what *they* want or need. Neither can they start the course when it is most convenient for them. In other words, it is not flexible enough to accommodate marked differences in student experience, ability, needs or aspiration. *Resource-based learning* was designed to accommodate such differences.

Moreover, the content and the delivery of the course is not in the student's control with class teaching, which can create demotivation and the problems of *learned dependency* and *passive learning* described in Chapter 5 on motivation. *Self-directed learning* should not have such problems. RBL and self-directed learning were designed to overcome the shortcomings of conventional class teaching.

The best whole-class teachers make use of RBL and self-directed learning to achieve 'personalisation', 'inclusion', 'differentiation' and to deal with 'diversity' – in other words, to make sure everybody learns. We used to teach courses, now we teach students! So read on, even if it doesn't seem relevant to you immediately.

Resource-based learning (RBL)

Examples: Students with different computer experience learning how to use a personal computer effectively. History students being taught library research skills. Science students being taught maths for physics.

An RBL course is usually embodied in workbooks which contain explanations and exercises designed to develop the students' knowledge and skills. The workbooks could be 'on computer' as a computer-based learning course. The learners work at their own pace through these workbooks, perhaps starting at different points.

Students take tests or provide some other evidence of their learning at various stages in the course, or when they or their teacher think they are ready. A diagnostic assessment discovers each student's prior learning, to ensure each student starts the programme at the appropriate point.

Each student's progress is usually monitored by some or all of the following:

- competences (formal competences or informal ones devised by you), for which the students provide the evidence
- individual record sheets for each student, which record previous experience on entry to the course, progress by date through the workbooks, competences achieved, test results, individual targets set by you (e.g. 'Make sure your next piece of work is spell-checked'), and so on
- tests.

Student records are usually 'open', that is, available for perusal by the student concerned or, exceptionally, available to the whole class of students. In order to encourage students to take an interest in, and some responsibility for, their own progress, records of progress and attendance may be kept by the students themselves. If so, the teacher usually keeps their own record of progress. Best of all, ask students to record their own progress and targets on record sheets kept by you. Keep a 'class-at-a-glance' record, as shown below. Also keep individual records for your students, perhaps in the competence form, also shown below, or in the form shown at the end of this chapter – or both! (Other record-keeping approaches are shown at the end of the chapter.)

Module:	One				Two	
Exercise	**1**	**2**	**3**	**4**	**1**	**2**
Jill Davies	✔	✔				
Peter Eaves	✔	✔	✔	✔	✔	
Jon Everett	✔	✔	✔			
Paula Francis		*not needed*			✔	✔
Tim Harroway	✔					

You could put the date instead of ticks

Name: Ian Walker   **Computer competences**

Word processing   **Initials**

1. Type in a 'file'   ✔   *IW*

2. Print out a file   ✔   *IW*

3. Save a file to a CD-ROM   ✔   *IW*

4. Use bold and underline   ✔   *IW*

5. etc.

These are informal competences made up by the teacher

Many teachers using RBL do not make lesson plans, arguing that the learning activities are already decided and embodied in the workbooks. However, it is usually a mistake to hand over the responsibility for teaching entirely to your workbooks. Many RBL teachers collect their class together occasionally, say at the start of sessions, for explanations, demonstrations or discussions. In this case, lesson plans are useful.

In addition to student records, teachers usually keep a 'monitoring copy' of the student workbooks (if they were devised in-house), annotated to record the sections students often find difficult and any suggested improvements, etc.

It is usual for the teacher to have a brief chat with each student about their progress every few hours of tuition. Then short-term 'actions plans' can be agreed, and student targets can be negotiated and recorded.

If you use RBL, you will need to think through the following:

* Will your students leave the course on completion of the workbooks, or when they have met the assessment requirements? Alternatively, will they stay on with the slower students, doing stretching tasks or extra work? What extra work will they do?
* How will you make sure that shy students who are reluctant to ask for help are not left to flounder alone?
* Is the programme of work in the workbooks complete and sufficient to meet the needs of both the course and your students? This is unlikely. You may need to devise assignments, give input, etc.

The most common mistake is to abdicate the responsibility of teaching to the workbooks. A related mistake is to talk to students only when they ask for help, and not to monitor their progress, praise them, and talk to them about difficulties they may have encountered in using the programme. Asking students if they are 'okay' is not enough; look at their work, and use problem-finding questions, such as 'What have you found most difficult so far?' If you have time, it is valuable just to sit with each student for a few moments to observe, encourage and interact.

What have you found most difficult?

The advantages of RBL are that students can work at their own pace, and can start the programme at any point, and at any time. Many managers are attracted to RBL because they assume minimum teacher support is needed, enabling small classes or even individual students to be accommodated economically. But if students are working at a challenging rate, they get stuck and ask questions, so it becomes hard to manage a class of 25.

A common problem with RBL is that in order to ensure students can work with the minimum of assistance, the tasks in the workbooks are made highly directive, very detailed and unchallenging. Solitary work on low-level tasks soon demotivates students, and creates low-quality surface learning, as we saw in chapter 1. Able students can get bored by the slow pace and low level of such workbooks, and weak students can be daunted by their length. Another problem is that many students, especially weak ones, do not like working alone. Students of all abilities often greatly miss the social contact and informal peer tutoring available in class teaching, especially if their work is mainly paper-based.

Set some more challenging tasks that involve peer work: '*In pairs, one of you find out how to insert a picture from clip art, the other how to insert a picture from a file. Then tell your partner how you did it*'. RBL courses often do badly in inspections because students are working in isolation on unchallenging tasks, there is not enough variety, and the teacher does not ask the students what they are finding difficult. Instead, they just wait for students to ask for help.

If you are aware of these weaknesses, you can of course do something to avoid them – for example, by designing pair work, peer tutoring and some whole-class teaching into your programme. Especially for academic subjects, try to find high-quality, multimedia RBL material. Writing your own material is *very* time consuming, though it may save you time over several years.

If students work on an RBL-type course, but away from the teacher except for occasional tutorial support, this is sometimes called *distance learning, flexible learning, open learning* or a *correspondence course*. The Open University, Open College, National Extension College and learndirect make use of such an approach.

If instruction and tasks are given by computer rather than by workbooks, then it is sometimes called *computer-based learning* (CBL), *information and learning technology (ILT)* or *e-learning*. Colleges and teachers vary in their use of all these terms, so beware! Bear in mind that in some circumstances independent learning (Chapter 33) is a preferable alternative to RBL.

Self-directed learning

Examples: An adult education recreational course in photography. Improving students' essay-writing skills on an A-level history course. Fine art students learning to paint.

In 'self-directed learning', what is to be learned and/or the student's activities are negotiated with the student to produce an individualised *learning contract* or *action plan* which describes long-term objectives, along with the next few weeks' work. This approach may not be familiar to you, but it is very commonly used in the training and teaching of adults, and in progressive schools and courses. It may surprise you that research into the effectiveness of this humanistic approach shows it to be appropriate for learners of all ages. However, it is demanding for the teacher, and if you have not met this approach as a student, it may seem strange to you at first. The reasons for the use and the effectiveness of self-directed learning will be considered later in this chapter.

The approach does not need to be 'all or nothing'. For example:

- A single topic on an otherwise conventional course might be taught through self-directed learning. Thus experimental design on a science course may be 'taught' by each student negotiating an experiment that they wish to design and carry out. Again, the amount of self-direction needs to be considered: will there be guidelines about the procedure or the format of the final report?
- A topic or an assignment need not be entirely self-directed, but could involve some choice. For example:
  - On an architecture course: 'Research a building you admire ...'
  - On a teacher training course: 'Investigate an educational topic that interests you ...'
  - On a social studies course: 'Write a critical appreciation of a social campaign ...' The degree of self-direction in such assignments can vary greatly, from being quite closely defined, to being completely free for both the topic and the mode of presentation.
- Certain times on the course could be left to self-directed learning – for example, one period a week or one a fortnight. The student may or may not be restricted in the subject or topic studied, and they may or may not be allowed to choose to study nothing at all!
- Even a preconceived course or qualification can be approached in a self-directed way. In National Vocational Qualifications, for example, the assessment and knowledge requirements are fixed, but everything else is, in principle, negotiable. On some courses, students have considerable control over the order in which topics are studied or assessed, what resources or support they would find helpful, and so on.
- It is very common to use self-directed learning to encourage students to develop complex skills such as learning how to learn, creative skills, management skills, etc.

The above shows that you can dabble in self-directed learning even on conventional courses, but some courses are entirely organised in this way, especially in recreational education. Art and design students working on a design brief are often managed in this way.

Why use self-directed learning? The adult learning approach

Let's take as our example an adult education evening class in photography. Those who attend such a course may be of very varied experience and ability and have very different aspirations and reasons for enrolling on the course. Forcing all learners into a series of teacher-devised activities will be a recipe for disaster, and a large drop-out rate will result. It is better to negotiate with each course partici-pant in turn to discover their reasons for enrolling, what they hope to learn and, perhaps, how they prefer to learn. A questionnaire may help this process. What is their previous experience? Do they have a preference for black and white or colour, or for landscape, portrait or still-life photography? etc.

Individual action plans can then be negotiated which plan the next few weeks' activities. These should be revised periodically. Alternatively, groups may be formed with similar interests – for example, landscape and portrait groups. The cycle and methods described in Chapter 34 on self-directed learning will be most helpful here.

Malcolm Knowles suggests that adults have a different view of learning than younger learners, rooted in their very nature as adults. Adults, by definition, have a self-concept of being an independent and self-directed personality. Consequently, says Knowles, they learn best in an independent and self-directed way.

Changing to self-directed learning is not easy for students. Adults may have a memory of being disempowered and dependent as a learner in their youth, so they may associate education with a feeling of powerlessness, and may feel alienated from learning as a result. Alternatively, they may expect the teacher to use class teaching and be irritated if the teacher refuses the role of leader, and challenges the students' dependency.

Although adults are typically not prepared for self-directed learning, they may experience release and exhilaration when they realise they can take control over their learning in the same way that they take control over the rest of their lives. However, recent criticism of Knowles's ideas has stressed that adults often lack confidence in their ability as learners at first, and feel lost if not given direction. If you experience this difficulty with your students, then move towards self-directed learning gradually – for example, by using independent learning (Chapter 33). As Chapter 34 on self-directed learning stresses, it is a mistake to give students much more freedom than they can manage.

It is a more common mistake to over-constrain adult learners. As adults, we define ourselves by what we have done, by our experience. If this experience is denied, or ignored, we feel ignored as a person. Teachers must see adults as a resource, not as empty vessels. The experience of adults means they have much to contribute to the learning of others. Consequently, adults prefer experiential learning: discussion, consultation, case study, simulations, role-play, etc. They also prefer collaboration rather than competition, and they enjoy taking control over their learning if they are helped to do this effectively.

Adult learners are often problem-centred, not subject-matter-centred. They need to know how to apply their learning in their lives. They look on learning most positively when it is focused on meeting their personal needs, so their learning becomes self-development. This requires that their teachers be 'person-centred' rather than 'subject-centred'.

> '*It is in fact nothing short of a miracle that the modern methods of instruction have not yet entirely strangled the holy curiosity of inquiry; for this delicate little plant, aside from stimulation, stands mainly in need of freedom; without this it goes to wrack and ruin without fail.*'
>
> Albert Einstein

Self-directed learning contract

Name: Cynthia Pearson   **Course:** Child Development

Relevant aspect of self-evaluation: I have had problems coping with unco-operative behaviour on my work placement.

Negotiated goals and/or question: 'Is it possible to explain moral rules and the virtue of cooperation to nursery school children? If so, how should it be done?'

Activities: Structured interview with two experienced nursery teachers. Literature search. Internet search, review my notes on moral development in children.

Time taken per week: 2 hrs

Length of project: Complete by Dec 12th.

How will this be self-evaluated and presented? I will do a short presentation to the class, giving them a one-page summarising handout. I will get feedback on the usefulness and the rigour of my ideas with a structured student evaluation at the end of the presentation.

Resources: Library, Internet, notes, my mentor at St Clare's and her colleague.

Next scheduled tutorial: 10:30am, Nov 14th.

By next tutorial I will: Have read my moral development notes and designed questions for the structured interview. I may have started reading and used the Internet.

Signed (student) ....

Signed (lecturer) ....

Self-directed learning with younger students

Carl Rogers, in *Freedom to Learn*, makes a passionate and well-argued case for self-directed learning in schools and colleges of every type, arguing that it increases curiosity, encourages students to take responsibility for their own development and learning, and promotes personal and academic growth. Humanistic psychologists believe in self-control, self-help and personal power within the context of caring relationships, and in the necessity for individuals to explore their own interests and curiosities if they are to grow into fully functioning, self-trusting, independent people. They see education as a means of freeing individuals so they can follow their own intrinsic interests, and so grow to their full personal potential, and they criticise traditional education for being too heavy-handed in imposing the expectations of society on students.

The humanistic approach is often criticised for being woolly-minded and trendy. But Rogers quotes an overview of hundreds of research projects comparing self-directed learning with traditional learning, which shows that self-directed learning produces the same academic achievements, but with improved self-concept, attitude towards school, creativity and curiosity. Students also show more cooperation, less anxiety and more self-control. Students are often found to be highly motivated by self-directed learning.

Using self-directed learning in practice

The use of self-directed learning, which can be seen as a cycle, as shown on page 451, is described in more detail in Chapter 34.

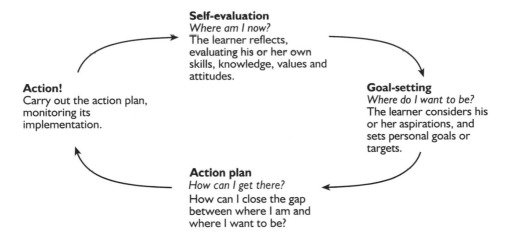

Self-directed learning delivers the considerable educational advantages of independent learning described in Chapter 33, but while independent learning gives the student responsibility only for *how* they learn, self-directed learning also gives the student at least some responsibility and control over *what* they learn. This is not a soft option. Self-evaluation requires the students to face up to their own strengths and weaknesses, and goal-setting requires students to give themselves responsibility for development. Self-directed learning is a difficult skill, crucial for higher education and for work, and many people can't make the vital transition from teacher-directed to self-directed learning without coaching. Self-directed teaching is not trendy and odd, it's life. It's the way most people learn most of the time.

> The 'Catch them before they fall' strategy summarised on page 550 adapts self-directed learning to provide one-to-one tutorial support on a course.

What records should I keep for self-directed learning?

Often lesson plans are not produced, except as a courtesy to observers; instead, individual student records are kept, by the student, and probably by you, of:

*   Student learning contracts and/or action plans, and perhaps the long-term learning programme agreed with each student. This should be renegotiated or at least checked occasionally. Old learning contracts are useful models for new students.
*   Activities carried out, progress and/or competences achieved, etc., for each learner.
*   Success of activities carried out in terms of learning achieved, i.e. an 'evaluation'.

In addition:

*   Students may keep a diary where they self-evaluate, reflect on goals and learning activities, and record their triumphs and disasters.
*   Other records may be required if a qualification is being pursued.

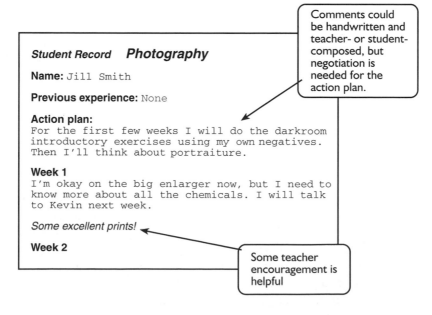

Example of an individual student record for self-directed or resource-based learning

Mixing modes for flexibility, inclusion and personalisation

It is usually better to use a mix of modes in order to overcome the weaknesses of any given mode if it is used in isolation. I will describe how to make whole-class teaching more flexible by mixing in the other two modes. However, any mode can be improved by mixing.

Making whole-class teaching more flexible

As we have seen, the main weakness of whole-class teaching is that it tends to treat all students the same, and so can fail to meet their individual needs. These unique needs can be met in part by mixing in some resource-based learning (RBL) and/or self-directed learning. The example below shows how a computing teacher mixes modes; see if you can guess her reasons for doing so.

Lessons on Mondays, Tuesdays & Fridays

Whole-class teaching

The main content is taught using whole-class teaching, e.g. theory of computing etc. Work is assessed by assignments.

Lessons on Wednesdays

Resource-based learning (learning from resources at your own pace)

Students improve their use of spreadsheets and databases by using workbooks.

Students learn to programme using an online tutor.

Progress is monitored by short end-of-chapter tests, taken when the student is ready.

Lessons on Fridays

Self-directed learning

For the first eight weeks of the second term, students complete a self-chosen 'personal project' associated with their hobbies or interests. It is assessed by a presentation at the end of the course.

This teacher mixes in RBL because she knows from experience that new students differ greatly in their spreadsheet and database skills, so she diagnoses what they can do with a questionnaire, and then places each student at an appropriate place in the workbook. None of her students can programme when they start the course, but she knows some learn programming much faster than others. Using RBL enables students to learn at their own pace. The aim of the personal project is to motivate students and to use computer skills in a context that is exciting for them – creating a database of fashion outlets, or a website for a local rock band. Self-directed learning personalises the course for students.

The teacher keeps RBL and self-directed learning records, as explained earlier in this chapter, alongside her whole-class learning records. Students keep personal action plans as part of their individual learning plan, the teacher has summaries.

Here are more examples of RBL being used to personalise whole-class teaching:

- Assessing learner's needs followed by tutorial action planning. This is a form of self-directed learning or RBL. This is described in detail in Chapters 47 and 48. These chapters will help you use RBL and self-directed learning effectively.
- Students could be given a topic to learn at their own pace from resources outside of class. This is called independent learning and is explained in Chapter 33.
- A student with dyslexia could be given a target to make notes using mind-maps assisted by an explanatory handout and a peer who is good at this.

Fixing differences in prior learning

- A science teacher teaches maths for physics using RBL. This helps her deal with the very different maths skills of her students.
- Art students who have not done silk-screen printing before follow an online course followed by two practical assignments.
- A student with behaviour difficulties is given a target not to call out in class. 'Call-out rate' is monitored by a peer, who records improvement on a teacher's record.

Fixing differences in intellectual and physical skills

- A childhood studies teacher finds her students differ hugely in their ability to learn independently. She uses a competence questionnaire (page 365) to diagnose weaknesses and set targets. See Chapter 33.
- An art and design teacher develops students' use of the creative process or design process by using the 'ICEDIP' competency questionnaire on www. geoffpetty.com/evidence_based_downloads.htm
- Sports students practise specified ball skills until they pass a practical test. This test is peer assessed, but the results are recorded by the teacher.

In the above cases, students' prior learning is assessed to diagnose where they are now, then appropriate targets or action plans are agreed; these are worked on, with support if necessary. There are frequent checks on student progress when new action plans are agreed. This process is described in Chapters 47 and 48.

Mixing in self-directed learning for further personalisation

Here are some examples of self-directed learning being mixed in with whole-class teaching. Chapter 34 deals with self-directed learning in detail.

- In an adult painting course, students study a painter of choice and record their reactions in a diary format.
- Sports science students choose a sport, self-assess a related skill or form of fitness, and work towards a target for improvement.

- Adult computing students are asked to set goals based on their reason for enrolling on the course. These goals are worked on for the first 10 minutes of every class. This accommodates different personal needs – and late arrivers!
- In A-level English literature and French, students set themselves background reading tasks, including one book from a prescribed list.
- Hairdressing students do a project on their favourite hair stylists, creating a personal exhibition space in the corridor.
- A student with learning and behaviour difficulties wants to make more friends and negotiates targets to improve his social behaviour.

> How could you use resource-based learning and self-directed learning to make your teaching more flexible, personalised, differentiated and inclusive? What records would you, or preferably your students, need to keep?
>
> There are other ways of responding to the individual needs and aspirations of your students; see the differentiation summary in Appendix 2.

Students with moderate or specific learning difficulties, or with behavioural difficulties, are very often taught in classes of students who don't share their difficulties. Most teachers set such students individual learning or behaviour targets. These are diagnosed individually, based on a combination of prior learning, previous behaviour, diagnostic assessment, specialist assessments and teacher judgement. These targets are negotiated and monitored in a near identical way to that described here and in Chapters 47 and 48.

RARPA: recognising and recording progress and achievement

This is a highly flexible approach which uses self-directed learning and, if they help meet students' needs efficiently, whole-class teaching and resource-based learning as well. It is required on courses that don't lead to recognised qualifications, but do attract government funding. However, a similar approach is used in other contexts – for example, teaching students with learning difficulties or gifted students, though with less bureaucratic scrutiny.

This approach works whenever individual needs rather than course objectives are paramount. If this is not true for you, you might not find it helpful. Chapters 47 and 48 describe a similar approach. Chapter 34 describes self-directed learning in more detail.

Some teachers see RARPA as a time-consuming bureaucratic burden imposed by funding and inspection bodies. But funders and inspectors insist that the learners' needs should be paramount and that teachers are free to design the method of implementation so that students and teachers see the process as useful rather than intrusive.

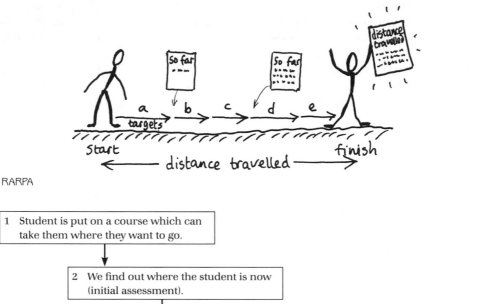

RARPA

```
┌─────────────────────────────────────────┐
│ 1   Student is put on a course which can │
│     take them where they want to go.     │
└─────────────────────────────────────────┘
              │
              ▼
     ┌─────────────────────────────────────────┐
     │ 2   We find out where the student is now │
     │     (initial assessment).                │
     └─────────────────────────────────────────┘
                   │
                   ▼
          ┌──────────────────────────────────────────┐
          │ 3   We set a series of challenging targets:│
          │     a, b, etc.                            │
          └──────────────────────────────────────────┘
                        │
                        ▼
               ┌─────────────────────────────────────────┐
               │ 4   Formative assessment, self-assessment │
               │     and feedback ascertain progress       │
               │     through targets. This progress is     │
               │     recorded by the learner, or possibly by│
               │     you, using audio, video, photographic,│
               │     written or online records, etc.       │
               └─────────────────────────────────────────┘
                             │
                             ▼
                    ┌─────────────────────────────────────────┐
                    │ 5   End point and distance travelled is  │
                    │     decided.                             │
                    └─────────────────────────────────────────┘
```

Find out what other teachers do, and what managers advise. The intention at every stage is to ensure the learner gets what they want and knows the distance they have travelled; if this is achieved, you should encounter no official or student objections. If your approach doesn't give learners what they want, change it. Let's look at the process in detail, then look at ways in which students can record their own progress.

Students need to understand the 'how' and 'why' of this process, and you must make time and opportunities to achieve this. Don't 'protect your back' by over-interpreting the process, which should be appropriate to the length of the course. When you are dealing with students one-to-one, make the meetings informal and natural, and ensure the other students have something productive and relevant to do.

At every stage, you explain, consult, listen and negotiate with your students until they understand, appreciate and agree each step. They have a right to suggest changes, and even to opt out if they want to.

'Never let your fears make your decisions.'

The RARPA process

1 Before enrolment, describe your course with integrity, explaining the purpose, work and level clearly. Avoid jargon and use translations or translators if necessary and check understanding. Some teachers use pre-programme meetings or 'taster' or 'drop-in' sessions. Every student should understand the purpose of the course before they enrol, and be inspired to participate.

2 To discover the distance travelled, we must first know the students' starting point. Initial assessment (Chapter 47) can be very informal. You could do it by chat, questionnaire, portfolio, online or formal screening test, depending on what best meets student needs. Students usually record their own starting points using paper, portfolio, audio, video or online mediums. The learner has access to this initial assessment, and knows if anyone else has access. Extra support might be arranged at this stage. The initial assessment often forms part of the student's learning agreement or individual learning plan (ILP). The aim is to discover what the student knows and can do already, but only well enough for the next stages.

3 Students now negotiate and agree a target appropriate to their starting point and their needs and aspirations. They must understand this well, ideally explaining it in their own words. Targets should explain what students will be able to do, think, feel or say, and should be assessable, as described in point 5 below. They need not be 'SMART' targets if they don't want these. Ensure the target is realistic and the student knows roughly the time and effort required to attain them.

Your course or 'programme' is now planned to achieve these targets – it doesn't just cover what you expected or fancy doing! If students want different things – and they usually will – you will need to use the flexible methods described earlier in this chapter, choosing carefully. Whole-class teaching might be entirely appropriate too, whenever all targets overlap and starting points are similar.

4 Periodically, your students, and you, will want to know how they are getting on. Students should self-assess first, perhaps using criteria provided by themselves or you. The criteria should, of course, be closely related to the targets from point 3 above. Ask what they have found most difficult. Ask for 'unintended' outcomes too – self-confidence, enjoyment, something surprising learned by watching other students. Students often need to discuss how to go about a self-assessment.

Have a look at this self-assessment, then give your own assessment, preferably in 'medal and mission' format (Chapter 43). Targets might now be renegotiated and agreed.

If a student does not want to take part in this stage, they have the option not to participate – funding bodies and inspectors are entirely happy about this, but might be interested in reasons.

This should not be too time-consuming or burdensome, which is not easy to achieve on a short course, but ensure self-assessment and self-target-setting take most of the load. If you visit students one-to-one during your normal teaching, these discussions can take place then. Again, records can be student-produced, in any medium. Chapter 48 looks at this process in more detail.

5   Very near the end of your students' course or programme, you conclude the RARPA process by determining how much each student has learned – their 'distance travelled'. Look at their initial assessment (2) and their challenging goals (3). How have they done compared to these? Has there been any unanticipated learning, including attitudes to learning, self-belief etc.?

Students record their progress in their own words and in their own style and in any appropriate medium: e.g. video, audio, photo, paper, online.

Many teachers ask students to create demonstrations or exhibitions to celebrate anticipated and unanticipated achievement. Some award home-made certificates, stressing the value of the learning to the individual, but also to work, family and community.

This stage is often completed just before the end of the programme, so students have a little time for catching up.

You can now discuss what learners might do next, and evaluate the programme. Remember, you are in control of exactly how you use RARPA. The aim is to help the learner, not the institution; don't allow it to become too burdensome, time-consuming or bureaucratic. Keep your focus on the learner and learning, and be brave. Find out how other teachers do this and talk over what you intend to do with them and your manager.

Chapters 47 and 48 look at the process of assessing learners' needs and action planning in the context of a conventional full-time course. These chapters suggest strategies also appropriate to the RARPA process. See, in particular, 'can you do this?' questionnaires, and how to carry out effective one-to-ones.

Record-keeping for RARPA or other flexible teaching

You can, of course, use any of the records described earlier in this chapter, but there are more ideas below. Get students to fill in records themselves, even if you store them. It helps give them 'ownership' and responsibility for their learning and makes them reflect.

The competency approach: You or your students list competences, knowledge, skills, exercises or criteria, etc.

These are written in informal student language. Students self-assess against these by placing a number in the appropriate column. They use a '1' for indicating their first self-assessment, and a '2' for their next self-assessment. If they use the same assessment sheet, then any progress, or coasting, is clear. Self-assessments are discussed and negotiated – 'you did better than that' – and used to set targets.

Photography I Name: Vinder Singh			
	Work on this	Okay	Good
Composition	I	2	
Use of contrast	I	2	
Use of colour		I, 2	
(etc.)			
Targets: September: exercises 7 & 9 November: exercise II – try to make my backgrounds plainer			

Page 362 shows competences being used to develop independent learning skills.

Assessment proformas: This is similar to competences, but more detailed comments are expected. Students can self-assess each piece of work and use this to set new targets. See pages 384–5 for some examples. Again, the self-assessments are discussed and negotiated, at least some of the time. See pages 490–2.

Student journal: Students can write reflections on their learning and use these to set themselves targets. See Chapter 46 on how you do this as a trainee teacher. Chapter 31 deals with learning by reflection.

The aspirational approach: Here, students state an aspiration in an area of personal interest, and negotiate with you a set of personal challenges that are stepping stones towards that aspiration. Ideally, challenges are worded in ways that allow the learner to assess whether they have been achieved.

Interest: Baroque violin music	Name: Julia Tseling
Aspiration: to play Bach suite or partita	Progress
Stepping stones:	
Improve detache bowing – exercises 17–21	
practice first 16 bars of the Allemande of the Dnaing Partita	
My learning notes	

Some questions on coasting

Some adult learners see their course as a club, providing regular social contact and a chance to dabble in an area of interest. Some students with learning difficulties see their course as a 'safe house' that exists solely to care for and protect them. However, funding bodies want to see progress for the public money spent. It is not always easy to reconcile these differences, but when you manage it, everybody often wins: taxpayer, learner and teacher. How can you use the approaches in this chapter, and others, to care for learners, but also to challenge them to learn? Are there circumstances when learning takes a back seat?

Other approaches to designing courses for adults are considered in the next chapter, under 'Designing your own course'.

Further reading

*Boud, D. (1988) *Developing Student Autonomy in Learning* (2nd edition), London: Kogan Page. Mainly HE-focused.

Knowles, M. S. (1975) *Self-Directed Learning*, Cambridge University Press.

Knowles, M. S. (1990) *The Adult Learner: A Neglected Species*, Houston, TX: Gulf Publishing.

Race, P. (1994) *The Open Learning Handbook*, London: Kogan Page.

Rogers, C. (1994) *Freedom to Learn* (3rd edition), New York: Merrill.

Rogers, J. (2001) *Adults Learning*, Maidenhead: Open University Press.

*Rowntree, D. (1992) *Exploring Open and Distance Learning*, London: Kogan Page.

42

Planning courses

If there is a syllabus, unit specification, a set of competences or any other documentation which defines the content of your course, then you can use this to devise a scheme of work. If not, you must decide the course content yourself, a process which we will leave until a little later in this chapter.

The scheme of work

Course content can be defined in terms of a syllabus of topics, unit specifications, a programme of study or a list of learning outcomes or competences; but this content is rarely set out in a suitable teaching order. It may also ignore skills such as essay writing or evaluating.

The scheme of work is a plan which organises course content and the learning of important skills such as reasoning and assignment writing, breaking them up into teaching weeks or lessons and putting them into a logical teaching order. The best schemes suggest active teaching and learning strategies that require the students to develop an understanding of the content, but also make them use important skills.

Schemes of work guide lesson planning, telling you 'what comes next' and whether you are on target to finish the course in the time available. Schemes should already have been devised for existing courses, though you may want to change them (if so, make sure this is permissible).

A scheme can take many forms, from non-existence to fat folders where elaborate detailed breakdowns of every lesson are provided, along with all teaching materials. Usually, however, it consists of a brief outline of the course, along with references for finding worksheets, assignments, etc.

Schemes may (or may not!) include the following information:

- *General information*, e.g. the course title, awarding body, length of course, duration of sessions, venue, previous experience of students, prerequisites for the course.
- *Aims, general objectives and learning outcomes or specific objectives*, broken down into a teaching order.
- *Content* of the course, organised in sequence, usually with some indication of the time taken for each section of the course. This should allow time for revision, assessments, trips, etc.
- *Teaching/learning methods* – though these may be omitted or scant. Activities and teaching methods may be suggested; and worksheets and assignments may be included, or reference given as to where to find them.

- *The student group*, e.g. their age, previous knowledge, experience and attainment.
- *Organisational factors*, e.g. course structure and methods, work experience, course team meetings and work-based assignments may all be referred to.
- *Assessment methods*, along with tests or exams (or references for them). A time-table of deadlines for the completion of assignments may also be included.
- *Evaluation methods*. (Assessment and evaluation are referred to in later chapters.)

Schemes of work may seem very rigid, but this is not usually their intention. It is expected that you will adapt the scheme to respond to your learners' needs.

There is an extract from a Scheme of Work on page 472.

While the scheme of work should tackle topics in a logical order, there is a grave danger in isolating topics and then teaching each in turn. You may find that this results in students forgetting topics 1 and 2 while you teach them topic 3; it may also produce a lack of coherence in students' understanding. The main problem with this approach, however, is that students must learn skills high on Bloom's taxonomy, not just content. Try to make use of earlier learning while developing new learning, as explained in Chapter 23 on learning for remembering. When devising a scheme of work, make sure the teaching order is logical, and that allow-ance is made for revision, exams, work experience, holidays, etc.

Embedding skills into your scheme of work

It is a common mistake to fill your scheme of work entirely with content, hardly teaching skills such as how to evaluate or write essays. Skills are difficult to learn and need lots of practice. It simply doesn't make sense to teach the easy stuff, avoid the hard stuff and then blame your students for lacking the skills you haven't taught them.

You can teach skills separately and this works quite well, but rarely provides suffi-cient practice. The best way to teach skills is to habitually embed them into your ordinary teaching. Chapters 21 and 24 of *Evidence Based Teaching* look at this in detail; what follows will get you started.

In trials, embedding learning to learn skills raised students' performance by more than a grade.

The skills you might need or want to embed come in three overlapping categories:

- *Functional skills (key skills, or core skills)*: These include mathematics/numeracy; English/literacy/communication; ICT and computer skills (see Chapter 36). These are often obligatory parts of courses assessed by exam and/or by portfolio of work.

- *Learning-to-learn skills*: for example, underlining, highlighting or annotating text; summarising and note-making; creating graphic organisers; essay writing and the ability to tackle a specific exam-style question, such as data analysis or comprehension questions.
- *Intellectual skills*: for example, reasoning, evaluating or critically appraising; problem-solving (e.g. in maths); ability to critique a hypothesis or point of view, e.g. in science or history; ability to use 'spectacles' to look at something from different perspectives or points of view (pages 153–4).

You could add other skills you think important – good behaviour, aesthetic appreciation, etc.

www.qca.org.uk has guidance and information on functional skills, key skills etc.

To embed skills, do the following:

1   Study the standards and assessment requirements for the skills your examining body requires you to embed. For example, functional skills are required for the new Diploma qualifications at levels 1, 2 and 3. (This does not apply on adult recreational courses and other courses without examining bodies.)

2   Identify the skills you want to embed because summative assessment or the nature of your subject requires it. For example, a business studies teacher might choose to embed 'how to evaluate' into their course, and 'how to do data analysis questions'.

3   Decide roughly how much practice is needed for each skill, and how much portfolio evidence is required, if any, for any functional or key skills, etc.

4   Look at the content in your scheme of work. Look for opportunities to use these skills on the content, so students can learn both the skill and the content in the same lesson. This is then a double-decker lesson, as described in Chapter 38.

For example, the business studies teacher mentioned earlier might decide that three topics involving evaluation would be about right for the module she is planning. Looking at the module, she decides her students could learn about business plans, marketing strategies and market research questionnaires in separate lessons, by evaluating examples of these. This will require her to devise scenarios and example business plans, etc. for them to evaluate, but she has some from past-paper questions and others in a textbook.

She also notices that the functional skill of reading has not been used much so far in her schemes. So she decides to teach some other topics by asking students to read, highlight, establish key points and then summarise the text with a graphic organiser. She will use old handouts and photocopies of sections of a textbook for this task. Students will self-assess their summary against a model summary provided by her.

When students learn content by practising skills on it, you must review the content and the skill separately, or students only notice the content (marketing questionnaire) not the skill (evaluation). Skills are reviewed by bridging, as described in Chapter 38.

Here are some more examples of double-decker lessons:

- Students plan an essay on the House of Lords as a class activity in groups. This active learning requires them to understand the content, but also teaches them how to essay-plan. The essay need not necessarily then be written.
- Students use desktop publishing to produce a leaflet on health and safety, in order to improve their computer skills and learn about health and safety.
- Students calculate percentage heat loss from a building to learn about heat loss rates and percentage calculations.

Your institution or tutor might require you to use a specific format for your scheme of work. If not, devise your own format. The example below has a 'skill tracker' column to help you see how well you are embedding skills. Most standard formats omit this, but you can often split a column to create one, or highlight the embedded skills.

Page 3 Scheme of Work Business Studies Year 1				
Teaching week	**Content: Syllabus reference & objectives**	**Student activity and resources**	**Skill tracker** (These skills are reviewed in double-decker lessons)	**Assessment**
7	3.1 Marketing displays. Students should be able to: explain the use and purpose of marketing displays.	Design a marketing display for their case study and justify their design. Need copies of case study.	Justification Word processing	Functional skill ICT 2.2 2.7 The justification can go in their portfolio if word-processed
8	3.2, 3.3 Marketing plans: The purpose, design & uses of marketing plans. Costing marketing plans. Students should be able to: criticise marketing plans constructively.	Students evaluate marketing plans. Use of spreadsheet to compute alternative costings. Need plans to evaluate pages 17–19 in handbook.	Evaluation Computation with a spreadsheet	Functional skills ICT 1.4, 1.6, 1.7 Spreadsheet document goes into their ICT portfolio

The spiral curriculum

Most people design a scheme of work to cover each topic only once. But this often means students forget their early learning.

An alternative approach, devised by Bruner, is the spiral curriculum. Here, a topic is encountered two or three times, each time to a greater depth. For example, our business studies teacher could teach students about different methods of marketing during one term, then, in a later year or term, students could devise and criticise marketing plans.

Learners' needs analysis

Courses are often designed, and even implemented, without any reference to the students who take them. This is almost never satisfactory, and can be a disaster. No doctor prescribes without consultation and diagnosis! But how can the course designer develop a profile of the learners? This process is usually carried out very early in the course or, if possible, before the course begins. It is explained in full in Chapters 47 and 48.

Designing your own course

Some teachers – for example, those in recreational adult education, or teachers and trainers in industry, commerce and the public sector – often need to devise their own courses from scratch, without competences, syllabus or other external requirements. We have already seen one approach to this in Chapter 41 (RARPA). We will now consider others.

It is impossible to be prescriptive about this essentially creative process, but in addition to a learners' needs analysis, explained in Chapter 47, the following may help to ensure that the course satisfies the demands of the learner and the client:

- a task analysis
- a topic analysis
- a workplace needs analysis.

These are described below. If you carry out a workplace needs analysis along with others, then the workplace analysis should come first.

Task analysis

This involves a careful study of a task for which training is being devised, in order to break it down into components. The components can then be sequenced and given priorities, with the aim of developing a logically ordered series of objectives or learning outcomes. If the course is to be of real practical use rather than an academic exercise, this usually requires careful consultation with those who carry out the task in practice.

Suppose, for example, that one of the tasks thrown up by the needs analysis is that sales staff should be able to 'use the new computer system'. Task analysis may reveal the information shown in the diagram below.

A task analysis may break down to many levels of analysis. Each component of the analysis can be used to develop at least one objective. For example, the components 'Coding by product type' and 'Entering sales data' may suggest the following objectives, along with some others:

Staff should be able to:

- state the eight major product types, giving the correct code for each
- enter and cancel a sales record …

Task analysis: Sales staff use of the new computer system

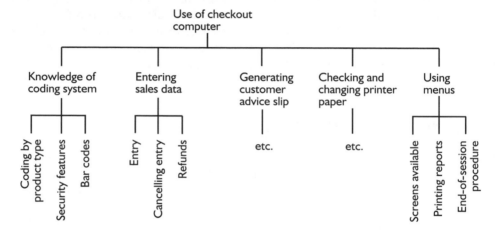

Topic analysis

Topic analysis is very much like task analysis, except that it breaks down a topic into its component parts. Again, this analysis can be used as a starting point for developing objectives. Like task analysis, it can be displayed in a 'tree' structure like the one above, or as an indented list of the kind shown below and on the following page.

Teaching Today is a detailed topic analysis of teaching.

The QTS standards are a very detailed task analysis of teaching (they can be found in Appendix 3).

```
EXTRACT FROM A TOPIC ANALYSIS ON MOTIVATION
success
        setting the level of work to ensure success
                setting individualised targets
                        formal targets
                        informal targets
        praise and criticism
                praise
                        importance of praise
                        how and when to praise
                        ensuring praise is not devalued
                criticism
                        being constructive
                        mixing with praise
purpose
        long-term purpose
                careers and employment
                development of transferable skills
        short-term purpose
                tests and exams
[etc.]
```

Affective considerations

Do you want your course to develop in students an appreciation of some matter or other? Are there any attitudes or opinions you want to foster or to change? These should be added to your topic and/or task analysis, and should find their way into your course objectives. Here are some examples of affective requirements for courses.

- *On a sign language course:* Learners should develop an appreciation of a deaf person's everyday difficulties.
- *On a woodworking course:* Course participants should value the employment of safe practices when using woodworking machinery.
- *On a sales staff course:* Staff should appreciate the impact of security lapses on company profit.

Do not undervalue the affective domain. Knowledge and skills may enable learners to do something – but it is often affect which makes them want to do it!

Resources

After your consultations and analyses, you will be almost ready to start devising the scheme of work described at the beginning of this chapter. However, other considerations may affect course design, and chief amongst these will be resource constraints. What equipment, personnel and money will be available to support the course? It is necessary to discover this before even beginning to design it in detail.

Workplace needs analysis

The workplace needs analysis which follows is sometimes simply called a 'needs analysis'. It aims to discover the training needs of the organisation which is initiating the training. You need read this only if you are designing training for your employer or a client; skip to the coda if you are not.

Trainers can, in principle, help to remedy deficiencies in job performance, such as low productivity, high wastage rates, high staff turnover, or poor quality. However, one must first discover, of course, whether such underperformance is due to inadequate training or to other factors.

It is fatal for training designers to attempt course design *in vacuo* (in a vacuum). They must consult widely – with those doing the job for which the training is being devised, and with their supervisors, unions, quality circles, colleagues, clients and customers.

This consultation process may lead to a working party of interested staff, who then determine a first guess at the training needs by stating goals or aims. For example:

> To improve sales staff familiarity with the new computer system.

Aims or goals should not contain hidden solutions. For example, the following aim is not legitimate:

> To improve staff familiarity with the new computer system by training all staff with the ATS package.

All aims should be achievable by training, of course, and may be suggested by a brainstorming session. These goals or aims can then be circulated for consultation, so that all those concerned can contribute their views on priorities – and possibly suggest additional goals or aims. Questionnaires like the one below may be useful.

EXCERPT FROM A WORKPLACE NEEDS ANALYSIS SURVEY

	strongly agree				strongly disagree
12. All sales staff are familiar with the new computer system.	1	2	3	4	5
13. All sales staff should be familiar with the new computer system.	1	2	3	4	5
14. All sales staff are familiar with new product development.	1	2	3	4	5
15. All sales staff should be familiar with new product development.	1	2	3	4	5

Please add below any training needs not mentioned above which you feel should be addressed, or any other comments about staff development.

Once any questionnaires have been answered, priority goals are decided. The views obtained on 'where we are now' (e.g. item 12 in the survey above) are compared with those on 'where we ought to be' (item 13). A large discrepancy in the numerical scores for the two types of question may well indicate an area where there is a training need.

If a sufficient number of new goals is suggested in responses to the survey, it may well be necessary to circulate another workplace needs analysis survey before deciding the priority these new goals should have. This new survey should contain both old and new goals, so that a fair comparison can be made between them.

When the training needs have been established, in the form of goals allotted, high-priority 'performance indicators' can be devised for each goal. For example, one performance indicator for the goal 'All sales staff should be familiar with the new computer system' might be a reduction in the number of erroneous computer sales records which sales staff produce, as detected by the accounts department. Performance indicators show whether goals have been met, and can be used later to check on the effectiveness of the training.

> *Even if you decide not to carry out a full-blown needs analysis, complete with questionnaires, make sure you still consult widely in the workplace. You will almost certainly find that the comments you receive are helpful, and that people appreciate being consulted. When making a recommendation for training, try to compare the cost of training with the cost of not training.*

The needs analysis should produce a list of high-priority training goals in the form of *tasks* (e.g. 'Using the new computer system') or topics (e.g. 'New product development'). These topics and tasks can be subjected to further analysis in order to produce objectives for the course, as described above.

Coda

I know what you're thinking. 'This course planning stuff is all very well, but I haven't the time to go through all that palaver.' But I can hear the chorus of your students, complaining as a result of hasty course design:

> 'From the moment he opened his mouth I didn't understand a single word. I asked the others at coffee, but they didn't understand either.'

Or perhaps:

> 'It was all very well, but I wanted to know the practical aspects of the subject, not just the theory.'

Or:

> 'I left the course after the first session. I've kept a horse for three years, and she was telling me which way up to fasten the saddle!'

Or:

'All I got was theory; all I wanted was how to do it.'

Or:

'So I arrived at work after the computer course with my briefcase full of handouts, and then to my horror it dawned on me – she never told us how to switch it on!'

Or:

'I couldn't understand the maths bit at all.'

Complaints like those above are common; you may well have made similar ones yourself about courses you have attended. Each complaint is important; some of them suggest that the effectiveness of the course was entirely undermined. Each could have been avoided by an analysis described in this chapter. (Which kind of analysis would have avoided the need for each of the above complaints?)

Don't underestimate the importance of course design.

Further reading

If your students are working towards a qualification, check the examining body's website for the qualification.

Most of the general teaching books in the bibliography deal with this topic; for example:

Reece, I. and Walker, S. (2007) *A Practical Guide to Teaching, Training and Learning* (6th edition), Tyne and Wear: Business Education Publishers.

Walklin, L. (1990) *Teaching and Learning in Further Education*, Cheltenham: Nelson Thornes.

43

Assessment

Assessment measures the breadth and depth of learning. It has been criticised as being inaccurate and unreliable, and for distorting both teaching and the curriculum; it is also true that assessment results are notoriously poor at predicting future performance. And yet society and teachers are unable to manage without it. In the right hands, assessment can inspire, motivate and provide the feedback which is essential for targeting prompt corrective help. But it can also lead us to ignore what cannot easily be measured.

Purposes of assessment

Assessment serves many different purposes. It can grade the attainment of learners, help to select candidates for jobs or future courses, contribute to evidence on the effectiveness of courses and teachers, and provide a long-term goal for learners. But this applies mainly to the *final* or *summative assessment* of a course, which aims to sum up the learners' achievements.

The main use of assessment for teachers is the ongoing or *formative assessment*. This is used throughout the course to form judgements on whether, and to what extent, learning has been successful; and to pinpoint difficulties so that remedial action can be taken. Initial and diagnostic assessment have similar 'formative' roles. They are carried out at the beginning of a course, and are dealt with in Chapter 47.

As summative and formative assessment have very different aims, they are usually carried out in radically different ways. Before we look at assessment in more detail, the difference between norm-referenced and criterion-referenced assessment must be understood.

Norm-referenced and criterion-referenced assessment

Suppose I gave 300 army recruits a test, choosing the best 30 per cent to be trained as engineers, and the next 30 per cent to be trained as technicians. This is *norm-referenced assessment*; it compares candidates with each other, and rewards the best. The marks show how the candidate does compared with the norm, or average, for all the candidates. (For statistical reasons, norm-referenced assessment works effectively only for examinations with at least a few hundred candidates.) The percentage of candidates getting each grade remains unchanged, regardless of their marks, unless a conscious decision is made to change those percentages. This has the advantage that variations in the difficulty of exams from year to year do not affect grades, but is potentially unfair, as students may be better one year than the next. Norm referencing is used, at least in part, for deciding A-level and GCSE grades. It is appropriate for developmental rather than mastery objectives.

By contrast, *criterion-referenced assessment* measures what the candidate can do, awarding a pass if they can do it and a fail if they cannot. The driving test is a good example. Assessment is only reliable if the criteria are well defined – for example, in a checklist, or a list of competences, or a mark scheme. Otherwise different markers will apply different standards, or the same marker may apply different standards on different days or to different candidates. This is true of any assessment. Criterion referencing is appropriate for mastery objectives.

A third alternative is student-referenced assessment or 'medal and mission' assessment, considered below. The learner's own standard is taken as the reference and the assessment involves telling the learner of important criteria they have met, and others they need to meet, but which are attainable in a relatively short time.

Formative assessment: using assessment to improve learning

Formative assessment is informative feedback to learners while they are still learning the topic. But to be truly formative, this information must be used by the learner to improve. The teacher can provide the formative assessment, but the learners can also formatively assess themselves and each other. Research shows that this feedback while you learn has more effect on student achievement than any other single factor, so it's worth getting right!

> *Researchers have compared teaching in the USA with teaching in Japan and elsewhere in Asia. The Asian teachers were much more effective. The researchers concluded that a major reason for this was that the Western teachers emphasised aptitude and ability, while the Asian teachers put emphasis on effort and persistence. Another reason suggested was that Asian teachers were allowed more preparation time out of the classroom.* (Scientific American, *December 1992*)

Two top-flight professors at King's College London carried out a review of research on formative assessment. Black and Wiliam (1998) found that the most effective formative strategies could add the equivalent of up to two grades to a student's achievement, and that it had the greatest effect on the weakest learners. They also discovered that, on the whole, teachers did not use the strategies that researchers had found most powerful.

What strategies were these, and why did they work? Let's find out with a thought experiment. Please do this before reading on.

EXERCISE

I want you to imagine you are about to have an extension built on your own house or flat. Two building firms have quoted about the same for doing this work. You were just about to toss a coin when you thought: No! I'll ask them for their quality systems. These are given below. Your questions are:

1 Which building firm would you choose?
2 Why would you choose that builder? Think of as many reasons as you can.

BILL OR SID?

Which builder would you choose to build your new extension?

SID'S HIGH-GRADE GRAFTERS

Quality-control system

- Sid grades each worker's efforts at the end of each day, informing them of this grade.
- He praises work of above-average standard.
- He draws attention to errors and deficiencies.
- He constructively criticises work that is not of an acceptable standard.
- He moves on to the next day's work to guarantee speedy completion.

BILL'S TROUBLESHOOTERS

Quality-control system

- Bill asks each worker to inspect their own work and fix errors and deficiencies as they go.
- He inspects work at the end of each day, praising work of an entirely acceptable standard.
- He gets workers to put right any errors and deficiencies and checks these corrections have been made.
- He constructively criticises work that is not of an acceptable standard.
- He moves on to the next day's work to guarantee speedy completion.

Formative assessment must be informative assessment

In Chapter 6 we looked at praise and criticism and concluded that every learner needs three important pieces of information if they are to learn to maximum effect (Sadler 1989). Keep in mind that this information can come from the teacher, from the learner's own self-assessment or from a peer assessment:

Clear goals

If learners don't know what they are trying to do, they are most unlikely to do it! Students must understand the tasks – for example, the differences between 'evaluate', 'analyse' and 'describe'. They must also understand the criteria for a good piece of work, which includes the 'assessment criteria'. They need to know what they are aiming for.

A medal

Information about what they have done well and what is good about it. You simply can't learn if you never discover when you have succeeded. Many people think the main advantage of the medal is that it is encouraging, but this has been found to be a secondary issue. What students need most is an informative view on what they have done well. It is better for learning if the learner discovers they have succeeded with one of their goals, than that they have your approval.

Medals can refer to the student's work – the *product* – or how they approached the work – the *process* (for example, 'You used the right method there, well done' or 'You really persisted with that'). They can also refer to progress: 'That's much quicker than last time.'

A mission

Information about what needs improving and how to improve it. This needs to be 'constructive', which means forward-looking and positive, showing how to improve, not just what is wrong.

Missions can be targets for the next piece of work, or improvements for the existing piece of work. Simple grades or marks are not missions.

EXERCISE
QUESTION 1

The following are alternative comments on the same graph completed by a student. Which contain medals, missions or both? In which are the missions forward-looking and positive? Re-read the definitions of medals and missions above before deciding.

a 7/10 Quite good!
b Good points and line. Units?
c Your line is an excellent fit to the points.
   You missed the units off the axes!
d Always give the units on your axes!
e This is a very good attempt.
f Points and line accurate, always check axes for label and units.
g *Axes:* units please
   Points: all correct
   Line: very good fit

QUESTION 2

These comments are on different pieces of work. Which are the best?

1   Well done, John, that's brilliant! 9/10
2   Good graph, Martha. Nice and neat. All the points are well plotted.
3   Better than last week. Rather thick lines though! Keep improvement up.
4   Better standard. A sharper pencil improves accuracy. Keep improvement up!
5   Good scales, good line, but some points missing! Nice and neat.
6   Good standard. No title. Neat writing. 8/10
7   Good axes, points and line.
8   Well done, you handed it in! Please finish it now. Keep this improvement up.

Bill or Sid? Whom did you choose?

Which builder did you choose and why? If you haven't decided, please do so before reading on.

Most people choose Bill for the following reasons:

- Bill expects his workers to self-assess their own work, so problems are fixed as they work, and before they cause more problems. Self-assessment will also help his workers learn better than Sid's.
- Bill's workers don't need to be above average to earn praise, so all his workers will be encouraged by recognition for their efforts.
- Not only does Bill *find* the errors and deficiencies, he also makes sure they are put right and checks this has been done. Sid only points the errors out. Bill's strategy is 'find faults, fix and follow up' (to check that the fix has been made). This strategy, along with self-assessment, makes his workers feel responsible and accountable for their own work – after all, *they* will have to fix it if they get it wrong.

Those who choose Sid are often concerned that Bill might accept low standards, but Bill can be even more challenging than Sid, as we will see.

The good news is that most teachers choose Bill in this thought experiment; the bad news is that many teachers work like Sid. There is a culture and set of assumptions in education that encourage teachers to:

- Point out learning errors and omissions, but not to require the learner to fix these, or to check these fixes have been made. Teachers are often not encouraged to use work diagnostically in order to set targets.
- Give even formative (practice) work grades or marks, but not give clear missions stating how to improve.
- Always mark work themselves, rather than requiring their students to mark their own work, or each other's, using model answers or assessment criteria.

So how should teachers formatively assess? If you teach practical skills, you could hardly do better than follow Bill's approach. If students present work in written form, then you must work out your own way, but let's look at a few very effective strategies: assessment proformas; mastery tests; and self-, peer or spoof assessment. You will find other useful approaches in Chapter 6 on praise and criticism. Chapter 19 of my *Evidence Based Teaching* has many more methods.

Assessment proformas to teach skills

Many teachers now use assessment 'proformas' like those below to ensure the learner gets good informative feedback on their essays, assignments, practicals and homeworks, etc. The proformas are given to students before they attempt the task. You need not use these proformas for every piece of work your students do if you cannot make time.

The criteria need to be taught. An excellent way to do this is to get the students to develop them themselves. Suppose you wanted to teach the criteria for essay writing, as shown in the first proforma below. You could first ask students to work in groups to identify what they think are the criteria for a good essay. Then you could use their answers to develop the criteria, using an 'assertive questioning' approach, as in Chapter 24. You can also illustrate the criteria with examples of good and mediocre work. Then they understand the goals or criteria, and will be ready to use the proforma.

The proformas are usually a full sheet of A4 paper, which leaves plenty of space for comments. If self-assessment is required, the learner does this before handing the work in, this further improves their understanding of goals.

Essay-writing assessment proforma: 2nd year A-level history		
Title: **Name:**		
Criteria	**Self-assessment**	**Teacher assessment**
Did you relate each of your arguments to the essay question?		
Criteria	**Self-assessment**	**Teacher assessment**
Did you give arguments both 'for' *and* 'against' both: • the proposition in the essay question? • any major points or conclusions you made?		
Did you give enough evidence, examples and illustrations for each of your arguments?		
Did you prioritise the arguments for and against, and evaluate them?		
Did you draw a justified conclusion related directly to the essay title?		
Main strengths:		
Improvements needed for this essay: (*Note: usually improving the content, but could be the criteria above*)		
Targets for the next essay:	(*Note: usually one or two of the criteria above*)	

Maths assessment proforma	
Exercise:	**Name:**
Assessment criteria	**Teacher, peer or self-assessment**
Methods: Aim to make these appropriate, and as simple or elegant as possible.	
Methods justified: The principles or formulae used are made clear.	
Working: Aim to make working clear, complete and easy to follow.	
Care taken: Read the question more than once! Check your work for errors, and present work neatly.	
Main strengths:	
Remember: • It's OK if you don't fully understand a concept first time; learning takes time. • If this work has a mark or grade, aim to beat your own record, not someone else's. • What counts is whether you understand the problem and solution, not whether you made any silly slips. • If you got something wrong, that's fine. It's how we learn. • You will learn from mistakes if you find out how to avoid mistakes next time, and really understand this.	
Corrective work on this exercise: *(Note: usually a task to redo or improve one of the questions)*	
Target for your next piece of work: *(Note: usually one or two of the criteria above)*	

Source: Based on an 'Assessment for Learning' report on the QCA website

Practical task:	Name:
Strengths	
Opportunities for development	
General comments	

Much more important than the design of these particular assessment proformas is that they require the student to tackle the most important goals, and that they require self-assessment. Also they involve a 'find faults, fix, then follow up' approach. One way of doing this is 'learning loops', where there is a 'target box' at the beginning of the *next* piece of work:

[Next piece of homework or essay]	
Please write your target from the last piece of work below. Work on this target for this piece of work.	Student and teacher comments on whether the target has been met.
I need to work on showing my working, and on asking for help when I'm stuck	`Clear working shown for questions 1 to 6, 7 and 8 need more detail.` `You did ask for help!`

Students write their skill target in the first box *before* starting the work, and then work towards the target. When they hand in the work, you note that student's personal target, mark the work with this in mind, and then comment in the second box on whether their target was met, or any improvement shown.

This is a good differentiation or personalisation strategy, as every learner is working towards a target diagnosed personally for them. But don't expect instant success; skill-based targets often take some time to achieve.

The proformas shown on the previous pages are all for skills that are high on Bloom's taxonomy. These skills are 'transferable', so the same criteria can be used for every essay or assignment. For example, whatever the topic of a history essay, the student will still need to justify their points of view.

However, your proforma can address lower-order skills, such as comprehension, with criteria like 'clearly and accurately labelled diagram of the heart'. To do this, you must provide different assessment criteria for different pieces of work.

> *You can download many more proformas from the feedback page of www.geoffpetty.com, but don't use these exactly as you find them. Devise your own criteria and designs to suit your subject and your students.*

Notice that none of the assessment proformas above require marks or grades. Black and Wiliam's review mentions well-supported research evidence which shows that grades degrade learning (Butler 1988). Marks and grades, and even some comments like 'above average', compare students with each other, rather than focus on the task and on improvement. Butler found that weak students are discouraged and demotivated by low grades and their interest in the topic is undermined.

Able students get good grades, and this makes them complacent, reducing their struggle to improve, though they still remain interested in the topic. 'I got a B grade, that's good enough for me; I don't need to improve. Butler also found that if you grade students' work they tend to notice only their grade (and those of their peers!), but not your comments about how to improve.

If grades stop students striving to improve, then the whole purpose of formative assessment is undermined. A mix of medals and missions prevents both complacency and despair, and ensures that all learners are striving to improve.

When learning something challenging and useful, we never get it right first time. Errors and omissions are inevitable. Indeed, they are helpful; learning is a trial-and-error process, with success achieved by recognising errors and omissions and correcting them to obtain a closer and closer approximation to the goal. Yet many learners are crippled by seeing learning errors as blameworthy. Encourage your students to take responsibility for correction, without blaming themselves for mistakes.

Some teachers, such as those teaching adult basic skills, never give grades or marks. But some qualifications require the frequent grading of coursework, and it is not easy to see what to do here. Some teachers give only medal and mission feedback, keeping the grades to themselves until a termly or half-termly review. Others give students their grades one or two assignments later. Others only grade examination work.

Students must usually have summative grades and marks occasionally, say, every term or half-term on a full-time course. They naturally want to 'know how I'm doing', in part to plan their progression: 'Will I get the B grade I need for Newcastle University?' If students are informed of why grades are being temporally withheld, they usually accept this readily, or even with relief.

Mastery tests and other mastery methods

We are so used to the concept of a 20–30% failure rate that we are in danger of being blinded to the alternative view of education, which sees it as capable of developing every individual. This view is not wishful thinking: take the example of the driving test. It is not easy to learn to drive; many fail first time, and yet almost all of those who attempt it pass eventually.

How is this achieved? Principally, by defining very carefully what needs to be learned, allowing people as much practice as they need, and telling people who don't pass what they need to work on. These 'find faults, fix and follow up' principles are common to all effective formative assessment and to the constructivism we saw in Chapter 1.

'The essence of mastery-learning strategies is group instruction supplemented by frequent feedback and individualised corrective help *as each student needs it.'*

B. S. Bloom, *Evaluation to Improve Learning*
(Bloom's emphasis)

Black and Wiliam's research review found that mastery learning was capable of adding the equivalent of at least one grade to students' achievements. It also made students feel more positive about their learning and increased their self-esteem, yet it is not commonly used. It only applies to mastery objectives, that is, to learning that is low on Bloom's taxonomy; typically it focuses on essential knowledge, comprehension and simple application. It must not be used alone, but in tandem with other assessment methods directed at high-order skills. Otherwise there is a clear danger of the surface learning we saw in Chapter 1.

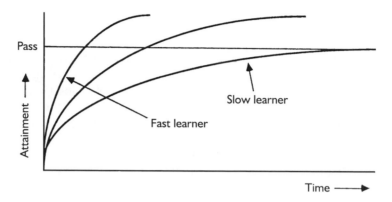

There are five stages in mastery learning:

1   You define precisely what students must know and be able to do. Only essential learning low on Bloom's taxonomy is considered – for example, the ability to explain the meaning of new technical terms.

2   Tell students what they should know and be able to do in order to pass the mastery test. Give them plenty of learning activities, including corrected practice to develop the knowledge and skills. Don't test them until they say they are ready.

3   Set tests that are very *short* (say, five minutes long) and very *frequent* (at least every week or two, or every five to eight hours of instruction). The students mark these tests *themselves*, from a mark scheme with either model answers or worked solutions provided by you. The good news for the students is that the questions are predictably based on vital material, are easy and the learning has already been practised. The bad news is that the pass mark is very high for this vital material: 80 or 85%.

4   Students get a 'P' for a pass, but their percentage is not recorded. If they do not pass, then the space on the record sheet is left blank until they do.

5   The students who did not pass look carefully at what they got wrong and work on this for a day or two in their own time, preparing for a retest. They keep doing remedial work and then taking retests, which are very similar but not the same as the original test, until they get a pass. If the topic splits neatly into subtopics, then the student only retakes the subtopic that they did not pass. Teachers do not wait during this remedial work; they teach the next topic.

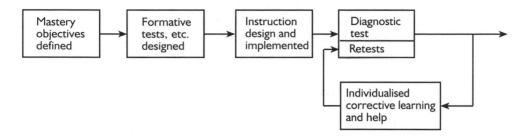

Most teachers make their mastery tests far too hard. The purpose is not to stretch students, but to check they know the very basics. When I first used mastery tests myself, I thought the tests were so easy that the students would laugh. Yet, to my surprise, quite a few did not pass (the others were cock-a-hoop!). I remember one student saying, 'I thought I knew that until I tried to write it down.' He had not checked his learning – for example, with a study–cover–write–check approach – but as I continued with mastery learning, he soon learned to!

> There is a widespread belief that the educational systems in Hong Kong and Japan are successful because they depend in part on their 'zero tolerance of failure'. They adopt mastery learning-style 'diagnostic testing', followed by corrective action.

Mastery marking

If students are doing worksheets or exercises that are mastery, you can use mastery marking. This involves giving students a 'PASS!' if they get a mark of 8/10 or better, and asking them to improve their answers to the questions they got wrong until they do get this mastery mark.

Students who would be depressed and discouraged by red-pen comments such as 'This work is not up to standard – 4/10' are content to find 'Please do questions 4 and 5 again for a mastery mark'. Most students welcome the opportunity to put their work right; they do not usually resent the time it takes, and they learn a great deal from the process.

Mastery marking is hard work for my students – but not as hard for me, as you might expect! Students soon learn to check their work as they do it, comparing it with their peers' and clearing up troubles with them or me before presenting it. They begin to accept responsibility for their learning. It is not in their interests to have to redo work, so few hand in work that is below the '8/10' standard. I check resubmitted work after lessons with the student present – they only have to redo the questions they did badly, so it doesn't take long. Resubmitted work is usually up to standard.

For GCSE students, I have a worksheet (a set of questions) for each topic, and when students have achieved a mastery mark on a worksheet, they tick it off on a personal 'mastery sheet' that they keep in their folder. They enjoy having a record of their success, and they don't like gaps in their record! They work hard to pass all the topics. (See below for an example of the kind of thing I have in mind.) An alternative scheme for recording students' mastery would be a large wall poster in the form of a table for the classroom noticeboard, with all the worksheets along the top and students' names down the side.

Part of a student's mastery record

Mastering GCSE physics		Name: Sarah Austin
Worksheet/Topics	**Mastery mark**	**Mastery test**
Measurement	P	P
Forces and elasticity	P	P
Energy transformations	P	P
Work, energy and power	P	P

WHAT DO THE FOLLOWING TWO PEOPLE HAVE IN COMMON?

Ruth Lawrence of Huddersfield (b. 1971) went to Oxford University aged 12 to study mathematics, and gained the best first-class degree of all entrants in 1985, aged 14.

Mrs Fannie Turner (b. 1903) of Arkansas passed her written test for drivers on her 104th attempt when aged 75.

Answer: They both took the time they needed to pass.

Self-assessment, peer assessment and spoof assessment

Were you surprised that Bloom required students to mark their own mastery tests? I was, until I saw my students mark their first one, on sines and cosines. There was intense concentration and absolute silence, punctuated by the slap of palms on foreheads as they recognised their own errors. I could see straight away that they were having a very vivid learning experience, and were peering at the model solutions and their own work with unusual intensity.

Whether or not you use mastery learning, get your students to mark their own work against a set of model answers or worked solutions. Alternatively, they can assess their work against assessment criteria which they create, or which you provide in advance of doing the work they will mark.

Students can also mark each other's work, called 'peer assessment'. The following example, based on a strategy developed by Graham Gibbs and quoted in Biggs (2007), almost doubled attainment on a university engineering course, but it can be adapted for use at any educational level.

1   Students do a worksheet of questions and put their name on it.

2   They hand these to the teacher, who gives them out to other students to mark. Students do not know who is marking their work.

3   Students mark their peer's work using 'model answers' or 'worked solutions', including a mark scheme provided by the teacher. Alternatively, they could use clear criteria, perhaps with marks for each criterion. For example, a criterion for a good graph might be 'fully labelled axes: three marks'.

4   The work is handed back to its rightful owner and students each keep the model answers, worked solutions or assessment criteria. Most students will probably check the quality of the peer's marking, but the teacher does not.

In the case Gibbs reports, the teacher did not even take down the marks that the students obtained, though *you* could of course. The average mark on the unit rose from around 45% to around 75% as a result of this strategy!

Spoof assessment involves you in producing a 'spoof' piece of work especially for this purpose. This can be a real piece of work kept, with the student's permission, from a previous year. You hand this out and ask your students to mark it; you may want to provide a mark scheme, assessment criteria or model answers. When they have finished, you can discuss the marks with the class. 'What did you give her for question 3? … Well, she only deserves one, because …'

An interesting approach to spoof assessment is to give students two pieces of work for the same task, one that is superficially impressive but poor, and another that is good but will not impress your students. For example, one essay could be long, with complex vocabulary, convoluted sentences and impressive diagrams, but it fails to answer the question. The other could be shorter and answer the question very well. Students nearly always give the worse work the better mark! This can be a valuable lesson that helps students clarify their goals.

> *If you ask students to spoof-assess good work with your assessment proforma, they will clarify the meaning of your criteria and learn how to meet the criteria in practice.*

Research reviews such as Black and Wiliam's show that the advantages of self- and peer assessment are considerable, especially when the learner must use what they have learned to plan action for improvement.

Why are self-, peer and spoof assessment sometimes able to even double attainment?

*   They help students to clarify goals. Model answers, mark schemes and assessment criteria must be studied closely, and all help the students to know and to *understand* 'what I should be aiming to do'.
*   They give students medal and mission information.
*   Making judgements about their own or a peer's work clarifies their understanding of the subject matter.

- In peer and spoof assessment, students see 'other ways of doing it'.
- They help students attribute success to doing the right thing, rather than to their innate talent or flair. This 'attribution training' is thought to have a massive effect on weak learners especially. They teach students that they can succeed. See Chapter 5 on motivation, or my *Evidence Based Teaching*, chapter 3.
- They put students in charge of their own improvement, that is, they develop in students a sense of 'ownership', responsibility and accountability.
- They increase students' effort and persistence.
- They help students develop a self-critical and reflective habit of mind.
- They save you time for more productive activities.
- Learning by induction from concrete examples of good practice is an easier way to learn than interpreting abstract assessment criteria.

If you don't like the idea of peers marking each other's work, or if your students aren't mature or confident enough to do it, use self- and spoof assessment instead.

Diagnostic questioning

Almost everything you do as a teacher in the class can be formative. For example, compare the following two alternative approaches to questioning the same student.

Teacher	'Is 7 a prime number?'		**Teacher**	'Is 7 a prime number?'
Student	'Yes.'		**Student**	'Yes.'
			Teacher	'Why?'
			Student	'Because it's odd.'

The first question, being factual, low on Bloom's taxonomy and closed, has not diagnosed that the student is suffering the misunderstanding that prime numbers are the same as odd numbers. The 'why?' question, because it requires explanation, discovers the misunderstanding. Further questioning and explanation can then be used to diagnose the misconception more fully if necessary, and then to correct it, as we saw in Chapter 14.

Similarly, the use of quizzes and the production of mind-maps can be made formative, by using the activity to diagnose weaknesses in the student's learning, and then to require the student to correct this, either in the lesson or in their own time. Then you or a peer can check on this improvement.

Try to be formative in everything you do, diagnose difficulties and opportunities for improvement, require that the learner works on these, and then confirm any improvement.

Discussion of Black and Wiliam's review

How do Black and Wiliam's findings differ from conventional practice?

Conventional practice: 'Teach, test, grade and move on' (assessment is summative).

Too often the teacher teaches a topic, sets some work, grades it, criticises it in a more or less constructive way, but does not check that the student has made good any deficiencies. Then the teacher moves on to the next topic.

A common assumption behind this approach is that learning quality and quantity depend on talent or *ability*, and that the role of assessment is to measure this ability. If learning is wanting, this is attributed to a lack of ability, flair or intelligence.

Best practice: 'Find faults, fix and follow up' (assessment is diagnostic).

Black and Wiliam's review suggests a different approach. A topic is taught and some work is set. The student *and* the teacher use this work to diagnose deficiencies and set targets for improvement. This improvement is itself reviewed.

The assumption is that learning quality and quantity depend on *time and effort* spent on improvement, and that the role of assessment is to diagnose deficiencies so that time and effort can be focused on improvement. Indeed, weaknesses are the very areas where the greatest improvement can be made with least effort. If learning is wanting, you need to try harder for longer.

Common practice: teach, test, grade and move on

Best practice: 'find faults and fix'

Research is very much in favour of the time and effort assumption rather than the talent assumption, even in areas like music where you might expect talent to be important. 'Talent' is learned, and is increased by time and effort directed at improvement, as we will see in Chapter 45.

> 'If a student fails to learn it is the teacher's fault. With appropriate instruction all pupils should get A grades.' (B. F. Skinner, behaviourist psychologist, 1955) Discuss!

Knowledge of results

Some teachers find it hard to say nice things to their students! They should work on this, of course. But they can take comfort from the fact that informing students of exactly what they have done well is encouraging to students, and rarely sounds patronising.

So you could use a quiz or short test to show students what they know and can do. Do this regularly for maximum effect and give warning of it. A three-minute test at the end of every lesson is an excellent review technique. You will sometimes see students punching the air in delight if they do reasonably well.

Of course, if they do badly this may not motivate. So consider using tests and quizzes 'formatively'. That is, give students a second chance to get right those questions they got wrong, perhaps the next day. Tell them about this, of course, so they can bone up on their weaknesses. Give them the test again, but tell them just to do the questions they got wrong. Then nearly everyone does well.

Reinforcement

Competences and self-assessment as reinforcement

Any acknowledgement of learning success is reinforcement. You could set students a set of informal competences and ask them to tick these off themselves as they achieve the, or ask them to self-assess against clear criteria. Almost any learning can be 'packaged' in the competence or criteria format. It is even possible to have criteria for behaviour, and ask students to self-assess or claim competence from you for this. Let your imagination off the leash and you will find a way to make it work for you!

Certification for reinforcement

Some programme managers give students Open College Network (OCN) certificates, in, say, first aid or customer care, very early on in their programme. If students have had official success by the end of their first term or soon after, this can be a great motivator.

Further reading

Biggs, J. (2007) *Teaching for Quality Learning at University* (3rd edition), Buckingham: Open University Press.

Black, P. and Wiliam, D. (1998) 'Assessment and classroom learning', *Assessment in Education*, 5(1): 7–74.
(Find their summary at www.pdkintl.org/kappan/kbla9810.htm)

Bloom, B. S., Madaus, G. F. and Hastings, J. T. (1981) *Evaluation to Improve Learning*, New York and London: McGraw-Hill.

Butler, R. (1988) 'Enhancing and undermining intrinsic motivation; the effects of task-involving and ego-involving evaluation on interest and performance', *British Journal of Educational Psychology*, 58: 1–14.

Rowntree, D. (1987) *Assessing Students: How Shall We Know Them?* (2nd edition), London: Kogan Page.

Sadler, R. (1989) 'Formative assessment and the design of instructional systems', *Instructional Science*, 18: 119–44.

See www.geoffpetty.com for more on this chapter, including more assessment proformas.

44

Summative assessment

Summative, or terminal, assessment takes place at the end of a module, course or academic year. As mentioned at the beginning of the previous chapter, the aim may be to sum up what the candidate can do (criterion referencing). This might be done with the aid of a checklist of skills or competences, and/or by reports or profiles. Alternatively, the aim may be to grade candidates, or place them in a rank order (norm referencing). This is usually done by means of an examination, designed to differentiate between candidates on the basis of the breadth and depth of their learning.

Summative assessment in school and post-school education is in the middle of a turbulent revolution at present. Practice varies from subject to subject, but it also varies from year to year for any given subject. I will give only a brief outline of the basic methods here. It is vital that you discover the detailed requirements of assessment for the courses on which you teach, and any personal responsibility you may have in this respect. Do this as soon as you know what you are teaching, and ask experienced teachers for advice.

Methods used for summative assessment: a brief outline

Profiles

Everyone is familiar with the school or college report. Profiles and records of achievement extend reporting to include a systematic coverage of the learner's achievements, abilities, skills, experiences and qualities. As mentioned in the section on self-appraisal in the previous chapter, they can be used formatively, as well as summatively, and are commonly used for both. Like any report or reference they are subjective, but they give information which cannot be measured objectively. They typically report only positively, and are written by the learner, but drafts are agreed by the teacher. They give information on the learner's:

- personal and social development, self-awareness and social skills
- attainment progress and motivation
- career aspirations
- interests and hobbies, both in and out of school or college
- achievement in key skills such as problem-solving, communication, information technology, numeracy or other skills, such as manual dexterity, etc.

Ideally, the students should be self-assessing and setting themselves targets for improvement as described in Chapter 34, with the profile acting as the outcome of this process. Profiles are the property of the learners, and can be used, if they wish, when seeking employment or educational progression.

Some profiles are in a grid format, listing core skills and achievement in those skills in terms of hierarchically ordered descriptors. This may mislead readers of the profile into believing the assessment was more objective than it really was, and the format is too restrictive to allow adequate description of more subjective criteria. Ticking a box labelled 'Can present a logical argument' is meaningless unless the context is clear, as everyone can present a logical argument at some level.

Other profiles are in an open-response format: effectively, they are a series of headings under which the student records their accomplishments. Combinations of the grid and open formats are common, and profiling design and practice vary markedly from institution to institution.

Profiles have been criticised by teachers for the work they generate; for lacking validity and being unreliable; and for giving unrealistic impressions, in that they report only positively. Some commentators doubt whether employers read the longer grid-style profiles. However, since the learner's academic achievements often make it very clear what the learner cannot do, it seems fair to redress the balance with a profile, especially as the self-assessment involved is so valuable. If you use profiling, make sure the learners do as much of the work as possible!

Competences

Assessment can also be carried out on the basis of checklists or a set of competences; this is a widely used method where a criterion-referenced assessment is required. The achievement of these competences is usually on a 'passed' or 'not passed' basis. Re-attempts are encouraged when a pass is not attained.

Competences are the method used to define the content and organise the assessment of National Vocational Qualifications (NVQs). Let's take as an example an NVQ in horticulture, which addresses the 'key purpose' of 'providing ornamental beds and borders'. The units of competence in this NVQ might be:

- Produce plants from seed.
- Establish ornamental beds and borders.
- Maintain ornamental beds and borders.

Each of these 'units of competence' has a number of 'elements of competence'. For example, the unit 'Maintain ornamental beds and borders' might have the following elements:

- Weed a bed and/or a border by hand, with or without the aid of tools.
- Maintain the appearance and health of plants.
- Maintain the soil condition and physical appearance of the bed or border.

Each of these competences can be assessed separately, or in any combination, at any convenient time by an accredited assessor. The assessment of each competence is then checked by an external verifier from the awarding body offering the qualification, such as City & Guilds.

The 'scope' of a competence is usually given. For example, a competence such as 'Assist with planting ornamental plants' might be given the following 'scope': 'Container-grown shrubs, herbaceous plants, bedding plants and bulbs'.

The learner, or 'candidate', submits evidence to an assessor in an attempt to demonstrate the attainment of a particular competence or competences. This might involve the candidate being observed. If the assessor agrees that the competence has been achieved, it is 'signed off' by the assessor; if not, any further work required to demonstrate the competence adequately is usually made clear.

Such competence-based schemes have the advantage that they set realistic work-based standards, agreed by experts in the vocational field (the industry's 'lead bodies'). Hence they ought to have the support of the relevant industry. They are accessible to learners in work, in that they encourage (indeed, may even require) work-based evidence and do not require the candidate to attend a course. Past evidence of skills can be used to meet competences by a process called 'Accreditation of Prior Learning and Experience' (APL/E) – though this can be a time-consuming and costly process.

Criticisms of NVQs include the suggestion that the lack of grading means both that the able are not stretched, and that potential employers have no means of using NVQs to differentiate between candidates with the same qualification. Some say they lower standards, and put too little emphasis on the candidate's understanding of the skills and techniques assessed, but good teaching can overcome this difficulty.

NVQs are overseen and 'kite-marked' by the QCA (Qualifications and Curriculum Authority). There are five levels:

Level 5: professional
Level 4: for people in a supervisory role
Level 3: roughly A-level standard
Level 2: roughly GCSE standard
Level 1: basic level – introductory.

Do not let yourself be tyrannised by competences. It is almost never a good idea to teach a course competence by competence, or even unit by unit. Teach first, get your candidates to do real work in a real context, then look for evidence for assessment. If your tasks and course are well designed, the assessment will fall into place quite easily. For example, some horticultural students could be given the task to design, stock and maintain a flower bed. Photographic records could be taken and they might write about their experience, putting references in the margin as to the competences they are claiming for each part of the job. This holistic experience is much more natural and meaningful than picking off competences one by one in the order given in documentation.

Continuous assessment or coursework

This is the process by which work done during a course is assessed as part of the learner's summative assessment. Most full-time vocational courses, and part of some GCSEs and A-levels are assessed in this way. Like most developments in education, this 'internal assessment' is more work for the teacher, though it does have the advantage of increasing student motivation considerably. In many instances, the assessment conditions, and therefore its findings, are much more realistic – who, for example, would want to write a poem or complete an engineering design in one time-constrained sitting?

> *Don't assess key or 'common' skills such as 'problem-solving' or 'working with others' without teaching these skills!*

In order to ensure that internal assessment has been carried out in the prescribed manner – and to the same standard – in different schools and colleges, an external verifier or moderator will usually view all or part of the marked coursework (see Chapter 49). Again, procedures vary greatly, and it is imperative to ascertain quickly exactly what is expected of you. For example, when must coursework be submitted to the moderator or verifier?

The examination board or validating body will provide written guidance on such matters, but some of this material is famously voluminous and opaque. Seek guidance from an experienced teacher in the first instance.

Examinations

Make sure you are aware of the form of the final examination, and ensure students have had some months of practice in answering papers of the appropriate type. Past papers are available from the appropriate board and are an excellent homework source. Examiners' reports on past papers are published by some examining boards, and these give valuable information on common mistakes and omissions made by candidates.

If students find past-paper questions daunting, it is often because they find the language used to frame the questions difficult. Give them a glossary, and play 'decisions, decisions' games to develop their ability to tell an evaluation from a description. Work through past-paper questions yourself on the board; then do some as worked examples with the class volunteering the answers; then let them loose on a few questions in pairs. Make use of spoof and peer assessment. Even so, they may take some months to gain confidence. If the first time they see a past paper is in their mock or practice examination, their marks will be a big disappointment.

Graded tests

Graded tests use the mastery-learning philosophy for summative assessment. A pioneer in this field has been the Graded Objectives in Modern Languages (GOML) movement, with tests similar in principle to the music examinations of the Associated Board of the Royal Schools of Music. The GOML tests are criterion referenced, taken when the learner is ready, and can be retaken. They have been popular with students, aiming to provide the frequent positive reinforcement of certificated success through the setting of attainable short-term goals.

Psychometric tests

Psychologists have devised special tests to measure intelligence quotients, verbal reasoning, non-verbal reasoning, manual skills, basic skills in reading and arithmetic, etc. Other tests measure aptitude – for example, the candidate's aptitude for learning how to use a computer, or their mechanical aptitude. Yet more tests claim to measure personality, and to indicate whether a candidate would be suitable for management training. Such tests can be expensive, and most require special training in their use.

It is generally recognised that there is a danger in relying too heavily on the results of such tests since, for example, they do not take motivation into account. Moreover, the results, are not as stable as is sometimes claimed; education can raise IQ scores by as much as 30%. Research reviews, like that of Ericsson *et al.* (1993), have shown that potential or aptitude is very hard to measure and that ability is more learned than innate (Chapter 45).

Question styles

Here is some advice if you are about to write examination questions. Don't, if you can possibly help it! Writing examination questions, especially objective test items (multiple-choice questions), is very time-consuming. Why reinvent the wheel? Try to obtain a store of past papers, and also to find internal papers used in your school or college in previous years; rifle textbooks or books of questions. Adapting these saves time.

Be clear on the purpose of your examination. Is it to grade and differentiate, or to diagnose learning problems? Are your questions fit for your purpose? All questions should be clear, concise and unambiguous, and written in everyday language. This is harder than it sounds, and it's easy to make a slip, so if you adapt or write questions, it is worth getting them checked by another teacher. The diagram below shows issues related to the type of questions you use.

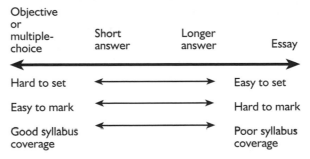

Characteristics of question types

Problems with assessment

Validity

The validity of an assessment depends on whether it actually measures the knowledge or skills it is designed to assess. For example, an objective test cannot measure a candidate's practical skill, or his or her ability to develop a coherent argument.

'To be valid, an assessment must also sample across a large proportion of the topics on the syllabus, and sample all the appropriate levels in Bloom's taxonomy. The breadth and depth of learning sampled by the assessment must be correctly weighted in the marking.

Validity is also compromised if questions are difficult for the candidates to understand, or are culturally biased. It is common for teachers to confuse poor learning with a student's difficulty in understanding examination questions.

Reliability

In public examinations, different examiners should award the same mark to the same script, and each year's paper should award the same grade to a student of a given standard. In addition, the same examiner should give the same mark if they unknowingly mark a script twice on different days. In practice, perfect reliability is impossible to achieve, and, in particular, essay questions are less reliable than objective test questions.

> *'During the 1960s schools were regularly putting pupils in for the same subject with different boards and getting totally different results.'*
>
> Peter Newsom, *Times Educational Supplement,*
> 16 October 1992

> *The 11-plus was (is, in a few areas) a much more reliable examination than most. Yet the definitive research published by the National Foundation for Educational Research in England and Wales in 1957 showed that, with the same pupils taking the same examination after a period of a few days, something like 10% 'passed' on one occasion and 'failed' on the other, and vice versa.*

The reliability of examinations is considerably increased by the use of carefully designed marking schemes which allot marks on objective criteria, rather than leaving the mark to the general impression of the examiner.

> *'You will never amount to very much.'*
>
> Comment made by a Munich schoolmaster to a 10-year-old pupil
> called Albert Einstein

VACSAR

'VACSAR' stands for valid, authentic, current, sufficient and reliable. As well as valid and reliable, as discussed above, assessments need to be:

- *authentic* – if you want to measure a student's ability to design, it would not be realistic to give them a design problem to solve in half an hour. That's not how designers work.
- *current* – an electrician may be used to out-of-date regulations, but can he or she work to the new ones? I could give mouth-to-mouth resuscitation last year – can I do it now?
- *sufficient* – how much writing must a student do before we can make a judgement on their ability to spell?

Developing an assessment strategy

Every course needs an assessment strategy. This should be related to the aims and objectives for the course, and should respond to considerations such as:

- What are the purposes of your assessment: to grade or to diagnose? (You may also assess to motivate, get feedback, acknowledge progress, certificate, select learners, evaluate courses or some combination of these.)
- What is to be assessed? How is it to be done?
- Who will assess whom, and when? Are marks required for reports or moderators?
- What will happen as a result of the assessment, particularly to those who have done badly or very well?

Once the strategy has been decided, methods appropriate to this strategy, and to the aims and objectives of the course, need to be devised. For example, a computer training course for adults of varied experience may choose to use a checklist of competences that learners tick off for themselves. A school mathematics teacher may decide on a series of mastery tests and a grading examination at the end of the year. A course to develop counselling skills may use learning journals, and have periodic one-to-one tutorial sessions where issues in the journal are discussed.

As always in education, the choice is made on the basis of fitness for purpose and value for effort.

Devise mark schemes along with the tests, and keep them safe for use next year, along with a monitoring copy of the paper, on which you can write suggested amendments. This enables you to improve the assessment process, and allows comparison of students from year to year. Saving and amending tests and mark schemes takes organisation, but it saves many precious hours of work.

MARK SCHEMES

- Contrary to fable, it is unusual to give most marks for the more difficult parts of a question or paper, as this strongly biases the test in favour of the most able. It is usual to apportion marks on the basis of the likely time taken by the candidate to complete the answer.

- Candidates should be aware of how marks are allocated.
- Work out solutions to numerical problems in advance, to ensure the questions are possible and valid.
- Mark a very good script first to check the mark scheme, and your answers!
- If you wish to grade or discriminate, set a large number of moderately difficult questions, rather than a small number of very hard ones.

You will, of course, need to keep records of your assessments; find out what has been done before. Don't keep more records than you need. Chapter 41 shows different approaches.

Coda

Because only the measurable can be reliably assessed, much of importance is usually ignored by the assessment process – and therefore, all too often, by the teaching process. Both teachers and students tend to the pragmatic view: 'If it's not assessed – ignore it'. And so the assessment tail is rightfully accused of wagging the dog.

At least a third of young people emerge from school branded as failures. The emotional damage inflicted on our children and young people by this process can only be guessed at by people like you and me, who for the most part have succeeded in our learning. Some of these 'failures' go on to reject the norms of the society which has rejected them, and pass into a twilight world of Giros, drugs, petty crime and imprisonment. It is no accident that over 50% of those in prison are functionally illiterate, in many cases as a result of dyslexia that was not adequately diagnosed or attended to.

Failure also has its economic consequences. Advanced economies like ours cannot compete on the world market with cheap labour, but only with the skills passed on by education and training.

In 1993, the Audit Commission reported that less than 50% of 17-year-olds were in full-time education. They found that one-third of those in education either dropped out of their courses or failed them. The situation has improved slightly since, but the introduction of new vocational qualifications has not been as helpful as you might think. These qualifications are vocational by name, but academic by nature, and so offer little to students in search of an alternative to 'book and biro'-based education.

This social, psychological and economic damage is due in large part to a curriculum which is heavily academic (see pages 125–6); to norm- rather than criterion-referenced assessment, with a consequent bias towards the achievements of the able; and to a tendency not to recognise and reward qualities which are difficult to measure. Try not to mirror these mistakes in your own assessment. Whatever the summative assessment of a course, for formative assessment consider using competence-based systems, profiles, graded tests and other mastery methods. These reward the effort and successes of every learner, and encourage the self-belief on which future learning relies. Remember that formative assessment has much more impact than summative on learning.

> 'Not everything that counts is countable, and not everything that is countable counts.'
>
> Albert Einstein

Checklist for your assessment system

- ☐ Is your assessment system related directly to the aims and objectives of the course?
- ☐ Do you use frequent diagnostic tests to discover weaknesses in learning?
- ☐ Do your students make efforts to overcome the above weaknesses?
- ☐ Are students allowed to improve and resubmit inadequate work?
- ☐ Do your methods recognise the efforts to learn which the less able are making?
- ☐ Do your methods stretch the able and recognise their achievements?
- ☐ Do your methods recognise and reward important qualities which are difficult to measure objectively?
- ☐ If you use mastery methods, are your tests easy enough?

EXERCISE

Compile a summary of the advantages and disadvantages of the main methods of assessment outlined in this and the previous chapter.

Further reading

Bloom, B. S., Madaus, G. F. and Hastings, J. T. (1981) *Evaluation to Improve Learning*, New York and London: McGraw-Hill.

Ericsson, K. *et al.* (1993) 'The role of deliberate practice in the acquisition of expert performance', *Psychological Review*, 100, 3: 363–406.

Gipp, C. and Stobart, G. (1993) *Assessment: A Teacher's Guide to Issues* (2nd edition), London: Hodder and Stoughton.

Rowntree, D. (1987) *Assessing Students: How Shall We Know Them?* (2nd edition), London: Kogan Page.

45

Values and what teachers can achieve

So far this book has concentrated on the classroom. It has focused on the nature of learning, and on how teachers can plan and deliver lessons that create high-quality learning. Now we need to step back from this detail and look at some new questions:

- How do we guide and recruit learners in their choice of subjects, courses or 'learning programmes'? We need to make sure these are appropriate for them and meet their needs.
- How do we discover what support they will need to succeed on these programmes, and then make sure they get it?
- How can we monitor the progress of learners, and act on this information to ensure their success?
- How do we design a course or programme to maximise the chance of success?
- How do we improve our courses and our teaching, and adapt them to experience and to the needs of our students?

It may seem strange at first, but a good place to start answering these questions is with your own values. Why do you teach? What are your ultimate professional purposes and expectations? These two questions are not 'just' theoretical or philosophical. Your answers to these questions inspire and underpin everything you do. They will, consciously or unconsciously, decide your strategies and priorities, and how vigorously you pursue them.

> *A recent publication by Runshaw College, a Beacon College, was subtitled 'Values drive behaviour'. The college attributes its huge success to the primacy given to values within the institution.*

Study the diagram on the next page and I hope you will agree that your values are very influential. They often decide your strategies, your tactics and ultimately your behaviour.

For example, suppose a teacher 'went the extra mile' to prepare a really helpful handout, and thought out a really interesting and useful student activity. If you asked them, '*Why* did you do that?' you might get the answer, 'To improve the lesson'. But if you asked them, '*Why* did you want to improve the lesson?', and kept asking 'why' questions like this, eventually you would get an answer in terms of ultimate values. 'Because it is important to me that … that's why.'

Values drive behaviour

Values, e.g.
- To value students as individuals
- To improve students' life chances
- To create an interest and curiosity in mathematics

how?   ⇓   ⇑   why?

Strategy, e.g.
- Course organisation
- Scheme of work
- Tutorial system

how?   ⇓   ⇑   why?

Tactic, e.g.
- Lesson plan
- Teaching method used
- Timetable

how?   ⇓   ⇑   why?

Behaviour, e.g.
- Your teaching
- Your attitudes to students in the classroom and in the corridor

Examples of these ultimate values might be:

> 'I want to make sure the weaker students succeed: I want to give them a chance in life.'
> 'I want my students to see my subject as important, enjoyable and understandable.'

The teacher may also express ultimate beliefs and expectations:

> 'I know that if I teach it right they can all understand it.'

Such values are the fuel for our motors: they provide the motive force for many things that we do.

We are not always 'value-driven' in this way; sometimes we are just doing what we are told to do, or what we have to do. We are not very motivated when we are just meeting our obligations like this. However, if we see these obligations in terms of values – perhaps because they were 'sold to us' in that way – we can be value-driven even here.

Whenever you are acting freely, autonomously and rationally, you are pursuing your values. Before we consider what these values are and what they should be, I will look at another fundamental question. How much of a difference are teachers able to make? Is student success largely determined by factors beyond the control of teachers, or do we really make a difference?

Teaching is very consequential

As a teacher, you can touch people's lives for ever. If you teach someone very well, they might get a qualification they would not have got without your excellent teaching. Then they might go on and get a higher qualification that they would not have got without your support. They might then get a job, indeed a whole career, indeed a whole life, just because of your excellent teaching. They will be more fulfilled, happier and more productive members of the community because of your teaching – and less likely to turn to crime or drugs! Not many careers are so consequential and confer such responsibility.

Some teachers deny that they make such a big difference. They believe that student success depends on factors such as resources, the quality of their managers, the government, or on social factors and the nature of the students themselves. There is some truth in this, of course. However, summaries of research on school effectiveness and improvement, and Professor John Hattie's reviews of research on the factors that affect student achievement, all agree that teachers make by far the biggest difference to student achievement. They have even quantified this, and conclude that teachers have three to four times the effect on achievement of any other school or college factor. Researchers talk of the 'proximity effect': the closer you are to the learner, the greater your effect on their achievement.

Paul Martinez points out, in his excellent 'Raising achievement' (2000) and elsewhere, that it is important to remember that in post-compulsory education, unlike in schools, the college can ensure that the student is enrolled on the most appropriate academic level for them. In schools, nearly all learners are aiming to jump the same bar: GCSE grade C; and so some don't make it. In the post-compulsory sector, *teachers* can set the height of the bar for each student individually during initial guidance and enrolment. Colleges have a lot of bars to offer too, everything from pre-entry or below, to degree level and above. And if that isn't enough, we can devise more; it is the college which decides the qualifications it offers, and colleges can devise their own qualifications – for example, using the Open College Network (OCN). The college is also in the position to diagnose the support that each student needs, to monitor their progress to ensure this support is adequate, and to increase it until it is sufficient.

This flexibility explains in part why some colleges, even though they serve the most socially and economically deprived areas, have an audited average achievement rate (pass rate) of over 90 per cent (Martinez 2000).

Many teachers believe that whether students pass or fail depends on their innate characteristics, such as their IQ, talent, aptitude or genes. Many students agree: 'I can't do maths.' Note that these factors are considered fixed, so neither the teacher nor the student believes they have any control over them. Dweck's theory of motivation mentioned in Chapter 5 pointed out that such beliefs were often self-fulfilling. This 'talent' view is very common in the West, but not in the East, where Confucian and other cultures see talent as learned. Research favours the Eastern, not the Western view.

The importance of self-belief in teachers

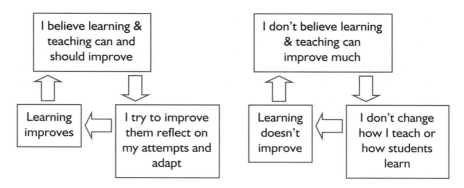

The above self-fulfilling cycles show that a teacher's beliefs are very consequential. When discussing improvements with colleagues, appeal to your common values, and to the evidence that improvement is possible. The improvability of teaching is what can make it indefinitely absorbing, vital and worthwhile. If it were possible to perfect teaching, we would soon bore ourselves by forever repeating our perfect lessons!

'Are you an active or a passive teacher' in Chapter 50 considers attitudes to improvement further.

Intelligence can be taught

The Israeli educationalist Reuven Feuerstein developed a hugely successful course for learners with moderate learning difficulties and very low IQs. They started his course with a mental age three years behind their real age, and an IQ of about 70 or 80. Such people sometimes need constant supervision and are not able to look after themselves. There was a 'control group', enabling Feuerstein to measure his students' progress against that of students who were matched for ability, but then taught in a conventional way. They were taught by the same or similar teachers in the same-sized groups.

The course involved special tuition for one hour per day for two years, and required teachers to use special materials and methods, for which they were specially trained. Two years after the programme had ended, the students were found to have average IQs (around 100) and to be quite independent. They had started Feuerstein's programme with a mental age three years behind the average and had now caught up! Some of his ex-students have since become university lecturers and professors. The control group had not shown this development. Intelligence and other gifts are teachable and learnable. We looked very briefly at one of Feuerstein's powerful teaching methods, called 'bridging', in Chapter 31 on learning from experience.

Feuerstein is not a lone voice. A most influential research review by K. Anders Ericsson *et al.* (1993) summarised research into how people become very expert musicians, chess players, athletes or academics. It showed that ability, talent, flair or expertise are learned, and are not innate gifts. Ability developed slowly even in the case of childhood prodigies, and was found to depend on 'deliberate practice' (see the graphs below). This is not just 'doing it again', but a deliberate attempt to learn and to improve by attending to skills not yet developed, or those in need of improvement. IQ hardly figured in predicting career achievements, even that of academics, and Dweck cites a Nobel Prize winner in science with a very unremarkable IQ.

I am not arguing that there is no such thing as ability or talent, but that these attributes are largely learned. This is a difficult message to accept in the West, where our culture assumes that exceptional ability is a gift. However, the evidence is emphatic that ability can be learned and can be taught, up to the very highest levels of achievement. See Chapters 21 and 24 of my *Evidence Based Teaching*.

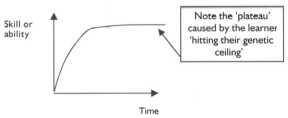

The 'talent model' (discredited by Ericsson's review)

Erricsson's 'deliberate practice' model

I am convinced that in a century or so people will marvel at our naive belief that skills 'plateau'. They will say: 'How could they not have realised that if you keep practising in a deliberate way, you will keep getting better?'

Cognitive acceleration has successfully taught intelligence:

www.kcl.ac.uk/schools/sspp/education/research/projects/cognitive.html

www.standards.dcsf.gov.uk/research/themes/thinkingskills/6553/

Motivation can improve

Other teachers blame poor achievement on their students' lack of motivation. There can be some truth in this view, but never forget that motivation is not a fixed characteristic of the student: it is an emotional response to their previous experience of learning. Change their experience of learning, and their motivation will also change. We saw in Chapters 1 and 5 that 'nobody learns for nothing', and that learners must see that their efforts to learn have a clear and immediate purpose. They must experience success and get rewards if learning is to be successful. It is not easy to change students' perception of learning, but good teachers do it all the time.

The challenge for education today is that Feuerstein, Ericsson and others have shown us that huge improvement is possible. You will play a part indeed – as a teacher, the most important part of all – in realising this potential. What values should guide, inform and inspire you as you square up to this challenge?

EXERCISE

1 Work alone for a few minutes and write down the main values you bring to teaching. The following questions may help you:

  a Why do you want to teach, and what do you hope to do for your students?

  b What have good teachers done for you?

  c What values are most important to you?

  Once you have considered these questions, try to write down some key values. Your teacher or tutor can take this further with you.

2 Join up in a pair and share your answers to question 1. Try to combine them into an agreed list.

3 Join up in groups of four and share your values statements. Again, try to combine them into an agreed set.

4 Share your point of view with the other groups in the class. Can you all agree some class value statements?

(This method is called 'snowballing'; it is a good way to explore deep questions. Could you use it with your students?)

Standards and values

There have been some recent attempts to codify the values and aspirations of teachers. Lifelong Learning UK has done this for the post-compulsory sector, and this is set out immediately below. In the box below and overleaf are values suggested by the government's Standards and Effectiveness Unit. These are for all teachers, not just schoolteachers.

Have a look at these. Did they get them right? This isn't a joke! Can there be anything more important than *your* values? After all, they are your inspiration and guidance in everything that you do freely. For this reason, it is always worth questioning and improving your values, so have a look at those below and see if you can use them to improve your own values.

Teachers in the lifelong learning sector value:

- *All learners*, their progress and development, their learning goals and aspirations and the experience they bring to their learning.
- *Learning*, its potential to benefit people emotionally, intellectually, socially and economically, and its contribution to community sustainability.
- *Equality, diversity and inclusion* in relation to learners, the workforce and the community.
- *Reflection and evaluation* of their own practice and their continuing professional development as teachers.
- *Collaboration* with other individuals, groups and/or organisations with a legitimate interest in the progress and development of learners.

They are committed to:

- The application of agreed codes of practice and the maintenance of a safe environment.
- Improving the quality of their practice.
- Maintaining an inclusive, equitable and motivating learning environment.
- Applying and developing their own professional skills to enable learners to achieve their goals.
- Communicating effectively and appropriately with learners to enhance learning.
- Collaboration with colleagues to support the needs of learners.
- Using a range of learning resources to support learners.

Download the full version from www.lluk.org.uk and search for a document called 'New overarching professional standards for teachers, tutors and trainers in the lifelong learning sector'.

The Standards and Effectiveness Unit of the DfES devised the following core principles for teaching and learning across the education system:

- Ensure every learner succeeds: set high expectations.
- Build on what learners already know: structure and pace teaching so that they understand what is to be learnt, how and why.
- Make learning of subjects and the curriculum vivid and real.

- Make learning an enjoyable and challenging experience: stimulate learning through matching teaching techniques and strategies to a range of learning styles and needs.
- Develop learning skills and personal qualities across the curriculum, inside and outside the classroom.
- Use assessment for learning to make individuals partners in their learning.

Core principles – school improvement

- Focus systematically on the priority for improvement that is likely to have the greatest impact on teaching and learning.
- Base all improvement activity on evidence – particularly data about relative performance against benchmarks.
- Build collective ownership through leadership development.
- etc. (the rest of the values lie outside the scope of this book)

These are draft principles at the time of writing (2008), downloaded from www.standards.dfes.gov.uk/seu/coreprinciples1/core-principles.doc

Notice the following themes:

Collegiality and collaboration: Teaching needs teamwork. We need to learn from each other, help each other and act in consort if our students are to benefit fully.

The centrality of learning and learner autonomy: Never mind the teaching, never mind the system, never mind the college – it's the *learner* and the *learning* that count! The rest should be a means to this end.

Entitlement, equality and inclusiveness: All learners are entitled to equal concern and respect, and to every opportunity, regardless of any aspect of their nature. Equality does not mean treating people the same; we considered this in Chapter 7. We must adapt to the diverse nature of our students. We should go to special trouble to include learners by discovering, respecting and meeting their individual needs. After all, one of them might be your son or daughter. If it can help them learn, let's deliver it if at all possible.

Using an evidence-based approach: Rather than relying exclusively on hunches, we should use evidence to discover the factors that will bring the biggest improvement.

It is important for our sanity to accept the difference between aspirations and actuality. Despite the improvability of students in general, and despite my every effort, I have certainly had failures with some students, and I expect you will too! The only failures a teacher can be guilty of are the failure to try and the failure to learn from previous failures.

> *'Education is the most powerful weapon which you can use to change the world.'*
>
> Nelson Mandela, Nobel Peace Laureate

adapt to the diverse nature of our students

Further reading

Adey, P. and Shayer, M. (1994) *Really Raising Standards: Cognitive Intervention and Academic Achievement*, London: Routledge. An overview of cognitivist approaches to 'teaching intelligence', including a useful section on Feuerstein.

Coles, A. (ed.) (2004) *Teaching in Post-Compulsory Education: Policy, Practice and Values*, London: David Fulton.

Dweck, C. (2000) *Self-Theories: Their Role in Motivation, Personality and Development*, Hove: Psychology Press, Taylor & Francis.

Ericsson, K. *et al.* (1993) 'The role of deliberate practice in the acquisition of expert performance', *Psychological Review*, 100, 3: 363–406. This is Ericsson's bombshell research review showing that talent and ability are learned. I have a summarising paper on this: do email from my website for a copy.

Gray, J. (1999) *Improving Schools: Performance and Potential*, Buckingham: Open University Press.

Hattie, J. A. (1999) Influences on student learning. This can be downloaded from Professor John Hattie's staff home page: www.uoa.auckland.ac.nz/education/staff/cfmj.hattie/j.hattie-homeeducation. See also www.geoffpetty.com

Martinez, P. (2000) 'Raising achievement: a guide to successful strategies', Learning and Skills Development Agency. This is a classic. Much of Paul Martinez's work can be downloaded using the author's name in the 'detailed search' at: www.lsneducation.org.uk/pubs/index.aspx

Martinez, P. (1998) '9000 voices: student persistence and drop-out in further education', LSDA online at: www.lsneducation.org.uk/pubs/index.aspx

Martinez, P. (2002) 'Raising achievement at levels 1 and 2', LSDA online at: www.lsneducation.org.uk/pubs/index.aspx

Petty, G. (2006) *Evidence Based Teaching*, Cheltenham: Nelson Thornes.

Sharron, H. and Coulter, M. (1994) *Changing Children's Minds: Feuerstein's Revolution in the Teaching of Intelligence*, Birmingham: Sharron Publishing Co. This is very readable and has an introduction by Feuerstein. Try also www.icelp.org (this is the 'official' site), www.lluk.co.uk (for the Lifelong Learning UK standards and values) www.standards.dfes.gov.uk/seu/coreprinciples2 (for the Core Principles for teachers).

Shayer, M. and Adey, A. (2002) *Learning Intelligence*, Buckingham: Open University Press.

46

Evaluating my teaching: the reflective practitioner

Questionnaire

If you have done some teaching already, please answer the following questions; if not, please leave the questionnaire until you have. The purpose of the questionnaire, and how to score it, will be made clear later. Record whether you agree or disagree with the following sentences, by marking each with a tick or a cross.

When I think about my teaching experience ✓ or ✗

A1 I don't think about past success and failures, I just get on with the job.

A2 I am careful not to jump to conclusions too quickly.

A3 I appreciate being able to talk things over after a lesson.

A4 I teach as well as I can; if students don't learn, it's their fault.

A5 I guard against bias in assessing my effectiveness.

A6 I don't mind admitting failure.

B1 Gut feelings are usually better than resorting to theory.

B2 I like to understand my actions in terms of a general principle.

B3 I enjoy puzzling out why things happened as they did.

B4 On the whole, intuition beats thorough analysis.

B5 I enjoy looking at things from the student's angle.

B6 I find theories about motivation and learning interesting.

C1 On the whole, it is best to find one effective technique and then stick to it.

C2 I like the challenge of trying out new ideas.

C3 I find it difficult to come up with new ideas.

C4 I prefer tried and tested ideas to newfangled ones.

C5 It is best to adopt the accepted way of teaching your subject.

C6 I am grateful for suggestions on new ways of teaching better.

Learning to teach from experience

Good teachers are not born, nor are they made by tutors. They make themselves. What's more, anyone can teach well. Research shows that there is no personality type that makes a good teacher. Whether you are a shy introvert or an enthusiastic extrovert, you can teach effectively, but only if you know how to learn from your mistakes and your successes.

Practice makes perfect? No. Some teachers have had 30 years of practice and still can't teach. Practice may be necessary, but it is not sufficient. So how exactly should we learn from experience?

In Chapter 31 we saw that the experiential or reflective learning cycle best describes how we learn from experience. This is true whether we are learning how to cook, how to drive or how to make successful human relationships. Whether consciously or not, we will learn how to teach with this same cycle:

1 *Concrete experience.* This is your experience of teaching. Sadly, it is not possible to learn to teach by lying on a beach in the Bahamas. We need practice. However, lack of practice is often not the major difficulty in learning to teach.

2 *Reflection on experience.* Here you evaluate your experience to discover in what areas you were effective or ineffective.

3 *Abstract conceptualisation.* Here you ask questions such as 'Why was the last half of that lesson so effective?' or 'Why did I fail to achieve my last objective?' You learn the nature and importance of concepts such as reinforcement, assessment and so on, and find generalised reasons for your successes or failures.

4 *Planning active experimentation.* Bearing in mind what you have learned from experience, you ask questions such as 'What would I do differently if I taught that lesson again?', 'What shall I do differently next lesson as a result of what I have learned?' and 'What new methods, styles or techniques should I try out in order to improve my teaching?'

Perhaps some people fail to learn how to teach effectively because they are unable or unwilling to cope with the difficult process of learning from experience. For example, if the reflection phase is to be effective, the evaluation must be honest and undefensive, however painful it may be. I don't need to remind you of the capacity for self-delusion in others. But what about yourself? The logic of the learning cycle suggests that we should accept knowledge of our weaknesses eagerly and gratefully, as this will help us to improve. But when we stagger out of our latest Friday-afternoon beating in room R101, this is unlikely to be our mindset. We feel angry and defensive, and anxious to protect our pummelled ego; so we cast around for scapegoats. They are not hard to find. The class, the room, the timetable, the head of department, the lack of resources … 'And anyway, it wasn't *that* bad, really …'

Only very rarely are learners genuinely to blame for an ineffective lesson, or course lessons. Learning and teaching strategies should be made to fit the students, not the other way round. After all, tailors don't blame their customers if their suits don't fit. Having said this, there are occasions when a teacher is given an impossible brief. For example, as was mentioned at the end of Chapter 9, the curriculum in schools is in many ways inappropriate for non-academic learners.

We should not blame our learners for an ineffective lesson, but neither should we blame ourselves. There is nothing wrong with a minor disaster, so long as you can learn from it. Mistakes are not only inevitable, they are a necessary part of your learning process. If you don't have the occasional failure, you are not experimenting enough. One must go too far to discover how far one can go.

But if some people fail to face up to their failures, then others do not acknowledge their successes. For them, tiny errors are blown up out of all proportion. If your lessons are evaluated by someone you trust, you will get a more objective view of your teaching skills.

The reflection phase is difficult to get right. It should be carried out on a no-blame basis, and it should be honest about both successes and failures.

Scoring the questionnaire

To learn successfully from experience, your mindset is crucial. You must be honest in reflection, determined in conceptualisation and daring in experimentation. This is not easy! The questionnaire at the beginning of this chapter was designed to discover what you will find most difficult about learning how to teach from experience. It is based on the reflective learning cycle.

- Score one point for each of the following if you marked it with a *cross*:

    A1, A4; B1, B4; C1, C3, C4, C5.

- All the others score one point if you marked them with a *tick*.

Work out a separate score out of 6 for the A, B and C sections of the questionnaire. A high score in section A means you find reflecting easy. Section B corresponds to abstract conceptualisation, and a high score means you find theoretical thinking easy. Section C corresponds to planning experimentation, and a high score means you like taking action. The higher your score in each category, the easier you are likely to find that phase of the learning cycle – though the questionnaire has not been scientifically validated. We all have a weak phase or phases; if you score less than three in any one phase, you may need to work on yourself in this area.

What's this learning journal all about?

I remember a trainee teacher I once taught – I will call him Jim – who did not believe in reflection or in theories of learning. He thought how to teach was common sense, that theories of learning were dreamed up by academics to justify their own existence, and that they made them as complicated as possible to try and make themselves look clever, and us stupid! For Jim, reflection and theory had nothing to do with the real-world experience of teachers in classrooms. He could not have been more wrong, and, to his credit, Jim's views changed considerably as he progressed on his course.

Every teacher and every learner has a theory about learning. You are no exception, and you will have a set of beliefs, ideas and assumptions about the nature of learning and teaching. You will believe that certain practices bring about learning, and certain others don't. You will use this theory, probably unconsciously, both to plan your lessons and to decide what to do while you teach. Schön called this your 'theory-in-use'. Never mind what you might write in an essay or tell your tutor, it is your 'theory-in-use' which guides what you do, and informs you as you plan and teach your lessons.

If you ask yourself 'How shall I teach this topic?' you will consider your 'theory-in-use' to help you decide. If a student started playing up in one of your lessons, you would use your 'theory-in-use' to decide what to do about it. If a lesson did not go well, it would be your 'theory-in-use' that you would use to explain to yourself why it went badly, and to decide how to make that lesson, or the next one, go better.

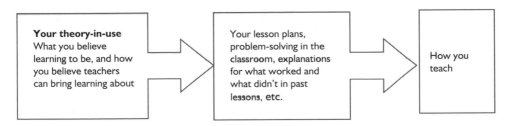

As your 'theory-in-use' guides your every action, it is clearly very important. If it faithfully describes the reality of how your students learn, then it will be an accurate guide for you, and you will be able to teach very well. If it doesn't describe that reality very well, then you will never teach effectively, except sometimes by accident! It is clearly crucial to get this 'theory-in-use' as right, and as comprehensive, as you can. So how can you go about that?

One way, of course, is to do what you are doing right now – to read about learning and teaching. Another is to attend an initial teacher training course. These can help, but in the end you must integrate this learning into your own 'theory-in-use' for it to affect what you do. This requires that you make your own sense of these learning experiences, and work out how to teach as a consequence. For example, to learn about Maslow's theory of motivation, and even to write about it, is one thing; to integrate it into your 'theory-in-use' is quite another. That would require you to work out what Maslow's theory means in practice for your students, and then to use this understanding to improve your student's motivation. That is very demanding, and will require much thought and practice!

In the end, you will only develop a fully effective 'theory-in-use' by teaching, and, most particularly, by reflecting on your experience of teaching. It is important, and difficult, to go right round the experiential learning cycle considered in Chapter 31; just doing and reviewing is not enough!

EXERCISE

Here are the 'theories-in-use' of Jim and Carole. How would these two teachers approach the problem of a learner who is finding the current topic hard to understand?

AN EXCERPT FROM JIM'S 'THEORY-IN-USE'

- A teacher needs to explain everything that they know about the topic very clearly.
- Learning takes place when students remember what they have been told.
- Some students are bright and motivated and they usually learn pretty well.
- If a student doesn't understand then you need to explain it again more slowly, but usually a student either 'gets' this subject or they don't, depending on their IQ.

AN EXCERPT FROM CAROLE'S 'THEORY-IN-USE'

- Learners need to apply their learning if they are to make sense of it.
- When they apply learning, students begin to make up their own 'story' of what the topic is all about, and use this understanding to answer questions and to do other tasks I set.
- You can use a student's work as a window into their current understanding.
- You can use question and answer to discover students' misunderstandings: a good start is to ask them how they arrived at an answer that they got wrong.

It is important to recognise that Jim's theory is not entirely 'wrong'. Some of it is partly right, but it is incomplete in important respects, and so it misleads Jim into using ineffective strategies – for example, blaming students who 'don't get it'. Carole's theory is nearer the truth, and so a better guide for her decision-making. She will be a better teacher than Jim, at least at present, not because she is more talented, but because she has a more truthful conception of how teachers bring about learning.

As you reflect, your 'theory-in-use' improves and so you become not only more effective, but also more adaptable and better able to solve problems. Effective teachers are always changing what they do; this is because they are continually learning how to teach better.

Learning and teaching are not simple, and if your experience is anything like mine, you will never arrive at a final decision about the nature of learning and teaching, but will continue to develop your understanding all through your career. You will never 'arrive', but that is not a problem, as the journey is so fascinating.

> *Pablo Casals, one of the world's greatest cellists, was asked why he still practised at the age of over 80. He answered, 'Because I think I am beginning to make progress'. Learning never stops, especially for the most able, and it was this inclination to learn that made them so able in the first place.*

Learning never stops

So how do we improve and add to our 'theory-in-use'? By high-quality reflection. And one of the best ways of encouraging high-quality reflection is to talk about your teaching with others, and to write your ideas down. This is where your reflective journal comes in. This is not a cunning means for your tutor to spy on your thoughts! It's a way to encourage you to learn from your experience, as we considered in Chapter 31.

EXERCISE

John Biggs characterises three common assumptions behind a teacher's 'theory-in-use'. These are that learning mainly depends on either:

1 the nature of the students: their intelligence, motivation, maturity, behaviour, etc., or
2 what the teacher does, or
3 what the learners do.

The more you think about learning, and experience teaching, the more you will realise that it is no. 3 that is much nearer the truth. But why? And why do many novice teachers think it is number 1 or number 2?

> *'Hostility to theory usually means … an oblivion of one's own.'*
>
> Terry Eagleton

How to reflect

You will probably begin to reflect the moment the lesson is over, if not before. Don't come to any fixed conclusions straight away, however, especially if the lesson has gone badly. You may well benefit from making some immediate notes, but will probably think more clearly after you have 'slept on it'.

Don't blame yourself if a lesson has gone badly. This is inevitable. Indeed, if all your lessons go well you are probably not taking enough risks. Mistakes are necessary if you want to learn at the maximum rate. Ineffective lessons are very helpful to you, and ultimately to your students, if you can work out why they didn't work and then make use of this insight. The same is true of effective lessons, of course, but, again, they are only helpful if you can work out why they worked, and use this insight in your future teaching.

Let's look at two examples to show what I mean. Notice that in the second example the teacher is learning general principles, which she then applies in new contexts. She does this by going right round the Kolb learning cycle:

Review	Reflect on experience
Learn	Abstract conceptualisation
Apply	Plan active experimentation
Do	Concrete experience
Review	She asks herself, 'What happened?'
Learn	She asks herself, 'Why did this happen?' and tries to learn some general principles of effective teaching.
Apply	She tries to use the general principle to see how she could have made the lesson better, but mainly how she can make future lessons better.
Do	She makes use of what she has learned in her future teaching.

This is 'bridging', as described in Chapter 31 on learning from experience. Note that a key result of this process is that she has improved her 'theory-in-use'.

Do	A teacher has just delivered a lesson which was quite successful. What went best was a 'decisions, decisions' game, where students had to classify examples of figures of speech such as 'metaphor' or 'simile' on cards.
Review	'That lesson went really well, and they really enjoyed the game.'

Example 1

Learn 1
'The game was effective. They were working away like beavers on it – I was really impressed.'
Apply 1
'I'll have to use that lesson plan again next year. It's the best one so far, I reckon.'
Do 1
The teacher applies the same lesson plan again next year.
Note that in this case there is no attempt to learn the general principles of effective teaching from the lesson.

Example 2

Learn 2
'I suppose the main reason the lesson was successful was the classification game. They enjoyed it, but it also enabled me to check their learning. And it made them think. It also made them apply their learning, but in a playful way. And they really had to make sense of figures of speech to play the game …'
Apply 2
'… I wonder if I could use a similar approach when I do tenses with them? What other games are there that could check learning? Perhaps a quiz? Or perhaps I could use decisions, decisions again. I could get them to classify sentences with different tenses or with mixed tenses …'

Do 2

(The teacher devises another game to check learning next week, and some more decisions, decisions games for later lessons.)

Note that in this case some general principles of good practice have been learned (e.g. games can be a good way to check learning) and the teacher then applied these principles in another lesson.

You will find that the internal dialogue that you go through when learning from your lessons will be much more detailed, complex and difficult than the example above. But the principles are the same. *Review*, then *learn* general principles (as general as possible), then *apply* these principles in new contexts.

In the chapter on praise and criticism, we looked at the idea that learners need:

- a medal which describes what they have done well
- a mission which describes what they could do to improve their performance.

Perhaps you are a learner as well as a teacher, and you need to give yourself medals and missions as well as your students!

Also, we discovered that grading students' work took their eye off the ball of how to improve it. The same goes when you think about your teaching: don't *evaluate* it ('That was/was not a good lesson'), *learn* from it!

Here are some more examples of teachers 'reflecting' to learn in their learning journals. One goes right round the learning cycle, but the other two miss out at least part of the cycle. Identify the review, learn and apply sections in these reflections to see which one is the most effective.

Reflections 1 and 2 are two possible reflections on the same lesson.

Reflection 1 (poor reflection)

'They really found that worksheet hard. I thought I explained it all really clearly, too, and I can't have done that badly as at least half of the class got the right idea. It was Jennifer's group that had most difficulty … again! They just aren't motivated and don't seem to remember anything from their GCSE. If they concentrated a bit more they would do a whole lot better.'

Reflection 2 (better reflection)

'They really found that worksheet hard. I explained the topic pretty well, too, so why couldn't they do it? Perhaps they just weren't listening. So how could I get them to listen? I suppose I could use more question and answer, perhaps ask a few of Jennifer's group especially. And just keep asking questions until I'm pretty sure they can do the questions on the worksheets. I'll give that a go.'

Reflections A and B are two possible reflections on an adult education lesson.

Reflection A (better reflection)

'The activity went pretty well in some respects – everyone got down to it and produced a still life of sorts, but there was lots of chatting about the problems with the new bus timetable and their approach was rather rushed and lacking in thought. With the exception of Phil, anyway. I need to find a way to make them think more, experiment more, set themselves higher standards. Actually it's interesting – they don't like me looking at their work, it's as if they know it's not as good as it could be. What if I got them to present their work to each other next time? That might make them take more pride in it. Also I could tell them to take the full half-hour, and if they finish do another quick one.'

Reflection B (poor reflection)

'The activity went pretty well, I suppose – they are all very polite and well behaved this lot, very mature. They took it at a cracking pace and at first I was pleased, but then it all seemed to look rushed and ill-considered. They don't seem to have very high expectations of themselves. They seem to think it is a social club, not an art class. I mean, I don't mind chatting and everything, but it ought to be about art, not the bloody bus service. They might learn something if they only talked about what they were doing. It's not fair really – they know I'm not as experienced or as confident as their normal teacher, and they are just taking liberties.

> *'The worst is not, so long as we can say, "This is the worst."'*
>
> Shakespeare, *King Lear*

Attribution

Who do you blame for a bad session? And who takes the credit if the learning goes well?

In the chapter on motivation, we looked at the active and passive learner, but we teachers can be active or passive too. Active teachers may understand that the nature of the students, such as their lack of prior learning, may be in part to blame for an ineffective lesson. But instead of blaming their students, they will concentrate on how to make the learning more effective.

Chapters 49 and 50 consider this in more detail.

Look at reflections 1, 2, A and B above. Who is being blamed for the difficulties?

If you attribute the problems to something outside your control, there is a danger you will not feel a need to change your practice to put the difficulties right.

But this lack of blaming works both ways. Don't blame yourself either. Instead, get busy thinking how the lesson could have been made to go well, and to learning general principles you can apply in the future to ensure it doesn't happen again.

> *'Our business in life is not to succeed, but to continue to fail in good spirits.'*
>
> Robert Louis Stevenson

Evaluating lessons

Lesson evaluation should be based on the lesson plan's clearly stated aims and objectives. You may also like to state your personal goals or aims, as considered in Chapter 10. These might include such factors as fostering interest in the subject and raising your students' sense of self-belief.

Evaluation may be done by a checklist, by filling in a proforma or by writing freely about the lesson. Most teachers use a combination of these methods. Similar methods are usually used when your lesson is evaluated by a tutor, a colleague or a fellow novice teacher. I suggest you design your own self-evaluation form, but leave space for generalised comments; there is a danger of over-categorising.

On the next page, you will find an example of a detailed evaluation proforma which could be photocopied on the back of your lesson plan proforma. The example has been filled in. (For your own form you might want to adjust the space for some sections, especially if you plan to handwrite the entries.

Alternative headings for a self-evaluation sheet might include: communication skills; introduction; teaching methods; teaching aids; student involvement; direction and control; timing; strengths and weaknesses; appearance of teacher; voice and mannerisms; teacher confidence; discipline; student interest in content; appropriateness of objectives; appropriateness of methods; worksheets and other resources; and so on.

As you become more experienced, you will find this or similar proformas too detailed for general use, and will usually rely on 'general comments' only. However, you may still want to concentrate on one feature of your teaching – for example, your use of a specific teaching method or your ability to produce motivation in your students. You could evaluate this feature of your teaching over a period of time, perhaps for only one group of students. This is a great way of problem-solving. The checklists at the end of each chapter in the 'Teacher's toolkit' section (Part 2 of this book) can be used to provide criteria for evaluating your use of a specific teaching method.

> *Try videoing or taping one of your lessons; or swap lesson observations with a fellow novice teacher. You could also ask your students to fill in an anonymous questionnaire, like that described in Chapter 49.*

LESSON EVALUATION

LESSON PLAN: aims and objectives, choice and variety of activities *(educare?)*, timing, pace, etc.

Seemed OK. Plenty of student activity – shame it didn't work! Review of last lesson worked well; they really enjoyed answering my questions. Not enough doing-detail, see note later.

ENVIRONMENT: seating, temperature, ventilation, lighting, safety, etc.

OK. Trailed OHP lead under desk – found my red pen in the process!

LEARNING AIDS: choice, design, and use

Using board and OHP at the same time worked well. Forgot to go to the back to check on clarity of OHT, but pretty sure it was OK.

IMPLEMENTATION OF PLAN: class management, use of teaching methods, start and close of lesson

Didn't really define the task clearly enough (again). They needed more doing-detail – I should have done one for them on board. They all got off on the wrong track at a blistering pace. Should have checked and corrected early in the lesson; instead sorted out Sam's and Anthony's homework queries. This could have been done later, after lesson if necessary.

COMMUNICATION: language, voice, body language, jargon, feedback, Q&A, explaining skills, summary

All right; more question and answer would have helped when I was explaining what they were supposed to do – might have picked up on misunderstandings.

TEACHER–STUDENT RELATIONSHIPS: empathy, rapport, discipline, humour, acknowledging student feelings

All right really – nice bunch. Sometimes hard to settle them when they have the Friday afternoon jitters. Spent some time talking to their regular teacher about this. She says I should wait longer for silence.

MOTIVATION: success, point, enjoyment, reinforcement, target-setting

Good, but must make sure they are mostly successful next lesson.

WERE OBJECTIVES ACHIEVED? test, homework

No, but should be next lesson. Must make students do more, me less.

GENERAL COMMENTS:

Try a settling activity to start their next Friday lesson.

Effectiveness of lesson (on a scale of 1–10): 7

Feedback rate (on a scale of 1–10): 6

Two successful things about the lesson were:

Good rapport is being developed. They worked quite hard eventually.

One suggestion for improvement:

Tell jokes at the end of a lesson, not the beginning.

One teaching principle demonstrated by this lesson was:

Showing is better than telling – exemplars help define doing-detail.

Keep your evaluations. They make interesting reading, and you will continue to learn a lot from them for some time. But most important, make sure you *do* learn from them, and change your teaching as a result.

If you find that you have a persistent problem, then ask for advice. There are always experienced teachers ready to help; they know that learning to teach is difficult. Asking for advice is not an admission of failure, but evidence of your desire to succeed. You may find it helpful to observe a lesson where an experienced teacher is dealing with a problem which is the same as, or similar to, the one that troubles you. Lonely anxiety is counter-productive and unnecessary, and experienced advice is priceless and free – seek it out!

> *Murphy's Law ('If anything can go wrong, it probably will') has recently been criticised by engineers as being too optimistic. It is soon to be changed to: 'If anything can go wrong, it already has'.*

The aim of evaluation is to make you into a 'reflective practitioner' – that is, someone who reflects on his or her teaching with the constant aim of improving it. The process is continuous throughout the career of the teacher. I'm still self-critical about my teaching, and still trying out new ideas. Have a look at the graph below, where would you place yourself?

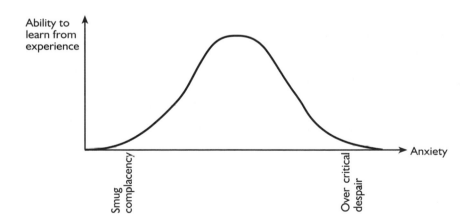

Checklist for using reflection to learn how to teach

☐ Do you always find time to reflect on your lessons?

☐ Do you consider what went right as well as what went less well?

☐ Do you ask yourself 'Why did it go like that?' and try to establish sound learning points that you can apply in future teaching?

❑ Do you deliberately try to learn from one lesson how to improve the next?

❑ Do you manage to avoid too much blaming of students, and of yourself?

❑ Do you seek out opportunities to talk about your teaching with those that might help?

❑ Are you able to give yourself a 'medal and a mission' after each lesson, however well or badly it went?

❑ Have you designed a comprehensive lesson evaluation form?

❑ Do you fill in an evaluation for every lesson?

❑ Do you make conscious use of the experiential learning cycle in improving your teaching?

❑ Have you taken concrete steps to improve your effectiveness in whichever phase of the experiential learning cycle you find most difficult?

Further reading

Argyris, C. and Schön, D. (1974) *Theory in Practice*, San Francisco: Jossey-Bass. (This suggests the idea of 'theory-in-use' on page 8.)

Biggs, J. (2007) *Teaching for Quality Learning at University* (3rd edition), Buckingham: Open University Press.

Brockfield, S. D. (1995) *Becoming a Critically Reflective Teacher*, San Francisco: Jossey-Bass.

Hillier, Y. (2005) *Reflective Teaching in Further and Adult Education* (2nd revised edition) London: Continuum.

Petty, G. (2006) *Evidence Based Teaching*, Cheltenham: Nelson Thornes.

Schön, D. (1983) *The Reflective Practitioner*, San Francisco: Jossey-Bass.

Schön, D. (1987) *Educating the Reflective Practitioner: Towards a New Design for Teaching and Learning in the Professions*, San Francisco: Jossey-Bass.

47

Initial and diagnostic assessment: assessing learners' needs

We saw in the previous chapter that teachers must believe in their ability to make a huge difference to students' lives, and that they will be most effective when they are inspired by values such as these:

- putting the learner and learning first
- believing that learning is not a privilege for the few, but an entitlement for all
- striving for equality of opportunity, and for inclusiveness.

But how are these values and aspirations to be achieved in practice? First, we must treat each learner as an individual, rather than as a member of a class of identical students. We must discover the needs of each individual learner, and then make sure these needs are met. This process is summarised by the diagram on page 533. Let's look at a few examples to see why this individual treatment is so necessary.

Why we use initial and diagnostic assessment

Suppose you are about to teach an A-level business studies module on accounting methods. It requires your students to understand percentages. They've all passed GCSE maths, so you assume they will have no problem …

I hope alarm bells are ringing! Some students may have got 50 per cent in their GCSE maths exam, and may never have understood percentages. And are percentages the only prior learning your students will require to succeed on your course?

Suppose you are an adult learner

Suppose you are an adult learner who has finally plucked up courage to attend a basic skills class. You want to be able to fill in your timesheet at work, and learn to read well enough to see what's on telly that evening. You are worried the teacher will just get you doing long division and reading childish fairy stories.

Suppose you are a dyslexic student who can cope well with support, but not without. How will your teacher discover your needs, and then meet them? How will your teacher ensure that your needs are indeed being met by the support provided?

Each learner is unique and has individual needs. If the needs of our learners are discovered and met, the chances of success are greatly increased. If you consider the examples above, you will see that it is not enough to guess the needs of the *average* student in your class. We need to discover and then meet *individual* needs, and this can make the difference between failure and success for many students.

> *We used to teach courses. Now we teach students.*

Education used to be a sieve: now it is a ladder. Poor teachers used to teach their courses with little consideration for initial and diagnostic assessment, waiting to see which students coped, and which didn't, and then perhaps dropped out. It was common for A-level teachers to feel pleased if the numbers in their classes dropped in the first few months: they said there was no point in having students in their class who 'weren't up to it'.

Education used to be a sieve …

There has been a huge culture change since these views were common. As we saw in the last section, the assumption now is that all students can learn if they are placed on the right programme, taught in the way they can learn, and given any help and support they might need.

But how do we get them on the right programme? How do we discover what they have learned so far? How do we discover the help they will need to succeed? By initial and diagnostic assessment, a process that is at the heart of inclusion.

Now it is a ladder

How this is done in practice depends hugely on the context. Those teaching adults basic skills such as numeracy and literacy will go about it in a radically different way from those teaching English in schools, or A-level business studies in a college. For example, the basic skills teacher will have control over what they teach, and can mould it to each individual learner's goals, as described in Chapter 34 on self-directed learning. If, for example, the learner only wants to learn how to fill in their work timesheet, then fine: that becomes the aim, and the focus for the learner's practice – at least at first.

But the English teacher and the A-level business studies teacher have a set syllabus to work to, so there is very little flexibility in course content. However, there are many other learners' needs these teachers can discover and respond to.

We use initial and diagnostic assessment for two main reasons: first, to help place them on the right course or programme, then to support the learner towards success on that programme.

Phase 1: 'Make the match'

The aim here is to get potential learners on the programme(s) that will suit them best. This includes choosing the right subjects for study at GCSE or A-level. The programmes must of course match the learners' short- and long-term goals, their present attainment, their interests, their availability for study and so on. At least a rough assessment of the student's needs must be made during this 'initial advice and guidance'. This is no easy task, especially in early September when many colleges enrol tens of thousands of students a week. Sometimes the decision is only provisional, awaiting the outcomes of the next phase.

Phase 2: 'Close the gap'

Once a programme has been decided, the aim is to close the gap between each student's characteristics and the characteristics and requirements of the programme. For example, if a student does not quite have the literacy skills necessary for a programme, then learning support could be arranged for that individual. In this way, the learner is moved closer to the ideal required by the programme.

But the *programme* can also be moved closer to the *student*. For example, if many of the learners on a programme do not have the literacy skills required for it, then the timetable may be altered to give more time for literacy. Learning support could be provided for all learners, say, one extra hour a week.

Also, if a chemistry teacher finds from a questionnaire that many new students can't calculate molar concentration, then she can plug that gap. Adaptations like these move the programme closer to the ideal required by the learners as a group.

Initial and diagnostic assessment in practice

Teachers carry out initial and diagnostic assessment, sometimes called 'assessing learners' needs', for a number of reasons – for example, to help them with initial advice and guidance, with enrolment, and to help them design the programmes they teach. This assessment is also an integral part of tutorial systems, learning support systems and so on.

Much of this activity is concentrated at the beginning of a course or programme of study, for the obvious reason that teachers need to know a good deal about their students if they are to place them on the right programme, and also to teach them well.

However, diagnostic assessment is really a continuous process. Teachers can assess needs when they look at a student's work, for example, and by questioning, tests and quizzes. This more informal approach to diagnostic assessment is covered in Chapter 43 on formative assessment and elsewhere in this book.

However you diagnose needs, they must also be addressed. Diagnosis is only the first part of the story!

How needs are assessed

In some cases, a programme manager, course leader, subject leader or other manager will lead the process of initial and diagnostic assessment. In other cases, teachers do the whole process for themselves. Often there is a shared responsibility, with teacher and manager taking on different aspects of the process.

1 Make a match
Match the learner's characteristics to a suitable programme or course or set of subjects.
The student is enrolled and a learning agreement form is produced.

2 Close the gap
Close the gap between the characteristics of the learner(s) and the characteristics of the programme. The gap varies from student to student, and is a measure of that student's need.

For example, produce an individual learning plan with an action plan to close the gap.

Adjust the teaching, and as far as possible the content of the programme, to meet the needs of the learner.

Learner's characteristics
What are the characteristics of the learner(s)?
e.g. aspirations, capabilities, preferences, etc.

Programme characteristics
What are the characteristics and requirements of this programme of study or subject, etc?
e.g. necessary prior learning, assessment methods, study skills required, time needed for homework, etc.

Move the learner closer to the programme requirements

Move the programme requirements closer to the learners' characteristics

You have ostiomyolitic emphesema

Treatment? I'm sorry, Mrs Gray – we only do diagnoses!

Whatever your role, initial and diagnostic assessment is a four-part process.

1 *Plan*: Decide what knowledge would help you to ensure your learners' success, and to teach them more effectively.

2 *Assess*: Find this information out. You will need to develop ways of discovering what you need to know, using, for example, references, interviews, questionnaires, tests, etc.

3 *Inform*: You need to tell your students and their teachers what you have found.

4 *Address*: You and others will need to do something constructive with the information.

That last bit is often forgotten! There is little point in diagnostic assessment if you do not use this information to improve their learning.

Many teachers and managers use standard procedures, documentation, tests and questionnaires. However, you may find this does not give you all the information you need to ensure the success of your learners. Then you will need to devise your own approach.

What do we need to find out about our students?

> **EXERCISE**
>
> Think of the sort(s) of teaching you do, or hope to do. As you read through the rest of this chapter, note the strategies that might be appropriate for assessing the needs of your learners. It is most unlikely that all the strategies will apply, though more could apply than you might realise. All of the strategies will need to be adapted to your particular context: that is, to your students, your subject, your course, etc. Sometimes this adaptation will require considerable effort. In teaching, context is always immensely important.

When we meet a new group of learners, there are lots of things we might need to know about them:

Why have my students enrolled on my subject/course? What do they hope to get out of it, and what are their medium-term and long-term aspirations?

What are my students' learning styles? We saw in the Introduction to Part 2 that learning styles are not fixed, and we shouldn't stereotype students or teach them in one style only. However, some teachers still find learning styles questionnaires useful.

What qualifications do my students have? This won't prove what students know, but it might be useful evidence of:

- what they definitely don't know or can't do (Philip hasn't got a first-aid certificate)
- what their average attainment has been (Philip has a high average GCSE grade; he is probably a capable learner).

What teaching methods will my students prefer, or learn best from? Do language students like reading round the class? Do students learn well from lectures? Do A-level mathematics students mind showing the rest of the class their solution to a problem?

Do my students have the study skills they will need? Can they, for example, do a logical search on the Internet, or use chapter headings and indexes to find relevant material in books? Can they plan writing or read difficult text?

What is my students' prior learning? The business studies students needed to be able to use percentages. This won't be the only vital 'prerequisite' learning they require.

Adult basic skills teachers, and teachers of recreational courses such as painting or horticulture, may be able to devise an individual programme for each student, as described in Chapters 41 and 42 on planning courses.

Do my students have any additional needs? For example, do they have:

- *Physical needs:* as a result of impaired sight or hearing, mobility problems or other relevant physical difficulties. For example, a deaf student might need to sit near the front to assist their lip-reading.
- *Psychological needs:* Do they have emotional or behaviour problems?
- *Health needs:* Do they have health problems that might affect attendance or their learning, such as eczema or asthma, or mental health problems?
- *Learning needs:* Do records show, or students believe, that they have specific learning difficulties such as dyslexia? Are there any emotional blocks or fears that might affect their learning? etc.
- *Care needs:* Are they in care, a client of the probationary service, or on a drugs rehabilitation scheme, etc.? If so, do the service providers concerned suggest any needs? For example, a student's probation officer may suggest what support will most help their client.
- *Other needs:* Are they a carer at home or do they have other family commitments that will make attending to their studies problematical, etc.?

Do they have constructive attitudes to learning? Do they believe in themselves as learners, and value what their programme can do for them?

The best practice in assessing learning needs is often in the field of teaching students with learning difficulties, or teaching adults basic skills. This is because such students often have very varied and profound needs. If you can, talk to someone in these areas and find out what they do, and look at the documentation they use. You may be able to adapt their approaches and documentation to your own use.

When we assess a learner's present educational attainment, we often do this against the national curriculum levels, or, in post-compulsory education, against the National Qualifications Framework. This is shown in the table on the next page; look at it carefully. Where are the courses you might teach? What qualifications might your students have on entry?

The national curriculum levels in the table describe attainment at school; this will be given in school records and in some school references.

Basic skills

In an international study in 1999, the Organisation for the Economic Cooperation and Development (OECD) found that 22% of British people were functionally illiterate, meaning unable to cope with the demands of modern life. The government commissioned a report from Sir Claus Moser (the Moser report), which was published in 1999 with great impact. Its opening paragraph is still relevant:

> Something like one adult in five in this country is not functionally literate, and far more people have problems with numeracy. This is a shocking situation and a sad reflection on past decades of schooling. It is one of the reasons for relatively low productivity in our economy, and it cramps the lives of millions of people. We owe it to them to remedy at public expense the shortcomings of the past. To do so should be a priority for Government, and for all those, in the business world or elsewhere, who can help.

The Basic Skills Agency describes basic skills as the ability to read, write and speak English or Welsh, and to be able to use mathematics at a level necessary to function and progress at work and in society in general.

Basic skills in literacy or numeracy are entry-level qualifications. Some learners on basic skills programmes may be below entry level 1, however.

The Qualifications and Curriculum Authority (QCA) produced for the government a set of national standards to form the basis of all literacy and numeracy qualifications and programmes of study. These standards explain in detail what is required in literacy (reading, writing, speaking and listening) and numeracy (interpreting, calculating and communicating mathematical information) at entry level and levels 1 and 2 of the National Qualifications Framework. They can be downloaded from the QCA's website (www.qca.org.uk).

Communication, application of number and information technology

Key skills and functional skills

There are three main key skills: *communication*, *application of number* and *information technology*. All full-time programmes in the post-compulsory sector at levels 1 to 3, and many other programmes, will include these. Key skills will soon be replaced by 'functional skills' in English, maths and ICT. Try an exam body's website, such as www.edexcel.com, and search for functional skills for up-to-date information.

The National Qualifications Framework

Initial and diagnostic assessment: assessing learners' needs

Level	National curriculum	Key skills and basic skills in literacy and numeracy		Occupational qualifications	Vocational qualifications	General qualifications
		Key skills	Literacy/numeracy			
Level 5		Key skills level 5		NVQ level 5		Degrees and other higher-level qualifications
Level 4		Key skills level 4		NVQ level 4		BTEC Higher Nationals: HNC, HND, City & Guilds 740, etc. First year of a degree
Level 3		Key skills level 3		NVQ level 3	Advanced Vocational Certificate of Education (AVCE) BTEC National Diploma (ND)	GCE A-levels AS and A2
Level 2		Key skills level 2	Literacy/numeracy level 2	NVQ level 2	GNVQ Intermediate BTEC First Certificate	GCSE grades A to C
Level 1	National curriculum level 5	Key skills level 1	Literacy/numeracy level 1	NVQ level 1	GNVQ Foundation	GCSE grades D to G
	National curriculum level 4					
Entry level	National curriculum level 3		Literacy/numeracy entry 3			Basic skills Entry Level Certificate
	National curriculum level 2		Literacy/numeracy entry 2			
	National curriculum level 1		Literacy/numeracy entry 1			

Source: Adapted from the framework on www.qca.org.uk

There are also three 'wider' key skills. These are optional for national qualifications, though some institutions make them obligatory for some courses: working with others, improving own learning performance and problem-solving.

Key skills were developed in the late 1980s, but there is still a lot of controversy about how to 'deliver' them. Ideally, they are integrated into a student's main academic or vocational studies. For example, students could learn the 'communication' key skill through their business studies homeworks and assignments. However, this integrated approach is not easy for teachers and colleges because:

- Teachers have to assess work 'twice', once for their subject, and once for the key skills.
- The key skills attainment of each individual student must be monitored and recorded, or 'tracked'. This is not easy when different students work towards different sets of qualifications, as they do for A-levels, for example.
- Some subject-specialist teachers lack confidence in their own key skills, and in their ability to teach at least one of them.

The alternative to integrating key skills is to teach them separately. The problem with this approach is that students tend to see them as an irksome irrelevance to their main course of study, and the teaching may not tailor the skills to their subject-specific needs. 'I came to college to do business studies, not English and maths'. Students are very wrong about this, of course! If business studies students learn to structure their essays or assignments, it can add over a grade to their attainment.

Integration may be a challenge, but it's well worth it. Students see the relevance of the skills, and learn to apply them in a meaningful context.

There is more detail about the content of key skills and related issues at www.qca.org.uk/keyskills/

DON'T ASSUME THAT LEVEL 3 STUDENTS HAVE LEVEL 3 KEY SKILLS

Dewsbury College screened their level 3 (Advanced) students:

- 6% were at or below level 1 in literacy.
- 17% were at or below level 1 in numeracy.

Other colleges find very similar results (Martinez 2000).

How to collect the information

How do we get all this information? Asking the student directly is not the only way. If you are about to teach some students who have already started their learning programme, then some of what is described below may already have been carried out. See if you can get hold of this information.

Common methods are listed below. As you read through this list, think of which ones would be most helpful in your own teaching situation. Remember that one can make do with relatively crude information in order to place a student on the right course:

'Has she got GCSE maths?' Once the student has started on the course, however, the teacher may need more detail: 'Can she do percentages?' It is much quicker and easier to collect crude information, of course, and speed is often a deciding factor during 'initial advice and guidance', when students are being placed on appropriate programmes. What works for 'making the match' may be insufficient for 'closing the gap'.

Some common methods are described below; many of them will then be described in greater detail later. Which ones would work for you? (I use the terminology of the Basic Skills Agency website, but these terms can have different meanings in some institutions.)

Screening tests

These simply discover whether there is a basic skills need. In other words, the tests find those learners who are below level 1 for numeracy and/or literacy.

Initial assessment

This places the learner against a level in the National Qualifications Framework. For example, a learner may be found to be at level 2 in numeracy.

Diagnostic assessment

This breaks down a key skill or basic skill, such as numeracy, into a number of sub-skills, and discovers which of these a student can and can't do. For example, it might show that a student at level 1 can do decimals but can't do percentages.

Diagnostic questionnaires

These can be used to diagnose study skills, learning style, preferred teaching methods, motivation and attitude to study, etc.

The 'diagnostic' assessment or questionnaire is only truly diagnostic if the information it finds is used to set targets, improve the students' skills, inform teaching, improve the course, or in some other constructive way.

'Can you do this?' questionnaire

This is a form of diagnostic questionnaire. Students are asked to state what they can do; here are some examples:

- Can you find the value of x in this equation? $x + 4 = 17$.
- Can you import a spreadsheet into a Microsoft Word® document?
- Could you book a hotel room in French?

Students can choose from three answers: 'Yes', 'I think so' and 'No'.

Such questionnaires are quicker and less intimidating than tests. There is more detail on this below.

Interview in a small group or one-to-one

This may involve asking set questions as well as a less structured discussion.

References, including school references

Some references are better than others, but if the referee knows the person well, you must have a good reason for ignoring what they say. Some colleges have found that a poor school reference is one of the best predictors of a student having difficulty in college (Martinez 2000).

College application form

These have standard questions on them.

Course questionnaire

Teachers can identify their own questions for this, of course.

GCSE or other qualifications attained

Research shows that the best measure of a student's ability to succeed is their average GCSE grade, not the number of GCSEs they have at grade C or above.

Record of achievement

Students who have recently left school will usually have one of these, which summarises their achievement, not just academic achievement.

Student's portfolio or other examples of their work

This can be very informative. My assumptions have often been demolished in seconds.

There are very many other informal methods. One teacher may hold a class discussion on note-taking with her students and find from their views that they really don't know how to take notes. Another might chat very informally with her learners one-to-one, finding out about them as individuals and discovering why they have enrolled on her computing course. The learners might think she is just being friendly, but she might make notes of each individual's learning goals after these discussions. A few lessons later, she might share these goals with her students and review them.

Finding out about them as individuals

As ever in teaching, it's not just what you do, it's also the way that you do it. It is not hard to imagine some spectacularly inappropriate methods for initial and diagnostic assessment. I knew of a school that invited its new intake to visit each summer. The new pupils lined up in the playground of their 'big school' for the first time, wide-eyed with awe and whispering in hushed excitement. They were then ushered into the gymnasium where they took a battery of tests in exam conditions. The school needed to know each learner's numeracy ability, along with their verbal and non-verbal reasoning scores, in order to put them into the correct sets for the following September. They didn't trust the information given them by their feeder schools. I bet you can guess the reactions of their new pupils. Suppose the basic skills teacher we considered at the start of this chapter adopted a similar strategy?

Some colleges can be every bit as intimidating as that school to some learners, at least during their first visit. Striking the balance between making a new student feel included and welcome, and finding out enough about them to ensure they succeed, requires real empathy and fine judgement.

Diagnostic assessment is not an event, it is a process. Some of it will take place at the first meeting with a potential learner, some will take place during 'induction', where students are made familiar with the programme, and some will be discovered later. In any case, diagnostic assessment is a continuous process; the teacher will always be cocking an ear in this direction, and devising activities to diagnose the needs of their learners.

'Can you do this?' questionnaires

When teaching A-level physics, I needed my students to understand basic algebra, but had no time to teach this. My students came from different schools and had studied maths at different levels. Some had excellent algebra, some had none. Their maths GCSE grade was too crude a measure to help me. Some had high grades but had studied no algebra at all on their course. Others had studied it in detail. What was I supposed to do? I didn't have time to teach algebra as well as physics.

I didn't want to set an algebra test as this would be an unsettling way to start the course. So I identified the algebra they would need to succeed at physics, which was stated explicitly in the syllabus, and turned this into a 'Can you do this?' questionnaire.

For example:

Could you solve the following for x? $2x + 4x = 3x - 72$ (answer 24)

Yes ☐ just about ☐ No ☐

If the students were not sure how to answer, they did the question and checked their answer with the one provided. There were about 25 questions altogether. Each question directed students who couldn't do it to a chapter in a maths textbook. This created an individual study programme for each student to fix weaknesses in their prior learning. This could go on their individual learning plan and be monitored by me and the tutor.

In addition, I ensured that the first few topics I taught required no algebra; this was not easy for me to do, but it ensured my students had time to fix their algebra before I made use of it.

A similar approach could be used on any course. Twenty or so well-chosen questions like this will give you a reasonable impression of your students' prior learning. You could devise a questionnaire to discover the extent of their previous knowledge, experience, attitudes and expectations. Example questions are given below for students about to start an improvers' French class; for those beginning a course on the use of a sales computer system; and for those about to start an A-level science course in a new college:

Knowledge. For example:

- 'Do you know the French for glass, soup and lorry?'
- 'Do you know the company's complaints procedure?'
- 'Could you define molar concentration?'

Skills and abilities. For example:

- 'Could you translate the following letter?'
- 'Are you able to make use of the computer's back-up procedure?'
- 'Could you prepare a microscope slide to view a … ?'

Experience. For example:

- 'Have you ever read a French novel?'
- 'Have you ever used a computer before?'
- 'Have you used computers in the laboratory to measure temperature?'

Attitudes and expectations. For example:

- 'How many hours of set reading are you prepared to do per week?'
- 'What is your main reason for enrolling on this course?'
- 'Are you used to weekly homeworks?'

Preferred learning styles. For example:

- 'Do you enjoy reading round the class?'
- 'Would you like informal tests?'
- 'Which of the following do you enjoy: working in groups … ?'

Of course, such questions can be asked informally during discussion or during one-to-one conversation, but the questionnaire is likely to produce the most honest and representative student profile.

The individual learning plan

In many schools and colleges, students have an individual learning plan (ILP). This plan responds to initial and diagnostic assessment, and to the student's goals and aspirations, and is drawn up by negotiation between the tutor and the student.

Practice varies very widely, but an ILP for a full-time student may contain:

Outcomes of diagnostic tests

This might include: key skills and/or basic skills, learning styles, study skills, course specific questionnaires and so on. (This information may be in the student's records rather than in the ILP itself.)

Long-term goals

For example, the student's career aspirations, and what they hope to achieve in their hobbies and interests.

Medium-term goals

This would include the qualification(s) the learner is working towards. For example, for a science student with an interest in working in a laboratory, and also becoming a part-time football referee, this might include a first-aid certificate as well as their science qualifications.

Short-term goals

These are, in effect, an action plan to address the learner's needs. They should respond to the findings of any diagnostic tests. For example, a science student found to have weak algebra might have an action plan point that specifies what they will do to improve this. There may be separate action points for the development of each key/basic skill, study skills, and for each subject or unit studied.

Clearly the student's short-, medium- and long-term goals should all be 'aligned', that is, pulling in the same direction.

Support

This would include learning support (e.g. help with writing assignments), learner support (e.g. support from a counsellor) and additional support (e.g. a student who has a hearing impairment may be supported by ensuring her teachers use an induction loop system linked to her hearing aid).

Whether or not students have an ILP, they will certainly have other student records, including previous educational attainment and a learning agreement form. This may record some or all of the information above instead of the ILP, and will also contain monitoring information about attendance, work-rate, progress and achievement, etc.

The purpose of an individual learning plan is to help create a well-planned, 'tailor-made' programme of activities for each student that meets their individual needs and aspirations. ILPs are negotiated in a one-to-one tutorial or series of tutorials with the student, in a similar manner to that described in the next chapter. See the diagram on page 550 which summarises this and the next chapter. Out of this comes a first action plan. This can be a very effective way to ensure that all learners are included and supported, and so succeed. Usually the institution also benefits. For example, results improve, and college funding is dependent on 'retention' (the proportion of students who are retained rather than drop out) and 'achievement' (the proportion of students who pass).

Induction

During the first few days or weeks of a course, students are introduced to the course, the qualification, the college, etc. This is called an induction. Induction is best thought of as a process rather than an event. You will have experienced an induction on the teacher training course you are attending, or perhaps on some other course.

What happened, and how did it help you? Is there anything else that could have been done to help you? Many of the activities described in this chapter take place during induction. The activities in the next chapter often begin during induction.

CASE STUDIES IN ASSESSING LEARNER'S NEEDS: AN EXERCISE

Ellen was a trainee teacher, and for teaching practice she was about to take a series of lessons on 'the short story' with an AS English language and literature group. All her students had GCSE English grade C or above, and she had already observed a lesson of a parallel group which gave her some idea of the standard her students would be working towards.

When I asked her how she assessed the prior learning of her students she looked blank at first, and only identified one or two of the actions listed below, though she had actually done them all. She did pretty well, I think, but with more time she would have liked to do more.

Question 1: What did she do well?

Question 2: What else could she have done if she had more time?

1 Ellen got advice from Mary, the class's regular teacher, about the needs of the group as a whole, and about the needs of two students in particular who had English as a second language.
2 She looked at Mary's records, paying particular attention to the students' GCSE results, their reading habits, and the outcomes of their key skills diagnostic assessments. She noticed that many of the learners had poor literacy scores; this surprised her for a language course.
3 She looked at one piece of marked work that the students had just completed, and was surprised by the range of abilities this showed.
4 She discussed with Mary and her tutor whether her provisional lesson plan ideas were suitable for her students.
5 She decided to ask her students to complete an anonymous questionnaire after her second lesson, asking them what they had learned that day; what they had most enjoyed about the lesson; and what they found most difficult or least enjoyable about the lesson.
6 She looked at the induction programme and talked to Mary about this. She discovered that the students would know all about the AS assessment procedures already.
7 She thought about what prior learning they would need and concluded they would need to understand metaphor, simile and other literary devices. At first she thought of devising a diagnostic test, but decided she didn't want to scare them to death in her first lesson! She wondered about a 'Can you do this?' questionnaire, but eventually decided on a class activity for her first lesson. This was a 'decisions, decisions' game (see page 247), which involved the students classifying phrases as metaphor, personification, etc. In the event, some students did quite badly with this activity, but completed it successfully with support from their peers. She was sure it helped them a great deal with the subsequent lessons.

References and further reading

Look carefully at documents and procedures produced by your college or school. Practice varies and you need to know what is expected of you, and what is available to you as a teacher.

Further Education Funding Council (1998) *Inclusive Learning Quality Initiative Materials*, Coventry: FEFC. These materials run to seven folders and were created by the predecessor of the Learning and Skills Council. At least one copy was delivered to all post-compulsory institutions. The first (orange) folder is probably the most useful for you, and is called 'Understanding and Managing the Individual Learning Process'. See section 4, part 2 of this folder, 'Conducting a curriculum skills analysis'.

Martinez, P. (1998) '9000 voices: student persistence and drop-out in further education', LSDA free download at www.lsneducation.org.uk/pubs/index.aspx (type the author's name into the 'detailed search').

Moser, C. (1999) *A Fresh Start* ('The Moser Report'), London: DfEE.

Useful websites

www.qca.org.uk/qca_6444.aspx is useful to explore for key skills.

www.keyskills4u.com has excellent key skills teaching material.

48

Providing learners with support

Let's suppose you have now enrolled your students on subjects or programmes that suit their aspirations, and that you have assessed their learning needs for these programmes. The task now is to monitor their progress, and develop for each student an action plan to meet their individual needs. It is important to involve your students as much as possible in this process, so that they take responsibility and control over their action plan and feel motivated to complete it. The diagram on page 550 summarises the process, and that described in the previous chapter.

Remember that learning support is not a last-ditch stand. The Basic Skills Agency (1997) found that students on learning support were more likely to achieve than those who did not need the support in the first place. This is in part because learning support employs the most powerful teaching method yet discovered: one-to-one teaching. In a famous article, B. S. Bloom (1984) showed that students who had one-to-one teaching could do massively better than similar students experiencing conventional group instruction.

The person responsible for monitoring each student's progress and the support they might need is usually called the student's 'tutor' or 'personal tutor'. Tutors usually teach the students they tutor, but not always.

Students who have one-to-one teaching can do massively better

Skills and qualities of tutors: the importance of interpersonal skills

When students are asked what they most value about FE – for example, in Paul Martinez's '9000 voices' research – many report it is their relationship with their tutor. The same is true in schools. As part of the Inclusive Learning Quality Initiative, The Professional in Practice, students on 40 courses in nine colleges were asked by a researcher: 'What skills and qualities make a good tutor?' Student responses included:

- 'A tutor who has time for me when I go and see them.'
- 'Someone who will listen to me.'
- 'A person who doesn't make me feel stupid.'
- 'Someone who is not rushing round all the time and taking things out on us.'
- 'A person who takes us as we are.'
- 'Someone who'll help me when I've got a problem.'

Notice that students most value interpersonal skills. But when the researchers asked tutors the same question, they mentioned subject knowledge, and stressed skills such as time management, liaison, communication, organisation, planning, etc. These management skills are clearly vital, but it's your interpersonal communication skills that your students really notice. And these skills can often make the difference between the student leaving and staying.

THE ROLE OF THE TUTOR

The role of the tutor varies greatly, but the following are commonly expected of a tutor on a full-time course. Less would be expected of a tutor on a part-time course.

STUDY SUPPORT

- Agree a programme of study and an individual learning plan with each student.
- Review each student's progress every six or eight weeks, or more often if necessary, producing reports twice a year.
- Ensure students reflect on their own progress and achievements, and take responsibility for their own learning.
- Agree targets and individual action plans for each student and review these periodically in 'one-to-one' or small-group tutorial sessions.
- Maintain individual student records and individual learning plans.

PASTORAL SUPPORT

Ensure the delivery of an active and useful whole-class tutorial programme, to include induction, careers, pastoral issues, study skills, etc.
This support is usually provided by a combination of whole-class tutorials and one-to-one tutorials.

EXERCISE: MEETING THE EMOTIONAL NEEDS OF LEARNERS

Think of your own experience on the course you are now on, or on one you did recently. Alternatively, imagine you are a learner on a course you know well. What *information*, *reassurance* and other *emotional needs* would you need at each stage below? Think particularly of the emotional needs you felt. If it helps, imagine a learner who lacks confidence enrolling on this course. Think of as many needs as you can under each category, and make them as concrete as you can. There are some answers given on page 561, but you should be able to think of many more.

Pre-enrolment

I need the best course for me, so …

- I need to know about the alternative qualifications I might study.
- etc.

Induction and the first few weeks

I need to feel valued, respected and wanted, and have my fears allayed, so …

- I need to meet my teachers and tutor on the first day.
- etc.

I need to believe that I can do it, so …

- I need some achievable tasks.
- etc.

I need the programme to adapt to me personally, so …

- I need the teacher to identify what help I need to complete the course successfully.
- etc.

I need to adapt to the programme, so …

- I need to know more about what the course requires of me.
- etc.

Monitoring for inclusion: tutorial action planning

Part of the tutor's role is to assess the learning needs of each student; negotiate an individual learning plan; monitor each learner's progress on the course, ensuring they are attending, completing their work and meeting other important requirements; and, in response to all this, negotiate an action plan with each learner. Then, of course, the tutor must ensure the learner has the support they need to learn effectively and to complete their action plan.

'Catch them before they fall'

This process is shown on the diagram opposite. See also the self-assessment forms. Don't worry if you don't understand all this straight away; it is all explained later.

Student self-assessment forms

The form on page 551 is adapted from those used at Sutton Coldfield College for full-time students aged 16–19. Other criteria would appear in the columns for adult learners. Can you think what these criteria might be?

Tutorials: evidence-based action planning

Both the teacher and the tutor can provide students who need it with support. What follows describes how tutors might do this, but a teacher could do something very similar, though it will usually be much less elaborate.

The 'Catch them before they fall' diagram shows the 'big picture', the first three stages of which were described in the last chapter.

Assess learner's needs

The needs of each learner are identified.

Negotiate an individual learning plan (ILP)

The ILP is negotiated in a one-to-one with the student in a manner similar to that described later in this chapter. This ILP contains an action plan which is the first stab at addressing the student's needs.

'Make the match and close the gap'

The stages above should help the learner adapt to the needs of the programme. However, the tutor may also be able to adjust the programme to better meet the needs of the students.

Do an on-programme assessment

A few weeks or so into the course, the teacher does an 'on-programme assessment' to find out how the student is doing. This includes the views of teachers and a student's self-assessment.

One-to-one review

The student and tutor meet 'one-to-one', or in a small group, to review progress and the old action plan in the ILP. Students are informed of their successes. They are encouraged to suggest items for a new action plan.

An action plan is set

The assessment of the learner's needs and the on-programme assessment usually identify weaknesses. An action plan is negotiated to address these, and to challenge the student with high expectations.

Assess learner's needs

Identify the learner's aspirations and needs
What are the learner's goals and what do they want to learn?
Screening and/or initial diagnostic testing, e.g. of key/basic skills; learning style, study skills and attitudes, other prior learning, etc.

Identify any additional needs
e.g. needs due to sensory or mobility impairment, behaviour problems, physical or mental health problems, etc.

- Disability guidance
- etc.

Negotiate an individual learning plan (ILP)
Agree appropriate programme(s) along with action plan points and any support needed.

'Make the match and close the gap'

Do an on-programme assessment
Self-assessment: Students self-assess their: work rate and motivation, attendance, punctuality, strengths and weaknesses, completion of any previous action plan, etc.

Teacher assessments: Every four to six weeks or so the teachers report on the student to the tutor: e.g. progress, marks and grades, attendance and the other criteria used under self-assessment above, general comments, etc.

'FATE' process (see page 556)
Find the real difficulties
Agree an action plan
Targets are set for action
Evaluate completion of the targets

The student works on the action plan
Learner may get support from student services, learning support or from:

- Peers
- Family
- Library
- Study centres
- Welfare officer
- Counselling
- Referral agencies e.g. for a drug addiction problem
- Careers advice, Connexions, etc.
- Crèche
- Modified materials and exam requirements
- Specialist equipment e.g. an induction loop

Do

Review

Apply

Learn

Tutor has a 'one-to-one' review with the student
Was the previous action plan completed?
Medals: 'What are your strengths?'
'What has gone well?'

Facilitation: 'What do you find worrying or difficult?'
'What could you do about that?'
'Could you make that a SMART target?'
'What help or support do you need?'
'Is your ILP still okay?'

Missions: 'What needs to go on your action plan?'

An action plan is set
Both the tutor and the student and ideally the teachers have copies of this plan

Targets are justified in terms of the student's own long and medium term goals

Tough love:

High regard
High expectations
High support

Catch them before they fall

MANAGING YOUR TIME AND RESOURCES   Name: ....   Date: ....

Please complete this form before your next one-to-one tutorial. Take it to your tutor for use during that session. Put a ring round all the categories that apply. You should be above the grey line in all categories. If you are not, it would be a good idea to have some suggestions for moving above the line; these can then become targets for your action plan. Use the bottom row for comments and explanations.

Weekly attendance for all classes	Punctuality for all classes	Work submitted to deadlines	Private study per week (hours)	Time spent in learning centre or library	Maths: additional support (include Skillbuilder exercises)	English: additional support (include Skillbuilder exercises)	Other additional support	Part-time employment per week (hours)	Social life: evenings out per week	Effective time management in place?
100%	100%		12 or more	4 or more	100%	100%	100%	3	1	
95%	95%		10	3	95%	95%	95%	6	2	
90%	90%	100%	8	2	90%	90%	90%	9	3	Yes
			6	1				12	4	No
			5	0				18	5	
			4					24	6	
			3					26	7	
Comment	Comment	Comment	Comment	Comment	Cross out if not applicable	Cross out if not applicable	Cross out if not applicable	Comment	Comment	Comment

I have analysed the above and set targets for improvement. I have achieved in .... categories out of 10.
I am **ON TARGET/CLOSE TO TARGET/OFF TARGET** (Cross out those which do not apply)

Student signature: ....   Tutor signature: ....

Source: Adapted from a form used at Sutton Coldfield College.

The student works on the action plan

This is done with or without support, depending on the student's need.

Another on-programme assessment

A few weeks later, or sooner if necessary, there is another on-programme assessment, and the cycle repeats. It is not just the student's learning that needs to be monitored, but also the support they are being given. If the support is inadequate, it is improved or increased.

This 'find faults, fix and follow up' approach is vital for inclusion; without it, the needs of learners cannot be met.

Note that a key principle here is to ensure that the support is determined by the need. If one of your students is struggling despite support, you must discover this, and ensure support is increased. Then the student can still succeed. The whole process is very responsive, and certainly not 'sink or swim'! But despite this meticulous attention, learners are encouraged to take as much responsibility for their own learning as possible. This is achieved in part by self-assessment, by the FATE approach explained later, and by holding learners responsible for carrying out their action plan.

Ideally, you encourage and challenge each of your students to improve and to develop, but arrange just enough support for them to meet this challenge, and no more. This 'challenge with support' or 'tough love' approach develops your students' independence and self-reliance, so in time the student is better able to manage without your help.

Some courses, where students learn by carrying out individual projects, such as art and design courses, use one-to-ones at every class meeting, both for teaching and for this inclusive monitoring process.

Students really value your undivided attention in one-to-ones, but you haven't that much time to give – so how is the time best spent? As ever, it is important to keep your aims in view.

What are one-to-ones for?

The aims of one-to-ones are:

To encourage and inspire the student

- To listen to the student's experience
- To value the student as an individual
- To reward their progress
- To challenge them with high regard and high expectations
- To inspire students to set themselves challenging action plan points that help them to both realise their personal goals and meet their individual needs

To solve problems, and teach students to solve problems for themselves

- To discover the real problems or blocks to progress, not just the symptoms (or ideally, help students to discover these for themselves)

- To encourage the student to develop an action plan to deal with any problems or blocks to progress *before* these impede progress
- To discover any assistance that may help them with their work or with their action plan
- To ensure they have completed their last action plan
- To ensure students are committed to their action plans

Reward their progress

A study of 48 young adults asked them to perform standard tests of mental alertness and vigilance. Those getting less than six hours' sleep each night failed to spot how badly they performed and didn't report feeling sleepy.

Getting less than six hours of sleep a night for just two weeks impairs your mental abilities as much as not sleeping for two days.

(University of Pennsylvania School of Medicine at Philadelphia, published in the journal Sleep)

How to carry out a successful 'one-to-one' tutorial

As the 'Catch them before they fall' diagram shows, the meeting is not just a cosy chat; it results in action and is informed by evidence. This means you will have to ensure that the student has self-assessed, and that other teachers have informed you of their views before the meeting.

Once you have this information, you may be tempted to simply tell students what to do, and persuade them what is in their own best interests:

'You are just not keeping up with Unit 3. Mr Evans says you need learning support for the maths. So, from now on, *every* Friday ...'
'You *must* keep up with coursework. So from now on I want you to show me your completed work before handing it in so I can ...'

Would this work? Even if the student is compliant, they would feel judged and bullied, and so resentful, reluctant and uncooperative. Few people like to be told what to do, least of all when they see it as a punishment for poor performance. So this 'directive approach' risks alienating learners from you – and from their learning.

But there are even more fundamental problems. This directive approach does not discover the real problems. Why is the student behind with coursework? Is it too hard for her? Is she working in a supermarket every evening? Is she just not getting round to it? Neither does this 'directive approach' teach the student to deal with her own difficulties.

The non-directive approach

This approach aims not to direct and control students, but to facilitate and *to teach them how to solve their own problems*.

Problem-finding questions are asked:

'What do you find most difficult about this course?'
'Why is that a difficulty?'

The tutor waits for the student to suggest a solution, but if they don't, the tutor asks:

'What could you do about that?'

A second approach is for the teacher to ask the student:

'In what direction would you like to develop? If you were really proud of yourself in a year's time, what would you have done?'

The tutor listens and then asks:

'So how are you going to get there? What could be your first step?'

This second approach can be carried out whether or not the student has a problem. Note that both these techniques involve asking students for a goal, and then asking *them* how they will achieve it.

Getting success with the non-directive approach

Preliminaries

Find a place that is as private and as quiet as possible. Set a provisional time limit of, say, five minutes, to encourage best use of the time you have. Face your body

What could you do about that?

slightly away from the student, but use plenty of eye contact, and give him or her your undivided attention.

Attitude: listening, empathising, being accepting and non-judgemental

The most critical success factor is your attitude. This attitude is shown not just by what you say, but by your tone of voice, body language, facial expression, gestures and so on. Extensive research carried out by Carl Rogers (1961), the most influential psychotherapist of the last century, shows that you need to listen, empathise and be accepting and non-judgemental.

Listening

Put aside you own agenda for now, and genuinely try to understand students from their own point of view – even if you think that point of view is scandalously unreasonable!

Show interest and concern and show that you value the student as a person, by nodding as they speak, by not interrupting, by waiting if they stumble over words, by smiling appropriately, etc. Do not overuse eye contact if the student is shy.

Empathising

Try to see things from *their* point of view. How do they see it? How do they feel? What are their values and motives? Even if you think their views are very unreasonable, you can still empathise. Empathy reduces defensiveness and obstinacy, and makes it more likely that the student will admit and face up to reality. However, it needs to be done genuinely, not adopted as a cunning ploy to manipulate the student.

Open questions

Ask open questions such as:

> 'What do you find most difficult?'
> 'Can you tell me more about how that made you feel?'
> 'Can you tell me why that was important to you?'
> 'Why do you find that so hard?'
> 'What part of the course most interests you?'

Avoid closed questions: 'What's your best subject?'

Avoid leading questions also: 'It sound like you find practicals hard.'

Reflecting

Also try to 'reflect' the views they have just stated to show you understand:

> 'So you're telling me that Unit 4 is really getting you down?'
> 'Let's see if I understand you here, you're up to date but ...'

Being accepting and non-judgemental

Rogers discovered the paradox that if you accept and understand someone, they are then most likely to change. Controlling, criticism and blaming, and attempts at persuasion are most likely to bring about a defensive, unchanging behaviour. The desire to change must come from within the student, not from your exhortations to do better.

A defensive, unchanging behaviour

So don't blame or criticise. If students are self-critical or negative, try to make them forward-looking and positive by, for example, looking for how the problem could be avoided in the future. But at this stage, try to concentrate on empathy and understanding. The chapter on formative assessment considered the gains of this non-judgemental approach, which is also entirely in line with the values mentioned in Chapter 45.

If students do not have a problem, then find in what direction they want to develop, and challenge them to do so.

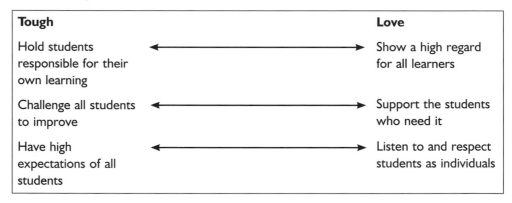

Tough		**Love**
Hold students responsible for their own learning	⟷	Show a high regard for all learners
Challenge all students to improve	⟷	Support the students who need it
Have high expectations of all students	⟷	Listen to and respect students as individuals

One-to-one tutorials in practice: the 'FATE' approach

Before the meeting, examine information from initial diagnostic testing, self-assessment, progress and attendance reports, etc. Recognise and praise achievement and effort, even if this is not great.

Find out *what* is wrong and *why*, using the non-directive, listening approach. Alternatively, find in what direction the learner wants to develop. Don't give advice, make judgements or 'tell off' the student in response to these questions.

Ask open, problem-finding questions:

'How do you think you are doing?'
'What do you find most difficult?'
'In what direction do you want to develop?'

Consider including some feelings-based questions:

'What worries you most about your college work?'
'How do you feel about … ?'

Explore issues with 'why' questions:

'Why do you find that difficult?'
'Why do you find it difficult to find the time?'

Confront complacency by asking the student what challenges they could set themselves.

Ask for action

'What could you do about that?'
'How could you overcome this difficulty, or meet that challenge?'
'What support might help you?'

Only if the student can't or won't suggest action do you make a suggestion yourself.

Targets for completion of action are negotiated and agreed:

'When could you do that by?'

Record who will do what, by when, and ensure both you and the student have written records.

Evaluation: progress towards the action plan is checked at the next one-to-one, or before.

'So you'll tell me on Monday how you got on?'

Ideally, this process remains *non-directive* throughout, but the disadvantages of the non-directive approach are overcome by setting a target which is evaluated. Use your judgement: a target may not always be appropriate; knotty problems may need talking over a few times before the student is committed to change. See 'facilitating change' on page 559.

Aspects of successful one-to-ones

Make sure that students get 'medals and missions' and that the mission expresses high expectation. Other aspects of successful one-to-ones often include the following.

Referrals

You will not be able to get students to solve all their own difficulties. Get to know and use your institution's student services or pastoral support system: it exists to support your students, and you, so do refer students where it is appropriate or when you feel uncomfortable. However, do follow up whether the student has acted on the referral.

Valuing education

Pointing out the material and personal gains of making a success of education is often important, especially if this message is not often heard at home. Role models of former students who have been successful can be inspiring.

Dealing with silence

If they are thinking, just remain silent and wait for them to speak. If they are stuck, try to help them clarify what they are trying to say. 'What's the key issue for you?'

Dealing with emotions

This is rarely a problem, but you must trust your professional judgement here. Stay calm. Try to reassure them, and ask if they need a break or a glass of water. Try to listen and empathise with extra care. If you feel you cannot cope, you have the right and the responsibility to leave the situation and seek assistance. If you close the meeting, arrange another before parting company.

Approaching persistent problems: facilitating change

> *'Given the choice between changing, and proving that change is not necessary, most people get busy with the proof.'*
>
> John Galbraith

Imagine a persistent problem, such as poor attendance, where action plans have not worked. Sometimes students are lazy, but sometimes it will take them time to change. Only simple difficulties will be solved by an agreed action plan after a single one-to-one session. What follows is based on 'motivational interviewing' (see below). Use your own professional judgement as to when the approach is applicable.

Some students need to go through the following process over a series of conversations with you:

- accepting they have a problem
- contemplating the problem and thinking about doing something about it
- deciding they want to do something – but wondering what, and only then …
- taking action.

Start with the non-directive approach and don't assume that you will get an action plan out of the meeting. Start off with:

- empathetic, non-judgemental listening
- trying to identify barriers
- focusing on the advantages of change.

EXERCISE

Facilitating change

Imagine a challenging and frightening or difficult change you might consider making in your own life, such as giving up smoking or tackling a problem with a relationship. Which strategy would be most likely to work?

- Being listened to non-judgementally during a truthful exploration of the issues, including a non-persuasive exploration of the alternatives and their consequences.

- Being challenged and persuaded.

Avoid trying to persuade the student. The change needs to come from within if it is going to happen, so forcing the student often fails.

Here is a sequence of questions that may help:

'What's the problem doing this? Why do you find it difficult?'
'Could you do with some help over this?' (Consider pairing the student up with a fellow student who is prepared to help them if this is appropriate.)
'How are you going to make sure you do it this time?'

If the problem persists:

'What's going to happen if you never sort this out?' – getting an answer and then:
'Are you happy with that? Is that what you want?'
'Are you letting yourself down here? Are you being your own best friend?'
'Do you think you have the strength of character to deal with this? Because I believe you have.'

MOTIVATIONAL INTERVIEWING

If you would like to follow up this approach to persistent problems in detail, take a look at the Entry To Employment – 'e2e' Standards Unit materials. Have a look in your institution's library.

The model of change

Most people who are faced with change are not ready to take action (70%) – for example, giving up smoking.

- Several stages must be passed through before action occurs.
- The object is to move people from one stage to the next, not directly to action.
- Stage-specific communication skills and strategies are required.

The stages of change are:

Precontemplation: 'unaware, unwilling, too discouraged'
Contemplation: 'open to information, thinking about trying something'
Preparation: 'getting ready to try out new behaviours'
Action: 'taking steps, needing will power, habituating behaviours'
Maintenance: 'has engaged for at least six months'

Other strategies to ensure inclusion

Inclusion, diversity, entitlement, differentiation, ensuring equal opportunities and personalised learning all require teachers to treat students as individuals. We have seen how course design ('making the match') and tutorial systems ('catch them before they fall') can help ensure every student succeeds. Here are some other ways, along with the chapter where you can learn more.

Inclusion in the classroom: some key strategies:

Strategy	Chapter where you can learn more
Establish good rapport and equal opportunities by *showing* respect	7
Help students with special needs such as dyslexia	7
Agree ground rules and enforce these	8 & 9
Set open, challenging, constructivist tasks	1
Use high-effect size methods	Intro. to Part 2
Ensure feedback is 'medal and mission'	6 & 43
Use inclusive questioning methods such as assertive questioning	14 & 24
Motivate students with tasks they value	5 & 41
Use whole-brain, varied student activities to meet all learning styles	Intro. to Part 2
Plan well-structured, active lessons	38 & 40
Most of all, listen and reflect with the right values	45 & 46
Use initial diagnostic testing and tutorial monitoring	47 & 48
Integrate study skills: see *Evidence Based Teaching*, Geoff Petty, chapters 21 and 24	

Ensure students know what to expect on the course, and give good initial guidance: see *Evidence Based Teaching*, Geoff Petty, page 360.

SOME ANSWERS FOR THE EXERCISE 'MEETING THE EMOTIONAL NEEDS OF LEARNERS'

Pre-enrolment

I need the best course for me

- I need to know about alternative qualifications, courses and programmes that might suit me.
- I need to have thought about the nature of the programme and what it will require of me.
- I need to appreciate how the programme meets my long-term aims and adds value to my life.
- I need to understand the consequences of doing the programme: costs, study time, effort, working conditions, extra commitments required for me to be successful.
- I need to be valued and feel I am wanted.
- I need to be 'kept warm' after first contact.

Induction and the first few weeks

I need to feel valued, respected and wanted and have my fears allayed

- I need to meet my teachers and tutor on the first day.
- I need to meet my fellow students and begin to bond with them and begin to belong. We need to discuss and agree fair ground rules.
- I need to feel secure about getting the support I might need to succeed.

I need to believe that I can do it

- I need achievable tasks as well as challenging tasks.
- I need to succeed early on.
- I need someone to discover whether I need support and to provide it.
- I need to learn in the ways that suit me.

I need the programme to adapt to me personally

- I need to know more about what the course requires of me.
- I need my teacher to listen to my queries and fears.
- I need my teacher to 'find faults and fix' regarding my 'match' with the course.

References and further reading

Look at the documents and procedures produced by your college or school. Practice varies and you need to know what is expected of you, and what is available to you as a teacher.

Basic Skills Agency (1997) 'Staying the course: the relationship between basic skills support, drop-out, retention and achievement – further education colleges', London: BSA. Shows that students on support are more likely to pass than those who don't even need the support in the first place.

Bloom, B. S. (1984) 'The 2 sigma problem: the search for methods of group instruction as effective as one-to-one tutoring', *Educational Researcher*, June/July: 4–16. Shows that one-to-one teaching is about four grades better than whole-class teaching.

Further Education Funding Council (1998) *Inclusive Learning Quality Initiative Materials*, Coventry: FEFC. See note in the bibliography of Chapter 47.

Green, M. (2002) *Improving One-to-One Tutorials*, London: Learning and Skills Development Agency. This is an excellent pack which includes a video. All post-16 institutions were given a free copy.

Martinez, P. (1998) '9000 voices: student persistence and drop-out in further education', LSDA free download at www.lsneducation.org.uk/pubs/index.aspx (type the author's name into the 'detailed search').

Rogers, C. (1961) *On Becoming a Person*, London: Constable.

Rogers, C. (1995) *On Becoming a Teacher: A Therapist's View of Psychotherapy*, Boston, MA: Marriner Books.

Useful websites

www.qca.org.uk/qca_6444.aspx is useful to explore for key skills.

www.keyskills4u.com has excellent key skills teaching material.

49

Evaluating courses and quality improvement

Monitoring, evaluation and review of courses

Like your teaching, the courses or 'subjects' you teach should be subjected to self-corrective feedback; it is the only way they will improve. I have seen even well-established and successful courses substantially improved by this process.

Monitoring

Monitoring is the day-to-day checking and improving of a course, with the aim of making relatively minor changes and improvements. It can be carried out informally, but best practice is to have weekly or fortnightly 'course team meetings', attended by all the tutors on the course and a few student representatives. The day-to-day running of the course is discussed, and improvements agreed. For example, business at my last meeting included two requests by student representatives: one for more coordination of assignments, so that they were more evenly spread over the course; and the other for more copies of a certain coursebook to be placed in the library. Arrangements were made by tutors for a chemistry assignment to be 'written up' on computer to give the students more information technology experience, and there was plenty of routine administrative business. What could be done to improve the performance of problem students was discussed without the student representatives present.

> Some teachers advocate having an open course diary, or an open suggestion folder for assignments, worksheet activities, etc. Students are invited or requested to write comments and suggestions for the improvement of the course or course materials, as the course progresses.

Less formally, knowledge of students' work and learning rate, and of the ideas and irritations of students and tutors, all helps in monitoring a course. Monitoring is a natural improvement process that any professional would undertake without thinking, but the most substantial changes result from an evaluation and review.

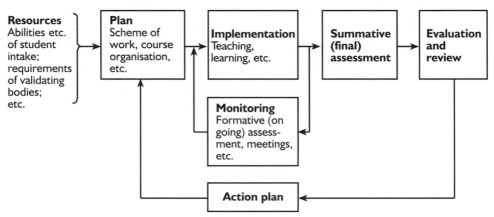

Flow diagram to show monitoring, evaluation and review of courses

Evaluation and review

An evaluation and review is carried out at the end of a course; the aim is to arrive at an informed decision about the course's effectiveness, or some aspect of it, and to use this to make suggestions for improvement. (A short course may be evaluated by asking students to write down one positive aspect of the course, and one way in which they felt it could have been improved.) Your institution's quality system or self-assessment/evaluation system will usually state what *must* be reviewed, but you can of course go further. The following topics are amongst those commonly considered (though clearly any aspect of the course may be evaluated):

• aims and objectives
• teaching strategies
• assignments, worksheets, textbooks, etc.
• course organisation
• course documentation (e.g. student coursebook or handbook)
• resources
• assessment
• learning outcomes, including a comparison of students' entry qualifications etc., with their subsequent performance on the course, drop-out rate, etc.

It would often take too long to consider all these points in detail in any one year, so the evaluation may only cover key and troublesome aspects. A more systematic approach is to draw up a timetable, so that every aspect of the course is evaluated over, say, four years. Evidence for the evaluation can come from:

- students' performance on assessment tasks and coursework
- reports from verifiers, moderators or similar external scrutiny (see below)
- the opinion of teachers, support staff (e.g. technicians) and students on the course – including those who dropped out of the course
- minutes of course team meetings, and other monitoring information
- consultation with industry or commerce if it is a vocational course (especially if it involves work experience)
- consultation with those initiating the training, if the course has been commercially commissioned
- consultation with other members of staff who do not actually teach on the course – for example, the appropriate head of department, and possibly also library staff and those responsible for quality control or equal opportunity policy.

Opinions may be collected by discussion, memo, questionnaires or by structured interview.

Questionnaires and structured interviews

A student questionnaire is a popular 'evaluation instrument'. It is usually completed anonymously, and ideally includes students who have left the course, if there are any. Your institution may use a standard questionnaire; if not, devise your own.

There are three commonly used methods for collecting the students' responses. A space may be left under the question in which the student is invited to write; alternatively, one of the following methods may be adopted – both have the advantage that the responses can be easily quantified:

- *The question may invite a yes/no or a tick/cross response.* For example: Did you find the section on computer programming useful? Yes/No
- *The student is asked to agree or disagree with a statement on a given scale.* For example:

	strongly agree			strongly disagree
The computer programming section was useful.	1	2	3	4	5

Often questionnaires mix response styles. The questions asked should, of course, be related to the main aims of your course, so you must devise the questions yourself.

Your questionnaire should aim to discover whether you are meeting the aims and objectives of the course, and any other priorities that you set for it (e.g. cost, enjoyment, student progression). Also, you should try to uncover any problems with the course. Typical topics and questions are shown below.

- *Admission.* Were you given sufficient guidance in choosing this course? Was it the right course for you? Did the course differ in any way from what you expected?

- *Resources*. Were the classrooms adequate? Did you have adequate access to library, computers, refectory, lavatories, sports facilities … ?
- *Course content*. Can you give an example of an activity you thought particularly interesting/useful? Was there enough student activity? Were activities sufficiently varied? Did you enjoy the assignments/practical work? Were they sufficiently work-related? Were you clear what was expected? Was adequate time given? Was adequate work set? Was content sufficiently challenging, or was it too easy or too hard? Were you actively involved in your own learning? Did you enjoy the teaching methods chosen? Would you have preferred others?
- *Learning*. Questions on the students' feelings about their learning are sometimes useful, e.g. Do you now feel confident enough to book a hotel room in French?
- *Assessment*. Was work fairly marked? Do you feel you were kept aware of how you were doing on the course?
- *Course management*. Do you feel the course was reasonably well organised? Was the course literature adequate? Was the induction useful/satisfactory?
- *General*. Do you feel the teachers on the course were effective? Have you enjoyed the course? State two things that were particularly good about the course. State two things about the course that could be improved. Please give the course an overall mark out of 10.

It is important to choose your questions to suit the learners – for example, younger learners may need simple, direct questions. Mature learners can themselves suggest questions for the questionnaire, and contribute valuable ideas for improvement. Whatever you do, make sure you include the last four 'general' topics from the list above, and leave some space for unstructured responses (e.g. inviting 'Any general comments?' under each heading in the questionnaire).

An alternative to the questionnaire is the structured interview, a one-to-one interview based on prepared questions. This may be a useful method for obtaining the opinion of former students, employers, etc.

Customer satisfaction is important, but it is learning that really counts. So don't always take the student responses too literally; their opinion needs to be interpreted – but not ignored!

> '*Success is overrated. Everyone craves it despite daily proof that man's real genius lies in quite the opposite direction. Incompetence is what we are good at: it is the quality that marks us off from animals and we should learn to revere it.*'
>
> Stephen Pile, *Heroic Failures*

Action plan

Once the course has been evaluated, suggestions are drawn up for its improvement.

This is called the action plan; without it, the evaluation would have been largely a waste of time. Ideally, someone should be made responsible for carrying out or overseeing each improvement, and a deadline should be set for the implementation of the improvement.

Then, in your next evaluation, you will find you have a *different* set of problems!

Verification and moderation – how fair is my marking?

We need to be sure marking is fair and consistent. This is not easy, especially if there is more than one teacher marking work on the same course.

Standards need to be consistent between institutions too. It would not be fair on students if a pass in one institution would have gained a merit in another, or if assessment procedures such as the time and help students had to complete coursework varied. Also, students need helpful and informative feedback on their work in order to improve, not just grades or marks.

These are 'Quality Assurance' issues which are usually addressed by 'moderation', 'verification' or 'standardisation', terms which are often interchangeable in practice.

- To 'moderate' means to make sure marks given are not too high or low.
- To 'verify' means to ensure marks and procedures are true and correct.
- To 'standardise' means to ensure marking and procedures conform to a standard.

But how do you do it? Here are some common approaches; decide which would be best for the courses on which you teach or are a student, then compare this with what actually happens.

In each case below, teachers teaching the same subject or course meet together to consider assessment procedures and marks. They might look over a random sample of students' work, perhaps some weak, some average and some strong work. They might discuss work on a grade borderline. They are probably from the same institution, but might come from different ones.

They might use the following strategies:

a Discuss procedures and how to interpret assessment tasks or criteria.

b Look at each other's marked work to consider the accuracy of the marks given and the quality of the feedback (students need 'medal and mission' feedback – see Chapters 6 and 43).

c Use blind second marking: a marked piece of work, but not the assessment decisions or comments, is given to another teacher to mark. The marks and comments are then compared.

d An experienced teacher in the institution with a verifier's or moderator's qualification looks carefully at marked work and reports on the quality of the teachers' responses.

e An external moderator or verifier might visit an institution to do the same as 'd' above. They might visit a number of institutions and so have experience of procedures, standards and good practice elsewhere.

> *You might consider getting a moderator's or verifier's qualifications yourself when you have sufficient experience. It's a short course.*

It is common to complain of the above procedures and to find them burdensome. However, with the right attitude you can learn a great deal. Don't be afraid to ask questions of other teachers – 'What exactly does "justify" mean in the context of this question?' 'Would you expect a graph for question 10?'

Merit or distinction.

Benchmarking – how am I doing?

How well do you teach compared to other teachers? Would your students have done better or worse if they had studied at a different institution, with another teacher at your own institution, or if they had studied with you last year? There is a mass of data to help you answer these questions, but the data is harder to interpret than most people realise.

A common approach is to compare your results with those of other teachers, using a figure such as your pass rate, or the percentage of your students who stayed the course and completed (retention rate). Such figures indicate how well you and your students performed and so are called 'performance indicators'. They are very crude measures, but very important ones for students, their families and college managers. Funding is often affected by institutional performance indicators, and continued underperformance can force a course, or even a school or college, to close.

Performance indicators are expressed in percentages and the most common are:

In schools:

- the percentage of GCSE students who get 5 grade Cs or better
- the percentage achieving level 5 in the SATs
- the contextual value-added figure (see the box on page 572).

In colleges and school sixth forms:

- the *retention rate* – the percentage of students who are retained and so complete the course
- the *achievement rate* – the percentage pass rate of those who completed the course
- the *success rate* – the percentage of students who passed, out of all those who started the course. Those who leave the course count as failed.

In both schools and colleges, inspection grades act as performance indicators – see the box below (page 572).

For full definitions of these and other statistical measures, visit the Learning and Skills Council (LSC) website (www.lsc.gov.uk/providers/data/statistics/success). Here you will find links to 'FE Qualification Level Success Rates Data'. Google the phrase in quotes if you have difficulty. Other data here will help you, including documents explaining the meanings of terms and other background information.

For 'school and college achievement and attainment tables', Google the phrase in quotes or go to www.dcsf.gov.uk/performancetables

Once you have performance indicators for your course or subject, you can compare your performance with how successful the same course was last year, or with average figures in your institution. This is called 'internal benchmarking'. For example:

> 'My pass rate this year is 80%, but last year it was 78%.'
> 'Our pass rate is not as good as other courses in our institution.'

If you compare your performance indicators with the average for *other* institutions, it is called 'external benchmarking'. For example, a school could compare its GCSE results with these 2007 national average results:

- 46.5% pupils got 5 GCSEs grade C or above, including English and maths.
- 51% of girls and 42.1% of boys reached the above benchmark.
- In Sutton, 64.9% reached this benchmark, while in Knowsley the figure was only 26.3%.
- In 1997, 37% of pupils achieved this same benchmark.

Note the improvement over the last 10 years, and that there is regional variation.

> A 'benchmark' is a surveyor's mark, on a wall on a building site, for example. It is used as a datum to compare heights. By analogy, figures used for comparison are also called 'benchmarks'.

Below I have quoted the 2005–6 average performance indicators (i.e. benchmarks) for qualifications in the post-compulsory or lifelong learning sector (FE colleges, sixth form colleges, art colleges, etc.):

- retention rate   87.0%
- achievement rate   87.6%
- success rate   76.2%

Like school performance indicators for students aged 11–16, these figures have improved remarkably over the last decade, but almost a quarter of students starting a course still do not complete it successfully. We have a lot of work to do! Later we will see how performance indicators and benchmarking can help or hinder your own and your institution's improvement, so this story is not over yet.

> 'You must be the change you wish to see in the world.'
>
> Mahatma Gandhi

The self-assessment of courses and institutions

Institutions learn and improve in just the way that people do! In Chapter 31, we saw that in order to learn from experience we need to use the Kolb cycle:

- *Do* it.
- *Review* how it went.
- *Learn* how you might do it better, in theory.
- Apply what you have learned, then *do* it again.
- *Repeat* the cycle.

We saw that it is easy to miss a part of the cycle and so not to learn. The problem is not just forgetfulness, but also a failure to review critically and honestly, and a failure to apply what you have learned because it takes courage to change. There can also be a failure to believe in the possibility of improvement affecting the whole cycle.

Chapter 46 applied Kolb's cycle to learning to teach and to writing your reflective learning journal. Chapter 48 applied the cycle to tutoring. In this chapter, we see how the Kolb cycle is used to improve a course or institution.

Institutions learn just like people

All post-compulsory institutions, such as school sixth forms, FE colleges, sixth form colleges and specialist colleges such as colleges of art, agriculture or colleges for blind students, are required to 'self-assess'. Schools go through a near-identical process called 'self-evaluation'. These terms are something of a misnomer, as they actually require the institution to go round the entire Kolb cycle, not just to review. The requirement comes from the Inspectorate and, in the case of the post-16 sector, also from the Learning and Skills Council, which funds such institutions. If you work in a school, take 'self-assessment' below to also mean 'self-evaluation'.

'Self-assessment' is usually a yearly cycle. Almost every aspect of the institution should self-assess: courses; support services; tutorial systems; resourcing; management; yes, even caretakers. Objective data are used to review performance and to track improvement whenever possible. Are more students using the resource centre? Are more passing maths?

When an institution is inspected, the first interest is the institution's ability to self-assess or self-evaluate. This determines its capacity to improve. A post-16 institution prepares a self-assessment using the inspectors' 'Common Inspection Framework', which asks five questions and grades the whole institution (and its parts, such as curriculum areas) on a scale of 1 to 4. Schools fill in a 32-page self-evaluation form which contains the same questions, and many others, including some on health and wellbeing of pupils. Colleges provide detailed data on student achievement in a similar way.

The Common Inspection Framework questions and grades are:

1. How well do learners achieve? 2. How effective are teaching, training and learning? 3. How well do programmes and activities meet the needs and interests of learners? 4. How well are learners guided and supported? 5 How effective are leadership and management in raising achievement and supporting all learners?	Each question is graded separately: Grade 1 Outstanding Grade 2 Good Grade 3 Satisfactory Grade 4 Inadequate

Notice the great emphasis on learning and learners' needs and support. Even leaders and managers are held to account exclusively on this issue.

So the institution inspects itself, then an inspection checks the quality of this self-assessment or self-evaluation. This will include whether old action plans have been well attended to, and whether the new one is sound.

> *Institutions learn just like people, by going round the Kolb cycle. Why is this?*

Creating and interpreting performance indicators

Whether you work in a school or a college, you will play a part in collecting data for the self-assessment or self-evaluation, and for other planning and review cycles. You may be required to collect and to provide data on attendance, student achievement, student action-planning cycles, the take-up of learning support and so on. Institutions differ in what data are collected and how they are recorded and processed; find out how it is done where you are.

There are problems with performance indicators that are not well understood, even by government ministers or the media. The problems are avoidable though, as we will see.

First, institutions differ so much that you would expect their performance indicators to differ too. For example, even if you correct for prior achievement, the performance indicators for schools are known to be affected by issues including:

- Whether the school selects students, overtly or otherwise.
- Social class – students with professional parents do better than those from a 'working-class' background.
- The degree of social deprivation. The proportion of students entitled to free school meals is one measure of this. (Deprivation overlaps with social class above.)
- The ethnicity mix – for example, students of a Chinese or Indian origin do better than 'white' students, who do better than those with a Bangladeshi origin. This is probably largely due to the extent to which the student's family/ culture values education, and believes that academic success is possible.
- The proportion of students who do not have English as their first language.
- The gender mix – girls do better than boys at GCSE.
- The proportion of pupils with special educational needs.
- Mobility – proportion of students who have moved school at a non-standard time.
- In care – proportion of students who are in care.
- Etc.

> *The government's education department acknowledges the above factors affect performance indicators. They have developed a 'contextual value added' (CVA) system for schools to try to adjust for all but the first one or two issues above. Type CVA into the search box at www.dcsf.gov.uk*
>
> *A post-16 CVA is being piloted: www.dcsf.gov.uk/performancetables/ pilotks5_07/a2.shtml*

> *'Remember no one can make you feel inferior without your consent.'*
> Eleanor Roosevelt

Post-16 institutions suffer all these issues except possibly the first one. However, they can enrol students on a course that is appropriate to their prior learning, so the prior learning of their intake has less impact on whole-college achievement than it does in schools, where pretty much all students work for the same qualifications – GCSEs.

Below are some big problems with performance indicators being used as an *external* benchmark.

- *They ignore context.* Because the factors bullet-pointed above affect achievement, it is not always easy to know whether your pass rate is good or bad mostly because of these factors, or mostly because of your good, or bad, teaching and tutoring. Only CVA performance indicators consider context; however, they do suffer the problems below.

- *They can create complacency*. Roughly half of teachers will find that their pass rate or CVA, for example, is better than the national average, and so they might think, 'That's okay then, no improvement is necessary'.
- *They can create disempowerment*. Consider the other half of teachers who find their pass rate is worse than average. How will they respond? They might excuse themselves by saying the problem is not their teaching, but the type of student they get, the deprived social neighbourhood, or the bad senior management at their institution, poor resourcing, etc. So they might argue that there is no point improving their teaching or tutoring as the real problem lies elsewhere. This is a false assumption, as we will see. (Chapter 43 describes why complacency and disempowerment occur with students when they are graded.)
- *They don't tell you how to improve*. They might indicate whether your greatest weakness is retention or achievement. Or they might tell an institution which courses or subjects do least well, and so where it needs to improve. But they don't say how.

> *External benchmarking can also detrimentally affect institutions, which might spend more effort fiddling the indicator than in improving overall performance.*

For all these reasons, the best performance indicator for a teacher is their own data from last year, and similar data in their own institution. The social and other issues bulleted on page 572 usually don't change much from one year to the next. So, if your teaching and tutoring improves, your results should improve too – and vice versa!

> *Hurworth School in Darlington increased the proportion of students who got five grade Cs or better at GCSE from 38% to 96% in nine years. The percentage of students achieving level 5 SATs results increased from 60% to about 90%. They concentrated on teaching and learning which inspection showed was 97% satisfactory or better, and particularly on 'assertive mentoring', rather like 'catch them before they fall' in Chapter 48. Darlington has its share of socially and economically deprived households.*

This doesn't solve all the problems, as year groups differ, and last year's data do not usually tell you how to improve. However, one's own data are probably a better benchmark than other people's data. A better approach still is to focus on how to improve rather than on the data.

Don't let benchmarking distract you from the key question – how to improve. Teaching and tutoring are too damned difficult to get perfect, and every teacher and every course can improve, whatever their performance indicators.

> *'Big shots are only little shots who keep shooting.'*
>
> Christopher Morley, writer

How to improve

Teachers are learners too! Like your students, you learn most from informative 'medal and mission' feedback, as described in Chapters 6 and 43. No matter how good or bad we are, we need a 'medal', informing us what we do well, and a 'mission', telling us how we could improve. We get these mainly from:

* reflecting carefully
* self-assessment and quality reports
* lesson observations
* inspection reports
* student surveys
* moderator or verifier reports
* our own gut feelings
* appraisal and managers' opinions.

The evidence is overwhelming (Petty 2006) that some factors have an exceptionally high effect on student achievement. These factors include:

* Active teaching methods that set open, challenging tasks, requiring reasoning rather than only reproduction. (Chapter 1)
* Informative feedback to the student and the teacher on how well that task was done. (Chapters 6, 43 and 24)
* 'Catch them before they fall' strategies to monitor student progress better and provide personalised action plans, with support for those who need it, as described in Chapter 48 and summarised on page 550.

Professor John Hattie has looked at masses of evidence to show that the first two factors have much greater effects than any of those that differ between institutions. See the box on Hurworth School on page 574 to see the power of the third factor.

> *'God doesn't require us to succeed; he only requires that you try.'*
>
> Mother Teresa

The next chapter 'Are you an active or a passive teacher?' considers attitudes to improvement further.

Your contribution to self-assessment or self-evaluation

Remember self-assessment or self-evaluation are improvement processes that go right round the Kolb cycle. Looking back over this chapter, what's your role?

- Take part in internal verification and ask questions of verifiers, etc., to clarify your understanding of tasks and of marking.
- Ask your students to do questionnaires that ask them about your teaching. Institutional questionnaires won't go into enough detail to help you improve.
- Evaluate and reflect on your own teaching, and on the courses you teach (see Chapters 46 and 49).
- Have a look at performance indicators, but pay more attention to your own institution's data from last year than to national averages.
- Pay most attention of all to how you could improve – even if your results are brilliant. *Teaching Today* and *Evidence Based Teaching* both have a lot of detail on this.
- Remember that the biggest influences on achievement are setting challenging tasks (Chapter 1); giving, getting or ensuring informative feedback (Chapters 6 and 43); and 'catching them before they fall' (tutorial monitoring and action planning, etc. – Chapter 48).

> *'A positive attitude may not solve all your problems, but it will annoy enough people to make it worthwhile.'*
>
> Herm Albright, writer

Continual professional development (CPD)

Once you have drawn up an action plan about how to improve, think about what support might help. Do you need to know more about integrating key skills into a programme, or more about effective study skills teaching? There might be courses you could go on, books you could read, Internet sites you could study or other teachers in your institution you could ask for advice. You might want to observe another teacher doing something you would like to develop, or visit a similar course to your own in another institution. This is called continual professional development (CPD). Some CPD will be to meet institutional needs – a course on the new quality system, for example – but ideally *you* should direct most of it. It's what you do that makes the difference; what improves this will make the biggest difference. Teaching is a continual learning experience, and that's what keeps it fresh and interesting.

Are you a team player?

Evaluating and improving courses is very much a team effort, and being part of a teaching team can be one of the great pleasures of teaching, and one of its greatest challenges! When I first started teaching, I had a very senior member of staff on my teaching team and I had to ask him for progress reports on my students. He was sometimes very late in providing these and I wondered for years how I should have approached him about this, as I never had the nerve to confront him with the difficulties he was causing me, and my students. Then I gradually began to realise that most of the principles of teaching applied to managing team members as well.

Good managers give medals and missions to their team, as we considered in Chapters 6 and 43; they require them to self-assess and to set themselves targets, as we considered in Chapter 48. Team members often need to be helped to learn from experience, as we considered in Chapters 31, 34 and 46, and so on.

If you find it hard to persuade team members to pull their weight or come up with the goods in time, then try to appeal to the values we considered in Chapter 45. Which of the following stances do you think is most persuasive?

- I need the reports by Monday.
- The quality system says the reports should be in by Monday.
- I want my students to have a full report book and the benefit of your comments.

The student experience has more authority than you, or college systems.

You might think it is difficult to give a medal and a mission to a teacher, especially if they are senior to you. But suppose you ask everyone on your team to self-assess their teaching on your course, and how your course is going in general (there will almost certainly be an institutional expectation that this takes place). Your team are bound to come up with strengths and weaknesses, and these should suggest medals and missions to you. You will probably have your own ideas too, and the students certainly will have.

Do tell each teacher on your team what you appreciate about what they have done for your students. They will not think this patronising if you are specific about the strengths of their teaching, as described in Chapter 6. They will feel valued and appreciated and this is hugely important to us all. Consider whether you should do this informally and privately, or formally and publicly. But do it.

Then suppose you give a frank self-criticism of your own teaching and of the course, from the students' point of view. And then you ask each teacher in your team to think about some ideas for improving their own teaching, and the course in general. If they feel valued by you they will not feel criticised and defensive of the status quo, but forward-looking and positive, and, taking the lead from you, focused on the students.

If you appeal to values, and especially to the student experience, then it gives you a special authority, and if you always justify your decisions from the point of view of the benefits to students, you will build a cohesive, effective and even inspired team of teachers around you. There is much more on managing teaching teams in my *Evidence Based Teaching*.

Checklist for evaluating lessons and courses

❏ Have you found out about the system for evaluating the courses you teach on?

❏ Are you going to evaluate your contribution to the courses you teach on?

❏ Have you used internal benchmarking to see whether you are improving?

❏ Have you included the student voice in the evaluation system?

❏ Have you ideas on how to improve?

❏ Do you appeal to values when working in a team?

Further reading

Martinez, P. (2001) *College Improvement: The Voice of Teachers and Managers*, London: LSDA free download at www.lsneducation.org.uk/pubs/index.aspx (type the author's name into the 'detailed search').

O'Connell, B. (ed.) (2002) *The Runshaw Way: Values Drive Behaviour*, Leyland: Runshaw College. This document was produced to disseminate Runshaw College's approach, as part of the Beacon College scheme.

Petty, G. (2006) *Evidence Based Teaching*, Cheltenham: Nelson Thornes.

Reece, I. and Walker, S. (2007) *A Practical Guide to Teaching, Training and Learning* (6th edition), Tyne and Wear: Business Education Publishers.

50

How to teach and remain sane

Most novice teachers expect teaching to be difficult – and then find it is impossible! It is impossible to give your best to every student all the time; impossible to avoid ever making mistakes; and impossible always to understand why students behave as they do. It is impossible to teach every student everything, and impossible to remain calm, reasonable and professional at all times.

There have been times during the writing of this book when I have found myself feeling guilty. It describes best practice, as a book of this sort should, but it is a counsel of perfection. Don't assume that you will be able to meet its every suggestion at all times. You will be fortunate indeed if you are given the preparation time and the other resources required to do the job as well as you would like.

Try to use your time as efficiently as possible. Save and improve your worksheets, games and lesson plans from year to year. Organisation saves a great deal of time, but it might take you two or three years to get what you need even roughly sorted out. Can you share some of this work with a colleague? For at least some of your needs, is suitable material already available in the department or on the Internet?

Efficient use of time

Your time is your life, so spend it wisely. Try to prioritise tasks on the basis of both urgency *and* importance. Make time for what you know is really important, like talking to your students, and pursuing those personal goals you outlined after reading Chapter 10.

Organisation saves time. The ideal teacher organiser is a set of folders which contains:

- a timetable
- seating plans for all your classes
- schemes of work
- a set of topic plans, or an 'ideas bank' of teaching strategies for each topic you teach – e.g. games, activities and experiments to try, interesting things to mention
- lesson plans
- monitoring copies of worksheets, tests and assignments, etc., on which you can write improvements for next year
- assessment strategies and mark schemes
- a folder of resources, such as notes, handouts and OHTs
- a year planner with dates for submission of coursework, term dates, dates for reports and so on.

> ## TO LOOK AFTER YOUR VOICE:
> * Drink water, as this lubricates your larynx.
> * Don't talk or shout over noisy classes. Attract attention by clapping, then wait for silence, as explained in Chapter 8.
> * Coughing puts a strain on the larynx, so do it gently, or, better still, drink or just swallow.
> * Use 'teaching without talking'! See the active learning page of www.geoff-petty.com

Are you an active or a passive teacher?

In Chapter 5 on motivation, we looked at passive and active learners, but there are passive and active teachers too! If you are an active teacher, your mottoes are 'Take control' and 'I can make a difference'. You take responsibility by actively searching for difficulties and problems, and by trying to put these right. If 'things don't work out', you try harder, and if this doesn't work, *you change your strategy*.

For example, if you are having trouble getting work in from students, you talk to the class about it, and stress the importance of handing work in on time. If this doesn't work, you try an alternative strategy; for example, you might ask students why they have the problem and put more pressure on them. Then you might try splitting the assignments to make them shorter and starting them off in class. You might try monitoring the students' work halfway through the assignments, and asking other staff for advice, and so on. In short, you are adaptive, responsive and continually looking for improvement.

If you are a passive teacher, your mottoes are 'It's not my fault' and 'There's nothing I can do'. You believe the problems depend on factors beyond your control, such as the students' innate capabilities or attitudes, the nature of your subject or the resources put at your disposal. If 'things don't work out', you blame such external factors as your students, your manager or limited resources, and say there is nothing you can do.

Research shows that while thinking about difficulties, active and passive people have a very different focus:

Active people are focused on:	*While passive people are focused on:*
the process: 'What should I do next?'	**likely negative outcomes:** 'It'll be a disaster.'
improvement: 'How could we do it better?'	**perfection:** 'We'll never get this right.'
the positive: 'At least that worked well.'	**the negative:** 'That was awful.'
learning: 'What can we learn from this?'	**blaming:** 'It was the student's fault.'

You can be active or passive towards difficulties at work; in relationships; in child-rearing; in personal problems; in every imaginable field! Not surprisingly, research shows that taking control with the 'active' approach is a hugely important factor, deciding effectiveness, creativity and your happiness in all these fields. There is a strong link between the passive approach and unhappiness, or even depression.

You have a choice whether to be active or passive, but the former is much better for you and for your students. That is not to say that some problems are not caused by others, and by circumstances beyond your control. Some are. But whatever caused these problems, *all* those with influence need to take an active response to addressing them. You should make your views known to people who are making your job difficult, but you also need to explore what you can do to limit the damage caused by these difficulties.

Remaining active in your response to persistent difficulties is not easy, and some teachers sink into cynicism. This is a corrosive state of mind of no use to teacher or student. So talk to others about your problems. If they are experiencing the same difficulties, then that is reassuring; if they are not, then you may have something to learn from them. It is not an admission of weakness to seek advice and support, it is a measure of your active professionalism. I do it often.

In Freedom to Learn, *Carl Rogers quotes research which shows that when teaching your heartbeat rises by 12 beats per minute.*

Your first year of full-time teaching is very likely to be the hardest year's work you ever do. Don't do more than you need in the classroom; remember, the students should be doing the work – not you! Teaching is acknowledged to be a very stressful job, so make sure you get plenty of exercise, and don't rely on temporary solutions like smoking or drinking to unwind. Allow yourself time to relax without feeling guilty about it; put tasks into an order of priority; and learn to say 'no' when you know you already have too much on your plate. And don't forget to talk about your problems with others.

Being active is one thing; having unreasonable expectations of yourself is quite another. If you were an employer of teachers, what would you expect of them? Expect no more of yourself than this. You have a duty to yourself and to your family, as well as to your students.

All that can be expected of you is that you do your best in the circumstances, especially when you are not responsible for the circumstances!

Further reading

Adair, J. (1996) *Effective Time Management: How to Save Time and Spend It Wisely*, London: Pan Books.

*Argyle, M. (1987) *The Psychology of Happiness*, London: Routledge. Shows how taking control is important to happiness and effectiveness.

*Nelson-Jones, R. (1996) *Effective Thinking Skills*, London: Cassell. On using thinking skills to help with difficulties of any kind.

O'Connell, B. (ed.) (2002) *The Runshaw Way: Values Drive Behaviour*, Leyland: Runshaw College. This document was produced to disseminate Runshaw College's approach, as part of the Beacon College scheme.

Appendix 1

Standards for the lifelong learning sector

These apply in the lifelong learning, post-compulsory or further education sector standards. See Appendix 3 if you work in a school.

How to use this table: Please download from **www.lluk.org/3066.htm** a document called: 'New overarching professional standards for teachers, tutors and trainers in the lifelong learning sector'. This gives the standards that teacher qualifications are designed to meet. The tables below give only the numbers of the standards; the text can be found in the downloaded document.

Key to these tables: In the 'Chapters' column, the most relevant chapters are given first.

In refers to the introduction to part 2. **Own** refers to your own institution or your own specialist area.

Domain A: Professional values and practice	Chapters
AS 1	7, 47, 48, 41, 11, 43
AS 2	45, 47, 48,
AS 3	7, 47, 48, 45, 41, In
AS 4	46, 49
AS 5	47, 48, 7
AS 6	7
AS 7	46, 49

Domain A: Professional knowledge and understanding	Chapters	Professional practice	Chapters
AK 1.1	5	AP 1.1	41, 47, 48, 33, 34
AK 2.1	45, 33, 34	AP 2.1	5, 45, 7
AK 2.2	45, 34	AP 2.2	46, 43, 45
AK 3.1	In, 7, 41, 48, 49	AP 3.1	46, 49, 7
AK 4.1	43, 1, 2, 3, 4	AP 4.1	1–4, 43

Domain A: Professional knowledge and understanding	Chapters	Professional practice	Chapters
AK 4.2	45	AP 4.2	46, 49
AK 4.3	46, 49	AP 4.3	46, 49
AK 5.1	47, 48	AP 5.1	47, 48, 49
AK 5.2		AP 5.2	43, 47
AK 6.1	7	AP 6.1	7
AK 6.2		AP 6.2	7
AK 7.1	46, 49	AP 7.1	41
AK 7.2	49	AP 7.2	49
AK 7.3	49 + whole book!	AP 7.3	49

Domain B: Learning and teaching	Chapters
AS 1–5	See above
BS 1	7, 5, 47, 48, In
BS 2	46 + whole book!
BS 3	4, 11–15
BS 4	49
BS 5	In, 19, 35, 36

Domain B: Learning and teaching	Chapters	Professional practice	Chapters
BK 1.1	7, 8, 9	BP 1.1	7, 8, 9
BK 1.2	7, 8, 9	BP 1.2	7, 8, 9
BK 1.3	5	BP 1.3	43, 33, 34
BK 2.1	1–4, 38	BP 2.1	37–40, In
BK 2.2	39	BP 2.2	33, 25–34
BK 2.3	33, 16–33	BP 2.3	In, 33
BK 2.4	In	BP 2.4	11, 34, 41
BK 2.5	41	BP 2.5	11, 34, 47
BK 2.6	11, 47	BP 2.6	46, 49
BK 2.7	46, 49	BP 2.7	46
BK 3.1	4, 35, 36	BP 3.1	In, 35, 36
BK 3.2	24, 14	BP 3.2	14, 24
BK 3.3	11, 14	BP 3.3	11–15
BK 3.4	7–12	BP 3.4	7, 46

Domain B: Learning and teaching	Chapters	Professional practice	Chapters
BK 3.5	Own	BP 3.5	Own, 36
BK 4.1	48	BP 4.1	48
BK 5.1	35, 36	BP 5.1	35, 36
BK 5.2	35, 36	BP 5.2	35, 36

Domain D: Planning for learning	Chapters
AS 1–5	See above
DS 1	7, 47, 48, In
DS 2	46, 47, 48
DS 3	46, 49

Domain D: Planning for learning	Chapters	Professional practice	Chapters
DK 1.1	41, 47, 48, In	DP 1.1	41, 47, 48, 7
DK 1.2	37–40	DP 1.2	37–40, 36
DK 1.3	41	DP 1.3	41
DK 2.1	47, 48, 34	DP 2.1	46, 49
DK 2.2	47, 48, 34	DP 2.2	47, 48
DK 3.1	46, 49	DP 3.1	46
DK 3.2	49	DP 3.2	49

Domain E: Assessment for learning	Chapters
AS 1–5	See above
ES 1	6, 43, 44, 47
ES 2	6, 43, 44
ES 3	6, 43
ES 4	6, 43, 47
ES 5	48, 49

Domain E: Assessment for learning	Chapters	Professional practice	Chapters
EK 1.1	43, 47, 44	EP 1.1	43, 47, 44
EK 1.2	43, 47, 44	EP 1.2	43, 47, 44
EK 1.3	36, 43	EP 1.3	36, 43
EK 2.1	43, 44	EP 2.1	43, 44, 47
EK 2.2	43, 44, 49	EP 2.2	49
EK 2.3	Own	EP 2.3	Own
EK 2.4	49	EP 2.4	49
EK 3.1	43	EP 3.1	43
EK 3.2	7, 43, 44	EP 3.2	7, 43, 47, 48
EK 4.1	6, 43, 24, 14	EP 4.1	24, 43
EK 4.2	49	EP 4.2	49
EK 5.1	49	EP 5.1	49
EK 5.2	44	EP 5.2	48, 49
EK 5.3	44, 48	EP 5.3	43, 41

Domain F: Access and progression	Chapters
AS 1–5	See above
FS 1	48
FS 2	48
FS 3	Own
FS 4	48

Domain F: Access and progression	Chapters	Professional practice	Chapters
FK 1.1	48	FP 1.1	47, 48
FK 1.2	48	FP 1.2	48
FK 2.1	48, 7	FP 2.1	48
FK 3.1	Own	FP 3.1	Own
FK 4.1	48	FP 4.1	48
FK 4.2	48	FP 4.2	48, 49

Postscript. It is dismaying to note that some of the most vital chapters in this book, from the point of classroom teaching, do not figure in these standards tables. The standards barely address the effective use of teaching methods described in Chapters 11–34, and give over much attention to the institutional preoccupations in Chapters 45–49. The evidence is overwhelming that Part 2 has huge effects on achievement.

Appendix 2

Differentiation strategies

Differentiation used to be called 'mixed-ability teaching'; then they discovered that it was not just ability that could be 'mixed'! Differentiation is adopting strategies that ensure success in learning for all, by accommodating individual differences of any kind. This includes whole-class strategies specifically designed to engage weak or demotivated learners.

What follows outlines the main differentiation strategies and refers to where these can be found in the book, with the chapter number(s) given in brackets for each strategy. See also www.geoffpetty.com. There is hardly a chapter in this book that does not deal with differentiation in some way, so this is by way of a summary of key points only.

Differentiation by task, by outcome and by time allowed

It is what the *learner* does, not what the teacher does, that creates learning, so the task is key. Remember that some students need more time than others.

- Using constructivist methods that require all learners (even the demotivated ones!) to form constructs (1)
- Building ladders of tasks (1 and 28)
- Breaking down high-order tasks and teaching them by bridging (31 and 28)
- Using a mix of mastery and developmental tasks (37 and 1)
- Stretching the more able learners, at least towards the end of activities, lessons and worksheets, by setting:
  - some open (rather than closed) questions and tasks (14 and 18)
  - some high-order tasks (1 and 37)
- Allowing students to take the time they need by making use of resource-based learning (41), mastery learning (43), independent learning (33), information and learning technology (ILT) (36) and self-directed or individualised learning (34 and 42)
- Differentiating resources – for example, recommending and using a range of resources, from level 2 to level 4, on a level 3 course (12)
- Allowing students to present work on a given topic in different ways – for example, as a written piece of work, as a presentation, mind-map or web page (36)
- Using high-order questioning on Bloom's taxonomy (1 and 14)
- Using simple high-order tasks to ensure that weak students have 'all Bloom's bits' (1), and, for example, using 'decisions, decisions' (19)

- Holding all students accountable for their learning (24, 14 and others)

Differentiation by accommodating different learning styles and support needs

- Using methods that suit a wide range of learning styles and individual preferences in teaching methods (Introduction to Part 2 and 32)
- Using group work, and setting tasks where students can help each other (18)
- Making explicit use of peer assessment and peer support (43)
- Diagnosing individual needs and setting individual targets to meet them (41, 47 and 48; also learning loops in 43)
- Accommodating the needs of students with specific learning difficulties such as dyslexia (4, 7 and 32)
- Valuing all individuals (7, 4, 45 and many other chapters)
- Buddying up students who can help each other, or using 'learning teams' of students given the goal of helping each other (33)
- Integrating learning support into your classes (48)

Differentiation by setting individual tasks and targets

This involves treating each learner as an individual, not just as a member of a class.

- Using learning loops (6 and especially 43)
- Using self-assessment to develop targets (43)
- Setting individualised, challenging but attainable targets (48)
- Individualising instruction (41)

Appendix 3

QTS standards for those training to teach in schools

For Qualified Teacher Status, you must prove competence in the standards below. Don't treat them as a tick-box exercise, but integrate them into your everyday practice. These standards, and others that will become relevant later in your career, can be downloaded from www.tda.gov.uk

The table below shows which chapters are relevant to each standard – the most relevant are in bold. Other chapters will be useful too (see the checklists at the end of each chapter).

QTS Standards 2007 onwards		
Relationships with children and young people		
Q1	Have high expectations of children and young people including a commitment to ensuring that they can achieve their full educational potential and to establishing fair, respectful, trusting, supportive and constructive relationships with them.	Chs **1**, **6**, 7 (note its end-of-chapter checklist), 14, 43, **45**, 48,
Q2	Demonstrate the positive values, attitudes and behaviour they expect from children and young people.	Chs **6**, **7**, **8**, 9, 10, 43, 45
Frameworks		
Q3	a) Be aware of the professional duties of teachers and the statutory framework within which they work. b) Be aware of the policies and practices of the workplace and share in collective responsibility for their implementation.	Chs 7, 49. You need to be aware of your placement school's policies for behaviour, assessment, health and safety, and their means of implementing government policies.

Communicating and working with others		
Q4	Communicate effectively with children, young people, colleagues, parents and carers.	Chs 1, **4**, 12, **13**, 14, 18 (useful on group work and student talk), **21**, 24
Q5	Recognise and respect the contribution that colleagues, parents and carers can make to the development and well-being of children and young people, and to raising their levels of attainment.	Chs 21, **48**
Q6	Have a commitment to collaboration and co-operative working.	Chs 30, 45, **49**
Professional Personal Development		
Q7	a) Reflect on and improve their practice, and take responsibility for identifying and meeting their developing professional needs. b) Identify priorities for their early professional development in the context of induction.	Chs 10, Intro. to Part 2, 24, 34, **46**, 49
Q8	Have a creative and constructively critical approach towards innovation, being prepared to adapt their practice where benefits and improvements are identified.	Chs **14**, **24**, **46**, 49
Q9	Act upon advice and feedback and be open to coaching and mentoring.	Chs 11, **46**, 49
Teaching and learning		
Q10	Have a knowledge and understanding of a range of teaching, learning and behaviour management strategies and know how to use and adapt them, including how to personalise learning and provide opportunities for all learners to achieve their potential.	Chs 1, **8**, **9**, Intro. to Part 2, 33, 37, 47, 48, **Appendix 2** Useful diagram page 127

Assessment and monitoring		
Q11	Know the assessment requirements and arrangements for the subjects/ curriculum areas they are trained to teach, including those relating to public examinations and qualifications.	Chs 43, 44
Q12	Know a range of approaches to assessment, including the importance of formative assessment.	Chs 6, 14, **43**, **44**
Q13	Know how to use local and national statistical information to evaluate the effectiveness of their teaching, to monitor the progress of those they teach and to raise levels of attainment.	Chs 41, **46**, read **49** first
Subjects and curriculum		
Q14	Have a secure knowledge and understanding of their subjects/ curriculum areas and related pedagogy to enable them to teach effectively across the age and ability range for which they are trained.	Chs 1, **5**, 13, 24, **Appendix 2**
Q15	Know and understand the relevant statutory and non-statutory curricula and frameworks, including those provided through the National Strategies, for their subjects/curriculum areas, and other relevant initiatives applicable to the age and ability range for which they are trained.	www.nationalstrategies.org.uk www.standards.dcsf.gov.uk
Literacy, numeracy and ICT		
Q16	Have passed the professional skills tests in numeracy, literacy and information and communications technology (ICT).	These can be downloaded from www. dcsf.gov.uk and have to be taken at an authorised centre.
Q17	Know how to use skills in literacy, numeracy and ICT to support their teaching and wider professional activities.	Chs **28**, **35**, **36**

Achievement and diversity		
Q18	Understand how children and young people develop and that the progress and well-being of learners are affected by a range of developmental, social, religious, ethnic, cultural and linguistic influences.	Chs 1, **7**, 48 (page 561), 49
Q19	Know how to make effective personalised provision for those they teach, including those for whom English is an additional language or who have special educational needs or disabilities, and how to take practical account of diversity and promote equality and inclusion in their teaching.	Chs 1, **7**, **14**, 41, **47**, **48**, Appendix 2
Q20	Know and understand the roles of colleagues with specific responsibilities, including those with responsibility for learners with special educational needs and disabilities and other individual learning needs.	Chs 1, **7**, 48, **49**
Health and well-being		
Q21	a) Be aware of the current legal requirements, national policies and guidance on the safeguarding and promotion of the well-being of children and young people. (b) Know how to identify and support children and young people whose progress, development or well-being is affected by changes or difficulties in their personal circumstances, and when to refer them to colleagues for specialist support.	Ch. **7** You need to be aware of the Every Child Matters documentation and underlying philosophy. See www.everychildmatters.gov.uk Chs 1, **47**, **48**

Planning		
Q22	Plan for progression across the age and ability range for which they are trained, designing effective learning sequences within lessons and across series of lessons and demonstrating secure subject/curriculum knowledge.	Chs 1, 12, 17, **19**, **37**, **38**, 39, **40**, 41, 42
Q23	Design opportunities for learners to develop their literacy, numeracy and ICT skills.	Chs 35, 36, **42**
Q24	Plan homework or other out-of-class work to sustain learners' progress and to extend and consolidate their learning.	Chs 26, 27, 35
Teaching		
Q25	Teach lessons and sequences of lessons across the age and ability range for which they are trained in which they: a) use a range of teaching strategies and resources, including e-learning, taking practical account of diversity and promoting equality and inclusion b) build on prior knowledge, develop concepts and processes, enable learners to apply new knowledge, understanding and skills and meet learning objectives c) adapt their language to suit the learners they teach, introducing new ideas and concepts clearly, and using explanations, questions, discussions and plenaries effectively d) demonstrate the ability to manage the learning of individuals, groups and whole classes, modifying their teaching to suit the stage of the lesson.	Chs 1, 5, 7, 12, **13**, **14**, 17, **18**, 20, 21, 24, 29, 31, 33, 35, 36, 42, Appendix 2

	Assessing, monitoring and giving feedback	
Q26	a) Make effective use of a range of assessment, monitoring and recording strategies.	Chs 2, 7, 33, **41**, **43**, 44, **47**
	b) Assess the learning needs of those they teach in order to set challenging learning objectives	Chs **47**, **48**
Q27	Provide timely, accurate and constructive feedback on learners' attainment, progress and areas for development.	Ch **6**, 41, **43**, 44, 47, **48**
Q28	Support and guide learners to reflect on their learning, identify the progress they have made and identify their emerging learning needs.	Chs 2, 6, **34**, 41, **43**, **47**, **48**
Q29	Evaluate the impact of their teaching on the progress of all learners, and modify their planning and classroom practice where necessary.	Chs 10, Intro. to Part 2, 31, **46**, **49**
	Learning environment	
Q30	Establish a purposeful and safe learning environment conducive to learning and identify opportunities for learners to learn in out-of-school contexts.	Chs **5**, **6**, **7**, **8**, 25, **26**, 34
Q31	Establish a clear framework for classroom discipline to manage learners' behaviour constructively and promote their self-control and independence	Chs 6, **7**, **8**, 9, 10, 20, 43
	Team working and collaboration	
Q32	Work as a team member and identify opportunities for working with colleagues, sharing the development of effective practice with them.	Chs 42, **49**
Q33	Ensure that colleagues working with them are appropriately involved in supporting learning and understand the roles they are expected to fulfil.	Chs 7, 36, **49**

Bibliography

Abbs, P. (1976) *Root and Blossom*, London: Heinemann Educational.

Adair, J. (1996) *Effective Time Management: How to Save Time and Spend it Wisely*, London: Pan Books.

Adey, P. and Shayer, M. (1994) *Really Raising Standards: Cognitive Intervention and Academic Achievement*, London: Routledge.

Adey, P., Shayer, M. and Yates, C. (2001) *Thinking Science*, London: Nelson Thornes.

Argyle, M. (1987) *The Psychology of Happiness*, London: Routledge.

Argyle, M. (1994) *The Psychology of Interpersonal Behaviour*, Harmondsworth: Penguin.

Argyris, C. and Schön, D. (1974) *Theory in Practice*, San Francisco: Jossey-Bass.

Atkinson, J. W. (1978) *An Introduction to Motivation*, Princeton, NJ: Van Nostrand.

Attewell, J. (2002) *Distributed and Electronic Learning: A Review of the Literature*, LSRC Research Findings, available online from www.lsrc.org.uk

Ausubel, D. (1978) *Educational Psychology: A Cognitive View*, New York: Holt, Rinehart & Winston.

Baker, G. C. (1994) *Planning and Organizing for Multicultural Instruction*, New York: Addison-Wesley.

Ball, L. (1996) *Helping Students to Learn Independently in the Crafts*, Crafts Council Research Study, London: Crafts Council.

Basic Skills Agency (1997) 'Staying the course: the relationship between basic skills support, drop-out, retention and achievement – further education colleges', London: BSA.

Beard, R. and Hartley, T. (1984) *Teaching and Learning in Higher Education* (4th edition), London: PCP.

Biggs, J. (1987) *Student Approaches to Learning and Studying*, Camberwell: Australian Council for Educational Research.

Biggs, J. (2007) *Teaching for Quality Learning at University* (3rd edition), Buckingham: Open University Press.

Black, P. and Wiliam, D. (1998) 'Assessment and classroom learning', *Assessment in Education*, 5(1): 7–74.

Black, P. and Wiliam, D. (1999) 'Inside the black box', download from: www.pdkintl.org/kappan/kbla9810.htm

Black, P. *et al.* (2003) *Assessment for Learning: Putting it into Practice*, Maidenhead: Open University Press.

Bloom, B. S. (1984) 'The 2 sigma problem: the search for methods of group instruction as effective as one-to-one tutoring', *Educational Researcher*, June/July: 4–16.

Bloom, B. S. and Krathwohl, D. (1956) *Taxonomy of Educational Objectives. Handbook 1: Cognitive Domain*, London: Longman.

Bloom, B. S., Krathwohl, D. and Masica, B. (1964) *Taxonomy of Educational Objectives. Handbook 2: Affective Domain*, London: Longman.

Bloom, B. S., Madaus, G. F. and Hastings, J. T. (1992) *Evaluation to Improve Learning*, New York and London: McGraw-Hill.

Boud, D. (1988) *Developing Student Autonomy in Learning* (2nd edition), London: Kogan Page.

Bransford, J. D. *et al.* (2000) *How People Learn: Brain, Mind, Experience and School*, Washington, DC: National Research Council.

Brockfield, S. D. (1995) *Becoming a Critically Reflective Teacher*, San Francisco: Jossey-Bass.

Brown, G. and Atkins, M. (1988) *Effective Teaching in Higher Education*, London: Routledge.

Brown, G. and Hatton, N. (1982) *Explanations and Explaining: A Teaching Skills Workbook*, Basingstoke: Macmillan Education.

Bruner, J. S. (1966) *Toward a Theory of Instruction*, New York: W. W. Norton.

Bruner, J. S. (1971) *The Relevance of Education*, New York: W. W. Norton.

Bull, S., Solity, J. and Feldman, P. (1987) *Classroom Management: Principles to Practice*, London: Routledge.

Butler, R. (1988) 'Enhancing and undermining intrinsic motivation; the effects of task-involving and ego-involving evaluation on interest and performance', *British Journal of Educational Psychology*, 58: 1–14.

Buzan, T. (2003) *How To Mind Map*, London: HarperCollins.

Buzan, T. (2003) *The Mind Map Book* (2nd edition), London: BBC Books.

Buzan, T. (2003) *Use Your Memory* (2nd edition), London: BBC Books.

Canter, L. and Canter, M. (1992) *Assertive Discipline*, Los Angeles: Canter and Associates.

Capel, S., Leask, M. and Turner, T. (2005) *Learning to Teach in the Secondary School*, London: Routledge.

Caviglioli, O. and Harris, I. (2008) *Reaching Out to All Thinkers; How Teachers Can Help All Pupils Become Better Thinkers*, Stafford: Network Educational Press.

Caviglioli, O. and Harris, I. (2008) *Wiseguide to Visual Tools; A Practical Classroom Guide for Raising Achievement*, Stafford: Network Educational Press.

Child, D. (1993) *Psychology and the Teacher* (5th edition), London: Cassell.

Cole, M. and Walker, S. (eds) (1989) *Teaching and Stress*, Milton Keynes: Open University Press.

Coles, A. (ed.) (2004) *Teaching in Post-Compulsory Education: Policy, Practice and Values*, London: David Fulton.

Coles, M. J. and Robinson, W. D. (1989) *Teaching Thinking: A Survey of Programmes in Education*, Bristol: The Bristol Press.

Cooper, R. (1997) 'Learning styles and staff development', *Journal of the National Association for Staff Development*, 37: 38–46.

De Bono, E. (1978) *Teaching Thinking*, Harmondsworth: Penguin.

DELG (2002) *Report of the Learning and Skills Council's Distributed Electronic Learning Group*, online at http://excellence.qia.org.uk

Dennison, B. and Kirk, R. (1990) *Do, Review, Learn, Apply: A Simple Guide to Experiential Learning*, Oxford: Blackwell Education.

Desforges, C. (1989) *Testing and Assessment*, London: Cassell.

Desforges, C. and Fox, R. (2002) *Teaching and Learning: The Essential Readings*, Oxford: Blackwell.

Dickinson, C. and Wright, J. (1993) *Differentiation: A Practical Handbook of Classroom Strategies*, Coventry: National Council for Educational Technology.

Dunn, R. *et al.* (1989) 'Survey of research on learning styles', *Educational Leadership*, 46(6): 50–8.

Dweck, C. S. (2000) *Self-Theories: Their Role in Motivation, Personality, and Development*. Philadelphia: Psychology Press.

Ellington, H. and Race, P. (1993) *Producing Teaching Materials*, London: Kogan Page.

Entwistle, N. (1988) *Styles of Learning and Teaching*, London: David Fulton.

Ericsson, K. *et al.* (1993) 'The role of deliberate practice in the acquisition of expert performance', *Psychological Review*, 100(3): 363–406.

Farrar, E. and Judson, D. (2007) *Assertive Mentoring; A Practical Step-by-Step Guide for Mentoring that Really Works*, Brentwood: Model Learning Publications (www.modellearning.com).

Feather, N. (ed.) (1982) *Expectations and Actions*, Hillsdale, NJ: Erlbaum.

Feuerstein, R. (1980) *Instrumental Enrichment Intervention Programme for Cognitive Modifiability*, Baltimore, MD: University Park Press.

Fitz-Gibbon, C. T. (1988) 'Peer tutoring as a teaching strategy', *Educational Management and Administration*, 16: 217–29.

Further Education Funding Council (1998) *Inclusive Learning Quality Initiative Materials*, Coventry: FEFC.

Gibbs, G. (1988) *Learning by Doing: A Guide to Teaching and Learning Methods*, London: FEU.

Gibbs, G. (1992a) *Improving the Quality of Student Learning*, Oxford Centre for Staff Development, Technical and Educational Services.

Gibbs, G. (1992b) *Independent Learning with More Students. Teaching More Students Project No. 5*, Oxford Centre for Staff Development, PCFC.

Gibbs, G. and Habeshaw, T. (1990) *253 Ideas for Your Teaching*, (2nd revised edition), Bristol: Technical and Educational Services.

Ginnis, P. (2002) *The Teacher's Toolkit: Raise Classroom Achievement with Strategies for Every Learner*, Carmarthen: Crown House Publishing.

Gipp, C. and Stobart, G. (1993) *Assessment: A Teacher's Guide to Issues* (2nd edition), London: Hodder and Stoughton.

Good, T. L. and Brophy, J. E. (2002) *Looking in Classrooms* (9th edition), New York: Allyn & Bacon.

Gray, H. and Freeman, A. (1987) *Teaching Without Stress*, London: Paul Chapman.

Gray, J. (1999) *Improving Schools: Performance and Potential*, Buckingham: Open University Press.

Gray, J. and Richer, J. (1995) *Classroom Responses to Disruptive Behaviour* (in the series *Special Needs in Mainstream Schools*), London: Routledge.

Green, M. (2002) *Improving One-to-One Tutorials*, London: Learning and Skills Development Agency.

Groarke, J., Ovens, P. and Hargreaves, M. (1986) 'Towards a more open classroom', in D. Hustler, A. Cassidy and E. C. Cuff (eds) *Action Research in Classrooms and Schools*, London: Allen & Unwin.

Groisser, P. (1964) *How to Use the Fine Art of Questioning*, Englewood Cliffs, NJ: Teachers Practical Press.

Halpern, D. F. (1994) *Changing College Classrooms*, New York: Jossey-Bass.

Hargreaves, D. H. (1975) *Interpersonal Relations and Education*, London: Routledge.

Harris, D. and Bell, C. (1994) *Evaluating and Assessing for Learning* (2nd edition), London: Kogan Page.

Hattie, J. (2008) *Visible Learning: A Synthesis of Over 800 Meta-Analyses Relating to Achievement*, London: Routledge.

Hill, C. (2003) *Teaching Using Information and Learning Technology in Further Education*, Exeter: Learning Matters.

Hill, J. D. and Flynn, K. M. (2006) *Classroom Instruction that Works with English Language Learners*, Alexandria, VA: ASCD.

Hillier, Y. (2005) *Reflective Teaching in Further and Adult Education* (2nd revised edition), London: Continuum.

Hodson, D. (1990) 'A critical look at practical work in school science', *School Science Review*, 71(256): 33–40.

Hodson, D. (1992) 'A critical look at practical work in school science', *School Science Review*, 73(264): 65–78.

Hollis, A. W. (1935) 'The personal relationship in teaching', unpublished MA thesis, University of Birmingham.

Holt, J. (1995) *How Children Learn* (revised edition), Cambridge, MA: Da Capo Press.

Honey, P. (1989) 'Trials and tribulations', *Guardian*, 19 December.

Honey, P. and Mumford, A. (1992) *The Manual of Learning Styles*, London: Peter Honey.

Hopson, B. and Scally, M. (1989) *Life Skills Teaching Programme No. 4*, Otley Lifeskills Associates.

Inhelder, B. and Piaget, J. (1958) *The Growth of Logical Thinking from Childhood to Adolescence*, London: Routledge.

Jaques, D. (2000) *Learning in Groups* (3rd revised edition), London: Kogan Page.

Jarvis, P. (1995) *Adult and Continuing Education: Theory and Practice* (2nd revised edition), London: Routledge.

Jense, E. (2000) *Brain-Based Learning* (revised edition), Thousand Oaks, CA: Corwin Press.

Jensen, E. (2008) *Super Teaching* (4th edition), Thousand Oaks, CA: Corwin Press.

Jepson, R. W. (1948) *Clear Thinking: An Elementary Course of Preparation for Citizenship*, London: Longman.

Joyce, B. and Showers, B. (2002) *Student Achievement through Staff Development*, Alexandria, VA: ASCD.

Kerry, T. (1982) *Effective Questioning*, London: Macmillan.

Kerry, T. (2002) *Explaining and Questioning*, Cheltenham: Nelson Thornes.

Knowles, M. (1975) *Self-Directed Learning*, Cambridge University Press.

Knowles, M. (1988) *The Modern Practice of Adult Education: From Pedagogy to Andragogy* (revised edition), Cambridge Book Company.

Knowles, M. (1990) *The Adult Learner: A Neglected Species*, Houston, TX: Gulf Publishing.

Kyriacou, C. (1989) 'The nature and prevalence of teacher stress', in M. Cole and S. Walker (eds) *Teaching and Stress*, Milton Keynes: Open University Press.

Kyriacou, C. (1997) *Effective Teaching in Schools* (2nd edition), Cheltenham: Nelson Thornes.

Kyriacou, C. (1998) *Essential Teaching Skills* (3rd edition), Cheltenham: Nelson Thornes.

Kyriacou, C. and Marshall, S. (1989) 'The nature of active learning in secondary schools', *Evaluation and Research in Education*, 3: 1–5.

Laslett, R. and Smith, C. (1992) *Effective Classroom Management: A Teacher's Guide* (2nd edition), London: Routledge.

Levine, J. (2007) *The Internet for Dummies* (11th edition), Foster City, CA: IDG Books.

Lewis, R. and Mee, J. (1981) *Using Role Play: An Introductory Guide*, Cambridge: Basic Skills Unit.

Lloyd-Jones, R. (1988) *How to Produce Better Worksheets*, London: Hutchinson.

Lunzer, E. and Gardner, K. (1979) *The Effective Use of Reading*, Oxford: Heinemann Educational Books.

McGregor, D. (1985) *The Human Side of Enterprise* (revised edition), New York: McGraw-Hill.

McNaught, A. (2004) 'Exploring e-learning for literacy, numeracy and ESOL teachers', Coventry: Ferl/Becta.

Madsen, C. H. Jr, Becker, W. C. and Thomas, D. R. (1968), 'Rules, praise and ignoring', *Journal of Applied Behavioural Analysis*, 1: 139–50.

Marland, M. (2002) *The Craft of the Classroom* (3rd edition), London: Croom Helm.

Martinez, P. (1998) '9000 voices: student persistence and drop-out in further education', LSDA online at www.lsneducation.org.uk/pubs/pages/982288.aspx

Martinez, P. (2000) 'Raising achievement: a guide to successful strategies', Learning and Skills Development Agency online at www.lsda.org.uk/pubs

Martinez, P. (2002) 'Raising achievement at levels 1 and 2', LSDA online: www.lsda.org.uk/pubs.

Marton, M. and Saljo, R. (1976) 'On qualitative differences in learning' (two articles), *British Journal of Educational Psychology*, 46: 4–11, 115–27.

Marzano, R. J. (2006) *Classroom Assessment and Grading that Work*: Alexandria, VA: ASCD.

Marzano, R. J. (2007) *The Art and Science of Teaching*, Alexandria, VA: ASCD.

Marzano, R. J. *et al.* (2001) *Classroom Instruction that Works: Research-Based Strategies for Increasing Student Achievement*, Alexandria, VA: ASCD.

Marzano, R. J. with Marzano, S. and Pickering, D. J. (2003) *Classroom Management that Works*, Alexandria, VA: ASCD.

Maslow, A. (1993) *The Farther Reaches of Human Nature*, London: Penguin Arkana.

Maslow, A. H. (1987) *Motivation and Personality* (3rd edition), New York: Harper Collins.

Mitchell, D. (2008) *What Really Works in Special and Inclusive Education: Using Evidence-Based Teaching Strategies*, Abingdon: Routledge.

Moon, B. and Shelton Mayes, A. (eds) (1994) *Teaching and Learning in the Secondary School*, London: Routledge.

Moseley, D. *et al.* (2005) *Frameworks for Thinking*, Cambridge University Press.

Moser, C. (1999) *A Fresh Start* ('The Moser Report'), London: DfEE.

Muijs, D. and Reynolds, D. (2005) *Effective Teaching: Evidence and Practice* (2nd edition), London: Paul Chapman.

Murphy, R. and Torrance, H. (1988) *The Changing Face of Educational Assessment*, Milton Keynes: Open University Press.

Myers, K. (ed.) (1992) *Genderwatch!*, Cambridge University Press.

Nelson-Jones, R. (1996) *Effective Thinking Skills*, London: Sage.

Nisbet, J. and Schucksmith, J. (1986) *Learning Strategies*, London: Routledge.

O'Connell, B. (ed.) (2002) *The Runshaw Way: Values Drive Behaviour*, Leyland: Runshaw College.

Perrott, E. (1982) *Effective Teaching*, London: Longman.

Petty, G. (1997) *How to Be Better at Creativity*, London: Kogan Page.

Petty, G. (1997) 'Independent learning', *Journal of the National Association for Staff Development*, 37 (June): 28–37.

Petty, G. (2006) *Evidence Based Teaching*, Cheltenham: Nelson Thornes.

Pinker, S. (1997) *How the Mind Works*, London: Penguin.

Powell, R. (1997) *Active Whole-class Teaching*, Stafford: Robert Powell Publications.

Race, P. (1994) *The Open Learning Handbook*, London: Kogan Page.

Ramsden, P. (1992) *Learning and Teaching in Higher Education*, London: Routledge.

Reardon, K. K. (1991) *Persuasion in Practice* (2nd edition), London: Sage.

Reece, I. and Walker, S. (2007) *A Practical Guide to Teaching, Training and Learning* (6th edition), Tyne and Wear: Business Education Publishers.

Reises, R. and Mason, M. (1992) *Disability Equality in the Classroom: A Human Rights Issue* (2nd edition), London: ILEA/Disability Equality.

Riding, R. and Rayner, S. (1998) *Cognitive Styles and Learning Strategies: Understanding Style Differences in Learning and Behaviour*, London: David Fulton.

Robertson, J. (1996) *Effective Classroom Control: Understanding Pupil–Teacher Relationships* (3rd edition), London: Hodder & Stoughton.

Rogers, A. (1986) *Teaching Adults*, Milton Keynes: Open University Press.

Rogers, Carl (1961) *On Becoming a Person* (new edition, 2004), London: Constable.

Rogers, Carl (1994) *Freedom to Learn* (3rd edition), New York: Prentice Hall.

Rogers, Carl (1995) *On Becoming a Teacher: A Therapist's View of Psychotherapy*, Boston, MA: Marriner Books.

Rogers, Colin (1982) *A Social Psychology of Schooling: The Expectancy Process*, London: Routledge & Kegan Paul.

Rogers, Colin (1989) *Accelerated Learning*, Aylesbury: Accelerated Learning Systems.

Rogers, J. (1989) *Adults Learning* (3rd edition), Milton Keynes: Open University Press.

Rose, C. (1997) *Accelerated Learning for the 21st Century*, Buckingham: Accelerated Learning Systems.

Rosenthal, R. and Jacobson, L. (1968) *Pygmalion in the Classroom: A Human Rights Issue* (2nd edition), London: ILEA/Disability Equality.

Rowntree, D. (1987) *Assessing Students: How Shall We Know Them?* (2nd edition), London: Routledge.

Rowntree, D. (1992) *Exploring Open and Distance Learning*, London: Routledge.

Russell, B. (1992) Part 10 of *The Basic Writings of Bertrand Russell* (2nd edition), London: Routledge.

Schön, D. (1982) *The Reflective Practitioner*, New York: Basic Books Inc.

Schön, D. (1990) *Educating the Reflective Practitioner: Towards a New Design for Teaching and Learning in the Professions* (new edition), San Francisco: Jossey-Bass.

Sharron, H. and Coulter, M. (1994) *Changing Children's Minds: Feuerstein's Revolution in the Teaching of Intelligence*, Birmingham: Sharron Publishing Co.

Shayer, M. and Adey, A. (2002) *Learning Intelligence*, Buckingham: Open University Press.

Short, G. (1986) 'Teacher expectation and West Indian underachievement', *Educational Research*, 27(2): 95–101.

Skinner, B. F. (1953) *Science and Human Behaviour*, New York: Macmillan.

Smith, A. (1988) *Starting to Teach: Surviving and Succeeding in the Classroom*, London: Kogan Page.

Sperry, R. W. (1968) 'Hemispherical deconnection and unity in conscious awareness', *Scientific American*, 23: 723–33.

Stern, J. (1997) *Homework and Study Support: A Guide for Teachers and Parents*, London: David Fulton.

Sutton, C. (ed.) (1981) *Communicating in the Classroom*, London: Hodder & Stoughton.

Swann, Sir Michael (1985) *Education for All* ('The Swann Report'), Report of Committee of Enquiry into the Education of Children from Ethnic Minority Groups, London: HMSO.

Taylor, D. W. *et al.* (1958) 'Does group participation when using brainstorming facilitate or inhibit creative thinking?', *Administrative Science Quarterly*, 3: 23–47.

Thorpe, S., Deshpande, P. and Edwards, C. (eds) (1994) *Race, Equality and Science Teaching: A Handbook for Teachers and Educators*, Hatfield: Association for Science Education.

Thouless, R. (1990) *Straight and Crooked Thinking*, London: Hodder Arnold.

Tomlinson, J. (1995) *Inclusive Learning* ('The Tomlinson Report'), Coventry: FEFC.

Tummons, J. (2005) *Assessing Learning in the Lifelong Learning Sector* (2nd edition), Exeter: Learning Matters.

Vernon, P. E. (1970) *Creativity: Selected Readings*, London: Penguin Educational.

Walklin, L. (1990) *Teaching and Learning in Further Education*, Cheltenham: Nelson Thornes.

Wallace, S. (2005) *Teaching and Supporting Learning in Further Education: Meeting the FENTO Standards* (2nd edition), Exeter: Learning Matters.

Waterhouse, P. (1983) *Managing the Learning Process*, London: McGraw-Hill.

Weiner, B. J. (1972) *Theories of Motivation*, Chicago, IL: Markham.

Westwood, P. (2007) *Commonsense Methods for Children with Special Educational Needs: Strategies for the Regular Classroom* (5th edition), London: Routledge-Falmer.

Wheldall, K. and Glynn, T. (1989) *Effective Classroom Learning*, Oxford: Blackwell.

Wiggins, G. and McTighe, J. (2001) *Understanding by Design*, New Jersey: Prentice-Hall.

Wilson, B. (1987) *Methods of Training, Vol. 1: The Systematic Design of Training Courses*, London: HMSO.

Wilson, B. (1987) *Methods of Training, Vol. 2: Groupwork*, London: HMSO.

Wilson, B. (1987) *Methods of Training, Vol. 3: Individualised Instruction*, London: HMSO.

Wilson, B. (1987) *Methods of Training, Vol. 4: Resource Based and Open Learning*, London: HMSO.

Wittrock, M. C. (1974) 'Learning as a generative process', *Educational Psychologist*, 11: 87–95.

Wolf, A. (1995) *Competence-Based Assessment*, Buckingham: Open University Press.

Wragg, E. C. (ed.) (1984) *Classroom Teaching Skills*, London: Croom Helm.

Wright, C. F. and Nuthall, G. (1970) 'The relationship between teacher behaviour and pupil achievement', *American Educational Research Journal*, 7: 477–91.

Index

Page references in *italic* indicate figures or tables.

Index

Index